Napoleon at St. Helena
by John Stevens Cabot Abbott

Copyright © 2019 by HardPress

Address:
HardPress
8345 NW 66TH ST #2561
MIAMI FL 33166-2626
USA
Email: info@hardpress.net

Napoleon at St. Helena

John Stevens Cabot Abbott

Fr 1406.9.4

HARVARD COLLEGE
LIBRARY

THE GIFT OF
BERNARD BERENSON
Class of 1887
of Florence, Italy

N.G.B.
July, 18

N. G. B.
July, 1842

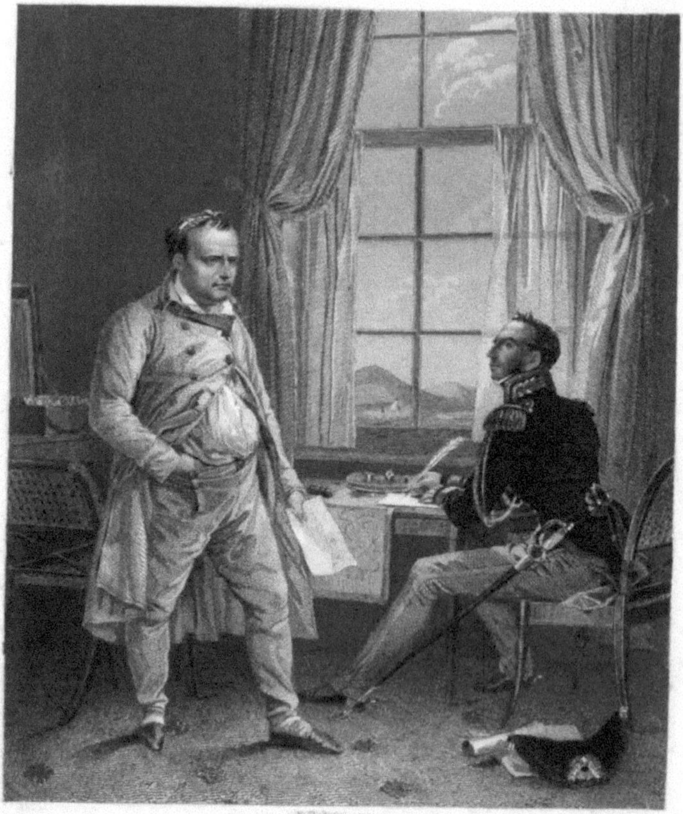

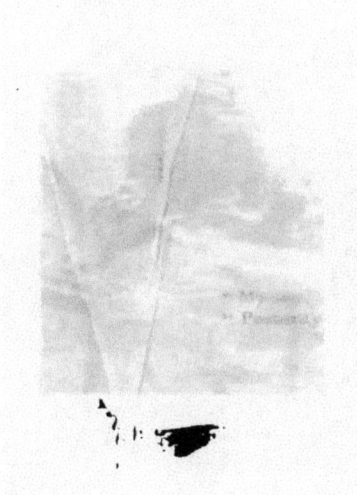

NAPOLEON AT ST. HELENA

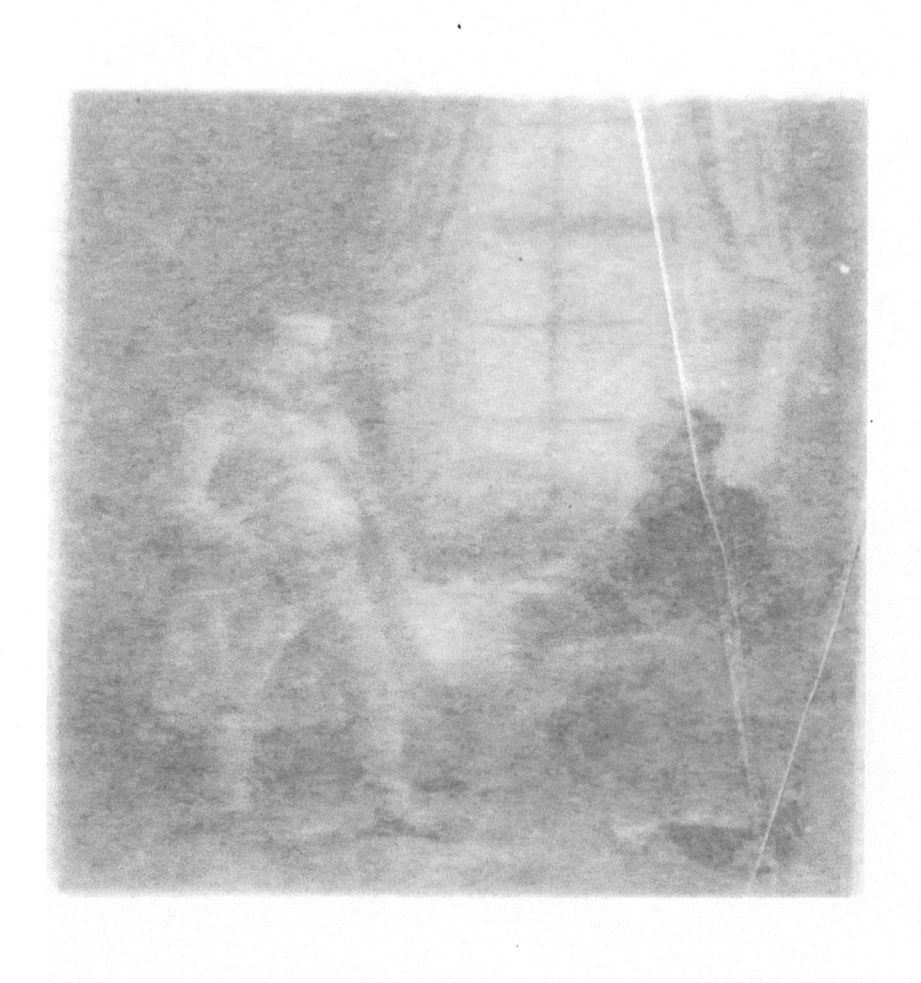

NAPOLEON AT ST. HELENA;

OR,

INTERESTING ANECDOTES AND REMARKABLE CONVERSATIONS OF THE EMPEROR

DURING THE FIVE AND A HALF YEARS OF HIS CAPTIVITY.

COLLECTED FROM THE MEMORIALS OF

Las Casas, O'Meara, Montholon, Antommarchi, and others.

BY JOHN S. C. ABBOTT.

With Illustrations.

"My son should not think of avenging my death"
"Posterity will do me justice."—NAPOLEON.

NEW YORK:
HARPER & BROTHERS, PUBLISHERS,
PEARL STREET, FRANKLIN SQUARE.

406.9.4

HARVARD COLLEGE LIBRARY
GIFT OF
BERNARD BERENSON

Entered, according to Act of Congress, in the year one thousand eight hundred and fifty-five, by

HARPER & BROTHERS,

in the Clerk's Office of the District Court of the Southern District of New York.

PREFACE.

THE Emperor Napoleon, by almost universal consent, is pronounced to be, intellectually, the most illustrious of mankind. Even his bitterest enemies are compelled to do homage to the universality and the grandeur of his genius. Lamartine declares him to be "the greatest of the creations of God." In the following terms, Sir Archibald Alison testifies to his gigantic intelligence:

"Never were talents of the highest, genius of the most exalted kind, more profusely bestowed upon a human being. The true scene of Napoleon's glory, and the most characteristic of the ruling passion of his mind, was his cabinet. Those who are struck with astonishment at the immense information and just discrimination which he displayed at the council-board, and the varied and important public improvements which he set on foot in every part of his dominions, will form a most inadequate conception of his mind, unless they are at the same time familiar with the luminous and profound views which he threw out on the philosophy of politics in the solitude of St. Helena. Never was evinced a clearer proof of the truth, which a practical acquaintance with men must probably have impressed upon every observer, that talent of the highest order is susceptible of any application, and that accident or Supreme direction alone determines whether their possessor is to become a Homer, a Bacon, or a Napoleon.

"It would require the observation of a Thucydides, directing the pencil of a Tacitus, to portray, by a few touches, such a character; and modern idiom, even in their hands, would probably have proved inadequate to the task. Equal to Alexander in military achievement, superior to Justinian in legal information, sometimes second only to Bacon in political sagacity, he possessed, at the same time, the inexhaustible resources of Hannibal, and the administrative powers of Cæsar."

The genius of Napoleon is astounding. All branches of human knowledge seemed alike familiar to his gigantic mind. His conversations at St. Helena, scattered through the numerous and voluminous memorials of those who gleaned them, are replete with intensest interest. During the long agony of his imprisonment and his death, he conversed with perfect freedom upon the events of his marvelous career, and upon all those subjects of morals, politics, and religion, which most deeply concern the welfare of our race. There is no mind which will not be invigorated by familiarity with these profound thoughts, expressed with so much glow of feeling and energy of diction.

The author of this volume performs mainly but the unambitious task of compilation. He desires to take the reader to St. Helena, and to introduce him to the humble apartment of the Emperor. He would give him a seat in the arm-chair, by the side of the illustrious sufferer reclining upon the sofa, or lead him to accompany the Emperor in his walk among the blackened rocks, and thus to listen to the glowing utterances of the imperial sage. The literature of our language affords no richer intellectual treat than the conversations of Napoleon. Hitherto widely scattered in many volumes, and buried in the midst of a multiplicity of details of but transient interest, they have been inaccessible to the mass of readers. By presenting them in one volume, they are within the reach of all who can appreciate the eloquence of words and of thought.

JOHN S. C. ABBOTT.

BRUNSWICK, Maine, 1855.

CONTENTS.

CHAPTER I.
THE VOYAGE.

The Emperor seeks the Hospitality of England—Doomed to St. Helena—His Trunks searched—Removed to the *Northumberland*—The Russian Campaign—Adieu to France—Habits on Shipboard—Threatening Aspect of the Russian Power—The French Navy—Captain Wright—Character of Kleber and of Desaix—Napoleon at Toulon—Anecdotes—Napoleon in Italy—Anecdotes—The Little Corporal—Dictation—Approach to St. Helena................... Page 13

CHAPTER II.
RESIDENCE AT THE BRIERS.

Description of St. Helena—The Ride to Longwood—Description of The Briers—The Youth of France—Deplorable Condition of the Exiles—Indignation of the Emperor—Note to the English Government—Overtures of the Bourbons—Suppression of the Tribunate—Character of the Senate—Anecdotes—Institute of Meudon—Candor of the Emperor—The Malay Slave—Popular Education—Fatality of the Emperor's Career—Treatment of the Spanish Princes............ 30

CHAPTER III
REMOVAL TO LONGWOOD.

Waterloo—Dangers of Military Commanders—Portraiture of Napoleon's Generals—The Spanish Princes—Political Prospects of France—Defense of Marshal Ney—Contrast between Ney and Turenne—Removal to Longwood—The Emperor's Apartments—Kindness of the Emperor—Political Views—The Emperor's Wounds—Calumnies 52

CHAPTER IV.
1816, JANUARY.

New-year's Day—Fowling-pieces—Colonel Wilks—The Disappointment—Visit to the Rooms—The drunken Sentinel—Social Reading—Goldsmith's Secret History—Conversation with Governor Wilks—Lodgings of Las Casas—The Emperor's Criticisms—Historical Remarks—The Ride—Mired Horse.. 67

CHAPTER V.
1816, FEBRUARY.

Scanty Resources of the Island—The Emperor's Progress in English—Learns the Death of Murat—Eloquent Parallel—Affairs of Spain—Dismal Days—Caricatures—French Politics—Picture of Domestic Happiness—The Emperor's Opinion of the French Poets—Public Contractors—Vigilance of the Emperor.. 85

CHAPTER VI.
1816, MARCH.

Invasion of England—Etiquette of the Emperor's Court—The Emperor's Levees—The Court and the City—The Anonymous Letter—Remarks on Medicine—Corvisart—Medical Practice in Babylon.. 97

CHAPTER VII.
1816, MARCH. Continued.

Trial of Ney—National Character of the French—The Emperor's Carriage taken at Waterloo—The Emperor at Dresden—Maria Louisa and Josephine—Alexander, Francis, and the King of Prussia—Eloquent Effusion of the Emperor—Testimony of B Constant................ 106

CONTENTS.

CHAPTER VIII.
1816, March. Continued.

New Insult to the Emperor—Execution of Marshal Ney—Message to the Prince Regent—Wretched Food—Remarks on the Gracchi—Sleep during Battle—Historians—Military Characters—Soult, Massena—Political Confessions—Marmont—Murat—Berthier—Danger in Battle—Bulletins—Summary of nine Months .... Page 117

CHAPTER IX.
1816, April.

Conspiracies—Measures that might have been adopted after Waterloo—Characteristic Fruits—The State of Europe—Ascendency of Liberal Opinions—Talleyrand—Fouché—Political Reflections—Arrival of Sir Hudson Lowe—Remarks on the Return from Elba—Introduction of the Governor—Character and Conduct of Sir George Cockburn................................. 129

CHAPTER X.
1816, April. Continued.

Convention between the Allied Powers—Declaration demanded of the Inmates of Longwood—Farewell Visit of Governor Wilks—Interesting Conversation on the Arts—Message to the Prince Regent—Portfolio lost at Waterloo—Cost of the Emperor's Toilet—Expenses in different Capitals—The Furnishing of the imperial Palaces—The Emperor's Mode of examining Accounts 147

CHAPTER XI.
1816, April. Continued.

Critique on Voltaire's Mohammed—Remarks on the Mohammed of History—Gretry—Napoleon's Proclamations—His Policy in Egypt—Confession of an illegal Act—The Domestics examined—The Emperor a Peace-maker—The Abbé de Pradt—The Russian War.................. 160

CHAPTER XII.
1816, May.

The Achievements of the Emperor—Inhumanity of the Governor—Conversation with Dr. O'Meara—Parallel between the Revolutions of France and England—The Emigrants—Concurrence of happy Circumstances in the Emperor's Career—The Spanish Bourbons—Arrival of the wooden Palace—The Iliad—Characteristic Remarks—Hoche and other Generals................ 174

CHAPTER XIII.
1816, May. Continued.

Ridiculous Invitation sent by Sir Hudson Lowe—Napoleon at the Institute—At the Council of State—On the Interior of Africa—The Marine Department—Decrés—The Dictionary of Weathercocks—The Reception—Angry Interview with the Governor—Remarks of the Emperor on his Family 192

CHAPTER XIV.
1816, May. Continued.

The Emperor sleeping—The Governor arrests a Servant at Longwood—The Bible—Princess Stephanie—Expulsion of Portalis—Political Reflections—Voltaire's Brutus—French Colony on the St. Lawrence—Carnot—French Manufactures—Physiognomy—The English Soldiers salute the Emperor—Corsica—Napoleon's Mother—Madam Chevreuse—The Conspirators—The Situation of England 214

CHAPTER XV.
1816, June.

Voltaire—Characteristic Difference between the English and the French—Affected Anger of the Emperor—Reflections on the Governor—Expenses of the Emperor's Household at the Tuileries—Finance—Dictation resumed—Military Schools—Female Schools—Gil Blas—General Biznet—Religious Opinions—Portraits of the Directors—Anecdotes—18th Fructidor 237

CONTENTS.

CHAPTER XVI.
1816, June. Continued.

English Diplomacy—Lord Whitworth—Chatham—Castlereagh—Cornwallis—Fox—Lacretelle's History of the Convention—Puns—Public Characters—Bailli—La Fayette—Monge—Grégoire—St. Domingo—Dictations on the Convention.. Page 254

CHAPTER XVII.
1816, June. Continued.

The War and Royal Family of Spain—Errors—Ferdinand at Valençay—Historical Sketch of the Events—The Moniteurs—The Liberty of the Press—The Conference at Tilsit—Anecdotes of the Emperor of Russia—Of the King and Queen of Prussia—Anecdote of Savary—The Emperor's Magnanimity 262

CHAPTER XVIII.
1816, June. Continued.

Arrival of the Commissioners—Etiquette established by Napoleon—Mode of dictating—The Return of the Monks—Departure of the *Northumberland*—Remarks on the History of the Russian Campaign—Lord Holland—Arrival of Books—Ideas on Political Economy—Annoyance by the Rats—Lord Castlereagh—French Heiresses—Allusion by Napoleon to his own History—Summary of three Months... 275

CHAPTER XIX.
1816, July.

Pillage in War—Character of the French Soldier—Anecdotes of Brumaire—Sièyes—Grand Elector—Cambacères—New Vexations—Little Tristam—Difficulty of judging Men—Junot: his Wife—Bernadotte—Lannes—Murat: his Character and Death....................... 291

CHAPTER XX.
1816, July. Continued.

The Works of Cherbourg—Designs of the Emperor—Audience given to the Governor—Faubourg St. Germain—Aristocracy—Democracy—The Emperor's Intention to marry a French woman—Difficulties in reforming Society—Etiquette at Longwood 301

CHAPTER XXI.
1816, July. Continued.

Establishments for Mendicity—Illyria—Prisoners of State—Freedom of the French People—Egypt—The Desert—Anecdotes—Paternal Advice—Remarkable Conversations—Cagliostro, Mesmer, Gall, Lavater, Madam de Balbi—Conversation with the Admiral—Commissioners—Santini—Nuns—Convents—Monks—The French Clergy 310

CHAPTER XXII.
1816, August.

Maria Antoinette—Manners of Versailles—The Father of a Family—Napoleon's Sentimental Journey—Spirit of the Times—The 10th of August—Piedmont—Canals of France—Plans for Paris—Versailles—Fontainebleau—History of Europe—Turkey—The Regency—Gustavus IV.—Bernadotte—Paul—Projects on India—War with Russia—Talleyrand—Madam de Staël...... 325

CHAPTER XXIII.
1816, August. Continued.

Avoiding the Governor—The Emperor's Birth-day—Present from Lord Holland—Remarks on Religion—Angry Interview with the Governor—Regrets of the Emperor—Libels—General Sarrazzin—The Hypocrite—Threats of Sir Hudson Lowe 342

CONTENTS.

CHAPTER XXIV.
1816, August. Continued.

Protest against the Treaty of 2d August, 1815—Remarks on Russia—The Burning of Moscow—Projects of Napoleon had he returned victorious—Decrees of Berlin and Milan—Political Defense—Remarks to Captain Poppleton .... Page 356

CHAPTER XXV.
1816, September.

Faded Dresses—The Campaign of Saxony—Reflections—The Massacres of the Third of September—Remarks on Revolutions—Unhappy Fate of Louis XVI.—Letters of Madam de Maintenon—Errors of the English Ministers—The Debt of England—The Emperor's Court at the Tuileries—The Emperor's Munificence—Guards of the Eagle—Lucien's Charlemagne 368

CHAPTER XXVI.
1816, September. Continued.

Scarcity of Food—The Emperor's Freedom from Animosity—The Bourbons—On Impossibilities—Statistical Calculations—Sale of Plate—Fresh Vexations—Debt of St. Domingo—Plans of Administration—On Sensibility—Holland and King Louis—The Emperor's Family—Business Habits of the Emperor—Treasures of Napoleon 385

CHAPTER XXVII.
1816, October.

Fatalism—The Governor seeks another Interview—New Demands and Restrictions—Remarks to Dr. O'Meara—Laws—Communication from Sir Thomas Reade—Reduction of Expenses—Influence of Public Opinion—The Emperor's Son—The Sacred Cause of Washington and of Napoleon—Great Grief of the Emperor 400

CHAPTER XXVIII.
1816, October. Continued.

The Declaration to be signed—Perplexity and Dismay—The Emperor proposes an Incognito—Remarks of the Emperor upon this Subject—Savary—Fouché—Sièyes—Conversation with Sièyes—Anecdotes of the Emperor—Enthusiasm of the Parisian Populace—New Vexations—Four removed from Longwood 414

CHAPTER XXIX.
1816, October. Continued.

Intellectual Employments—Sale of Plate—Madam de Staël—Baron Larrey—Remarks on the peculiar Situation of the Emperor—Expenses at St. Helena—Marshal Jourdan—The Russian War—The Chamber of Sickness—Lord Exmouth's Expedition—The Debt of England—Wellington and Waterloo—Sailors—Heartlessness of the Governor—Affecting Scene—Immorality—Want of Water—Playfulness of the Emperor—Thoughts on Italy 425

CHAPTER XXX.
1816, November.

Rupture of the Treaty of Amiens—Treatment of Prisoners—Exchange of Prisoners—Plan of employing Prisoners of War—Magnificent Views in reference to Antwerp—Reason for refusing the Terms offered at Chatillon—Confidence of the Emperor respecting the Verdict of Posterity—Disinthrallment of the Jews—Marriages—Freemasons—Illuminati—The Jesuits—The Affair of Mallet—The Emperor's Family—The Historical Atlas—Anecdotes 438

CHAPTER XXXI.
1816, November. Continued.

Remarks on Russia—Contrast between Pitt and Fox—Monopolies—Wants of the French Navy—Remarks on the Imperial Government—Troubles in La Vendée—Remarks on Tragedy—Anec-

CONTENTS.

dotes—Remarks on Religion; on Instinct—Blucher—The Treatment of Soldiers—The Neapolitans—On Peace with England—Sir Sydney Smith—The Regeneration of Spain—Sir Hudson Lowe—Duplicity of the English Government .... Page 450

CHAPTER XXXII.
1816, NOVEMBER. Continued.

Dumouriez—Leopold—The Tuileries—Monarchies and Republics—Hostility of the English Ministry—Designs of the Emperor—The Reorganization of Italy—Causes of the Emperor's Downfall—Bernadotte—Wounds of the Emperor—Devotion of his Soldiers—The Return from Elba—Plans after Waterloo—Talleyrand—The Sword of Frederick—The Second Marriage—Anecdote—Dismissal of the Servant of Las Casas—Causes of Success—Alexander the Great—Cæsar—Hannibal—Frederick the Great—The Conscription—Lawyers—The Clergy 469

CHAPTER XXXIII.
1816, NOVEMBER. Continued.

Longwood invested—Dramatic Readings—Lord Liverpool—Lord Sidmouth—Lord Bathurst—Lord Castlereagh—The Division of Europe—Remarks on Wellington and Waterloo—Character of the French Ministers—Duroc—Marmont—Gaming—Memorable Remarks—A Hereditary Nobility—Truth of History—The Bourbon Conspiracy—Pichegru—Moreau 484

CHAPTER XXXIV.
1816, NOVEMBER. Continued.

Secret Visit from the Servant of Las Casas—Arrest of Las Casas—His Imprisonment—Indignation of the Emperor—Fainting-fit of O'Meara 502

CHAPTER XXXV.
1816, DECEMBER.

Decision of Las Casas to return to Europe—Remarks of the Emperor upon the Conduct of the Governor—Remarks on Moreau, Desaix, Massena—Message to the Emperor from the Governor—Indignant Remarks of the Emperor—Character of Alexander—The Expedition to Copenhagen—The Call from Lady Lowe—Continued Imprisonment of Las Casas—Political Blunders of Lord Castlereagh—The Manufactures of France 509

CHAPTER XXXVI.
1816, DECEMBER. Continued.

Letter from the Emperor to Las Casas—Arrival of Sir Thomas Strange—Brutality of Colonel Reade—Death of Moreau—Anecdote—Continued Imprisonment of Las Casas—Relentings of the Governor—Views of the Emperor respecting his Situation—Las Casas forbidden to take leave of the Emperor—Departure of Las Casas—His subsequent Persecutions 516

CHAPTER XXXVII.
1817, JANUARY.

New-Year's Gifts—Representations of Chateaubriand and of Sir Robert Wilson—Annoyance from Rats—Secret Amours of Napoleon—The Invasion of England—Conduct of the Governor .. 527

CHAPTER XXXVIII.
1817, FEBRUARY.

Message from the Governor—Remarks of the Emperor upon his Treatment—Russia and the Emperor Paul—On the Invasion of India—Designs of Alexander—The Ambigu—The Return from Elba—Character of the French—Newspapers withheld from the Emperor—Vigilance with which the Emperor was guarded—Blunders of Lord Castlereagh—The Botanist who had seen Maria Louisa 531

CONTENTS.

CHAPTER XXXIX.
1817, MARCH.

False Assertion of Lord Castlereagh—O'Meara's previous Estimate of the Emperor—Napoleon's Confidence in the Verdict of Posterity—The Libels of Pelletier—The iron Railing—The Distress in England—Napoleon's Proposition to assume an Incognito—Warden's Book—Prince Regent—Montchenu—The Bookseller Palm—The New Testament—Conduct of the Governor—Talleyrand—Remarks on Egypt—Menou—The Secret Memoirs—Uniting the Nations ..... Page 539

CHAPTER XL.
1817, APRIL and MAY.

On Aristocracy—Cornwallis—False Documents—Lord Whitworth—Commendation of the English Seamen—Habits of Writing—Pleasant Interview with Admiral Malcolm—Remarks on receiving Lord Amherst—The Princess of Wales—Prince Leopold—The Re-establishment of Poland—Deplorable State of Louis XVIII.—Lord Bathurst's Speech 555

CHAPTER XLI.
1817, JUNE.

The marble Bust—Present from Lady Holland and others—Grand Lama—Murat—Waterloo—The Delivery of the Bust—The Mother of Napoleon—Testimony of Mrs. Abell—Necessity for the second Abdication—Arrival of Lord Amherst.. 566

CHAPTER XLII.
1817, JULY.

Arrival of the *Conqueror*—Malcolm—Validity of Napoleon's Title to the Crown—Breakfast with O'Meara—Story of the Bust—Letter to Mr. Radwick—The Presentation of Lord Amherst—Remarkable Conversation—Vigilance with which the Emperor was guarded—Captain Elphinstone—The Present—Cause of the War with Spain—Anecdote—Controversy with the Governor—Increasing Tyranny 572

CHAPTER XLIII.
1817, AUGUST.

Rumor of a Removal to Malta—Remarks upon the English Ministers—The Emperor's Birth-day—Fondness for Children—Blindman's Buff—Anecdotes—The Queen of Prussia—Malta—Interesting Remarks—Maria Louisa—The Restoration of the Bourbons—Dethronement of the Spanish Princes—Robespierre—Talleyrand—Fouché—Carnot 584

CHAPTER XLIV.
1817, SEPTEMBER.

Influence of Libels—St. Helena chosen by Wellington—Remarks on Sir Hudson Lowe—Society of Ladies—St. Domingo—The Manuscript from St. Helena—Anecdote of the lent Horse—Ross Cottage—The Earthquake—Remarks on the Restrictions—Aristocratic Pride............ 591

CHAPTER XLV.
1817, OCTOBER, NOVEMBER, and DECEMBER.

Alarming Symptoms—The Restrictions relaxed—The Duke of Reichstadt deprived of his Inheritance—Napoleon's Command of himself—Libels—Continued Crimes of the Governor—The new House 597

CHAPTER XLVI.
1818.

Sad Condition of the Emperor—Remarks on the French Revolution—O'Meara insulted by the Governor—Contrast between Lowe and Cockburn—New Instructions from Lord Bathurst—Portraits of Napoleon's Son—Dr O'Meara again insulted by the Governor—Plans in the Invasion of England—Death of Cipriani—Gourgaud's Return to Europe—Departure of the Balcombes—O'Meara Imprisoned—O'Meara sent from the Island—Extension of Liberty—Dr. Stockoe.. 600

CHAPTER XLVII.
1819.

New Outrages—Departure of Madam Montholon—Noble Protest—Arrival of Dr. Antommarchi and the Ecclesiastics—Conversation with Antommarchi—The Books and the Portrait—Protest of Dr. Antommarchi—Corsica as a Retreat—Amiability of the Emperor—The Ancestry of Napoleon .... Page 612

CHAPTER XLVIII.
1820.

New-year's Day—Gardening Operations—Journal of the orderly Officer—Remarks on Waterloo and the Holy Alliance—Interview with the Daughter of Sir Hudson Lowe—Scenes at Fontainebleau—The Emperor's filial Affection—Birth-day Presents—Proposal for Escape—Aversion to Medicine—Public Works of the Emperor—The Fish-basin—Death of the Princess Eliza—Remarks on the Divorce—The Close of the Year 626

CHAPTER XLIX.
1821, JANUARY to MAY.

Completion of the new House—Lady Holland—Phrenology—Departure of Buonavita—Progress of the Disease—Remarks to Dr. Arnott—The Emperor's Will—Atheism—The last Letter—The Dying-scene—Burial—Departure of the Companions of Napoleon 635

LIST OF ILLUSTRATIONS.

	Page
1. Napoleon's Reception on board the Bellerophon	13
2. Searching the Emperor's Trunks	16
3. Farewell to France	17
4. Kleber Assassinated	22
5. The Trial Shot	24
6. Napoleon appealing to Gasparin	25
7. Napoleon and Junot	27
8. The First Dictation	28
9. The First Sight of St. Helena	29
10. The Northumberland and Myrmidon approaching St. Helena	29
11. The Rock of St. Helena	31
12. View of The Briers	31
13. Napoleon's Room	32
14. The Emperor and Las Casas at The Briers	37
15. Respect the Burden	40
16. Madam Montesquieu and the King of Rome	41
17. The Infernal Machine	47
18. Napoleon and poor Toby	50
19. Portrait of Josephine	51
20. View of Longwood	56
21. Plan of Longwood	58
22. Napoleon and the Farmer	61
23. The Emperor wounded at Ratisbonne	63
24. Napoleon descending the Ravine	66
25. The Sailors of the Northumberland visiting their Shipmate	69
26. The Drunken Sentinel	72
27. Battle of Austerlitz	80
28. Death of Lannes	81
29. Death of Duroc	82
30. The Emperor on the Cliff	84
31. Death of Murat	87
32. "Tyrannical Act of a Usurper"	89
33. The English Soldiers saluting the Emperor	91
34. Napoleon examining the Accounts	96
35. The Emperor and the Peasant Woman	100
36. The Game of Chess	104
37. Portrait of Marshal Ney	106
38. Portrait of the Empress Maria Louisa	111
39. The Emperor's Return to the Tuileries	115
40. Execution of Marshal Ney	118
41. The Emperor asleep at Wagram	121
42. Portrait of Marshal Soult	123
43. The Fanatic of Shoënbrunn	131
44. Portrait of Talleyrand	138
45. Napoleon receiving the Command from the Convention	140
46. The Emperor's Residence at Elba	144
47. Napoleon and Metternich in Council	153
48. The Emperor crossing Poland	157
49. The golden Acorn	159
50. "And yet they have dared to say that I could not write"	162
51. Interview with the Abbé de Pradt at Warsaw	165
52. The Retreat from Russia	168
53. The Bosphorus	170
54. The Birth-house of Napoleon	173
55. Napoleon's Apartment at Longwood	177
56. Interview with Sir Hudson Lowe	179
57. The Return of the Bourbons	182

LIST OF ILLUSTRATIONS.

	Page
58. The Returned Emigrant	184
59. Portrait of Charles Bonaparte, the Father of Napoleon	186
60. Napoleon and Hoche	189
61. The Captive and his Jailer	202
62. Portrait of Louis Bonaparte, the Brother of Napoleon	209
63. Portrait of Hortense, the Daughter of Josephine	210
64. Portrait of Madam Letitia, the mother of Napoleon	211
65. Portrait of Jerome Bonaparte, the Brother of Napoleon	213
66. Malmaison	222
67. Portrait of Carnot	223
68. Bay of Ajaccio, Corsica	226
69. Portrait of Lucien Bonaparte, the Brother of Napoleon	228
70. Arrest of George Cadoudal	232
71. The Emperor at Breakfast	262
72. Interview with the Spanish Princes	266
73. Torture-room of the Spanish Inquisition	268
74. The three Sovereigns at Tilsit	273
75. The Emperor dictating	276
76. Scenery at St. Helena	277
77. The Retreat from Waterloo	278
78. Napoleon chosen Corporal	288
79. The Sentinel and the Little Corporal	289
80. Honor to unfortunate Courage	292
81. The Emperor and Little Tristam	297
82. Portrait of Murat	301
83. The March through the Desert	316
84. The Ruins of Egypt	317
85. The Attack upon the Tuileries	328
86. Napoleon descending the Alps	334
87. Valley at St. Helena	339
88. The Coronation	348
89. The Conflagration of Moscow	363
90. The Emperor's Bivouac	367
91. Eylau after the Battle	372
92. The Emperor in the Wagoner's Shop	373
93. The Emperor dictating	388
94. Portrait of Joseph Bonaparte, the Brother of Napoleon	393
95. Napoleon incognito	421

	Page
96. The Emperor and the Market-woman	423
97. Baron Larrey	427
98. Portrait of Pauline the Sister of Napoleon	449
99. The Emperor contemplating Constantinople	452
100. The Infernal Machine	462
101. Napoleon at Montereau	465
102. The Bomb-shell	476
103. The Emperor examining the Fortifications	485
104. The Governor and his Aids	504
105. Arrest of Las Casas	505
106. Examining the Papers of Las Casas	507
107. The Fall of Moreau	520
108. Death of Bessières	521
109. Death of Poniatowski	535
110. Interview with Lord Whitworth	556
111. Napoleon	573
112. Adieu to O'Meara	610
113. Napoleon receiving the Portrait of his Son	618
114. The Emperor a Gardener	624
115. The Emperor Gardening	627
116. The Fish-basin	629
117. Portrait of Eliza, the Sister of Bonaparte	633
118. Napoleon with his Wife and Child	634
119. The embarrassed Interview	635
120. The new House	636
121. Chamber of Sickness	640
122. Napoleon dictating his last Letter	647
123. The Emperor receiving the Sacrament of the Lord's Supper	649
124. The Storm	651
125. The Dying-scene	652
126. Napoleon's Grave	656

LIST OF MAPS.

	Page
1. Siege of Toulon	26
2. The Turkish Empire	109
3. Map of Waterloo	279
4. St. Helena	290
5. Lower Egypt and Syria	550

NAPOLEON AT ST. HELENA.

CHAPTER I.

THE VOYAGE.

The Emperor seeks the Hospitality of England—Doomed to St. Helena—His Trunks searched—Removed to the *Northumberland*—The Russian Campaign—Adieu to France—Habits on Shipboard—Threatening Aspect of the Russian Power—The French Navy—Captain Wright—Character of Kleber and of Desaix—Napoleon at Toulon—Anecdotes—Napoleon in Italy—Anecdotes—The Little Corporal—Dictation—Approach to St. Helena.

ON the 15th of July, 1815, the Emperor Napoleon, pursued as an outlaw by all the combined monarchs of Europe for the crime of allowing himself to be chosen sovereign of France, and for heroically defending, in that capacity, the independence of his country, sought refuge under the protection of the laws of Great Britain. He was received by Captain Maitland on board the *Bellerophon*, and, with every mark of respect, was conveyed to England. The British ministry, trampling upon the English Constitution, and regardless of justice and humanity, without any trial, without any judicial accusation even, condemned the illustrious foreigner to imprisonment for life upon the dreary rock of St. Helena.

NAPOLEON'S RECEPTION ON BOARD THE BELLEROPHON.

On the 30th of July, Admiral Keith and Sir Henry Bunbury, under secretary of state, came on board the *Bellerophon*, which was then at anchor in the harbor of Plymouth, and informed the Emperor of his awful doom. Napoleon listened patiently to the reading of the atrocious document, which, in contempt of England's boasted laws, sentenced him, without a hearing, to the most dreadful punishment, and with calm dignity replied,

"I am the guest of England, not her prisoner. I have come of my own accord to place myself under the protection of English *law*. In my case, the government has violated the laws of its own country, the laws of nations, and the sacred duty of hospitality. I protest against their right to act thus, and appeal to British honor."

The friends of Napoleon who had accompanied him on board the *Bellerophon*, anticipating a peaceful retreat with their beloved Emperor either in England or America, were almost frantic with grief. Napoleon alone seemed calm, though very sad. Arrangements were energetically adopted by the English government to collect a squadron to convey the illustrious captive to his prison, and to guard him there.

August 3. The Emperor was conversing in his cabin with Las Casas. "What kind of a place is St. Helena?" said he. "Is it possible to endure life upon that island?" And then he added slowly, in solemn, thoughtful tones, "After all, am I quite sure of going there? Is a man dependent on others when he wishes that his dependence should cease?"

For some time, absorbed in silent anguish, he walked up and down the floor of his small cabin, and then continued,

"My friend, I have sometimes the wish to leave you. And that is not very difficult. It is only necessary to create a little mental excitement, and I shall soon have escaped. All will be over, and you can then tranquilly rejoin your families. This is the more easy, since my internal principles do not oppose any bar to it. I am of those who conceive that the pains of the other world were only imagined as a counterpoise to those inadequate allurements which are offered to us there. God can never have willed such a contradiction to his infinite goodness, especially for an act of this kind. And what is it, after all, but wishing to return to him a little sooner?"

Las Casas, with deep emotion, replied, "Poets and philosophers have said that it is a spectacle worthy of the Divinity to see men struggling against misfortune. Reverses and constancy have their glory. What will become of those who still place their hopes in you? Besides, who can tell the secrets of time, or dare assert what the future may produce?"

"Some of these suggestions have their weight," the Emperor mournfully replied, "but what can we do in that desolate place?"

"Sire," Las Casas replied, "we will live on the past. There is enough of it to satisfy us. Do we not enjoy the life of Cæsar and that of Alexander?"

"Be it so," the Emperor replied. "We will write our memoirs. Yes, we must be employed. Occupation is the scythe of time. After all, a man ought to fulfill his destinies; this is my grand doctrine. Let mine be accomplished."

From this moment the Emperor was himself again. These unworthy thoughts, so naturally suggested by anguish and despair, immediately passed away entirely and forever.

The English *people* were making great efforts to rescue the Emperor from the despotic lawlessness of the ministers, and to bring him under the protection of British law. The ministers, to frustrate their endeavors, ordered the *Bellerophon* to leave the harbor of Plymouth, and to anchor off Start Point. Here, upon the rough sea, where there was no shelter, the Emperor and his friends were kept waiting the arrival of the *Northumberland* and her convoy, by which they were to be conveyed six thousand miles to St. Helena.

August 5. The *Northumberland*, and several frigates filled with soldiers, arrived, and Admirals Keith and Cockburn came on board the *Bellerophon* to communicate to the Emperor the instructions they had received respecting his transportation to the island of his imprisonment. The Emperor was permitted to take, as the companions of his exile and captivity, Count Las Casas and Count Montholon, General Bertrand and General Gourgaud, with their families and servants. Dr. O'Meara, an Irish gentleman, surgeon on board the *Bellerophon*, with alacrity volunteered his services as the Emperor's physician. The wives and children of some of these gentlemen, and twelve servants of the household, increased the party of exiles to twenty-four.

The English government, refusing to recognize the right of popular suffrage, insisted upon stigmatizing the Emperor Napoleon, the elected monarch of France, as a *usurper*. They therefore ordered that his imperial title should never be acknowledged, but that he should be styled *General Bonaparte*. This insult to France, and to her Emperor, Napoleon constantly opposed with a calm and quiet dignity, which commanded the general respect and admiration even of his enemies.

Admiral Sir George Cockburn, who was in command of the squadron, a rough sailor, without any delicacy of character, is not ashamed to record,

"I went again to the *Bellerophon* to examine the baggage of the general, and of those who were to accompany him. At this proceeding he was extremely indignant. I, however, in conformity with my instructions, caused every thing to be inspected before I permitted an article to be sent on board the *Northumberland*. I detained four thousand Napoleons in gold ($20,000), which I delivered to Captain Maitland, to be by him transmitted to the Lords Commissioners of the Treasury."

August 7. The Emperor, however, was to-day transferred from the *Bellerophon* to the *Northumberland*. He appeared calm and even cheerful. He requested that the officers of the ship might be introduced to him, and greeted them with cordiality. At the dinner-table he ate with his accustomed appetite, and, conversed with perfect ease and freedom. Alluding to the Russian campaign, he said,

"I meant only to have refreshed my troops at Moscow for four or five days, and then to have marched for Petersburg. But the destruction of Moscow subverted all my projects. Nothing could be more horrible than this campaign. For several days together it appeared to me as if we were

SEARCHING THE EMPEROR'S TRUNKS.

marching through a sea of fire, owing to the constant succession of villages in flames, which arose in every direction as far as the eye could reach. This has by some been attributed to the French troops, but it was always done by the Russians. Many of our soldiers, however, lost their lives by endeavoring to pillage in the midst of the flames. The cold was so severe, that one night, after I had left the army to return to Paris, an entire half of my guard were frozen to death."

The subject of the French navy was introduced. The Emperor said,

"Before going to Elba, I had made preparations for having a navy of one hundred sail of the line. I had established a conscription for the navy, and the Toulon fleet was entirely manned and brought forward by people of this description. I ordered them positively to get under weigh and maneuver every day when the weather would permit, and to stand out occasionally to exchange long shots with the English ships. This was much remonstrated against by those about me, and cost me, at first, a great deal of money to repair the accidents which occurred from the want of maritime knowledge, such as the ships getting foul of each other, splitting their sails, and springing their masts. But even these accidents, I found, tended to improve the crews, and, therefore, I determined to continue to pay my money and to oblige them to persevere in that exercise."

"He appeared in good humor," says Admiral Cockburn, "chatted in a very good-natured mood with every body, and retired to his bed-room apparently as much at his ease as if he had belonged to the ship all his life."

August 9. The convoy set sail to-day for St. Helena. As the ships were making their way out of the British Channel, the coast of France for a moment emerged from the clouds which had concealed it. A spontaneous cry of "France! France!" burst from the lips of the grief-stricken exiles. The Emperor was silently and thoughtfully walking the deck. He stopped, gazed for a moment upon the dim outline of his beloved country, now fading from his eyes forever, and then, uncovering his head, bowed to the distant hills, and said, with deep emotion, "Land of the brave! I salute thee! Farewell! France, farewell!"

The emotion excited in every heart was electric. Even the English officers, moved by this sublime adieu, involuntarily uncovered their heads, respecting the grief of their illustrious captive.

FAREWELL TO FRANCE.

The voyage occupied sixty-seven days. The Emperor, as was his custom, adopted regular habits for the employment of his time. He breakfasted in his room, and passed the day, until five o'clock in the afternoon, in reading.

writing, or conversing with those of his companions whom he had invited to his cabin. He then dressed for dinner, and entered the saloon, where he frequently amused himself for half an hour with a game of chess. At five o'clock the admiral came to invite him to dinner. The Emperor had no taste for conviviality. He had seldom, during his extraordinarily laborious life, allowed himself more than fifteen minutes at the dinner-table. He ate very frugally, and of the most simple dishes. He was not a wine-drinker. The English custom of loitering away hour after hour at the wine was repugnant to him. Out of respect to the company, the Emperor remained at the table through the regular courses, which lasted for an hour. He then, after taking a cup of coffee, rose from his seat and went on deck. As the Emperor retired, the whole company rose, and continued standing until he had left the room. Some one of his suite, in turn, each day, accompanied him to the deck. He walked for an hour or two, conversing freely with his friends, and with any others whom he happened to encounter on board the ship.*

August 10. At the dinner-table the subject was introduced of the last war between England and the United States.

"Mr. Madison," said the Emperor, "was too late in declaring war. He never made any requisition on France for assistance. I would very readily have lent any number of line-of-battle ships Mr. Madison might have desired, if American seamen could have been sent to man them and carry them over. But the affairs of France beginning to go wrong about that period, it was out of my power to afford any other material assistance to the Federal government."

On another occasion, speaking of the Emperor Alexander, he said,

"Russia is much to be feared if Poland is not preserved as an independent nation, to be a barrier between that empire and the rest of Europe. I do not, however, think that Russia will succeed in making Poland an appendage to the empire. The Poles are too brave and too determined ever to be brought to submit quietly to what they considered a personal disgrace and a national humiliation.

"The only object I had in view in my Russian expedition, and all I should have asked had I been successful, was the independence of Poland. To that nation I intended leaving the free choice of their king, only recommending Poniatowski to them as worthy of such distinction. I intended, however, to make the Emperor of Russia engage to join firmly in the Continental system against commercial intercourse of any sort with England, until its government should be brought to agree to the independence of the seas."

One day the Emperor entered into conversation with the *master* of the vessel, whose rank as pilot did not admit him to the society of the admiral

---

* Sir George Cockburn records the event in the following terms, characteristic of the man : " Immediately after dinner to-day, the general got up, rather uncivilly, and went upon deck as soon as he had swallowed his coffee, and before all the rest of us were even served. This induced me to request particularly the remainder of the party to sit still; and he went out attended only by his mareschal, without the slightest further notice being taken of him. It is clear he is still inclined to act the sovereign occasionally ; but I can not allow it, and the sooner, therefore, he becomes convinced it is not to be admitted, the better."—*Diary of Rear-Admiral Sir George Cockburn,* p. 24.

and the general officers. Napoleon was much pleased with the character and intelligence of the man, and in conclusion said, "Come and dine with me tomorrow."

The astonished *master* replied, "The admiral and my captain will not be willing that a master should sit at their table."

"Very well," answered the Emperor; "if they do not, so much the worse for them. You shall dine with me in my cabin."

When the admiral rejoined the Emperor, and was informed of what had passed, he very courteously remarked that any one invited by General Bonaparte to the honor of sitting at his table was, by this circumstance alone, placed above all the rules of etiquette. The master was accordingly informed that he would be welcome to dinner the next day. This incident, so characteristic of the Emperor, at once won the affection of the whole ship's company.

September 1. The squadron was passing the Cape de Verd islands, though not in sight of the land. The Emperor was speaking to the admiral of his efforts to supply France with a navy suitable to the importance of its commercial relations.

"Unfortunately," said he, "I found nobody who understood me. During the expedition to Egypt I had cast my eyes on Decrés; his intelligence pleased me. I reckoned upon him for understanding and executing my projects with regard to the navy. I was mistaken. His passion was to form a police, and find out, by means of the smugglers, every web which your ministers or the intriguers of Hartwell were weaving against me. And then he always proceeded on a system of coterie, the navy of Brest against that of Toulon; no enlarged ideas; always the spirit of locality and of insignificant detail paralyzing my views. I was obliged to give myself great trouble in order to send a small squadron of frigates to drive your commerce from India and from the Antilles. The old routine always obtained the upper hand. I should have done you a great deal of mischief had I been obeyed; but I was too much taken up with land affairs to be able to think of the navy otherwise than occasionally. What I have done will be known if ever my correspondence with Decrés is published.

"The navy of Louis XVI. was no longer in existence when I took the government into my hands. The republic possessed only four vessels of the line. The taking of Toulon, the battle of the River Jenes in 1793, of Rochefort in 1794, and, finally, the battle of Aboukir, had given the death-blow to the navy. Well, notwithstanding the disaster of Trafalgar, which I owe solely to the disobedience of Admiral Villeneuve, I left to France one hundred vessels of the line, eighty thousand sailors and soldiers, and all this in a reign of ten years, and while I had to struggle with a coalition of the great powers of Europe.

"I ceded to England the sceptre of the seas, but I required that she should respect the French flag on the sea, as an Emperor of Austria and of Russia had learned from me to respect it on land. The treaty of Paris has destroyed all that I did for the navy. Centuries will perhaps elapse before my work is recommenced. Your power on sea no longer experiences any control. And if it is true that Louis XVIII. said that he owed his crown to the Prince Regent, the latter might say, with as much truth, ' I owe the empire of the seas to the Count d'Artois, who, at the instigation of Talleyrand, signed, without any necessity, the sacrifice of the finest squadrons France ever had.' In short, the treaty of Paris is such a betrayal of the French interest, that Louis XVIII. executed it as a thing done, but never ratified it with his signature."

Every day, when the weather permitted, the captain of one of the vessels of the squadron was invited to dine on board the *Northumberland.* There was a Captain Wright in command of the brig Griffin.

" Are you a relation," inquired the Emperor, " of the Captain Wright whom your libelers accuse me of having strangled ?"

" Yes, sire," he replied; " and I am curious to know the circumstances of his death."

" Well, I will tell you," the Emperor replied. " Captain Wright commanded the brig which, during four months, had been landing, on the steep shores of Biville, the accomplices of Georges, who had already figured in the plot of the infernal machine. They concealed themselves by day in farms or country houses, forming stations between Paris and the coast. They had a great deal of money, paid largely, and easily corrupted poor peasants. One named Makee de la Fouche, whom your ministers paid to favor conspiracies, but who had sold himself to my police, gave the first information respecting these disembarkments, and the secret object of the cruise of Captain Wright's brig.

" I was weary of all these intrigues, and resolved to put an end to them. I ordered the records of the police to be brought. One evening, when I was turning them over, I remarked, I know not why, the name of a young man called Gueral, who was a student of medicine. I ordered him to be immediately brought before a council of war, to be watched with care, and notice taken of all his words. My foresight was just. He confessed every thing after his condemnation to death, and, in order to gain his pardon, detailed all the smallest particulars of the plot. Savary received orders to proceed to the places indicated, accompanied by disguised gens d'armes. He surprised a party disembarking. At the same time, Captain Wright, a description of whom had been sent to all the different points of the coast, ventured to set his foot on land. He was immediately arrested, conducted to Paris, and imprisoned in the Temple.

" I might have had him included in the number of accomplices of Georges, and have had him judged and condemned along with them. I did not do it. I would have kept him in prison till the peace, but grief and remorse overwhelmed him; he committed suicide. And you English ought to be less astonished than any other people at such an occurrence, because, among you, suicide is almost a national habit. Your ministers seized this opportunity to accuse me of crime, as in the case of Pichegru, although they knew very well that Pichegru's presence before a criminal tribunal would have been a hundred times more advantageous to my cause than his death. But it mattered little to them to be false to their own consciences. It was one calumny more.

"Your ministers will not always be able to impose on the English people with respect to me. Sooner or later your nation will render me justice, and the English will be the first to take my part, and avenge the savage hatred of their ministers. Notwithstanding all their libels, I fear nothing for my renown. Posterity will render me justice. It will compare the good I have done with the faults which I have committed. I do not fear the result. If I had succeeded, I should die with the reputation of being the greatest man who ever existed. From being nothing, I became, by my own exertions, the most powerful monarch in the universe, without committing any crimes. If crime had been in accordance with my opinions, neither Louis XVIII. nor Ferdinand would now reign. Many times have their heads been offered me for a price, and their deaths have daily been put forward to me as advisable. I refused. I do not regret it. My ambition was great, I confess it, but it rested on the opinion of the masses. I have always thought that sovereignty resides in the people. The Empire, as I had organized it, was but a great republic. Called to the throne by the voice of the people, my maxim has always been, '*A career open to talent without distinction of birth.*' And it is for this system of equality that the European oligarchy detests me. And yet, in England, talents and great services raise a man to the highest rank. You should have understood me."

On another occasion the Emperor was speaking upon the influence of chance. "I am well aware," said he, "of the influence which chance usurps over our political determinations; and it is the knowledge of that circumstance which has always kept me free from prejudice, and rendered me very indulgent with regard to the party adopted by individuals in our political convulsions. To be a good Frenchman, or to wish to become so, was all I looked for in any one. The confusion of our troubles was like battles in the night time, when every man attacks his neighbor, and friends are often confounded with foes; but when daylight returns and order is restored, every one forgives the injury which he has sustained through mistake.

"Even for myself, how could I undertake to say that there might not have existed circumstances sufficiently powerful, notwithstanding my natural sentiments, to induce me to emigrate—the vicinity of the frontier, for instance, a friendly attachment, or the influence of a chief? In revolutions we can only speak with certainty of what we have done. It is silly to affirm that we could not have acted otherwise."

One day, speaking of Egypt, the Emperor regretted exceedingly that it had not remained in the hands of the French. "This would infallibly have been the case," said he, "had the country been defended by Kleber or Desaix. These were my most distinguished lieutenants. Both possessed great and rare merits, though their characters and dispositions were very different. Kleber's was the talent of nature. Desaix's was entirely the result of education and assiduity. The genius of Kleber was only called forth at particular moments, when roused by the importance of the occasion; and then it immediately slumbered again in the bosom of indolence and pleasure. The talent of Desaix was always in full activity. He lived only for noble ambition and true glory. His character was entirely unique. His death was the greatest loss I could have sustained. Their conformity of education and principles would always have preserved a good understanding between them. Desaix would have been contented with a secondary rank, and would have remained ever devoted and faithful. Had he not been killed at the battle of Marengo, I would have given him the command of the army of Germany, instead of continuing it to Moreau. A very extraordinary circumstance in the destiny of these two lieutenants was, that on the very day, and at the very hour when Kleber was assassinated at Cairo, Desaix was killed by a cannon ball at Marengo."

KLEBER ASSASSINATED

Speaking of his early career, the Emperor said, "My success at Toulon did not much astonish me. I enjoyed it with a lively satisfaction, unmingled with surprise. I was equally happy the following year at Saorgia, where my operations were admirable. I accomplished in a few days what had been attempted in vain for two years. Vendemiaire, and even Montenotte, never induced me to look upon myself as a man of a superior class. It was not till after Lodi that I was struck with the possibility of my becoming a decided actor on the scene of political events. Then was enkindled the first spark of a lofty ambition."

September 6. The Emperor related the following anecdote in reference to the capture of Toulon:

"On my arrival at head-quarters, I waited on General Cartaux, a haughty man, covered with gold lace from head to foot, who asked me what duty I had been sent upon. I presented him with the letter which directed me, under the general's command, to superintend the operations of the artillery.

"'This is quite unnecessary,' said the general, twisting his whiskers. 'We want no assistance to retake Toulon. But still you are welcome. You may share the glory of burning the town to-morrow, without having experienced any of the fatigue.'

"He invited me to sup with him. A party of thirty sat down at the table. The general alone was served like a prince, while every one else was almost dying of hunger; a circumstance which, in those days of equality, strangely shocked me. The next morning, at break of day, the general took me out in his cabriolet, to admire, as he said, the preparations for attack. As soon as he had crossed the height, and came within sight of the road and harbor, we got out of the carriage and threw ourselves down among some vines. I there perceived some pieces of ordnance and some digging, for which it was really impossible for me in the slightest degree to account.

"'Dupas,' said the general, haughtily, turning to his aid-de-camp, 'are those our batteries?'

"'Yes, general,' was the reply.

"'And where is our park?'

"'There, close at hand.'

"'And our red-hot balls?'

"'In yonder houses, where two companies have been employed all the morning heating them.'

"'But how shall we be able to carry these red-hot balls?'

"This consideration seemed to puzzle them both completely; and they turned to me to know whether, through my scientific knowledge, I could not explain how the thing was to be managed. I should have been much tempted to take the whole for a hoax had my interrogators evinced less simplicity, for the guns were more than a league and a half from the object of attack. I summoned, however, to my aid all the gravity I was master of, and endeavored to persuade them, before they troubled themselves about red-hot balls, to try the range of the shot with cold ones. After much trouble, I at length prevailed on them to try my advice, but not till I had very luckily made use of the technical term *coup d'epreuve*, which took their fancy and brought them over to my opinion. They then made the experiment, but the shot did not reach to a third of the distance required. The general and Dupas then began to abuse the aristocrats, who, they said, had maliciously spoiled the powder.

THE TRIAL SHOT.

"In the mean time, the representative of the people came up on horseback. This was Gasparin, an intelligent man, who had served in the army. Perceiving how things were going on, I immediately decided upon the course to pursue, and, assuming great confidence of manner, I urged the representative to intrust me with the whole direction of the affair. I exposed, without hesitation, the unparalleled ignorance of all who were about me, and from that moment took upon myself the entire direction of the siege."

"Cartaux," said Napoleon, "was a man of such limited intellect that it was impossible to make him understand that, to facilitate the taking of Toulon, it would be necessary to make the attack at the outlet of the road. When I sometimes pointed on the map to Little Gibraltar at this outlet, and told him there was Toulon, Cartaux suspected that I knew very little of geography; and when, in spite of his opposition, the authority of the representative decided upon the adoption of this distant point of attack, the general was haunted with the idea of treasonable designs, and would often remark, with great uneasiness, that Toulon did not lie in that direction.

"All my disputes with Cartaux usually took place in the presence of his wife, who uniformly took my part, saying to her husband, with great naïveté,

"'Let the young man alone. He knows more about it than you do, for he never asks your advice. Besides, are not you the responsible person? All the glory will be yours.'

"This woman," continued Napoleon, "was not without some share of good sense. On her return to Paris, after the recall of her husband, the Jac-

NAPOLEON APPEALING TO GASPARIN.

obins gave a splendid fête. In the course of the evening, the conversation happened to fall on the commandant of artillery at Toulon, who was enthusiastically praised.

" 'Do not reckon on him,' said she; 'that young man has too much understanding to remain long a *sans culotte*.'

" The general exclaimed, with the voice of a stentor, 'Woman Cartaux, would you make us all fools, then?'

" 'No, I don't say that, my dear; but I must tell you he is not one of your sort.'

" We were in possession of the town," continued the Emperor, "before the army had scarcely dreamed of it. After taking the Little Gibraltar, which I always looked upon as the key of the whole enterprise, I said to old Dugommier, who was worn out with fatigue, ' Go and rest yourself. We have taken Toulon. You may sleep there the day after to-morrow.' When Dugommier found the thing actually accomplished—when he reflected that the young commandant of artillery had always foretold exactly what would happen, he became all enthusiasm and admiration. He was never tired of praising him.

" It is true," continued Napoleon, " that Dugommier informed the committees of Paris that he had with him a young man who merited particular notice; for that, whichever side he might adopt, he was certainly destined to throw great weight into the balance. When Dugommier joined the army of the Eastern Pyrenees, he wished to take me with him; but this he was unable to do. He, however, spoke of me incessantly. At a subsequent period, when this army was sent to re-enforce the army of Italy, of which I soon after became general-in-chief, I found, on my arrival, that, in consequence of all Dugommier had said, the officers had scarcely eyes enough to look at me.

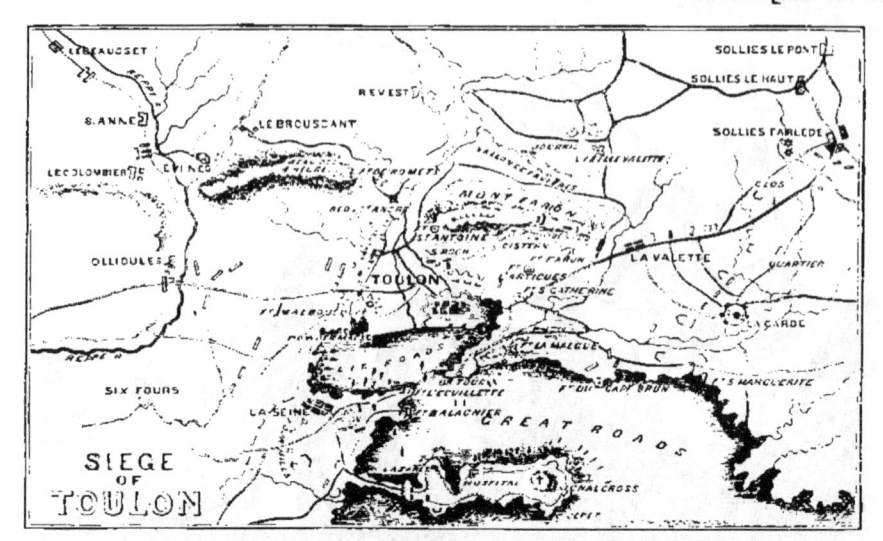

"At the army of Nice," said the Emperor, "there was a representative whose wife was an exceedingly pretty and fascinating woman. She shared and even usurped his authority. Both husband and wife became extremely fond of me, and treated me in the handsomest manner. This was to me, at that time, during the absence or the inefficiency of the laws, a great advantage. A representative of the people was a man of immense power. I was very young when I first knew this lady. I was proud of the favorable impression I had made on her, and seized every opportunity of showing her attention. I will mention one circumstance, to show for what trivial causes men sometimes abuse the authority on which the fate of their fellow-creatures depends, for I am no worse than the rest. I was walking about, one day, with the representative's wife, inspecting our positions, when the idea occurred to me of giving her the spectacle of a skirmish, and I ordered the attack of an advanced post. We were conquerors, it is true, but the affair could be attended by no advantage. The attack was a mere whim, and yet it cost the lives of several men. Whenever the memory of that deed recurs to me, I reproach myself bitterly.

"During the erection of one of the first batteries against the English," continued the Emperor, "on my arrival at Toulon, I asked whether there was a sergeant or corporal present who could write. A man advanced from the ranks, and wrote to my dictation on the epaulement. The note was scarcely ended, when a cannon ball, which had been fired in the direction of the bat-

NAPOLEON AND JUNOT.

tery, fell near the spot, and the paper was immediately covered by the loose earth thrown up by the ball. 'Well,' said the writer, 'I shall have no need of sand.' This remark, together with the coolness with which it was made, fixed my attention, and made the fortune of the sergeant. This man was Junot, afterward Duke of Abrantes. He died the victim of the intemperance which destroyed both his health and his reason.

"On taking the command of the army of Italy," continued the Emperor, "Napoleon, notwithstanding his extreme youth, immediately impressed the troops with a spirit of subordination, confidence, and the most absolute devotedness. The army was subdued by his genius rather than seduced by his popularity. He was, in general, very severe and reserved. During the whole course of his life, he uniformly disdained to court the favor of the multitude by unworthy means. A singular custom was established in the army of Italy in consequence of the youth of the commander, or from some other cause. After each battle, the oldest soldiers used to hold a council and confer a new rank on their young general, who, when he made his appearance in the camp, was received by the veterans and saluted with his new title. They made him *corporal* at Lodi, and sergeant at Castiglione. Hence the name of *Little Corporal*, which was for so long a time applied to Napoleon by the soldiers. How subtile is the train which unites the most trivial circumstances to the most important events! Perhaps this very nickname contributed to his miraculous success on his return from Elba. While he was haranguing the first battalion, which he found it necessary to address, a voice from the ranks exclaimed, 'Long live our Little Corporal. We will never fight against him.'"

September 9. The Emperor determined to beguile the weary hours by dictating a memoir of his campaigns. To-day he called Las Casas into his cabin, and dictated, for the first time, some details respecting the siege of Toulon. "When the Emperor," Las Casas afterward wrote, "commenced his daily dictations, he always complained that the circumstances to which he wished to recur were no longer familiar to him. After considering a few moments, he would rise and walk about, and then begin to dictate. From that moment he was quite another man. Every thing flowed smoothly. He spoke as if by inspiration. Places, phrases, dates—he stopped at nothing."

THE FIRST DICTATION.

October 15. On the evening of the 14th the island of St. Helena was dimly discerned in the distant horizon. The ship lay to all night. The Emperor went to the bows of the ship early the next morning, and gazed long and in silence upon the gloomy shores of his prison. As they drew nearer, the blackened crags, hove from the ocean by volcanic fires, towered in sombre majesty to the clouds. A straggling village was seen planted upon rocks, and surrounded by bleak, precipitous, verdureless hills. Every platform among the rocks, every aperture, the brow of every hill, was planted with cannon. "I stood behind him," says Las Casas. "My eyes were constantly fixed on his countenance, in which I could perceive no change. And yet he saw before him perhaps his perpetual prison—perhaps his grave! How much then remained for me to feel and to witness! The Emperor soon left the deck. He desired me to come to him, and we proceeded to our usual occupation."

THE FIRST SIGHT OF ST. HELENA.

The vessels of the squadron had been scattered during the voyage, and the *Northumberland*, with but one accompanying ship, approached the island. At noon on the 15th of October, 1815, they cast anchor in the little harbor of Jamestown.

THE NORTHUMBERLAND AND MYRMIDON APPROACHING ST. HELENA.

CHAPTER II.

RESIDENCE AT THE BRIERS.

Description of St. Helena—The Ride to Longwood—Description of The Briers—The Youth of France—Deplorable Condition of the Exiles—Indignation of the Emperor—Note to the English Government—Overtures of the Bourbons—Suppression of the Tribunate—Character of the Senate—Anecdotes—Institute of Meudon—Candor of the Emperor—The Malay Slave—Popular Education—Fatality of the Emperor's Career—Treatment of the Spanish Princes.

ON the 16th of October, in the dusk of the evening, the Emperor landed at St. Helena. He had chosen that hour to avoid the gaze of the curious crowd. Before leaving the ship, he bade a friendly adieu to the captain, and requested him to convey his thanks to the officers and the crew. The whole ship's company assembled, with respectful and friendly feelings, upon the gangway and the quarter-deck, to witness his departure. Tears of sympathy were in many eyes. In the gloom of the approaching night he was rowed to the shore, and walked through the craggy streets of the miserable village of Jamestown to a small unfurnished room which had been obtained for him. His friends had brought from the ship his camp bedstead and a few other articles of furniture. The inhabitants of Jamestown crowded the streets. Sentinels, with their muskets, guarded the windows and door of the prisoner. The Emperor, weary and sad, soon dismissed his attendants, and was left to the solitude of his own thoughts.

St. Helena is one of the most dreary of the rocks of the ocean. Bleak, blackened, storm-battered crags pierce the clouds. Wild ravines, desolate and verdureless, wind along among the overhanging cliffs. The island is six thousand miles from Europe, and twelve hundred miles from the nearest point of land. The rock is ten miles long and six broad, and every craggy projection, every aperture, and the brow of every hill, seemed planted with cannon. The island at this time contained about five hundred inhabitants, about two hundred of whom were soldiers. There were also three hundred slaves. The imprisonment of Napoleon upon the island increased the population to between four and five thousand. Nearly three thousand soldiers were thought necessary to guard his room, while a squadron of ships, well manned with sailors and marines, cruised around the shores.

October 17. At an early hour this morning, the Emperor, accompanied by Las Casas and Sir George Cockburn, rode to an elevated plain, called Longwood, fifteen hundred feet above the level of the sea, which he was informed had been selected as the place of his future residence. Hardly any thing can be conceived more cheerless and repulsive than was the scene here presented. A small and dilapidated one-story house, which had originally been a cowshed, but which had been subsequently fitted up as a summer retreat for the governor for a few weeks during the year, was the mansion which was to be

THE ROCK OF ST. HELENA.

prepared for Napoleon and his twenty-two companions and servants. The Emperor gazed sadly and silently upon his awful doom.

As he was returning, in extreme dejection, to his miserable lodgings in the

VIEW OF THE BRIERS.

narrow street of Jamestown, where a crowd was continually gazing at his window, he passed a small farm-house, occupying a very solitary position in a secluded valley. Eagerly he inquired if he could not obtain accommodations there until the dilapidated hut at Longwood had received those repairs which were essential to render it habitable. A very worthy man, Mr. Balcombe, resided at this place, which was called The Briers. Though his little cottage contained but five rooms, all of which were needed for the accommodation of his family, he cheerfully offered the hospitality of his house to the illustrious captive. A few yards from the dwelling-house there was, in the garden, a little arbor or summer-house, consisting of one room on the ground floor and two small garrets. Napoleon, unwilling to incommode the family, selected this humble room for his abode.

The room was square, having two doors facing each other on two of its sides, and two windows, one on each of the other sides. These windows had neither curtains nor shutters. As the Emperor took possession of this empty apartment, night was again darkening over the island. Soon his valets brought in his iron bedstead and one or two chairs. It was necessary for the Emperor to go out of doors while they were preparing his room. At last the Emperor retired. Las Casas, with his son, climbed to one of the garrets, which was seven feet square. The two valets, wrapped in their cloaks, slept upon the ground before the doors. Such was the first night at the Briers.

NAPOLEON'S ROOM.

The mode of life immediately instituted at the Briers was as follows: The Emperor rose very early, and took a short walk before his door, and then read till breakfast, about ten o'clock. Las Casas usually breakfasted with him. Las Casas then read over what had been dictated the preceding day. The Emperor corrected the copy, and then continued his dictation until five o'clock. The Emperor usually then descended, with his secretary, to the lower walk, and, slowly pacing up and down for one hour, engaged in social conversation. He was, at such times, very frank and unreserved. At six he returned again to his room to dine. Some of his friends were generally present, and the conversation was prolonged after dinner until bedtime. "The days," says Las Casas, "were very long, and the evenings still longer." Occasionally, the Emperor, to beguile an hour of the evening, would call in at Mr. Balcombe's and converse with the amiable family.

October 20. The Emperor invited the son of Las Casas to dine with him. In examining some ancient medals, he requested the young Las Casas to translate the inscription. The well-educated lad did it without difficulty. Napoleon was highly gratified, and turning to his father, said, "What a rising generation I leave behind me! This is all my work. The memory of the French will be a sufficient revenge to me. On beholding the work, all must do justice to the workman, and the perverted judgment or bad faith of declaimers must fall before my deeds. If I had thought only of myself and securing my own power, as has been continually asserted, I should have endeavored to hide learning under a bushel, instead of which, I devoted myself to the propagation of knowledge. And yet the youth of France have not enjoyed all the benefits which I intended they should. My university, according to the plan I had conceived, was a masterpiece in its combinations, and would have been such in its national results. But an evil-disposed person spoiled all, and in so doing he was actuated by the worst of feelings, and, doubtless, by a calculation of consequences."

October 23. The deprivations and sufferings to which the Emperor was exposed were very great, and though he generally endured them in silence, he felt them severely. He had but one room, a few feet square, and he was obliged to go out when he had the wretched apartment cleaned. His meals were brought to him a mile and a half from Jamestown. Good articles of food could not be obtained. He was separated from his friends and servants, and their intercourse was interrupted by a vexatious system of passports. This morning several of his friends were gathered around him, and all felt the oppression of their dreadful lot. The Emperor exclaimed, "This is the anguish of death. To injustice and violence they now add insult and protracted torment. If I were so hateful to them, why did they not get rid of me? A few musket balls in my heart or my head would have been sufficient. There would, at least, have been some energy in the crime. Were it not for you, and, above all, for your wives, I would receive nothing from them but the pay of a private soldier. How can the monarchs of Europe permit the sacred character of sovereignty to be violated in my person? Do they not see that they are, with their own hands, working their own destruction at St. Helena? I entered their capital victorious, and, had I cherished such sentiments, what would have become of them? They styled me their brother, and I had become so by the choice of the people, the sanction of victory, the character of religion, and the alliances of their policy and their blood. Do they imagine that the good sense of nations is blind to their conduct? And what do they expect from it? At all events, make your complaints, gentlemen. Let indignant Europe hear them. Complaints from me would be beneath my dignity and character. I must command or be silent."

October 24. An English officer gently opened the door of the Emperor's single room, and, without further ceremony, entered. His intentions, however, were kind. He was about to return to Europe, and came to inquire if the Emperor had any commands. The Emperor requested him to communicate the following sentiments to the British government. Las Casas made a memorandum of the glowing remarks thus uttered, and placed them in the hands of the British officer:

"The Emperor desires, by the return of the next vessel, to receive some account of his wife and son, and to be informed whether the latter is still living. He takes this opportunity of repeating, and conveying to the British government, the protestations which he has already made against the extraordinary measures adopted toward him.

"1st. That government has declared him a prisoner of war. The Emperor is not a prisoner of war. His letter to the Prince Regent, which he wrote and communicated to Captain Maitland before he went on board the *Bellerophon*, sufficiently proves to the whole world the resolutions and the sentiments of confidence which induced him freely to place himself under the English flag.

"The Emperor might, had he pleased, have agreed to quit France only on stipulated conditions with regard to himself. But he disdained to mingle personal considerations with the great interests with which his mind was constantly occupied. He might have placed himself at the disposal of the Emperor Alexander, who had been his friend, or of the Emperor Francis, who was his father-in-law; but, confiding in the justice of the English nation, he desired no other protection than its laws afforded, and, renouncing public affairs, he sought no other country than that which was governed by fixed laws independent of private will.

"2d. Had the Emperor really been a prisoner of war, the rights which civilized governments possess over such a prisoner are limited by the law of nations, and terminate with the war itself.

"3d. If the English government considered the Emperor, though arbitrarily, as a prisoner of war, the right of that government was then limited by public law, or else, as there existed no cartel between the two nations during the war, it might have adopted toward him the principle of savages, who put their prisoners to death. This proceeding would have been more humane, and more conformable to justice, than that of sending him to this horrible rock. Death, inflicted on board the *Bellerophon* in the Plymouth Roads, would have been a blessing compared with the treatment to which he is now subjected.

"We have traveled over the most desolate countries of Europe, but none is to be compared to this barren rock. Deprived of every thing that can render life supportable, it is calculated only to renew perpetually the anguish of death. The first principles of Christian morality, and that great duty imposed on man to pursue his fate, whatever it may be, may withhold him from terminating with his own hand a wretched existence. The Emperor glories in being superior to such a feeling. But if the British ministers should persist in their course of injustice and violence toward him, he would consider it a happiness if they would put him to death."

October 31. In conversation, allusion was made to the report that the Emperor had at one time made proposals to the Bourbons to abdicate the throne in his favor, which statement had been widely circulated through Europe. The Emperor remarked,

"The truth is, I never bestowed a thought on the princes. You who were abroad seemed to have no idea of the opinions of those at home. Even if I had been favorably disposed toward the princes, it would not have been in my power to carry my intentions into execution. I, however, received overtures both from Mittau and London.

"The king wrote me a letter, which was conveyed to me by Lebrun, who had it from the Abbé de Montesquieu, the secret agent of the prince at Paris. This letter, which was written in a very labored style, contained the following paragraph:

"'You delay long to restore me to my throne. It is to be feared that you may allow favorable moments to escape. You can not complete the happiness of France without me, nor can I serve France without you. Hasten, then, and specify the places which you would wish your friends to possess.'

"To this the First Consul replied, 'I have received your royal highness's letter. I have always felt deep interest in your misfortunes and those of your family. You must not think of appearing in France. You could not do so without passing over a hundred thousand dead bodies. I shall, however, be always eager to do every thing that may tend to alleviate your fate or to enable you to forget your misfortunes.'

"The overtures made by the Count d'Artois possessed still more elegance and address. He commissioned, as the bearer of them, the Duchess de Guiche, a lady whose fascinating manners and personal graces were calculated to assist her in the important negotiation. She easily got access to Madam Bonaparte, with whom all the individuals of the old court came naturally in contact. She breakfasted with her at Malmaison, and the conversation turning on London, the emigrants, and the French princes, Madam de Guiche mentioned that, as she happened, a few days before, to be at the house of the Count d'Artois, she had heard some person ask the prince what he intended to do for the First Consul in the event of his restoring the Bourbons, and that the prince replied,

"'I would immediately make him constable of the kingdom, and every thing else he might choose. But even that would not be enough. We would raise on the Carrousel a lofty and magnificent column, surmounted with a statue of Bonaparte crowning the Bourbons.'

"As soon as the First Consul entered, which he did very shortly after breakfast, Josephine eagerly repeated to him the circumstance which the duchess had related.

" 'And did you not reply,' said her husband, 'that the corpse of the First Consul would have been made the pedestal of the column?'

"The charming duchess was still present. The beauties of her countenance, her eyes, and her words, were directed to the success of her mission. She said that she was so delighted she did not know how she should ever be able sufficiently to acknowledge the favor which Madam Bonaparte had procured her, of seeing and hearing so distinguished a man, so great a hero. It was all in vain. The Duchess de Guiche received orders that very night to quit Paris. The charms of the emissary were too well calculated to alarm Josephine to induce her to say any thing very urgent in her favor, and the next day the duchess was on her way to the frontier.

"It is, however, absolutely false that I, on my part, made overtures to the princes touching the cession of their rights. How was such a thing possible? I, who could only reign by the very principle which excluded them—that of the sovereignty of the people—how could I have sought to possess through them rights which were proscribed in their persons? That would have been to proscribe myself. The absurdity would have been too palpable, too ridiculous. It would have ruined me forever in public opinion. The fact is, that neither directly nor indirectly, at home or abroad, did I ever do any thing of the kind. And this will, no doubt, in the course of time, be the opinion of all persons of judgment, who allow me to have been neither a fool nor a madman.

"The prevalence of this report, however, induced me to seek to discover what could have given rise to it, and these are the facts which I collected. At the period of the good understanding between France and Prussia, and while that state was endeavoring to ingratiate herself in our favor, she caused inquiry to be made whether France would take umbrage at her allowing the French princes to remain in the Prussian territories, to which the French government answered in the negative. Emboldened by this reply, Prussia next inquired whether we should feel any great repugnance to furnishing them, through her medium, with an annual allowance. To this our government also replied in the negative, provided that Prussia would be responsible for their remaining quiet, and abstaining from all intrigue. The affair being thus set on foot, and the negotiation in train, Heaven knows what the zeal of some agent, or even the doctrines of the court of Berlin, which did not accord with ours, may have proposed. This furnished, no doubt, the motive and pretext, if, indeed, any really existed, for the fine letter of Louis XVIII., to which all the members of his family so ostentatiously adhered. The French princes eagerly seized that opportunity of reviving the interest and attention of Europe, which had been, by this time, totally withdrawn from them."

In front of Mr. Balcombe's house there was a walk, as will be seen in the plate, bordered by a few stunted trees. The Emperor frequently descended by the steep path to this walk for an hour before dinner. Here he was sometimes joined by Mrs. Balcombe and her two little daughters. The servants took this opportunity to make his bed and put his room in order.

THE EMPEROR AND LAS CASAS AT THE BRIERS.

November 1. As the Emperor was slowly pacing the walk in front of the house with Las Casas, the subject of the suppression of the Tribunate was introduced.

"It is certain," said Napoleon, "that the Tribunate was absolutely useless, while it cost nearly half a million. I therefore suppressed it. I was well aware that an outcry would be raised against the violation of the law. But I was strong. I possessed the full confidence of the people, and I considered myself a reformer. This, at least, is certain, that I did all for the best. I should, on the contrary, have created the Tribunate had I been hypocritical or evil-disposed; for who can doubt that it would have adopted and sanctioned, when necessary, my views and intentions? But that is what I never sought after in the whole course of my administration. I never purchased any vote or decision by promises, money, or places. And if I administered favors to ministers, counselors of state, and legislators, it was because these were things to give away, and it was natural, and even just, that they should be dealt out among those whose avocations brought them in contact with me.

"In my time all constituted bodies were pure and irreproachable, and I can firmly declare that they acted from conviction. If those bodies were condemned, it was by persons who knew them not, or wished not to know them; and the reproaches which were leveled at them must be attributed to the discontent or opposition of the time, and, above all, to that spirit of detraction and ridicule which is so peculiarly natural to the French people.

"The Senate has been much abused. Great outcry has been raised against its servility and baseness; but declamation is not proof. What was the Senate expected to do? To refuse conscripts? Was it wished that the committees of personal liberty and the liberty of the press should have brought disgrace upon the government? The truth is, that we were placed in forced and unnatural circumstances. Men of understanding knew this, and accommodated themselves to the urgency of the moment. It is not known that, in almost every important measure, the senators, before they gave their vote, came to communicate to me privately, and sometimes very decidedly, their objections and even their refusal; and they went away convinced, either by my arguments, or by the necessity and urgency of affairs. If I never gave publicity to this fact, it was because I governed conscientiously, and because I despised quackery and every thing like it.

"The votes of the Senate were always unanimous, because the conviction was universal. Endeavors were made, at the time, to cry up an insignificant minority, whom the hypocritical praises of malevolence, together with their own vanity, or some other perversity of character, excited to harmless opposition. But did the individuals composing that minority evince, in the last crisis, either sound heads or sincere hearts? I once more repeat that the character of the Senate was irreproachable; the moment of its fall was alone disgraceful and culpable. Without right, without power, and in violation of every principle, the Senate surrendered France and accomplished her ruin. That body was the sport of high intrigues, whose interest it was to discredit and degrade it, and to ruin one of the great bases of the modern system. It may be truly said that they succeeded completely, for I know of no body that can be recorded in history with more ignominy than the French Senate. However, it is but just to observe, that the stain rests not on the majority, and that among the delinquents there was a multitude of foreigners, who will henceforth, at least, be indifferent to our honor and interests."

The incessant annoyances and absurd regulations to which the exiles were exposed led the Emperor to request Las Casas to draw up a note upon the subject, to be presented to the admiral. The grand marshal, General Bertrand, was commissioned to convey this protest to Sir George Cockburn, and to discuss its contents with him. General Bertrand, however, apprehending that the note would not accomplish the desired result, ventured not to fulfil his mission. A fortnight passed away, when the Emperor learned, to his astonishment, that the grand marshal had not delivered the note. The displeasure of the Emperor was visible, yet he said mildly to General Bertrand,

"Your not delivering the note, if you were dissatisfied with its tenor, or if you regarded it as dictated by an impulse of anger, was a proof of your devotion to my interests. But this should only have been a delay of some hours. After this delay, you ought to have spoken to me on the subject. You well know that I should have listened to you with attention, and should have agreed with your opinions if you had proved to me that you were in the right. But to delay a fortnight without telling me that you did not execute the mission, this is inexplicable. What have you to reply?"

The grand marshal only answered by the respectful assurance that he thought that he had done well in not delivering the note, which he disliked, both as to its composition and its intention. The Emperor, after a moment of profound and silent thought, replied,

"You are right, Bertrand! Let these gentlemen make their complaints. Mine are below my dignity and my character. I command or am silent."

November 6–8. The Emperor spoke of the generals of the army of Italy. "Massena," said he, "was endowed with extraordinary courage and firmness, which seemed to increase in excess of danger. When conquered, he was always as ready to fight the battle again as though he had been the conqueror. Augereau was a cross-grained character. He seemed to be tired and disheartened by victory, of which he always had enough. His person, his manner, and his language gave him the air of a braggadocio, which, however, he was far from being. He was satiated with honors and riches, which he had received at all hands and in all ways. Serrurier, who retained the manners and severity of an old major of infantry, was an honest and trustworthy man, but a bad general."

The Emperor could not ride out on horseback unless accompanied by a British officer in the capacity of a guard and a spy. Rather than submit to such an indignity, he silently relinquished the healthful exercise. Las Casas, alarmed in view of the declining health of the Emperor, inquired of the officer if it would be necessary for him to observe his instructions literally in case the Emperor merely took a ride round the house. The officer replied that his instructions were to follow General Bonaparte whenever he mounted his horse, but that he would take the responsibility of allowing him to ride unaccompanied in the paths immediately around the house. Las Casas, at the breakfast-table, communicated the conversation to Napoleon. He replied,

"I can not avail myself of the indulgence. It is not conformable with my sentiments to enjoy an advantage which may be the means of compromising an officer."

In this decision the Emperor acted with his accustomed wisdom, as well as in accordance with his instinctive magnanimity. The officer that very evening, much mortified, hastened to inform Las Casas that the admiral had ordered him to obey his instructions literally. Las Casas mentioned the incident to the Emperor. He seemed to have expected it, and mildly replied that the horses might as well be returned, as he could have no farther use for them. Las Casas could not conceal his indignation at such treatment on the part of the admiral, and said, with warmth, "I will go immediately and order them to be sent back."

"No, sir," the Emperor replied, with peculiar gravity of voice; "you are now out of temper. It rarely happens that any thing is done well under such circumstances. It is always best to let the night pass over after the offense of the day."

November 10. The Emperor, with his secretary, after his usual task of dictation was ended, walked out a short distance toward the town. As he was returning, he met Mrs. Balcombe, and a Mrs. Stuart, an English lady, about twenty years of age, who was returning from Bombay to England. The Emperor conversed with her respecting the manners and customs of India, and the inconveniences of a sea voyage. As they were talking, some slaves, carrying heavy burdens, came along the narrow path. Mrs. Balcombe, in rather an angry tone, ordered them to keep back. But the Emperor interfered in their behalf, saying,

"Respect the burden, madam."

Mrs. Stuart, who had been attentively observing the Emperor's features, exclaimed, in a low tone of voice, to her friend, "What a countenance, and what a character! How different from what I had been led to expect!"

RESPECT THE BURDEN.

November 13. "Madam de Montesquieu," said the Emperor, "was a woman of singular merit. Her piety was sincere, and her principles excellent. She had the highest claims on my esteem and regard. I wanted half a dozen like her. I would have given them all appointments equal to their deserts. She discharged her duties admirably when with my son at Vienna.

"The apartments of the young prince at the Tuileries were on the ground floor, and looked out on the court. At almost every hour of the day, numbers of people were looking in at the window in the hope of seeing him. One day, when he was in a violent fit of passion, and rebelling furiously against the authority of Madam de Montesquieu, she immediately ordered all the shutters to be closed. The child, surprised at the sudden darkness, asked Maman Quieu, as he used to call her, what it all meant. 'I love you too well,' she replied, 'not to hide your anger from the crowd in the court-yard. You, perhaps, will one day be called to govern all those people, and what would they say if they saw you in such a fit of rage? Do you think they would ever obey you if they knew you to be so wicked?' Upon which the child asked her pardon, and promised never again to give way to such fits of anger.

"This," the Emperor continued, "was language very different from that addressed by M. de Villeroi to Louis XV. 'Behold all those people, my prince,' said he; 'they belong to you. All the men you see yonder are yours.'"

The Emperor had thought much upon the education of the King of Rome. For this purpose he had decided on the "Institute of Meudon." There he proposed to assemble the princes of the imperial house, particularly the sons

MADAM MONTESQUIEU AND THE KING OF ROME.

of those branches of the family who had been raised to foreign thrones. In this institution he intended that the princes should receive the attentions of private tuition, combined with the advantages of public education.

"These children," said he, "who were destined to occupy different thrones and to govern different nations, would thus have acquired conformity of principles, manners, and ideas. The better to facilitate the amalgamation and uniformity of the federative parts of the empire, each prince was to bring with him, from his own country, ten or twelve youths about his own age, the sons of the first families in the state. What an influence would they not have exercised on their return home! I doubted not but that the princes of other dynasties, unconnected with my family, would soon have solicited, as a great favor, permission to place their sons in the Institute of Meudon. What advantages would thence have arisen to the nations composing the European association! All these young princes would have been brought together early enough to obviate the fatal effects of rising passions, the ardor of partiality, the ambition of success, the jealousy of love.

"I wished to have the education of the princes founded on general information, extended views, summaries, and results. They should possess knowledge rather than learning, judgment rather than attainments. I prefer the application of details to the study of theories. Above all, I would not have them pursue any particular study too deeply; for perfection, or too great success in certain things, whether in the arts or sciences, is a disadvantage to a prince. A nation will never gain much by being governed by a poet, a virtuoso, a naturalist, a turner, a locksmith."

Speaking of Maria Louisa, the Emperor said,

"She confessed to me that, when her marriage was first proposed, she could not help feeling a kind of terror, owing to the accounts she had heard of me from the individuals of her family. When she mentioned these reports to her uncles the archdukes, who were very urgent for the marriage, they replied, ' That was all very true while he was our enemy, but the case is altered now.'

"To afford an idea of the sympathy and good-will with which the different members of the Austrian family were taught to regard me, it is sufficient to mention that one of the young archdukes frequently burned his dolls, which he called *roasting Napoleon*. He afterward declared he would not roast me any more, for he loved me very much, because I had given his sister Louisa plenty of money to buy him playthings."

In this connection Las Casas remarks,

"Since my return to Europe, I have had an opportunity of ascertaining the sentiments entertained by the house of Austria toward Napoleon. In Germany, a person of distinction informed me that, having had a private audience of the Emperor Francis during his tour in Italy in 1816, the conversation turned on Napoleon. Francis spoke of him in the most respectful terms. One might almost have supposed, said my informant, that he still regarded him as the ruler of France, and that he was ignorant of his captivity at St. Helena. He never alluded to him by any other title than the Emperor Napoleon. The Archduke John visited a rotunda, on the ceiling of which was painted a celebrated action of which Napoleon was the hero. As he raised his head to look at the painting, his hat fell off, and one of his attendants stooped to pick it up. 'Let it be,' said he; 'it is thus that I should contemplate the man who is there portrayed.' "

November 14. "Vanity," said the Emperor, "was the ruin of Marmont. Posterity will justly cast a shade upon his character. Yet his heart will be more valued than the memory of his career. The conduct of Augereau was the result of his want of information and of the baseness of those who surrounded him; that of Berthier, of his want of spirit and of the absolute nullity of character."

"Berthier," said Las Casas, "lost the best opportunity for rendering himself forever illustrious by frankly rendering his submission to the king, and entreating his majesty's permission to withdraw from the world."

"Yes," the Emperor replied; "but even this step, simple as it was, was beyond his power."

"His talents, his understanding," said Las Casas, "had always been a subject of doubt with us. Your majesty's choice, your confidence, your great attachment, surprised us exceedingly."

"Nevertheless," the Emperor replied, "Berthier was not without talents. I am far from wishing to disavow his merit, or my partiality for him. But his talent and merit were special and technical. Beyond a limited point he had no mind whatever; and then he was so undecided."

"He was, notwithstanding," said Las Casas, "full of pretensions and pride in his conduct toward us; he was very harsh and overbearing."

"Do you think, then," the Emperor added, "that the title of Favorite stands for nothing? But nothing is more imperious than feebleness that feels itself protected by strength. Look at women, for example.

"Berthier accompanied me in my carriage during my campaigns. As we drove along, I examined the order-book and the report of the positions, whence I formed my plans and arranged the necessary movements. Berthier noted down the directions, and at the first station, or during the first moments allotted to rest, whether by night or by day, he made out, in his turn, all the orders and individual details with admirable regularity, precision, and despatch. This was the special merit of Berthier. It was most valuable to me. No other talent could have made up for the want of it."

Las Casas records in this place, "And here I must observe, that since I have become acquainted with the Emperor's character, I have never known him to evince, for a single moment, the least feeling of anger or animosity against those individuals who have been most to blame in their conduct toward him. He gives no great credit to those who distinguished themselves by their good conduct; they had only done their duty. He is not very indignant against those who acted basely, attributing their conduct, in some measure, to existing circumstances, which he acknowledged were of a very perplexing nature, and threw the rest to the account of human weakness.

"He invariably speaks with perfect coolness, without passion, without prejudice, and without resentment, of the events and the persons connected with his life. He seems as though he could be equally capable of becoming the ally of his most cruel enemy, and of living with the man who had done him the greatest wrong. He speaks of his past history as if it had occurred three centuries ago; in his recitals and his observations he speaks the language of past ages. He is like a spirit discoursing in the Elysian Fields; his conversations are true dialogues of the dead. He speaks of himself as of a third person; noticing the Emperor's actions, pointing out the faults with which history may reproach him, and analyzing the reasons and the motives which might be alleged in his justification.

"He can never excuse himself, he says, by throwing blame on others, since he never followed any but his own decision. He may complain, at the worst, of false information, but never of bad counsel. He surrounded himself with the best possible advisers, but he always adhered to his own opinion, and he was far from repenting of so doing. 'It is,' said he, 'the indecision and anarchy of agents which produce anarchy and feebleness in results. In order to form a just opinion respecting the faults produced by the sole personal decision of the Emperor, it will be necessary to throw into the scale the great actions of which he would have been deprived, and the other faults which he would have been induced to commit by those very counsels which he is blamed for not having followed.'

"In viewing the complicated circumstances of his fall, he looks upon things so much in a mass, and from so high a point, that individuals escape his notice. He never evinces the least symptom of virulence toward those of whom it might be supposed he has the greatest reason to complain. His greatest mark of reprobation, and I have had frequent occasion to notice it, is to preserve silence with respect to them whenever they are mentioned in his presence. But how often has he not been heard to restrain the violent and less reserved expressions of those about him!

"'You are not acquainted with men,' he has said to us; 'they are difficult to comprehend, if one wishes to be strictly just. Can they understand or explain even their own characters? Almost all those who abandoned me would, had I continued to be prosperous, never, perhaps, have dreamed of their own defection. There are vices and virtues which depend on circumstances. Our last trials were beyond all human strength. Besides, I was forsaken rather than betrayed. There was more of weakness than of perfidy around me. *It was the denial of St. Peter;* tears and repentance are probably at hand. And where will you find, in the page of history, any one possessing a greater number of friends and partisans? Who was ever more popular and more beloved? Who was ever more ardently and deeply regretted? Here, from this very rock, on viewing the present disorders in France, who would not be tempted to say that I still reign there? The kings and princes, my allies, have remained faithful to me to the last; they were carried away by the people in a mass; and those who were around me found themselves overwhelmed and stunned by an irresistible whirlwind. No! human nature might have appeared in a more odious light, and I might have had greater cause of complaint.'"

November 17. The Emperor inquired of Las Casas respecting several officers of his household, of whom he had heard unfavorable reports. Las Casas affirmed that they had continued, through all changes, to evince an ardent devotion to the Emperor's interests.

"What do you tell me?" exclaimed Napoleon, eagerly interrupting him while he was speaking of one of them; "and yet I gave him so bad a reception at the Tuileries on my return! Ah! I fear that I have committed some involuntary acts of injustice. This comes of being obliged to take for granted the first story that is told, and of not having a single moment to spare for verification. I fear, too, that I have left many debts of gratitude in arrear. How unfortunate it is to be incapable of doing every thing one's self!"

Las Casas then alluded to the multitude of courtiers who hastened to meet the re-enthroned Bourbons. "Each individual," said he, "sought only to justify himself. Your majesty was, from that instant, disavowed and abjured. The ministers, the nobles, the intimate friends of your majesty, styled you simply *Bonaparte*, and blushed not for themselves or their nation."

"Here," said the Emperor, "we see a true picture of our national character. We are still the same people as our ancestors the Gauls. We still retain the same levity, the same inconstancy, and, above all, the same vanity. When shall we exchange this vanity for a little pride?"

"Many of the officers of your household," said Las Casas, "belonged to the first families, and were men of independent fortune. It was for them to have set an example which would have afforded us a claim on public esteem."

"Yes," said the Emperor; "if all the upper classes had acted in that way, affairs might have turned out very differently. The old editors of the public journals would not then have indulged in their chimeras of the good old times. We should not then have been annoyed with their dissertations on the straight line and the curve line; the king would have adhered honestly to his charter; I should never have dreamed of quitting the island of Elba; the head of the nation would have been recorded in history with greater honor and dignity; and we should all have been gainers."

November 18. At five o'clock in the afternoon the Emperor took his accustomed walk in the garden. The conversation turned on the French Revolution. "I did not know Robespierre," said the Emperor, "but I believe him to have been destitute of talent, energy, or system. He was the real *scape-goat* of the Revolution, sacrificed as soon as he endeavored to arrest it in its course—the common fate of all who, before myself, ventured to take that step. The Terrorists and their doctrine survived Robespierre; and if their successes were not continued, it was because they were obliged to bow to public opinion. They threw all the blame on Robespierre. But the latter declared, shortly before his death, that he was a stranger to the recent executions, and that he had not appeared in the committees for six weeks previously.

"While I was in the army of Nice, I saw some long letters addressed by Robespierre to his brother, condemning the horrors of the commissioners of the Convention, who, as he expressed it, were ruining the Revolution by their tyranny and atrocities. Cambacères, who must be good authority on subjects relating to that period, answered an inquiry which I one day addressed to him respecting the condemnation of Robespierre, 'Sire, that was a sentence without a trial;' adding, that Robespierre had more foresight and conception than was generally imagined; that after he should have succeeded in subduing the unbridled factions which he had to oppose, his intention was to restore a system of order and moderation. 'Some time previous to his fall,' added Cambacères, 'he delivered an admirable speech on this subject. It was not thought proper to insert it in the Moniteur, and all trace of it is now lost.'

"I am well acquainted," continued the Emperor, "with his brother, the younger Robespierre, the representative to the army of Italy. Had I followed him, how different might have been my career! On what trivial circumstances does human fate depend. Some office would doubtless have been assigned to me; and I might, at that moment, have been destined to attempt a sort of Vendemiaire. But I was then very young; my ideas were not fixed. It is probable, indeed, that I should not have undertaken any task that might have been allotted to me. But supposing the contrary case, and even admitting that I had been successful, what results could I have hoped for? In Vendemiaire the revolutionary force was totally subdued; in Thermidor it was still raging in its utmost fury and at its greatest height.

"Public opinion is an invisible and mysterious power which it is impossible to resist. Nothing is more unsteady, more vague, or more powerful. And capricious as it may be, it is nevertheless just and reasonable more frequently than is supposed. On becoming Provisional Consul, the first act of my administration was the banishment of fifty anarchists. Public opinion, which had, at first, been furiously hostile to them, suddenly turned in their favor, and I was forced to retract. But some time afterward, these same anarchists, having shown a disposition to engage in plots, were again assailed by that very public opinion, which had now returned to support me. Thus, through the errors that were committed at the time of the restoration, popularity was secured to the regicides, who, but a moment before, had been proscribed by the great mass of the nation.

"It belonged to me to shed a lustre over Louis XVI. in France, and to purify the nation of the crimes with which it had been sullied by frantic acts and unfortunate fatalities. The Bourbons, being of the royal family and coming from abroad, merely avenged their own private cause, and augmented the national opprobrium. I, on the contrary, being one of the people, should have raised the character of the nation by banishing from society, in her name, those whose crimes had disgraced her. This was my intention, but I proceeded prudently in the fulfillment of it. The three expiatory altars of St. Denis were but a prelude to my design. The Temple of Glory on the site of the Madeleine was to have been devoted to this object with still greater solemnity. There, near the tomb, and over the very bones of the political victims of our revolutions, human monuments and religious ceremonies would have consecrated their memory in the name of the French people. This is a secret that was not known to above ten individuals, though it would have been necessary to communicate a hint of the design to those who might have been intrusted with the arrangement of the edifice. I should not have executed my scheme in less than ten years; but what precautions had I not adopted! how carefully had I smoothed every difficulty, and removed every obstruction! All would have applauded my design, and no one would have suffered from it. So much depends on circumstances and forms, that, in my reign, Carnot would not have dared to write a memorial boasting of the death of the king, though he did so under the Bourbons. I should have leagued with public opinion in punishing him, though public opinion sided with him in rendering him unassailable."

November 28. The Emperor alluded to the numerous conspiracies which had been formed against him. "A hundred furious Jacobins,"* said he, "the real authors of the scenes of September and of the 10th of August, had resolved to get rid of the First Consul. For this purpose they invented a fifteen or sixteen pound howitzer, which, on being thrown into the carriage,

* *The Jacobin Club*, the most celebrated and powerful of all political sects, originated in France in 1789, under the denomination of the *Breton Club*, because it was established by the representatives from Brittany. Its numbers rapidly increased, and it assumed the more comprehensive name of *The Friends of the People*. Soon, however, their violent measures arrested the attention of France and of Europe, and they were universally known by the name of the place where they assembled, which was called the "Hall of the Jacobins," in the Rue St. Honore. It was so called because it belonged to some Dominican friars, who were thus denominated after their patron saint. In the meridian of its power, this society had twenty thousand affiliated clubs scattered through France. In its decay it took the name of the *Société du Manège*, from the *Manège*, or Riding House, where it held its sittings.

would explode by its own concussion, and hurl destruction on every side. To make sure of their object, they proposed to lay caltrops along a part of the road, which, by suddenly impeding the horses, would, of course, render it impossible for the carriage to move on. The man who was employed to lay down the caltrops, entertaining some suspicions of the job which he had been set upon, as well as of the good intentions of his employers, communicated the business to the police. The conspirators were soon traced, and were apprehended near the Garden of Plants, in the act of trying the effect of the machine, which made a terrible explosion. The First Consul, whose policy it was not to divulge the numerous conspiracies of which he was the object, did not give publicity to this, but merely imprisoned the criminals. He soon relaxed his orders for keeping them in close confinement, and they were allowed a certain degree of liberty. In the same prison in which these Jacobins were confined, some Royalists were also imprisoned for an attempt to assassinate the First Consul by means of air guns. These two parties formed a

THE INFERNAL MACHINE.

league together; and the Royalists transmitted to their friends out of prison the idea of the infernal machine, as being preferable to any other plan of destruction.

"It is remarkable that, on the evening of the catastrophe, the Emperor expressed an extreme repugnance to go out. Madam Bonaparte and some intimate friends absolutely forced him to go to the Oratorio. They roused him from a sofa, where he was fast asleep. One brought him his sword, and another his hat. As he drove along in his carriage he fell asleep again, and awoke suddenly, saying that he had dreamed that he was drowning in the Tagliamento. The illusion, however, was but momentary. A dreadful explosion immediately ensued. 'We are blown up!' exclaimed the First Consul to Lannes and Bessières, who were in the carriage with him. They proposed immediately to make arrests, but he desired them not to be too hasty. The First Consul arrived safe, and appeared at the Opera as though nothing had happened. He was preserved by the desperate driving of his coachman. The machine injured only a few individuals who closed the escort."

November 29. There was working in Mr. Balcombe's garden a poor old slave named Toby. He was a Malay Indian, and had been torn from his home by the crew of an English vessel, and sold at St. Helena. His countenance was frank and benevolent, and his whole appearance prepossessing. The Emperor became deeply interested in the story of his misfortunes, and made unavailing efforts to purchase his freedom and restore him to his country. When walking in the garden, the Emperor frequently stopped at Toby's hut, and entered into conversation with him, through an interpreter. The poor slave became exceedingly attached to the Emperor, always greeted him with a smile, and ever spoke of him as the *good gentleman*. He knew him by no other name.

"Poor Toby," said Napoleon one day, "has been torn from his family, from his country, from himself, and sold. Can there be greater misery for him, or a greater crime in others? If this crime be the act of the English captain alone, he is doubtless one of the vilest of men; but if it be that of the whole of the crew, it may have been committed by men perhaps not so base as might be imagined, for vice is always individual, scarcely ever collective. Joseph's brethren could not bring themselves to slay him, while Judas, a cool, hypocritical, calculating villain, betrayed his master. A philosopher has affirmed that men are born wicked. It would be very difficult and idle to attempt to discover whether the assertion be true. This, at least, is certain, that the great mass of society is not evil-disposed; for if the majority were determined to be criminal and to violate the laws, who would have the power to restrain or prevent them? This is the triumph of civilization, for this happy result springs from its bosom and arises out of its nature. Sentiments are, for the most part, traditionary. We feel them because they were felt by those who preceded us. Thus we must look to the development of the human reason and faculties for the only key to social order, the only secret of the legislator.

"Only those who wish to deceive the people, and rule them for their own selfish advantage, would desire to keep them in ignorance, for the more they are enlightened, the more they will feel convinced of the utility of laws, and of the necessity of defending them, and the more steady, happy, and prosperous will society become. If, however, knowledge should ever be dangerous in the multitude, it can only be when the government, in opposition to the interests of the people, drives them into an unnatural situation, or dooms the lower classes to perish for want. In such a case, knowledge would inspire them with a spirit to defend themselves or to become criminal.

"My code alone, from its simplicity, has been more beneficial to France than the whole mass of laws which preceded it. My schools and my system of mutual instruction are preparing generations yet unknown. Thus, during my reign, crimes were rapidly diminishing, while, on the contrary, with our neighbors in England, they have been increasing to a frightful degree. This alone is sufficient to enable one to form a decisive judgment of the respective governments.

"Look at the United States, where, without any apparent force or effort, every thing goes on prosperously, every one is happy and contented, and this is because the public wishes and interests are, in fact, the ruling power. Place the same government at variance with the will and interests of its inhabitants, and you would soon see what disturbance, trouble, and confusion, and, above all, what an increase of crime would ensue.

"When I acquired the supreme direction of affairs, it was wished that I might become a Washington. Words cost nothing; and, no doubt, those who were so ready to express the wish did so without any knowledge of times, persons, places, or things. Had I been in America, I would willingly have been a Washington, and I should have had little merit in so being, for I do not see how I could reasonably have acted otherwise. But had Washington been in France, exposed to discord within and invasion from without, I would have defied him to have been what he was in America, or, if he had attempted it, he would have been but a simpleton, and would only have prolonged the existence of evil. For my own part, I could only have been a *crowned Washington.* It was only in a congress of kings, in the midst of kings yielding or subdued, that I could become so. Then, and then only, I could successfully display Washington's moderation, disinterestedness, and wisdom. I could not reasonably attain to this but by means of the *universal dictatorship.* To this I aspired. Can that be thought a crime? Can it be believed that to resign this authority would have been beyond the power of human nature? Sylla, glutted with crimes, dared to abdicate, pursued by public execration. What motive could have checked me, who would have been followed only by blessings? But it remained for me to conquer at Moscow. How many will hereafter regret my disasters and my fall! But to require prematurely of me that sacrifice for which the time had not arrived was a vulgar absurdity, and for me to have proclaimed or promised it would have been taken for hypocrisy and quackery. That was not my way. I repeat it, it remained for me to conquer at Moscow."

On another occasion, pausing before Toby, he said,

"What, after all, is this poor human machine? There is not one whose exterior form is like another, or whose internal organization resembles the rest; and it is by disregarding this truth that we are led to the commission of so many errors. Had Toby been a Brutus, he would have put himself to death; if an Æsop, he would now, perhaps, have been the governor's adviser; if a Christian, ardent and zealous, he would have borne his chains in the sight of God, and blessed them. As for poor Toby, he thinks of none of this. He stoops and works in tranquillity."

NAPOLEON AND POOR TOBY.

After contemplating him a few moments in silence, the Emperor turned away, saying,

"It is certain that there is a wide distance between poor Toby and King Richard. And yet," he continued, as he walked thoughtfully along, "the crime is not the less atrocious, for this man, after all, had his family, his enjoyments, his liberty. It was a horrible act of cruelty to bring him here to die, under the fetters of slavery." Then, suddenly stopping, he said to Las Casas,

"But I read in your eyes that you think he is not the only example of the sort at St. Helena. My dear friend, there is not the least resemblance here. If the outrage is of a higher class, the victims also furnish very different resources. We have never been exposed to corporeal sufferings, or, if that had been attempted, we have souls to disappoint our tyrants. Our situation may even have its charms. The eyes of the universe are fixed upon us. We are martyrs in an immortal cause. Millions of human beings are weeping for us. Our country sighs, and glory mourns our fate. We here struggle against the oppression of the gods; and the prayers of nations are for us." After a pause of a few seconds, he continued,

"Besides, this is not the source of my real sufferings. If I considered only myself, perhaps I should have reason to rejoice. Misfortunes are not without their heroism and their glory. Adversity was wanting to my career.

Had I died on the throne, enveloped in the dense atmosphere of my power, I should, to many, have remained a problem; but now, misfortune will enable all to judge me without disguise."

A medical gentleman of much distinction was one day presented to the Emperor at the Briers. In the course of conversation, Napoleon remarked,

"I have no faith in medicine. My own remedies are starvation and the warm bath. At the same time, I have a higher opinion of the medical, or, rather, surgical profession, than of any other. The practice of the law is too severe an ordeal for poor human nature. He who habituates himself to the distortion of truth, and to exultation at the success of injustice, will at last hardly know right from wrong. So it is with politics; a man must have a conventional conscience. Of ecclesiastics too much is expected, and they consequently become hypocrites. As to soldiers, they are cut-throats and robbers, and not the less so because they are ready to send a bullet through your head if you tell them your opinion of them. But the mission of surgeons is to benefit mankind, not to mystify, destroy, or inflame them against each other. They have opportunities of studying human nature as well as of acquiring science."

Mr. Balcombe had a daughter Elizabeth, a mirthful, fun-loving girl of twelve or thirteen years, who became quite a favorite of the Emperor. She many years afterward, when a married woman, Mrs. Abell, published a narrative of what she could remember of her childish interviews with the Em-

PORTRAIT OF JOSEPHINE

peror. "On one occasion," she writes, "Madam Bertrand produced a miniature of the Empress Josephine, which she showed to Napoleon. He gazed at it with the greatest emotion for a considerable time without speaking. At last he exclaimed, it was the most perfect likeness he had ever seen of her, and told Madam Bertrand he would keep it, which he did, till his death. He has often looked at my mother for a length of time very earnestly, and then apologized, saying that she reminded him so much of Josephine. Her memory appeared to be idolized by him, and he was never weary of dwelling on her sweetness of disposition and the grace of her movements.

"'She was,' said the Emperor, 'the most truly feminine woman I have ever known. She was the most amiable, charming, and affable woman in the world. She was the goddess of the toilet. All fashions originated with her. Every thing she appeared in seemed elegant; moreover, she was so *humane*—she was the best of women. Although the Bourbons and the English allow that I did some good, yet they generally qualify it by saying that it was chiefly through the instrumentality of Josephine. But the fact was that she never interfered with politics. Nothing could have induced me to listen to such a measure as the divorce but political motives. No other reason could have persuaded me to separate myself from a wife whom I so tenderly loved. But I thank God that she died in time to prevent her from witnessing my last misfortunes.'"

A tent had been pitched adjoining the Emperor's single room, which somewhat enlarged his accommodations. When the weather was mild and dry, he frequently had his dinner-table spread in the tent, and the French gentlemen dined with him.

CHAPTER III.

REMOVAL TO LONGWOOD.

Waterloo—Dangers of Military Commanders—Portraiture of Napoleon's Generals—The Spanish Princes—Political Prospects of France—Defense of Marshal Ney—Contrast between Ney and Turenne—Removal to Longwood—The Emperor's Apartments—Kindness of the Emperor—Political Views—The Emperor's Wounds—Calumnies.

December 5. The weather had now become cold and very damp, and the Emperor was confined most of the time to his comfortless room. On this day, as the weather did not permit the usual walk after dinner, the conversation was continued at the table after the dishes were removed.

"The fate of a battle," observed the Emperor, "is the result of a moment —of a thought. The hostile forces advance with various combinations. They attack each other, and fight for a certain time. The critical moment arrives; a mental flash decides, and the least reserve accomplishes the object. At Waterloo, had I followed up the idea of turning the enemy's right, I should easily have succeeded. I preferred, however, to pierce the centre and separate the two armies. But all was fatal in that engagement. It even assumed the appearance of absurdity. Yet I ought to have gained the victory. Never had any of my battles presented less doubt to my mind. I am still at a loss to account for what happened. Grouchy had lost himself. Ney appeared bewildered. Derlon was useless. If, in the evening, I had been aware of Grouchy's position, and could have thrown myself upon it, I might, in the morning, with the help of that fine reserve, have repaired my ill success, and, perhaps, even have destroyed the allied force by one of those miracles, those turns of fortune, which were familiar to me, and which would have surprised no one. But I knew nothing of Grouchy, and, besides, it was not easy to act with decision among the wrecks of the army. It would be difficult to imagine the condition of the French army on that disastrous night. It was a torrent dislodged from its bed, hurling away every thing in its course."

Then turning the subject, he said, "The dangers incurred by the military commanders of ancient times are not to be compared with the perils which attend generals of our day. There are no positions in which a general may not now be reached by artillery. But anciently a general ran no risk except when he himself charged, which Cæsar did only twice or thrice.

"We rarely find combined together all the qualities necessary to constitute a great general. The object most desirable is that a man's judgment should be in equilibrium with his physical character or courage. This is what we may call being well squared both by base and perpendicular. If courage be in the ascendency, a general will rashly undertake that which he can not execute; on the contrary, if his character or courage be inferior to his judgment, he will not venture to carry any measure into effect. The sole merit of the Viceroy Eugene consisted in this equilibrium of character. This, however, was sufficient to render him a very distinguished man.

"With respect to physical courage, it was impossible for Murat or Ney not to be brave; but no man possessed less judgment than the former in particular. As to moral courage, I have rarely met with the *two hours after midnight* kind. I mean unprepared courage—that which is necessary on an unexpected occasion; and which, in spite of the most unforeseen events, leaves full freedom of judgment and decision. I do not hesitate to declare that I am eminently gifted with this *two hours after midnight courage.* In this respect I have met with but few persons who were equal to me. An incorrect idea is generally formed of the strength of mind necessary to engage in one of those great battles, on which depends the fate of an army or a nation, or the possession of a throne. Generals are rarely found eager to give battle. They choose their positions; establish themselves; consider their combinations; but then commences their indecision. Nothing is so difficult, and, at the same time, so important as to know when to decide.

"Kleber was endowed with the highest talent, but he was merely the man of the moment. He pursued glory as the only road to happiness. But he had no national sentiment, and he could, without any sacrifice, have devoted himself to foreign service. He commenced his youthful career among the Prussians, to whom he continued much attached. Desaix possessed, in a very superior degree, the important equilibrium above described. Moreau scarcely deserved to be placed in the first rank of generals. In him Nature had left her work unfinished. He possessed more instinct than genius. In Lannes courage first predominated over judgment. But the latter was every day gaining ground, and approaching equilibrium. He had become a very able commander at the period of his death. I found him a dwarf, but I lost him a giant.

"I know the depth, or what I call the draught of water, of all my generals. Some will sink to the waist, some to the chin, others over the head; but the number of the latter is very small, I assure you. Suchet was one whose courage and judgment had been surprisingly improved. Massena was a very superior man, and, by a strange peculiarity of temperament, he possessed the desired equilibrium only in the heat of battle. It was created in the midst of danger."

December 6. The Emperor passed the morning, as usual, in dictation. Some gentlemen called, with whom he had a long conversation. After they had withdrawn, he descended, with Las Casas, to the lower walk. His countenance expressed dejection and trouble.

"Well," said he, "we are to have sentinels under our windows at Longwood. They wished to force me to have a foreign officer at my table and in my drawing-room. I shall not be able to mount a horse without being accompanied. In a word, we shall not be able to do any thing without being exposed to insult."

"This," said Las Casas, "was not the treatment the Spanish princes experienced at Valençay, or the Pope at Fontainebleau."

"Certainly not," said the Emperor. "The princes hunted and gave balls at Valençay without being physically aware of their chains. They experienced respect and courtesy at all hands. Old King Charles IV. removed from Compiegne to Marseilles, and from Marseilles to Rome, whenever he wished. And yet how different are those places from this! The Pope at Fontainebleau, whatever may have been the reports circulated in the world, was treated in the same manner. And yet how many persons, in spite of all the indulgences which he enjoyed, refused to be appointed to guard him! a circumstance which gave me no offense, for I thought it perfectly natural. Such employments are subject to the influence of delicacy of feeling. Our European manners require that power should be limited by honor. For my own part, I should, as a private man and an officer, without hesitation, have refused to guard the Pope, whose removal to France was never ordered by me."

Perceiving that Las Casas manifested some surprise at this statement, he added,

"You are astonished; you did not know this; but it is nevertheless true, as well as many other similar facts, which you will learn in course of time. But, in reference to the subject upon which we have just been speaking, it is necessary to distinguish the conduct of the sovereign, who acts collectively, from that of the private man, whose sentiments are without constraint. Policy permits, nay, even pardons in the one what would be unpardonable in the other."

December 9. A ship arrived bringing newspapers from Europe down to the 15th of September. The Emperor read them with intensest interest, and remarked, in reference to the news which they contained,

"Three great events present themselves to the imagination, *the Division of France, the Reign of the Bourbons, or a New Dynasty.* Louis XVIII. might easily have reigned in 1814 by rendering himself a national monarch. Now, there remains to him but the chance, very odious and very uncertain, of excessive severity, a reign of terror. His dynasty may be permanently established, or that which is to succeed him may still be in the secret of futurity."

"The Duke of Orleans," said some one, "may be called to the throne."

"The Duke of Orleans," the Emperor replied, "will never wear the crown in the course of succession. It is the well-understood interest of all the sovereigns in Europe to prefer me to the Duke of Orleans coming to the throne by crime. For what is the doctrine of kings against the events of the present day? Is it to present a renewal of the example which I furnished against what they call legitimacy? But the example which I have set can not be renewed in ages, but that which the Duke of Orleans would give—near relative of the monarch on the throne—may be renewed daily, hourly, in every country. There is no sovereign who has not in his palace, and about his person, cousins, nephews, brothers, and other relations, ready to pursue a course which one day or other may cause them to be deposed."

These same papers contained a memorial of the defense urged in justification of Marshal Ney.

"The defense is most pitiable," said the Emperor. "It is not calculated to save his life, and by no means to maintain his honor."

In the defense the marshal's devotion to the king and estrangement from the Emperor were strenuously affirmed.

"An absurd plan," said Napoleon, "but one which has been generally adopted by those who have figured in the present memorable times, and who seem not to have considered that I am so entirely identified with our prodigies, our monuments, our institutions, and all our national acts, that to separate me from them is to do violence to France. The glory of France is to acknowledge me; and in spite of all the subtlety, evasion, and falsehood that may be employed to prove the contrary, my character will still be fairly estimated by the French nation.

"The political defense of Ney was all clearly defined. He was swept away by a general movement which appeared to him to be the will, and for the welfare of the country. He yielded without premeditation and without treason. Reverses followed, and he found himself cited before a tribunal. There remained nothing more for him to say upon the great event. As to the defense of his life, he had nothing to say except that he was protected by a solemn capitulation, which guaranteed to every individual silence and oblivion with respect to all political acts and opinions. Had he pursued that line of defense, and were his life, nevertheless, to be sacrificed, it would be, in the face of the whole world, a violation of the most sacred laws. He would leave behind him the recollection of a glorious character, carrying to the grave the sympathy of every generous mind, and covering those with reprobation and infamy who, in defiance of a solemn treaty, shamefully abandoned him. But this enthusiasm is probably beyond his moral strength. Ney is the bravest of men; there end all his faculties."

The Emperor then instituted a comparison between the situation of Ney and that of Turenne. "In 1649," said he, "Turenne commanded the royal army, which command had been conferred on him by Anne of Austria, the regent of the kingdom. Though he had taken the oath of fidelity, he bribed his troops, and declared himself for the Fronde, and marched on Paris; but when he was declared guilty of high treason, his repentant army forsook him, and Turenne took refuge with the Prince of Hesse to avoid the pursuit of justice.

"Ney, on the contrary, was urged by the unanimous wish and outcry of his army. But nine months had elapsed during which he had acknowledged a monarch who had been preceded by six hundred thousand foreign bayonets—a monarch who had not accepted the Constitution presented to him by the Senate as the formal and necessary condition of his return, and who, by declaring that he had reigned nineteen years, proved that he regarded all preceding governments as usurpations. Ney, whose education had taught him to respect the national sovereignty, had fought for five-and-twenty years to support that cause, and from a private soldier had raised himself to the rank of a marshal. If his conduct on the 20th of March was not honorable, it was at least explicable, and in some respects pardonable.

"But Turenne was absolutely criminal, because the Fronde was the ally of Spain, which was then at war with his sovereign, and because he had been prompted by his own interest and that of his family, in the hope of obtaining a sovereignty at the expense of France, and, consequently, to the prejudice of his country."

VIEW OF LONGWOOD.

December 10. The cottage at Longwood was now prepared for the captive and his accompanying friends. The Emperor was consequently this day, much to his regret, removed to this bleak and cheerless abode. He, however, appeared in cheerful spirits, and manifested no discontent. Many persons were assembled on the road to see him pass. As he rode along, his graceful figure and handsome countenance attracted much attention. When he arrived at the entrance of his dreary jail-yard, a guard, under arms, rendered the prescribed honors to the august prisoner. It was about four o'clock in the afternoon when the Emperor entered his new residence, where he was doomed to endure five and a half years of mortal agony, and then to die. He beckoned to Las Casas to follow him to his sleeping-room. Examining various articles of furniture, he inquired if his secretary was similarly provided. Upon being answered in the negative, he insisted that Las Casas should take the articles, saying, in the kindest manner,

"Take them. I shall want for nothing. I shall be better taken care of than you."

The accompanying cut will give the reader an idea of the house at Longwood, and of the plan of the rooms. The entrance was through a hall, which answered the double purpose of an antechamber and a dining-room. This hall opened into the drawing-room. Beyond this was a dark room, with but one small window, originally intended for the Emperor's books and maps, but which subsequently was converted into a dining-room. The Emperor's chamber opened into this room on the right.

His apartments consisted of two rooms, A and B, each fifteen feet long and twelve broad, and seven feet high. An indifferent carpet covered the floors, and pieces of nankeen were hung along the rough and unsightly walls. The bed-room contained the little camp bed in which the Emperor slept, and the couch on which he reclined the greater part of the day. The couch was usually covered with books. Beside the couch stood a small table, on which the Emperor breakfasted and dined when he took his meals in his own room, and on which, in the evening, was placed a candlestick with three branches. Between the two windows stood a chest of drawers, containing the Emperor's linen, and on the top of which stood his large dressing-case. Over the fire-place hung a very small glass, together with several pictures. In one corner of the room stood a large silver wash-basin, which the Emperor brought from the Elysée. On the right was a portrait of the King of Rome sitting on a lamb. On the left, as a pendant to it, there was another portrait of the young prince sitting on a cushion, and putting on a slipper. Lower down was a small marble bust of the King of Rome. Two candlesticks, two scent-bottles, and two cups of silver-gilt completed the decoration of the chimney-piece. At the foot of the couch, and directly in view of the Emperor, hung a portrait of Maria Louisa holding her son in her arms. The large silver watch of Frederick the Great, which was taken at Potsdam, hung on the right of the chimney. A small bathing-closet was attached to this room.

In the second room, B, which served as a sort of study, along the walls next the windows were several rough shelves, supported on brackets, on which were scattered a great number of books and manuscripts. Between the two windows was a book-case. On the opposite side stood another camp bedstead; on this the Emperor sometimes reposed in the daytime, when fatigued with dictating or walking about alone in his chamber. He occasionally, also, laid down upon it when he rose from the other in his frequent sleepless nights. In the middle of the room stood the writing-table, with marks indicating the places usually occupied by the Emperor and his amanuenses during his dictations.

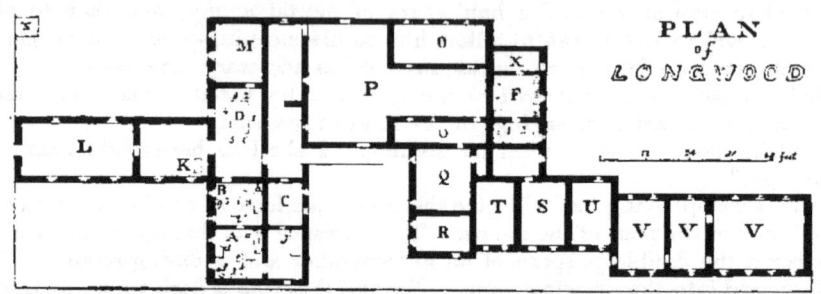

This plan is an exact copy of one drawn by young Las Casas, first for his mother, and afterward inclosed to Maria Louisa in a letter which was intercepted.

A. The Emperor's bed-room :—a. Small iron camp bedstead, on which the Emperor slept.—b. Sofa, on which the Emperor sat a great part of the day, turned toward the fire-place.—c. Small table, upon which the Emperor's breakfast was served. He often made my father come to it, particularly when he took his English lessons.—d. Chest of drawers between two windows.—e. Fire-place, over which are suspended two portraits of the Empress and five of the King of Rome, one of which was embroidered by Maria Louisa; also a small marble bust of him.—f. Large ewer, brought from the Elysée.

B. Study :—g. Library.—h. Second small bed. When the Emperor could not sleep, he removed from one bed to the other.—i. Table on which the Emperor wrote :—1. The Emperor's place.—2. That of my father.—3. Myself, to whom he dictated the campaigns of Italy. Each of us had our particular department, and different hours of study.

C. Closet, where the valet de chambre attended : —j. Bath, in which the Emperor bathed when there was not a scarcity of water.

D. Dining-room :—1. Place of the Emperor.—2. My father's.—3. My own.—4. Montholon.—5. Gourgaud.—6. Madam Montholon. Count and Countess Bertrand, living in another house at some distance from Longwood, only came to dine on Sundays. After dinner, which never lasted more than from fifteen to eighteen minutes, the Emperor dismissed all his attendants, exercising his English by telling them to "go out, go to supper." He would then turn to us, and ask us if we wished to visit the theatre, upon which I was sent to the library for a book; this the Emperor generally read aloud. One of our great authors was always chosen, generally Corneille, Racine, or Molière. When the reading was over, he withdrew to his bed-room. If he read till eleven o'clock or midnight, he considered himself fortunate, and called this a victory over time.

E. My father's bed-room : — 1. His bed. — 2. My own. The room was so small that there was scarcely space enough for two chairs.

F. Our study :—1. My father's desk.—2. Table, on which I wrote to you, my mother.—3. Table, on which All, the Emperor's valet, frequently transcribed for my father.—4. Sofa, on which my father lay a great part of the day. These rooms are so low that you can touch the ceilings with your hands; they are covered with tarred paper. If the sun were shining, we were almost suffocated; if it rained, we were almost drowned. How often have my father and I walked about here till a late hour, talking of you, my mother!

K. Small parlor, with a little table upon which the Emperor often played chess before sitting down to dinner.
L. Antechamber and waiting-room for visitors.   M. Library.
N. Tent, where the Emperor often breakfasted in fine weather and dictated during the day.
O. Servants' Hall.   P. Court-yard, always muddy.   Q. Kitchen.
R. First apartment of my father.   S. Room of General Gourgaud.   T. Room of the orderly officer
U. Lodgings of Dr. O'Meara.   V. Apartments of Count Montholon.   X. Chamber for our servant.
The second establishment of the grand marshal was four hundred yards from Longwood.

General Bertrand, wife, and children were placed in a little hut, called Hut's Gate, two miles distant from Longwood. A tent was spread for General Gourgaud, and another for Doctor O'Meara. The house was surrounded by bleak and uncultivated grounds, without shade-trees or flowers, which by courtesy were called *the garden*. In front of the house, and separated from it by a deep ravine, was encamped the fifty-third regiment of British troops. Parties of these troops were continually posted on all the surrounding heights. Such were the accommodations prepared for the captive Emperor of France.

The imperial household now consisted of the Emperor, Count Las Casas and son, Count Montholon, wife, and child, Count Bertrand, wife, and three children, Baron Gourgaud, and fourteen servants, three of whom were attached to the family of Count Bertrand at Hut's Gate.

"Our new residence," says Las Casas, "was fitted up with a bathing-machine, which the admiral had ordered the carpenters to prepare in the best way they could. The Emperor, who, since he quitted Malmaison, had been obliged to dispense with the use of the bath, which to him had become one of the necessaries of life, expressed a wish to bathe immediately, and directed me to remain with him. The most trifling details of our new establishment came once more under consideration, and as the apartment which had been assigned to me was very bad, the Emperor expressed a wish that, during the day, I should occupy what he called his topographic cabinet, which adjoined his own private closet, in order, as he said, that I might be nearer to him. I was much affected by the kind manner in which all this was spoken. He even went so far as to tell me that I must come the next morning and take a bath in his machine; and when I excused myself on the ground of the respect and the distance which it was indispensable should be observed between us,

"'My dear Las Casas,' said he, 'fellow-prisoners should accommodate each other. I do not want the bath all day, and it is no less necessary to you than to me.'

"One would have supposed," continues Las Casas, "that he wished to indemnify me for the loss I was about to sustain in being no longer the only individual about his person. This kindness delighted me, it is true, but it also produced a feeling of regret. The kindness of the Emperor was doubtless the reward of my assiduous attentions at the Briers, but it also gave me cause to anticipate the close of that constant intercourse with him for which I had been indebted to our profound solitude. The Emperor, not wishing to dress again, dined in his own chamber, and desired me to remain with him."

December 19. The conversation turned upon the inspection of letters under the government of Napoleon. The Emperor remarked, "The system of examining letters was adopted with the view of preventing, rather than discovering, dangerous correspondence. Since the reign of Louis XIV., there has existed an office of political police for discovering foreign correspondence; and since that period, the same family have managed the business of the office, though the individuals and their functions were alike unknown. It was, in all respects, an official post. The persons superintending this department were educated at great expense in the different capitals of Europe. They had their own peculiar notions of propriety, and always manifested great reluctance to examine French domestic correspondence. This matter, however, remained entirely at their own discretion. As soon as the name of any individual was entered upon the lists of this important department, his arms and seals were immediately engraved at the office, and with such a degree of accuracy that the letters, after being read, were closed up and delivered without any marks of suspicion. These circumstances, joined to the serious evils they might create, and the important results they were capable of producing, constituted the vast responsibility of the office of postmaster general, and required that it should be filled by a man of prudence, judgment, and intelligence.

"I am by no means favorable to the system of inspecting correspondence. With regard to the diplomatic information therein obtained, I do not consider it of sufficient value to counterbalance the expenses incurred, which were $120,000 annually. As to the examination of the letters of citizens, I regard that as a measure calculated to do more harm than good. It is rarely that conspiracy is carried on through such channels. And with respect to the individual opinions obtained from epistolary correspondence, they may be more dangerous than useful to a sovereign, particularly among such a people as the French. Of whom will not our national volatility and fickleness lead us to complain? The man whom I may have offended at my levee will write to-day that I am a tyrant, though but yesterday he overwhelmed me with praises, and perhaps to-morrow will be ready to lay down his life to serve me. The violation of the privacy of correspondence may therefore cause a prince to lose his best friends by wrongfully inspiring him with distrust and prejudice toward all, particularly as enemies capable of mischief are always sufficiently artful to avoid exposing themselves to that kind of danger. Some of my ministers were so cautious in this respect, that I could never succeed in detecting one of their letters.

"Upon my return from Elba, numerous letters and petitions were found in which the Emperor was spoken of most indecorously. They would have formed a most odious collection. For a moment I entertained the idea of inserting some of them in the Moniteur. They would have disgraced certain individuals, but they would have afforded no new lesson on the human heart; men are always the same."

December 20. The Emperor, after breakfast, mounted his horse for a ride. He directed his course toward some cultivated fields called the farm. The farmer, an intelligent Englishman, accompanied the Emperor on horseback over the whole of the grounds. "The Emperor," says Las Casas, "asked him a number of questions respecting his farm, as he used to do during his hunting excursions in the neighborhood of Versailles, where he discussed with the farmers the opinions of the Council of State, in order to bring forth to the council, in their turn, the objections of the farmers."

December 22. Las Casas records, "In our melancholy situation, every day brought with it some new cause of uneasiness. We were constantly receiving some new sting, which seemed the more cruel, as we were destined to endure it for a long futurity; yet, lacerated as our feelings undoubtedly were, each fresh wound was not the less sensibly felt. The motives which

NAPOLEON AND THE FARMER.

were assigned for our vexations frequently amounted to irony. Thus sentinels were posted beneath the Emperor's windows and before our doors; and this, we were informed, was for our own safety. We were cut off from all communication with the inhabitants of the island; we were put under a kind of close confinement; and we were told that this was done to free the Emperor from all annoyance. The passwords and orders were incessantly changed. We lived in the continual perplexity and apprehension of being exposed to some unforeseen insult. The Emperor, whose feelings were keenly alive to all these things, resolved to write to the admiral through the medium of Count Montholon.

"'Let not the admiral suppose,' said he, 'that I treat with him on any of these subjects. Were he to present himself to me to-morrow, in spite of my just resentment, he would find my countenance as serene, and my temper as composed as usual. This would not be the effect of dissimulation on my part, but merely the fruit of experience. I remember that Lord Whitworth once filled Europe with the report of a long conversation that he had held with me, scarcely a word of which was true. But that was my fault. It taught me to be more cautious in future. The Emperor has governed too long not to know that he must not commit himself to the discretion of any one who may have it in his power to say falsely, *The Emperor told me so and so*, while the Emperor may not have the means of either affirming or contradicting the statement. One witness is as good as another. It is necessary, therefore, to employ some one who may be enabled to tell the narrator that he speaks false, and that he is ready to set him right, which the Emperor himself can not do.'"

December 24. The Emperor was reading a publication in which he was represented as speaking in a very amiable strain. "How could they put these words into my mouth," said he. "This is too tender, too sentimental for me. Every body knows that I do not express myself in that way."

"Sire," said Las Casas, "it was done with a good intention. That reputation for amiability which you seem to despise might have exercised great influence over public opinion."

"What is the advantage," the Emperor replied, "of popularity and amiability of character? Who possessed the qualities in a more eminent degree than the unfortunate Louis XVI.? Yet what was his fate? His life was sacrificed. No; a sovereign must serve his people with dignity, and not make it his chief study to please them. The best mode of winning their love is to secure their welfare. Nothing is more dangerous than for a sovereign to flatter his subjects. If they do not afterward obtain every thing they want, they become irritated, and fancy that promises have been broken; and if they are then resisted, their hatred increases in proportion as they consider themselves deceived. A sovereign's first duty is, doubtless, to conform with the wishes of the people. But what the people say is scarcely ever what they wish. Their desires and their wants can not be learned from their own mouths so well as they are to be read in the heart of their prince.

"Each system may, no doubt, be maintained—that of mildness as well as that of severity. Each has its advantages and disadvantages; for every thing is mutually balanced in this world. If you ask me what was the use of my severe forms and expressions, I shall answer, to spare me the pain of inflicting the punishment I threatened. What harm have I done, after all? What blood have I shed? Who can boast that, had he been placed in my situation, he could have done better? What period of history, exhibiting any thing like the difficulties with which I was surrounded, presents such harmless results? What am I reproached with? My government papers and my private archives were seized, yet what has there been found to publish to the world? All sovereigns situated as I was, amid factions, disorders, conspiracies, are surrounded by murders and executions; yet, during my reign, what sudden tranquillity pervaded France!"

December 25. As the Emperor was dressing for dinner, Las Casas being present, he put his hand on his left thigh, where there was a deep scar, and said that it was the mark of a bayonet wound, by which he had nearly lost his limb at the siege of Toulon.

"Many persons," said he, "have wondered at my good fortune, which rendered me, as it were, invulnerable in so many battles. They were mistaken; the only reason was, that I made a secret of all my dangers. I had three horses killed under me at the siege of Toulon. I had several killed or wounded in the campaigns of Italy. I have been wounded several times. At the battle of Ratisbonne a ball struck my heel. At the battle of Wagram a ball tore my boot and stocking, and grazed the skin of my left leg. I lost my horse and hat at Arcis sur Aube. I have been frequently exposed to danger in my different battles, but it was carefully kept secret. I enjoined, once for all, the most absolute silence on all circumstances of that nature. It would be impossible to calculate the confusion and disorder which might have resulted from the slightest report or smallest doubt relative to my existence. On my life depended the fate of a great empire, and the whole policy and destinies of Europe. This habit of keeping circumstances of that kind secret has prevented me from relating them in my campaigns, and, indeed, they are now almost forgotten. It is only by mere accident, and in the course of conversation, that they can recur to me."

THE EMPEROR WOUNDED AT RATISBONNE.

December 29. Las Casas records, "An Englishman whom we frequently saw confessed to Napoleon, with the utmost humility of heart, and, as it were, by way of expiation, that he had to reproach his conscience with having once firmly believed all the abominable falsehoods related of him. He had given credit to all the accounts of stranglings, massacres, and brutal ferocity— in short, he even believed in the deformities of his person, and the hideous features of his countenance. 'And how,' said he, 'could I help crediting all this? Our publications were filled with these statements. They were in every mouth. Not a single voice was raised to contradict them.'

"'Yes,' said Napoleon, smiling, 'it is to your ministers that I am indebted for these favors. They inundated Europe with pamphlets and libels against me. Perhaps they may say in excuse that they did but respond to those which they received from France; and it must in justice be confessed, that those Frenchmen who have since been seen to exult over the ruins of their country, felt no hesitation in furnishing them with such articles in abundant supplies.

"'Be this as it may, I was repeatedly urged, during the period of my power, to adopt measures for counteracting this underhand work. But I always declined it. What advantage should I have gained by such a defense? It would have been said that I had paid for it, and that would only have discredited me still more. Another victory, another monument; these, I said are the best, the only answers I can make. Falsehood passes away and truth remains. The sensible portion of the present age, and posterity in particular, will form their judgment only from facts. Is it not so? Already the cloud is breaking. The light is piercing through, and my character grows clearer every day. It will soon become the fashion in Europe to do me justice. Those who have succeeded me possess the archives of my administration and police, and the records of my tribunals. They hold in their pay and at their disposal those who must have been the executors and the accomplices of my atrocities and crimes. Yet what proofs have they brought forward? What have they made known?

"'The first moments of fury being passed away, all honest and sensible men will render justice to my character; none but the stupid or the malicious will be my enemies. I may rest at ease. The succession of events, the disputes of opposing parties, their hostile productions, will daily clear the way for the correct and glorious materials of my history. And what advantage has been reaped from the immense sums which have been paid for libels against me? Soon every trace of them will be obliterated, while my institutions and monuments will recommend me to the remotest posterity. Now, however, it is too late to heap abuse on me. Calumny has exhausted all its venom upon my person; it can no longer hurt me; there is nothing left to operate against me but *the poison of Mithridates.*'"

December 30. Las Casas makes the following pleasing record of the events of this day:

"The Emperor desired to be called before eight o'clock. While he dressed, I finished reading to him the newspapers which I had begun to examine the day before. When dressed, he himself went to the stables, asked for his horse, and rode out with me alone, his attendants not being yet quite ready. We rode on at random, and soon arrived in a field where some laborers were engaged in plowing. The Emperor alighted from his horse, seized the plow, and, to the great astonishment of the man who was holding it, he himself traced a furrow of considerable length. He again mounted, and continued his ride through various parts of the neighborhood, and was joined successively by General Gourgaud and the grooms.

"On his return, the Emperor expressed a wish to breakfast under a tree in the garden, and desired us to remain with him. During the ride he had mentioned a little present that he intended for us. 'It is a trifle, to be sure,' said he, 'but every thing must be proportioned to circumstances, and to me this is truly *the widow's mite.*' He alluded to a monthly stipend which he had determined to settle upon each of us. It was to be deducted from an inconsiderable sum which we had contrived to secrete in spite of the vigilance of the English, and this sum was henceforth Napoleon's sole resource. It may well be imagined how precious this trifle had become. I seized the first moment, on finding myself alone with him, to decline his intended bounty. He laughed at this, and, as I persisted in my resolution, he said, pinching my ear, 'Well, if you do not want it now, keep it for me; I shall know where to find it when I stand in need of it.'

"After breakfast the Emperor went in-doors, and desired me to finish reading the newspapers. I had been some time engaged in reading, when M. de Montholon requested to be introduced. He had just had a long conversation with the admiral (Sir George Cockburn), who was very anxious to see the Emperor. I was directed to suspend my translations from the newspapers, and the Emperor walked about for some time as though hesitating how to proceed. At length, taking up his hat, he went into the drawing-room to receive the admiral. This circumstance afforded me the highest satisfaction, for I knew that it was calculated to put a period to our state of hostility. I was well assured that two minutes' conversation with the Emperor would smooth more difficulties than two days' correspondence with any one else.

"Accordingly, I was soon informed that his convincing arguments and amiable manners had produced the wished-for effect. I was assured that on his departure the admiral appeared enchanted. As for the Emperor, he was very well pleased at what had taken place. He is far from disliking the admiral; he is even somewhat prepossessed in his favor.

"'You may be a very good seaman,' said the Emperor to him, 'but you do not understand our situation. We ask for nothing. We can maintain ourselves without all these annoyances and privations. We can provide for ourselves; but still, our esteem is worth the obtaining.'

"The admiral referred to his instructions. 'But,' replied the Emperor, 'you do not consider the vast distance that intervenes between the dictation and the execution of these instructions. The very individual who issues them in a remote part of the world, would oppose them if he saw them carried into execution. Besides, it is certain that, on the least difference, the least opposition, the slightest expression of public opinion, the ministers would disavow their instructions, or severely blame those who had not given them a more favorable interpretation.'

"The admiral conducted himself wonderfully well. The Emperor passed high praises on him. All asperities were softened down, and good understanding prevailed. It was agreed that the Emperor should henceforth freely ride about the island, and that the officer who had been instructed to attend him should merely watch him from a distance, so that the Emperor might not be offended with the sight of a guard; that visitors should be admitted to the Emperor, not with the permission of the admiral as the inspector of Longwood, but with that of the grand marshal who did the honors of the establishment.

"To-day our little colony was increased by the arrival of Captain Piontkowsky, a native of Poland. He was one of those individuals whom we had left behind us at Plymouth. His devotedness to the Emperor, and his grief at being separated from him, had subdued the severity of the English ministers, and he received permission to proceed to St. Helena."

The Emperor went out with some of his companions for a ride on horseback. In attempting to descend a very steep and deeply-furrowed valley, they were compelled to dismount. General Gourgaud and the two grooms turned off with the horses, while Napoleon and Las Casas continued their rugged and precipitous journey on foot. The Emperor found much trouble in clambering over the ridges, and lamented the loss of his youthful activity. They at last got into a morass, where the Emperor found himself sinking in the mud, and he was compelled to creep out, with sadly soiled garments, upon his hands and feet. He looked for a moment in silence upon his bespattered boots, and then said,

"Las Casas, this is a dirty adventure. If we had been lost in the mud, what would have been said in Europe? The hypocrites would have proved beyond a doubt that we had been swallowed up for our crimes."

NAPOLEON DESCENDING THE RAVINE.

CHAPTER IV.
1816, January.

New-year's Day—Fowling-pieces—Colonel Wilks—The Disappointment—Visit to the Rooms—The drunken Sentinel—Social Reading—Goldsmith's Secret History—Conversation with Governor Wilks—Lodgings of Las Casas—The Emperor's Criticisms—Historical Remarks—The Ride—Mired Horse.

January 1. All the exiles of Longwood assembled at ten o'clock in the morning to present the compliments of the season to the Emperor. He received them with great kindness, accepted affectionately those congratulations which were blended with the intensest sympathy, and invited them all to breakfast and spend the day with him.

"We are but a handful," said he, "in one corner of the world, and all our consolation must be our regard for each other."

Notwithstanding the efforts which all made to appear cheerful, the gloom of the opening year settled heavily upon their hearts, and it was to them all a day of sadness. Some fowling-pieces belonging to the Emperor, and which had been detained by the admiral, were to-day returned to him. The Emperor remarked that they were quite useless, as *rats* were the only game to be found at Longwood. There were two or three guns, also, belonging to individuals of the Emperor's suite. These were also returned, but only on condition that they should be sent every evening to the tent of the English officer on duty. The French gentlemen, of course, refused to receive them on terms so degrading. As the exiles were guarded by armed sentinels, and surrounded by a regiment of English soldiers, and hemmed in by impregnable fortifications, and blockaded by several ships of war, the admiral, after much hesitation, ventured to intrust them with the dangerous weapons.

January 3. Las Casas was invited to dine with Governor Wilks at Plantation House. Governor Wilks was superseded in his authority by Admiral Cockburn. He was soon to return to Europe. He lived in genteel style, in by far the most agreeable residence upon the island, and was a gentleman of polished manners and of intellectual tastes. His amiable wife and lovely daughter contributed much to the attractions of his hospitable mansion. Las Casas rode to the governor's, over a rocky and precipitous road, in a carriage drawn by six oxen. In consequence of this engagement, Las Casas did not see the Emperor during the day.

January 4. It was a brilliant day, serene and clear. Though the heat was intense, ocean, rock, and sky seemed to rejoice in the beams of the cloudless sun. As Las Casas, in the morning, entered the apartment of the Emperor, Napoleon playfully pinched his ear, saying, in touching tones of affection,

"Well! you deserted me yesterday. I got through the evening very well, notwithstanding. Do not suppose that I could not do without you."

The Emperor, since his arrival at Longwood, had omitted his usual dictations. He now read every day, in his cabinet, until between three and four in the afternoon. He then dressed and rode out on horseback, accompanied by two or three of his friends. His rides were usually directed toward a favorite valley, which was solitary and sombre in the extreme. The roads were so bad that it was frequently necessary to dismount and clamber over piles of stones. The Emperor named this wild ravine the *Valley of Silence*. He frequently invited company to dine with him, whom he usually found assembled upon his return from his ride. These guests, thus honored, consisted of the colonel of the 53d regiment, several English officers and their ladies, Admiral Cockburn, and strangers of distinction who visited the island.

January 5. Sir George Cockburn dined at Longwood with the Emperor. During the conversation, the admiral remarked that the 66th regiment was coming to re-enforce the 53d. The Emperor smiled at this, and said,

"Do you not consider yourself strong enough already? An additional seventy-four would, however, be of more use than a regiment. Ships of war are the security of an island. Fortifications produce but delay. The landing of a superior force is a complete success, if the distance does not admit the arrival of succors."

The admiral inquired which, in the Emperor's opinion, was the strongest place in the world.

"It is impossible to point it out," the Emperor replied, "because the strength of a place arises partly from its own means of defense, and partly from extraneous and indeterminate circumstances. We may mention among the very strong fortresses, Strasburg, Lille, Metz, Mantua, Antwerp, Malta, and Gibraltar."

"You were suspected in England for some time," said the admiral, "of entertaining a design to attack Gibraltar."

"We knew better than that," the Emperor replied. "It was for our interest to leave Gibraltar in your possession. It is of no advantage to you. It neither protects nor intercepts any thing. It is only an object of national pride, which costs England very dear, and gives great umbrage to Spain. It would have been very injudicious in us to destroy such arrangements."

January 7. "I was walking one afternoon in the garden," Las Casas records, "when a sailor, about twenty-two or twenty-three years of age, with a frank and open countenance, approached us with gestures expressive of eagerness and joy, mingled with apprehension of being perceived from without. He spoke nothing but English, and told me, in a hurried manner, that he had twice braved the obstacle of sentinels and all the dangers of severe prohibition to get a close view of the Emperor. He had obtained this good fortune, he said, looking steadfastly at the Emperor, and should die content; that he offered up his prayers to Heaven that Napoleon might enjoy good health and be one day more happy. I dismissed him, and, on quitting us, he hid himself once more behind the trees and hedges, in order to have a longer view of us.

"We frequently met with such unequivocal proofs of the good-will of the sailors. Those of the *Northumberland*, above all, considered themselves as having formed a connection with the Emperor. While we were residing at the Briers, where our seclusion was not so close, they often hovered, on a Sunday, around us, saying that they came to take another look at their shipmate. The day on which we quitted the Briers I was with the Emperor in the garden, when one of the sailors presented himself at the gate, asking if he might step in without giving offense. I asked him of what country he was, and what religion he professed. He answered by making various signs of the cross, in token of his having understood me, and of fraternity. Then, looking steadfastly upon the Emperor, before whom he stood, and raising his eyes to heaven, he began to hold a conversation with himself by gestures, which his stout, jovial frame rendered partly grotesque and partly sentimental. Nevertheless, it would have been difficult to express more naturally admiration, respect, kind wishes, and sympathy, while big tears started in his eyes. 'Tell that dear man,' said he to me, 'that I wish him no harm, but all possible happiness. So do most of us. Long life and health to him!' He had a nosegay of wild flowers in his hand, which he seemed to wish to offer us, but either his attention was taken up, or he felt restrained by the Emperor's presence or his own feelings, and he stood wavering, as if con-

THE SAILORS OF THE NORTHUMBERLAND VISITING THEIR SHIPMATE.

tending with himself for some time, then suddenly he made us a bow and disappeared. The Emperor could not refrain from evincing emotion at these two circumstances, so strongly did the countenances, accents, and gestures of these two men bear the stamp of truth. He then said,

"'See the effect of imagination. How powerful is its influence! These are people who do not know me, who have never seen me; they have only heard me spoken of; and what do they not feel! What would they not do to serve me! And the same caprice is to be found in all countries, in all ages, and in both sexes. This is fanaticism. Yes, imagination rules the world!'"

January 9. The limits around Longwood allotted to the Emperor admitted of but half an hour's ride. He was, however, informed that he might extend his ride over a great part of the island, if he would submit to the escort of an English officer. The Emperor promptly decided that he could derive no pleasure and no benefit from a ride in which he was accompanied by his jailer. Admiral Cockburn, respecting these feelings, had consented, in communication with the friends of the Emperor, that the English officer should follow at such a distance as to occasion no embarrassment or annoyance to the Emperor in his conversation with his friends.

Napoleon was much gratified by this arrangement. He accordingly proposed to mount his horse at seven o'clock, to ride to the northern part of the island, to visit a spring, which in that vicinity gushed from beneath a beautiful grove in the midst of the rocks. From the bleak, barren, and verdureless exposure of Longwood, a ride to the cool fountain, the green grass, and the rich foliage presented great attractions. The sun rose brilliantly. The Emperor and his friends had partaken of their slight breakfast. The horses were at the door. All were in cheerful spirits, and were at the moment of mounting, when they were informed that the admiral had reconsidered his decision, and that the English officer on guard was ordered not to allow "General Bonaparte" to ride beyond his limits without keeping closely by his side.

The Emperor immediately relinquished his intended jaunt, and returned, deeply wounded and profoundly saddened, to his room. He threw off his riding-dress, put on his morning-gown, and, lying down upon the sofa, dismissed his attendants, and surrendered himself to silence, and solitude, and melancholy. His own spirit was, however, under perfect control, and he uttered not a word of anger or of reproach. His deep dejection, however, showed the anguish with which he yielded to wrongs so disgraceful to his oppressors, and, on his part, so utterly without remedy.

January 10. The Emperor passed the day, until four o'clock in the afternoon, reading alone in his room. He then dressed, and sent for Las Casas to accompany him in a walk in the garden. A sudden shower falling, he walked for some time up and down the rooms. He entered the drawing-room. Count Montholon and General Gourgaud were there, suspending a small mirror over the mantle-piece. The Emperor assisted them, and seemed much pleased at this improvement in his drawing-room furniture. He had but just left those palaces of France, which were embellished with all the luxuries Europe could afford, at a cost of more than eight millions of dollars.

The rain continuing, he relinquished his intended walk, and said, "Let us go and call upon Madam Montholon." Las Casas announced him. He entered her humble apartment and sat down, and requested Las Casas to do the same. The conversation turned upon furniture and housekeeping. He began to form an inventory of the articles, piece by piece, in Madam Montholon's room, and it was agreed that the whole was not worth more than one hundred and thirty dollars.

Leaving Madam Montholon's apartment, he continued his tour of observation from room to room till he came to the steep, almost perpendicular, and narrow stairs which led to the chambers of the servants.

"Let us look at Marchand's apartment," said the Emperor; "they say he keeps it like that of an elegant lady."

They climbed the stairs. Marchand, the Emperor's valet, was in his little room, and it was in a state of perfect neatness. He had pasted paper upon the walls, and painted the paper with his own hands. The drawers were opened which contained the Emperor's linen and other articles of clothing. The Emperor, taking up a pair of spurs, said,

"How many pairs of spurs have I, Marchand?"

"Four pair, sire," the valet replied.

"Are any of them more remarkable than the rest?" the Emperor inquired.

"No, sire."

"Well, then, I will give a pair of them to Las Casas. Are these old?"

"Yes, sire, they are almost worn out. Your majesty wore them in the campaign of Dresden, and in that of Paris."

"Here," said he to Las Casas, "these are for you."

"I could have wished," says Las Casas, "that he would have permitted me to receive them on my knees. I felt that I was really receiving something connected with the glorious days of Champaubert, Montmirail, Nangis, Montereau."

January 12. The Emperor took a short ride on horseback to-day within the limits allotted him. A drunken sentinel on one of the heights, mistaking his orders, shouted out and came running toward them, aiming his musket at the Emperor. General Gourgaud collared the wretch and secured him. This event caused the companions of the Emperor to tremble for his life, while Napoleon regarded it as an additional affront, and a fresh obstacle to the continuance of his exercise on horseback.

The Emperor now ceased giving further invitations to dinner, and, to beguile the melancholy hours, resumed his daily dictations. He thus worked diligently until dinner-time. The time after dinner was devoted to reading. The Emperor himself usually read aloud, accompanying his reading with profound criticism. Whenever the Emperor could protract this exercise till eleven or twelve o'clock at night, he seemed truly rejoiced. He called this making conquests over time.

Every three or four weeks a ship arrived from England with the European

THE DRUNKEN SENTINEL.

journals. These were devoured by the exiles with the most intense avidity. Some journals had recently been received. It was stated in them that England had desired the dismemberment of France, but that Russia had opposed it.

"I expected this," said the Emperor. "It is the natural system. Russia must be dissatisfied at seeing France divided. On the other hand, the English aristocracy must be desirous of reducing France to the extreme of weakness, and of establishing despotism upon her ruins. I can foresee nothing but catastrophes, massacres, and bloodshed."

January 15. Las Casas, having been sent for by the Emperor, entered his room immediately after breakfast, and found him reclining upon the sofa in his morning-gown. The conversation led him to inquire what Las Casas was reading. Las Casas replied that he was reading "The Secret History of the Cabinet of Bonaparte, by Goldsmith."* This was one of the most

* The following is the title-page of a royal octavo volume of over six hundred pages, published in London in the year 1810:

"*The Secret History of the Cabinet of Bonaparte*, including his Private Life, Character, Domestic Administration, together with the Secret Anecdotes of the different Courts of Europe, and of the French Revolution. With two Appendices, consisting of the State Papers and of Biographical Sketches of the Persons comprising the Court of St. Cloud. By LEWIS GOLDSMITH, Notary Public, Author of the 'Crimes of Cabinets,' 'An Exposition of the Conduct of France toward America.' '*The truth, and nothing but the truth*.' London, 1810."

The following are extracts from this work. We must implore pardon of our readers for thus sullying this page:

"Napoleon Bonaparte is the *reputed* son of the town clerk of Ajaccio, in Corsica. General Marbœuf was the *avowed protector* of the family. The meaning of this will be easily understood."

notorious and scurrilous libels published against the Emperor. Las Casas had, with much difficulty, borrowed it of Doctor O'Meara. He quoted to the Emperor some of its ridiculous and abominable stories.

The Emperor smiled at calumnies so incredible, and desired to see the work. Las Casas sent for it, and they glanced over its pages together. As they passed from one horrid calumny to another, the Emperor sometimes shrugged his shoulders in amazement, again he laughed heartily, but he nev-

"Our hero was placed at the military school at Brienne. He had an amour with a young girl of that place. Her disgrace was anticipated, and the disgrace of her paramour. The latter began his career of poisoning and murder by administering a dose to this unfortunate young woman. No positive proof being adduced, he was allowed to remain at school."

"In the year 1786, General Marbœuf died, and Napoleon was obliged to return to Corsica. From that period till he was sent off the island in 1793 by General Paoli, he was guilty of crimes of ev ery description."

"In the year 1793 he arrived at Marseilles, with his mother and sisters, who were sent off the island on account of these women having kept a house of accommodation, in which every species of vice was encouraged."

"One day he went to church, and having laid his hands on the hostie, emptied it of the conse crated wafers, and supplied the place with the refuse of his own body."

"It is the general opinion that both Kleber and Desaix were assassinated by the order of Na poleon."

"In his fits of passion he kicks those about him. He runs about the room foaming, raging, and swearing like a mad boy."

"Merely for amusement, he used to pinch his Josephine to that degree that the impression of his fingers on her body has been visible for days."

"He lived in a state of undisguised concubinage with his two sisters, Mesdames Murat (Caroline) and Borghese (Pauline). The former made a public boast of it. This voluptuous murderer has also established a seminary for young persons, daughters and orphans of the Legion of Honor. But it is nothing more than a nursery for his intended victims whom he wishes to debauch."

"Never was there, in one human being, such a combination of cruelty, tyranny, petulance, lewd ness, luxury, and avarice as there is in Napoleon Bonaparte. Human nature had not before pro duced such a frightful being."

"At the execution of the Duke d'Enghien, Bonaparte and his brother Louis were present. Louis fainted. This so enraged Napoleon that he kicked him as he would a dog."

"The new-made Emperor fell upon the grand judge, and beat him in the face in the most un merciful manner. He was taken out of the tyrant's presence, or he would have killed him. An eye-witness told me that it was truly laughable to see a grand judge, lying quietly on the sofa, suf fering himself to be beaten like a slave without making the least resistance. And when he was taken into the antechamber, he was weltering in his blood, his robe torn, and his wig pulled off,. while he was crying like a school-boy."

"The poison which Bonaparte administered to his victims is, I am very credibly informed, pre pared in the following manner : Arsenic is given to a pig, which they hang by its legs, and the sub stance which drops out of the mouth and nostrils is collected, and goes through a chemical process. When he means to have any one poisoned, he sends for the cook or valet-de-chambre of the intend ed victim, and, what with bribes and threats, they unfortunately never fail of attaining their bloody ends."

Such were the *histories* of Napoleon, which, during this conflict, were circulated through the aris tocratic circles of England. They were eagerly read and thankfully believed. For the masses of the people, sixpenny pamphlets of a similar character were issued. The following is the title of one of them : "*The Atrocities of the Corsican Demon ; or, A Glance at Bonaparte Do but observe the face of villainy.*"

These *histories* may be found in the Boston Atheneum, and probably in most other of the large libraries of our country. Being a little too strong for modern palates, they have been slightly di luted by Sir Walter Scott. his son-in-law Lockhart, and by Sir Archibald Alison. It is not strange that so many have risen from the reading of such volumes with the conviction that Napoleon was a "monster."

er betrayed the least sign of anger. When he read the recital of his reckless licentiousness and his enormous debaucheries, he said,

"The author doubtless wished to make me a hero in every respect; but I must leave him to settle this charge with those who, on the other hand, have accused me of impotency. They are, however, in the wrong to attack me on the score of morals, since all the world knows, that I have so singularly improved them. They can not but be ignorant that I was not at all inclined by nature to debauchery. Moreover, the multiplicity of my affairs would never have allowed me time to indulge in it."

When he came to the pages which heaped obscene and monstrous abuse upon his venerated mother, he exclaimed, in accents of blended grief and indignation,

"Ah, madam! poor madam! with her lofty character! If she were to read this! Great God!"

Doctor O'Meara was soon introduced. The Emperor, who was then shaving himself, turned to his physician and said,

"Doctor, I have just read one of your fine London productions against me. It is a very just remark that it is the truth only which gives offense. I have not been angry for a moment, but I have frequently laughed at it."

"It is an infamous and disgusting libel," the doctor replied, with embarrassment. "Nevertheless, persons may be found who will believe it from its not having been replied to."

"But how can that be helped?" said the Emperor. "If it should enter any one's head to put in print that I had grown hairy and walked on four paws, there are people who would believe it, and would say that God had punished me as he did Nebuchadnezzar. And what could I do? There is no remedy in such cases."

January 16. "The conversation," says Las Casas, "led me to observe that I had just given my son his first lesson in mathematics. It is a branch of knowledge which the Emperor is very fond of, and in which he is particularly skilled. He was astonished that I could teach my son so much without the help of any text-book. He said he did not know I was so learned in this way, and threatened me with examining, when I did not expect it, both master and scholar. At dinner he undertook what he called the Professor of Mathematics, who was very near being posed by him. One question did not wait for another, and they were frequently very keen. He never ceased to regret that the mathematics were not taught at a very early age in the Lyceums. He said that all the intentions he had formed respecting the universities had been frustrated, and that while he was obliged to be at a distance carrying on war, they spoiled all he had done at home."

January 20. The Emperor received Governor Wilks. The governor was a man of much intelligence, and the conversation was very animated upon the army, the sciences, government, and the Indies. Speaking of the organization of the English army, he expressed his surprise at the principles of promotion adopted therein, and that, in a country in which the equality of rights is maintained, the soldiers so seldom become officers.

"The English soldiers," said Governor Wilks, "are not capable of becoming officers. The English were astonished, in their turn, at the great difference in that respect which they had remarked in the French army, where almost every soldier showed the nascent talents of an officer."

"That," said the Emperor, "is one of the great results of the conscription. It has rendered the French army the best constituted that ever existed. It was an institution eminently national, and already strongly interwoven with our habits. It had ceased to be a cause of grief except to mothers. The time was at hand when a girl would not have listened to a young man who had not acquitted himself of this debt to his country, and it would have been only when arrived at this point that the conscription would have manifested the full extent of its advantages. When the service no longer bears the appearance of punishment or compulsory duty, but is become a point of honor, on which all are jealous, then only is the nation great, glorious, and powerful. It is then that its existence is proof against reverses, invasions, even the hand of time.

"Besides, it may be truly said that there is nothing that may not be obtained from Frenchmen by the excitement of danger. It seems to animate them. It is an inheritance they derive from their Gallic predecessors. Courage, the love of glory, are, with the French, an instinct, a kind of sixth sense. How often, in the heat of battle, has my attention been fixed on my young conscripts, rushing, for the first time, into the thickest of the fight, honor and valor bursting forth at every pore!"

The subject of chemistry was introduced, upon which Governor Wilks was peculiarly well informed.

"All our manufactures," said the Emperor, "have made immense progress by the aid of this science. Both England and France undoubtedly possess great chemists. But chemistry is more generally diffused in France, and more particularly directed to useful results. In England it has remained a science, while in France it has become thoroughly practical."

The governor admitted that these observations were correct, and also added that it was to the Emperor that all these advantages were due. "When science," he continued, "is led by the hand of power, it will produce great and happy effects upon the well-being of society."

"Of late," said the Emperor, "France has obtained sugar from the beet-root as good and cheap as that extracted from the sugar-cane. It is the same with woad, the substitute for indigo, and with almost all the colonial produce except the dyewoods. If the invention of the compass has produced a revolution in commerce, the progress of chemistry bids fair to produce a counter revolution."

The conversation then turned to the numerous emigration of artisans from France and England to America.

"That favored country," said the Emperor, "grows rich by our follies."

"Those of England," the governor replied, smiling, "will occupy the first place in the list, from the numerous errors of administration which led to the revolt and subsequent emancipation of the colonies."

"Their emancipation," the Emperor continued, "was inevitable. When children come to the size of their fathers, it is difficult to retain them long in a state of obedience."

Conversation now turned upon Madam de Staël's *Delphine*. The Emperor analyzed it with great critical acumen. The irregularity of mind and imagination which pervades it excited his censure. "There are throughout," said he, "the same faults which had formerly made me keep the author at a distance, notwithstanding the most pointed advances and the most unremitting flattery on her part. No sooner had victory immortalized the young general of the army of Italy, than Madam de Staël, from the mere sympathy of glory, instantly professed for him sentiments of enthusiasm worthy of her own *Corinne*. She wrote him long and numerous epistles, full of wit, imagination, and metaphysical erudition. It was an error, she observed, arising only from human institutions, that could have united him with the meek, the tranquil Madam Bonaparte. It was a soul of fire like hers (Madam de Staël) that nature had undoubtedly destined to be the companion of a hero like him.

"While at Geneva," continued the Emperor, "on my way to Marengo, I received a visit from Madam de Staël's father, M. Neckar. He made known, in an awkward manner enough, his desire to be admitted again to the administration. M. Neckar afterward wrote a dangerous work upon the policy of France, which he attempted to prove could no longer exist as a monarchy or a republic, and in which he called the First Consul the necessary man—*l'homme nécessaire*.

"The First Consul," continued the Emperor, "proscribed the work, which at that time might have been highly prejudicial to him, and committed the task of its refutation to the Consul Lebrun, who, in his excellent prose, executed prompt and ample justice upon it. The Neckar coterie was irritated, and Madam de Staël, engaging in some intrigues, received an order to quit France. Thenceforth she became an ardent and strenuous enemy. Nevertheless, on the return from Elba, she wrote, or sent to the Emperor, to express, in her peculiar way, the enthusiasm which this wonderful event had excited in her; that she was overcome; that this last act was not that of a mortal; that it had at once raised its author to the skies. Then, returning to herself, she concluded by hinting, that if the Emperor would condescend to allow the payment of the two millions, for which an order in her favor had already been signed by the king, her pen and her principles should be devoted forever after to his interest. The Emperor desired she might be informed that nothing could flatter him more highly than her approbation, because he fully appreciated her talents, but he really was not rich enough to purchase it at that price."

The room which Count Las Casas temporarily occupied had been intended as a topographical cabinet for the Emperor. New lodgings were now constructed for him. He thus describes them: "Upon a soil constantly damp had been placed a floor eighteen feet long by eleven wide. This was surrounded by a wall a foot and a half in thickness, composed of a sort of loam, and which might have been destroyed by a kick of the foot. At the height of seven feet it was covered with a roof of boards, defended by a coating of paper and tar. Such were the construction and outline of my new palace, divided into two apartments, one of which contained two beds separated by a chest of drawers, and would only afford room for a single chair. The other, at once my saloon and my library, had a single window, strongly fastened on account of the violence of the winds and rain. On the right and left of it were two writing-tables, for me and my son; on the opposite side, a couch and two chairs. This was the whole of the furniture and the accommodations. Add to this that the aspect of the two windows is toward a wind constantly blowing from the same quarter, and generally accompanied with rain, often very heavy, and which, previous to our taking possession, had already forced its way through the cracks, or soaked through the walls and the roof."

Las Casas, with a heavy heart, entered this cheerless room. Weary and sick, he passed a sleepless night. To his amazement, early in the morning, before he had risen, the Emperor, in a playful mood, came bustling into his chamber, threw open the curtains, and, with an assumed air of authority, said that it was time to shake off sloth, and to be up and out. Then, struck with the extreme smallness and closeness of the apartment, he said,

"You must not be suffered to sleep huddled together in this way. It is far too unwholesome. You must return to the bed in the topographical cabinet. If you occasion any inconvenience there, you shall be told of it."

The Emperor then went out and mounted his horse for a ride. Las Casas soon dressed and overtook him. The conversation turned on the long audience the Emperor had given Governor Wilks the day before. Las Casas was an author of much celebrity, and was treated with great deference by the governor. Napoleon alluded to this in a vein of pleasantry, and said,

"Of course it is understood that these sentiments are to be mutual; the usual regard and fraternity of authors, as long as they do not criticise each other. And is he aware of your relationship to the venerable Las Casas?"

General Gourgaud replied that he was.

"And how do you know it yourself?" said the Emperor, turning to Las Casas. "Are you not romancing with us? Let us hear all about it. Come, Sir Castellan, Sir Knight Errant, Sir Paladin, let us see you in your glory; unroll your old parchments; come enjoy yourself."

Las Casas then gave the evidence that he was a descendant of the illustrious Spaniard, Barthelemi de Las Casas.

January 26. Several days of incessant rain had confined the captive and his friends to their rooms. The Emperor read and wrote with great diligence, apparently never experiencing any fatigue from intellectual exertion. He often read aloud to his companions. He also engaged earnestly in the study of the English language. He read, with many comments, the letters of Madam de Sevigné, and the History of Charles XII.; and also, with great rhetorical effect, the pathetic story of Paul and Virginia.

"The most touching passages," said the Emperor, "are always the most simple and natural. Those which abound with abstract and false ideas, so much in fashion when the work was published, are all cold, bad, spoiled. I was infatuated with this book in my youth, but I have little personal regard for its author. I can never forgive him for having imposed on my generosity on my return from the army of Italy. The sensibility and delicacy of Bernardin Saint Pierre were little in harmony with his charming picture of Paul and Virginia. He was a bad man. He used his wife, the daughter of Didot, the printer, very ill. He was always ready to ask charity without the least shame. On my return from the army of Italy, Bernardin came to see me, and almost immediately began to tell me of his wants. I, who in my early youth had dreamed of nothing but Paul and Virginia, and felt flattered by a confidence which I imagined was reposed in me alone, and which I attributed to my great celebrity, hastened to return his visit, and, unperceived by any one, left on the corner of his chimney-piece a little rouleau of five-and-twenty Louis ($112). But how was I mortified in seeing every one laugh at the delicacy of my proceeding, and on learning that such ceremony was entirely superfluous with M. Bernardin, who made it his trade to beg of all comers, and to receive from every body. I always retained some little resentment toward him for having thus imposed upon me. It was otherwise with my family. Joseph allowed him a large pension, and Louis was constantly making him presents."

The *Studies of Nature*, by the same author, the Emperor considered contemptible. "Bernardin," said he, "though versed in Belles Lettres, was very little of a geometrician. This last work was so bad that scientific men disdained to answer it. Bernardin complained loudly of their not answering him. The celebrated mathematician, Lagrange, when speaking on this subject, always said, alluding to the Institute,

"'If Bernardin were one of our class, if he spoke our language, we would call him to order. But he belongs to the Academy, and his style is out of our line.'

"Bernardin was complaining, as usual, one day, to the First Consul, of the silence of the learned with respect to his work. 'Do you understand the differential method, M. Bernardin?' Napoleon asked. 'No,' was the reply. 'Well,' added Napoleon, 'go and learn it, and then you will be able to answer it yourself.'"

In reading Vertot's Roman Revolutions, the Emperor highly commended the work, on the whole, though he thought the declamations much too diffuse. He amused himself in striking out the superfluous phrases, thus giving the work much more energy and animation.

"It would certainly be," said he, "a most valuable and successful labor, if any man of taste and discernment would devote his time to reducing the principal works in our language in this manner. I know of no one but Montesquieu who would escape these curtailments." He thought Rollin diffuse and too credulous. Crevier, his continuator, he pronounced detestable. He condemned the French historians generally.

"I can not bear," said he, "to read any of them. Velly is rich in words and poor in meaning. His continuators are still worse. Our history should be either in four or five volumes, or in a hundred. I was acquainted with Garnier, who continued Velly and Villaret. He lived in the basement of Malmaison. He was an old man of eighty, and lodged in a small set of apartments on the ground floor, with a little gallery. Struck with the officious attention which this good old man always evinced whenever I was passing, I inquired who he was. On learning it was Garnier, I comprehended his motives. He no doubt imagined that a First Consul was his property as historian. I dare say, however, he was astonished to find consuls where he had been accustomed to see kings. I laughingly told him so one day, and settled a good pension upon him. From that time the good man, in the warmth of his gratitude, would gladly have written any thing I pleased with all his heart."

January 27. The conversation at dinner and afterward turned on various deeds of arms. "One of the finest maneuvers," said the Emperor, "which I remember, I executed at Eckmühl. Success in war depends so much on quick-sightedness, and on seizing the right moment, that the battle of Austerlitz, which was so completely won, would have been lost if I had attacked six hours sooner. The Russians showed themselves on that occasion such excellent troops as they have never appeared since. The Russian army of Austerlitz would never have lost the battle of Moscow.

"Marengo was the battle in which the Austrians fought best. Their troops behaved admirably there. But that was the grave of their valor. It has never since been seen.

"The Prussians at Jena did not make such a resistance as was expected from their reputation. As to the multitudes of 1814 and 1815, they were a mere rabble compared to the real soldiers of Marengo, Austerlitz, and Jena.

"The night before the battle of Jena I ran the greatest risk. I might then have disappeared without my fate being clearly known. I had approached the bivouacs of the enemy in the dark to reconnoitre them. I had only a few officers with me. The opinion which was then entertained of the Prussian army kept every one on the alert. It was thought that the Prussians were particularly given to nocturnal attacks. As I returned, I was fired at by the first sentinel of my camp. This was a signal for the whole line. I had no resource but to throw myself flat on my face until the mistake was discovered. My principal apprehension was that the Prussian line, which was very near me, would act in the same manner.

"At Marengo, the Austrian soldiers had not forgotten the conqueror of Castiglione, Arcola, and Rivoli. His name had much influence over them, but they were far from thinking that he was present. They believed he was dead. Care had been taken to persuade them that he had perished in Egypt. This report had gained so much credit every where, that I was under the necessity of appearing in public at Milan in order to refute it.

"Two of the circumstances," continued the Emperor, "which most affected me on the field of battle, were the deaths of young Guibert and General Corbineau. At Aboukir a bullet went quite through the heart of the former.

BATTLE OF AUSTERLITZ.

without killing him instantly. After saying a few words to him, I was obliged by the violence of my feelings to leave him. General Corbineau was carried away, crushed, annihilated by a cannon ball at Eylau, before my face, while I was giving him some orders."

The Emperor spoke of the last moments of his devoted friend Lannes, the Duke of Montebello.

"I had the highest esteem for him," said the Emperor. "He was for a long time a mere fighting man, but he afterward became an officer of the first talents."

Some one remarked that he should like to know what line of conduct Lannes would have pursued in these latter times if he had lived.

"We have learned," the Emperor replied, "not to take our oath to any thing. Yet I can not conceive that it would have been possible for him to deviate from the path of duty and of honor. Besides, it is hard to imagine that he could have existed. With all his bravery, he would unquestionably have got killed in some of the last affairs, or, at least, sufficiently wounded to be laid up out of the centre and influence of events. And if he had remained disposable, he was a man capable of changing the whole face of affairs by his own weight and influence."

DEATH OF LANNES.

The Emperor then entered upon a glowing eulogy of the private life and character of Duroc. "He had," said the Emperor, "lively, tender, and concealed passions, little corresponding with the coldness of his manner. It was long before I knew this, so exact and regular was his service. It was not until my day was entirely closed and finished that Duroc's work began.

F

Chance, or some accident, could alone have made me acquainted with his character. He was a pure and virtuous man, entirely disinterested and extremely generous.

"On the opening of the campaign at Dresden I lost two men who were extremely valuable to me, Bessières and Duroc. When I went to see Duroc after he had received his mortal wound, I attempted to hold out some hopes to him. But Duroc was not deceived, and only replied by begging them to give him opium. I could not endure the distressing spectacle, and tore myself away."

One of the company then reminded the Emperor that, upon leaving Duroc, he went alone to his tent, and that no one ventured to accost him. But at last some one, impelled by the urgency of the case, went to him and inquired where the battery of the guard was to be placed. "Ask me nothing till to-morrow," was the reply.

The Emperor struggled against the grief which these mournful recollections introduced, and, with much apparent effort, abruptly changed the conversation.

DEATH OF DUROC.

January 31. "Our days passed," says Las Casas, "as may be supposed, in an excessive stupid monotony. Ennui, reflection, and melancholy were our formidable enemies; occupation, our great and only refuge. The Emperor followed his pursuits with great regularity. English was become an affair of importance to him. It was now near a fortnight since he took his first lesson, and from that moment he had devoted some hours every day, beginning at noon, to that study.

"Let any one form the idea of what the scholastic study of conjugations, declensions, and articles must have been to him. He often asked me whether he did not deserve the ferula, of which he now comprehended the vast utility in schools. He declared, jestingly, that he should have made much greater progress himself had he stood in fear of correction. He complained of not having improved, but, in reality, the progress he had made would have been extraordinary in any one. The Emperor thus procured the pleasure of reading English, and he could make himself understood by writing in that language."

Every day the Emperor passed some hours dictating the campaigns of Egypt to General Bertrand, and revising, with Las Casas, the campaigns of Italy. He also occasionally dictated to Messrs. Gourgaud and Montholon. On the 30th, after several days of rain, he went on horseback to the secluded vale which he had named the Valley of Silence. An apparently trifling event took place, which pleasantly illustrates the domestic character of the Emperor. Las Casas thus records it:

"We were near the middle of the vale. The passage was stopped up with dead bushes, and a kind of bar to restrain cattle. The servant dismounted to clear the way for us. We passed on, but while the servant was engaged in assisting us, his horse had strayed from him, and when he attempted to catch him, ran away. A great quantity of rain had fallen, and the horse sank into a quagmire. The servant ran after us to say that he must remain for the purpose of disengaging his horse. We were in a very difficult and narrow road, riding one by one. It was not until some time after that the Emperor heard us mention to one another the accident of the servant. He found much fault because we had not waited for him, and desired the grand marshal and General Gourgaud to return to his aid.

"The Emperor dismounted to wait for them, and ascended a little elevation, on which he looked like a figure on a pedestal in the midst of ruins. He had the bridle of his horse passed around his arm, and began to whistle an air. Mute nature echoed the strains, but only to a barren desert. 'Yet,' thought I, 'a short time ago, how many sceptres he wielded! how many crowns belonged to him! how many kings were at his feet! It is true,' said I, 'that in the eyes of those who approach him, who daily see and hear him, he is still greater than ever. This is the sentiment, the opinion of all about him. We serve him with no less ardor, we love him with greater affection than ever.'

"Soon the grand marshal and Gourgaud arrived. They assisted the Emperor to mount again, and we went on. They acknowledged that without their assistance the horse could not have been saved. The united efforts of

THE EMPEROR ON THE CLIFF.

all three had barely been sufficient to disengage him. A short time afterward, in turning an elbow of the road, the Emperor observed that the servant had not followed, and said that they ought to have remained till he was in a condition to come on. They thought he had staid behind to clean his horse a little. In the course of our ride, at several other turnings the Emperor repeated the same observation. We arrived at the grand marshal's at Hut's Gate, went in, and rested there a few minutes. As we came out, the Emperor asked if the servant had passed on. No one had seen him. When we arrived at Longwood, his first question was whether the man had returned. He had been at home some time, having taken a different road.

"I may perhaps have dwelt," says Las Casas, "somewhat too much upon this trifling circumstance, but I did so because it appeared to me perfectly characteristic. In this domestic solicitude the reader will find it difficult to recognize the insensible, obdurate, wicked, cruel monster, the tyrant of whom he has so often and so long been told."

CHAPTER V.
1816, February.

Scanty Resources of the Island—The Emperor's Progress in English—Learns the Death of Murat—Eloquent Parallel—Affairs of Spain—Dismal Days—Caricatures—French Politics—Picture of Domestic Happiness—The Emperor's Opinion of the French Poets—Public Contractors—Vigilance of the Emperor.

February 1. A pleasant morning dawned upon the inmates of Longwood. The Emperor, cheered by the invigorating air, appeared tranquil and contented. As he walked with Las Casas in the garden, he surrendered himself to that wise philosophy which looks upon the "brightest side," and pleasantly remarked,

"After all, as a place of exile, St. Helena is perhaps the best that could be selected. In high latitudes we should have suffered greatly from cold. In any other island of the tropic we should have dragged out a miserable existence under the scorching rays of the sun. This rock is wild and barren, no doubt. The climate is monotonous and unwholesome, but the temperature, it must be confessed, is mild and agreeable."

"Meanwhile," says Las Casas, "in order to afford a correct idea of our place of exile and the scantiness of its resources, it is only necessary to observe that we were this day informed it would be necessary to economize various articles of our daily consumption, and, perhaps, even to make a temporary sacrifice of some. We were told that the store of coffee was rapidly diminishing, and that it would soon be entirely exhausted. For a considerable time we have denied ourselves the use of white sugar. There was but very little, and that very bad, which was reserved exclusively for the Emperor's use; and there is now every prospect of this little supply being exhausted before more can be obtained. It is the same with various other necessaries. Our island is like a ship at sea; our stores are speedily exhausted. But of all the privations with which we are threatened, that which surprises us, and which is most of all vexatious, is the want of writing-paper. We are informed that, during our three months' residence here, we have consumed all the paper in the island. In addition to this, our physical and moral privations must be taken into account. It must be recollected that we were not in the full enjoyment of even the few resources which the island affords, and of which arbitrary feeling and caprice in part deprive us, for we are not permitted to regale our eyes with the sight of the grass and foliage in places at a certain distance from Longwood. The admiral had promised that the Emperor should be free to ride over the whole island, and that he would make arrangements with respect to his guard, so as to free him from all annoyance. The admiral, however, broke his engagement; and by his order, an officer insisted on accompanying the Emperor in his rides. The Emperor consequently renounced the idea of taking any excursion whatever, and we now remained cut off from any communication with the inhabitants.

"With respect to physical comforts, our situation was most miserable, either through unavoidable circumstances or mismanagement. Scarcely any of the provisions were eatable. The wine was execrable. The oil was unfit for use. The coffee and sugar were almost at an end; and, as I have already observed, we had almost bred a famine in the island. Of course, we could endure all these privations, and might have contrived to exist under many more. But when it is asserted that we were treated in a style of magnificence, we are induced to unfold our real situation, and to show that we were destitute of every comfort."

February 8. For several days the weather had been most dismal. The rain fell in torrents, and the howling gale swept fiercely over the bleak and craggy rock. The water soaked through the roof and the ceilings of tarred paper, and a chill dampness pervaded all the apartments. Irresistible gloom oppressed the spirits of all the inmates of this dreary prison. In the driving storm, no one could leave the house. The Emperor, however, far surpassed any of his companions in patience and fortitude. Perceiving the dejection which Las Casas in vain endeavored to conceal, he said to him, playfully, one morning,

"What is the matter with you? You seem quite altered for these few days past. Is your mind ailing? Are you conjuring up *dragons*, like Madam de Sevigné?"

The Emperor resolutely devoted four and five hours a day to the study of English. He prized very highly the knowledge he was thus acquiring, as it enabled him to read fluently the English papers. He was very methodical in the employment of his time, and toiled with most exemplary patience through the drudgery of acquiring the rudiments of a new tongue. He said to Las Casas,

"I stand in need of excitement. Nothing but the pleasure of advancement can bear me through; for, between you and me, it must needs be confessed that there is nothing very amusing in all this. Indeed, there is but very little of diversion in the whole routine of our present existence."

To-day a frigate arrived bringing newspapers from Europe. One of these journals contained the intelligence that Murat had landed in Calabria with a few troops, and had been seized and shot. As this unexpected intelligence was read to the Emperor, he exclaimed, "The Calabrians were more humane and generous than those who sent me here." The Emperor was then silent, lost in painful musing, and for some time there was a pause, during which nothing was said. Afterward he remarked,

"Murat was doomed to be our bane. He ruined us by forsaking us, and he ruined us by too warmly espousing our cause. He observed no sort of discretion. He himself attacked the Austrians without any reasonable plan and without adequate forces, and he was subdued without striking a blow."

"Endeavors have been made," says Las Casas, "to represent Napoleon

DEATH OF MURAT.

as a man of furious and implacable temper; but the truth is that he was a stranger to revenge, and he never cherished any vindictive feeling, whatever wrong he might have suffered. His anger was usually vented in violent transports, and was soon at an end. Murat had scandalously betrayed him, had twice ruined his prospects, and yet he came to seek an asylum at Toulon."

"I should have taken Murat with me to Waterloo," said the Emperor, "but such was the patriotic and moral feeling of the French army, that it was doubtful whether the troops could surmount the horror and disgust which they felt for the man who had betrayed and lost France. I did not consider myself sufficiently powerful to protect him. Yet he might have enabled us to gain the victory. How useful would he have been at certain periods of the battle! He would have broken three or four English squares. Murat was admirable in such a service as this. He was precisely the man for it. At the head of a body of cavalry, no man was ever more resolute, more courageous, more brilliant.

"As to drawing a parallel," continued the Emperor, "between the circumstances of Napoleon and Murat, between the landing of the former in France and the entrance of the latter into the Neapolitan territory, no such parallel exists. Murat had no good argument to support his cause except success. His enterprise was purely chimerical, both as to the time and manner of its commencement. Napoleon was the chosen ruler of a people; he was their legitimate sovereign, according to modern doctrines; but Murat was not a Neapolitan; the Neapolitans had not chosen Murat. How, therefore, could it be expected that he would excite any lively interest in his favor? Thus his proclamation was totally false and void of facts. Ferdinand of Naples could view him in no other light than as a supporter of insurrection. He did so, and treated him accordingly.

"How different was it with me! Before my arrival, one universal sentiment pervaded France, and my proclamation was imbued with that sentiment. Every one found that it echoed the feelings of his own heart. France was discontented; I was her resource. The evil and the remedy were immediately in unison. This is the whole history of that electric movement which is unexampled in history. It had its source solely in the nature of things. There was no conspiracy, and the impulse was general. Not a word was spoken, and a general understanding prevailed throughout the country. Whole towns threw themselves at the feet of their deliverer. The first battalion which I gained over to me immediately placed the whole army in my power. I found myself borne on to Paris. The existing government and its agency disappeared, without efforts, like clouds before the sun. And yet, had I been subdued, had I fallen into the hands of my enemies, I was not a mere insurrectionary chief; I was a sovereign, acknowledged by all Europe. I had my title, my standards, my troops, and I was advancing to wage war on my enemy."

February 9. Las Casas read to the Emperor, from an English paper, an account of the Spanish general Porlier, who had endeavored to rouse his countrymen against the tyranny of Ferdinand. He failed, was arrested, and hanged.

"I am not in the least surprised," said the Emperor, "that such an attempt should have been made in Spain. Those very Spaniards, who proved themselves my most inveterate enemies when I invaded their country, and who acquired the highest glory by the resistance they opposed to me, immediately appealed to me on my return from Elba. They had, they said, fought against me as their tyrant, but they now came to implore my aid as their deliverer. They required only a small sum to emancipate themselves and to produce in the Peninsula a revolution similar to mine. Had I conquered at Waterloo, it was my intention immediately to have assisted the Spaniards. This circumstance sufficiently explains to me the attempt that has lately been made. There is little doubt but that it will be renewed again. Ferdinand, in his madness, may grasp his sceptre as firmly as he will, but one day or other it will slip through his fingers like an eel."

February 11. It was a calm and beautiful Sabbath. The sun shone serenely upon the solitude of St. Helena. In the afternoon the Emperor walked out with several of his companions, and remarked upon the peacefulness and loneliness of the scene. "We can not, at least," said he, "be accused of dissipation, or of the ardent pursuit of pleasure."

"The Emperor," says Las Casas, "endures this mode of life admirably. He surpasses us all in equanimity and serenity of temper. He says himself that it would be difficult to be more philosophic and tranquil than he is. He retires to bed at ten o'clock, and does not go out before five or six in the afternoon, so that he is never more than four hours out of doors, like a prisoner who is led from his cell once a day to breathe the fresh air. But then how intense is the occupation of each day! how various are the thoughts which occupy his mind!"

"With regard to mental exertion," said the Emperor, "I feel as capable of bearing it as I have ever been. I never feel any exhaustion or weariness. I am astonished myself at the slight impression of all the great events of which I have lately been the object. They are as lead which has glided over marble. Weight may compress a spring, but can not break it. It rises again with its own elasticity. I do not think that any one in the world knows better than myself how to yield to necessity. This is the true empire of reason, the true triumph of the soul."

The hour for the calash had now arrived. In going to it the Emperor saw little Hortense, the daughter of Madam Bertrand. She was a lovely child, and quite a favorite of the Emperor. He called her to him, embraced her two or three times tenderly, and took her out in the carriage to ride along with little Tristan Montholon. During the ride, General Bertrand, who had been looking over the papers, gave an account of several witticisms and caricatures which he had met with.

One in the Emperor's favor represented him giving to the Princess of Hats-

"TYRANNICAL ACT OF A USURPER."

field, to commit to the flames, the letter whose disappearance would save the life of her husband by destroying the proof of his guilt. Underneath was written, "*Tyrannical Act of a Usurper.*" Connected with this was another caricature representing Madam Labédoyère and her son imploring, at the feet of Louis XVIII., the life of the husband and father. The king rudely repulses her. At a little distance some soldiers are drawn up to shoot M. Labédoyère. Underneath were inscribed the words, "*Paternal Act of a Legitimate King.*"

This led to a general conversation upon the subject of caricatures. There were many mentioned which afforded the Emperor much amusement. One of them caused him to laugh very heartily. There was a representation of the grand palace of the Tuileries. A herd of geese and unwieldy swine were waddling and wallowing in by the great entrance gate of the palace, driven by a group of soldiers of all nations and of all arms. At the same moment, an imperial eagle from one of the upper windows, with outspread wings, soared away in a bold and rapid flight. Upon the front of the palace there was inscribed these simple words, "*Change of Dynasty.*"

Another one the Emperor applauded very much as quite ludicrous and in very good taste. It represented George III. a corpulent old man standing upon the English coast, and in great rage hurling at the head of Napoleon, upon the opposite shores of France, an immense beet-root, saying, "*Go and make yourself some sugar.*"

"If caricatures," said the Emperor, "sometimes avenge misfortune, they form a continual annoyance to power; and how many have been made upon me! I think I have had my share of them."

February 17. At six o'clock in the morning the Emperor mounted his horse and rode through the valley. A party of about two hundred sailors and soldiers from the *Northumberland* were at work upon the road. As soon as they saw the Emperor approaching, they immediately formed into line to salute him. The Emperor spoke to the officers and smiled with pleasure upon the men. He appeared highly gratified in again seeing them.

Continuing his ride, he remarked upon the intelligence which he had recently received from Europe.

"The Bourbons," said he, "have now no other resource than severity. Four months have already elapsed, the allied forces are about to be withdrawn, and none but half measures have been taken. The affair has been badly managed. A government can exist only by its principle. The principle of the French government evidently is to return to its old maxims. It should do this openly. In present circumstances, the chambers, above all, will be fatal. They will inspire the king with false confidence, and will have no weight with the nation. The king will soon be deprived of all means of communication with them. They will no longer follow the same religion nor speak the same language. No individual will henceforth have a right to undeceive the people with regard to any absurdities which may be propagated, even if it should be wished to make them believe that all the springs of water are poisoned, and that trains of gunpowder are laid under ground.

THE ENGLISH SOLDIERS SALUTING THE EMPEROR.

"There will be some juridical executions, and an extreme desire of reaction, which will be sufficiently strong to irritate but not to subdue. Sooner or later a volcanic eruption will ingulf the throne, its courtiers, and its partisans. If destiny has decreed that the Bourbons should reign, many ages must pass before they can be sure of that fact. At present they are undoubtedly much worse situated than they were last year. Then one could, as a desperate resort, represent them as mediators between the coalesced powers and their country. They had not then directly contributed to the abasement of France, to the degradation of our national glory, but now they are the allies of our enemies. They have returned over the carnage and the conflagrations which they have provoked, and over which they exult. They have ruined the nation, its forces, its glory, its monuments, and have not hesitated to share its spoils with the enemy, and have thus reserved for themselves shame and contempt. In the eyes of all France they have ceased to be Frenchmen. They have proscribed themselves.

"As to Europe, it appears to me as violently agitated as it has ever been. The Allies have destroyed France, but her resurrection may some day be caused by the uprising of the masses of the people in Europe whom the policy of the sovereigns is calculated to alienate. France may also rise again in consequence of a quarrel among the Allies, which will probably take place.

"As to our personal prospects here at St. Helena, they can only be improved through the medium of England, and she can only be induced to favor us by some political interest, some change of the ministry, the death of the sovereign, or still more probably by a sentiment of national glory excited by an outburst of popular opinion. As for political interests, circumstances may bring them about. The change of individuals depends on accidents. As to the sentiment of national glory, so easily understood, the present ministry has disavowed it, but another may not be so insensible."

February 18. The Emperor, after studying English several hours, at five o'clock went into the garden, accompanied by most of his devoted companions. He began to describe the happiness of a private individual, of irreproachable character and easy circumstances, peacefully enjoying life in his native province, in the house and surrounded by the lands which he had inherited from his ancestors. " Happiness of this kind," said he, " is now unknown in France except by tradition. The Revolution has destroyed it. The old families have been deprived of this enjoyment. The new ones have not yet been long enough established to appreciate it. The picture which I have sketched has now no real existence.

" To be driven from one's natal chamber, from the garden where one has played in childhood, to have no paternal mansion, is, in reality, to be deprived of one's country."

February 23. Las Casas, in conversation, alluded to an atrocious act of cruelty perpetrated by Louis XVIII., and quoted ironically a phrase which had become proverbial, "*The hereditary kind-heartedness of the Bourbons.*" The Emperor repeated the adage, and exclaimed,

" Yes, how powerful is the empire of words when they have once been received. A historian will hazard a phrase which presents itself to him as fine. Others repeat it through adulation. The multitude seize upon words which fill all mouths even in the midst of facts the most contrary. Behold the proof of the falsehood of this adage. It is to be found in Henry IV., undeniably the best of the Bourbons, offering life to Marshal Byron, his companion in arms, his bosom friend, if he would confess his fault, and who yet left him heartlessly to his executioner because he remained firm. It is to be found in Louis XIII., who, at the moment of the execution of his favorite, immolated by an implacable minister, said, looking at his watch, '*Our good friend must be passing a very uncomfortable quarter of an hour.*' It is to be found in the conduct of Louis XIV., who, upon being informed, while setting out for the chase, of the inevitable and immediate death of his mistress, but eighteen years of age, expressed no other regret than the cold remark, '*She dies very young.*' It is to be found in the character of the Regent, who, during the dying agonies of Cardinal Dubois, the companion of his debaucheries, the confidant of his thoughts, and his prime minister, wrote to one of his boon companions, exiled by the dying cardinal, '*Hasten; I expect you to supper to-night. Dead dogs do not bite.*' It is to be found in Louis XV., who, losing his mistress, the friend, the confidante of twenty years, said to his companions, because it rained during the funeral, ' *The marquise has a very unpleasant day for her journey.*' In fine, a hundred other things, of the same sort, would not finish the catalogue. And, nevertheless, the adage continues its career. Such is history to the unreflecting."

February 28. The Emperor, in twenty-five lessons, had become so familiar with the English that he could read any book without difficulty. He was much interested in reading tragedies of a high character.

"The Emperor," records Las Casas, "likes them particularly, and takes pleasure in analyzing them, which he does with singular logic and much taste. He remembers a great quantity of poetry which he learned in his childhood, at which time, he says, he knew much more than he does at present. The Emperor is delighted with Racine; in him he finds true beauty. He greatly admires Corneille(but thinks very little of Voltaire, who, he says, is full of bombast and trickery, always false, neither acquainted with men, or things, or truth, or the grandeur of the passions.)

"At one of the evening levees at St. Cloud, the Emperor analyzed a piece which had just been brought out. It was *Hector*, by *Luce de Lancival*. This piece pleased him much. It had warmth, energy; he called it a *head-quarter* piece, saying that one would meet the enemy more resolutely after hearing it, and that he wished more were written in that spirit.

"Then adverting to the dramas which he called *waiting-maids' tragedies*, he said they could survive but one representation. A good tragedy, on the contrary, gains every day. 'High tragedy,' said he, 'is the school of great men. It is the duty of sovereigns to encourage and disseminate it. It is not necessary to be a poet to appreciate its merits. It is sufficient to know men and things, to have elevation of character, and to be a statesman. Tragedy fires the soul, warms the heart, and creates heroes. In this view, perhaps, France owes to Corneille a part of her great actions. Gentlemen, had he lived in my time, I would have made him a prince.'

"On a similar occasion he analyzed and condemned the *Etats de Blois*, which had just been presented, for the first time, at the Theatre of the Court. Perceiving among the company present the arch-treasurer Lebrun, who was distinguished for his literary acquirements, he asked his opinion of it. Lebrun, who was undoubtedly in the author's interest, contented himself with remarking that the subject was a bad one.

"'That,' replied the Emperor, 'was M. Renouard's first fault. He chose it himself. It was not forced upon him. Besides, there is no subject, however bad, which great talents can not turn to some account; Corneille would still have been himself even in one like this. As for M. Renouard, he has totally failed. He has shown no other talent but that of versification. Every thing else is bad—very bad. His conception, his details, his results, are altogether deficient. He violates the truth of history; his characters are false, and their political tendency is dangerous, and, perhaps, prejudicial. This is an additional proof of what, however, is very well known, that there is a wide difference between the reading and the representation of a play. I thought at first that this piece might have been allowed to pass. It was not until this evening that I perceived its improprieties. Of these, the praises lavished on the Bourbons are the least. The declamations against the Revolutionists are much worse. M. Renouard has made the chief of these Sixteen the capuchin Chabot of the Convention. There is matter in this piece for all parties and all passions. Were I to allow it to be represented in Paris, I should probably be informed of half a hundred people murdering one another in the pit. Besides, the author has made Henry IV. a true Philinte, and the Duke of Guise a Figaro, which is much too great an outrage on history. The Duke of Guise was one of the most distinguished men of his time; and if he had but ventured, he might have established the fourth dynasty. Besides, he was related to the Empress; he was a prince of the house of Austria, with whom we are in friendship, and whose embassador was present this evening at the representation. The author has, in more than one instance, shown a strange disregard of propriety.' "

" Talma," continues Las Casas, " the celebrated tragedian, had frequent interviews with the Emperor, who greatly admired his talent, and rewarded him magnificently. When the First Consul became Emperor, it was reported all over Paris that he had Talma to give him lessons in attitude and costume. The Emperor, who always knew every thing that was said against him, rallied Talma one day upon the subject, and, finding him look quite disconcerted, said, 'You are wrong; I certainly could not have employed myself better if I had had leisure for it.' On the contrary, it was the Emperor who gave Talma lessons in his art. 'Racine,' said he to Talma, 'has loaded his character of Orestes with imbecilities, and you only add to their extravagance. In the death of Pompey you do not play Cæsar like a hero. In Britannicus you do not play Nero like a tyrant.' Every one knows the corrections which Talma afterward made in his performances of these celebrated characters."

February 29. It was a dark and stormy night, and the exiles of Longwood remained at the table conversing for several hours after the cloth was removed. The conversation turned upon what were termed the *agents* during the Revolution, and the great fortunes which they acquired.

" Scarcely had I become First Consul," said the Emperor, " ere I found myself at issue with Madam Recamier. Her father had been placed in the Post-office Department. I had found it necessary to sign in confidence a great number of appointments, but I soon established a very rigid inspection in every department. A correspondence was discovered with the Chouans, going on under the connivance of M. Bernard, the father of Madam Recamier. He was immediately dismissed, and narrowly escaped trial and condemnation to death. His daughter hastened to me, and upon her solicitations I exempted M. Bernard from taking his trial, but was resolute respecting his dismissal. Madam Recamier, accustomed to obtain every thing, would be satisfied with nothing less than the reinstatement of her father. Such were the morals of the times. My severity excited loud animadversions. It was a thing quite unusual. Madam Recamier and her party, which was very numerous, never forgave me.

" The contractors and the agents, above any other class, excited my uneasiness. They were the scourge and the plague of the nation. The whole of France would not have satisfied the ambition of this class who were in Paris. When I came to the head of affairs they constituted an absolute power. They were most dangerous to the state, whose resources they obstructed and corrupted by their intrigues, and by those of their agents and numerous dependents. In truth, they could never be regarded as any thing but sources of corruption and ruin, like Jews and usurers. They had discredited the Directory, and they wished, in like manner, to control the Consulate. At that period they enjoyed the highest rank and influence in society.

"One of the principal retrograde steps which I took, with the view of restoring the past state and manners of society, was to throw all this false lustre back into the crowd. I never would raise any of this class to distinction. Of all aristocracies, this appeared to me the worst. The party always disliked me for this. But they were still less inclined to pardon the rigid inquiry which I instituted into their accounts with the government.

"In this business I turned the service of the Council of State to the best account. I used to appoint a committee of four or five members of the council, men of integrity and intelligence. They made their report to me, and if the case required farther investigation, I wrote at the bottom of the report, *Referred to the grand judge, to be submitted to his laws.* The individuals implicated generally endeavored to compromise the affair when it arrived at this point. They would disgorge one, two, three, or four millions of francs rather than suffer the business to be legally investigated. I well knew that all these facts were misrepresented in the different circles of the capital; that they created me many enemies, and drew down upon me the reproach of being arbitrary and tyrannical; but I thus acquitted a great duty to the mass of society, who must have been grateful to me for the measures I adopted toward these bloodsuckers of the public.

"Men are always the same. Since Pharamond, contractors have always acted thus; and they have always occupied the same place in the opinions of the people. But at no period of the monarchy were they ever attacked in so legal a form, or assailed so energetically and openly, as by me. Even among the contractors themselves, the few individuals who possessed honesty and integrity found, in this extreme severity, a new guarantee for their own conduct.

"I enjoyed singular reputation among the heads of offices and accountants. The examination of accounts I understood very well. The circumstance that first gained me reputation in this way was that, while balancing a yearly account during the Consulate, I discovered an error of four hundred thousand dollars to the disadvantage of the Republic. M. Dufresne, who was then Secretary of the Treasury, and who was a perfectly honest man, at first would not believe that the error existed. However, it was an affair of figures. The fact could not be denied. At the Treasury several months were occupied in endeavoring to discover the error. It was at length found in an account of the contractor Seguin, who immediately acknowledged it on being shown the accounts, and restored the money, saying that it was a mistake.

"On another occasion, while examining the accounts of the pay of the garrison of Paris, I observed a charge of some twelve thousand dollars set down to a detachment which had never been in the capital. The minister made a note of the error merely from complaisance, but was convinced, in his own mind, that the Emperor was mistaken. I, however, proved to be right, and the sum was restored."

NAPOLEON EXAMINING THE ACCOUNTS.

Speaking of the *Cadastre*, the Emperor said, "According to the plan which I had drawn up, it might be considered the real constitution of the Empire. It was the true guarantee of property, and the security for the independence of each individual; for the tax being once fixed and established by the Legislature, each individual might make his own arrangements, and had nothing to fear from the authority or arbitrary conduct of assessors, which is always the point most sensibly felt, and the surest to enforce submission.

"I had succeeded in creating a system of government doubtless the purest and most energetic in Europe. I had the details so much at my command, that I am sure I could now, merely with the help of the Moniteurs, trace the complete history of the financial administration of the Empire during my reign."

CHAPTER VI.
1816, March.

Invasion of England—Etiquette of the Emperor's Court—The Emperor's Levees—The Court and the City—The Anonymous Letter—Remarks on Medicine—Corvisart—Medical Practice in Babylon.

March 3. The Emperor had passed a restless night, and was quite unwell and depressed in spirits. At two o'clock he sent for Las Casas, and beguiled the time for two hours in listening to his remarks upon London.

"Were the English much afraid of my invasion?" inquired the Emperor. "What was the general opinion at the time?"

"I can not inform you," Las Casas replied. "I had then returned to France. But in the saloons of Paris we laughed at the idea of the invasion of England, and the English who were in Paris at the time did so too."

"Well," replied the Emperor, "you might laugh in Paris, but Pitt did not laugh in London. He soon calculated the extent of the danger, and, therefore, threw a coalition upon my shoulders at the moment when I raised my arm to strike. Never was the English oligarchy exposed to greater danger.

"I had taken measures to preclude the possibility of failure in my landing. I had the best army in the world. I need only say that it was the army of Austerlitz. In four days I should have been in London. I should have entered the British capital, not as a conqueror, but as a liberator. I should have been another William III., but I would have acted with greater generosity and disinterestedness. The discipline of my army was perfect. My troops would have behaved in London the same as they would in Paris. No sacrifices, not even contributions, would have been exacted from the English. We should have presented ourselves to them, not as conquerors, but as brothers, who came to restore to them their rights and liberties. I would have assembled the citizens, and directed them to labor themselves in the task of their regeneration, because the English had already preceded us in political legislation. I would have declared that our only wish was to be able to rejoice in the happiness and prosperity of the English people, and to these professions I would have strictly adhered.

"In the course of a few months, the two nations, which had been such determined enemies, would have henceforward composed only one people, identified in principles, maxims, and interests. I should have departed from England in order to effect from south to north, under republican colors (for I was then first consul), the regeneration of Europe, which at a later period I was on the point of effecting from north to south under monarchical forms. Both systems were equally good, since both would have been attended by the same results, and would have been carried into execution with firmness, moderation, and good faith. How many ills that are now endured, and how

G

many that are yet to be experienced, would not unhappy Europe have escaped? Never was a project so favorable to the interests of civilization conceived with more disinterested intentions, or so near being carried into execution. It is a remarkable fact, that the obstacles which occasioned my failure were not the work of men, but proceeded from the elements. In the south the sea frustrated my plans. The burning of Moscow, the snow and the winter, completed my ruin in the north. Thus water, air, and fire, all nature, and nature alone, was hostile to the universal regeneration which nature herself called for. The problems of Providence are insoluble."

The Emperor was for a few moments silent, absorbed in thought. He then added,

"It was supposed that my scheme was merely a vain thought, because it did not appear that I possessed any reasonable means of attempting its execution. But I had laid my plans deeply, and without being observed. I had dispersed all our French ships, and the English were sailing after them to different parts of the world. Our ships were to return suddenly and at the same time, and to assemble in a mass along the French coasts. I would have had seventy or eighty French or Spanish vessels in the Channel.* I calculated that I should continue master of it for two months. Three or four thousand little boats were to be ready at a signal. A hundred thousand men were every day drilled in embarking and landing as a part of their exercise. They were full of ardor and eager for the enterprise, which was very popular with the French, and was supported by the wishes of a great number of the English. After landing my troops, I could calculate upon only one pitched battle, the result of which could not be doubtful, and victory would have brought us to London. The nature of the country would not admit of a war of maneuvering. My conduct would have done the rest.

"The people of England groaned under the yoke of an oligarchy. On feeling that their pride had not been humbled, they would have ranged themselves on our side. We should have been considered only as allies come to effect their deliverance. We should have presented ourselves with the magical words of *liberty* and *equality*."

March 5. The Emperor, in his conversations, frequently spoke of himself in the third person, as of an historical personage who had passed from the stage of action. To-day, in this mood of mind, he spoke with great frankness about his court and the etiquette observed in it.

"At the period of the Revolution," said he, "the courts of Spain and Naples still imitated the ceremony and grandeur of Louis XIV., mingled with the pomp and exaggeration of the Castilians and Moors. The court of St. Petersburg had assumed the tone and forms of the drawing-room. That of Vienna had become quite citizen-like. There no longer remained any vestige of the wit, the grace, and the good taste of the court of Versailles.

"When, therefore, Napoleon obtained the sovereign power, he formed a court according to his own taste. He was desirous of adopting a national medium by accommodating the dignity of the throne to modern customs, and

* Spain was then in friendly alliance with France, and at war with England.

particularly by making the creation of a court contribute to improve the manners of the great, and promote the industry of the mass of the people. It certainly was no easy matter to reconstruct a throne on the very spot where a reigning monarch had been judicially executed, and where the people had constitutionally sworn their hatred of kings. It was not easy to restore dignities, titles, and decorations among a people who, for the space of fifteen years, had urged a war of proscription against them.

"Napoleon, however, who seemed always to possess the power of effecting what he wished, perhaps because he had the art of wishing for what was just and proper, after a great struggle surmounted all these difficulties. When he became Emperor he created a class of nobility and founded a court. Victory seemed, all on a sudden, to do her utmost to consolidate and shed a lustre over this new order of things. All Europe acknowledged the Emperor. At one period it might have been said that all the courts of the Continent had flocked to Paris to add to the splendor of the Tuileries, which was the most brilliant and numerous court ever seen. There was a continued series of parties, balls, and entertainments, and the court was always distinguished for extraordinary magnificence and grandeur. The person of the sovereign was alone remarkable for extreme simplicity, which, indeed, was a characteristic that served to distinguish him amid the surrounding splendor. He encouraged all this magnificence from motives of policy, and not because it accorded with his own taste. It was calculated to encourage manufactures and national industry. The ceremonies and fêtes which took place on the marriage of the Empress and the birth of the King of Rome far surpassed any which had preceded them, and probably will never again be equaled.

"The Emperor endeavored to establish in his foreign relations every thing that was calculated to place him in harmony with the other courts of Europe, but at home he constantly tried to adapt old forms to new manners. He established the morning and evening levees of the old kings of France; but with him these levees were merely nominal, and did not exist in reality as in former times. Instead of being occupied with the details of the toilet and the conversations which might naturally ensue, these levees under the Emperor were, in fact, appropriated to receiving in the morning, and dismissing in the evening, such persons of his household as had to obtain orders directly from him, and who were privileged to pay their court to him at those hours. The Emperor also established special presentation to his person and admission to his court; but instead of making noble birth the only means of securing these honors, the title for obtaining them was founded solely on the combined basis of fortune, influence, and public services.

"Napoleon, moreover, created titles, the qualifications for which gave the last blow to the old feudal system. These titles, however, possessed no real value, and were established for an object purely national. Those which were unaccompanied by any prerogatives or privileges might be enjoyed by persons of any rank or profession, and were bestowed as rewards for all kinds of services. Abroad they had the useful effect of appearing an approximation to the old manners of Europe, while, at the same time, they served as a toy for amusing the vanities of many individuals at home; for how many really clever men are children more than once in their lives!

"The Emperor revived decorations of honor, and distributed crosses and ribbons, but, instead of confining them to particular and exclusive classes, he extended them to society in general, as rewards for every description of talent and public service. The value of these privileges was enhanced in proportion to the number distributed. About 25,000 decorations of the Legion of Honor were conferred, and the desire to obtain this distinction increased until it became a kind of mania. After the battle of Wagram the Emperor sent the decoration of the Legion of Honor to the Archduke Charles, and, by a refinement of compliment, he sent him merely the silver cross which was worn by the private soldiers.

"It was only by acting strictly and voluntarily in conformity with these maxims that the Emperor became the real national monarch. An adherence to the same course would have rendered the fourth dynasty the truly constitutional one. Of these facts the people of the lowest ranks frequently evinced an instinctive knowledge. On returning from his coronation in Italy, as the Emperor approached the environs of Lyons he found all the population assembled on the roads to see him pass, and he took a fancy to ascend the mountain of Tarare alone. He gave orders that nobody should follow him. Mingling with the crowd, he accosted an old woman, and asked what all the bustle meant. She replied that the Emperor was expected. After some little conversation, the Emperor said to her,

"'My good woman, formerly you had Capet the tyrant, now you have Napoleon the tyrant; what have you gained by the change?'

"The force of the argument disconcerted the old woman for a moment, but, immediately recollecting herself, she replied,

"'Pardon me, sir, there is a great difference. We ourselves have chosen Napoleon, but we got Capet by chance.'

THE EMPEROR AND THE PEASANT WOMAN.

"The old woman was right," continued the Emperor. "She exhibited more instinctive good sense than many men who are possessed of great information and talents.

"The Emperor surrounded himself with great crown officers. He established a numerous household of chamberlains and grooms. He selected persons to fill these offices indiscriminately from among those whom the Revolution had elevated, and from the ancient families which it had ruined. The former considered themselves as standing on an estate which they had acquired, the latter on one which they thought they might recover. The Emperor had in view, by this mixture of persons, the extinction of hatreds and the amalgamation of parties. He, however, was not displeased at seeing a variety of manners. The individuals belonging to the ancient families performed their duties with the greatest courtesy and assiduity. A Madam de Montmorency would have stooped down to tie the Empress's shoes; a lady of the new school would have hesitated to do this, lest she should be taken for a real waiting-woman; but the Madam de Montmorency had no such apprehension.

"These posts of honor were, for the most part, without emolument; they were even attended with expense; but they brought the individuals who filled them daily under the eye of the sovereign, of a very powerful sovereign, the source of honor and favor, and who declared that he would not have the lowest officer in his household solicit benefits from any one but himself.

"At the time of his marriage with the Empress Maria Louisa, the Emperor made an extensive recruit of chamberlains from among the highest ranks of the old aristocracy. This he did with the view of proving to Europe that there existed but one party in France, and of rallying around the Empress those names which must have been familiar to her. The Emperor even hesitated whether or not to select the lady of honor from that class; but his fear lest the Empress, with whose character he was unacquainted, might be imbued with prejudices respecting birth that might too much elate the old party, led him to make another choice.

"From this moment until the period of our disasters, the most ancient and illustrious families eagerly solicited places in the household of the Empress. And how could it be otherwise? The Emperor had raised France and the French people above the level of other nations. Power, glory, constituted his retinue. Happy were they who inhaled the atmosphere of the imperial court. To be immediately connected with the Emperor's person furnished, both abroad and at home, a title to consideration, homage, and respect.

"It is the custom to talk of the influence of the tone and manners of the court upon those of the nation. I was far from having succeeded in bringing about any such result; but it was the fault of circumstances and of several unperceived combinations. I had reflected much on the subject, and think that it would have been accomplished in time.

"The court, taken collectively, does not exert this influence. It is only because its elements, those who compose it, go to communicate, each in his own sphere of action, that which they have collected from the common source.

The tone of the court is thus infused into a whole nation only through intermediate societies. Now we had no such societies, nor could we yet have them. Those delightful assemblies, where one enjoys so fully the advantages of civilization, suddenly disappear at the approach of revolutions, and are reestablished but slowly when the tempests dissipate. The indispensable bases of society are leisure and opulence. But we were all still in a state of agitation, and great fortunes were not yet firmly established. A great number of theatres, a multitude of public establishments, moreover, presented pleasures more ready, less constrained, and more exciting. The women of the day, taken collectively, were young. They liked better to be out, and to show themselves in public, than to remain at home and to compose a narrower circle. But they would have grown old, and, with a little time and tranquillity, every thing would have fallen into its natural course.

"And then, again, it would perhaps be an error to judge of a modern court by the remembrance of the old ones. The *power* certainly resided in the old courts. They said the *court and the city*. At the present day, if we desire to speak correctly, we are obliged to say *the city and the court*. The feudal lords, since they have lost their power, seek to make themselves amends in their enjoyments. Sovereigns themselves appear to be, for the future, subjected to this law. The throne, with our liberal ideas, has insensibly ceased to be a seigniory, and has become purely a magistracy. The prince, having only a simple practical character to maintain, always sufficiently dull and tedious in the long run, must seek to withdraw from it, to come, as a mere citizen, and take his share in the charms of society."

In continuation of this long conversation, the Emperor remarked upon a great number of new measures which he had projected for the tranquil future which he was ever so earnestly desiring.

"My favorite idea," said he, "had been, peace being obtained and repose secured, to devote my life to purifying the administration, and to local ameliorations; to be occupied in perpetual tours in the departments. I would have visited, not hurried over; sojourned, not posted through. I would have used my own horses, and would have been surrounded by the Empress, the King of Rome, my whole court. At the same time, it was my intention that this great equipage should not be burdensome to any, but rather a benefit to all. A suit of tapestry hangings and all the other appendages, following in the train, would have furnished and decorated his places of rest. The other persons of the court would have been extremely welcome to the citizens, who would have looked upon their guests as a benefit rather than as a burden, because they would always have been the sure means of their acquiring some advantage or some favors. It is thus that I should have been able, in every place, to prevent frauds, punish misappropriations, direct edifices, bridges, roads, drain marshes, and fertilize lands. If Heaven had then granted me a few years, I would certainly have made Paris the capital of the world, and all France a real fairy land."

March 6. Some East Indiamen arrived at the island, returning to England from China. Dr. O'Meara purchased for $150 a very massive set of chessmen, elaborately carved in ivory. The Emperor considered them quite useless, saying pleasantly, "Every piece will require a crane to move it." The day was excessively hot, and the Emperor remained in his room. Many of the officers of the China fleet were sauntering around the house at Longwood, intensely desirous of getting a glimpse of the Emperor. When Napoleon was informed of the ardor of their curiosity, he with great kindness ordered them all to be admitted. For half an hour, with perfect affability, he conversed with them respecting China, its commerce, its revenue, its missionaries. These English officers and seamen were delighted with the Emperor, and gave enthusiastic utterance to their admiration. When Napoleon was informed of these friendly expressions, he said,

"I believe it. Do you not perceive that they are our friends? All that you have observed in them belongs to the commons of England, the natural enemies, perhaps without giving themselves credit for it, of their old and insolent aristocracy."

March 7. The Emperor, at an early hour, mounted his horse for a ride. He was accompanied by Las Casas and his son. The Emperor had particularly requested that the young Las Casas should go with them. The evening before, seeing the lad on horseback, he had said to his father,

"Do you have Immanuel taught to groom his own horse? Nothing is more useful. I gave particular orders that the students should do this in the military school of Saint Germain."

Las Casas immediately adopted the plan, and his son appeared in the morning upon a horse which he himself had groomed. When the Emperor was informed of this, he was quite pleased, and made the lad pass through an examination of his knowledge and skill.

After a ride of two hours, the Emperor dismounted at his door, and the whole party of exiles breakfasted together under a gum-tree, upon the green turf. The Emperor then returned to his room and to his intellectual avocations. He now understood English so well that he could read and write in that language with much facility. To test his skill, he playfully wrote an anonymous letter to Las Casas, who was an author of some celebrity, and who had the usual sensitiveness of authors respecting their works. Las Casas thus records this incident:

"A short time before dinner, I presented myself as usual in the drawing-room. The Emperor was playing at chess with the grand marshal. The valet de chambre in waiting at the door of the room brought me a letter, on which was written *very urgent*. Out of respect to the Emperor, I went aside to read it. It was in English. It stated that I had written an excellent work; that, nevertheless, it was not without faults; that if I would correct them in a new edition, no doubt the work would be more valuable for it; and then went on to pray that God would keep me in his gracious and holy protection.

"Such a letter excited my astonishment and made me rather angry. The color rushed to my face. I did not, at first, give myself time to consider the writing. In reading it over again, I recognized the hand, notwithstanding its being much better written than usual, and I could not help laughing a good deal to myself. But the Emperor, who cast a side glance at me, asked me from whom the letter came that was given to me. I replied that it was a paper that had caused a very different feeling in me at first from that which it would leave permanently. I said this with so much simplicity, the mystification had been so complete, that he laughed till tears came in his eyes. The letter was from him. The pupil had a mind to jest with his master, and try his powers at his expense. I carefully preserve this letter. The gayety, the style, and the whole circumstance render it more valuable to me than any diploma the Emperor could have put into my hands when he was in power."

THE GAME OF CHESS.

March 8. The Emperor was quite unwell during the night, and not being able to sleep, he rose and amused himself in writing another letter in English to Las Casas. General Gourgaud was also quite sick, and the admiral sent the surgeon of the *Northumberland*, Dr. Warden, to visit him. The Emperor detained the surgeon to dinner. The conversation turned upon medical practice, and the Emperor manifested so much accuracy of knowledge upon the subject as to surprise exceedingly his auditor. Napoleon had no faith in medicine, and could seldom be induced to take any.

"Doctor," said he, "our body is a machine for the purpose of life. It is organized to that end; that is its nature. Leave the life there at its ease; let it take care of itself; it will do better than if you paralyze it by loading it with medicines. It is like a well-made watch, destined to go for a certain time. The watchmaker has not the power of opening it. He can not meddle with it but at random, with his eyes bandaged. For one who, by dint of racking it with his ill-formed instruments, succeeds in doing it any good, how many blockheads destroy it altogether!"

The celebrated Corvisart* was a great enemy to medicines, and employed them very sparingly. "Do you not believe," said the Emperor to him one day, "that, seeing the uncertainty of the art itself, and the ignorance of those who practice it, its effects, taken in the aggregate, are more fatal than useful to the people? Have you never killed any body yourself? that is to say, have not some patients died evidently in consequence of your prescriptions?"

"Undoubtedly," Corvisart replied; "but I ought no more to let that weigh upon my conscience than would your majesty if you had caused the destruction of some troops, not from having made a bad movement, but because their march was impeded by a ditch or a precipice which it was impossible for you to be aware of."

"What is life?" continued the Emperor; "when and how do we receive it? Is that still any thing but mystery? Madness is a vacancy or incoherence of judgment between just perceptions and the application of them. The dangerous madman is he in whom this vacancy or incoherence of judgment occurs between perceptions and actions. It was he who cut off the head of a sleeping man, and concealed himself behind a hedge to enjoy the perplexity of the dead body when he should awake. And what is the difference between sleep and death? Sleep is the momentary suspension of the faculties which are within the power of our volition. Death is the lasting suspension, not only of these faculties, but also of those over which our will has no control."

The conversation then turned upon the plague. "It is communicated," said the Emperor, "by inspiration as well as by contact. It is rendered most dangerous, and is most extensively propagated, by fear. Its principal seat is in the imagination. In Egypt, all those in whom the imagination was affected perished. The most prudent remedy was moral courage. I touched with impunity some infected persons at Jaffa, and saved many lives by deceiving the soldiers, during two months, as to the nature of the disease. It was not the plague, they were told, but a fever accompanied with ulcers. Moreover, the best means to preserve the army from it were to keep them on the march, and give them plenty of exercise. Fatigue, and the occupation of the mind upon other subjects, were found the surest protection.

"If Hippocrates," continued the Emperor to the doctor, "were on a sudden to enter your hospital, would he not be much astonished? Would he adopt your maxims and your methods? Would he not find fault with you? On your part, would you understand his language? Would you at all comprehend each other?" He concluded by pleasantly extolling the practice of medicine in Babylon, where the patients were exposed at the door, and the relations, sitting near them, stopped the passengers to inquire if they had ever been afflicted in a similar way. "One had at least the certainty," said he, "of escaping all those whose remedies had killed them."

* The Emperor's family physician.

CHAPTER VII.

1816, March.   Continued.

Trial of Ney—National Character of the French—The Emperor's Carriage taken at Waterloo—The Emperor at Dresden—Maria Louisa and Josephine—Alexander, Francis, and the King of Prussia—Eloquent Effusion of the Emperor—Testimony of B. Constant.

March 10–12. The weather was dismal. High winds and pelting rains confined the exiles within doors. Fortunately, some papers arrived from England, which enabled them to beguile the weary hours. These journals contained an account of the atrocious trial of Marshal Ney, which was then in progress, in defiance of the terms of the capitulation of Paris. As the Emperor sadly perused the proceedings of the narrative, he said,

"The horizon is indeed gloomy. The unfortunate marshal is certainly in great danger. We must not, however, despair. The king undoubtedly believes himself quite sure of the Peers. These are, it is true, violent enough, firmly resolved, highly incensed; but for all that, suppose the slightest accident, some new rumor, or I know not what, then you would see, in spite

PORTRAIT OF MARSHAL NEY

of all the efforts of the king, and of what they believe to be the interest of their cause, the Chamber of Peers would, all on a sudden, take it into their heads not to find him guilty, and thus Ney may be saved."

Then, turning his thoughts to the volatile character of the French nation, the Emperor said,

"All the French are turbulent and disposed to rail, but they are not addicted to seditious combinations, still less to actual conspiracy. Their levity is so natural to them, their changes so sudden, that it may be said to be a national dishonor. They are mere weathercocks, the sport of the winds, it is true; but this vice is with them free from the calculations of interest, and that is their best excuse. But we must only be understood here to speak of the mass—of that which constitutes public opinion; for individual examples to the contrary have swarmed in our latter times, that exhibit certain classes in the most disgusting state of meanness.

"It was this knowledge of the national character which always prevented my having recourse to the High Court. This court was instituted by our Constitution. The Council of State had decreed its organization. But I felt all the danger and bustle that such spectacles always produce. Such a proceeding was, in reality, an appeal to the public, and was always highly injurious to authority when the accused gained the cause. A ministry in England might sustain, without inconvenience, the effects of a decision against it under such circumstances, but a sovereign like me, and situated as I was, could not have suffered it without the utmost danger to public affairs. For this reason, I preferred to have recourse to ordinary tribunals. Malevolence often started objections to this; but, nevertheless, among all those whom it was pleased to call victims, which of them, I ask you, has retained his popularity in our late struggles? They have taken care to justify me. All of them are faded in the national estimation."

The journals contained an article relative to the carriage which the Emperor lost at Waterloo. A very minute description was given of this vehicle, and an inventory of its contents. As the Emperor rode night and day, and ate, slept, read, and wrote in his carriage, the interior was arranged for such conveniences. The carriage itself was, however, perfectly plain and unostentatious, and without any of the appliances of luxury. The captious English editor, in alluding to a small liquor-case, observed that the Emperor never forgot *himself*. In describing the Emperor's compact dressing-case, he added, sneeringly, "It may be seen that he made his toilet *comme il faut*." Napoleon, as he heard this read, shrugged his shoulders, and exclaimed, with a mingled expression of disgust and sadness,

"How is this? Do these people of England, then, take me to be some wild animal? Have they really been led so far as this? Or their Prince of Wales, who is a kind of ox Apis, as I am assured, does he not pay that attention to his toilet that is considered proper by every person of any education among us?"

In commenting upon this, Las Casas adds, "It is known that the Emperor, of all people in the world, set the least value on his personal convenience, and studied it the least; but, on the other hand, and the Emperor ever acknowledged it with pleasure, there never was one for whom the devotion and attention of servants had been so diligent in that particular. As he ate at very irregular hours, they contrived, in the course of his journeys and campaigns, to have his dinner, similar to what he was accustomed to at the Tuileries, always ready within a few paces of him. He had but to speak and he was instantly served. He himself said it was magic."

The conversation turned upon the celebrated interview at Dresden, when Napoleon, upon the eve of the Russian campaign, met the associated European monarchs who were friendly to his cause. Las Casas informed him that at Dresden he had not a single French soldier near him, and that his court was sometimes not without apprehension for the safety of his person. The Saxon body-guard was his only protection.

"It is all one," said the Emperor. "I was then in so good a family that I ran no risk. I was beloved by all. And at this very time I am sure that the good King of Saxony repeats every day a *Pater* and an *Ave* for me.

"But I ruined the fortunes of his daughter, the poor Princess Augusta, and I acted very wrong in so doing. Returning from Tilsit, I received at Marienwerder a chamberlain of the King of Saxony, who delivered me a letter from his master. He wrote, 'I have just received a letter from the Emperor of Austria, who desires my daughter in marriage. I send this to you, that you may inform me what answer I ought to return.' I replied that I should be in Dresden in a few days. On my arrival, I set my face against the match, and prevented it. I was very wrong. I was fearful that the Emperor Francis would withdraw the King of Saxony from me. On the contrary, the Princess Augusta would have brought over the Emperor Francis on my side, and I should not now have been here."

Speaking of Maria Louisa, the Emperor said, "The reign of Maria Louisa was very short, but it must have been full of enjoyment for her. She had the world at her feet."

The Empress of Austria was Maria Louisa's mother-in-law, and was supposed to regard with much jealousy the splendor of her step-daughter. Las Casas took the liberty to inquire, "Was not the Empress of Austria the sworn enemy of Maria Louisa?"

"Nothing more," replied the Emperor, "than a little regular court hatred, a thorough detestation in the heart, but glossed over by daily letters of four pages, full of coaxing and tenderness. The Empress of Austria has, however, address and ability, and that sufficient to embarrass her husband, who had acquired the suspicion that she entertained a poor opinion of him. Her countenance was agreeable, engaging, and had something very peculiar in it. She was a pretty little nun. As to the Emperor Francis, his good nature is well known, and makes him constantly the dupe of the designing. His son will be like him.

"The King of Prussia, as a private character, is an honorable, good, and worthy man, but in his political capacity he is naturally disposed to yield to necessity. He is always commanded by whoever has power on his side, and seems about to strike.

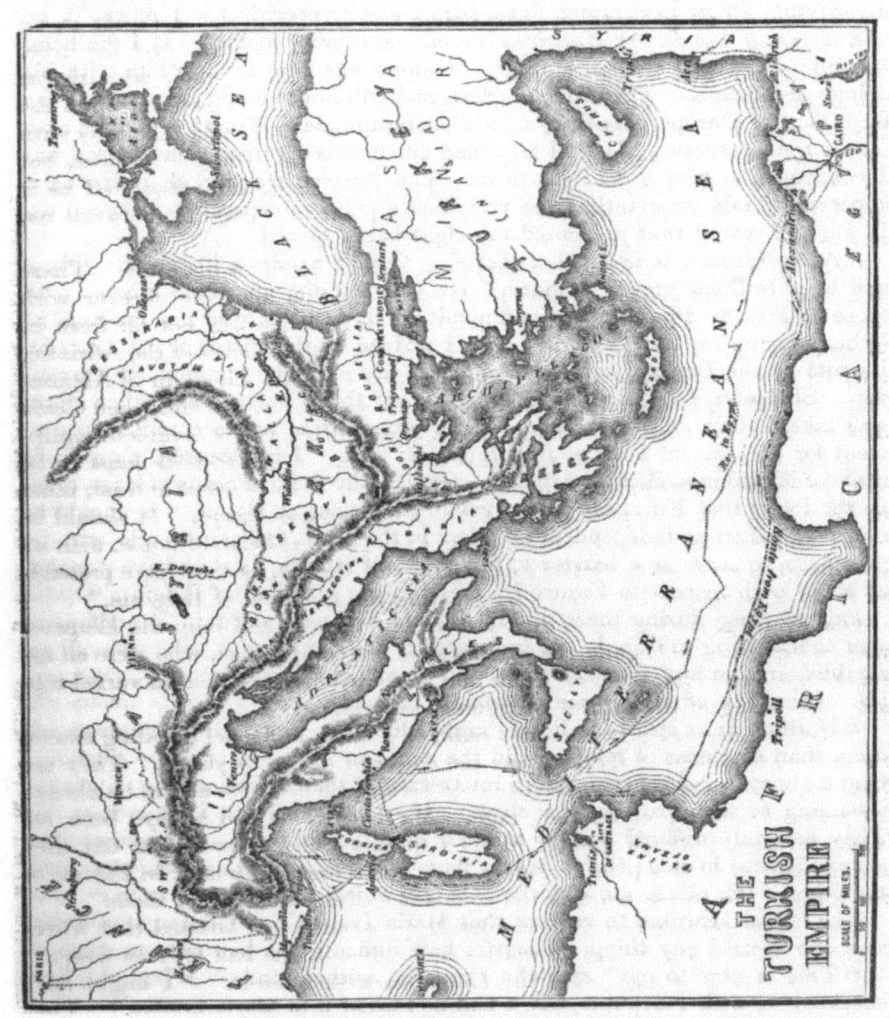

"As to the Emperor of Russia, he is a man infinitely superior to these. He possesses wit, grace, information, and is fascinating, but he is not to be trusted. He is devoid of candor, a true *Greek of the Lower Empire*. At the same time, he is not without ideology, real or assumed; after all, it may be only a smattering derived from his education and his preceptor. Would you believe what I had to discuss with him? He maintained that *inheritance* was an abuse in monarchy, and I had to spend more than an hour, and employ all my eloquence and logic, in proving to him that this right constituted the peace and happiness of the people. It may be, too, that he was mystifying, for he is cunning, false, adroit, and hypocritical. I repeat it, he is a *Greek of the Lower Empire;* he can go a great length. If I die here, he will be my real heir in Europe. I alone was able to stop him with his deluge of Tartars. The crisis is great, and will have lasting effects upon the Continent of Europe, especially upon Constantinople. He was solicitous with me for the possession of it. I have had much coaxing upon this subject, but I constantly turned a deaf ear to it. The Turkish Empire, shattered as it appeared, would constantly have remained a point of separation between us. It was the marsh that prevented my right being turned.

"As to Greece, it is another matter. Greece awaits a liberator. There will be a brilliant crown of glory. He will inscribe his name forever with those of Homer, Plato, and Epaminondas. I, perhaps, was not far from it. When, during my campaign in Italy, I arrived on the shores of the Adriatic, I wrote to the Directory that I had before my eyes the kingdom of Alexander. Still later, I entered into engagements with Ali Pacha; and when Corfu was taken, they must have found there ammunition and a complete equipment for an army of forty or fifty thousand men. I had caused maps to be made of Macedonia, Servia, Albania. Greece, the Peloponnesus at least, must be the lot of that European power which shall possess Egypt. It should be ours; and then an independent kingdom in the north, Constantinople, with its provinces, to serve as a barrier to the power of Russia, as they have pretended to do with respect to France by creating the kingdom of Belgium."

One evening, during these dreary days of darkness and rain, the Emperor was endeavoring to beguile the weariness of his companions, who were all assembled around him, by very frank and animated conversation on varied topics. Speaking of the caprice of women, he said,

"Nothing more clearly indicates rank, education, and good breeding among them than evenness of temper, and the constant desire to please. They are bound always to show themselves mistresses of themselves, and to be always attending to their part on the stage. My two wives had always been so. They certainly differed greatly in their qualities and dispositions, but they always agreed in this point. Never have I witnessed ill humor in the one or the other. To please me was the constant object with both of them."

Las Casas ventured to remark that Maria Louisa had boasted that whenever she desired any thing, no matter how difficult, she had only to weep.

"This is new to me," said the Emperor, with a smile. "I might have suspected it with Josephine, but I had no idea of it in Maria Louisa." Then addressing himself to Madam Bertrand and Madam Montholon, he said, playfully, "Thus it is with you all, ladies. In some points you all agree."

During this conversation the Emperor inquired the day of the month. "It is the 11th of March," some one replied. It was the anniversary of the Emperor's triumphant entrance into Lyons on his return from Elba.

"Well," added the Emperor, in earnest tones, "it is a year ago to-day; it was a brilliant day; I was at Lyons. I reviewed some troops, and had

PORTRAIT OF THE EMPRESS MARIA LOUISA.

the mayor to dine with me, who, by-the-way, has boasted since that it was the worst dinner he ever made in his life."

The Emperor became animated, and, pacing the chamber rapidly, continued: "I was again become a great power. I had founded the finest empire in the world, and I was so necessary to it, that, notwithstanding all the last reverses, here, upon my rock, I seem still to remain the master of France. Look at what is going on there; read the papers, you will find it so in every line. Let me once more set my foot there, and you will see what France is, and what I can do. What a fatality that my return from the island of Elba was not acquiesced in—that every one did not perceive that my reign was desirable and necessary for the balance and repose of Europe! But kings and people both feared me. They were wrong, and may pay dearly for it. I returned a new man; they could not believe it. They could not imagine that a man could have sufficient strength of mind to alter his character, or to bend to the power of circumstances. I had, however, given proofs of this, and some pledges to the same effect. Who is ignorant that I am not a man for half measures? I would have been as sincerely the monarch of the Constitution and of peace as I had been of absolute sway and great enterprises.

"Let us reason a little upon the fears of kings and people on my account. What could the kings apprehend? Did they still dread my ambition, my conquests, my universal monarchy? But my power and my resources were no longer the same; and, besides, I had only defeated and conquered in my own defense. This is a truth which time will more fully develop every day. Europe never ceased to make war upon France, her principles, and me, and we were compelled to destroy to save ourselves from destruction. The coalition always existed, openly or secretly, avowed or denied. It was permanent. It only rested with the Allies to give us peace. For ourselves, we were worn out. The French dreaded making new conquests. As to myself, is it supposed that I am insensible to the charms of repose and security when glory and honor do not require it otherwise? With our two Chambers, they might have forbidden me, in future, to pass the Rhine, and why should I have wished it? For my universal monarchy? But I never gave any convincing proof of insanity. And what is its chief characteristic but a disproportion between our object and the means of attaining it? If I have been on the point of accomplishing this universal monarchy, it was without any original design, and because I was led to it step by step. The last efforts wanting to arrive at it seemed so trifling, was it very unreasonable to attempt them? But, on my return from Elba, could a similar idea, a thought so mad, a purpose so unattainable, enter the head of the most rash man in the world? The sovereigns then had nothing to fear from my arms.

"Did they apprehend that I might overwhelm them with anarchical principles? But they knew by experience my opinion on that score. They have all seen me occupy their territories. How often have I been urged to revolutionize their states, give municipal functions to their cities, and excite insurrection among their subjects! However I may have been stigmatized in their name as *the modern Attila, Robespierre on horseback*, &c., they all know better at the bottom of their hearts; let them look there. Had I been so, I might, perhaps, still have reigned, but they most certainly would have long since ceased to reign. In the great cause of which I saw myself the chief and the arbitrator, one of two systems was to be followed—to make kings listen to reason from the people, or to conduct the people to happiness by means of their kings. But it is well known to be no easy matter to check the people when they are once set on. It was more rational to reckon a little upon the wisdom and intelligence of rulers. I had a right always to suppose them possessed of sufficient intellect to see such obvious interests. I was deceived. They never calculated at all, and in their blind fury they let loose against me that which I withheld when opposed to them. They will see.

"Lastly, did the sovereigns take umbrage at seeing a mere soldier attain a crown? Did they fear the example? The solemnities, the circumstances that accompanied my elevation, my eagerness to conform to their habits, to identify myself with their existence, to become allied to them by blood and by policy, closed the door sufficiently against new-comers. Besides, if there must needs have been the spectacle of an interrupted legitimacy, I maintain that it was much more for their interest that it should take place in my person, one risen from the ranks, than in that of a prince, one of their own family; for thousands of ages will elapse before the circumstances accumulated in my case draw forth another from among the crowd to reproduce the same spectacle, while there is not a sovereign who has not, at a few paces distant, in his palace, cousins, nephews, brothers, and relations, to whom it would be easy to follow such an example, if once set.

"On the other side, what was there to alarm the people. Did they fear that I should come to lay waste and to impose chains on them? But I returned the messiah of peace and of their rights. This new maxim was my whole strength. To violate it would have been ruin. But even the French mistrusted me. They had the insanity to discuss when there was nothing to do but to fight; to divide, when they should have been united on any terms. And was it not better to run the risk of having me again for master than to expose themselves to that of submitting to a foreign yoke? Would it not have been easier to rid themselves of a single despot, of one tyrant, than to shake off the chains of all the nations united? And, moreover, whence did they derive this mistrust of me? Because they had already seen me concentrate every effort in myself, and direct them with a vigorous hand? But do they not learn at the present day, to their cost, how necessary that was? Well, the danger was, in any case, the same; the contest terrible, and the crisis imminent.

"In this state of things, was not absolute power necessary, indispensable? The welfare of the country obliged me even to declare it openly on my return from Leipsic. I ought to have done so again on my return from Elba. I was wanting in consistency, or, rather, in confidence in the French, because many of them no longer placed any in me, and it was doing me great wrong. If narrow and vulgar minds only saw, in all my efforts, the care of my own power, ought not those of greater scope to have shown that, under the circumstances in which we were placed, my power and the country were but one? Did it require such great and incurable mischiefs to enable them to comprehend me? History will do me justice. It will signalize me as a man of self-denial and disinterestedness. To what temptations was I not exposed in the army of Italy? England offered me the crown of France at the time of the treaty of Amiens. I refused peace at Chatillon. I disdained all personal stipulations at Waterloo. And why? Because all this had no reference to my country, and I had no ambition distinct from hers—that of her glory, her ascendency, her majesty. And there is the reason that, in spite of so many calamities, I remain so popular among the French. It is a sort of instinct of after-justice on their part.

"Who in the world ever had greater treasures at his disposal? I have had many hundred millions in my vaults; many other hundreds composed my extraordinary domain. All these were my own. What is become of them? They were poured out in the distresses of the country. Let them contemplate me here. I remain destitute upon my rock. My fortune was wholly in that of France. In the extraordinary situation to which Fate had raised me, my treasures were hers. I had identified myself completely with her destinies. What other calculation was consistent with the height I had risen to? Was I ever seen occupied about my personal interests? I never knew any other enjoyment, any other riches, than those of the public; so much so, that when Josephine, who had a taste for the arts, succeeded, under the sanction of my name, in acquiring some masterpieces, though they were in my palace, under my eyes, in my family apartments, they offended me; I thought myself robbed; *they were not in the Museum.*

"Ah! the French people undoubtedly did much for me—more than was ever done before for man. But, at the same time, who ever did so much for them? Who ever identified himself with them in the same manner? But to return: after all, what could be their fears? Were not the Chambers and the new Constitution sufficient guarantees for the future? Those Additional Acts, against which so much indignation was expressed, did they not carry in themselves their own corrective—remedies that were infallible? How could I have violated them? I had not myself millions of arms; I was but one man. Public opinion raised me up once more. Public opinion might equally put me down again; and, compared with this risk, what had I to gain?

"But as to surrounding states, England in particular, what could be her fears, her motives, her jealousies? We inquire in vain. With our new Constitution, our two Chambers, had we not adopted her creed for the future? Was not that the sure means of coming to a mutual understanding, to establish in future a community of interests? The caprice, the passions of their rulers once fettered, the interests of the people move on, without obstacle, in their natural course. Look at the merchants of hostile nations. They continue their intercourse and pursue their business, however their governments may wage war. The two nations had arrived at that point. Thanks to their respective Parliaments, each was become the guarantee for the other. And who can ever tell to what extent the union of the two nations and of their interests might be carried? what new combinations might be set at work? It is certain that, on the establishment of our two Chambers and our Constitution, the ministers of England held in their hands the glory and the prosperity of their country, the destinies and the welfare of the world. Had I beaten the English army and won my last battle, I would have caused a great and happy astonishment. The following day I would have proposed peace, and for once it would have been I who scattered benefits with a prodigal hand. Instead of this, perhaps the English will one day have to lament that they were victorious at Waterloo.

"I repeat it, the people and the sovereigns were wrong. I had restored thrones and an inoffensive nobility; and thrones and nobility may again find themselves in danger. I had fixed and consecrated the reasonable limits of the people's rights. Vague, peremptory, and undefined claims may again arise. Had my return, my establishment on the throne, my adoption been freely acquiesced in by the sovereigns, the cause of kings and of the people would have been settled. Both would have gained. Now they are again to try it. Both may lose. They might have concluded every thing; they may have every thing to begin again. They might have secured a long and certain calm, and have already begun to enjoy it ; but, instead of this, a spark may now be sufficient to reproduce a universal conflagration."

These are certainly remarkable utterances, and indicate the movements of a serious, earnest, and far-reaching intellect. M. Benjamin Constant, one of the most illustrious of writers and of men, and a zealous Republican, records an interview he held with Napoleon at the Tuileries immediately after the Emperor's return from Elba. It was with the Emperor an hour of exultation. He was again seated upon the throne of France. But the profound political maxims which the Emperor expressed in the day of his prosperity were the same with those he cherished in the period of adversity.*

THE EMPEROR'S RETURN TO THE TUILERIES.

" I went to the Tuileries," says M. Constant. " I found Bonaparte alone. He began the conversation. It was long. I will only give an analysis of it, for I do not propose to make an exhibition of an unfortunate man. I will not amuse my readers at the expense of fallen greatness. I will not give up to malevolent curiosity him whom I have served, whatever might be my motive, and I will not describe more of his discourse than is indispensable, but in what I shall transcribe I will use his own words.

" He did not attempt to deceive me either as to his views or the state of affairs. He did not present himself as one corrected by the lessons of adver-

* *Minerve Français*, 94 liv., tome viii., *Second Letter on the Hundred Days*. By M. B. Constant.

sity. He did not desire to take the merit of returning to liberty from inclination. He investigated coolly as regarded his interest, and with an impartiality, too, nearly allied to indifference, what was possible and what was preferable.

" 'The nation,' said he, 'has rested for twelve years from all political agitation, and for a year it has been undisturbed by war. This double repose has begotten a necessity for motion. It desires, or fancies it desires, a public rostrum and assemblies. It has not always desired them. It cast itself at my feet when I came to the government. You must remember, you who made trial of its opinion. Where was your support, your power? Nowhere. I took less authority than I was invited to take. Now all is changed. A weak government, opposed to the interests of the nation, has given these interests the habit of taking up the defensive, and of caviling at authority. The taste for constitutions, debates, harangues, seems to return. However, it is only the minority that desires it. Do not deceive yourself. The people, or, if you like it better, the mob, desire me alone. Have you not seen them, this mob, crowding after me, rushing from the tops of the mountains, calling me, seeking me, saluting me?

" 'On my return here from Cannes I did not conquer, I administered. I am not only, as has been said, the Emperor of the soldiers, I am the Emperor of the peasants, the lower ranks in France. Thus, in spite of all that is past, you see the people return to me. There is a sympathy between us. It is not so with the privileged classes. The nobility have served me, have rushed in crowds into my antechambers. There are no offices which they have not accepted, solicited, pressed for. I have had my Montmorencies, my Noailles, my Rohans, my Beauveaus, my Mortemarts, but there was no sympathy between us. The steed curveted; he was well trained, but I perceived that he fretted. With the people it is another thing. The popular fibre responds to mine. I am come from the ranks of the people. My voice has influence over them. Observe these conscripts, these sons of peasants; I did not flatter them, I treated them with severity. They did not the less surround me, they did not the less shout '*The Emperor forever.*' It is because between them and me there is an identity of nature. They look to me as their support, their defender against the nobles. I have but to make a sign, or, rather, to turn away my eyes, and the nobles will be massacred in all the departments: they have carried on such intrigues for these last six months. But I will not be the king of a mob. If there are any means of governing with a Constitution, well and good. I desired the empire of the world, and to insure it, unlimited power was necessary to me. To govern France only, a Constitution may be better. I desired the empire of the world, and who, in my situation, would not? The world invited me to govern it. Sovereigns and subjects vied with each other in hastening beneath my sceptre.

" 'I have rarely found any opposition in France; but I have, however, met with more from some obscure unarmed Frenchmen, than from all these kings, so vain at present of no longer having a popular man for their equal.

Consider, then, what seems to you to be possible. Give me your ideas. Free elections, public discussions, responsible ministers, liberty, all this is my wish; the liberty of the press in particular. To stifle it is absurd. I am satisfied upon this point. I am the man of the people. If the people sincerely wish for liberty, I owe it them. I have recognized their sovereignty. I am bound to lend an ear to their desires, even to their caprices. I never desired to oppress them for my own gratification. I had great designs. Fate has decided them. I am no longer a conqueror; I can no more become so. I know what is possible and what is not. I have now but one charge, to relieve France and give her a government suited to her. I am not inimical to liberty. I set it aside when it obstructed my road, but I comprehend it; I have been educated in its principles. At the same time, the work of fifteen years is destroyed. It can not begin again. It would require twenty years, and the sacrifice of two millions of men. Besides, I am desirous of peace, and I shall obtain it only by dint of victories. I will not hold out false hopes to you. I abstain from telling you that there are negotiations in train; there are none. I foresee a difficult contest, a long war. To maintain it, the nation must support me; but, in return, she will require liberty; she shall have it. The situation is new. I desire no better than to receive information. I grow old; one is no longer at forty-five what one was at thirty. The repose of a constitutional monarch may be well suited to me. It will assuredly be still more suitable for my son.'"

CHAPTER VIII.

1816, March. Continued.

New Insult to the Emperor—Execution of Marshal Ney—Message to the Prince Regent—Wretched Food—Remarks on the Gracchi—Sleep during Battle—Historians—Military Characters—Soult, Massena—Political Confessions—Marmont—Murat—Berthier—Danger in Battle—Bulletins—Summary of nine Months.

March 15. The Emperor had requested the grand marshal to write to the admiral to ascertain if a letter which he should write to the Prince Regent would be forwarded. It was the Emperor's intention to employ this method, the only one which seemed compatible with his character, to write to his wife and obtain tidings of his son.

Sir George Cockburn insultingly replied to General Bertrand that he knew no person by the title of *Emperor* at St. Helena, and that he should not allow any letter to leave the island without first examining it himself. The Emperor, of course, decided that he could not submit to such an indignity. His heart was lacerated in being thus barbarously deprived of all intercourse, even by letter, with his wife and his idolized son. His desire to correspond with them was so great, that he was willing to submit to send the open letters to the reigning King of England, but he would endure any agony of a crushed spirit rather than open his letters to the insolent officials of St. Helena. The world will do homage to this spirit.

A frigate arrived, bringing European papers to the 31st of December. They contained information of the execution of Marshal Ney, and of the escape of Lavalette.

"Ney," said the Emperor, "as ill attacked as he was ill defended, has been condemned by the Chamber of Peers in the teeth of a formal capitulation. His execution has been allowed to take place. That is another error. From that moment he became a martyr. That Labédoyère should not have been pardoned, because the clemency extended to him would seem only a predilection in favor of the old aristocracy, might be conceived, but the pardon of Ney would only have been a proof of the strength of the government and the moderation of the prince. It will be said, perhaps, that an example was necessary; but the marshal could become so, much more certainly, by a pardon, after having been degraded by a sentence. It was to him, in fact, a moral death that deprived him of all influence, and, nevertheless, the object of authority would be obtained, the sovereign satisfied, the example complete.

EXECUTION OF MARSHAL NEY.

The refusal of pardon to Lavalette, and his escape, are new subjects of animadversion equally unpopular.

"But the saloons in Paris exhibit the same passions as the clubs. The nobility are a new version of the Jacobins. Europe, moreover, is in a state of complete anarchy. The code of political immorality is openly followed. Whatever falls under the hands of the sovereigns is turned to the advantage of each of them. At least, in my time, I was the butt of all the accusations of this kind. The sovereigns then talked of nothing but principle and virtue; but, now that they are victorious and without control, they practice unblushingly all the wrongs which they themselves then reprobated. What resource and what hope are then left for nations and for morality? Our countrywomen, at least, have rendered their sentiments conspicuous. Madam Labédoyère is on the point of dying from grief. These papers show us that Madam Ney exhibited the most courageous and determined devotion. Madam Lavalette has become the heroine of Europe."

March 16. The captain of a frigate which was about to sail for England was presented to the Emperor. Napoleon was deeply depressed in spirits, but was roused by the question if he had any letters to send to Europe. He requested Las Casas to ask the captain if he should see the Prince Regent. On being answered in the affirmative, the Emperor directed Las Casas to interpret to the captain the following message to the Prince Regent:

"I was desirous of writing to the Prince Regent, but, in consequence of the observation of the admiral that he would open the letter, I have abstained from it, as being inconsistent with my dignity and that of the Prince Regent himself. I have, indeed, heard the laws of England much boasted of, but I can not discover their benefits any where. I have only now to expect, even to desire, an executioner. The tortures they make me endure are inhuman, savage. It would have been more open and energetic to put me to death."

March 17. At four o'clock in the afternoon, an English colonel, on his return to Europe from the Isle of France, was presented to the Emperor. The isle had been ceded by the Bourbons to the English, and its prosperity had suffered materially by the change.

"The person of the Emperor," said the colonel, "remains very dear to the inhabitants of the Isle of France. The name of Napoleon is never pronounced there but with commiseration. It was on the day of a great festival that they learned of the fall of the Emperor after the disaster of Waterloo. The theatre that evening was to be unusually attractive, but the sympathy and grief were so strong that not a single colonist appeared at the entertainment. There were some English there, who were exceedingly confused and irritated by the circumstance."

The Emperor was for a moment silent after listening to this recital. He then said, "It is quite plain. This proves that the inhabitants of the Isle of France have continued French. I am the country; they love it. It has been wounded in my person; they are grieved at it."

It was remarked that, in consequence of a change of dominion, they did not dare to propose his health publicly, but they never neglect it, notwithstanding. They drink to "*Him.*" This word is consecrated to Napoleon.

The Emperor seemed much touched by these proofs of continued affection. "Poor Frenchmen! poor people! poor nation!" he exclaimed. "I deserved all that; I loved thee! But thou, thou surely didst not deserve all the ills that press upon thee! Ah! thou didst merit well that one should devote himself to thee! But it must be confessed what infamy, what baseness, what degradation I had about me!"

Journals which had recently arrived contained many tokens of the affection with which Napoleon was still regarded by the people. The English who took possession of the desert island of Ascension found engraved upon a rock upon the beach, "*May the great Napoleon live forever.*" There was also in the papers, in several languages, a *jeux de mots*, " Paris will never be happy till his Helena shall be restored to him." "These," says Las Casas, " were a few drops of honey in our cup of wormwood."

March 18–19. The Emperor was suffering much in health for want of exercise. He seldom rode on horseback in consequence of the very limited space to which he was confined. "After dinner," says Las Casas, "we could not help reverting to the meal we had just made; literally nothing was fit to eat; the bread bad; the wine not drinkable; the meat disgusting and unwholesome. The Emperor could not refrain from saying with warmth,

"No doubt there are some individuals whose physical situation is still worse than ours, but that circumstance does not deprive us of the right of giving an opinion on our condition, or of the infamous manner in which we are treated. The injustice of the English government has not been contented in sending us hither; it has selected the individuals to whom our persons and our supplies are intrusted. For my part, I should suffer less if I were sure that our treatment would be one day divulged to the world in such a way as to brand with infamy those who are guilty of it. But let us talk of something else."

March 22. The Emperor read to his companions some pages on Roman history. Speaking of the Gracchi, he said,

"History presents these Gracchi, in the aggregate, as seditious people, revolutionists, criminals, and nevertheless allows it to appear in detail that they had virtues—that they were gentle, disinterested, moral men; and, besides, they were the sons of the illustrious Cornelia, which, to great minds, ought to be a strong primary presumption in their favor. How, then, can such a contrast be accounted for? It is thus:

"The Gracchi generously devoted themselves for the rights of the oppressed people against a tyrannical senate. Their great talents and noble character endangered a ferocious aristocracy, which triumphed, murdered, and calumniated them. The historians of a party have transmitted their characters in the same spirit. Under the emperors it was necessary to continue in the same manner. The bare mention of the rights of the people, under a despotic master, was a blasphemy, a downright crime. Afterward the case was the same under the feudal system, which was so fruitful in petty despots.

Such, no doubt, is the fatality which has attended the memory of the Gracchi. Throughout succeeding ages, their virtues have never ceased to be considered crimes; but at this day, when, possessed of better information, we have thought it expedient to reason, the Gracchi may, and ought, to find favor in our eyes.

"In that terrible struggle between the aristocracy and the democracy, which has been renewed in our time—in that exasperation of ancient territory against modern industry, which still ferments throughout Europe, there is no doubt but that, if the aristocracy should triumph by force, it would point out many Gracchi in all directions, and treat them, in future, with as little mercy as its predecessors have done the Gracchi of Rome."

Continuing his criticisms, the Emperor remarked upon what he called historical follies, ridiculously exalted by translators and commentators.

"Such things prove, in the first place," said he, "that the historians formed erroneous judgments of men and circumstances—for instance, when they applaud so highly the *continence of Scipio*, and fall into ecstasies at the calmness of Alexander, Cæsar, and others, for having been able to sleep on the eve of battle. Even a monk debarred from women, whose face brightens up at the very name, who neighs behind his barrier at their approach, would not give Scipio much credit for forbearing to violate the females whom chance threw into his power, while he had so many others entirely at his disposal. A famished man might as well praise the hero for having quietly passed by a table covered with victuals without greedily snatching at them. As to sleeping just before a battle, there is not one of our soldiers or generals who has not twenty times performed that miracle. Their chief heroism lay in supporting the fatigue of watching the day before."

General Bertrand remarked, "I can safely say that I have seen your majesty sleep, not only on the eve of an engagement, but even during the battle."

THE EMPEROR ASLEEP AT WAGRAM.

"I was obliged to do so," said Napoleon, "when I fought battles that lasted three days. Nature was also to have her due. I took advantage of the smallest intervals, and slept when and where I could. Independently of the necessity of obeying nature, these slumbers afford a general commanding a very great army the important advantage of enabling him to await calmly the relations and combinations of all his divisions, instead of, perhaps, being hurried away by the only event which he himself could witness."

The Emperor then reverted to the Gallic war as narrated by Cæsar and by Rollin: "I can not comprehend," said he, "the invasion of the Helvetii, the road they took, the object ascribed to them, the time they spent in crossing the Rhine, the diligence of Cæsar, who found time to go into Italy, as far as Aquileia, to seek the legions, and overtook the invaders before they had passed the Saone. It is equally difficult to comprehend what is meant by establishing winter quarters that extended from Treves to Vannes.

"Ancient history, however," he continued, "embraces a long period, and the system of war often changes. In our days it is no longer that of the time of Turenne and Vauban. Campaign works are growing useless. Even the system of our fortresses have become problematical or ineffectual. The enormous quantity of bombs and howitzers change every thing. It is no longer against the horizontal attack that defense is requisite, but also against the curve and the reflected lines. None of the ancient fortresses now afford shelter; they have ceased to be tenable; no country is rich enough to maintain them. The revenue of France would be insufficient for her lines of Flanders, for the exterior fortifications are not now above a fourth or fifth of the necessary expense. Casements, magazines, places of shelter secure from the effects of bombs, are now requisite, and they are too expensive.

"Modern masonry is exceedingly defective in strength. The engineer department is radically weak in this point. It cost me immense sums, which have been wholly thrown away. To meet this difficulty, I invented a system altogether at variance with the axioms hitherto established. It was to have metal of an extraordinary calibre to advance beyond the principal line toward the enemy, and to have the principal line itself, on the contrary, defended by a great quantity of small, movable artillery. Hence the enemy would be stopped short in his sudden advance. He would have only weak pieces to attack powerful ones with. He would be commanded by this great calibre, round which the resources of the fortress, the small pieces, would form in groups, or even advance to a distance as skirmishers, and might follow all the movements of the enemy by means of their lightness and mobility. The enemy would then stand in need of battering cannon. He would be obliged to open trenches. Time would be gained, and the true object of fortification accomplished. I employed this method with great success, and to the great astonishment of the engineers, in the defense of Vienna and in that of Dresden. I wished to employ it in that of Paris, which city can not, I think, be defended by any other means. But of the success of this method I have no doubt."

March 23–26. For five days the rain fell in floods, and none of the inmates of Longwood could leave their damp and gloomy apartments. The Emperor read, with much disgust, a calumnious work by Miss Williams, on the return from the island of Elba. It was merely a collection of all the malevolent rumors circulated by the Royalists in those times. The evenings, even when the weather was pleasant, were invariably spent in the house, as at 9 o'clock the dwelling was surrounded by sentinels, and the Emperor could not pass them unless under the guard of an English officer. He sat down to dinner at 8 o'clock, and never remained at the table more than half an hour, frequently not more than fifteen minutes. He then returned to the drawing-room, where he conversed with his friends till half past nine or ten o'clock. When cheerful, and the conversation became animated, the social interview was continued until eleven o'clock.

One of these evenings the conversation turned upon the trials, which were then going on in France, of the friends of Napoleon, who, upon his return from Elba, had deserted the Bourbons. He spoke of Marshal Soult.

PORTRAIT OF MARSHAL SOULT.

"Soult," said he, "I know to be innocent. And yet, were it not for that fact, were I a juror in Soult's case, I have no doubt that I should declare him guilty, so strongly are appearances combined against him. Soult even acknowledged to me that he had taken a real liking to the king. The authority he enjoyed under him, he said, so different from that of my ministers, was a very agreeable thing, and had quite gained him over."

"Massena is another person whom they will perhaps condemn as guilty of treason. Appearances are overwhelming against him, and yet he fulfilled his duty up to the very moment of declaring himself openly. The truth is, that all the commanders did their duty; but they could not withstand the torrents of opinion, and no one had sufficiently calculated the sentiments of the mass of the people, and the national impetuosity. Carnot, Fouché, Maret, and Cambacères confessed to me at Paris that they had been greatly deceived on this point; and no one understands it well even now.

"Had the king," Napoleon continued, "remained longer in France, he would probably have lost his life in some insurrection. But had he fallen into my hands, I should have thought myself strong enough to have allowed him every enjoyment in some retreat of his own selection, as Ferdinand was treated at Valençay."

Immediately after this conversation, the Emperor engaged in a game of chess with Las Casas. His king having accidentally fallen from the board, he exclaimed,

"Ah! my poor king, you are down!"

Las Casas picked the piece up, and restored it to him in a mutilated state.

"Horrid!" said the Emperor; "I certainly do not accept the omen, and I am far from wishing any such thing. My enmity does not extend so far."

In reference to this characteristic incident, Las Casas writes, "I would not, on any account, have omitted this circumstance, trifling as it may appear, because it is, in many respects, characteristic. We ourselves, when the Emperor had retired, reverted to the incident. What cheerfulness! what freedom of mind in such dreadful circumstances! we said. What serenity in the heart! what absence of malice, irritation, or hatred! Who could discover in him the man whom enmity and falsehood have depicted as a monster? Even among his own followers, who is there that has well understood him, or taken sufficient pains to make him known?"

Another evening the Emperor was speaking of the companions of his early years. Reference was made to one whom Napoleon, when first placed in command of the army of Italy, had loaded with favors, but who soon afterward abandoned his general to attach himself to the Directory. He did not venture afterward to seek the favor of one whom he had forsaken.

"Nevertheless," said the Emperor, "when once I was seated on the throne, he might have done much with me if he had known how to set about it. He had the claim of early friendship, which never loses its influence. I could certainly never have withstood an unexpected overture in a hunting-party, for instance, or half an hour's conversation on old times at any other opportunity. I should have forgotten his conduct. It was no longer important whether he had been on my side or not. I had united all parties. Those who had an insight into my character were well aware of this. They knew that, with me, however well I might have been disposed toward them, it was like the game of prison-bars. When once the point was touched, the game was won. In fact, if I wished to withstand them, I had no resource but that of refusing to see them."

March 27. The Emperor was walking in the garden with Count Las

Casas and Count Bertrand, when the following interesting conversation took place between them.

"I was a very warm and sincere Republican," said the Emperor, "at the commencement of the Revolution. I cooled by degrees, in proportion as I acquired more just and solid ideas. My patriotism sunk under the political absurdities and monstrous domestic excesses of our Legislatures. Finally, my Republican faith vanished on the violation of the choice of the people by the Directory at the time of the battle of Aboukir."

"For my part," said the grand marshal, "I was never a Republican. I was a very warm Constitutionalist until the 10th of August. The horrors of that day cured me of all illusion. I came very near being massacred in defending the king at the Tuileries."

"As for me," added Las Casas, "it was notorious that I commenced my career a pure and ardent Royalist."

"Why, then," said the Emperor, with vivacity, "it seems, gentlemen, that I am the only one among us who has been a Republican."

"And something more, sire," both Las Casas and Bertrand exclaimed.

"Yes," repeated the Emperor, "Republican and patriot."

"And I have been a patriot, sire," repeated Las Casas, "notwithstanding my royalism; but, what is still more extraordinary, I did not become so till the period of the imperial reign."

"How! you rogue!" rejoined the Emperor; "are you compelled to own that you did not always love your country?"

"Sire," replied Las Casas, "we are making our political self-examination, are we not? I confess my sins. When I returned to Paris by virtue of your amnesty, could I at first look upon myself as a Frenchman, when every law, every decree, every ordinance that covered the walls constantly added the most opprobrious epithets to my unlucky denomination of emigrant? Nor did I think of remaining when I first arrived. I had been attracted by curiosity, yielding to the invincible influence of one's native land, and the desire of breathing the air of one's country. I now possessed nothing there. I had been compelled, at the frontier, to swear to the relinquishment of my patrimony, to accede to the laws which decreed its loss. I looked on myself as a mere traveler in that land, once mine. I was a true foreigner, discontented, and even malevolent. The Empire came. It was a great event. 'Now,' said I, 'my manners, prejudices, and principles triumph; the only difference is in the person of the sovereign. When the campaign of Austerlitz opened, my heart, with surprise, found itself once more French. My situation was painful. I was divided between blind passion and national sentiment. The triumph of the French army and their general displeased me, yet their defeat would have humbled me. At length the prodigies of Ulm and the splendor of Austerlitz put an end to my embarrassment. I was vanquished by glory. I admired, I acknowledged, I loved Napoleon. From that moment I became French to enthusiasm. Henceforth I have had no other thoughts, spoke no other language, felt no other sentiments; and here I am by your side.'"

"It must be admitted," said the Emperor, "that our being assembled at St. Helena from political causes is certainly a most extraordinary circumstance. We have come to a common centre by roads originally in very different directions. We have, however, traveled through them with sincerity. Nothing more clearly proves the sort of chance, the uncertainty, and the fatality which usually, in the labyrinth of revolutions, direct upright and honest hearts, nor can any thing more clearly prove how necessary indulgence and intelligent views are to recompose society after long disorders. This disposition and these principles made me the most suitable man for the circumstances of *Brumaire*. These views, without doubt, render me the most suitable person for the present state of France. On this point I have neither distrust, prejudice, nor passion. I constantly employed men of all classes, of all parties, without ever looking back, without inquiring what they had done, what they had said, what they had thought, only requiring that they should pursue in future, and with sincerity, the common object—the welfare and the glory of all—that they should show themselves true and good Frenchmen. Above all, I never made overtures to leaders in order to gain over parties. On the contrary, I approached the mass of the parties, that I might be in a situation to despise their leaders. Such has ever been the uniform system of my internal policy, and, in spite of the last events, I am far from repenting of it. If I had to begin again, I should pursue the same course.

"It is totally unreasonable to reproach me with having employed nobles and emigrants. It is a trite and vulgar imputation. The fact is, that under me there existed in France only individual opinions and sentiments. The nobles and the emigrants have not brought about the restoration; it is rather the restoration which has raised the nobles and the emigrants. They have not contributed more particularly to our ruin than others. Those really in fault are the intriguers of all parties and all opinions. Fouché was not a noble. Talleyrand was not an emigrant. Augereau and Marmont were neither. To conclude, do you desire a final proof of the injustice of blaming whole classes when a revolution like ours has operated in the midst of them? Look at yourselves here. Among four, you find two nobles, one of whom was even an emigrant. The excellent M. de Ségur, in spite of his age, at my departure offered to follow me. I could multiply examples without end.

"It is with as little reason that I have been blamed for *neglecting* certain persons of influence. I was too powerful not to despise with impunity the intrigues and the known immorality of the greater part of them. Neither had that any thing to do with my downfall, but only unforeseen and unheard-of catastrophes, compulsory circumstances, five hundred thousand men at the gates of the capital, a revolution still recent, a crisis too powerful for French heads, and, above all, a dynasty too recent. I would have risen, even from the foot of the Pyrenees, could I have been my own grandson. And, moreover, what a fascination there is respecting past times! It is most certain that I was chosen by the French. Their new worship was their own work. Well, immediately upon the return of the old forms, see with what facility they have recurred to idols!

"And, after all, how could another line of policy have prevented that which ruined me? I have been betrayed by Marmont, whom I might call my son, my offspring, my own work. To his hand I had committed my destinies by sending him to Paris at the very moment that he was putting the finishing hand to his treason and my ruin. I have been betrayed by Murat, whom I had raised from a soldier to a king, who was my sister's husband. I have been betrayed by Berthier, a mere goose, whom I had converted into a kind of eagle. I have been betrayed in the senate by those very men of the national party who owe every thing to me. My fall, then, did not in any way depend upon my system of internal policy. Undoubtedly one might accuse me of having employed too readily old enemies, whether nobles or emigrants, if a Macdonald, a Valence, a Montesquieu had betrayed me; but they were faithful. If one objects to me the stupidity of Murat and Berthier, I oppose to this the judgment of Marmont. I have, then, no cause to repent of my interior system of policy."

March 28. At the dinner-table it was remarked that one in thirty of the ships engaged in the China trade were lost at sea.

"The dangers of battle," said the Emperor, "are less than that. At Wagram we were one hundred and sixty thousand. I do not think that the killed were more than three thousand. That is only a fiftieth. At Essling, where we were forty thousand, about four thousand were killed. This was a tenth; but it was one of the most severe battles. The others were incomparably below."

The conversation then turned upon the correctness of bulletins. The Emperor declared that his were very correct. "Except," said he, "when the proximity of the enemy compelled me to disguise, that when they came into their hands they might not derive any information prejudicial to me from them, all the remainder were very exact. If they have acquired an ill reputation in our armies, if it was a common saying '*as false as a bulletin*,' it was personal rivalship, party spirit, that had established it. It was the wounded self-love of those whom it had been forgotten to mention in them, and who had, or fancied they had, a right to a place there, and, still more than all, our ridiculous national defect of having no greater enemies to our successes and our glory than we were ourselves."

The rain was falling in torrents. After dinner the Emperor played a game of chess, and retired early to his bed.

March 29–31. The weather was damp and dismal. Dense fog enveloped the island, accompanied by drizzling rain. The Emperor's health was visibly declining. "We all suffered," says Las Casas; "besides, we are absolutely infested with rats, fleas, and bugs. Our sleep is disturbed by them, so that our troubles by night are in perfect harmony with those by day. Yet never do we hear a complaint from the Emperor. His great soul suffers nothing to overcome it." In the course of conversation the Emperor observed, speaking of Egypt and Syria,

"If I had taken St. Jean d'Acre, as ought to have been the case, I should have wrought a revolution in the East. The most trivial circumstances lead to the most serious events. The weakness of a captain of a frigate, who stood out to sea instead of forcing a passage into the harbor, some trifling impediments with respect to some shallops or light vessels, prevented the face of the world from being changed. Possessed of St. Jean d'Acre, the French army would have flown to Damascus and Aleppo. In a twinkling it would have been on the Euphrates. The Christians of Syria, the Druses, the Christians of Armenia, would have joined it. Nations were on the point of being shaken."

"You would soon," said Las Casas, "have been re-enforced by four hundred thousand men."

"Say rather," the Emperor replied, "by six hundred thousand. Who can calculate what it might have been? I should have reached Constantinople and the Indies. I should have changed the face of the world."

Nine months had now elapsed since Napoleon left France. Las Casas gives the following summary of its events:

"On quitting France, we remained for a month at the disposal of the brutal and ferocious English ministry. Then our passage to St. Helena occupied three months. On our landing we occupied the Briers nearly two months. Lastly, we have been three months at Longwood.

"All the time of our stay at Plymouth, Napoleon remained thoughtful and merely passive, exerting no power but patience. His misfortunes were so great and so incapable of remedy, that he suffered events to take their course with a stoical indifference. During the whole of our passage he constantly possessed a perfect equanimity; he expressed no wish, manifested no disappointment. It is true, the greatest respect was paid to him. He received it without noticing it. He spoke little, and the subject was always foreign to himself. Any one who, coming suddenly on board, had witnessed his conversation, would undoubtedly have been far from guessing with whom he was in company. I can not better picture him in this circumstance than by comparing him to those passengers of high distinction who are conveyed with great respect to their destination.

"Our abode at the Briers presented another shade of difference. Napoleon, left almost entirely to himself, receiving nobody, constantly employed, seeming to forget events and men, enjoyed, apparently, the calm and the peace of a profound solitude, either from abstraction or contempt not condescending to notice the inconveniences or privations with which he was surrounded. If he now and then dropped an expression relative to them, it was only when roused by the importunity of some Englishman, or when excited by the recital of the outrages his attendants suffered. His whole day was occupied in dictation; the rest of the time was dedicated to the relaxation of familiar conversation. He never mentioned the affairs of Europe, spoke rarely of the Empire, very little of the Consulate, but much of his situation as general in Italy; still more, and almost constantly, of the minutest details of his childhood and early youth. The latter subjects especially seemed at this time to have a peculiar charm for him; it was almost exclusively with these objects that he employed the many hours of his nightly walks by moonlight.

"Finally, our establishment at Longwood was a fourth and last change. All our situations hitherto had been but short and transitory; this was fixed, and threatened to be lasting. There, in reality, were to commence our exile and our new destinies. History will take them up there. There the eyes of the world were to be directed to consider us. The Emperor, seeming to make this his calculation, regulates all about him, and takes the attitude of dignity oppressed by power. He traces around him a moral boundary, behind which he defends himself, inch by inch, against indignity and insult. He no longer compromises any thing with his persecutors. He shows himself sensibly jealous in respect to forms, and hostile to all encroachments.

"It was no small surprise to us, nor a slight satisfaction, to have to observe among ourselves that, without knowing how or why, it was nevertheless perceptible that the Emperor now stood higher in the opinion and the respect of the English than he had hitherto done. We could even perceive that this sentiment was every day increasing. With us, the Emperor entered fully into the affairs of Europe. He analyzed the projects and the conduct of the sovereigns. He compared them with his own; weighed, separated, spoke of his reign, of his deeds; in a word, we once more found the Emperor, and *all* Napoleon. Not that he had ever ceased to be so for an instant as regarded our devotion and our attention, nor that we, on our side, had any thing to endure. Never did we experience a more even temper, a more constant kindness, a more unaltered affection.

"The Emperor's health," continues Las Casas, "visibly declines, but never do we hear a complaint from him. His great soul suffers nothing to overcome it, and even contributes to deceive him with respect to his own state. But we can see him decay very perceptibly."

CHAPTER IX.
1816, April.

Conspiracies—Measures that might have been adopted after Waterloo—Characteristic Fruits—The State of Europe—Ascendency of Liberal Opinions—Talleyrand—Fouché—Political Reflections—Arrival of Sir Hudson Lowe—Remarks on the Return from Elba—Introduction of the Governor—Character and Conduct of Sir George Cockburn.

April 1. Las Casas was present as the Emperor was making his toilet. His skin was peculiarly soft and white, and the moulding of his limbs was feminine in beauty. As he was drawing on his flannel waistcoat, Las Casas gazed steadfastly at him with an expression of countenance which arrested the attention of the Emperor.

"Well," said Napoleon with a smile, "what is *your excellency* thinking of this moment?"

"Sire," Las Casas replied, "in a pamphlet which I lately read, I found it stated that your majesty was shielded by a coat of mail for the security of your person. A report of the same kind was circulated among certain classes in Paris. In support of the assertion, allusion was made to your majesty's sudden *embonpoint*, which was said to be quite unnatural. I was just thinking that I could bear positive evidence to the contrary, and that at St. Helena, at least, all precautions for personal safety have been laid aside."

"This," rejoined the Emperor, "is one of the thousand absurdities which have been published respecting me. But the story you have just mentioned is the more ridiculous, since every individual about me knows how careless I am in regard to self-preservation. Accustomed, from the age of eighteen, to be exposed to the cannon ball, and knowing the inutility of precautions, I abandoned myself to my fate. When I came to the head of affairs, I might still have fancied myself surrounded by the dangers of the field of battle, and I might have regarded the conspiracies which were formed against me as so many bomb-shells; but I followed my old course. I trusted my lucky star, and left all precautions to the police. I was, perhaps, the only sovereign in Europe who dispensed with a body-guard. Every one could freely approach me without having, as it were, to pass through military barracks. The sentinels at the outer gate being passed, all had free access to every part of my palace.

"Maria Louisa was much astonished to see me so poorly guarded, and she often remarked that her father was surrounded by bayonets. For my part, I had no better defense at the Tuileries than I have here. I don't even know where to find my sword. Do you see it?" said he, looking around. "I have, to be sure, incurred great dangers. Upward of thirty plots were formed against me. These have been proved by authentic testimony, without mentioning many that never came to light. Some sovereigns invent conspiracies against themselves. For my part, I made it a rule carefully to conceal them whenever I could. The crisis most serious to me was during the interval from the battle of Marengo to the attempt of Georges, and the affair of the Duke d'Enghien."

As they were descending to the garden, after the Emperor had finished dressing, he remarked,

"The two designs on my life which placed me in the most imminent danger were those of Cerachi the sculptor, and the fanatic of Schoenbrun. Cerachi and some other desperate wretches had laid a plan for my assassination. Cerachi had formerly adored the First Consul; but he vowed to sacrifice me, when, as he pretended, I had proved myself a tyrant. This artist, who had executed my bust, I had loaded with favors. When he entered into the plot against me, he endeavored, by every possible means, to procure another sitting, under pretense of making an essential improvement on the bust. Fortunately, I had not a single moment of leisure, and thinking that *want* was the real cause of the urgent solicitations of the sculptor, I sent him six thousand francs. But how was I mistaken! His real motive was to stab me at the sitting.

"This conspiracy was disclosed by a captain of the line, who was himself an accomplice. This was a proof of the strange modifications of which the human mind is susceptible, and shows to what lengths the combinations of folly and stupidity may be carried. This officer regarded me with horror as

1816, April.]   RESIDENCE AT LONGWOOD.   131

First Consul, though he had adored me as a *general*. He wished to see me driven from my post, but he rejected the idea of any attempt upon my life. He wished that I should be secured, but would not have me injured in any way. He proposed that I should be sent back to the army, to face the enemy and to defend the glory of France. The rest of the conspirators laughed at these notions; but when he found that they were distributing poniards, and going far beyond his intentions, he disclosed the whole.

"The fanatic of Schoenbrun was the son of a Protestant minister of Erfurth. He had passed the sentinels, and had been twice or thrice driven back, when General Rapp, in the act of pushing him aside with his hand, felt something concealed under his coat. This proved to be a knife a foot and a half long, pointed, and sharp at both edges. I shuddered to look at it. It was merely rolled up in a piece of newspaper. The assassin was brought into my closet, and I called Corvisart, and directed him to feel the criminal's pulse while I questioned him. The assassin stood unmoved, confessing his intended crime, and frequently making quotations from the Bible.

THE FANATIC OF SCHOENBRUN.

"'What was your purpose here?' I inquired.
"'To kill you,' he replied.
"'What have I done to offend you, and by what authority do you constitute yourself my judge?'
"'I wish to put an end to the war.'
"'And why not address yourself to the Emperor Francis?'
"'To him!' he replied; 'wherefore? he is a mere cipher. Besides, if he

were dead, another would succeed him; but when you are gone, the French will immediately retire from Germany.'

"I vainly endeavored to appeal to his feelings. 'Do you repent?' I inquired. 'Would you again attempt the perpetration of your intended crime?'

"'Yes,' he replied.

"'What! if I were to pardon you?'

"Here nature for an instant resumed her sway. The man's countenance and voice underwent a momentary change.

"'Even though *you* do,' said he, '*God* will not forgive me.'

"But he immediately resumed his ferocious expression. He was kept in solitary confinement, and without food, for four-and-twenty hours. He still remained the same man, or, to speak more properly, the same ferocious brute. He was left to his fate."

April 3. The day dawned beautifully clear and serene. The lovely weather enticed the Emperor out of doors, and he dictated in the garden, under the shade of a tree. He had been reading the account of Alexander's expedition in Rollin's History.

"It affords," he said, "no just idea of the grand designs of Alexander. I should like myself to write an account of that expedition."

At five o'clock, having finished his dictation, he was walking in the garden, attended by all the gentlemen. As Las Casas joined the company, the Emperor said,

"Come, we must have your opinion on a point which we have been discussing for the last half hour. On my return from Waterloo, do you think that I could have dismissed the Legislative Body, and have saved France without it?"

"No, sire," Las Casas replied, "it would not have been dissolved voluntarily. You would have found it necessary to employ force, which would have been regarded as scandalous. The dissatisfaction excited in the Legislative Body would have spread through the whole nation. Meanwhile, the enemy would have arrived, and your majesty must have surrendered, accused by all Europe, accused by foreigners, and even by Frenchmen; perhaps loaded with universal malediction, regarded merely as an adventurer carrying every thing by violence; but as it was, your majesty issued pure and unsullied from the conflict, and your memory will be everlastingly cherished in the hearts of those who respect the cause of the people. Your majesty has, by your moderation, insured to yourself the brightest character in history, while, by a different line of conduct, you might have incurred the risk of reprobation. You have lost your power, it is true, but you have gained the summit of your glory."

"Well," rejoined the Emperor, "this is partly my own opinion. But, after all, am I certain that the French people will do me justice? Will they not accuse me of having abandoned them? History will decide. Instead of dreading, I invoke its decree. I have often asked myself whether I have done for the French people all that they could expect of me, for that people did much for me. Will they ever know all that I suffered during the night which preceded my final decision?

"In that night of anguish and uncertainty I had to choose between two great courses. The one was to endeavor to save France by violence, and the other to yield to the general impulse. The measure which I pursued was, I think, the most advisable. Friends and enemies, the good and the evil-disposed, were all against me, and I stood alone. I surrendered. My decision, being once adopted, could not be revoked. I am not one who takes half measures, and besides, sovereignty is not to be thrown off and on like one's cloak. The other course demanded extraordinary severity. It would have been necessary to arraign great criminals and to decree great punishments. Blood must have been shed, and then who can tell where we should have stopped? But what scenes of horror might not have been renewed!

"By pursuing this line of conduct, should I not have drowned my memory in the deluge of blood, crimes, and abominations of every kind with which the libelists have already overwhelmed me? Should I not thereby have seemed to justify all that they have been pleased to invent? Posterity and history would have viewed me as a second Nero or Tiberius. If, after all, I could have saved France at such a price, I had energy sufficient to carry me through every difficulty. But is it certain that I should have succeeded? All our dangers did not come from without. The worst existed in our internal discord. Did we not see an insensate crowd eager to dispute about the shade before we had secured the triumph of the color? How would it have been possible to persuade them that I was not laboring for myself alone, for my own personal advantage? How could I convince them of my disinterestedness, or prove that all my efforts were directed to save the country? To whom could I point out the dangers and miseries from which I sought to rescue the French people? They were evident to me, but the vulgar mass will ever remain in ignorance of them until they are crushed beneath their weight.

"What answer could be given to those who exclaimed, 'Behold the despot! the tyrant! again violating the oaths which he took but yesterday?' And who knows whether, amid this tumult, this inextricable complication of difficulties, I might not have perished by the hands of a Frenchman in the civil conflict? Then, how would France have appeared in the eyes of a universe, in the estimation of future generations? The glory of France is to identify herself with me. I could not have achieved so many great deeds for her honor and glory without the nation and in despite of the nation. I repeat, history will decide."

After these remarks, he reverted to the plans and details of the campaign of Waterloo, dwelling with pleasure upon its glorious commencement, and with agony upon the terrible disaster in which it terminated.

"Nevertheless," said he, in conclusion, "I should have considered the state of affairs by no means desperate had I obtained the aid which I had a right to expect. Our only resources were in the Chambers. I hastened to Paris to convince them of this. But they immediately rose against me, under the pretense that I was come to dissolve them. What absurdity! From that moment all was lost. It would, perhaps, be unjust to condemn the majority of the Chambers; but such is the inevitable tendency of these numerous bodies, that they perish without unity. Chiefs are as necessary to them as to armies. In armies, chiefs are appointed, but great talents and eminent genius seize hold of assemblies and govern them. We were wanting, however, in all this. Therefore, in despite of the good spirit which might have animated the majority, the whole body found itself in an instant in confusion, vertigo, and tumult. Perfidy and corruption stationed themselves at the doors of the Legislative Body, while incapacity, disorder, and perversity prevailed in its bosom. Thus France became the prey of foreigners.

"For a moment I entertained the idea of resistance. I was on the point of declaring myself in permanence at the Tuileries in the midst of the ministers and the Council of State; to call around me the six thousand men of the Guard whom I had at Paris, augmenting them with the best-disposed portion of the National Guard, who were very numerous, and with all the federate troops of the faubourgs; of adjourning the Legislative Body to Tours or to Blois; of reorganizing before the walls of Paris the wrecks of the army, and thus to work alone, as dictator, for the safety of the country.

"But would the Legislative Body have obeyed? I might have enforced obedience, it is true, but then what scandal, and what new complication! Would the people have made common cause with me? The army even, would it have obeyed me with constancy? In the crises continually arising, might it not separate from me? Might not plans have been formed to my prejudice? Would it not have been a plausible pretext that so many efforts and dangers had but me for their object? The facilities which every one had found the preceding year in gaining favor with the Bourbons, might they not have become decisive inducements?

"Yes, I hesitated long; weighed the *for* and the *against*, and at last concluded that I could not resist the coalition without and the Royalists within, the numerous parties which the violence done the Legislative Body would have created, that portion of the multitude which must be driven by force, and, in fine, that moral condemnation which imputes to you, when you are unfortunate, all the evils which ensue. There remained for me absolutely, then, but abdication. All was lost. I foresaw this; I foretold it; but I had no other alternative.

"The Allies had always pursued against us the same system. They began it at Prague, continued it at Frankfort, at Chatillon, at Paris, at Fontainebleau. They conducted themselves with much judgment. The French might have been their dupes in 1814, but posterity will find it difficult to conceive how they could have been deceived in 1815. History will forever condemn those who suffered themselves to be misled. I told them their fate when I was departing to join the army.

"'Do not resemble,' said I, 'the Greeks of the Lower Empire, who amused themselves in debating while the battering-ram was leveling the walls of their city.' Again I said to them, when they forced me to abdicate, 'The enemy wish to separate me from the army. When they shall have succeeded, they will separate the army from you. You will then be but a helpless flock, the prey of ferocious beasts.'"

"Do you think," one of his companions inquired, "that, with the concurrence of the Legislative Body, you could have saved France?"

"I would confidently," he promptly replied, "have undertaken to do so, and would have answered for success. In less than a fortnight, that is to say, before the masses of the enemy would have been able to present themselves before Paris, I should have completed the fortifications. I would have collected under the walls, from the wreck of the army, eighty thousand good troops, and three hundred pieces of horse artillery. After a few days' firing, the National Guard, the federal troops, and the inhabitants of Paris, would have sufficed to defend the intrenchments. There would then have remained under my hand eighty thousand disposable troops. It is well known how advantageously I was capable of employing this force. The remembrance of 1814 was still fresh. Champaubert, Montmirail, Craone, Montereau, were still present in the imagination of our enemies. The same places would have revived the recollection of the prodigies of the preceding year. They then surnamed me the *one hundred thousand men*. The rapidity, the force of our blows, gave rise to this name. The conduct of the French troops was most admirable. Never did a handful of brave men accomplish such marvels. If their heroic exploits have never been well known to the public, in consequence of our disasters, they have, at least, been duly appreciated by our enemies, who counted our attacks by our victories. We were truly the *Briairées* of fable.

"Paris would, in a few days, have become impregnable. The appeal to the nation, the magnitude of the danger, the excitement of the public mind, the grandeur of the spectacle, would have drawn multitudes from all parts to the capital. I should undoubtedly have assembled more than four hundred thousand men, and I think that the allied force did not exceed five hundred thousand. Thus the affair would have been brought to a single combat, which would have been as perilous to the enemy as to us. The enemy would have hesitated, and the confidence of the multitude would have been restored to me.

"Meanwhile, I should have surrounded myself with a national senate or junta, selected from among the members of the Legislative Body—men distinguished by national names and worthy of general confidence. I should thus have fortified my military dictatorship with all the force of civil opinion. I should have had my tribune, which would have promulgated the talisman of my principles through Europe. The sovereigns would have trembled to behold the contagion spread among their subjects. Terrified, they must have treated with me, or have been vanquished."

"But, sire!" one exclaimed, "why did you not attempt what would infallibly have succeeded? Why are we here?"

"Now," resumed the Emperor, "you are blaming and condemning me; but if you took a view of the contrary chances, you would soon change your language. Besides, you forget that we reasoned on the hypothesis that the Legislative Body had joined me, and you know the course it adopted. I had the power to dissolve it, it is true. France and Europe perhaps blame, and posterity will doubtless blame, my weakness in not breaking up the Legislative Body after its insurrection. I should have devoted myself, it will be said, to the destinies of a people who had done all for me; but by dissolving the Assembly, I could, at the most, but have obtained a capitulation from the enemy. In that case, I again repeat, blood must have been shed, and I must have shown myself a tyrant. I had, however, arranged a plan on the night of the 20th, and on the morning of the 21st measures of the most rigid severity were to have been adopted. But, ere the return of day, the dictates of humanity and prudence warned me that such a course was not to be thought of; that I should fail in my enterprise, and that every one was merely seeking blindly to accommodate himself to circumstances. But I must not begin again. I have already said too much on a subject which always revives painful recollections. I repeat once more that history will decide." Thus saying, the Emperor retired to his chamber.

April 5-8. Under this date Las Casas makes the following record. "During these four days the Emperor invariably rode out on horseback about six or seven in the morning, accompanied only by me and my son. I am enabled to affirm that I never saw Napoleon swayed either by passion or prejudice; that is to say, I never knew him to pronounce judgment on men and things that was not dictated by reason. Even when he displays what may perhaps be called anger, it is merely the effect of transitory sensation, and never influences his actions; but I can truly say that during the eighteen months in which I have had the opportunity of observing his character, I never knew him to act in contradiction to reason.

"Another fact which has come to my knowledge is, that, either from nature, calculation, or the habit of preserving dignity, he for the most part represses and conceals the painful sensations which he experiences, and still more, perhaps, the kind emotions of his heart. I have frequently observed him repressing feelings of sensibility as if he thought they compromised his character. The following characteristic trait so perfectly corresponds with the object of this journal, namely, that of showing the man as he really is, and seizing nature in the fact, that I can not refrain from mentioning it.

"For some days past Napoleon seemed to have something deeply at heart. A domestic circumstance had pained him exceedingly. He was deeply wounded. For three days during which we every morning rode in the park, he on each occasion alluded to the subject with much feeling. At one time the following observations escaped him:

"'I know well that I am fallen; but to be reminded of this by one of my friends! Ah!'

"These words," says Las Casas, "his gesture, his tone, pierced my heart. I was ready to throw myself at his feet and to embrace his knees."

"'I know,' he continued, 'that man is exacting and sensitive, and frequently unreasonable. Thus, when I am distrustful of myself, I ask, should I have been treated so at the Tuileries? This is my sure test.'

"He then," says Las Casas, "spoke of himself, of us, of our reciprocal relations, of our situation in the island, and of the influence which our individual circumstances might enable us to exercise. His reflections were numerous, forcible, and just. In the emotion with which this conversation inspired me, I exclaimed,

"'Sire, permit me to take this affair upon myself. It certainly never could have been viewed in this light. If the matter were explained, I am sure that it would excite deep sorrow and repentance. I only ask permission to say a single word.'

"No, sir,' the Emperor replied, with dignity, ' I forbid it. I have opened my heart to you. Nature has had her course. I shall think of it no more, and you must seem never to have known it.'"

April 9. A ship arrived from England bringing papers to the 21st of January. These journals announced the continued agitation of France and of all Europe. Upon hearing the recital read of the deluge of evils which afflicted all the departments of France, the Emperor rose in nervous agitation from his sofa, and exclaimed with fervor,

"Ah! what a misfortune that I was not able to proceed to America! From the other hemisphere I might have protected France against reaction. The fear of my reappearance would have held in check their violence and their folly. My name would have sufficed to bridle their excess and to fill them with terror."

In earnest utterance, he continued for some time upon the same subject, and said in conclusion,

"The counter revolution, even had it been allowed to proceed, would inevitably have been lost in the grand revolution. The atmosphere of modern ideas is sufficient to stifle the old feudalists, for henceforth nothing can destroy or efface the grand principles of our revolution. These great and excellent truths can never cease to exist, so much have we blended them with our fame, our monuments, our prodigies. We have washed away their first stains in floods of glory, and henceforth they will be immortal. Created in the French Tribune, cemented by the blood of battles, adorned with the laurels of victory, saluted with the acclamations of the people, sanctioned by the treaties, the alliances of sovereigns, made familiar to the ears as well as to the mouths of kings, they can never again retrograde.

"They live in Great Britain, they illuminate America, they are nationalized in France. Behold the tripod from whence issues the light of the world! They will yet triumph. They will be the faith, the religion, the morality of all people; and this memorable era, whatever may be advanced to the contrary, will be inseparably connected with my name.

"For, after all, I kindled the torch and consecrated the principle, and now persecution renders me, of those principles, the messiah. Friends and enemies, all must acknowledge that I am, of them, the chief soldier, the grand representative. Thus, when I am in my grave, I shall still be, for the people, the polar star of their rights. My name will be the war-cry of their efforts, the signet of their hopes."

April 12. Napoleon, speaking of the fickleness of the French people, said, "This levity, this inconsistency, has descended to us from antiquity. We still remain Gauls, and our character will never be complete until we learn to substitute principles for turbulence, pride for vanity, and, above all, the love of institutions for the love of places. But the excuse may perhaps be found in the nature of things and in the power of circumstances. Democracy raises up sovereignty, aristocracy preserves it. Mine had neither taken deep enough root nor sufficient spirit. At the moment of the crisis, it was still connected with the democracy. It mingled with the multitude, and yielded to the impulse of the moment, instead of becoming an anchor of safety against the tempest, and a light to guide them in their darkness."

Speaking of Talleyrand, the Emperor said,

" M. de Talleyrand waited two days and nights at Vienna for full powers to treat for peace in my name; but I should have been ashamed to have thus prostituted my policy. And yet, perhaps, it has cost me my exile to St. Helena, for I can not but allow that Talleyrand is a man of singular talent, and capable at all times of throwing great weight into the scale. He was always in a state of treason, but it was in participation with fortune. His circumspection was extreme. He treated his friends as if they might, in future, become his enemies, and he behaved to his enemies as if they might, some time or other, become his friends. Talleyrand had always been, in my opinion, hostile to the Faubourg St. Germain. In the affair of the divorce, he was for the Empress Josephine. It was he who urged the war with Spain, though

PORTRAIT OF TALLEYRAND.

in public he had the art to appear averse to it. In short, Talleyrand was the principal instrument and the active cause of the death of the Duke d'Enghien.

"Mademoiselle Raucourt, a celebrated actress, described him with great truth. 'If you ask him a question,' said she, 'he is an iron chest, whence you can not extract a syllable; but if you ask him nothing, you will soon be unable to stop his mouth; he will become a regular gossip.' This was a foible which, at the outset, destroyed my confidence in Talleyrand. I had intrusted him with a very important affair, and, a few hours after, Josephine related it to me word for word. I instantly sent for the minister to inform him that I had just learned from the Empress a circumstance which I had told in confidence to himself alone. The story had already passed through four or five intermediate channels. The countenance of Talleyrand is so immovable that nothing can ever be read in it. Lannes and Murat used jocularly to say of him, that if, while he was speaking to you, some one should come behind and give him a kick, his countenance would betray nothing.

"M. de Talleyrand is mild and even endearing in his domestic habits. His servants, and the individuals in his employment, are attached and devoted to him. With his intimates he speaks willingly and good-humoredly of his ecclesiastic profession, which he embraced by compulsion, constrained by his parents, though he was the eldest of many brothers. He one day expressed dislike of a tune which was played in his hearing. He said he had a great horror of it; it recalled to his recollection the time when he was obliged to practice church music and to sing at the desk. On another occasion, one of his intimate friends was telling a story during supper, while M. de Talleyrand was engaged in thought, and seemed inattentive to the conversation. In the course of the story, the speaker happened to say, in a lively manner, of some one whom he had named, 'That fellow is a comical rogue; he is a married priest.' Talleyrand, roused by these words, seized a spoon, plunged it hastily into the dish before him, and, with a threatening aspect, called out to him, 'Mr. ——, will you have some spinach?' The person who was telling the story was confounded, and all the party burst into a fit of laughter, M. de Talleyrand as well as the rest.

"Fouché," said the Emperor, "was the Talleyrand of the clubs, and Talleyrand was the Fouché of the drawing-rooms. Intrigue was to Fouché a necessary of life. He intrigued at all times, in all places, in all ways, and with all persons. Nothing ever came to light but he was found to have had a hand in it. He made it his sole business to look out for something that he might be meddling with. His mania was to wish to be concerned in every thing—always in every body's shoes. The remark which he made, or which is attributed to him in the affair of the Duke d'Enghien, is well known, and shows the character of the man. 'It is worse than a crime,' said he, 'it is a fault.' I was to blame for having employed him in 1815, when, indeed, he basely betrayed me. I was not ignorant of his disposition, but I also knew that the danger depended more on the circumstances than on the individual. If I had been victorious, Fouché would have been faithful. He took great care, it is true, to hold himself in readiness for whatever might happen. I ought to have conquered."

April 13. It was a pleasant morning, and the Emperor breakfasted in the garden, with all his companions around him. One of the company read the papers which had recently arrived.

"On the 13th Vendemiaire,"* said the Emperor, "the inhabitants of Paris were completely disgusted with the government, but the whole of the army, the great majority of the population of the departments, the lower class of citizens, and the peasantry remained attached to it. Thus the Revolution triumphed over this grand attack of the counter revolution, though it was only four or five years since the new principles had been promulgated. Most frightful and calamitous scenes had been witnessed, and a happier future was anticipated.

NAPOLEON RECEIVING THE COMMAND FROM THE CONVENTION.

"But to-day what a difference! The immense majority of the French hold in abhorrence the government which is imposed upon them by force, for it deprives them of their glory, their prosperity, their customs. It wounds their pride, their principles, their maxims. It places under the yoke of foreigners that France which for twenty years had given laws to others. This government, hostile to every thing dear to the people, has no support in France. It is sustained only by the will and the power of foreigners. This government is extended over a people nearly all of whom have been born under the Revolution, and who cherish the principles which the government wishes to destroy. Who can foresee the end of all this? Who can predict the result? In 1814, the entire nation could have been carried over to the king. This is now impossible; then it was a peaceable succession.

* October 5, 1795, when Napoleon defeated the attack of the Sections on the Convention.

To-day it is a conquest terrible, outrageous. If the government should undertake to form a national army, it would immediately stand in fear of that army.

"A soldier in his tiresome march, in the weary monotony of his barracks, has need to speak of war; but he can not speak of Fontenay or Prague, which he did not witness. He must speak of the victories of Marengo, Austerlitz, and Jena—of him who gained them—in short, of me, whose fame fills every mouth and lives in all imaginations. Such a situation is unexampled in history. On whichever side it is viewed, nothing but misfortunes present themselves. What will be the result of this? Two classes of people upon the same soil, exasperated, irreconcilable, will be incessantly contending, and will finally, perhaps, exterminate each other. The same fury will soon spread through Europe. The whole Continent will be composed of but two hostile parties. It will be no longer divided by nations and territories, but by party colors and opinions. Who can foresee the crisis, the duration, the details of so many storms? The event can not be doubtful. The present enlightened age will not retrograde in knowledge. How unfortunate was my fall! I had imprisoned the winds; hostile bayonets have released them. I could have proceeded tranquilly in the universal regeneration; it can henceforth be effected only amid tempests. My object was to amalgamate; others, perhaps, will extirpate."

April 15. It was a dark and gloomy day, and the rain fell in torrents. "After dinner, the Emperor," says Las Casas, "described to us the contents of some French papers which he had by him, and which, he said, gave an account of the shipwreck of La Perouse, his different adventures, his death, and which also contained his journal. The narrative consisted of the most curious, striking, and romantic details, and interested us exceedingly. The Emperor observed how highly our curiosity was excited, and then burst into a fit of laughter. This story was nothing but an impromptu of his own, which he said he had invented merely to show us the progress he had made in English."

April 16. The rain still continued, and a ship arrived at the island bringing the new governor, Sir Hudson Lowe. Without any regard to decorum, this ill-bred man sent an impertinent message to Longwood that he should call the next morning at nine o'clock to see General Bonaparte.

"Let him come as soon as he pleases," said the Emperor to Count Montholon; "I will receive him only when he asks to be received in a proper manner."

A little before nine, in a driving storm of wind and rain, Sir Hudson Lowe, accompanied by Sir George Cockburn and a numerous staff, rode up to the door of Longwood, and demanded admission to see his prisoner. He was informed that the Emperor was indisposed, and could not receive any visitors that morning. The insolent official was quite confounded by this unanticipated repulse, and after angrily walking for a few moments up and down before the windows of the drawing-room, demanded at what hour on the following day he could be introduced. Two o'clock was appointed for the interview. The governor again mounted his horse in high dudgeon, and, with his retinue, disappeared in the rain and the mist.

April 17. About the middle of the day the Emperor sent for Las Casas, to converse with him confidentially upon some of their family matters. This frank and private conversation affords a valuable development of Napoleon's real character.

"There occasionally arose among us," says Las Casas, "transient misunderstandings and disputes, which gave much pain to the Emperor. He adverted to this topic. He analyzed our situation with his ordinary perspicuity. He appreciated the misery and the uneasiness of our exile, and pointed out the best alleviations. He said that we ought to make mutual sacrifices and overlook many grievances; that man can only enjoy life by controlling the character given to him by nature, or by creating to himself a new one by education, and learning to modify it according to the obstacles which he may encounter."

"You should endeavor to form here but one family," said Napoleon. "You have followed me only with the view of assuaging my sorrow. Ought not this feeling to subdue every other consideration? If sympathy alone is not sufficiently powerful, let reason be your guide. You should learn to calculate your sorrows, your sacrifices, and your enjoyments, in order to arrive at a result, just as we make additions or subtractions in every kind of calculation. All the circumstances of our lives should be submitted to this rule. We must learn to conquer ill temper. It is natural enough that little misunderstandings should arise among you, but they should be followed by explanation, and not succeeded by ill humor. The former will produce a result; the latter will only render the affair more complicated. Reason and logical inference should, in this world, be our constant guides."

"He then proceeded to show," says Las Casas, "how he had sometimes acted up to these principles and sometimes departed from them. He added that we ought to learn to forgive, and to avoid that hostility and acrimony which must be offensive to our neighbors and prejudicial to our own happiness; that we ought to make allowance for human frailties, and conform ourselves to them rather than oppose them."

"What would have become of me," said the Emperor, "had I not followed these maxims? It has often been said that I have been too good-natured, and not sufficiently cautious; but it would have been much worse for me had my disposition been the reverse of what it is. I have been twice betrayed, it is true, and I may be betrayed a third time; but still, it was my knowledge of human character, and the spirit of reasonable indulgence which I had adopted, that enabled me to govern France, and which still, perhaps, render me the fittest person to rule that nation, under existing circumstances. On my departure from Fontainebleau, did I not say to all who requested me to point out the line of conduct they should pursue, '*Go to the king; serve him?*' I wished to grant them lawful authority for doing what many would not have hesitated to do of their own accord. I did not wish to have some ruin themselves by persisting in fidelity to me, and, above all, I did not wish to have any one to censure on my return."

"Here," says Las Casas, "I ventured, contrary to my constant custom, to call the Emperor in some measure to account. 'How, sire,' I exclaimed, 'had your majesty any idea of returning when you left Fontainebleau?'"
"Yes, certainly," the Emperor replied, "and by the simplest reasoning. If the Bourbons, said I, intend to commence a fifth dynasty, I have nothing more to do here—I have acted my part; but if they should obstinately attempt to recontinue the third, I shall soon appear again. It may be said that the Bourbons had then my memory and my conduct at their disposal, if they had been contented to be the magistrates of a great nation: had they consented to this, I should have been regarded by the mass of mankind as an upstart, a tyrant, a firebrand, and a scourge. How much good sense and calm reflection would have been necessary to appreciate my real character, and render me justice!

"But they persisted in returning feudal lords; they preferred to be but the odious chiefs of a party hateful to the whole nation. But the men by whom the Bourbons were surrounded, the erroneous line of conduct they pursued, rendered my return desirable. The Bourbons themselves restored my popularity and decreed my return. But for them, my political mission would have been consummated, and I should have ended my days on the island of Elba; and, without any doubt, this would have been better both for them and for me, for I did not return for the sake of ascending the throne, but to pay a great debt. Few will comprehend it, but no matter. I undertook a strange charge, but it was a duty I owed the French people. Their cries reached me; how could I remain insensible?

"My situation upon the island of Elba was, on the whole, sufficiently enviable, sufficiently agreeable. I should soon have created for myself a new sort of sovereignty. All that was most distinguished in Europe was about to pass in review before me. I should have presented a spectacle unknown in history—that of a monarch descended from his throne beholding the civilized world defile eagerly before him. It may be said, it is true, that the Allies would have removed me from my island, and I admit that this circumstance hastened my return; but if the Bourbons had governed France wisely, if the French people had been contented, my influence would have been at an end; I should thenceforth have belonged only to history, and they would not have thought, at Vienna, of displacing me. It was the agitation, created and maintained in France by the Bourbons and by those who surrounded them, which led them to think of my removal."

While the Emperor was thus talking the hour of two arrived, and the grand marshal entered to announce the arrival of the governor, who was accompanied by the admiral, and escorted by the whole of his staff. The governor and his suite were assembled in the ante-chamber. The Emperor was to grant them an audience in his drawing-room.* The valet de chambre, Novarrez, who stood at the door to announce the persons introduced, was devoted to the Emperor with deathless fervor. As the Emperor entered the drawing-room, the valet de chambre summoned the governor, and he was ad—

* See the plan of Longwood.

THE EMPEROR'S RESIDENCE AT ELBA.

mitted; the admiral followed close behind, intending to present the governor. But the valet, not having heard the admiral's name called, shut the door in his face, and refused to admit him. Sir George Cockburn, regarding this as an insult, retired in a towering passion. The governor's staff was then announced. In about a quarter of an hour the Emperor took leave of his visitors. The whole affair appears to have vexed both the governor and the admiral exceedingly. The Emperor was not at all disposed to submit to the insolent manners of these vulgar men. He effectually opposed to their impertinence the shield of his lofty character and his renown.

Soon after the presentation the Emperor joined his friends in the garden. Speaking of Sir Hudson Lowe, he said,

"That man is malevolent. While looking at me, his eye was like that of a hyena taken in a trap. Put no confidence in him. We complain of the admiral; we shall perhaps regret him, for, in truth, he has the heart of a soldier, while the general only wears the dress. His appearance and expression recall to my mind those of the constables of Venice. Who knows? perhaps he will be my executioner. Let us not, however, be hasty in forming our judgment. His disposition may, however, after all, atone for his unfavorable appearance."

The Emperor knew nothing of the repulse which the haughty admiral had received. When informed of it he was exceedingly diverted, and rubbing his hands with glee, he said,

"Ah! my good Novarrez, you have done a clever thing for once in your life. He had heard me say that I would not see the admiral again, and he thought that he was bound to shut the door in his face. But this honest Swiss may perhaps carry the joke too far. If I were unfortunately to say we must get rid of the governor, he would be for assassinating him before my eyes.

"But, after all," he added, in a more serious tone, "it was entirely the governor's fault. He should have requested that the admiral might be admitted, particularly as he had informed me that he could be presented only by him. And why did he not request the admiral's admission when he presented his officers to me? He is solely to blame. But the admiral has lost nothing by the mistake. I should, without hesitation, have apostrophized him in the presence of his countrymen. I should have told him that, by the sentiment attached to the honorable uniform which we had both worn for forty years, I accused him of having, in the eyes of the world, degraded his government, his nation, his sovereign, in failing, without necessity and without discretion, in respect to one of the oldest soldiers in Europe. I should have reproached him with having landed me at St. Helena just as he would have landed a convict at Botany Bay. I should have assured him that a man of true honor would have shown me more respect on my rock than if I were still on my throne and surrounded by my armies."

Las Casas, in the following summary, expresses his views of the character and conduct of Sir George Cockburn.

"As I have thus alluded to the admiral, and as he is now about to quit us, I will, once for all, sum up the insults with which we have to reproach him with as much impartiality as our situation and the state of our feelings will admit.

"We can not pardon the affected familiarity with which he treated us, though our conduct afforded but little encouragement to it; still less can we forgive him for having endeavored to extend this familiarity to the Emperor. We can never forget the haughty and self-complacent air with which he addressed Napoleon by the title of *general.* The Emperor, it is true, has immortalized that title; but the tone and intention with which it was applied were sufficiently insulting.

"On our arrival at St. Helena, he lodged the Emperor in a little room a few feet square, where he kept him for two months, though other residences could have been procured, and there was one which the admiral had himself fixed upon. He indirectly prohibited the Emperor from riding on horseback even in the grounds surrounding the Briers, and the individuals of the Emperor's suite were loaded with embarrassments and humiliations when they came to pay their daily visits to him in his little cell.

"On our removal to Longwood, he stationed sentinels under the very windows of the Emperor; and then, by an evasion which savored of the bitter-

K

est irony, he alleged that this step had been taken only with a view to the *general's* own advantage and protection. He suffered no one to come near us without a note from him, and, having thus placed us in close confinement, he declared that these arrangements had been made only to secure the Emperor against importunity, and that he (the admiral) was merely acting the part of *grand marshal.* He gave a ball, and sent a written invitation to *General Bonaparte* in the same manner as he did to every individual in the suite. He replied with the most unbecoming jeers to the notes of the grand marshal, who used the title of Emperor, saying that he knew no *Emperor* at the island of St. Helena, nor any such sovereign in Europe or elsewhere who was not in his own dominions. He refused to forward a letter from the Emperor to the Prince Regent unless it were delivered to him open, or he were permitted to read it. He even stifled the sentiments and expressions of respect which other individuals manifested to Napoleon. We were assured that he had put persons of inferior situations under arrest merely for having used the title of *Emperor*, or other similar expressions, which, however, were frequently employed by the 53d regiment, doubtless, as the Emperor observed, through an irresistible sentiment with which these brave men were inspired.

"From his own personal caprice he had limited the extent of our rides and walks. He had, moreover, neglected the most ordinary forms of decorum, always fixing upon unsuitable hours for his own visits, and directing strangers who arrived at the island to select the same unseasonable periods for visiting the Emperor. This was no doubt done with the view of preventing people from gaining access to Napoleon, who constantly refused to be seen on these occasions.

"However, if we were required to pronounce an impartial opinion on him, making allowance for the irritability of our own feelings, and the delicacy of his situation, we should not hesitate to declare that our grievances rested in forms rather than facts. We should say with the Emperor, who had, after all, a natural predilection for him, that Admiral Cockburn is far from being an ill-disposed man ; that he is even susceptible of generous and delicate sentiments ; but that he is capricious, irascible, vain, and overbearing ; that he is a man who is accustomed to authority, and who exercises it ungraciously, frequently substituting energy for dignity. To express in a few words the nature of our relations with respect to him, we should say that, as a *jailer*, he was mild, humane, and generous, and that we have reason to be grateful to him ; but that, as a *host*, he was generally impolite, often something worse, and that, in this character, we have cause to be displeased with him."

CHAPTER X.
1816, April. Continued.

Convention between the Allied Powers—Declaration demanded of the Inmates of Longwood—Farewell Visit of Governor Wilks—Interesting Conversation on the Arts—Message to the Prince Regent—Portfolio lost at Waterloo—Cost of the Emperor's Toilet—Expenses in different Capitals—The Furnishing of the imperial Palaces—The Emperor's Mode of examining Accounts.

April 18. Dr. O'Meara brought some European journals to the Emperor. In the course of conversation, the name of Admiral Cockburn was mentioned.

"I believe," said the Emperor, "that he was rather ill-treated the day he came up with the new governor. What does he say about it?"

Dr. O'Meara, kindly disposed to apologize for his countryman, replied, "The admiral conceived it as an insult offered to him, and certainly felt greatly offended at it. Some explanation has, however, been given by General Montholon upon the subject."

"I shall never see him with pleasure," added the Emperor. "But he did not announce himself as being desirous of seeing me."

"He wished," said Dr. O'Meara, "to introduce officially to you the new governor, and thought, as he was to act in that capacity, it was not necessary to be previously announced."

"He should have sent me word," replied the Emperor, "by General Bertrand, that he wanted to see me. But he wished to embroil me with the new governor, and for that purpose persuaded him to come up here at nine o'clock in the morning, though he well knew that I never had received any person, and never would at that hour. It is a pity that a man who really has talent, for I believe him to be a very good officer in his own service, should have behaved in the manner he has done to me. It shows the greatest want of generosity to insult the unfortunate. To insult those who are in your power, and who, consequently, can not make any opposition, is a certain sign of an ignoble mind."

"I am confident," said Dr. O'Meara, "that the whole was a mistake, and that the admiral had not the smallest intention of embroiling your majesty with the governor."

"I, in my misfortunes," the Emperor resumed, "sought an asylum. Instead of that, I have found contempt, ill treatment, and insult. Shortly after I came on board his ship, as I did not wish to sit at the table two or three hours guzzling down wine to intoxicate myself, I rose from the table and walked out upon the deck. While I was going out, he said, in a contemptuous manner, 'I believe the *general* has never read Lord Chesterfield,' meaning that I was deficient in politeness, and did not know how to conduct myself at table."

Dr. O'Meara, still apologizing for the rudeness of the admiral in not applying for an audience, said, "The English, and, above all, naval officers, are not in the habit of going through many forms. The omission of the customary etiquette was quite unintentional on the part of the admiral."

"But if," Napoleon replied, "Sir George had wished to see Lord St. Vincent or Lord Keith, would he not have sent beforehand and asked at what hour it might be convenient to see him? And should not I be treated with at least as much respect as either of them? Putting out of the question that I have been a crowned head, I think," said he, with a smile, "that the actions which I have performed are at least as well known as any thing they have done."

Just at this moment Count Montholon came in with the following communication from Sir Hudson Lowe. It was a copy of instructions which the governor had received from Lord Bathurst relative to the inmates of Longwood:

"Downing Street, January 10th, 1816.

"It is my duty to inform you that it is the pleasure of his Royal Highness the Prince Regent, that on your arrival at St. Helena you should communicate to all the persons forming the suite of Napoleon Bonaparte, including his domestic servants, that they are at liberty immediately to quit the island and return to Europe; adding that none will be permitted to remain at St. Helena except such as declare in writing, to be deposited in your hands, that it is their desire to remain on the island, and to submit to such restrictions as it may be necessary to impose upon Napoleon Bonaparte personally.

"(Signed),   BATHURST."

Napoleon read this communication, and, after a short conference with his friends, calmly dictated to Count Montholon the following paper, to be presented to the household:

"We, the undersigned, desiring to remain in the service of the Emperor Napoleon, consent, however frightful the abode in St. Helena may be, to remain there, submitting ourselves to the restrictions, however unjust and arbitrary, which are imposed upon his majesty and the persons in his service."

"There," said the Emperor; "let those who please sign that, but do not attempt to influence them either one way or the other."

Though the members of the household were informed that those who decided not to leave would be compelled to remain upon the island during the lifetime of *General Bonaparte*, every member of the household promptly signed the paper excepting General Bertrand. He had near relatives in Europe to whom he was tenderly attached. The idea of cruel exile from them for perhaps twenty or thirty years for a moment shook his resolution.

"Bertrand is always the same," said the Emperor. "Although he constantly speaks of going, when the time comes he will not have the courage to leave. One must be able to love one's friends with all their faults. In him, as in the unfortunate Louis XVI., domestic virtues form the basis of his organization. I do not, however, believe that he will ever leave me."

There was something unutterably ignoble and cruel in this attempt to drive Napoleon's companions from him, and thus to leave Napoleon, friendless and alone, to grope through the glooms of his captivity and death. History would be recreant to its task in neglecting to consign the authors of such inhumanity to contempt and infamy.

April 18. The Convention of the allied sovereigns, relative to the captivity of Napoleon, was presented to him. It was as follows:

"*Convention between Great Britain, Austria, Russia, and Prussia, signed at Paris, August 20th, 1815.*

"Napoleon Bonaparte, being in the power of the allied sovereigns, their majesties the King of the United Kingdom of Great Britain and Ireland, the Emperor of Austria, the Emperor of Russia, and the King of Prussia, have agreed, by virtue of the stipulations of the treaty of the 25th of March, 1815, on the measures best calculated to preclude the possibility of his making any attempt to disturb the peace of Europe.

"*Art.* I. Napoleon Bonaparte is considered by the powers who signed the treaty of the 25th of March last as their prisoner.

"*Art.* II. His safeguard is specially intrusted to the British government. The choice of the place, and the measures which may best insure the object of the present stipulation, are reserved to his Britannic majesty.

"*Art.* III. The imperial courts of Austria and Russia, and the royal court of Prussia, shall appoint commissioners to reside in the place which his Britannic majesty's government shall assign as the residence of Napoleon Bonaparte, and who, without being responsible for his security, shall assure themselves of his presence.

"*Art.* IV. His most Christian majesty (Louis XVIII.) is invited, in the name of the four courts above mentioned, also to send a French commissioner to the place of Napoleon Bonaparte's detention.

Art. V. His majesty, the King of the United Kingdom of Great Britain and Ireland, pledges himself to fulfill the engagements assigned to him by the present Convention."

The Emperor, after having heard this read, remarked, with perfect composure of spirit,

"If the people, whose interests have been conquered at Waterloo, submit to the iron yoke imposed upon them by the Congress of Vienna, we shall not be worth the money which it will cost England to keep us here, and they will get rid of us; but our captivity may still be prolonged for some years, perhaps three, four, or five. Otherwise, setting aside the fortuitous events which are beyond the reach of human foresight, I see, my friends, but two chances, very uncertain, for our liberation from this place; first, that the *sovereigns* may stand in need of me to put down rebellion among their subjects; and, secondly, that the *uprising people* may demand my aid in their conflict with the kings; for, in this immense strife of the present against the past, I am the natural arbitrator and mediator. I have always aspired to be the supreme judge in this cause. All my administration at home, all my diplomacy abroad, tended to this great end. The issue might have been brought about more easily and promptly, but fate has ordained otherwise.

"Finally, there is a last chance, which is, perhaps, the most probable of all. I may be wanted to check the power of the Russians. In less than ten years all Europe may perhaps be overrun with Cossacks, or all under republican government. Such are the statesmen who have brought about my overthrow. At Waterloo I ought to have been victorious. The chances were one hundred to one in my favor; but Ney, the bravest of the brave, at the head of forty-two thousand men, suffered himself to be delayed a whole day by some thousands of Nassau troops.* Had it not been for this inexplicable inactivity, the English army would have been taken *flagrante delicto*, and annihilated without striking a blow. Grouchy, with forty thousand men, suffered Bulow and Blucher to escape from him; and, finally, a heavy fall of rain had made the ground so soft, that it was impossible to commence the attack at daybreak. Had I been able to commence early, Wellington's army would have been trodden down in the defiles of the forest, before the Prussians could have had time to arrive. It was lost without resource. The defeat of Wellington's army would have been peace, the repose of Europe, the recognition of the interests of the masses and of the democracy."

After a few moments of absorption in intense thought, the Emperor added, "It is difficult to account for the style of this document—for the malignant spirit which pervades it.

"*Francis!* he is religious, and I am his son.

"*Alexander!* we are friends. We once loved each other.

"*The King of Prussia!* I have undoubtedly done him much injury, but I could have injured him more. And is there no glory, no true happiness in ennobling one's self by magnanimity?

"As to *England*, it is to the animosity of her ministers that I am indebted for all this treatment. But still, may it not be that the Prince Regent will see the necessity of interfering, under penalty of being considered senseless, or the protector of vulgar malignity?"

Then turning to Count Montholon, he said, "Send no answer. Do not acknowledge the receipt of the communication. There is time enough to do that. I shall probably reply to it by a protest, which I shall send to Vienna and Petersburg at the same time as to London."

April 19. For many days the weather had been disagreeable in the extreme. The Emperor said to Dr. O'Meara, "In this wretched island there is neither sun nor moon to be seen for the greater part of the year. Constant rain and fog."

Allusion was made to some absurd falsehoods published in the ministerial papers respecting Napoleon.

"Is it possible," said he, "that the English can be so foolishly credulous as to believe all the stuff they publish against me?"

April 20. Colonel Wilks, the former governor of the island, who was now about returning to England, requested permission to take leave of the Emperor before his departure from St. Helena. He had been formerly diplomatic

* The Emperor, Count Montholon says, was not aware, at that time, of the cause of Ney's *forced* inaction at Quatre Bras.

agent of the East India Company, and was a man of extensive information and distinguished talents. He had attained celebrity as a soldier, author, diplomatist, and chemist. The exiles, however, had seen but little of him, as the gout had confined him to his bed most of the time since their arrival. His daughter was as remarkable for the grace and the beauty of her person as for her rich intellectual accomplishments. She spoke French with Parisian fluency and purity, and served as an interpreter for her father in his intercourse with the French gentlemen.

The Emperor with great cordiality received the father and daughter, and expressed his regret at their departure. The interview continued for more than two hours, and the conversation was lively and varied. Speaking of the English dominion in India, the Emperor said,

"You lost America by enfranchisement. You will lose India by invasion. The first loss was perfectly natural. As children advance in years, they break their parental bonds; but for the Hindoos, they are not advancing at all; they still remain children. The catastrophe can only proceed from without. You are not aware of the dangers with which you were threatened by my arms or my negotiations. As for my Continental system, you perhaps laughed at it."

"Sire," replied Governor Wilks, "we affected to do so, but all men of judgment felt the full force of it."

"Well," continued the Emperor, "I stood alone in my opinion on the Continent, and I was forced, for the moment, to employ violence every where. At length my plan began to be understood. The tree already bears its fruit. I made the beginning; time will do the rest. Had I not fallen, I should have changed the face of commerce as well as the route of industry. I had naturalized in the midst of us sugar and indigo. I should have naturalized cotton, and many other articles of foreign produce. They would have seen me displace the colonies, if they had obstinately refused to grant us a share in them. With us the impulse was most powerful. National prosperity and science advanced beyond measure. Yet your ministers proclaimed through all Europe that the French were overwhelmed with misery, and were retrograding to a state of barbarism. Thus the vulgar mass of the Allies were strangely surprised at the sight of our interior, and you even were disconcerted. The strides of knowledge in France were gigantic. The ideas of the French people were every where properly directed and extended. We took pains to render science popular. I have been informed that your countrymen are distinguished for their knowledge of chemistry. I am, however, far from deciding on which side of the water the most able chemists will be found."

"In France," said Governor Wilks, promptly.

"It is of little importance," continued the Emperor; "but I maintain that in the mass of the French people there is ten, and perhaps a hundred times more chemical knowledge than in England, because the manufacturing classes now employ it in their daily labor. This was one of the characteristics of my school. Had I been allowed sufficient time, there would soon have been no such things as *trades* in France; they would all have been converted into *arts*.

"England and France held in their hands the fate of the world, particularly that of European civilization. How much injury we did each other! how much good might we not have done! Under the school of Pitt we have desolated the world, and with what result? You imposed on France a tax of three hundred millions of dollars, and raised it by means of Cossacks; I laid a tax of fourteen hundred millions on you, and made you raise it with your own hands by means of your Parliament. And to-day, even after your victory, is it certain that you may not, sooner or later, sink beneath the weight of such a burden? With the system of Fox, we should have understood each other; we should have accomplished and maintained the emancipation of the peoples, the reign of principles. There would have been in Europe but a single fleet, a single army. We should have united our interests and our efforts; we should have yoked together to advance with more certainty to the same end; we might have governed the world; we might every where have established peace and prosperity, either by force or persuasion. Yes, I repeat, what mischief have we done! what good might we not have effected!"

After a short pause the Emperor continued:

"I have always wished sincerely for peace, and always offered it after a victory. I have never asked it after a reverse, because a nation more readily repairs its resources and finds new troops than recovers its honor. I am wrongfully accused of having refused peace at Dresden. When history shall give publicity to the negotiations of Prague, the policy of Metternich will be unmasked, and justice will be done me. I wished for a general peace, honorable to all parties, and such as would secure the repose of Europe. As the price of her mediation, Austria wished, by a stroke of the pen, to demolish the ramparts of Dantzig, Custrin, Magdeburg, Wesel, Mayence, Antwerp, Alexandria, and Mantua—in short, of all the strongest places in Europe, of which my troops were still in possession, and the keys of which had cost me thirty victories. She dared to propose to me, with arms in my hands, to evacuate the half of Germany, and to wait, like an idiot, behind the Rhine, till the allied armies, having recovered the losses which they had sustained in so many battles, should be in condition to put forward new pretensions. It was in the name of my father-in-law, before Austria had drawn the sword, that they flattered themselves with inducing me to sign their insulting proposal. I said to Metternich, with indignation, 'Is it my father-in-law who entertains such a project? Is it he who sends you to me? In what an attitude does he wish to place me before the French people! He is strangely mistaken if he supposes that a throne so mutilated as that could afford a refuge for his daughter and his grandson in France. How much has England given you to induce you to play this game against me? Have not I done enough for your fortune? It is of no consequence—be frank—what is it you wish? If twenty millions will not satisfy you, say what you wish?'

"The sudden paleness of Metternich, and his silence, recalled me to myself; but the blow was mortal, and from that moment I had no further belief

NAPOLEON AND METTERNICH IN COUNCIL.

in peace. On the same evening, however, my minister for foreign affairs signed a convention, by which I accepted the mediation of Austria, which, on her part, engaged to obtain from the Allies that a congress should be assembled in Prague before the 10th of August, in order to negotiate a general peace. My plenipotentiaries went thither, and their declarations, as recorded in the minutes, prove that I wished for peace at all cost, provided French honor was respected.

"I have always been of opinion that the rivalries between great nations have been the results of misunderstanding, and from the moment that I was balked in my project of making a descent upon England by the fault of Admiral Villeneuve, I never desired any thing but peace. As long as the negotiations on your part were conducted by Fox, they were honorably conducted, and had he lived, England and France would have been united in the closest alliance since 1806. Unfortunately for both nations, Fox died, and the ministry which succeeded him adopted the shade of Pitt for its ægis.

"In short, I have always wished for peace with England by all means reconcilable with the dignity of the French nation. I have desired peace at the cost of all sacrifices consistent with national honor. I had neither prejudice, hatred, nor jealousy of ambition against England. It was of little consequence to me that England was rich and prosperous, provided that France was so also. I should not have contested with her the dominion of the sea, I repeat, if at sea she had been ready to respect the French flag, as the Emperors of Austria or Russia would have respected our standards on land. Had I been conqueror at Waterloo, I should have made no change in the message sent to London before passing the Sambre. You are about to go to London. Tell your fellow-citizens what you have heard, and that in going on board the *Bellerophon* of my own accord, I gave the English people the highest proof of my esteem."

Four ships arrived during the day, bringing another regiment to guard the Emperor. After dinner, Napoleon good-humoredly related the remark of an old soldier of the 53d, who, having yesterday, for the first time, seen the Emperor, went back to his comrades and said,

"What lies they told me about Napoleon's age. He is not old at all. The rogue has at least sixty campaigns in his body yet."

This led to the recital of many anecdotes respecting the feeling of the French soldiers upon the Emperor's return from Elba. One pleased Napoleon highly. Immediately after the Emperor's landing, there was a grand review at Lyons of the king's troops. Count d'Artois, apprehensive of the attachment of his men to their old chieftain, said to them,

"You are well clothed and well fed. Your wages are punctually paid."

"Yes, certainly," replied an old grenadier.

"Well," continued the count, "it was not so under Bonaparte. Your pay was in arrears. He was in your debt."

"And what did that signify," the grenadier boldly replied, "if we were willing to trust him?"

April 21. Captain Hamiton, of the frigate *Havana*, who was the next day to sail for England, called, by appointment, at four o'clock in the afternoon, to take leave of the Emperor. The audience took place under a tree in the garden, where the Emperor, with his companions around him, received the captain. In the course of a very friendly conversation, Napoleon, having inquired of the captain if he should probably see the Prince Regent, and being answered in the affirmative, said to him,

"Tell the Prince Regent that I have but one thing to ask, my liberty or an executioner. I am not the prisoner of England, and the government has, in my case, most unworthily violated the sacred laws of hospitality, which even savages respect."

Captain Hamiton ventured to observe that the Emperor was not the prisoner of England alone, but of all the allied powers.

"I am not the prisoner," the Emperor replied, "of Russia, Austria, or Prussia. I freely, and of my own accord, gave myself up to England, because I had confidence in the sacred faith of the law, and in the honor of the English people. I have been cruelly deceived. The justice of God will avenge me. Already that of man has set an indelible mark of disgrace upon the conduct of your government.

"Had I given myself to Russia, I should have been well received, for Alexander and I are friends. Had I surrendered to Austria, I should have been equally well treated. The Emperor Francis would not have wished to inflict disgrace upon the husband of his daughter and the father of his grandson. Undoubtedly Metternich's police would have watched my most trifling actions. But what would his police have been to me, when I had renounced all concern in political affairs, and wished to live politically a stranger to all intrigues? I would have occupied the whole of my time in the education of my son, and in the peaceful enjoyment of family happiness. If, finally, I had thrown myself into the hands of the Prussians, the king would have received me with the recollection of his own misfortunes and my generosity ; for, if I did him much evil, it was the result of his own conduct, and it depended entirely upon myself to do him much more. The King of Prussia is an honest man, a man of honor, who would not have violated the sacred laws of hospitality. I must do him that justice. The hatred which your ministers bear to me has left a stain upon English honor. If the Prince Regent is really powerless against the decisions of his ministers, he should avow it, and protest before the nation. He is but a contemptible or wicked king who sympathizes with the vulgar passions of his inferiors when he is able to repress them."

The Emperor returned to his room and sent for Las Casas. Together they perused an English publication containing the official documents found in the portfolio, which was taken from Napoleon at Waterloo. The Emperor himself was astonished at the number of orders which he had issued at the same moment, and at the countless details which he had directed in all quarters of the empire.

"This publication," he said, "after all, can do me no harm. It will at least satisfy every one that its contents are not the production of a sluggard. They will compare me with the legitimate sovereigns, and I shall not suffer by the comparison."

After dinner the Emperor conversed freely upon many unconnected subjects. In speaking of his embassadors, he said,

"I consider Count de Narbonne as the only one who fully deserved that title, and who really fulfilled the duties of his office. This arose not only from his mind, which was subtle and observing, but from his polished manners and his illustrious name, which opened to him every door among the old aristocracy. When an embassador has but to fulfill a prescribed duty, any one may fill the post; one person is just as good as another; perhaps an aid-de-camp is the best man that can be chosen; but when it is necessary to negotiate, it is a different thing; then, to the old aristocracy of the courts of Europe, it is necessary to send none but the elements of that same aristocracy, for this is a kind of freemasonry. An Otto, an Andreossi, were they to enter the saloons of Vienna, immediately the free interchange of opinions would be restrained, and habitual manners would cease; they would be regarded as intruders, profaners, and the mysteries would be suspended. But how different would it be with a Narbonne, possessing the advantages of affinity, sympathy, identity!

"I was strongly attached to M. de Narbonne, and regretted him exceedingly. Until the period of his embassy, we had been duped by Austria. In less than a fortnight he penetrated all the secrets of the Vienna cabinet, and M. de Metternich was deeply mortified at the appointment. From the very moment of his arrival, he succeeded, by means of the friendship of one of the first ladies at court, in removing the veil which had concealed the whole truth from his predecessor. His mother had been lady of honor to the sisters of Louis XVI., and, as such, during the emigration had contracted a great intimacy with this lady, who looked upon Narbonne in no other light but as the son of her old friend. The embassador was forgotten in the agreeable recollections of the heart, and the impressions given by the mistress of the house produced an electrical effect on the frequenters of her saloon; hence they conversed in the presence of Narbonne as they would have done fifteen years before, and thus he knows all. However, by a singular fatality, perhaps even the success of M. de Narbonne thwarted my views. I found that his talent was no less fatal than useful. Austria, thinking her designs were guessed, threw aside the mask and precipitated measures. Had less penetration been evinced on our part, she would have acted with greater reserve and deliberation; she would have prolonged her natural indecision, and, in the interim, other chances might have risen up.

"I had occasion to see the same result when I removed Talleyrand from the office of foreign affairs. There were still some aristocratical affinities with Champagny, for he was an ancient noble, but there were none whatever with Maret; and still, the latter had all the courtliness of the old *régime*, and the Duchess of Bassano, his wife, was, without contradiction, as graceful in her deportment as she was beautiful. It was, however, natural, after all. *The barrel still smells of the herring.*"

Count Montholon alluded to the French embassadors at Dresden and Berlin, and censured their conduct. The Emperor defended them, saying,

"The fault was not to be attributed to persons, but to things. At a single glance, one might have foreseen what would have happened. For my part, I was not deceived for a moment. I did not conduct the army in person back to Wilna and into Germany through the apprehension of not being able to reach France myself. I wished to obviate this danger by the boldness of my movement in crossing Germany rapidly and alone. I was, however, on the point of being taken in Silesia, but luckily the Prussians were deliberating at the moment when they ought to have been acting. Their conduct in this respect was like that which the Saxons observed toward Charles XII., who said, when he quitted Dresden on a similar occasion, 'You will see that they will deliberate to-morrow whether they ought to have detained me to-day.'"

Just before dinner the Emperor had called Las Casas into his room to speak about replenishing his wardrobe. He said that he had just been calculating the expenses of his toilet, and that it cost him about twenty dollars a month. He spoke of ordering clothes, boots, shoes, &c., from tradesmen in Europe who had his measure. Las Casas, however, suggested that his enemies would not permit this.

"It is, however," said the Emperor, "extremely vexatious to be thus de-

THE EMPEROR CROSSING POLAND.

prived of money, and I wish to come to some settlement on this point. As soon as the bill, which is to determine our situation here, shall be notified to me, I intend to make arrangements for receiving an annual loan of thirty-five or forty thousand dollars from Eugene. He can not refuse me. He has received from me, perhaps, upward of eight millions. It would be doing injustice to his personal sentiments to doubt his readiness to serve me; besides, we have long accounts to settle together. I am sure, if I had appointed a committee of my councilors of state to draw up a report upon this subject, they would have presented me with a balance of at least two or three millions on Eugene."

A branch of this subject was renewed at the dinner-table, and the Emperor asked the gentlemen present their opinions respecting the sums necessary to enable a bachelor to live in a European capital, or for the support of a plain family establishment, or for the maintenance of a family in a style of elegance. "He is fond," says Las Casas, "of these questions. He treats them with great shrewdness, and enters into the most curious details. We each presented our budgets, and agreed that a residence in Paris would cost a bachelor three thousand dollars (15,000 francs), a plain family establishment eight thousand dollars, and a family in elegance twenty thousand. The

Emperor dwelt much on the prices of various articles, and even on the prices of the same articles as they are charged to different persons and under different circumstances."

"When I was about to leave the army of Italy," said he, "to return to Paris, Madam Bonaparte wrote to inform me that she had furnished, in the best possible style, a small house that we had in the Rue de la Victoire. The house was not worth more than eight thousand dollars. What was my surprise and vexation to find that the drawing-room furniture, which, after all, appeared to me nothing out of the way, was charged at the enormous price of about twenty-five thousand dollars! In vain did I remonstrate. I was obliged to pay the amount. The upholsterer showed me the directions he had received, and which required that every article should be the very best of its kind. Every thing had been made after new designs, and the designs themselves had been invented expressly for the fitting up of my house. Any judge of the case must have condemned me."

The Emperor then adverted to the extravagant charges made for furnishing the imperial palaces, and the vast economy which he had introduced on this point. The following particulars will show some of the methods he adopted for ascertaining the correctness of the accounts that were presented to him.

"On one occasion when he returned to the Tuileries, which had been magnificently fitted up during his absence, the individuals who attended him eagerly drew his attention to all the new furniture and decorations. After expressing his satisfaction at every thing he saw, he walked up to a window overhung by a rich curtain, and asking for a pair of scissors, he cut off a superb gold acorn which was suspended from the drapery, and coolly putting it into his pocket, continued his inspection, to the great astonishment of all present, who were unable to guess his motive. Some days afterward, at his levee, he drew the acorn from his pocket, and gave it to the individual who superintended the furnishing of the palace.

"'Here,' said he; 'Heaven forbid that I should think you rob me; but some one has doubtless robbed you. You have paid for this at the rate of one third above its value. They have dealt with you as if you had been the steward of a great nobleman. You would have made a better bargain if you had not been known.'

"The fact was that Napoleon, having walked out one morning in disguise, as he was often in the habit of doing, visited some of the shops in the Rue St. Denis, where he priced ornaments similar to that which he had cut from the curtain, and inquired the value of various articles of furniture like those provided for the palace, and thus, as he said, he arrived at the result in its simplest form. Every one knew his habit in this respect. Those, he remarked, were his grand plans for insuring domestic economy, which, notwithstanding his extreme magnificence, were carried to the utmost degree of precision and regularity.

"In spite of his numerous avocations, he himself revised all his accounts; but he had his own method of doing this, and they were always made out to

THE GOLDEN ACORN.

him in their details. He would cast his eye on the first article—sugar, for example—and finding some millions of pounds set down, would take a pen, and say to the person who drew up the accounts,

"'How many individuals are there in my household?'

"'Sire, so many,' would be the reply; and it was necessary to give the answer immediately.

"'And how many pounds of sugar do you suppose they consume in a day, on an average?'

"'Sire, so many.'"

The Emperor immediately made his calculation, and having satisfied himself, he would give back the paper, saying,

"Sir, I have doubled your estimate of the daily consumption, and yet you are enormously beyond the mark. Your account is faulty. Make it out again, and let me have greater correctness."

This reproof would be sufficient to establish the strictest regularity. Thus he sometimes said of his private as of his public administration,

"I have introduced such order, and employed so many checks, that I can not be much imposed upon. If I am wronged at all, I leave the guilty person to settle the matter with his own conscience. He will not sink under the weight of his crime, for it can not be very heavy."

CHAPTER XI.
1816, April.   Continued.

Critique on Voltaire's Mohammed—Remarks on the Mohammed of History—Gretry—Napoleon's Proclamations—His Policy in Egypt—Confession of an illegal Act—The Domestics examined—The Emperor a Peace-maker—The Abbé de Pradt—The Russian War.

April 22–25. Dismal days darkened over the island, and the inmates of Longwood, enveloped in fogs and rain, were imprisoned in their narrow chambers. The Emperor devoted himself with great regularity to his studies, and to the dictation of the campaign of 1814. In the evening the group assembled round the Emperor, and he read to them from the plays of Voltaire. Napoleon was an admirable reader, and the interest of the entertainment was vastly enhanced by those observations and criticisms which gush from the soul of genius.

Mohammed was the subject of profound criticism.

"Voltaire," said the Emperor, "in the character and conduct of his hero, is alike false to history and to the human heart. He has degraded the grand character of Mohammed by making him descend to the lowest intrigues. He has represented an illustrious man, who changed the face of the world, acting like a worthless wretch deserving the scaffold. He has no less absurdly travestied the lofty character of Omar, which he has drawn like the cut-throat of a melodrama.

"Voltaire committed a fundamental error in attributing to intrigue that which was solely the result of opinion. Men who have wrought great changes in the world have never done it by gaining the chiefs, but always by moving the masses. The first measure is the resort of intrigue, and produces secondary results; the second is the march of genius, and transforms the face of the world."

The Emperor, then reverting to the truth of history, expressed his disbelief of what was recorded respecting Mohammed.

"He must doubtless have been," said he, "like all chiefs of sects. The Koran, having been written thirty years after his death, may have recorded many falsehoods. The empire of the Prophet, his doctrine, and his mission, being established and fulfilled, people might, and must, have spoken accordingly. Still, it remains to be explained how the prodigious event which we are certain did take take place, namely, the conquest of the world, could have been effected in the short space of fifty or sixty years. By whom was it brought about? By the hordes of the desert, who, as we are informed, were few in number, ignorant, unwarlike, undisciplined, and destitute of system. And yet they opposed the civilized world, abounding in resources. Fanatacism could not have accomplished this miracle, for fanatacism must have had time to establish her dominion, and the career of Mohammed lasted only thirteen years. Independently of the fortuitous events by which miracles are sometimes produced, there must have been, in this case, some hidden circumstance which has never been transmitted to our knowledge. Europe doubtless sunk beneath the results of some first cause of which we are ignorant. The different races of men, who suddenly issued from the desert, had perhaps been engaged in long civil wars, in which men of heroic character and great talent might have risen up, and irresistible impulses have been created.

"But to return to Voltaire," said he, "it is astonishing how ill his dramas are adapted for reading. When criticism and good taste are not cheated by pomp of diction and scenic illusion, he immediately loses a thousand per cent. It will scarcely be believed that, at the time of the Revolution, Voltaire had superseded Corneille and Racine. The beauties of these two great dramatists lay dormant until the First Consul again ushered them into notice."

"The Emperor spoke truly," said Las Casas. "It is very certain that when he brought us back to civilization, he at the same time restored us to good taste. He revived our dramatic and lyric *chefs d'œuvres*, even those pieces which had been proscribed for political reasons. Thus *Richard Cœur de Lion* was again brought upon the stage, though a tender interest had, as it were, consecrated it to the Bourbons."

"Poor Gretry," said the Emperor, "had long urged me to permit the performance of the opera of Richard. It was rather a dangerous experiment, and a violent uproar was predicted. The representation, however, went off without any unpleasant circumstances, and I ordered it to be repeated for a week and a fortnight in succession, until the public were completely tired of it. The charm being broken, Richard continued to be played like any ordinary piece until the time when the Bourbons, in their turn, prohibited it because it excited an interest in *my* favor."

April 26. Sir Hudson Lowe sent to Las Casas two books, with a note, in which he expressed the hope that their perusal would be gratifying to the Emperor. One of these works was the Abbé de Pradt's Embassy to Warsaw, a malignant libel upon Napoleon. The other was a collection of all the proclamations and official documents of Napoleon, published by the infamous libelist Goldsmith. Though some of the finest bulletins were suppressed and others mutilated, the collection was still a noble monument to the political wisdom and genius of the Emperor. It is uncertain whether Sir Hudson Lowe, in this act, was guilty of an intentional insult, or whether it was the stupid blunder of a coarse and vulgar man. After dinner, the Emperor amused himself in reading some of his own proclamations to the army of Italy. As, reclining upon the sofa, he perused the glowing periods, his spirit was roused by the fire of his own youthful eloquence.

"And yet," he exclaimed, "they have dared to say that I could not write."

He then turned to the proclamations to the army in Egypt, in which he had spoken of his mission to Egypt as one which Providence had appointed, and of himself as an agent of the Deity.

"This is charlatanry, it is true," said he," but it is charlatanry of the
L

"AND YET THEY HAVE DARED TO SAY THAT I COULD NOT WRITE."

highest order. Besides, the proclamation was composed only for the purpose of being translated into high-flown Arabic verse by one of the cleverest of the sheiks. My French troops merely laughed at it. And such was their disposition in this respect, both in Italy and in Egypt, that, in order to induce them to listen to the bare mention of religion, I was myself obliged to speak very lightly upon the subject—to place Jews by the side of Christians, and rabbis beside bishops.

"The assertion, however, made by Goldsmith, of my having assumed the Mussulman's dress, is totally false. If I ever entered a mosque, it was always as a conqueror and not as a worshiper; but, after all, it would not have been so very extraordinary even though circumstances had induced me to embrace Islamism. But I must have had good reasons for my conversion; I must have been secure of advancing as far as the Euphrates, at least. Change of religion, inexcusable for private interests, may perhaps be pardoned in consideration of immense political results. Henry IV. said '*Paris is well worth a mass*.' Will it then be said that the dominion of the East, and perhaps the subjugation of all Asia, were not worth *a turban and a pair of trowsers*? And, in truth, the whole matter was reduced to this. The grand sheiks had studied how to render it easy to us. They had smoothed down the greatest obstacles; allowed us the use of wine, and dispensed with all corporeal formalities. We should, therefore, have lost only our small clothes and hats. I say *we*, for the army, in the disposition in which it then was, would have entertained few scruples on the subject, and would have made it a mere matter of jest and laughter; but what would have been the consequence? I should have turned my back on Europe, and the old civilization of the Continent would have been bound up; and who would then have troubled themselves about the course of the destinies of our France, or the regeneration of the age? Who would have attempted it? who could have succeeded?"

The Emperor, continuing his examination of Goldsmith's book, by chance cast his eye on the act of the consuls by which the commandant of Mantua was cashiered for the surrender of that fortress.

"This," said the Emperor, "was, without doubt, an illegal and tyrannical act, but it was a necessary evil. It was the fault of the laws. The general was a hundred and a thousand times guilty, and yet it was doubtful whether we ought to have condemned him. His acquittal would have produced the most fatal effects. We therefore struck him with the arm of public opinion; but I repeat, it was a tyrannical act—one of those severe strokes which are sometimes indispensably necessary in a great nation, and under important circumstances."

During the day Dr. O'Meara called in, and was speaking of a ship which was daily expected. The Emperor inquired if the vessel was furnished with a chronometer, and, on receiving an answer in the negative, he said,

"The vessel may probably miss the island through the want of one. How shameful it is for your government to put three or four hundred men on board of a ship destined for this place without a chronometer, thereby running the risk of losing ship and cargo, of the value of perhaps half a million, together with the lives of so many poor creatures, for the sake of saving a hundred dollars for a watch! I ordered that every ship employed in the French service should be supplied with one. It is a weakness in your government not to be accounted for."

Then turning to another subject, the Emperor inquired, "Is it true that a court of inquiry is now holding upon some officer for making too free with the bottle? Is it a crime for the English to get intoxicated? If that were the case, you would have nothing but courts-martial every day. —— was merry on board every day after dinner."

April 27. At two o'clock the governor came to Longwood, and demanded permission to summon all the domestics before him, that he might ascertain whether their signatures had been spontaneously given. The Emperor said to Count Montholon, who had the superintendence of the servants,

"Inform Sir Hudson Lowe, in my name, that I had not imagined that there could be any pretense for interference between me and my *valet de chambre*. If my permission is asked, I decidedly refuse it. If the governor's instructions require the adoption of this measure, the power is in his own hands, and he may use it. This will only be adding another outrage to those which the English ministers have already accumulated upon me."

The governor persisted. He assembled the servants, and, by an examination of each individual, found that they all wished to remain at St. Helena with the Emperor.

About five o'clock the Emperor went out to ride in his plain barouche. As he was entering the carriage, he said to his companions, in a tone of irony, and yet of gayety,

"Gentlemen, but for one man I should have been master of the world! And who do you think this one man was?"

All were eager to know.

"The Abbé de Pradt," continued the Emperor; "the almoner of the God of war."

This excited a general burst of laughter.

"I am serious," the Emperor continued. "The abbé thus expresses himself in his 'Embassy to Warsaw.' You may read it yourselves. The work is altogether a wicked attack on me, an absolute libel, overwhelming me with insults and calumnies. Whether I happened to be in a particular good humor at the time, or whether it was because only truth offends, I know not, but, at all events, it only made me smile. It truly amused me."

"Misunderstandings," says Las Casas, "occasionally occurred between two individuals of the Emperor's suite. This circumstance would not have been mentioned here but that it serves to introduce some characteristic traits of the mind and heart of him to whom we are devoted. When I entered the drawing-room to wait until the announcement for dinner, I found the Emperor speaking with the utmost warmth on this subject, which troubled him exceedingly. His language was energetic and moving."

"You followed me," said he, "with the view of cheering my captivity. *Be brothers*, otherwise you do but annoy me. Do you wish to render me happy? Be united, then; otherwise you are to me but a punishment. You speak of fighting even before my very eyes. Am I, then, no longer the object of your regard? Are not the eyes of foreigners fixed upon us? I wish that each one here may be animated by my spirit. I wish that each one around me may be happy—that each one in particular may share the few enjoyments which are yet left for us. Even down to little Immanuel there, I wish you all to have your due share."

The announcement of dinner put an end to the reprimand.

April 28. The Emperor again recurred to the work of the Abbé de Pradt. "In the first page," said he, "he states himself to be the only man who arrested Napoleon's career. In the last, he shows that the Emperor, on his way back from Moscow, dismissed him from the embassy, which is true. And this fact his self-love would fain misrepresent or revenge. This is the whole work.

"But the abbé did not fulfill at Warsaw any of the objects which had been intended. On the contrary, he did a great deal of mischief. Reports against him poured in upon me from every quarter. Even the young men, the clerks attached to the embassy, were surprised at his conduct, and went so far as to accuse him of maintaining an understanding with the enemy, which, however, I by no means believed. But he certainly had a long conversation with me, which he misrepresents, as might be expected. And it was at the very moment when he was delivering a long, prosing speech, which appeared to me a mere string of absurdity and impertinence, that I wrote upon the chimney-piece the order to withdraw him from his embassy, and to send him, as soon as possible, to France—a circumstance which was the cause of a good deal of merriment at the time, and which the abbé seems very desirous of concealing."[*]

---

[*] The abbé, in his "Embassy to Warsaw," gives an interesting account of the Emperor Napoleon's court at Dresden. "You," he says, "who wish to form a just idea of the omnipotence exer-

INTERVIEW WITH THE ABBÉ DE PRADT AT WARSAW.

"They are distorted facts and mutilated conversations. Surely," continued the Emperor, as he read the abbé's adulation of the Allies and denunciation of himself, "this is not a French bishop, but an Eastern magician, a worshiper of the rising sun."

Speaking of the Russian war, Napoleon said, "No events are trifling with regard to nations and sovereigns, for their destinies are controlled by the most inconsiderable circumstances. For some time a misunderstanding had risen up between France and Russia. France reproached Russia with the

cised in Europe by the Emperor Napoleon—who wish to fathom the depths of terror into which almost every European sovereign has fallen, transport yourselves in imagination to Dresden, and there contemplate that superb prince at the period of his highest glory, so nearly bordering on his fall. The Emperor occupied the grand apartments of the chateau, whither he had transported a considerable portion of his household. Here he gave grand dinner-parties, which were always attended by the sovereigns and the different members of their families, according to the invitations issued by the grand marshal of the palace. Some private individuals were admitted on these occasions. I enjoyed that honor on the day of my appointment to the embassy of Warsaw. The Emperor's levees were held here, as at the Tuileries, at nine o'clock. Then, with what timid submission did a crowd of princes, mingling with the courtiers, and often scarcely perceived among them, anxiously await the moment for presenting themselves before the new arbitrator of their destinies!"

violation of the Continental system, and Russia required an indemnification for the Duke of Oldenburg, and raised other pretensions. Russian troops were approaching the duchy of Warsaw, and a French army was forming in the north of Germany. Yet we were far from being determined on war, when, all of a sudden, a new Russian army commenced its march toward the duchy, and, as as ultimatum, an insolent note was presented at Paris by the Russian embassador, who, in the event of its non-acceptance, threatened to quit Paris in eight days. I considered this as a declaration of war. It was long since I had been accustomed to this sort of tone. I was not in the habit of allowing myself to be anticipated. I could march to Russia at the head of the rest of Europe. The enterprise was popular. The cause was one which interested Europe. It was the last effort that remained to France. Her fate, and that of the new European system, depended on the struggle. Russia was the last resource of England. The peace of the whole world rested with Russia. The event could not be doubtful. I commenced my march, but when I reached the frontier, I, against whom Russia had declared war by withdrawing her embassador, still considered it my duty to send mine to the Emperor Alexander, who was at Wilna. My embassador was rejected, and the war commenced.

"Yet, who would credit it? Alexander and myself were in the situation of two bullies, who, without wishing to fight, were endeavoring to terrify each other. I would most willingly have maintained peace. I was surrounded and overwhelmed with unfavorable circumstances, and all that I have since learned convinces me that Alexander was still less eager for war than myself. M. de Romanzoff, who had maintained communications at Paris, and who, some time after, when the Russians experienced reverses, was very severely treated by Alexander for the course he had induced him to pursue, had assured the Russian emperor that the moment was come when Napoleon, in his embarrassments, would readily make some sacrifices to avoid war; that the favorable opportunity should not be allowed to escape; that it was only necessary to assume a bold attitude and a tone of firmness; that indemnity would be obtained for the Duke of Oldenburg; that Dantzic would be gained, and that Russia would thus acquire immense weight in Europe.

"Such was the cause of the movement of the Russian troops, and of the insolent note of Prince Kurakin, who, doubtless, was not in the secret, and who had been foolish enough to execute his instructions in too literal a way. The same mistaken notions, and the same system also, occasioned the refusal to receive Lauriston at Wilna. This was an instance of the errors and misfortunes which attended my new diplomacy. It stood insulated, without affinity or contact, in the midst of the objects which it had to direct. Had my minister for foreign affairs been a member of the old aristocracy, and a man of superior ability, there is no doubt but that he must have observed the cloud that was gathering, and might have prevented our going to war. Talleyrand, perhaps, might have done this, but it was above the powers of the new school. I could not make the discovery myself; my dignity precluded personal explanations. I could form my judgment only from documents;

and in vain did I turn them over and over, for I was sure at last to arrive at a point where they could make no reply to my inquiries.

"Scarcely had I opened the campaign when the mask fell, and the real sentiments of the enemy were developed. In the course of two or three days, Alexander, alarmed at our first successes, dispatched a messenger to me to say that, if I would evacuate the invaded territory, and fall back as far as the Niemen, he would enter upon negotiations. But I, in my turn, took this for a stratagem; I was elated with success; I had taken the Russian army in the critical moment; I had cut off Bagration, and I might have hoped to destroy him; I thought, however, that the enemy merely wanted to gain time for the purpose of rallying his forces. Had I been convinced of Alexander's sincerity, I should doubtless have acceded to his proposition of falling back to the Niemen. In that case, he would not have passed the Dwina, Wilna would have been neutralized, and there Alexander and myself, accompanied by a few battalions of our Guard, would have negotiated in person. How many arrangements should I not have proposed! Alexander would have had only to take his choice, and we should have separated good friends.

"Yet, in spite of the events which succeeded, and which left my enemy triumphant, is it quite certain that the measures I have just hinted at would have been less advantageous than those which have since been pursued? Alexander marched to Paris, it is true, but he came accompanied by the forces of all Europe. He has gained Poland, but what will be the result of the shock given to the whole European system; of the agitation into which every nation has been thrown; of the increase of European influence over the rest of Russia, through the accumulation of new acquisitions; the expeditions in which Russian troops are engaged in remote quarters, and the influence of the incongruous mass of men and knowledge which have taken refuge in Russia from foreign parts?

"Will the Russian sovereigns be content to consolidate what they have acquired? If, on the contrary, they should be influenced by ambition, what extravagant enterprises may they not attempt? And yet they have lost Moscow, her wealth and her resources, and those of many other cities! These are wounds which will bleed for half a century; but at Wilna we might have entered into arrangements for the advantage of all, subjects as well as sovereigns. What, then, has Alexander gained which he might not have secured to better advantage at Wilna?"

"He has conquered," Las Casas replied, "and he remains triumphant."

"That may be the vulgar opinion," exclaimed the Emperor, "but no sovereign should entertain such an idea. A monarch if he himself governs, or his counselors if they govern him, must, in vast enterprises of this nature, attach less importance to the victory than to its results; and, even though the case be limited to vulgar considerations, still I maintain, that the wished-for object has not been attained; even here the palm must be awarded to the vanquished party. Who will pretend that my victories in Germany were equaled by the successes of the Allies in France? Will any thinking man, will any historian, pronounce such an opinion?

THE RETREAT FROM RUSSIA.

"The Allies advanced, with all Europe in their train, against a force which might almost be counted as nothing. They had six hundred thousand men in the line, and nearly an equal number in reserve. If they had been beaten, they had nothing to fear; they could have fallen back. I, on the contrary, in Germany, fifteen hundred miles from home, had hardly a force equal to my enemy's; I was surrounded by sovereigns and people repressed only by fear, and who, on the first disaster, were ready to rise against me. But I triumphed amid dangers constantly increasing; I was incessantly compelled to exercise an equal degree of address and energy. In all these enterprises, I found it necessary to maintain a strange character; to evince singular acuteness of perception, and great confidence in my own plans, though they were, perhaps, disapproved by every one around me."

"What deeds on the part of the Allies can be compared with these? If I had not conquered at Austerlitz, I should have had all Prussia on me. If I had not proved victorious at Jena, Austria and Spain would have assailed me in my rear. If I had not triumphed at Wagram, which, by-the-by, was a less decisive victory, I had to fear that Russia would abandon me, that Prussia would rise against me; and, meanwhile, the English were already before Antwerp. Yet what was my conduct after the victory? At Austerlitz I gave Alexander his liberty, though I might have made him my prisoner. After Jena, I left the house of Prussia in possession of a throne which I had conquered. After Wagram, I neglected to parcel out the Austrian monarchy.

"If all this be attributed merely to magnanimity, cold and calculating politicians will doubtless blame me; but, without rejecting that sentiment, to which I am not a stranger, I had higher aims in view. I wished to bring about the amalgamation of the great European interests in the same manner as I had effected the union of parties in France. My ambition was one day to become the arbiter in the great cause of nations and kings. It was therefore necessary that I should secure to myself claims on their gratitude, and seek to render myself popular among them. This I could not do without losing something of the estimation of others. I was aware of this; but I was powerful and fearless. I concerned myself but little about transient popular murmurs, being very sure that the result would infallibly bring the people over to my side.

"I committed a great fault, after the battle of Wagram, in not reducing the power of Austria still more. She remained too strong for our safety, and to her we must attribute our ruin. The day after the battle, I should have made known by proclamation that I would treat with Austria only on condition of the preliminary separation of the three crowns of Austria, Hungary, and Bohemia. Will it be credited? A prince of the house of Austria several times hinted to me the idea of transferring one of the two last-mentioned crowns to him, or even raising him to the throne occupied by his own family, on pretense that it was only thus that Austria could be induced to act sincerely with me. He even proposed to give me, as a kind of hostage, his son for an aid-de-camp, and all other imaginable guarantees.

"I even turned this idea over in my own mind. I hesitated about it for some time previous to my marriage with Maria Louisa, but after that event it became impracticable. On the subject of marriage my notions were too citizen-like. Austria had become a portion of my own family, and yet my marriage ruined me. If I had not thought myself safe and protected by this alliance, I should have delayed for three years the resurrection of Poland. I should have waited until Spain was subdued and tranquil. I set my foot upon an abyss concealed by a bed of flowers."

Again the Emperor said, in reference to Constantinople, "I might have shared with Russia the possession of the Turkish empire. We had, oftener than once, contemplated the idea, but Constantinople was always the obstacle that opposed its execution. The Turkish capital was the grand stumbling-block between us. Russia wanted it, and I could not resign it. Constantinople is an empire of itself. It is the real key-stone of power, for he who possesses it may rule the world."

THE BOSPHORUS

April 29. The Emperor, languid and depressed, passed the whole day reading alone in the solitude of his room. About nine o'clock in the evening he sent for Las Casas. An atlas happened to be lying beside him. He opened it to the map of the world, and as his eye fell upon Persia, he said,

"I had laid out some excellent plans with regard to that country. What a happy resting-point it would have been for my lever, whether I wished to disturb Russia or to make an incursion on India! I had set on foot relations with Persia, and I hoped to bring them to a point of intimacy, as well as those with Turkey. It might have been supposed that these animals would have understood their own interests sufficiently well to have acceded to my propositions, but both Persians and Turks evaded me at the decisive moment. English gold proved more powerful than my plans. Some treacherous minister, for a few guineas, sacrificed the prosperity of their country, which is usually the case under seraglio monarchs or imbecile kings."

To cheer the Emperor in these dark hours of the night, Las Casas entered into a recital of sundry anecdotes of the court. The Emperor perceived the motive, and was gratified with the attention. At the conclusion of one of the amusing stories, Napoleon, playfully pinching Las Casas's ear, said,

"I have read a story in your Atlas of a northern monarch who was immured in a prison, and one of his soldiers solicited and obtained permission to be imprisoned with him, in order that he might cheer his spirits, either by inducing him to converse, or by relating amusing stories to him. My dear Las Casas, you are that soldier."

Among others, Las Casas related the following anecdote: "It was reported, sire, that one day your majesty, being much dissatisfied with the perusal of a dispatch from Vienna, said to the Empress, in a moment of ill-humor, '*Votre père est une ganache*' (your father is a blockhead). Maria Louisa, who was unacquainted with many French phrases, turned to the person nearest her, and, observing that the Emperor had called her father a *ganache*, asked what the term meant. The courtier, embarrassed at this unexpected interrogatory, stammered out that the word signified a wise man, a man of judgment, and a good counselor. Some time afterward, the Empress, with her newly-learned term fresh in her memory, was present at the Council of State, and the discussion becoming somewhat warm, in order to put a stop to it, she called on M. Cambacères, who was yawning by her side: 'You must set us right on this important point; you shall be our oracle; for I consider you as the greatest *ganache* in the empire.'"

The Emperor laughed very heartily at this, and said, "What a pity that this anecdote is not true! Only imagine the scene—the offended dignity of Cambacères, the merriment of the whole council, and the embarrassment of poor Maria Louisa, alarmed at the success of her unconscious joke!" The conversation was thus prolonged until near midnight, when the Emperor retired in a very cheerful mood.

April 30. The rain fell in floods, and the Emperor did not leave his room. In an undress, he spent the day reading upon his sofa. The governor called and was admitted. The Emperor was undressed, and was unable to rise from his couch. In a long conversation, Napoleon spoke of protesting against the treaty of the second of August, in which the allied sovereigns declared him an exile and a prisoner.

"What right," said he, "have these sovereigns to dispose of me without my consent? Had I thought proper to withdraw to Russia, Alexander, who styled himself my friend, and who never had any but political disputes with me, would, if he had not upheld me as king, at least have treated me as one. Had I thought to take refuge in Austria, the Emperor Francis could not, without disgracing himself, have denied me not only his empire, but even his house and his family, of which I was a member. Lastly, if, relying on my own individual interests, I had persisted in defending them in France by force of arms, there is no doubt that the Allies would have formally granted me immense advantages, perhaps even dominion."

The governor, after a little hesitation, said, "It is altogether probable that a sovereignty might have thus been easily obtained."

"I did not wish it," continued the Emperor. "I determined on abandoning public affairs; indignant at beholding the leading men in France betraying their country, or, at least, committing the grossest errors with regard to her interests; indignant at finding that the mass of the representatives preferred disgrace to death, and stooped to barter with that sacred independence, which, like honor, should be *a rocky and inaccessible island*. In this state of things, what did I determine on? What resolution did I adopt? I sought an asylum in a country which was supposed to be governed by laws, among a people of whom for twenty years I had been the greatest enemy. But what did you do? Your conduct will not honor you in history. Yet there is an avenging Providence. Sooner or later you will meet your reward. It will not be long before your prosperity, your laws, will expiate your crime.

"Your ministers, by their instructions, have sufficiently proved that they wish to get rid of me. Why did not the kings who proscribed me openly decree my death? One act would have been as legal as the other. A speedy termination to my sufferings would have shown more energy than the lingering death to which they have doomed me. The Calabrians have been more humane, more generous than the allied sovereigns or your ministers.* I will not die by my own hands. That would be an act of cowardice. It is courageous and noble to triumph over misfortune. Each one is bound to fulfill his destiny; but if it be intended to keep me in this imprisonment, you will be doing me a kindness in depriving me of life, for here I daily suffer the agonies of death. This island is too small for me, who was every day accustomed to ride ten, fifteen, or twenty leagues on horseback. The climate is not like ours. Neither the sun nor the seasons are like what we have been accustomed to. Every thing here is hostile to happiness and comfort. The situation is disagreeable and unwholesome. This part of the island is totally barren, and has been deserted by the inhabitants."

The governor stated that his instructions required that the Emperor should be restricted to certain limits in his rides, and that an officer should always accompany him.

"If they had been thus observed," replied the Emperor, "I should never have left my chamber. If your instructions will not admit of greater latitude, you can henceforth do nothing for us. However, I neither ask nor wish for any thing. Convey these sentiments to the English government."

"This," replied the governor, "is the consequence of transmitting instructions from so great a distance, and with regard to a person of whom those who draw up the instructions know so little. But on the arrival of the new wooden house, which is now on its way to St. Helena, better plans may, perhaps, be adopted. The vessel which is expected is bringing furniture and stores of provisions, which it was supposed would be agreeable. The English government is making every exertion to render your situation comfortable."

"All their efforts," said the Emperor, "amount to but little. I have requested to be furnished with the Morning Chronicle and the Statesman,† that I might read what relates to myself in the least disagreeable forms; but my request has never been complied with. I have asked for books, which are my only consolation; but nine months have passed away, and I have not received any. I have desired to obtain intelligence of my wife and son, but this has been withheld from me.

"As to the provisions, the furniture, and the house that are intended for

---

* This has reference to the execution of Murat.
† London papers which were opposed to the British ministry.

me, you and I, sir, are soldiers; we appreciate those things at their true value. You have been in my native city, perhaps in the very house occupied by my family. Though it was not the worst upon the island—though I have no reason to be ashamed of my family circumstances, yet you know what they were. But, though I have occupied a throne, and have disposed of crowns, I have not forgotten my first condition. My couch and my camp bed, you see, are still sufficient for me."

THE BIRTH-HOUSE OF NAPOLEON.

"Still," the governor observed, "the wooden palace and its accompaniments are, at least, not to be disregarded."

"Probably not," replied the Emperor, "for your own satisfaction in the eyes of Europe, but to me they are matters of perfect indifference. It is not a house, nor furniture, that should have been sent to me, but an executioner and a coffin. The former are a mockery, the latter would be a favor. I say again, the instructions of your ministers tend to this result, and I invoke it. The admiral, who is not an ill-disposed man, appears to me now to have softened these instructions. I do not complain of his acts. His forms alone offended me."

"Have I," inquired the governor, "unconsciously committed any faults?"

"No sir," said the Emperor; "we complain of nothing since your arrival. Yet one act has offended us, and that is your inspection of our domestics. It was insulting to M. de Montholon, by appearing to throw a suspicion on his integrity; and it was petty, disagreeable, and insulting toward me, and, perhaps, degrading to the English general himself, who thus came to interfere between me and my valet de chambre."

As the Emperor related the incidents of this interview to Las Casas, he said, "The governor was seated in an arm-chair on one side of me; I remained reclining upon the sofa. It was dark; the evening was drawing in, and it was not easy to distinguish objects, therefore it was in vain that I endeavored to watch the play of his features, and to observe the impression which my words made on him." After a moment of silent reflection, he added, "How mean and disagreeable is the expression of the governor's countenance! I never saw any thing like it in my life. I should be unable to drink my coffee if this man were beside me. My dear Las Casas, they have sent me worse than a jailer."

CHAPTER XII.
1816, May.

The Achievements of the Emperor—Inhumanity of the Governor—Conversation with Dr. O'Meara—Parallel between the Revolutions of France and England—The Emigrants—Concurrence of happy Circumstances in the Emperor's Career—The Spanish Bourbons—Arrival of the wooden Palace—The Iliad—Characteristic Remarks—Hoche and other Generals

May 1. The Emperor still confined himself to his room. About seven o'clock in the evening he sent for Las Casas. He had been reading Goldsmith's mutilated collection of his proclamations and speeches. Laying down the book, he said, in calm and serious tones,

"After all, let them abridge, suppress, and mutilate as much as they please, they will find it very difficult to throw me entirely into the shade. The historian of France can not pass over the Empire, and, if he have any honesty, he will not fail to render me my share of justice. His task will be easy, for the facts speak of themselves; they shine like the sun.

"I closed the gulf of anarchy and cleared the chaos. I purified the Revolution, ennobled the people, and established kings. I excited every kind of emulation, rewarded every kind of merit, and extended the limits of glory. This is, at least, something. And on what point can I be assailed on which a historian could not defend me? Can it be for my intentions? But even here I find absolution. Can it be for my despotism? It may be demonstrated that the dictatorship was absolutely necessary. Will it be said that I restrained liberty? It can be proved that licentiousness, anarchy, and the greatest irregularities still haunted the threshold of freedom. Shall I be accused of having been too fond of war? It can be shown that I always received the first attack. Will it be said that I aimed at universal monarchy? It can be proved that this was merely the result of fortuitous circumstances, and that our enemies themselves led me, step by step, to this determination. Lastly, shall I be blamed for my ambition? This passion I must doubtless be allowed to have possessed, and that in no small degree; but, at the same time, my ambition was of the highest and noblest kind that, perhaps, ever existed—that of establishing and consecrating the empire of reason, and the full exercise and the complete enjoyment of all the human faculties. And here the historian will probably feel compelled to regret that such ambition should not have been fulfilled and gratified. This is my whole history in a few words."

May 2. For four days the Emperor had now not left his room. He complained of great debility, and said that his legs refused to support him. He endeavored to walk a few times up and down his chamber, but was so much fatigued that he threw himself upon his bed. He spent much of the day reading from the libelist Goldsmith and from the historical Moniteur the records of his past career.

"It is certainly," said he to Las Casas, "a very remarkable circumstance, and one of which few besides myself can boast, that I made my way through the Revolution at so early an age, and with so much notoriety, without having to dread the Moniteur. There is not a sentence in it which I could wish to obliterate. On the contrary, the Moniteur will infallibly serve me as a justification whenever I may have occasion for it."

May 3. Another day of languor and dejection dawned darkly upon the Emperor. He said to Las Casas that he felt melancholy and restless; that the days seemed long, and the nights still longer. Sir Hudson Lowe came to Longwood, apparently greatly alarmed lest the Emperor had escaped. He walked around the house several times, inquired of Dr. O'Meara very particularly respecting the captive, and laid the plan of a ditch to be dug around the house, as he said, to prevent the cattle from trespassing.

May 4. This was the sixth day of the Emperor's seclusion. He had expressed the intention of riding out, about four o'clock, on horseback. Rain, however, prevented. Sir Hudson Lowe again drove up to Longwood in great trouble.

"He went," says Dr. O'Meara, "to see Count Bertrand, with whom he had an hour's conversation, which did not appear to be of a nature very pleasing to him, as, on his retiring, he mounted his horse muttering something, and evidently out of humor. Shortly afterward, I learned the purport of his visit. He commenced by saying that the French made a great many complaints without any reason; that, considering their situations, they were well treated, and ought to be thankful instead of making any complaints; that he was determined to assure himself of General Bonaparte's actual presence daily by the observation of an officer appointed by him, and that this officer should visit him at fixed hours for such purpose. During the whole conversation, he spoke in a very authoritative, and, indeed, contemptuous manner, frequently referring to the great powers with which he was invested."

Immediately after this interview, the grand marshal called and reported the conversation to the Emperor. At eight o'clock in the evening, the Emperor sent for Las Casas to dine with him.

"The governor," said the Emperor, "has called on the grand marshal, and remained with him more than an hour. His conversation was disagreeable and sometimes even offensive. He spoke on a variety of topics in a tone of ill-humor and disrespect, reproaching us particularly with being loud and unreasonable in our complaints. He maintained that we were well provided for, and ought to be contented, and that we seemed to be strangely mistaken with regard to what was due to our persons and situations. He added, at least so he was understood, that he was desirous of being assured every day, by ocular testimony, of the existence and presence of the Emperor."

"Several days," says Las Casas, "had passed away without the governor having been able to receive any report from his officer or spies, as the Emperor had not gone out, and no one had been admitted to his presence. But what measures would the governor adopt? This consideration occupied us all in turn. The Emperor would never submit, even at the peril of his life, to a regular visit, which might be capriciously renewed at any hour of the day or night. Would the governor employ force or violence to dispute with the Emperor a few hours of repose, and a last asylum of a few feet in circumference? His instructions must have been drawn up in anticipation of the case that had now occurred. No outrage, no want of respect, or act of barbarity could surprise me.*

May 5. For a week the Emperor had not left his chamber; he was languid and depressed; sick both in body and in mind. The communication of Sir Hudson Lowe of his determination to have, every day, ocular evidence of the presence of his captive, annoyed the Emperor excessively, and he had no heart to go out or to meet his friends. About nine o'clock in the morning he sent for Dr. O'Meara.

"I was introduced," says the doctor, "by the back door into his bed-room. It was fourteen feet by twelve, and ten or eleven feet in height. The walls were lined with brown nankeen; two small windows looked out toward the camp of the 53d regiment; one of them was thrown up, and fastened by a piece of notched wood; window curtains of white long-cloth; a small fire-place, a shabby grate, and fire-irons to match, with a paltry mantle-piece of wood painted white, upon which stood a small marble bust of his son. Above the mantle-piece hung the portrait of Maria Louisa, and four or five of young Napoleon, one of which was embroidered by the hands of the mother. A little more to the right hung also a miniature picture of the Empress Josephine, and to the left was suspended the alarm chamber-watch of Frederick the Great, obtained by Napoleon at Potsdam; on the right hung the consular watch, engraved with the cipher B, hung by a chain of the plaited hair of Maria Louisa, from a pin stuck in the nankeen lining. The floor was covered with a second-hand carpet, which had once decorated the dining-room of a lieutenant of the St. Helena artillery; in the right-hand corner was placed the little plain iron camp bedstead, with green silk curtains, upon which its master had reposed on the fields of Marengo and Austerlitz. Between the

---

* Sir Hudson Lowe, in his official account of this interview with General Bertrand, says:
"The result was the establishment of three points, which had been either before not sufficiently specific, or had fallen into partial disuse.

"1. The necessity of General Bonaparte showing himself twice a day, morning and evening, or giving, by some other means, certain indications of his actual presence at the house.

"2. The prohibition of communication with merchants, shopkeepers, and tradesmen, except through the medium of a third person.

"3. The prevention of any stranger seeing him except with the governor's previous authority.

"Sir George Cockburn, *after* my conference, told me he had suffered General Bertrand to give passports, but considered himself as guarded from any ill consequences by the officer of the guard being compelled to report every person who passed, and send the passport to him. I was not aware of General Bertrand's authority having extended to any thing more than the invitations to dinner, when I entered upon the conversation with him; but have not, on such account, regretted the precise line now established by my conversation with him."

windows there was a paltry second-hand chest of drawers; an old book-case, with green blinds, stood on the left of the door leading to the next apartment. Four or five cane-bottomed chairs, painted green, were standing here and there about the room. Before the back door there was a screen covered with nankeen, and between that and the fire-place an old-fashioned sofa covered with white long-cloth.

"Napoleon reclined upon the sofa clothed in his white morning-gown, white loose stockings and trowsers all in one. A checkered red Madras handkerchief was bound around his head, and his shirt collar open, without a cravat. His air was melancholy and troubled. Before him stood a little round table, with some books, at the foot of which lay, in confusion upon the carpet, a heap of those which he had already perused. In front of the fire-place stood Las Casas, with his arms folded over his breast, and some papers in one of his hands. Of all the former magnificence of the once mighty Emperor of France, nothing was present except a superb wash-hand-stand, containing a silver basin, and water-jug of the same metal, in the left-hand corner."

NAPOLEON'S APARTMENT AT LONGWOOD.

"You know," said Napoleon, "that it was in consequence of my application that you were appointed to attend upon me. Now I wish to know from you, precisely and truly, as a man of honor, in what situation you conceive yourself to be; whether as my surgeon, as M. Maingaud was, or the surgeon of a prison-ship and prisoners. Whether you have orders to report every trifling occurrence or illness, or what I say to you, to the governor. Answer me candidly."

"As your surgeon," O'Meara replied, "and to attend upon you and your suite. I have received no other orders than to make an immediate report in case of your being taken seriously ill, in order to have promptly the advice and assistance of other physicians."

"First obtaining my consent to call in others," demanded the Emperor; "is it not so?"

"I should certainly," O'Meara answered, "first obtain your consent."

"If you were appointed," continued the Emperor, "as surgeon to a prison, and to report my conversation to the governor, whom I take to be the head of the spies, I would never see you again. Do not suppose that I take you for a spy. On the contrary, I have never had the least occasion to find fault with you; and I have an esteem for you, and a friendship for your character, a greater proof of which I could not give you than by asking you candidly your own opinion of your situation, as you, being an Englishman, and paid by the English government, might, perhaps, be obliged to do what I have asked."

Dr. O'Meara replied that in his professional capacity he did not consider himself as belonging to any country.

"If I am taken seriously ill, then," continued the Emperor, "acquaint me with your opinion, and ask my consent to call in others. This governor, during the few days that I was melancholy, and had a mental affliction in consequence of the treatment I receive, which prevented me from going out, that I might not weary others with my afflictions, wanted to send his physician to me, under the pretext of inquiring after my health. I desired Bertrand to inform him that I had not sufficient confidence in his physician to take any thing from his hands; that, if I were really ill, I would send for you, in whom I have confidence, and that I only wished to be left alone. I understand that he proposed that an officer should enter my chamber if I did not go out. Any person," the Emperor continued, with much emotion, "who endeavors to force his way into my apartment, shall be a corpse the moment he enters it. If he ever eats bread or meat again, I am not Napoleon. This I am determined on. I know that I shall be killed afterward, as what can one do against a *camp?* I have faced death too many times to fear it. I am convinced that this governor has been sent out by Lord ———.* I told him, a few days ago, that if he wanted to put an end to me, he could have a very good opportunity by sending somebody to force his way into my chamber; that I would immediately make a corpse of the first that entered, and then I should be, of course, dispatched, and he might write home to his government that '*Bonaparte*' was killed in a brawl. I also told him to leave me alone, and not to torment me with his hateful presence. I have seen Prussians, Tartars, Cossacks, Calmucks, but never before in my life have I beheld so ill-favored and so forbidding a countenance. He carries the demon impressed upon his face."

"I endeavored," says O'Meara, "to convince him that the English ministry could never be capable of what he supposed, and that such was not the character of the nation."

"I had reason," the Emperor continued, "to complain of the admiral, but, though he treated me roughly, he never behaved in such a manner as this Prussian. A few days ago he insisted upon seeing me, when I was undress-

* O'Meara leaves a blank. It was doubtless Lord Bathurst

INTERVIEW WITH SIR HUDSON LOWE.

ed in my chamber, and a prey to melancholy. The admiral never asked to see me a second time when it was intimated to him that I was unwell or undressed. He knew that, although I did not go out, I was still to be found."

After O'Meara had withdrawn, the Emperor took a short ride on horseback, and called at Hut's Gate. He returned much fatigued, and his friends observed, with great solicitude, the evident change in his health. He undressed, threw himself upon the sofa, and had a fire kindled in his room. Las Casas and General Bertrand sat by his side. The evening had now come. No candles were brought into the room, and by the glimmer of the fire alone the weary exiles endeavored to beguile the hours with conversation. The two great revolutions of England and France became the topics of discourse.

"There are many points, both of resemblance and difference," said the Emperor, "between these two great events. They afford inexhaustible subjects for reflection. Both in France and England the storm gathered during the two feeble and indolent reigns of James I. and Louis XV., and burst over the heads of the unfortunate Charles I. and Louis XVI. Both these sovereigns fell victims. Both perished on the scaffold, and their families were proscribed and banished. Both monarchies became republics, and, during that period, both nations plunged into every excess which can degrade the human heart and understanding. They were disgraced by scenes of madness, blood, and outrage. Every tie of humanity was broken, and every principle overturned.

"Both in England and France, at this period, two men vigorously stemmed the torrent and reigned with splendor. After these, the two hereditary families were restored, but both pursued an erroneous course. They committed faults. A fresh storm suddenly burst forth in both countries, and expelled the two restored dynasties, without their being able to offer the least resistance to the adversaries who overthrew them.

"In this singular parallel, Napoleon appears to have been in France at once the Cromwell and the William III. of England; but as every comparison with Cromwell is in some degree odious, I must add that, if these two celebrated men coincided in one single circumstance of their lives, it was scarce possible for two beings to differ more in every other point. Cromwell appeared on the theatre of the world at the age of maturity. He attained supreme rank only by dint of address, duplicity, and hypocrisy. Napoleon distinguished himself at the very dawn of manhood, and his first steps were attended by the purest glory. Cromwell obtained supreme power opposed and hated by all parties, and by fixing an everlasting stain on the English Revolution. Napoleon, on the contrary, ascended the throne by obliterating the stains of the French Revolution, and through the concurrence of all parties, who, in turn, sought to gain him as their chief. All the glory of Cromwell was bought by English blood. His triumphs were all so many causes of national mourning, but Napoleon's victories were gained over the foreign foe, and they filled the French nation with transport. Finally, the death of Cromwell was a source of joy to all England. The event was regarded as a public deliverance. The same can not exactly be said of Napoleon's fall.

"In England, the Revolution was the rising of the whole nation against the king. The king had violated the laws and usurped absolute power, and the nation wished to resume her rights. In France, the Revolution was the rising of one portion of the nation against another—that of the third estate against the nobility. It was the reaction of the Gauls against the Franks. The king was attacked, not so much in his character of monarch as in his quality of chief of the feudal system. He was not reproached with having violated the laws, but the nation wished to emancipate and reconstitute itself. In England, if Charles I. had yielded voluntarily, if he had possessed the moderate and undecided character of Louis XVI., he would have survived. In France, on the contrary, if Louis XVI. had openly resisted, if he had had the courage, activity, and ardor of Charles I., he would have triumphed.

"During the whole conflict, Charles I., isolated in his kingdom, was surrounded only by partisans and friends, and was never connected with any constitutional branch of his subjects. Louis XVI. was supported by a regular army, by foreign aid, and by two constitutional portions of the nation —the nobility and the clergy; besides, there remained to Louis XVI. a second decisive resolution which Charles I. had it not in his power to adopt, namely, that of ceasing to be a *feudal chief* in order to become a *national chief*. Unfortunately, he could not decide on either the one or the other. Charles I., therefore, perished because he resisted; Louis XVI. perished because he did not resist. The one had a perfect conviction of the privileges of his prerogative, but it is doubtful whether the other had any such conviction, any more than he felt the necessity of exercising its privileges. In England, the death of Charles I. was the result of the artful and atrocious ambition of a single man. In France, it was the work of the blind multitude —of a disorderly popular assembly. In England, the representatives of the people evinced a slight shade of decorum by abstaining from being the judges and actors in the murder which they decreed: they appointed a tribunal to try the king. In France, the representatives of the people presumed to be at once the accusers, judges, and executioners. In England, the affair was managed by an invisible hand: it assumed an appearance of reflection and calmness. In France it was managed by the multitude, whose fury was without bounds. In England, the death of the king gave birth to the republic. In France, on the contrary, the birth of the republic caused the death of the king. In England, the political explosion was produced by the most ardent religious fanaticism. In France it was brought about amid the acclamations of cynical impiety; each according to its age and manners.

"The English Revolution was ushered in by the excesses of the gloomy school of Calvin. In France, the loose doctrines of the modern school conjured up the storm. In England, the Revolution was mingled with civil war. In France, it was attended by foreign wars; and to the efforts and hostility of foreigners the French justly attribute their excesses. The English can advance no such excuse for theirs. In England, the army proved itself capable of every act of outrage and fury: it was the scourge of the citizens. In France, on the contrary, we owed every benefit to the army; its triumphs abroad either diminished or caused us to forget our horrors at home. The army secured independence and glory to France. In England, the Restoration was the work of the English people, who hailed the event with the most lively enthusiasm. The nation escaped slavery and seemed to have recovered freedom. In France, on the contrary, the Restoration was the work of foreign powers. It carried humiliation and despair to the souls of the French. The nation saw its glory tarnished, and all were plunged into slavery. In England, a son-in-law hurled his father-in-law from the throne. He was supported by all Europe, and the memory of the act is revered and imperishable. In France, on the contrary, the chosen sovereign of the people, who had reigned for the space of fifteen years with the assent of his subjects and foreigners, reappeared on the theatre of the world to seize a sceptre which he regarded as his own. Europe rose in a mass and outlawed him. One million one hundred thousand men marched against him. He surrendered. He was thrown into captivity; and now efforts are made to tarnish the lustre of his memory."

May 6. The Emperor, at nine o'clock in the morning, sent for Las Casas.

THE RETURN OF THE BOURBONS.

He was sorely annoyed by the threat of the governor to violate his last humble sanctuary. He preferred death rather than to submit to this insult. "They are determined," said he, "to bring about my death, and only seek a plausible pretense. I am resolved not to evade it. I am prepared for every thing. They will kill me, it is certain."

Again he sent for Dr. O'Meara, and questioned him particularly respecting his position.

"Are you," said he, "my surgeon, or the surgeon of a galley; and are you expected to report what you observe and hear? All that I wish is, that you should act the part of a gentleman—as you would do were you surgeon to Lord St. Vincent. I do not mean to bind you to silence, or to prevent you from repeating any idle chat you may hear me say; but I wish to prevent you from allowing yourself to be cajoled, or made a spy of, unintentionally on your part, by this governor. After your duty to your God, your next duty is to be paid to your own country and sovereign, and then to your patients.

"During the short interview that this governor had with me in my bedchamber, one of the first things which he proposed was to send you away and take his own surgeon in your place. This he repeated twice; and so earnest was he to gain his object, that, although I gave him a most decided refusal, when he was going out he turned about and again proposed it. I never saw such a horrid countenance. He sat on a chair opposite to my sofa, and on the little table between us there was a cup of coffee. His physiognomy made such an unfavorable impression upon me, that I thought his looks had poisoned it, and I ordered Marchand to throw it out of the window. I could not have swallowed it for the world."

Dr. O'Meara assured the Emperor that he would regulate his conduct with respect to conversations by the rules which existed to that effect among gentlemen, and as he would do were he attached in a similar capacity to an English nobleman.

General Gourgaud then came in, and the Emperor, for a few hours, found the oblivion of present griefs in dictating the events of the fierce strife of the campaign of Waterloo. About three o'clock the Emperor walked out into the garden with Las Casas. The conversation turned upon the emigrants. Las Casas was one of the nobles who had fled from France to escape the horrors of the Revolution, and who had returned under the protection which Napoleon nobly extended to this proscribed class.

"Were you not," said the Emperor, "shocked at the word *amnesty?*"

"No, sire," Las Casas replied; "we knew all the difficulties which the First Consul had experienced in this respect. We knew that all the advantages of the measure were due to him; that he alone was our protector, and that every evil originated with those with whom he had been obliged to contend in our favor. Subsequently, on our return to France, we found indeed that the consul might have treated us better with respect to our property, and this without much difficulty, merely by assuming a silent and passive attitude. This, we conceived, would have sufficed in every case to have produced amicable arrangements between the old proprietors and the purchasers."

"Doubtless I might have done so," said the Emperor; "but could I have trusted sufficiently to the emigrants? Answer me this question."

"Sire," Las Casas replied, "now that I have more knowledge of public affairs, and take a more comprehensive view of things, I can readily conceive that policy required you to act as you did. Recent circumstances have proved how wise was the course you pursued. It would have been bad policy thus to disinterest the nation. The question of national property is one of the first bulwarks of public spirit and of the national party."

"You are right," observed the Emperor. "But I might nevertheless have granted all that was wished. For a moment I cherished the idea of doing so, and I committed a fault in not fulfilling this idea. I intended to form a mass or a syndicate of all the unsold property of the emigrants, and, on their return, to distribute it in certain proportions among them. But, when I came to grant property to individuals, I soon found that I was creating too many wealthy men, and that they repaid my favors with insolence. Those who, by dint of petitioning and cringing, had perhaps obtained an annual income of from twenty-five to fifty thousand dollars, no longer lifted their hats to me. Far from evincing the least gratitude, they had the impertinence to pretend that they had paid, in an underhand way, for the favors they enjoyed. This

THE RETURNED EMIGRANT.

was the conduct of the whole Faubourg St. Germain. I restored the fortunes of these people, and they still remained no less hostile and anti-national.

"Then, notwithstanding the act of amnesty, I prohibited the restitution of the unsold forests whenever they should exceed a certain value. This was doubtless an act of injustice according to the letter of the law, but policy imperiously called for it. The fault was in the drawing up of the law, and the improvidence which dictated it. This reaction on my part counteracted all the good effects of the recall of the emigrants, and robbed me of the attachment of all the great families. I might have guarded against this evil, or I might have neutralized its effects by my *syndicate*. For one great family alienated, I might have secured the attachment of a hundred provincial nobles; and thus I should, in reality, have strictly conformed with justice, which required that the emigrants, who had all run the same risk, embarked their fortunes in common on board the same ship, suffered the same wreck, and incurred the same penalty, should all receive the same indemnification. Here I committed an error, which was the more unpardonable, as I entertained an idea of the plan which I have just mentioned; but I stood alone, and was surrounded by opposition and difficulty. All parties were hostile to the emigrants; and, meanwhile, I was pressed by important affairs; time was running on, and I was compelled to direct my attention to other matters. Even so late as my return from Elba, I was on the point of executing a project of the same sort. If I had had time, I should have taken into consideration the case of the poor emigrants from the provinces, who were neglected by the court. It is rather a singular circumstance that this idea was suggested to me by an old ex-minister of Louis XVI., whose services had been but ill requited by the princes, and who pointed out to me the various plans by which evils of the same kind might have been advantageously remedied."

"Sire," said Las Casas, "the reasonable portion of the emigrants well knew that the few generous and liberal ideas that were cherished with respect to them originated only with you. They were aware that all who surrounded you wished for their destruction. They knew that the very idea of nobility was hateful to them, and they gave you credit for not being of that opinion.

"The great mass of the emigrants," continued Las Casas, "were far from being unjust to your majesty. The sensible part of the old aristocracy disliked you, it is true, but only because you proved an obstacle to their views; they knew how to appreciate your achievements and your talents, which they admired in spite of their inclination. Even the fanatics acknowledged that you had but one fault: '*Why is he not legitimate?*' they were frequently heard to say. Austerlitz staggered us, though it did not subdue us; but Tilsit prostrated every thing. Your majesty might yourself have judged of this, and have enjoyed, on your return, the unanimity of homage, acclamation, and good wishes."

"That is to say," observed the Emperor, smiling, "that if, at that time, I could or would have indulged in repose and pleasure; if I had resigned myself to indolence; if every thing had resumed its old course, you would have adored me. But if such had been my taste and inclination, and certainly nothing was more opposite to my natural disposition, circumstances would not have permitted me to act as I pleased."

The turn of conversation then led the Emperor to observe that he had frequently reflected on the singular occurrence of secondary circumstances which had brought about his wonderful career.

"1. If my father," said he, "who died before he had attained the age of forty, had survived some time longer, he would have been appointed deputy from the Corsican nobility to the Constituent Assembly; he was much attached to the nobility and the aristocracy, and, on the other hand, he was a warm partisan of generous and liberal ideas. He would therefore have been either entirely on the right side, or at least in the minority of the nobility; at any rate, whatever might have been my own personal opinions, I should have followed my father's footsteps, and thus my career would have been entirely deranged and lost.

"2. If I had been older at the time of the Revolution, I should perhaps myself have been appointed deputy. Being of an enthusiastic disposition, I should infallibly have adopted some opinion, and ardently followed it up; but, at all events, I should have shut myself out from the military service, and thus again my career would have been changed.

"3. Had my family been better known, more wealthy, or more distin-

PORTRAIT OF CHARLES BONAPARTE, THE FATHER OF NAPOLEON.

guished, my rank of nobility, even though I had followed the course of the Revolution, would have annulled and proscribed me; I could never have obtained confidence; I could never have commanded an army; or, if I had attained such a command, I could not have ventured to do all that I did. Had my family circumstances been different from what they really were, I could not, with all my success, have followed the bent of my liberal ideas with regard to the priests and the nobles, and I should never have arrived at the head of government.

"4. The number of my sisters and brothers is also a circumstance which proved of great use to me, by multiplying my connections and means of influence.

"5. My marriage with Madam Beauharnais placed me on a point of contact with a party whose aid was necessary in my system of amalgamations, which was one of the chief principles of my government, and that by which it was especially characterized. But for my wife, I should not have obtained any natural connection with this party.

"6. Even my foreign origin, though in France an endeavor was made to raise an outcry against it, was not unattended with advantage. The Italians regarded me as their countryman, and this circumstance greatly facilitated my success in Italy. This success being once obtained, inquiries were set on foot respecting our family history, which had long been buried in obscurity. My family was acknowledged by the Italians to have acted a distinguished part in the events of their country; it was viewed by them as an Italian family. Thus, when the question of my sister Pauline's marriage with the Prince Borghese was agitated, there was but one voice in Rome and Tuscany among the members of that family and their adherents. 'Well,' said they, 'the union is among ourselves; they are our own connections.' Subsequently, when it was proposed that the Emperor should be crowned by the Pope at Paris, great obstacles were, as circumstances have since proved, thrown in the way of that important event. The Austrian party in the conclave violently opposed the measure, but the Italian party decided in its favor by adding to political considerations a little consideration of national self-love. 'We are placing,' said they, 'an Italian family on the throne to govern these barbarians; we shall thus be revenged on the Gauls.'

"It is certain," continued the Emperor, "that Rome will afford a natural and favorable asylum for my family. There they may find themselves at home. Finally," added he, smiling, "even my name, Napoleon, which in Italy is uncommon, poetic, and sonorous, contributed its share in the great circumstances of my life."

May 6. In continuation of the conversation, the Emperor adverted to the numerous difficulties with which he had been incessantly surrounded and controlled. Alluding to the Spanish war, he said,

"That unlucky war ruined me. It divided my forces, obliged me to multiply my efforts, and caused my principles to be assailed. And yet it was impossible to leave the Peninsula a prey to the machinations of the English, the intrigues, the hopes, and the pretensions of the Bourbons. Besides, the Spanish Bourbons were not calculated to inspire much fear. Nationally, they were foreign to us, and we to them. At the Castle Marrach and at Bayonne, I have known Charles IV. and the queen unable to distinguish between Madam de Montmorency and ladies of the new nobility. The names of the latter were indeed rendered more familiar to them through the medium of the gazettes and public documents. The Empress Josephine, who had the most delicate tact on matters of this sort, never ceased alluding to the circumstance. The Spanish royal family implored me to adopt a daughter, and to create her a princess of the Asturias. They pointed out Mademoiselle de Tascher, afterward Duchess of Aremberg. But I had personal reasons for objecting to this choice. For a moment I decided on Mademoiselle de la Rochefoucault, afterward Princess of Aldobrandini. But I wanted some one sincerely devoted to my interest; a true Frenchwoman, possessing talent and information; and I could not fix on one endowed with all the qualities I wished for."

During the day a transport arrived from England, bringing the frame of a wooden house for the Emperor, and materials for its construction. Even Sir Hudson Lowe deemed the wretched hut in which the Emperor was imprisoned totally unfit for his occupancy.

May 7. The day was fine, but the Emperor, suffering from a headache, did not leave his room. About five o'clock in the afternoon he sent for Las Casas. The subject of literature was introduced. The Emperor took up an edition of Homer, and read several cantos of the Iliad.

"I greatly admire the Iliad," said he; "it is like the books of Moses, the token and the pledge of the age in which it was produced. Homer, in his epic poem, has proved himself a poet, an orator, an historian, a legislator, a geographer, and a theologian. He may justly be called the encyclopedist of the period in which he flourished. I have never been so struck with the beauties of the Iliad as at this moment. The sensations with which it now inspires me fully convince me of the justice of the universal approbation bestowed upon it. One thing which particularly strikes me is the combination of rudeness of manners with refinement of ideas. Heroes are described killing animals for their food, cooking their meat with their own hands, and yet delivering speeches distinguished for singular eloquence, and denoting a high degree of civilization."

The Emperor took his dinner alone in his room, and then sent for all his suite to join him. They remained engaged in conversation until ten o'clock.

May 8. About four o'clock in the afternoon the Emperor rode out in his calash. He then received to an audience several English gentlemen, who had touched at the island on their voyage to China. After dinner, one of the Emperor's suite remarked that he had been painfully excited in the morning, when writing out a fair copy of his dictation on the battle of Waterloo, to find that the result had depended, as it were, on a hair's breadth. The Emperor was for a moment silent. Then turning to young Immanuel Las Casas, he said, in his usual mode of addressing him, but in tones expressive of deep emotion,

"My son, go and get Iphigenia in Aulis. It will be a more pleasing subject."

He then read that beautiful drama to his companions.

May 9. The Emperor was describing the evils attendant upon weakness and credulity in a sovereign. "A sovereign," said he to Las Casas, "distinguished for these qualities, must inevitably become the dupe of courtiers and the victim of calumny. Of this I will give you a proof. You yourself, who have sacrificed every thing to follow me—you, who have evinced such noble and affecting devotedness—how do you think that your conduct is viewed? How do you imagine that your character is estimated? You are regarded merely as one of the old nobility, an emigrant, an agent of the Bourbons, maintaining correspondence with the English. It is said that you concurred in betraying me to them, and that you followed me hither only to be a spy upon me, and to sell me to my enemies. The aversion and animosity which you evince toward the governor are affirmed to be only false appearances, agreed upon between you for the purpose of disguising your treachery. You may smile," continued he, "but I assure you that I am not inventing; I am merely echoing the reports that have reached my ears. And can you imagine that a silly, feeble, and credulous being would not be influenced by such stories and contrivances? My dear Las Casas, if I had not been superior to the majority of *legitimates*, I might already have been deprived of your services here, and your upright heart would perhaps have been doomed to suffer the cruel stings of ingratitude. How wretched is the lot of man! He is the same every where, on the summit of a rock, or within the walls of a palace. Man is always man!"

May 10. It was a dark and rainy day. The Emperor, not being able to go out, walked for a time up and down the dining-room. He afterward ordered a fire to be kindled in the drawing-room, and read to his companions the history of Joseph from the Bible. Afterward, in the course of conversation, the name of Hoche was mentioned. Las Casas said that at a very early age he had inspired great hope.

NAPOLEON AND HOCHE.

"And what is still better," said the Emperor, "you may add that he fulfilled that hope. We have seen each other, and conversed together two or three times. I do not hesitate to say that I possessed over Hoche the advantages of extensive information and the principles of a good education. There was, in other respects, a great difference between us. Hoche endeavored to raise a party for himself, and gained only servile adherents. For my part, I created for myself an immense number of partisans without in any way seeking popularity. Hoche possessed a hostile, provoking kind of ambition. He was the sort of man who could conceive the idea of coming from Strasburg with twenty-five thousand men to seize the reins of government by force; but my policy was always of a patient kind, led on by the spirit of the age and the circumstances of the moment. Hoche would ultimately either have yielded to me, or he must have been subdued. As he was fond of money and pleasure, I doubt not that he would have yielded.

"Moreau, in similar circumstances, knew not how to decide. I attached but little importance to him. I regarded him as totally wanting in ability, without, however, extending this opinion to his military talent. But he was a weak man, guided by those who surrounded him, and slavishly subject to the control of his wife. He was a general of the old monarchy.

"Hoche died suddenly, and under singular circumstances; and as there existed a party who seemed to think that all crimes belonged to me of right, endeavors were made to circulate a report that I had poisoned him. There was a time when no mischief could happen that was not imputed to me. Thus, when in Paris, I caused Kleber to be assassinated in Egypt; I blew out Desaix's brains at Marengo; I strangled and cut the throats of persons who were confined in prisons; I seized the Pope by the hair of his head; and a hundred similar absurdities were affirmed. However, as I paid not the least attention to all this, the fashion passed away, and I do not see that my successors have been very eager to revive it; and yet, if any of the crimes imputed to me had any real existence, the documents, the perpetrators, and the accomplices might have been brought forward. Yet such is the influence of report, that these stories, however absurd, were credited by the vulgar, and are, perhaps, still believed by a numerous body of individuals. Happily, the statements of the historian who reasons are divested of this pernicious effect.

"What a number of great generals rose suddenly during the Revolution! Pichegru, Kleber, Massena, Marceau, Desaix, Hoche, and almost all, were originally private soldiers. But here the efforts of Nature seem to have been exhausted, for she has produced nothing since, or, at least, nothing so great. At that period, every thing was submitted to competition among thirty millions of men, and Nature necessarily asserted her rights; subsequently, we were again confined within the narrower limits of order and the forms of society. I was even accused of having surrounded myself in civil and military posts with men of inferior ability, the better to display my own superiority; but now, when the competition will not certainly be renewed, it remains for those who are in power to make a better selection. We shall see what they will do.

"Another circumstance no less remarkable was the extreme youth of some of those generals, who seem to have started ready-made from the hands of Nature. Their characters were perfectly suited to the circumstances in which they were placed, with the exception of Hoche, whose morals were by no means pure. The others had no object in view save glory and patriotism, which formed their whole circle of rotation; they were men after the antique model. Desaix was surnamed by the Arabs *Sultan the Just.* At the funeral of Marceau, the Austrians observed an armistice on account of the respect which they entertained for him; and young Duphot was the emblem of perfect virtue.

"But the same commendations can not be bestowed on those who were further advanced in life, for they belonged in some measure to the era that had just passed away. Massena, Augereau, Brune, and many others, were merely intrepid depredators. Massena was, moreover, distinguished for the most sordid avarice. It was asserted that I played him a trick which might have proved a hanging matter; that, being one day indignant at his depredations, I drew on his banker for five or six hundred thousand dollars. Great embarrassment ensued, for my name was not without its due weight. The banker wrote to intimate that he could not pay the sum without the authority of Massena; on the other hand, he was urged to pay it without hesitation, as Massena, if he were wronged, could appeal to the courts of law for justice. Massena, however, resorted to no legal steps, and consoled himself as well as he could for the payment of the money. Such was the story.

"Oudinot, Murat, and Ney were commonplace kind of generals, having no recommendation save personal courage. Moncey was an honest man. Macdonald was distinguished for firm loyalty. Soult also had his faults as well as his merits. The whole of his campaign of the south of France was admirably conducted. It will scarcely be credited that this man, whose deportment and manners denoted a lofty character, was the slave of his wife. When I learned, at Dresden, our defeat at Vittoria, and the loss of all Spain through the mismanagement of poor Joseph, whose plans and measures were not suited to the present age, and seemed rather to belong to a Soubise than to me, I looked about for some one capable of repairing these disasters, and cast my eyes on Soult, who was near me. He said that he was ready to undertake what I wished, but entreated that I would speak to his wife, by whom, he said, he expected to be reproached. I desired him to send her to me. She assumed an air of hostility, and decidedly told me that her husband should certainly not return to Spain; that he had already performed important services, and was now entitled to a little repose.

"'Madam,' said I to her, 'I did not send for you with the view of enduring your scolding. I am not your husband; and if I were, I should not be the more inclined to bear with you.'

"These few words confounded her, and she became pliant as a glove, turned quite obsequious, and was only eager to obtain a few conditions. To these, however, I by no means acceded, and merely contented myself with congratulating her on her willingness to listen to reason. 'In critical circumstances, madam,' said I, 'it is a wife's duty to endeavor to smooth difficulties. Go home to your husband, and do not torment him by your opposition.'"

The Bengal fleet arrived. The Countess of Loudon and Moira, wife of Earl Moira, the governor general of India, was among the passengers.

CHAPTER XIII.
1816, May. Continued.

Ridiculous Invitation sent by Sir Hudson Lowe—Napoleon at the Institute—At the Council of State—On the Interior of Africa—The Marine Department—Decrés—The Dictionary of Weathercocks—The Reception—Angry Interview with the Governor—Remarks of the Emperor on his Family.

May 11. As Las Casas, at four o'clock in the afternoon, was conversing with the Emperor, the grand marshal entered with a note. Napoleon glanced his eye over it, and, shrugging his shoulders, exclaimed, "This is too absurd. There is no answer. Give it to Las Casas."

The note was from the governor to the grand marshal, inviting *General Bonaparte* to dine at Plantation House, to meet Lady Loudon. This note, though undoubtedly kindly intended, showed the blundering indelicacy of this soulless man. To address Napoleon as *General Bonaparte* was insulting him with the declaration that he had been a *usurper*. He knew that his captive must expose himself to the degradation of being conducted to the dinner-table and from it as a prisoner, under the guard of a British officer. The law was imperative that the Emperor could not pass beyond the very narrow limits of his jail unless thus accompanied. He had declared that he would never subject himself to that ignominy. The grand marshal, in the following terms, acknowledged the receipt of the note:

"Count Bertrand has the honor to present his compliments to General Sir Hudson Lowe, and to thank him for the trouble he has been pleased to take to inform him of the arrival in this island of the Countess Loudon. He will be happy to pay his respects to her. Count Bertrand has communicated the note of Sir Hudson to the Emperor, who has not made any reply to it."

The Emperor, however, sent a verbal message to the countess, saying that it would have afforded him much satisfaction to pay his respects to her, if she had been within his limits. He also sent some sweetmeats for her children.

The Emperor, while walking in the garden with his friends, entered into a long and very frank conversation respecting the events of his life. Las Casas gives the following record of his remarks:

"When I took my place," said he, "in the Institute, on my return from the army of Italy, I might consider myself as the tenth member of my class, which consisted of about fifty. Lagrange, La Place, and Monge were at the head of this class. It was rather a remarkable circumstance, and one which attracted considerable notice at the time, to see the young general of the army of Italy take his place in the Institute, and publicly discuss profound metaphysical subjects with his colleagues. He was then called the geometrician of battles and the mechanician of victory."

"On becoming First Consul," says Las Casas, "Napoleon caused no less sensation in the Council of State. He constantly presided at the sittings for drawing up the civil code. 'Tronchet,' said the Emperor, 'was the soul of this code, and I was its demonstrator. Tronchet was gifted with a singularly profound and correct understanding, but he could not descend to developments. He spoke badly, and could not defend what he proposed. The whole council at first opposed his suggestions.'

"But Napoleon," says Las Casas, "with his shrewdness and great facility of seizing and creating luminous and new relations, arose, and, without any other knowledge of the subject than the correct basis presented by Tronchet, developed his ideas, set aside objections, and brought every one over to his opinions. The minutes of the Council of State have transmitted to us the extempore speeches of the First Consul on most of the articles of the civil code. At every line we are struck with the correctness of his observations, the depth of his views, and particularly with the liberality of his sentiments. Thus, in spite of the opposition that was set up to it, we are indebted to him for that article of the Code which enacts that *every individual born in France is a Frenchman.*"

"I should like to know," said the Emperor, "what inconvenience can possibly arise from acknowledging every man born in France to be a Frenchman. The extension of the French civil laws can only be attended by advantageous consequences. Thus, instead of ordaining that individuals born in France of a foreign father shall obtain civil privileges only when they declare themselves willing to enjoy them, it may be decreed that they will be deprived of those privileges only when they formally renounce them. If individuals born in France of a foreign father were not to be considered as enjoying the full privileges of Frenchmen, we can not subject to the conscription, or other public duties, the sons of those foreigners who have married in France through the events of the war. I am of opinion that the question should be considered only with reference to the interests of France. Though individuals born in France possess no property, they are, at least, animated by French spirit, and they follow French customs. They cherish that attachment which every one naturally feels for the country that gave him birth. Finally, they help to maintain the public burdens."

"The First Consul distinguished himself no less by his support of the article which *preserves the privileges of Frenchmen to children born of Frenchmen settled in foreign countries,* and this law he extended in spite of powerful opposition. 'The French people,' said he, 'who are a numerous and industrious people, are scattered over every part of the world, and in course of time they will be scattered about in still greater numbers; but the French visit foreign countries only to make their fortunes. The acts by which they seem momentarily to attach themselves to foreign governments have for their object only to obtain the protection necessary for their various speculations. If they should intend to return to France after realizing a fortune, would it be proper to exclude them? If it should happen that a country in the possession of France was to be invaded by the enemy, and afterward ceded to him by a treaty, would it be just to say to those of the inhabitants who might come to settle on the territory of the republic that they had forfeited their rights of Frenchmen for not having quitted their former country at the moment it was ceded, and because they had sworn temporary allegiance to a new sovereign, in order to gain time to dispose of their property and transfer their wealth to France?'

"In another debate on the decease of soldiers, some difficulties having arisen relative to those who might die in a foreign country, the First Consul exclaimed, with vivacity, 'The soldier is never in a foreign land when he is under his flag; where the flag is, there is France!'

"On the subject of divorce, the First Consul was for the adoption of the principle, and spoke at great length on the ground of incompatibility, which it was attempted to repel.

"'It is pretended,' said he, 'that divorce is contrary to the interests of women and children, and to the spirit of families; but nothing is more at variance with the interests of married persons, when their humors are incompatible, than to reduce them to the alternative of either living together or of separating with publicity. Nothing is more opposite to domestic happiness than a divided family. Separation had formerly, with regard to the wife, the husband, and the children, nearly the same effect as divorce, and yet it was not so frequent as divorce now is. It was attended with this additional inconvenience, that a woman of bad character might continue to dishonor her husband's name because she was permitted to retain it.'

"When opposing the drawing up of an article to specify the cases for which divorce would be admissible, he said, 'But is it not a great misfortune to be compelled to expose these causes, and reveal even the most minute and private family details?

"'Besides, will these causes, even in the event of their real existence, be always sufficient to obtain divorce? That of adultery, for instance, can only be successfully maintained by proofs which it is always very difficult, and sometimes even impossible to produce. Yet the husband who should not be able to bring forward these proofs would be compelled to live with a woman whom he abhors and despises, and who introduces illegitimate children into his family. His only resource would be separation from bed and board, but this would not shield his name from dishonor. Marriage is not always, as is supposed, the result of affection. A young female consents to marry for the sake of conforming to the fashion, and obtaining independence and an establishment of her own. She accepts a husband of a disproportionate age, and whose tastes and habits do not accord with hers. The law, then, should provide for her a resource against the moment when, the illusion having ceased, she finds that she is united in ill-assorted bonds, and that her expectations have been deceived. Marriage takes its form from the manners, customs, and religion of every people. Thus its forms are not every where alike. In some countries, wives and concubines live under the same roof, and slaves are treated like children. The organization of families is, therefore, not deduced from the law of nature. The marriages of the Romans were not like those of the French.

"The precautions established by law for preventing persons from contracting unthinkingly, at the age of fifteen or eighteen, an engagement which extends to the whole of their lives, are certainly wise, but are they sufficient?

"That, after ten years passed in wedlock, divorce should not be admitted but for very weighty reasons, is also a proper regulation. Since, however, marriages contracted in early youth are rarely the choice of the parties themselves, but are brought about by their families for interested views, it is proper that, if the parties themselves perceive that they are not formed for one another, they should be enabled to dissolve a union on which they had no opportunity of reflecting. The facility thus afforded them, however, should not tend to favor either levity or passion; it should be surrounded by every precaution, and every form calculated to prevent its abuse. The parties, for example, might be heard by a secret family council, held under the presidency of the magistrate. In addition to this, it might, if thought necessary, be determined that a woman should only once be allowed to procure divorce, and that she should not be suffered to remarry in less than five years after, lest the idea of a second marriage should induce her to dissolve the first; that, after married persons have lived together for ten years, the dissolution should be rendered very difficult. To grant divorce only on account of adultery publicly proved, is to proscribe it completely; for, on the one hand, few cases of adultery can be proved; and, on the other, there are few men shameless enough to expose the infamy of their wives; besides, it would be scandalous, and contrary to the honor of the nation, to reveal the scenes that pass in some families; it might be concluded, though erroneously, that they afford a picture of our French manners."

"The first lawyers of the council," says Las Casas, "were of opinion that civil death should carry along with it the dissolution of the civil contract of marriage. The question was warmly discussed. The First Consul, with great animation, opposed it in these terms:

"'A woman is then to be forbidden, though fully convinced of her husband's innocence, to follow in exile the man to whom she is most tenderly united; or, if she should yield to her conviction and to her duty, she is to be regarded only as a concubine! Why deprive an unfortunate married couple of the right of living together under the honorable title of lawful husband and wife? If the law permits a woman to follow her husband without allowing her the title of wife, it permits adultery. Society is sufficiently avenged by the sentence of condemnation, when the criminal is deprived of his property, and torn from his friends and connections. Is there any need to extend the punishment to the wife, and violently to dissolve a union which identifies her existence with that of her husband? Would she not say, You would better have taken his life; I should then have been permitted at least to cherish his memory; but you ordain that he shall live, and you will not allow me to console him in his misery? Alas! how many men have been led into guilt only through their attachment for their wives! Those, therefore, who have caused their misfortunes, should at least be permitted to share them. If a woman fulfill this duty, you esteem her virtue, and yet you are allowing her no greater indulgence than would be extended to the infamous wretch who prostitutes herself."*

In the evening the conversation chanced to turn upon Africa. "I regret very much," said the Emperor, "that I had not time, during my stay in Egypt, to make an exploration of the interior. I possessed troops calculated in every respect to brave the dangers of the desert. I had received presents from the Queen of Darfour, and had sent her some in return. Had I remained longer, I intended to have carried to a great extent our geographical investigations in the northern district of Africa, and that, too, by the simplest means—merely by placing in each caravan some intelligent officers, for whom I would have procured hostages."

Speaking of the marine department, the Emperor remarked, "I can not say that I was entirely satisfied with Decrès. I am not sure that the confidence which I reposed in him was fully merited. The difficulty of finding persons better qualified maintained him in his post, for, after all, Decrès was the best I could find. Gantheaume was merely a sailor, and was destitute of every other talent. Caffarelli forfeited my good opinion because I had been informed that his wife intrigued in political affairs, which I regarded as an unpardonable offense. Missiessi was not a man to be depended upon, for his family had been one of those who had surrendered up Toulon. For a mo-

* "After the Restoration," says Las Casas, "as I was conversing with M. Bertrand de Molleville, former minister of the marine under Louis XVI., a man of great abilities, and who has distinguished himself in more ways than one, he said:

"'Your Napoleon was a very extraordinary man, it must be confessed. How little did we know him on the other side of the water! We could not but yield to the conviction of his victories and his invasions, it is true; but Genseric, Attila, and Alaric were as victorious as he. Thus he produced on me an impression of terror rather than of admiration. But since I have been here I have taken the trouble to look over the debates on the civil code, and I have ever since been imbued with profound veneration for him. But where in the world did he collect all his knowledge? I discover something new every day. Ah! sir, what a man you had at the head of your government! Really he was nothing short of a prodigy.'"

Our own illustrious statesman, Henry Clay, in the following terms expresses his opinion of the political wisdom of this "prodigious man." In a speech upon the tariff, in the House of Representatives, in 1844, he says:

"The principle of the system under consideration has the sanction of some of the best and wisest men in all ages, in foreign countries as well as our own—of the Edwards, of Henry the Great, of Elizabeth, of the Colberts, abroad; of our Franklin, Jefferson, Madison, and Hamilton, at home. But it comes to us recommended by a higher authority than any of these, illustrious as they unquestionably are—by the master spirit of the age, that extraordinary man who has thrown the Alexanders and Cæsars infinitely farther behind him than they stood in advance of the most eminent of their predecessors; that singular man, who, whether he was seated on his imperial throne deciding the fate of nations, and allotting kingdoms to the members of his family with the same composure, if not with the same affection, as that with which a Virginia father divides his plantation among his children, or on the miserable rock of St. Helena, to which he was condemned by the cruelty and injustice of his unworthy captors, is equally an object of intense admiration. He appears to have comprehended, with the rapidity of intuition, the true interests of a state, and to have been able, by the turn of a single expression, to develop the secret springs of the policy of cabinets."

ment I cast my eye on Emériau, but, on consideration, I did not think that he possessed adequate capabilities. I had asked myself if Truguet might not have filled the post, but decided that he was not qualified for it. He was a good man of business, it is true, but he had plunged very deeply into the affairs of the Revolution. I was confirmed in my disapproval of him by having subsequently seen some of his private letters, by which it was evident that he still adhered to his old Jacobinical sentiments.

"I had rendered the duties of all my ministerial posts so easy that almost any one was capable of discharging them, if he possessed only fidelity, zeal, and activity. I must, however, except the office of minister of foreign affairs, in which it was frequently necessary to exercise a ready talent for persuasion.

"In fact, in the marine department, but little was required, and Decrés was perhaps, after all, the best man I could have found. He possessed authority. He discharged the duties of his office scrupulously and honestly. He was endowed with a good share of understanding, but this was evinced only in his conversation and private conduct. He never conceived any plan of his own, and was incapable of executing the ideas of others on a grand scale. He could walk, but he never could be made to run. He ought to have passed one half of his time in the sea-ports or on board the exercising squadrons. He would have lost none of my favor by so doing; but, as a courtier, he was afraid to quit his portfolio. This shows how little he knew me. He would not have been the less protected by removing from my court. His absence would have been a powerful circumstance in his favor.

"I very much regretted Latouche Treville, whom I regarded as a man of real talent. I am of opinion that that admiral would have given a different impulse to affairs. The attack on India, and the invasion of England, would by him have been at least attempted, and perhaps accomplished. I blame myself for having employed the pinnaces at Boulogne. It would have been better had I employed actual ships at Cherbourg. I am of opinion that, had Villeneuve manifested more vigor at Cape Finisterre, the attack might have been rendered practicable. I had made arrangements for the arrival of Villeneuve with considerable art and calculation, and in defiance of the opinions and the routine of the naval officers by whom I was surrounded. Every thing happened as I had foreseen, when the inactivity of Villeneuve ruined all. But," added the Emperor, "Heaven knows what instruction he might have received from Decrés, or what letters might have been privately written to him which never came to my knowledge. I was very powerful, and was fond of searching into every thing, yet I am convinced that I was far from knowing all that was passing around me.

"The grand marshal said the other day that it used to be remarked in the saloon of the household that I was never accessible to any one after I had had an audience with the minister of marine. The reason was because he never had any but bad news to communicate to me. For my part, I gave up every thing after the disaster of Trafalgar. I could not be every where, and I had enough to occupy my attention with the armies of the Continent. I had long meditated on a decisive expedition to India, but my plans had been constantly frustrated. I intended to have fitted out a force of sixteen thousand troops on board ships of the line ; each seventy-four to have taken five hundred troops on board, which would, of course, have required thirty-two ships. I proposed that they should take in a supply of water for four months, which supply might have been renewed at the Isle of France, or in any habitable spot of the desert of Africa, Brazil, or the Indian Ocean. In case of need, they might have taken in water wherever they chose to cast anchor. On reaching the place of their destination, the troops were to be put ashore, and the ships were immediately to depart, making up the number of their crews by the sacrifice of seven or eight of the vessels, which might be condemned as unserviceable, so that an English squadron arriving from Europe immediately after would have found no trace of ours. As for the army, when abandoned to itself, and placed under the command of a clever and confidential chief, it would have renewed the prodigies that were familiar to us, and Europe would have beheld the conquest of India, as she has already seen the conquest of Egypt."

"I knew Decrés well," said Las Casas. "We both commenced our career together in the marine. No sooner had your majesty returned to the Tuileries, than Decrés and I ran to embrace each other, exclaiming, 'He has returned. We have him again.' His eyes were suffused with tears. I must bear this testimony to his feelings. 'Well,' said he to me, in the presence of his wife, 'I am now convinced that I have often done you wrong, and I owe you reparation ; but your old habits and connections so naturally brought you in contact with the Bourbons, that I doubted not that you would, sooner or later, be perfectly reconciled with them, though you were, perhaps, often offended at the expression of my real sentiments.'"

"And did you believe this, you simpleton ?" said the Emperor, laughing. "This was an excellent piece of courtier-like art—a touch for La Bruyère. It was really a good idea on the part of Decrés ; for if, during my absence, any thing offensive to me had chanced to escape him, he would, you see, by these means, have atoned for it once for all."

"Well, sire," continued Las Casas, "what I have just told you is perhaps only amusing, but what I will now communicate is of a more important nature. During the crisis of 1814, before the taking of Paris, Decrés was sounded, in a very artful way, as to his inclination to conspire against your majesty, and he honestly repelled the suggestion. Decrés was easily and often roused to discontent, and he possessed a certain air of authority in his language and manners which rendered him a useful acquisition to any party he might espouse. He happened, at the unhappy period I just have mentioned, to visit a person of celebrity, the hero of the machinations of the day. The latter advanced to Decrés, and, drawing him aside to the fire-place, took up a book, saying,

"'I have just now been reading something that struck me forcibly. You shall hear it. Montesquieu, in such a chapter and page, says, "When the prince rises above the laws, when tyranny becomes insupportable, the oppressed have no alternative but—"'

"'Enough!' exclaimed Decrés, putting his hand before the mouth of the reader; 'I will hear no more. Close the book.' The other coolly laid down the volume as though nothing particular had occurred, and began to talk on a totally different subject."

"The Emperor," continues Las Casas, "maintained the conversation for nearly two hours in the bath. He did not dine till nine o'clock, and he desired me to stay with him. We discoursed about the military school in Paris. I left the school only a year before Napoleon entered it, and therefore the same officers, tutors, and comrades were common to us both. He took particular pleasure in reverting with me to this period of our youth— in reviving the recollection of our occupations, our boyish tricks, and our games.

"In this cheerfulness of humor he called for a glass of Champagne, which was a very unusual thing. Such is his habitual abstinence, that a single glass of wine is sufficient to flush his face and to animate him. It is well known that he seldom sits longer than a quarter of an hour or half an hour at table, but to-day we sat upward of two hours. He was very much surprised when Marchand informed him it was eleven o'clock. 'How rapidly,' said he, with an expression of satisfaction, 'has time slipped away! Why can I not always pass my hours thus agreeably! My dear Las Casas, you leave me happy.'"

May 12. Sir Hudson Lowe issued a proclamation prohibiting "any person from receiving or being the bearer of any letters or communications from General Bonaparte, the officers of his suite, his followers, or servants, of any description, or to deliver any to them, under pain of being arrested immediately and dealt with accordingly."

May 13. Dr. Warden, the surgeon of the *Northumberland*, had an audience with the Emperor, and remained for two hours. The Emperor, in conversation, took a review of the acts of his government which had drawn on him the greatest share of calumny, and concluded his remarks with the following words:

"I concern myself but little about the libels which have been written against me. My acts and the events of my reign refute them more completely than the most skillful arguments that could be employed. I seated myself on an empty throne. I arrived at supreme power unsullied by the crimes that have usually disgraced the chiefs of dynasties. Let history be consulted; let me be compared with others. If I have to fear the reproaches of posterity and history, it is not for having been too wicked, but perhaps for having been too good."

After dinner the Emperor looked at a humorous book called "The Dictionary of Weathercocks." It consisted of an alphabetical collection of living characters who had figured since the Revolution, and whose language and conduct had varied with the political winds. Weathercocks were affixed to their names, with abstracts of the speeches or acts which had procured them the distinction. On opening the work the Emperor said,

"Are any of us mentioned in it?"

"No, sire," replied Las Casas, laughing, "none save your majesty. The name of Napoleon is recorded because it is affirmed that he first sanctioned the republic, and then he assumed the prerogative of royalty."

The Emperor read several articles, and often laughed most heartily at the coolness and effrontery with which the transitions were made. After reading a few pages, however, he closed the book with an expression of regret and disgust, saying,

"After all, the publication is a disgrace to society, a code of turpitude, and a record of our dishonor."

He seemed deeply affected in reading the recital of the apostacy of Bertholet. This man was one of the most eminent theoretical chemists of the day. He had accompanied Napoleon in the Egyptian expedition, and had returned with him. The Emperor, highly appreciating his scientific endowments, had loaded him with favors. Bertholet at one time sustained losses which involved him in difficulties. The Emperor heard of this, and immediately sent him one hundred thousand crowns, adding, "I have reason to complain of you. You seem to have forgotten that I am always ready to serve my friends." But when days of disaster were darkening around the Emperor, Bertholet ungratefully abandoned him, and with eagerness returned to the Bourbons. Such ingratitude wounded the generous heart of the Emperor. He exclaimed, in saddened tones, "What! Bertholet! my friend Bertholet! on whom I thought I could rely with so much confidence!"

May 14. A large number of distinguished gentlemen and ladies, who had arrived at St. Helena in the East India fleet, were presented to the Emperor. He received them in the garden. The grand marshal conducted them to his presence. The Emperor met them with that grace and that captivating smile which ever exercised such irresistible power. He conversed with each individual, and, with that tact peculiar to himself, seized upon the topics in which each was interested. With the supreme judge he discoursed on legislation and the administration of justice; with the officers of the East India Company, on trade and the internal affairs of India; with the military gentlemen, on their wounds and campaigns; while he complimented the ladies upon their fair appearance, remarking that the climate of India had not injured their complexions. To one of the gentlemen he said,

"The grand marshal has informed me that Lady Loudon is on the island. Had she been within my limits, it would have afforded me much pleasure to pay my compliments to her; but as she happens to reside beyond the boundaries which have been prescribed to me, I have no more opportunity of seeing her than if she were still at Bengal."

During the interview, one of the English gentlemen remarked to Las Casas, "What grace and what dignity of manner! He is too great and too gifted a man! We have too much cause to dread and fear him! I can scarcely form a conception of the strength of mind necessary to enable him to endure such wonderful reverses." The English gentlemen, as they left, expressed much mortification in contemplating the wretched apartments and shabby furniture of the Emperor.

After dinner the Emperor asked his companions what they would like to read. One proposed the "Dictionary of Weathercocks."
"No," said the Emperor, "that serves but to render my evenings more unpleasant. Rather let us amuse ourselves with fiction." He then called for "Jerusalem Delivered," and read aloud several cantos of that poem, occasionally translating paragraphs into French. He then read a large part of Phedre and Athalie, always expressing his great admiration of the writings of Racine.

May 14. The Emperor was unwell, and said to Dr. O'Meara, "I have promised to see a number of people to-day, and, though I am indisposed, I shall do so."

At this moment some of the visitors, who were walking around the house, came close to the window of his dressing-room, which was open, and tried to push aside the curtain and peep in. The Emperor made no remark upon this impertinence, but calmly closed the window, and, continuing his conversation, said,

"The governor sent an invitation to Bertrand for *General Bonaparte* to come to Plantation House to meet Lady Loudon. I told Bertrand to return no answer to it. If he really wanted me to see her, he would have put Plantation House within the limits; but to send such an invitation, knowing that I must go in charge of a guard if I wished to avail myself of it, was an insult. Had he sent me word that Lady Loudon was sick or fatigued, I would have gone to see her, although I think that, under all the circumstances, she might have come to see me, or Madam Bertrand or Montholon, as she was free and unshackled. The first sovereigns in the world have not been ashamed to pay me a visit. It appears that this governor was with Blucher, and is the writer of some official letters to your government descriptive of the operations of 1814. I pointed them out to him the last time I saw him, and asked him, 'Is it you, sir?' He replied, 'Yes.' I told him they were full of falsehoods and nonsense. If those letters were the only accounts he sent, he betrayed his country."

May 16. Under this date Las Casas makes the following record: "The governor presented himself at Longwood about three o'clock, with his military secretary, and desired to see the Emperor on business. The Emperor was unwell, and not dressed; he said, however, he would see the governor as soon as he had finished dressing. In the course of a few minutes he entered the drawing-room, and I introduced Sir Hudson Lowe. As I was waiting in the ante-chamber with the military secretary, I could hear, from the Emperor's tone of voice, that he was irritated, and that the conversation was maintained with great warmth. The audience was long and stormy. On the governor's departure I went to the garden, whither the Emperor had sent for me. He had not been well for the last two days, and this affair completely upset him.

"'Well, Las Casas,' said he, on perceiving me, 'we have had a violent scene; I have been thrown quite out of temper. They have now sent me worse than a jailer! Sir Hudson Lowe is a downright executioner! I re-

THE CAPTIVE AND HIS JAILER.

ceived him to-day with my stormy countenance—my head inclined, and my ears pricked up. We looked most furiously at each other. My anger must have been powerfully excited, for I felt a vibration in the calf of my left leg. This is always a sure sign with me, and I have not felt it for a long time before.'

"The governor had opened the conversation with an air of embarrassment, and in broken sentences. He said some planks of wood had arrived. The newspapers must have made Napoleon acquainted with this circumstance. They were intended for the construction of a residence for him. He should be glad to know what he thought of it.

"To this the Emperor replied only by a very significant look; then, adverting hastily to other subjects, he told the governor with warmth that he asked him for nothing, and that he would receive nothing at his hands; and that he merely desired to be left undisturbed. He added that, though he had much cause to complain of the admiral, he had never had reason to think him totally destitute of feeling; that, though he found fault with him, he had, notwithstanding, received him always in perfect confidence; but that, during the month that Sir Hudson Lowe had been on the island, he had experienced more causes of irritation than during the six preceding months.

"The governor observed that he did not come to receive a lesson.

"'But that, sir,' the Emperor hastily replied, 'is no proof that you do not stand in need of one. You tell me, sir, that your instructions are much more rigid than those that were given to the admiral. Do they direct that I should suffer death by the sword or poison? No act of atrocity would surprise me on the part of your ministers! If my death is determined on, execute your orders! I know not how you will administer the poison, but as to putting me to death by the sword, you have already found the means of doing that. If you should attempt, as you have threatened, to violate the sanctuary of my abode, I give you fair warning that the brave 53d shall only enter by trampling over my corpse.

" 'On hearing of your arrival, I congratulated myself on the hope of meeting with a general who, having spent some portion of his life on the Continent, and having taken part in important public affairs, would know how to act in a becoming way to me; but I was grossly deceived.'

"The governor here said that, as a soldier, his conduct had been conformable with the interests and forms of his country.

" 'Your country, your government, and yourself,' the Emperor replied, 'will be overwhelmed with disgrace for your conduct to me; and this disgrace will extend to your posterity. Was there ever an act of more refined cruelty than yours, sir, when, a few days ago, you invited me to your table under the title of *General Bonaparte*, with the view of rendering me an object of ridicule or amusement to your guests? Would you have proportioned the extent of your respect to the title you were pleased to give me? I am not General Bonaparte to you. It is not for you, or any one in the world, to deprive me of dignities which are fairly my own. If Lady Loudon had been within my boundaries, I should undoubtedly have visited her, because I do not stand upon strict etiquette with a woman; but I should nevertheless have considered that I was conferring an honor upon her. I have been told that you propose that some of the officers of your staff should accompany me in my rides about the island, instead of the officer established at Longwood. Sir, when soldiers have been christened by the fire of the battlefield, they have all one rank in my eyes. It is not the sight of any particular uniform that offends me here, but the obligation of seeing soldiers at all, since this must be regarded as a tacit concession of the point which I dispute. I am not a prisoner of war, and I can not, therefore, submit to the regulations required in such a situation. I am placed in your power only by the most horrible breach of confidence.'

"The governor, on taking leave, said, 'There is an officer of my staff with me whom I am desirous, on this occasion, of presenting to you.'

" 'I can not receive him at present,' the Emperor replied. 'No social relationship can exist between jailers and prisoners.'

"The grand marshal now joined us. He came from his own house, where the governor had alighted both before and after his visit to the Emperor. He gave a detailed account of both his calls. He said that the governor, on his return, had shown great ill-humor, and had complained very much of the Emperor's temper. Not relying sufficiently on his own wit, he had recourse to that of the Abbé de Pradt, whose work had just then passed through our hands. He had said 'that Napoleon was not content with having created to himself an imaginary France, an imaginary Spain, and an imaginary Poland, but that he now wished to create *an imaginary St. Helena.*' On hearing this, the Emperor could not refrain from laughing.

"He then drove out in the calash, and on our return the Emperor took a bath. He sent for me, and giving directions that he would not dine till nine o'clock, kept me with him. He talked over the affairs of the day, and dwelt on the abominable treatment he suffered, the atrocious malignity by which it was dictated, and the brutality by which it was executed. After a few moments of silence, he exclaimed, as he frequently does, 'My dear Las Casas, they will kill me here! It is certain.'"

Under this date Dr. O'Meara writes,

"Saw Napoleon walking in the garden, in a very thoughtful manner, a few minutes subsequent to the governor's departure. He said,

"'Here has been this jackanapes to torment me. Tell him that I never wish to see him again, and that I desire that he may not come again to annoy me with his hateful presence. Let him never again come near me, unless it be with orders to dispatch me. He will then find my breast ready for the blow; but, till then, let me be free of his odious countenance. I cannot accustom myself to it.'"*

May 17. The Emperor was very ill all the night, and in the morning was dull and melancholy. He breakfasted with Las Casas in the garden, and then, for some time, walked up and down the narrow path without uttering a word. At ten o'clock, the heat of the blazing sun, from which there was no shade, drove him into the house. Dr. O'Meara called.

"What is the news?" inquired the Emperor.

"The ladies," said O'Meara, "who were received a few days ago, were highly delighted with your majesty's manners, especially as, from what they had read and heard, they had been prepossessed with opinions of a very different nature."

"Ah! I suppose," said the Emperor, with a smile, "that they imagined that I was some ferocious horned animal."

Dr. O'Meara then spoke of the gross misrepresentations and calumnies of Sir Robert Wilson, and said, "As these assertions have never been fully contradicted, they are believed by numbers of the English."

"Bah!" replied Napoleon; "those calumnies will fall of themselves, especially now that there are so many English in France, who will soon find out that they are all falsehoods. Were Wilson himself not convinced of the untruth of the statements which he had once believed, do you think that he would have assisted Lavalette to escape out of prison?"†

"After dinner, the Emperor," says Las Casas, "who had scarcely eaten any thing, attempted to read to us the Sitting of the Academy from Anacharsis. His voice and his whole frame had lost their wonted vigor and spirit. Contrary to his custom, he ended without analysis or observation. He retired to rest as soon as the chapter was concluded."

---

* The official account which Sir Hudson Lowe gives of this interview is almost exactly the same with that recorded above. The Emperor has not colored the scene at all in his own favor.

† Count Lavalette, immediately after the capitulation of Paris in 1815, notwithstanding the solemn pledge of amnesty, was condemned by the Bourbons to death as an accomplice of Napoleon. On the day before the one appointed for his execution, his wife and daughter called to take leave of him. Exchanging garments with Madam Lavalette, the count escaped from prison. He concealed himself in Paris for a fortnight, eluding the utmost vigilance of the police. In the uniform of a British officer, he got into a cabriolet with Sir Robert Wilson, and passed the barriers. For his escape he was indebted to three British officers, Messrs. Bruce, Hutchinson, and Wilson. These men detested the tyranny of the Bourbons, and had become warm advocates of that liberty which Napoleon had so nobly advocated. The Bourbons, irritated at the escape of their victim, treated Madam Lavalette with such inhumanity that she became a confirmed lunatic.

May 18. The Emperor continued quite unwell, and dined in his room with Las Casas. The faithful secretary, endeavoring to beguile the sadness of his illustrious friend, related several anecdotes of the court. Among others, he adverted to an instance of courtesy in a certain individual, who, being originally a private soldier, attained the rank of marshal. One day, during his newly-acquired splendor, he assembled together at a family dinner his former colonel and four or five officers of the regiment, whom he received in his original uniform of a private, and he addressed his guests in the same terms which he had been in the habit of employing before he attained his elevated rank.

"And this," observed the Emperor, "was the only way to soften down the fury of the times. Such acts as these must necessarily have created mutual feelings of kindness between the opposite parties. And we may naturally suppose that, during recent events, the persons thus obliged will have returned the obligations they have received, were it only for the sake of being great."

This remark reminded Las Casas of a characteristic anecdote. A general had been guilty of irregularities in his department, which, had they been brought before a military tribunal, must have cost him his honor, perhaps his life. Now this general had rendered the most important services to Napoleon on the day of Brumaire. The Emperor sent for him, and reproached him with his misconduct. "However," said he, "you have laid me under obligations which I have not forgotten. I am, perhaps, about to transgress the laws and to fail in my duty. I pardon you, sir. Leave me. But know that, from this day forward, we are *quit*. Take care of yourself for the future. I shall look sharply after you."

May 19. Dr. O'Meara found the Emperor better and in very cheerful spirits. Conversation turned upon Sir Hudson Lowe.

"This governor," said the Emperor, "is an imbecile. He asked Bertrand the other day if he ever had asked any of the passengers bound to England whether they intended to go to France, as, if he had done so, he must not continue such a practice. Bertrand replied that he certainly had, and, moreover, had begged of some to tell his relations that they were in good health.

"'But,' said this imbecile, 'you must not do so.'

"'Why,' said Bertrand, 'has not your government permitted me to write as many letters as I like? and can any government deny me the liberty of speaking?'

"Bertrand," continued the Emperor, "ought to have replied that galley-slaves and prisoners under sentence of death were permitted to inquire after their relations."

He then observed how unnecessary and vexatious it was to require that an officer should accompany him, should he be desirous of visiting the interior of the island.

"It is all right," continued he, "to keep me away from the town and the seaside; I would never desire to approach either the one or the other. All that is necessary for my security is to guard well the sea-borders of this rock.

Let him place his pickets round the island close by the sea, and in communication with each other, which he might easily do with the number of men he has, and it would be impossible for me to escape. Can not he, moreover, put a few horsemen in motion when he knows I am going out? Can not he place them on the hills, or where he likes, without letting me know any thing about it? *I will never appear to see them.* Can not he do this without obliging me to tell Poppleton that I want to ride out? Not that I have any objection to Poppleton. I love a good soldier of any nation, but I will not do any thing which may lead people to imagine that I am a prisoner. I have been forced here contrary to the law of nations, and I will never recognize their right to detain me. My asking an officer to accompany me would be a tacit acknowledgment of it. I have no intention to attempt to escape, although I have not given my word of honor not to try; neither will I ever give it, as that would be acknowledging myself a prisoner, which I will never do. Can not they impose additional restrictions when ships arrive; and, above all, not allow any ship to sail until my actual presence is ascertained, without inflicting such useless, and, because useless, vexatious restrictions? It is necessary for my health that I should ride seven or eight leagues daily, but I will not do so with an officer or a guard over me.

"It has always been my maxim that a man shows more real courage in supporting and resisting the calamities and misfortunes which befall him than by making away with himself. *That* is the action of a losing gamester or a ruined spendthrift, and is a want of courage instead of a proof of it. Your government will be mistaken if they imagine that, by seeking every means to annoy me, such as sending me here, depriving me of all communication with my nearest and dearest relatives, so that I am ignorant if one of my blood exists, isolating me from the world, imposing useless and vexatious restrictions, which are daily getting worse, sending the dregs of society as keepers, they will weary out my patience and induce me to commit suicide. They are mistaken. Even if I ever had entertained a thought of the kind, the idea of the gratification it would afford them would prevent me from completing it.

"That *palace*," said he, laughing, "which they say they have sent out for me, is so much money thrown into the sea; I would rather that they had sent me four hundred volumes of books than all their furniture and houses. In the first place, it will require some years to build it, and before that time I shall be no more. All must be done by the labor of those poor soldiers and sailors. I do not wish it; I do not wish to incur the hatred of those poor fellows. They are already sufficiently miserable by having been sent to this detestable place, and harassed in the manner they are. They will load me with execrations, supposing me to be the author of all their hardships, and, perhaps, may wish to put an end to me."

"No English soldier," said Dr. O'Meara, "would become an assassin." Napoleon interrupted him, saying,

"I have no reason to complain of English soldiers or sailors. On the contrary, they treat me with every respect, and even appear to feel for me."

He then spoke of some English officers. "Moore," said he, "was a brave soldier, an excellent officer, and a man of talent. He made a few mistakes, which were probably inseparable from the difficulties with which he was surrounded, and caused, perhaps, by his information having misled him."

This eulogium he repeated more than once, and observed that he had commanded the reserve in Egypt, where he had behaved very well, and displayed talent.

"Moore," said Dr. O'Meara, "was always in the front of the battle, and was generally unfortunate enough to be wounded."

"Ah!" said the Emperor, "it is necessary sometimes. He died gloriously! he died like a soldier. Menou was a man of courage, but no soldier. You ought not to have taken Egypt. If Kleber had lived, you never would have conquered it. Kleber was an irreparable loss to France and to me. He was a man of the brightest talents and the greatest bravery. I have composed, while at the Briers, the history of my own campaigns in Egypt and of yours."

The conversation then turned upon French naval officers. "Villeneuve," said he, "when taken prisoner and brought to England, was so much grieved at his defeat, that he studied anatomy that he might destroy himself. For this purpose, he bought some anatomical plates of the heart, and compared them with his own body, in order to ascertain the exact situation of that organ. On his arrival in France, I ordered that he should remain at Rennes, and not proceed to Paris. Villeneuve, afraid of being tried by a court-martial for disobedience of orders, and consequently losing the fleet—for I had ordered him not to sail or to engage the English—determined to destroy himself, and accordingly took his plates of the heart, and compared them with his breast. Exactly in the centre of the plate he made a mark with a large pin, then fixed the pin as near as he could judge in the same spot in his own breast, shoved it in to the head, penetrated his heart, and expired. When the room was opened he was found dead, the pin in his breast, and a mark in the plate corresponding with the wound in his breast. He need not have done it, as he was a brave man, though possessed of no talent.

"Barré, whom you took in the *Rivoli*, was a very brave and good officer. When I went to Egypt, I gave directions, after I had disembarked and had taken Alexandria in a few hours, to sound for a passage for the fleet. A Venetian sixty-four got in, which I suppose you have seen there, but it was reported that the large ships of the line could not. I ordered Barré to sound. He reported to me that there was a sufficiency of water in one part of the channel. Brueys, on the contrary, said there was not enough of water for the eighty-gun ships. Barré insisted that there was. In the mean time, I had advanced into the country after the Mamelukes. All communication with the army from the town by messengers was cut off by the Bedouins, who took or killed them all. My orders did not arrive, or I would have obliged Brueys to enter, for you must know that I had the command of the fleet as well as of the army. In the mean time, Nelson came and destroyed Brueys and his fleet.

Sir Stamford Raffles, governor of Java, with his suite, arrived at St. Helena. At three o'clock they were presented to the Emperor in the garden. About six o'clock the Emperor returned to his study, and sending for Las Casas, and Count Bertrand and lady, he conversed with great familiarity until dinner-time on various subjects relating to his family and his minutest domestic affairs. Speaking of the Empress Josephine, he said,
"We lived together like a private citizen and his wife. We were most affectionate and united, having for a long period occupied but one chamber and one bed. These are circumstances which exercise great influence over the happiness of a family, securing the reputation of the wife and the confidence of the husband, and preserving union and good conduct on both sides. A married couple may be said never to lose sight of one another when they pass the night together; otherwise they soon become estranged. Thus, as long as this practice was continued, none of my thoughts or actions escaped the notice of Josephine. She observed, seized, and comprehended every thing. This circumstance was sometimes not altogether without its inconveniences to myself and to public affairs. A son by Josephine would have completed my happiness, not only in a political point of view, but as a source of domestic felicity. As a political result, it would have secured to me the possession of the throne. The French people would have been as much attached to the son of Josephine as they were to the King of Rome, and I should not have set my foot on an abyss covered with a bed of flowers. But how vain are all human calculations! Who can pretend to decide on what may lead to happiness or unhappiness in this life?

"During the Reign of Terror, Josephine was thrown into prison, while her husband perished on the scaffold. Her son Eugene was bound apprentice to a joiner, which trade he actually learned. Hortense had no better prospects. She was, if I mistake not, sent to learn the business of a seamstress.

"Josephine would willingly have seen Maria Louisa. She frequently spoke of her with great interest, as well as of the young King of Rome. Maria Louisa, on her part, behaved wonderfully well to Eugene and Hortense, but she manifested the utmost dislike and even jealousy of Josephine. I wished one day to take her to Malmaison, but she burst into tears when I made the proposal. She said that she did not object to my visiting Josephine, only she did not wish to know it; but, whenever she suspected my intention of going to Malmaison, there was no stratagem which she did not employ for the sake of annoying me. She never left me. And as these visits seemed to trouble her exceedingly, I did violence to my own feelings, and scarcely ever went to Malmaison. Still, however, when I did happen to go, I was sure to encounter a flood of tears and a multitude of contrivances of every kind.

"Josephine," Napoleon continued, "possessed a perfect knowledge of all the different shades of the Emperor's character, and she evinced the most perfect tact in turning this knowledge to the best account. For example, she never solicited any favor for Eugene, or thanked me for any I conferred on him. She never even showed any additional complaisance or assiduity at the moment when the greatest honors were lavished on him. Her grand aim was to prove that all this was my affair and not hers, and that it tended to my advantage. Doubtless she entertained the idea that one day or other I would adopt Eugene as my successor. I am well convinced that I was the person whom Josephine loved best in all the world. She never failed to accompany me on all my journeys. Neither fatigue nor privation could deter her from following me. She employed importunity and even artifice to gain her point. If I stepped into my carriage at midnight to set out on the longest journey, to my surprise I found Josephine already prepared, though I had had no idea of her accompanying me. But I would say to her,

"'You can not possibly go. The journey will be too long, and will be too fatiguing to you.'

"'Not at all,' Josephine would reply.

"'Besides, I must set out instantly.'

"'Well, I am quite ready.'

"'But you must take a great deal of luggage.'

"'Oh no! every thing is packed up.'"

"I was generally obliged to yield. In a word, Josephine rendered her husband happy, and constantly proved herself his sincerest friend. At all times and on all occasions she manifested the most perfect submission and

PORTRAIT OF LOUIS BONAPARTE, THE BROTHER OF NAPOLEON.

devotedness. I shall never cease to remember her with tenderness and gratitude. Josephine ranked the qualities of submission, obedience, and complaisance in her sex on a level with political address. She often condemned the conduct of her daughter Hortense and her relation Stephanie, who lived on very bad terms with their husbands, frequently indulging in caprice, and pretending to assert their independence.

"Louis had been spoiled by reading the works of Rousseau. He contrived to agree with his wife only for a few months. There were faults on both sides. On the one hand, Louis was too teasing in his temper; and, on the other, Hortense was too volatile. They were attached to each other at the time of their marriage, which was agreeable to their mutual wishes. The most ridiculous reports were circulated respecting an improper intercourse between Napoleon and Hortense. Such a connection would have been wholly repugnant to my ideas; and those who knew any thing of the morality of the Tuileries must be aware that I need not have been reduced to so unnatural and revolting a choice.

"But Hortense, the virtuous, the generous, the devoted Hortense, was not entirely faultless in her conduct toward her husband. This I must acknowledge, in spite of all the affection I bore her, and the sincere attachment which

PORTRAIT OF HORTENSE, THE DAUGHTER OF JOSEPHINE.

I am sure she entertained for me. Though Louis's whimsical humors were, in all probability, sufficiently teasing, yet he loved Hortense. In such a case, a woman should learn to subdue her own temper, and endeavor to return her husband's attachment. Had she acted in the way most conducive to her interests, she might have avoided her late lawsuit, secured happiness to herself, and followed her husband to Holland. Louis would not then have fled from Amsterdam, and I should not have been compelled to unite his kingdom to mine, a measure which contributed to ruin my credit in Europe. Many other events might also have taken a different turn.

"Pauline was too careless and extravagant. She might have been immensely rich, considering all that I gave her; but she gave all away in her turn. Her mother frequently lectured her upon this subject, and told her that she would die in some house of charity. *Madam*, however, carried her parsimony much too far. It was even ridiculous. I offered to furnish her with a very considerable monthly income on condition that she would spend it. She, on the other hand, was very willing to receive the money, provided she were permitted to hoard it up. This arose, not so much from covetousness as from excess of foresight. All her fear was that she might one day be reduced to beggary. She had known the horrors of want, and they now

PORTRAIT OF MADAME LETITIA, THE MOTHER OF NAPOLEON.

constantly haunted her imagination. It is, however, but just to acknowledge that she gave a great deal to her children in secret. She is, indeed, a kind mother.

"Nevertheless, this woman, who was so reluctant to part with a single crown, would willingly have given me her all on my return from the island of Elba; and, after the battle of Waterloo, she would have surrendered to me all she possessed in the world, to assist me in re-establishing my affairs. This she offered to do; and she would, without a murmur, have doomed herself to live on brown bread. Loftiness of sentiment still reigned paramount in her heart. Elevation of character and a noble ambition moved in advance of parsimony. I still have present in my memory the lessons of magnanimity which I had received from my mother in childhood, and which have influenced my conduct through life. The naturally powerful mind of *Madam mother* had been exalted by the great events of which she had been a witness. She had seen five or six revolutions. Her house had been thrice burned to the ground by factions in Corsica.*

"Joseph rendered me no assistance, but he is a very good man. His wife, Queen Julia, is the most amiable creature that ever existed. Joseph and I were always attached to each other, and kept on very good terms. He loves me sincerely, and I doubt not that he would do every thing in the world to serve me; but his qualities are only suited to private life. He is of a gentle and kind disposition, possesses talent and information, and is altogether a most amiable man. In the discharge of the high duties which I confided to him, he did the best he could; his intentions were good, and therefore the principal fault rested not so much with him as with me, who raised him above his proper sphere. When placed in important circumstances, he found his strength unequal to the task imposed upon him.

"The Queen of Naples (Caroline) had chiefly formed herself amid great events. She had solid sense, strength of character, and boundless ambition. She must naturally suffer severely from her reverses, more particularly as she may be said to have been born a queen. She had not, like the rest of us, moved in the sphere of private life. Caroline, Pauline, and Jerome were still in their childhood when I had attained supreme rank in France. Thus they never knew any other estate than that which they enjoyed during the period of my power.

* Las Casas remarks, "How justly did the Emperor paint his mother's character! On my return to Europe, I was delighted to witness the literal confirmation of all he had said respecting her. As soon as I disclosed to Madam mother the Emperor's real situation, and declared my resolution to exert all my efforts to alleviate his misery, the answer returned to me by the courier was, that her whole fortune was at her son's disposal, and that she would gain her subsistence by entering into service She, at the same time, authorized me, though I was not personally known to her, to draw immediately in her name any sum that I might think necessary for the Emperor's use. Cardinal Fesch also tendered his services in the most affectionate way; and I must take this opportunity of mentioning that all the different members of the Emperor's family evinced equal love, zeal, and devotedness. So long as my health permitted me to maintain correspondence with them, I received a multitude of letters, which form altogether a most interesting collection. They reflect honor on the hearts of the writers, and they would have proved a source of consolation to the Emperor had the restrictions of the English government permitted me to submit them to his perusal."

"Jerome was an absolute prodigal. He plunged into boundless extravagance and the most odious libertinism. His excuse may perhaps be in his youth, and the temptations by which he was surrounded. On my return from Elba he appeared to be much improved, and to afford great promise. One remarkable testimony in his favor was the love with which he had inspired his wife, whose conduct was admirable, when, after my fall, her father, the despotic and harsh King of Wurtemberg, wished to procure her divorce. The princess then, with her own hand, honorably inscribed her name in history."

PORTRAIT OF JEROME BONAPARTE, THE BROTHER OF NAPOLEON

The conversation was thus continued until midnight. The Emperor, on retiring, said,
"What is doing at this moment in France and in Paris, and what shall we ourselves be doing on this day twelvemonth?"

CHAPTER XIV.
1816, May. Continued.

The Emperor sleeping—The Governor arrests a Servant at Longwood—The Bible—Princess Stephanie—Expulsion of Portalis—Political Reflections—Voltaire's Brutus—French Colony on the St. Lawrence—Carnot—French Manufactures—Physiognomy—The English Soldiers salute the Emperor—Corsica—Napoleon's Mother—Madam Chevreuse—The Conspirators—The Situation of England.

May 20. Under this date Las Casas makes the following record:

" Mr. Balcombe had intimated to me that he was appointed to supply us with what we wanted at the expense of the English government; but I wrote to inform him that, as my own pecuniary circumstances enabled me to dispense with this favor, I was resolved not to avail myself of it. I therefore begged that he would obtain permission from the government to receive from me a bill drawn on some person in England, which could not be transmitted without special permission. I wished to remain free of all obligations, so that nothing might impede me in freely exercising the just and sad privilege of venting my reproaches and imprecations.

" The Emperor rode out in the calash very early. On his return, about three o'clock, he desired me to follow him to his chamber.

" 'I am low-spirited, unwell, and fatigued,' said he; 'sit down in that chair and bear me company.'

" He threw himself on his couch and fell asleep, while I watched beside him. I sat within a few paces of him. His head was uncovered, and I gazed on his brow—that brow on which were inscribed Marengo, Austerlitz, and a hundred other immortal victories. What were my thoughts and sensations at that moment! They may be imagined, but I can not attempt to describe them.

" In about three quarters of an hour the Emperor awoke. He took a few turns in his chamber, and then took a fancy to visit the apartments of all the individuals of his suite. When he had minutely considered all the inconveniences of mine, he said, with a smile of indignation,

" ' Well, I do not think that any Christian on earth can be worse lodged than you are.'

" After dinner the Emperor attempted to read a part of the *Caravansérail de Sarrazin*. After glancing over a few of the tales, and reading a page from one of them, he said,

" ' The moral of this story doubtless is, that *men never change*. This is not true. They change to better and worse. A thousand other maxims which authors attempt to establish are all equally false. They affirm that *men are ungrateful;* but no, they are not so ungrateful as is supposed. And if ingratitude be frequently a subject of complaint, it is because the benefactor requires more than he gives.

"'It is also said, that *when you know a man's character, you have a key to his whole conduct;* but this is a mistaken notion. A man may commit a bad action though he be fundamentally good. He may be led into an act of wickedness without being himself wicked. This is because man is usually actuated, not by the natural bent of his character, but by a secret momentary passion which has lain dormant and concealed in the inmost recesses of his heart. Another error is to suppose that *the face is the mirror of the mind.* The truth is, that it is very difficult to know a man's character. To avoid being deceived on this point, it is necessary to judge a person by his actions, and it must be by his actions of the moment, and merely for that moment.

"'In truth, men have their virtues and their vices, their heroism and their perversity. Men are neither generally good or generally bad, but they possess and practice all that is good and bad in this world. This is the principle. Natural dispositions, education, and accidental circumstances are the applications. I have always been guided by this opinion, and I have generally found it correct. However, I was deceived in 1814, when I believed that France, at the sight of her dangers, would make common cause with me; but I was not deceived in 1815, on my return from Waterloo.'

"The Emperor felt unwell, and retired very early."

May 21. The Emperor continued quite unwell, but was able to take a short ride in the calash. On his return, he was informed that Sir Hudson Lowe had been to Longwood, and had himself arrested one of the servants of General Montholon, who had recently left the service of deputy governor Skelton. On hearing this, the Emperor exclaimed,

"What turpitude! what meanness! A governor, an English lieutenant general, himself to arrest a servant! Really, this conduct is too disgusting!"*

After dinner the Emperor asked what book he should read, and all decided for the Bible.

"This is certainly very edifying," said the Emperor; "it would never be imagined in Europe."

He read the book of Joshua, observing, at almost every town or village that he named,

"I encamped there; I carried that place by assault; I gave battle here."

May 22. At dinner to-day conversation turned upon Madam Campan's establishment, the young persons who had been educated in it, and the fortunes which the Emperor had conferred upon some of them. He particularly alluded to Stephanie de Beauharnais, afterward Princess of Baden. She was the cousin of Josephine, and the Emperor was much attached to her. Speaking of himself in the third person, the Emperor said,

"Princess Stephanie, of Baden, lost her mother in her childhood. She

---

* The servant was arrested because he had entered into the service of General Montholon without having first obtained permission of the governor. The servant was a Persian, and waited at the Emperor's table. Sir Hudson Lowe arrested him, "seizing him," says Count Montholon, "with his own hands by the throat, and then giving him in charge to a dragoon." Respecting this arrest, Sir Hudson Lowe says, "The hire of servants without my permission was a thing attempted to be established, and this put a stop to it."

was left in the care of an English lady, her mother's intimate friend, who was very rich and without children, and who confided the education of her *protegée* to some old nuns in the south of France, I believe at Montauban. Napoleon, during his consulship, one day heard Josephine mention this circumstance, while alluding to her young relation, Stephanie.

" 'How can you permit this?' said he; 'how can you suffer one of your name to be supported by a foreigner, an English woman, who must, at this moment, be regarded as our enemy? Are you not afraid that your memory will one day suffer by this?'

"A courier was immediately dispatched to bring the young lady to the Tuileries, but the nuns refused to part with her. Napoleon, however, instituted the necessary legal forms, and a second courier was speedily sent to the prefect of the district, with orders instantly to seize the person of the young lady in the name of the law.

" Owing to the circumstances of the times, such was the influence of certain systems, and of the opinions which they inspired, that Stephanie's removal was to herself a source of deep regret; and she beheld, not without terror, him who declared himself her relative, and who was about to become her benefactor. She was placed in the establishment of Madam Campan, at St. Germain. All sorts of masters were appointed to superintend her education; and, on her introduction to the world, her beauty, wit, accomplishments, and virtues rendered her an object of universal admiration.

" The Emperor adopted her as his daughter, and gave her in marriage to the hereditary Prince of Baden. This union was for several years far from being happy. In course of time, however, the causes of difference gradually vanished; the prince and princess became attached to each other, and from that moment they had only to regret the happiness of which they had deprived themselves during the early years of their marriage.

" At the conferences of Erfurth, the Princess of Baden received the most flattering attentions from her brother-in-law, the Emperor Alexander. During our disasters in 1813, persons who were at the head of political affairs, dreading the result of an interview between Alexander and the Princess of Baden at Manheim, succeeded in depriving the princess of the regard of her august relative by circulating false reports to the prejudice of her character. Thus, when Alexander arrived at Manheim in his triumphant march to Paris, he by no means treated Princess Stephanie with due respect. His conduct was calculated to wound her feelings, but it could not humble her pride.

" On this occasion, the conduct pursued by the Prince of Baden reflected true glory on his character. The most august personages surrounded him, and urged him to repudiate the wife whom he had received from the hands of Napoleon; but the prince, with true nobleness of sentiment, rejected the idea, observing that he would never commit an act of baseness which would be as repugnant to his affections as to his honor. This generous prince, to whom we did not render sufficient justice in Paris, afterward fell a victim to a tedious and painful illness; the princess personally attended on her husband throughout the whole of his sufferings, performing with her own hands all the minute services that his situation required. Her devoted attachment gained for her the admiration of her relatives and subjects.

"Princess Stephanie, of Baden, shed a lustre over her exalted station. She conferred honor on her character as a wife and a daughter. She at all times professed the highest veneration for him who, when in the enjoyment of boundless power, had benevolently adopted her as his child."

May 23. The Emperor was quite ill, and had passed a sleepless night. He sat upon his sofa during the morning in an undress. During the conversation with Las Casas he remarked,

"A sovereign should be regarded only as the blessing of his people. His acts of severity should be overlooked in consideration of his acts of clemency. Mercy must still be held to be his chief attribute. In Paris I have sometimes been reproached for conversations and words which, in truth, ought not to have escaped me, but my personal situation, my extreme activity, and most of my acts, which really proceeded from myself, ought to have made amends for many things.

"I must reproach myself for the expulsion of Portalis from the Council of State. I was too severe. I should have checked myself before I ordered him to be gone. He attempted no justification, and, therefore, the scene should have ended merely by my saying *it is well*. His punishment should have awaited him at home. Anger is always unbecoming in a sovereign. But perhaps I was excusable in my council, where I might consider myself in the bosom of my own family. Or perhaps, after all, I may be justly condemned for this act. Every one has his fault. Nature will exert her sway over us all."

The following was the scene to which the Emperor here alludes:

A religious faction was fomenting civil discord in the state by secretly circulating bulls and letters from the Pope. They were shown to M. Portalis, a councilor of state, appointed to superintend religious worship, and who, if he did not himself circulate them, at least neither prevented nor denounced their circulation. This was discovered, and the Emperor suddenly challenged him with the fact in open council.

"What could have been your motive, sir?" said he. "Were you influenced by your religious principles? If so, why are you here? I use no control over the conscience of any man. Did I force you to become my councilor of state? On the contrary, you solicited the post as a high favor. You are the youngest member of the council, and, perhaps, the only one who has not some personal claim to that honor. You had nothing to recommend you but the inheritance of your father's services. You took a personal oath to me. How could your religious feelings permit you openly to violate that oath, as you have just now done? Speak, however; you are here in confidence. Your colleagues shall be your judges. Your crime is a great one, sir. A conspiracy for the commission of a violent act is stopped as soon as we seize the arm that holds the poniard; but a conspiracy to influence the public mind has no end. It is like a train of gunpowder. Perhaps at this very moment whole towns are thrown into commotion through your fault."

The councilor, quite confused, said nothing in reply. His guilt was undeniable. The members of the council, to the majority of whom this event was quite unexpected, were struck with astonishment, and observed profound silence.

"Why," continued the Emperor, "did you not, according to the obligation imposed by your oath, discover to me the criminal and his plots? Am I not at all times accessible to every one of you?"

"Sire," said the councilor, at length venturing to reply, "he was my cousin."

"Your crime is then the greater, sir," replied the Emperor, sharply. "Your kinsman could only have been placed in office at your solicitation. From that moment all the responsibility devolved on you. When I look upon a man as entirely devoted to me, as your situation ought to render you, all who are connected with him, and all for whom he becomes responsible, from that time require no watching. These are my maxims."

The accused member still remained silent, and the Emperor continued, "The duties which a councilor of state owes to me are immense. You, sir, have violated those duties, and you hold the office no longer. Leave me. Let me never see you here again."

The disgraced councilor, as he was withdrawing, passed very near the Emperor. The latter looked at him, and said,

"I am sincerely grieved at this, sir, for the services of your father are still fresh in my memory." When he was gone the Emperor added, "I hope such a scene as this may never be renewed. It has done me too much harm. I am not mistrustful, but may become so. I have allowed myself to be surrounded by every party. I have placed near my person even emigrants and soldiers of the army of Condé; and though it was wished to induce them to assassinate me, yet, to do them justice, they have continued faithful. Since I have held the reins of government, this is the first individual employed about me by whom I have been betrayed."

Then turning toward M. Locré, who took notes of the debates of the Council of State, he said, "You will write *betrayed*, do you hear?"

As the Emperor continued the conversation with Las Casas, he reproached himself very severely for another scene in which he allowed himself to give passionate utterance to his just indignation. The occurrence took place at the Tuileries, at one of the grand audiences, and in the presence of all the court.

"But in this instance," said the Emperor, "I was provoked to the utmost extreme. My anger burst forth against my inclination. I had given G——, a name very illustrious in the Faubourg St. Germain, the command of a legion of the capital, which was menaced. He undertook to defend it. I afterward learned that he rejoiced in our disasters, and invoked them; but I then did not know this. The enemy was advancing upon us. G—— coolly wrote to inform me that his health would not permit him to take the command; and, nevertheless, he dared to present himself to me as a courtier in perfect activity and good spirits. I was very indignant at his conduct, but

I repressed my anger, and resolved to take no notice of him. He, however, on three or four occasions, sought an opportunity of throwing himself in my way. I could no longer stifle my rage. The bomb exploded.

" 'How, sir!' said I, 'you write me that you are too sick to command the troops, and yet you appear here a courtier in perfect health! I, who believed that your name belonged to the country, I have done you the honor to give you one of the legions of the capital, to defend it against the enemy which is at its gates, and you refuse me! What do you wish me to think? I am perplexed. There is either cowardice here, or treason. Can there be treason? But I do not intrude my opinions upon any one, sir. It is not I who have sought you out. Remember all your eagerness and your sycophancy to throw yourself in my way. Lay aside that cross of honor which you have purloined from me; it is very much misplaced; and let me never again see you in the palace. These walls only proclaim your shame.'

"Can it be believed," continued the Emperor to Las Casas, "that after such an assault, for which I most severely reproach myself, he only occupied himself in sending to me his submission, his repentance, his new protestations? The poltroon! But I would listen to nothing from him."

"And you did wisely, sire," said Las Casas; "he justified to the end the opinion you had formed of him. When the Allies entered Paris, he was seen on the terrace of the Tuileries, in front of the hotel of Talleyrand, which the Emperor Alexander occupied, waving a white handkerchief in the midst of the crowd, and shouting, 'Come on, my lads! cheers for Alexander! our friend! our liberator!' The multitude were indignant, and, in spite of the Russian Guards who surrounded the hotel, they forced him to fly. He narrowly escaped with his life."

"But what distressed me most of all," continued the Emperor, "was the situation of G——'s son, who was my chamberlain, and of whom I had no reason to complain."

May 24. The Emperor rode out in his calash. As journals had recently been received from England, the conversation naturally turned upon politics.

"In France," said the Emperor, "I perceive that the patriots are emigrating rapidly; and there seems to be a wish to encourage their emigration, as their property has not been confiscated.

"I think, also, that I can perceive, from the debates in the English Parliament, a reserved idea respecting the division of France. This is dreadful. Every one possessing a true French heart must now be overwhelmed with despair. An immense majority of the population of France must be plunged in the deepest sorrow. Ah! why am I not placed in some remote sphere, on a soil truly free and independent, where no external influence could be dreaded! How would I astonish the world! I would address a proclamation to the French; I would say to them, 'You are lost if you are not united! The odious, the insolent foreigner is about to parcel you out and to annihilate you! Frenchmen, arise! make common cause at all hazards! Rally, if it must be so, *even around the Bourbons!* Let the existence, the safety of France, take place of every other consideration!'"

"Russia, however," continued the Emperor, "I think, must oppose this division. She would thereby have to fear the growing strength of Germany."

"Austria also," said Las Casas, "must oppose it, from the apprehension of wanting the necessary support in case of any attempts on the part of Russia. In such a case, Austria might possibly subserve the cause of the King of Rome by bringing him forward."

"Yes," replied Napoleon, "as an instrument of menace, perhaps, but never as the object of her good wishes. Austria must have too much cause to dread him. The King of Rome will be the man of the people—he will be the champion of Italy. Thus it will be the policy of Austria to take his life. This will probably not be attempted during the reign of his grandfather, who is a good man; but the Emperor Francis can not live forever. If, however, the manners of the present age should preclude the possibility of an attempt to murder him, they will endeavor to brutalize his faculties; or, finally, if he should escape both physical and moral assassination—if his mother's cares and his own natural endowments should rescue him from all those dangers, then—then—" he repeated several times, as if absorbed in reflection, "why, then—but who can calculate the destinies of any one?"

The Emperor then turned the conversation to England, and said, "England alone is interested in the destruction of France. She can not, however, increase the power of Belgium, for in that case Antwerp would become as formidable to her as it was under my reign. She must leave the Bourbons in the centre, with only eight or ten millions of inhabitants, and surround them with princes, dukes, or kings of Normandy, Brittany, Aquitaine, and Provence, so that Cherburg, Brest, Garonne, and the Mediterranean would be in the possession of different sovereigns. This would make the French monarchy retrograde several ages; would restore it to its situation under the first Capets; and would provide for the Bourbons a few centuries of new and laborious efforts. But, fortunately, before England can arrive at this point, she will have to surmount almost invincible obstacles—the uniformity of the division of the territory in departments, the similitude of language, the identity of manners, the universality of the Code, the generality of my lyceums, and the glory and splendor which I have left behind me. These are so many indissoluble knots and truly national institutions.

"A great nation like France can not easily be parceled out; and if it should be, it will be constantly reuniting, and seeking to recover its importance, like Ariosto's giant, who runs after his limbs, and even his head, as they are lopped off, and, after putting them on, begins to fight again."

"But, sire," said Las Casas, "the power of the giant depended on the plucking out of a single hair. In like manner, Napoleon may be said to be the hair on which depended the existence of France."

"No," resumed the Emperor, "my memory and my ideas would still survive; but England, on the contrary, would, in the course of time, have become a mere appendage to France, had the latter continued under my dominion. England was by nature intended to be one of our islands, as well as Oleron or Corsica. On what trifles does the fate of empires depend!

How petty and insignificant are our revolutions in the grand organization of the universe! If, instead of entering upon the Egyptian expedition, I had invaded Ireland, if some slight derangement of my plans had not thrown obstacles in the way of the Boulogne enterprise, what would England have been to-day? What would have been the situation of the Continent and of the whole political world?"

May 25. After dinner the Emperor read the Greek tragedy of Œdipus, which he admired exceedingly. He then took up Brutus, which he analyzed with remarkable skill.

"Voltaire," said he, "has not truly comprehended his subject. The Romans were guided by patriotism as we are by honor. Voltaire has not portrayed the real sublimity of Brutus, sacrificing his sons for the welfare of his country, and in spite of the pangs of paternal affection. He has made him a monster of pride, decreeing the death of his children for the sake of preserving his power, his name, and his celebrity. The other characters of the tragedy are equally misconceived. Tullia is described as a fury, who takes advantage of her situation, and not as a woman of tender sentiment, who might be led into crime by seduction and dangerous influence."

May 26. At two o'clock the Emperor sent for Las Casas. He was weary and sad. Together they looked over some of the European journals. It was there stated that Joseph Bonaparte had purchased an extensive tract of land on the River St. Lawrence, in the northern part of the State of New York.

"This establishment," said the Emperor, "will in a few years present a numerous population, distinguished for all sorts of useful knowledge. If they do their duty, they will transmit from their colony excellent writings, victorious refutations of the system which now triumphs in Europe.

"If I had gone to America, I intended to have collected all my relatives around me. I suppose that we might realize at least eight millions of dollars. This point would have become the nucleus of a national union, a second France. Before the conclusion of the year, the events of Europe would have collected around me twenty millions of dollars, and sixty thousand individuals, most of them possessing wealth, talent, and information. I should like to have realized that dream. It would have been a renewal of my glory.

"America was, in all respects, our proper asylum. It is an immense continent, presenting the advantages of a peculiar system of freedom. If a man be troubled with melancholy, he may get into a coach and drive a thousand leagues, enjoying all the way the pleasure of a common traveler. In America you may be on a footing of equality with every one. You may, if you please, mingle with the crowd without inconvenience, retaining your own language, your own manners, and your own religion. It is impossible that I could henceforth consider myself a private man in Europe; my name is too popular throughout the Continent. In some way or other, I am connected with every people, and belong to every country.

"As for you," said he to Las Casas, smiling, "your fate seemed naturally to lead you to the shores of the Orinoko or to Mexico, where the recollection of the good Las Casas is not yet obliterated. You would there have enjoyed all you could have wished. The destinies of some men seem to be marked out: Gregoire, for instance, has only to go to Hayti, and he would immediately be made a Pope."

In this connection Las Casas makes the following record:

"At the time of the Emperor's second abdication, an American in Paris wrote to him as follows: 'While you were at the head of a nation, you could perform any miracle, you might conceive any hopes; but now you can do nothing more in Europe. Fly to the United States; I know the hearts of the leading men, and the sentiments of the people of America. You will there find a second country, and every source of consolation.'

"The Emperor would not listen to such a suggestion. He might, doubtless, by dint of speed or disguise, have gained Brest, Nantes, Bordeaux, or Toulon, and in all probability have reached America; but he conceived that either disguise or flight would be derogatory to his dignity. He thought himself bound to prove to all Europe his full confidence in the French people, and their extreme attachment to him, by passing through his dominions

MALMAISON

at such a crisis merely in the quality of a private man, and unattended by any escort. But what, above all, influenced him at that critical moment was the hope that impending dangers would open the eyes of his subjects, that they would rally around him, and that he might save the country. This hope caused him to linger at Malmaison, and to postpone his departure after he reached Rochefort. If he is now at St. Helena, he owes his captivity to this sentiment, of which he was unable to divest himself. Subsequently, when he had no other resource than to accept the hospitality of the *Bellerophon*, it was not, perhaps, without a feeling of inward satisfaction that he found himself, by the force of circumstances, irresistibly led to fix his abode in England, where he might enjoy the happiness of being still but little removed from France. He was well aware that he could not be free in England; but he hoped to be heard, and then a chance would at least have been open to the impressions he might create."

"The English ministers," said he, "who are the enemies of their country, and who have sold her to foreigners, thought they had too much cause to dread my presence. They conceived that my opinion in London would be more powerful than the whole opposition; that it would have compelled them either to change their system or resign their places; and to keep themselves in place, they basely sacrificed the true interests of their country, the triumph, the glory of her laws, the peace of the world, the welfare of Europe, the happiness and the benedictions of posterity."

In the course of conversation, the Emperor adverted to Waterloo, and described the terrible anxiety and suffering he endured before he came to the resolution to abdicate.

"My speech to the ministers," said he, "was the literal prophecy of all that subsequently took place."

"Carnot was the only one who seemed to take a right view of the case. He opposed the abdication, which he said was a deathblow to France; and he wished that we should defend ourselves even to annihilation. Carnot was the only one who maintained this opinion; all the rest were for the abdication. That measure was determined, and Carnot, covering his face with his hands, burst into tears.

"I said, 'I am not a

PORTRAIT OF CARNOT.

God. I can not do all by my own single efforts. I can not save the nation without the help of the nation.' I am certain that the people then entertained these sentiments, and that they are now suffering undeservedly. It was the host of intriguers, and men possessing titles and offices, who were really guilty. That which misled them and ruined me was the mild system of 1814, the benignity of the Restoration. They looked for a repetition of this lenity. The change of the sovereign had become a mere joke. They all calculated on remaining just as they had been before, whether I should be succeeded by Louis XVIII. or any other. These stupid, selfish, and egotistical men looked upon the great event as merely a competition, about which they cared but little, and they thought only of their individual interest when a deadly war of principles was about to be commenced. And why should I disguise the truth? There were among the individuals whom I had elevated, and by whom I was surrounded, a number of wretched boasters!"

Then turning to Las Casas, he added, "I am not alluding to your Faubourg St. Germain, with respect to which the matter was totally different, and for which some excuse may be found. During my reverses in 1814, the greatest traitors were not the individuals connected with that party, of whom I had no great cause to complain, and who, therefore, on my return, were not bound to me by any particular ties of gratitude. I had abdicated. The king was restored. They had but returned to their old attachments, and had only renewed their allegiance."

May 27. It was a beautiful day, but the Emperor was very ill and very low-spirited. He walked out, with some of his friends, to the extremity of the wood, waiting for the calash. When it arrived, they entered it for their usual drive. Some one alluded in conversation to the state of manufactures in France.

"The Emperor," said Napoleon, "had brought them to a degree of prosperity hitherto unknown, and which was scarcely credited in Europe, or even in France. This was a subject of wonder to foreigners on their arrival. The Abbé de Montesquieu was constantly expressing his astonishment at this circumstance, the proofs of which he had in his own hands when he became minister of the interior. The Emperor was the first individual in France who said, '*Agriculture first, manufactures next, and, finally, trade, which must arise out of the superabundance of the two first.*' He also defined and put into practice, in a clear and connected way, the systems most conducive to the interests of our manufacturers and merchants. To him we were indebted for the cultivation of sugar, indigo, and cotton. He offered a reward of $200,000 to the individual who should discover a method of spinning flax like cotton, and he doubted not that this discovery would have been made. The fatality of circumstances alone prevented this grand idea from being carried into execution.

"The old aristocracy—those enemies to our prosperity—exhausted all their wit in stupid jokes and frivolous caricatures on these subjects. But the English had no cause to laugh. They felt the blow, and have not yet recovered from it."

A short time before dinner, the Emperor sent for Las Casas to attend him in his chamber. He was very unwell, and could converse but little. The turn of the conversation led him to express his surprise at the contrast between the character of the mind and the expression of the countenance which was observable in some individuals.

"This proves," said he, "that we must not judge of a man by his face. We can know him only by his conduct. What countenances have I had to judge of in the course of my life! What odd examples of physiognomy have come under my observation! And what rash opinions have I heard on this subject! Thus I invariably made it a rule never to be influenced either by features or by words. Still, however, it must be confessed that we sometimes find curious resemblances between the countenance and the character. For instance, on looking at the face of our *monseigneur* the governor, who would not recognize the features of a *tiger-cat?* I will mention another instance. There was a man in my service who was employed about my person. I liked him very much, but was obliged to dismiss him because I several times caught him with his hands in my pockets. He committed his thefts too impudently. Let any one look at this man, and they must admit that he has a *magpie's eye.*"

While they were conversing on the subject of physiognomy, Las Casas remarked that Mirabeau, speaking of Pastoret's face, said, "It is a compound of the tiger and the calf, but the calf predominates." At this the Emperor laughed heartily, and said it was strictly true.

He dined alone in his chamber. About ten o'clock in the evening he sent again for Las Casas. The Emperor was reclining upon the sofa, with many books scattered around him. He began to read Racine's Alexander, of which he expressed his dislike. He afterward took up Andromache, which was one of his favorite pieces.

May 28. The weather was exceedingly pleasant. The friends of the Emperor urged him to ride out on horseback, for his health was suffering from the want of exercise.

"I can not consent," said he, "to ride backward and forward within the limits marked out to me. It is like being confined in a riding-school. I can not endure it."

By much persuasion, however, they succeeded in inducing him to change his determination. They all accompanied him. On their return they passed in front of the English camp. This was the first time the Emperor had passed it. The soldiers immediately were thrown into commotion upon his approach. They abandoned their occupations, and formed themselves in a line to salute the Emperor. Napoleon was gratified. He bowed pleasantly to them, and said to his companions, "What European soldier would not be inspired with respect at my approach?"

The Emperor was aware of the sentiments of respect with which the English soldiers regarded him, and therefore had carefully avoided, in his usual rides, passing the English camp, lest he should be accused of wishing to excite this enthusiasm.

P

As the Emperor returned, he saw some skittles which the servants had made for their own amusement. He ordered them to be brought, and played several games. He won a Napoleon and a half from Las Casas, which he threw to the servant who ran after the ball.

May 29. At half past eight in the morning the Emperor went into the garden to enjoy the morning air. He sent for Las Casas, and the conversation, which turned upon Corsica, was continued more than an hour.

"Our native country," said he, "is always dear. Even St. Helena may have charms to those who are born here. Therefore Corsica presents to me a thousand attractions. The scenery of the country is very grand, and islanders always present originality of character, for their situation tends to protect them from invasion, and precludes that perpetual intercourse with foreigners which is experienced in Continental states. The inhabitants of mountainous regions always possess a degree of energy and a turn of mind peculiar to themselves. The charms of my native country, from my early recollections, are to me superior to those of any other spot in the world. I think that the very smell of the earth would enable me to distinguish my native land, even were I conducted blindfold to her shores. There was in it something peculiar which I have never observed elsewhere. Corsica was the scene of all my early attachments. I there passed the happy years of my childhood, freely roaming over the precipices, and among the hills and valleys. I recollect with pride that, when under twenty years of age, I accompanied Paoli on a grand excursion to Porte Nuovo. Paoli's retinue was numerous. He was escorted by upward of five hundred of his followers on horseback. I rode by his side, and, as he went along, he pointed out to me the different positions and the places which had been the scenes of resistance or triumph during the war for Corsican liberty. He related to me all the particulars of that glorious conflict, and on hearing the remarks and opinions which fell from his young companion's lips, he said, 'Oh, Napoleon! there is nothing modern in your character. You are formed entirely on Plutarch's model.'

BAY OF AJACCIO, CORSICA.

"When Paoli manifested his determination to surrender the island to the English, our family continued to head the French party, and had the fatal honor of being *threatened* with a *march* of the inhabitants of the island—that is to say, we were attacked by a levy in mass. Twelve or fifteen thousand peasants made a descent from the mountains of Ajaccio. The house occupied by our family was pillaged and burned, and the vines and flocks were destroyed. Madam, surrounded by a few faithful friends, wandered for some time on the sea-shore, and was at length obliged to fly to France. Our family had always been much attached to Paoli, and he, in his turn, had professed particular respect toward Madam. It is, however, but just to remark, that he employed persuasion before he resorted to force.

" 'Renounce this opposition,' said he. 'It will prove the ruin of yourself, your family, and your fortune. You will bring irreparable misery on yourself.'

"But for the chances of the Revolution, we could never have recovered from our misfortunes. Madam, like another Cornelia, heroically replied that she, her children, and her relatives would only obey two laws, namely, those of duty and honor. Had old Archdeacon Lucien been living at that time, his heart would have bled at the idea of the danger of his sheep, goats, and cattle, and his prudence would not have failed to allay the storm.

"*Madam*, the victim of her patriotism and her devotedness to France, expected to be received at Marseilles as an emigrant of distinction, but there she scarcely found herself in safety. To her astonishment, she discovered that the spirit of patriotism existed only among the very lowest classes of the people. In my youth I wrote a history of Corsica, which I dedicated to the Abbé Raynal. This production gained for me some flattering compliments and letters from the abbé, who was the fashionable author of the day.

"Paoli died in London at a very old age. He lived to see me First Consul and Emperor. I regret not having recalled him; that would have been highly gratifying to me. Such an act would have been a real trophy of honor; but my mind was absorbed in important affairs; I rarely had time to indulge in personal feelings.

"After my return in 1815, when Lucien arrived in Paris, Joseph advised me to appoint him Governor-general of Corsica. This measure was even determined upon. The importance and hurry of passing events alone prevented its execution. If Lucien had gone to Corsica, he would still have remained master of the island, and what resources would it not have presented to our persecuted patriots! To how many unfortunate families would not Corsica have afforded an asylum! I perhaps committed a fault at the time of my abdication in not reserving to myself the sovereignty of Corsica, together with the possession of some millions of the civil list, and in not having conveyed all my valuables to Toulon, whence nothing could have impeded my passage. In Corsica, I should have found myself at home. The whole population would have been, as it were, my own family. I might have disposed of every arm and of every heart. Thirty thousand, or even fifty thousand allied troops could not have subdued me. No sovereign in Europe would have undertaken such a task. But it was precisely the happy security of the situation which deterred me from availing myself of it. I would not have it said that, amid the wreck of the French people, which I plainly foresaw, I alone had been dexterous enough to gain the port."

PORTRAIT OF LUCIEN BONAPARTE, THE BROTHER OF NAPOLEON.

Las Casas observed that, according to the general opinion, he might, in 1814, have secured the possession of Corsica instead of the island of Elba.

"Certainly I might," replied the Emperor, "and those who were well acquainted with the affairs of Fontainebleau will be surprised that I did not. I might then have reserved to myself whatever I pleased. The humor of the moment led me to decide in favor of Elba. Had I possessed Corsica, it is probable that my return in 1815 would never have been thought of. Even at Elba, those whose interest it was to keep me there decreed my return by their own misgovernment and the non-fulfillment of the engagements which they had entered into with me."

"We now," says Las Casas, "reminded the Emperor of his intention of riding on horseback, but he said he would rather walk and chat. He ordered his breakfast, after which we conversed for some time on the old court, the nobility who composed it, their pretensions, and the king's equipages. All this was compared with what the Emperor had himself introduced."

"I found great difficulty," continued Napoleon, "in forming the court which I established at the Tuileries. On my arrival there, I was resolved to obliterate the recollection of the manners and conflicts of the period to which I had just succeeded. But I had hitherto passed my life in camps; I had just returned from Egypt, and had left France when young and inexperienced. I was a stranger to every one, and at first found this a source of great embarrassment. Lebrun acted as my guide during the first years of my consulship. Bankers and money-speculators were at that time persons of the first consequence. No sooner did I enter upon my functions than a host of these people crowded around me, and eagerly offered to advance me considerable sums of money. This conduct, though seemingly dictated by generosity, was not, however, without interested views. They were, for the most part, men of bad character, and their offers were rejected. I had a natural dislike of men of this profession. I had laid down the firm determination to act upon other principles than those of the Directory. I was anxious that probity should become the mainspring and feature of my new government. I was also immediately surrounded by the wives of these money-lenders, who were all beautiful and elegant women. Indeed, a money-lender at that time seemed to regard it as indispensably necessary that his wife should be a woman of fascinating manners; it was a circumstance that tended materially to assist his speculations. But the prudent Lebrun was at hand to direct the young Telemachus. It was resolved to exclude this sort of society from the Tuileries. It was, however, no such easy matter to assemble a suitable circle around me. Nobles were rejected in order to avoid giving offense to public opinion, and contractors were excluded with the view of purifying the morals of the new era. These two classes being shut out, of course no very distinguished society remained, and the Tuileries for some time presented a sort of magic lantern, very varied and changeable.

"At Moscow, the viceroy Eugene happened to meet with some letters written by Princess Dolgoruki, who had been at Paris at the period alluded to. This correspondence gave a very favorable picture of the Tuileries. The princess observed that it was not precisely a court, nor yet exactly a camp, but something perfectly new in its kind. She added that the First Consul did not carry his hat under his arm, nor wear a dress sword by his side, but that he was nevertheless a swordsman. However, such is the effect of evil report, that, owing to some such expressions as these having been misrepresented to me, Princess Dolgoruki was very unjustly treated. I ordered her at that time to quit France. We thought her hostile to the principles of our government; but we were, as it may be seen, mistaken. Madam Grant, the mistress of M. de Talleyrand—for he had not yet made her his wife—greatly contributed to alienate from us the regard of the Russians.*

---

* The Emperor was determined that his court should exhibit a model of morality and decorum. His refusal to admit to his saloons the dishonored wife of Talleyrand nearly produced a rupture between the Emperor and his renowned minister for foreign affairs. The following story is told of

"On my return from Elba, I experienced far less embarrassment in composing my court. It was, indeed, already formed by the ladies whom I termed my *widows*. These were Madam Duroc, Duchess of Istria; Mesdames Regnier, Lagrand, and all the other widows of my first generals. I told the princesses who consulted me on the method of recomposing their courts to follow my example. Nothing was more natural and proper. These ladies, though still young, were already experienced in the world, and among them were several beautiful and fascinating women. Most of them have now lost their fortunes. Some, I have been told, are remarried, and have changed their names; so that of all the wealth and rank founded by me, no traces will perhaps remain. Even names will disappear. If this should really be the case, will it not afford ground for saying that, after all, there must have been a radical error in the selections I made? But it will be all the worse for the parties themselves. They will by this means only furnish a triumph and a ground of insolence to the old aristocracy."

"We again," says Las Casas, "reminded the Emperor of his intended ride on horseback. We urged him not to neglect it, because we knew it to be absolutely necessary for his health; but we could not prevail on him to leave the garden."

"We are very well here," said he. "We will have some tents pitched on this spot."

"We began to talk," says Las Casas, "about the Faubourg St. Germain, and the Hotel de Luynes, which the Emperor termed its cathedral. He described to us the cause of the banishment of Madam de Chevreuse."

"I had frequently," said the Emperor, "threatened to visit her with this punishment, and for conduct of the most mischievous and insolent nature. One day, when urged to the utmost extremity, I addressed her as follows:

"'Madam! according to the feudal notions and doctrines entertained by you and your friends, you pretend to be the sovereigns of your estates. Now, on the same principle, I may style myself the sovereign lord of France. I may claim Paris as my village, and may banish from it every individual who is obnoxious to me. I judge you by your own laws. Leave Paris, and never venture to return.'

"On decreeing her exile, I was firmly resolved never to be prevailed on to recall her, because I had endured much before I decreed her punishment, and I found myself compelled to set an example of severity, to spare the necessity of repeating it on others. This was one of my grand principles."

"I have frequently visited," said Las Casas, "the Hotel de Luynes, and I was well acquainted with Madam de Chevreuse and her mother-in-law, for whom I always entertained a great regard. As for Madam de Chevreuse, who was a pretty, intelligent, and amiable woman, with a somewhat romantic turn of mind, she had doubtless been seduced by the charms of notoriety,

this lady: M. de Talleyrand having one day invited M Denon, the celebrated traveler, to dine with him, told his wife to read the work of their guest, indicating its place in his library. Madam de Talleyrand unluckily got hold, by mistake, of the adventures of Robinson Crusoe, which she ran over in great haste, and at dinner began to question Denon about his shipwreck, his island, and finally about his man Friday.

or urged on by her numerous flatterers and admirers, some of whom were little worthy of her regard."
"I know it," added the Emperor. "She hoped to recommence *the Fronde*. But I was not a minor sovereign."

The Emperor retired with Las Casas to his room. A ship had recently arrived from England, bringing European journals. He began to read the *Journal des Debats*. The grand marshal brought in a letter for the Emperor. Sir Hudson Lowe had broken the seal, that he might first peruse its contents. The Emperor received the letter, read it over once, and sighed heavily. He then read it over again, looked at the seal which Sir Hudson Lowe had insolently broken, and then tore the letter into fragments and threw them under the table. In silence he resumed the perusal of the journal. Suddenly stopping, he turned to Las Casas and said,

"That letter is from poor Madam; she is well, and wishes to come and reside with me at St. Helena."

"After this," says Las Casas, "he continued his reading. This, which was the first letter that the Emperor had received from any individual of his family, was in the handwriting of Cardinal Fesch. The Emperor was evidently much hurt by its having been delivered to him with the seal broken."

May 30. At two o'clock the Emperor laid aside his dictation, and walked out into the garden, accompanied by Las Casas, Gourgaud, Bertrand, and Montholon. One of the French journals had stated that the Bourbons contemplated erecting statues to the memory of Moreau and Pichegru.

"A statue to Moreau," said the Emperor, "whose conspiracy in 1803 is now so well proved! Moreau, who in 1813 died fighting under the Russian standard! A monument to the memory of Pichegru, who was guilty of one of the most heinous of crimes! who purposely suffered himself to be defeated, and who connived with the enemy in the slaughter of his own troops! But, after all," continued the Emperor, "history is only made up of reports which gain credit by repetition. Because it has been repeatedly affirmed that these were great men, who deserved well of their country, they will at length pass for such, and their adversaries will be despised."

The Emperor then entered quite at length into the celebrated conspiracy of the Bourbons for his assassination, in which Moreau and Pichegru were implicated with the inflexible desperado Georges Cadoudal.

"The man who first made the confessions," said Napoleon, "indicated, though without naming him, a person to whom Georges and the other leaders of the conspiracy never spoke without taking off their hats, and whom they treated with the utmost consideration and respect. It was at first supposed that this individual must have been the Duke de Berri. Some, however, concluded him to have been the Duke d'Enghien, during his momentary appearance. Charles d'Hosier, one of the conspirators, unexpectedly drew aside the veil. A few days after his arrest, he was seized with a fit of melancholy and hanged himself in prison. The alarm was, however, given, and he was cut down. Stretched on his bed, and while yet struggling between life and death, he vented repeated imprecations on Moreau, and accused him of having treacherously seduced many well-disposed men, and held out to them promises of assistance which he never realized. He likewise mentioned the names of Georges and Pichegru. This was the first circumstance which excited suspicion against these two men; there was previously no idea of either of them having been engaged in the conspiracy.

"This event created a great sensation. The public mind was wrought up to a high pitch of fermentation. Doubts were entertained of the truth of the statement made by the government respecting the extent of the conspiracy and the number of the conspirators. Of the latter, it was affirmed that there were about forty in Paris. Their names were published, and the First Consul pledged his honor to secure them. He summoned Bessières, and gave orders that he, with his corps, should surround and guard the walls of Paris. For the space of six weeks nobody was suffered to quit the capital without special permission; a general gloom prevailed through Paris; but every day the Moniteur announced the arrest of one or two of the individuals who, it was alleged, were concerned in the conspiracy. Public opinion took a turn in my favor, and indignation against the conspirators increased in proportion as they were secured. Not one escaped.

"The public papers of the period detail the particulars of the arrest of Georges, who killed two men before he could be secured. It appears that he was betrayed by his comrade, who drove the cabriolet in which they were both riding.

ARREST OF GEORGES CADOUDAL.

"As to Pichegru, he was the victim of the basest treachery. This circumstance was truly a disgrace to human nature. He was sold by his intimate friend—by a man whom I will not name, on account of the horror and disgust which his conduct is calculated to excite. This man, who was formerly a military officer, and who has since followed the business of a merchant at Lyons, offered to deliver up Pichegru for one hundred thousand crowns. On the day on which he made this proposition, he stated that they had, on the preceding evening, supped together, and that Pichegru, finding himself every day alluded to in the Moniteur, and being aware that the critical moment was fast approaching, said,

"'If I and a few other generals were boldly to present ourselves to the troops, should we not gain them over?'

"'No,' replied his friend. 'You form a wrong idea of the state of feeling in France. You would not gain over a single soldier.'

"He spoke truly. At night the faithless friend conducted the officers of the police to Pichegru's door, and he gave them a minute description of his chamber and of his means of defending himself. Pichegru had pistols on his bed-room table, and he kept a light burning while he slept. The officers gently unlocked the door by means of the false keys which the treacherous friend had procured for them, the table was overturned, the candle was extinguished, and the officers seized Pichegru, who immediately jumped out of bed. He was a very powerful man. He struggled desperately, and it was found necessary to bind him and convey him to prison without waiting till he could be dressed.

"On being placed at the head of the government, the First Consul was extremely anxious to tranquillize the western departments. He summoned nearly all the leading men of those districts, and succeeded in rousing several of them to a sense of the interests and glory of their country. He even drew tears from the eyes of some. Georges had his turn among the rest. The First Consul endeavored to touch every fibre of his heart. He passed over all the chords, but could produce no vibration. He found him lost to every generous feeling, and coldly intent on his own ambitious calculations. He persisted in his determination to command his cantons. The Consul, having exhausted every conciliatory argument, at length assumed the language of the first magistrate of France. He dismissed him, and recommended him to go home, and live quietly and submissively; and, above all, not to mistake the nature of the course he had that moment adopted, nor to attribute to feebleness what was only the result of his moderation and the consciousness of his power. He desired him to repeat to himself, and to all who were connected with him, that so long as the First Consul should hold the reins of authority, there would be no chance of safety for any who might dare to engage in conspiracy. Georges took his leave, but, as the event proved, not without having imbibed from this conference a feeling of respect for Napoleon, on whose destruction, however, he still continued bent.

"Moreau was the rallying-point and the centre of attraction to the conspirators who came from London to attack Paris. It appeared that Lajollais, his aid-de-camp, had deceived these men by addressing them in the name of Moreau, and telling them that the general was secure of popular favor throughout the whole of France, and could dispose of the whole army. Moreau constantly assured them that he could command no one, not even his aid-de-camp, but that if they killed the First Consul, they might do any thing.

Moreau, when left to himself, was a very good sort of man. He was easily led, and this accounts for his inconsistencies. He left the palace in raptures, and returned to it full of spleen and malice, having in the interim seen his mother-in-law and wife. The First Consul, who would have been very glad to have gained him over to his side, once made it up with him completely; but their friendship lasted only four days. The Consul then vowed that he would never renew it. In fact, attempts were afterward frequently made to reconcile them, but Napoleon never would agree to it. He foresaw that Moreau would commit some fault—that he would lose himself, and certainly he could not have done so in a way more advantageous to the First Consul.

"Some days previous to the battle of Leipsic, some carriages, containing property and papers belonging to Moreau, which were on their way to his widow in England, were intercepted at Wittemburg. Among those papers there was a letter from Madam Moreau herself, in which she advised her husband to lay aside his silly, wavering conduct, and to come boldly to a determination. She urged him to assist in the triumph of the legitimate cause—that of the Bourbons. In answer to this, Moreau wrote, a few days before his death, begging her not to trouble him with her chimeras. 'I have come near enough to France,' said he, 'to know all that is going forward there. I have got into a true wasp's nest.'

"The Emperor was on the point of publishing these intercepted papers in the Moniteur; but there still existed in France some persons blindly tenacious of the opinion they had always maintained of Moreau, and who persisted in regarding him as a victim to tyranny. The counter-revolution had not yet afforded an opportunity of making known those acts hitherto disavowed, and of claiming their recompense. The circumstance of personal enmity prevented the Emperor from executing his intention. He thought it would not be becoming to revive this enmity for his own advantage, and to tarnish the memory of a man who had just fallen on the field of battle.

"The trial of Moreau and Pichegru, which was protracted for such a length of time, violently agitated the public mind. What added to the notoriety and interest of this trial was its connection with the affair of the Duke d'Enghien, with which it became interwoven.

"I have," continued the Emperor, "been reproached with having committed a great fault in that trial. It has been compared with the affair of the necklace, in the reign of Louis XVI., which that monarch put into the hands of Parliament, instead of having it judged by a committee. Politicians have affirmed that I should have contented myself with consigning the criminals to the judgment of a military committee. It would have been ended in eight-and-forty hours. *I could have done it;* it was legal, and nothing more would have been required of me. I should have avoided the risks to which I was exposed. But I felt my power so unlimited, and I was, at the same time, so strong in the justice of my cause, that I was determined the affair should be open to the observation of the whole world. For this reason, the embassadors and agents of foreign powers were present during the proceedings."

One of the company present here observed to the Emperor that the course he then adopted had proved advantageous to history, and honorable to his own character. It had furnished three volumes of authentic documents relating to the trial.

Another individual of the Emperor's suite, who, at the time of this celebrated trial, was with the army at Boulogne, said that all these events, even the affair of the Duke d'Enghien, had there excited but little interest, and that, on his return to Paris some time after, he was astonished to observe the sensation which they had created in the capital.

"The public mind," the Emperor rejoined, "had indeed been highly excited, particularly on the occasion of the death of the Duke d'Enghien, which event still appears to be judged of in Europe with blindness and prejudice." He maintained his right of adopting the step he had taken, and enumerated the reasons which had urged him to do it. He then adverted to the many attempts that had been made to assassinate him, and observed that he was bound in justice to say that he had never detected Louis XVIII. in any direct conspiracy against his life, though such plots had been incessantly renewed in other quarters.

"If," continued he, "I had remained in France in 1815, I intended to have given publicity to some of the latter attempts that were made against me. The Maubreuil affair, in particular, should have been solemnly investigated by the first court of the Empire, and Europe would have shuddered to see to what an extent the crime of secret assassination could be carried."*

May 31. "At five o'clock," says Las Casas, "I went to join the Emperor in the garden. We were all assembled there. The conversation turned on politics. He described the melancholy situation of England amid her triumphs. He alluded to the immensity of her debt, the madness, the impossibility of her becoming a Continental power, the dangers which assailed her Constitution, the embarrassment of her ministers, and the great clamor of the people. England, with her one hundred and fifty or two hundred thousand men, made as many efforts as he, the Emperor, had ever made during the period of his great power, and perhaps even more. He had never employed beyond five hundred thousand French troops. The traces of his Continental system were followed by all the powers on the Continent, and would be pursued still farther in proportion as those powers became more settled. He did not hesitate to say, and he proved it, that England would have gained by remaining faithful to the treaty of Amiens; that such a line of conduct would have been to the advantage of all Europe, but that Napoleon himself,

---

* The Marquis of Maubreuil was so exultant at the downfall of Napoleon in 1814, that, it is said, he rode through the streets of Paris with the star of the Legion of Honor tied to his horse's tail. With an armed force he robbed the wife of Jerome Bonaparte as she was traveling in her carriage to Germany, with a passport from the Allies. Being imprisoned for this offense, he published a letter to his judges declaring that he had been employed by the government to assassinate Napoleon. This assertion he also repeated in a very severe letter to the embassadors of the allied powers. He escaped from prison, and, meeting Talleyrand, beat him with great severity. On his trial for this offense, he accused Talleyrand of having been the cause of all his sufferings by employing him to assassinate Napoleon. Talleyrand has made no reply to this, and the mystery must now forever remain unexplained.

and his glory, would have suffered by it. Yet it was England, and not he, who broke the treaty."

"There was only one course," the Emperor continued, "for England to pursue, namely, to return to her Constitution and abandon the military system; to interfere with the Continent only through her maritime influence, in which she is pre-eminent. It is easy to foresee that great calamities will assail her should she adopt any other course; but this she will inevitably do, because the folly, pride, or venality of her present ministry causes her to persist in the system she has been pursuing."

The conversation being concluded, the Emperor returned to his study, and desired Las Casas to follow him.

"A letter," said the Emperor, "has been sent to me from England by post. It is reported that the governor has refused to deliver it, because it was not addressed to him officially. It is also said that a letter for General Bertrand has been detained for the same reason. If this is true, there is something peculiarly cruel in the conduct of the governor in having sent back the letters without even mentioning them to us, and without affording us the consolation of knowing from whom they came. A neglect of form might easily be corrected in the island. It can not so easily be done at two thousand leagues' distance."

"I told the Emperor," says Las Casas, "that a circumstance nearly similar to that which he had just mentioned had occurred to me eight or ten days back. A person who was on his way to Europe had tormented me with his offers of service. I yielded to his solicitations, and commissioned him to order me some shoes, and to get a watch changed for me, for there is no person here who knows how to repair a watch. The governor has forbidden the execution of those commissions because they were not addressed to himself. I have said nothing on the subject to any one, sire, because it is a principle with me to conceal an insult for which I can not obtain redress. But I shall find an opportunity to tell the governor my mind. In the mean time, neither he nor the person to whom I gave the commission have been able to draw from me a line or a single word, though the latter has made several attempts to do so."

"After dinner," says Las Casas, "the Emperor, conversing on our situation and the conduct of the governor, who came to-day and took a rapid circuit round Longwood, reverted to the subject of the last interview they had had together, and made some striking observations respecting it."

"I behaved very ill to him, no doubt," said the Emperor, "and nothing but my present situation could excuse me. But I was out of humor, and could not help it. I should blush for it in any other situation. Had such a scene taken place at the Tuileries, I should have felt myself bound in conscience to make some atonement. Never, during the period of my power, did I speak harshly to any one without afterward saying something to make amends for it; but here I uttered not a syllable of conciliation, and I had no wish to do so. However, the governor proved himself very insensible to my severity. His delicacy did not seem wounded by it. I should have liked, for his sake, to have seen him evince a little anger, or shut the door violently as he went out. This would, at least, have shown that there was some spring and elasticity about him; but I found nothing of the kind."

"The Emperor then again," says Las Casas, "resumed his conversation on political affairs, which he maintained with so much spirit and interest that I could have forgotten for a time what part of the world I was in. I could have believed myself still at the Tuileries or in the Rue de Bourgogne."

CHAPTER XV.

1816, June.

Voltaire—Characteristic Difference between the English and the French—Affected Anger of the Emperor—Reflections on the Governor—Expenses of the Emperor's Household at the Tuileries—Finance—Dictation resumed—Military Schools—Female Schools—Gil Blas—General Bizanet—Religious Opinions—Portraits of the Directors—Anecdotes—18th Fructidor.

June 1. The Emperor remained in the bath three hours, engaged in reading Rousseau's New Eloise. At the Briers, where he first looked into this work, he expressed himself charmed with it; but now, after a more careful perusal, he condemned it with unsparing severity.

"The high estimate," said he, "which has been formed in France of the English character, is to be ascribed to the noble character given by Rousseau to Lord Edward, and to the impression produced by some of Voltaire's plays. The facility with which public opinion was governed in those days is surprising. Voltaire and Rousseau, who then guided public opinion as they pleased, would not, I think, be able to do so at the present time. Voltaire, in particular, exerted so powerful an influence over his contemporaries, and was considered the great man of the age, only because all around him were pigmies.

"The higher classes among the English," said he, "are proud; with us, unfortunately, they are only vain. In that consists the great characteristic distinction between the two nations. The mass of the people in France certainly possess a greater share of national feeling than any other now existing in Europe; they have profited by the experience of their twenty-five years' Revolution. But, unfortunately, that class which the Revolution has advanced have not been found equal to the station of life to which they have been elevated. They have shown themselves corrupt and unstable. In the last struggles they have not been distinguished either by talents, firmness, or virtue. In short, they have degraded the honor of the nation."

The Emperor read a speech of Chateaubriand on the propriety of allowing the clergy to inherit.

"It is an academical oration," said he, "rather than the opinion of a legislator. It has wit, but shows little judgment, and contains no views whatever. Allow the clergy to inherit, and nobody will die without being obliged to purchase absolution; for, whatever our opinions may be, we none of us know where we go on leaving this world. Then must we remember our last and final account, and no one can pronounce what his feelings will be at his last hour, nor answer for the strength of his mind at that awful moment. Who can affirm that I shall not die in the arms of a confessor, and that he will not make me acknowledge myself guilty of the evil I shall not have done, and implore forgiveness for it?"

In this connection, Las Casas mentions one or two anecdotes illustrative of the character of the Emperor.

"The Emperor would often censure whole bodies," he says, "in the person of one individual, and, in order to strike with greater awe, he did it in the most solemn and imposing manner. But the anger which he sometimes showed in public, and of which so much has been said, was only feigned and put on for the moment. The Emperor affirmed that by such means he had often deterred many from the commission of a fault, and spared himself the necessity of punishing.

"One day, at one of his grand audiences, he attacked a colonel with the utmost vehemence, and quite in a tone of anger, upon some slight disorders of which his regiment had been guilty toward the inhabitants of the country they had passed through in returning to France. During the reprimand, the colonel, thinking the punishment out of all proportion to the fault of which he was accused, repeatedly endeavored to excuse himself; but the Emperor, without interrupting his speech, said to him, in an under tone, 'Very well, but say nothing; I believe you; be tranquil.' When he afterward saw him in private, he said to him,

"'When I thus addressed you, I was chastening, in your person, certain generals whom I saw near you, and who, had I spoken to them direct, would have been found deserving of the lowest degradation, and perhaps of something worse.'

"But it sometimes happened, also, that the Emperor was publicly appealed to. I have witnessed several instances of this kind. Once, at St. Cloud, at a grand audience, which was held on each Sunday, a public officer of Piedmont, who was standing by my side, addressed the Emperor in a loud tone of voice and with the utmost emotion, calling for justice, asserting that he had been falsely accused, and unjustly condemned and dismissed from the service.

"'Apply to my ministers,' answered the Emperor.

"'No, sire,' said he, 'I wish to be judged by you.'

"'That is impossible,' the Emperor replied; 'my time is wholly absorbed with the general interests of the empire, and my ministers are appointed to take into consideration the particular causes of individuals.'

"'But they will condemn me,' said the officer; 'for every body is against me.'

"'Why?' inquired the Emperor.

"'Because I love you,' said the officer: 'to love you, sire, is a sufficient motive to inspire every one with hatred.'

"The Emperor with the utmost calmness replied, 'This is rather a strange assertion, sir; but I am willing to hope that you are mistaken.' And he passed on to the next person.

"On another occasion, also, on the parade, a young officer stepped out of the ranks, in extreme agitation, to complain that he had been ill used, slighted, and passed over, and that he had been *five years* a lieutenant without being able to obtain promotion.

"'Calm yourself,' said the Emperor; 'I was *seven years* a lieutenant, and yet you see that a man may push himself forward for all that.'

"Every body laughed, and the young officer, suddenly cooled by those words, returned to his place.

"It may be observed as a general principle, that however violent the Emperor's actions might appear, they were always the result of calculation."

"When one of my ministers," said the Emperor, "or some other great personage, had been guilty of a fault of so grave a nature that it became absolutely necessary for me to be very angry, I always took care, in that case, to have a third person present to witness the scene which was to ensue; for it was a general axiom with me, that, when I had resolved to strike a blow, it must be felt by many at the same time. The immediate object of my resentment did not feel more incensed against me on that account, and the bystander, whose embarrassed appearance was highly ludicrous, did not fail to run and circulate most discreetly, as far as he could, all he had seen and heard. A salutary terror ran thus, from vein to vein, through the body social; a new impulse was given to the march of affairs; I had less to punish, and a great deal of public good was obtained without inflicting much private hardship."

June 2. At eight o'clock in the morning the Emperor rode out on horseback, and, calling at the house of Madam Bertrand, made a long visit. He appeared to be in very cheerful spirits. With infinite humor, he alluded to the ridiculous behavior of the governor toward his prisoners; to his paltry measures, his total want of consideration, the absurd manner in which he conducted the affairs of the government of the island, and his total ignorance of the business and the manners of life.

"We had certainly some reason," said he, "to complain of the admiral; but *he*, at least, was an Englishman, and this man is nothing but a constable of Italy. We have not the same manners. We can not understand each other. Our feelings do not speak the same language. He probably can not conceive, for instance, that heaps of diamonds would be insufficient to atone for the affront he has offered in causing one of my domestics to be arrested almost in my presence. Since that day, all my household are in consternation."

Returning from the ride, the Emperor breakfasted in the garden. In the afternoon he took a short ride in the calash. The conversation led to some details respecting the Emperor's household at the Tuileries. "Two hundred thousand dollars were allowed for the table, and yet the expenses of the Emperor's own table did not exceed twenty dollars a day. It had never been found possible to manage to give him his dinner hot, for, when once engaged in his closet, it was impossible to know when he would leave it. Therefore, when the hour of dinner arrived, a fowl was put on the spit for him every half hour. It has at times happened that some dozen have been roasted before that which has finally been set before him."

The conversation then turned upon the importance of a skillful administration of the finances.

"M. Mollien and M. Labouillerie," said the Emperor, "exhibited talents of the highest order in that branch. M. Mollien, in particular, had put the treasury on the footing of a simple banking-house. I had continually under my eyes, in a small book for that purpose, a complete statement of the revenue, the receipt, expenditure, arrears, and resources. I had in my cellars at the Tuileries as much as four hundred millions of francs in gold, which were entirely my own property, so much so that no other account of it existed but in a small book in the hands of my private treasurer. All this treasure disappeared by degrees, and was applied to the expenses of the Empire, particularly at the time of our disasters. How could I think of keeping any thing for myself? I had identified myself with the nation. I had sent two thousand millions of specie into France, without taking into account what private individuals may have brought.

"I was, however," continued the Emperor, "much hurt at the conduct of M. Labouillerie, who, being at Orleans in 1814, in charge of several millions belonging to me, my own private property, took them to the Count d'Artois in Paris instead of carrying them to Fontainebleau, as he was in duty and in conscience bound to do. And yet Labouillerie was not a bad man. I had both loved him and esteemed him. On my return in 1815, he earnestly entreated me to see him and hear what he had to say in his own defense. He, no doubt, would have proved that his fault arose from his ignorance and not from his heart. He knew me. He was aware that, if he could approach me, the affair would have been settled with a few angry expressions on my part. But I also knew my own weakness. I was resolved not to take him into my service again, and therefore refused to admit him. It was the only way in which I could hope, at that moment, to hold out against him and several others. Esteve, the predecessor of Labouillerie, would not have acted in that manner. He was entirely devoted to my person. He would have brought my treasure to Fontainebleau at all hazards, or, if he had failed in the endeavor, he would have thrown it into a river, or distributed it in various places rather than give it up."

June 4. At four o'clock the Emperor sent for Las Casas and rode out in the calash.

"I have at last," said the Emperor, "commenced dictating again, and what I have done will not be found devoid of interest. During the whole morning I was very much out of humor. At one o'clock I attempted to go out, but found myself compelled to return to the house, pursued by disgust and ennui. Not knowing what to do, I thought of resuming my dictations."

For many weeks the Emperor had ceased to apply himself regularly to this occupation. Various circumstances had concurred to cause interruptions.

"I took advantage of what he had just said," Las Casas observes, "to represent to him that to dictate was for him the surest, the only remedy against ennui; the only way in which he could beguile the tedious hours, and for us the means of obtaining the inestimable advantage of being put in possession of treasures in the existence of which the honor and glory of France were equally interested. The Emperor replied that he would continue his memoirs, and consulted me as to the plan to be followed."

At the dinner-table the Emperor said playfully, "I have to-day been severely reprimanded on account of my idleness; I am, therefore, going to take to my task again, and embrace several periods at the same time. Each of you shall have his share. Did not Herodotus give to his books the names of the Muses? I intend that each of mine shall bear the name of one of you. Even little Immanuel shall give his to one of them. I will begin the history of the Consulate with Montholon; Gourgaud shall record the events of some other period, or detached battles; and little Immanuel shall prepare the documents and materials necessary to commemorate the period of the coronation."

June 5. It was a fine afternoon, and, though the Emperor felt very unwell, he rode out with some of his friends in the calash. Las Casas made some remarks upon the luxurious arrangements of the military school at Paris before the Revolution.

"I was anxious," said the Emperor, "to avoid falling into this error. I wished, above all, that my young officers, who were one day to command soldiers, should begin by being soldiers themselves, and learn by experience all the technical details of the service; a system of education which must ever prove an immense advantage to an officer in the course of his future career, by enabling him to watch over and enforce the observance of those details in others who are placed under his orders. It was according to this principle that at St. Germain the young students were obliged to groom their own horses, and were taught to shoe them. This same spirit presided over the regulations at St. Cyr. There several pupils were made to lodge together in one large apartment, and a common mess was provided for all indiscriminately. Yet the attention paid to these particulars was not suffered to interfere with the care bestowed upon the instruction necessary to qualify them for their future career. In short, they did not leave St. Cyr before they had really earned the rank of officer, and were found capable of leading and commanding soldiers; and it must be admitted, that if the young men who passed from that institution at its origin into different corps of the army were at first viewed with jealousy, ample justice was soon rendered to their discipline and to their abilities."

Napoleon established at Ecouen, St. Denis, and other places, institutions to be conducted on similar principles for the daughters of the members of the Legion of Honor. Many of the regulations for these institutions were drawn up by his own hand, and he marked out the course of study. He ordered that all the articles of female manufacture, for the use of each institution, should be made in the house, and by the pupils themselves. He forbade all luxury and extravagance in dress and amusements. "I wish," said he, "to make them virtuous and useful women. They will then be sufficiently agreeable."

Q

"Public opinion," says Las Casas, "had given to Napoleon, at the time of his elevation, the reputation of a man of harsh disposition, and one void of sensibility, yet it is certain that no sovereign ever acted more from the impulse of genuine feeling than he did. He had adopted all the children of the officers and soldiers killed at Austerlitz; and with him, such an act would not have been one of mere form. He would have provided for them all."

In the evening, the Emperor again sent for Las Casas. It was a chill and gloomy hour. A few sticks of wood, blazing upon the hearth, dimly illuminated the narrow apartment with flickering light. The Emperor sat in his arm-chair before the fire, silent and dejected. As Las Casas entered, he said to him, "This darkness is in harmony with my melancholy." Gradually, however, he entered into conversation. The habits of society in former times, and those of the present, were passed in review.

"I had thought much and often," said the Emperor, "upon the means of introducing variety into the pleasures of society. I had assemblies at court, plays, journeys to Fontainebleau, but they only produced the effect of inconveniencing the people at court, without influencing the circles of the metropolis. There was not yet a sufficient degree of adhesion in the heterogeneous parts to allow them to react upon each other with due effect; but this would have been brought about in course of time. It was observed to me that I had contributed much to shorten the evenings at Paris, as all persons employed by government, having a great deal to do, and being obliged to rise very early, were under the necessity of retiring early. It caused, however, great surprise in Paris, produced quite a revolution in manners, and almost stirred up a sedition in the circles of the metropolis when the First Consul required that boots should be abandoned for stockings, and that some little care should be bestowed upon dress to appear in company."

"The Emperor dwelt," says Las Casas, "with great pleasure upon the causes of the good-breeding and amiable manners which distinguished society in our younger days. He defined particularly those points which contributed to render intimacy agreeable, such as a slight tinge of flattery on both sides, or at least an opposition seasoned with delicacy and politeness."

June 6. The Emperor was quite unwell, and remained in his room all day without taking any food. Las Casas did not see him until six o'clock in the evening. "Dr. O'Meara," said Napoleon, "hearing that I was not well, claimed me as his prey by immediately advising me to take some medicine—medicine to me, who, to the best of my recollection, never took any in the whole course of my life!"

He had been reading, during the day, *Gil Blas.* "It is full of wit," said he, "but the hero and all his companions deserved to be sent to the galleys."

He then turned over a chronological register, and stopped at the brilliant affair of Bergen-op-Zoom, commanded by General Bizanet.

"How many gallant actions," said the Emperor, "have been either forgotten in the confusion of our disasters, or overlooked in the number of our exploits! The affair of Bergen-op-Zoom is one of these. A competent garrison for that town would have been, probably, from eight to ten thousand men.

But it did not then contain more than two thousand seven hundred. An English general, favored by the darkness of the night, and by the intelligence which he had kept up with the inhabitants, had succeeded in penetrating into it at the head of four thousand eight hundred chosen men. They are in the town, the inhabitants are on their side, but nothing can triumph over French valor. A desperate engagement takes place in the streets, and nearly the whole of the English troops are killed or remain prisoners. That is, undoubtedly, a gallant action. General Bizanet is a gallant officer."

June 7. Dr. O'Meara breakfasted with Napoleon in the garden. They had a long medical argument, in which Napoleon maintained that *his* practice in case of sickness, namely, to eat nothing, drink plenty of barley-water and no wine, and ride for seven or eight leagues to promote perspiration, was far superior to the drugs of the apothecary.

Some conversation ensued upon the mode of solemnizing marriage. Dr. O'Meara observed that in England, when a Protestant and Catholic were married, it was necessary that the ceremony should be performed first by a Protestant clergyman, and afterward by a Roman Catholic priest.

"That is wrong," said the Emperor; "marriage ought to be a civil contract; and on the parties going before a magistrate, in the presence of witnesses, and entering into an engagement, they should be considered as man and wife. This is what I caused to be done in France. If they wished it, they might go to the church afterward and get a priest to repeat the ceremony; but this ought not to be considered as indispensable. It was always my maxim that those religious ceremonies should never be above the laws, take the lead or upper hand (*prendre l'essor*). I also ordained that marriages contracted by French subjects in foreign countries, when performed according to the laws of those countries, should be valid on the return of the parties to France."

June 7–8. During a long private conversation this morning, the Emperor passed in review all the horrors to which he and his companions were subjected in their present situation, and enumerated all the chances which hope suggested of better days.

After having gone over these topics, he gave the rein to his imagination, and said, "The only countries in which I can reside for the future are England and America. My inclination would lead me to America, because *there* I should be really free; and independence and repose are all I now sigh for."

Then followed an imaginary plan of life. He fancied himself with his brother Joseph, in the midst of a little France in the New World.

"Yet policy," he observed, "might decide for England. I am bound, perhaps, to remain a slave to events. I owe the sacrifice of myself to a nation which has done more for me than I have done for it in return." Then followed another imaginary plan for the future.

In the course of the subsequent conversation, the Emperor remarked, "I can not sufficiently express my surprise at the conviction which I have obtained, that several of those who surrounded me, and formed my court, believed the greatest part of the many absurdities and idle reports which had been circulated respecting me, and that they even went so far as to doubt the falsehood of the enormities with which my reputation has been stained; such as, that I wore armor in the midst of my friends; was addicted to the superstitions of forebodings and fatality; that I was subject to fits of rage or of epilepsy; that I had strangled Pichegru, and caused a poor English captain's throat to be cut."

"We could not but admit," says Las Casas, "that his reproaches were merited. All we could allege in our defense was, that many circumstances had concurred to leave those who formerly surrounded his person as much in ignorance on the subject as the bulk of the nation could be. We frequently saw him, but we never held any communication with him. Every thing remained a mystery for us. Not a voice was raised to refute, while many in secret, and some that were nearest his person, either through perverseness or with bad intentions, seemed ever busy in dealing out insinuations. As for myself, I candidly confessed that I had not formed a just idea of his disposition before I came here, although I could congratulate myself that I had certainly guessed."

"And yet," said the Emperor, in reply, "*you* have often seen me and heard me in the Council of State."

In the evening, after dinner, the conversation turned upon religion. The Emperor dwelt upon the subject at length. The following is given by Las Casas as a faithful summary of his arguments:

"Every thing," said Napoleon, "proclaims the existence of a God. *That* can not be questioned. But all our religions are evidently the work of men. Why are there so many? Why has ours not always existed? Why does it consider itself exclusively the right one? What becomes, in that case, of all the virtuous men who have gone before us? Why do these religions revile, oppose, exterminate one another? Why has this been the case ever and every where? Because men are ever men; because priests have ever and every where introduced fraud and falsehood. However, as soon as I had power, I immediately re-established religion. I made it the groundwork and foundation upon which I built. I considered it as the support of sound principles and good morality, both in doctrine and in practice. Besides, such is the restlessness of man, that his mind requires *that something* undefined and marvelous which religion offers; and it is better for him to find it there than to seek it of Cagliostro, of Mademoiselle Lenormand, or of other soothsayers and impostors."

Las Casas ventured to say, "It is possible that, in the end, you, sire, may become devout."

"I fear not," the Emperor answered, with an air of deep seriousness; "and yet it is with regret that I say it, for faith is no doubt a great source of consolation. But my incredulity does not proceed from perverseness or licentiousness of mind, but from the strength of my reason; yet no man can answer for what will happen, particularly in his last moments. At present, I certainly believe that I shall die without a confessor, and yet there is such a one," pointing to one who was present, "who will, perhaps, receive my confession. I am assuredly very far from being an Atheist, but I can not believe all that I am taught, in spite of my reason, without being false and a hypocrite. When I became emperor, and particularly after my marriage with Maria Louisa, every effort was made to induce me to go with great pomp, according to the custom of the kings of France, to take the sacrament at the church of *Nôtre Dame;* but this I positively refused to do. I did not believe in the act sufficiently to derive any benefit from it, and yet I believed too much in it to expose myself to commit a profanation."

One of the company then alluded to a certain person who had boasted, as it were, that he had never taken his first communion.

"That is very wrong," said the Emperor; "either he has not fulfilled the intention of his education, or his education had not been completed."

Then resuming the subject, he said, "To explain where I come from, what I am, and whither I go, is above my comprehension; and yet all that is. I am like the watch, that exists without possessing the consciousness of existence. However, the sentiment of religion is so consolatory that it must be considered as a gift from Heaven. What a resource would it not be for us here to possess it! What influence could men and events exercise over me, if, bearing my misfortunes as if inflicted by God, I expected to be compensated by him with happiness hereafter? What rewards have I not a right to expect, who have run a career so extraordinary, so tempestuous as mine has been, without committing a single crime; and yet how many might I not have been guilty of? I can appear before the tribunal of God, I can await his judgment without fear. He will not find my conscience stained with the thoughts of murder and poisonings, with the infliction of violent and premeditated deaths, events so common in the history of those whose lives have resembled mine. I have wished only for the glory, the power, the greatness of France; all my faculties, all my efforts, all my moments were directed to the attainment of that object. These can not be crimes; to me they appeared acts of virtue. What, then, would be my happiness, if the bright prospect of futurity presented itself to crown the last moments of my existence!"

The Emperor paused for a moment, and no one ventured to disturb his silent meditations; then continuing the subject, he said,

"How is it possible that conviction can find its way to our hearts when we hear the absurd language, and witness the acts of iniquity of the greater number of those whose business it is to preach to us? I am surrounded by priests who repeat incessantly that their kingdom is not of this world, and yet they lay hands upon every thing that they can get. The Pope is the head of that religion from Heaven, and yet he thinks only of this world. What did the present chief pontiff, who is undoubtedly a good and a holy man, not offer to be allowed to return to Rome! The surrender of the government of the Church, of the institution of bishops, was not too high a price for him to give to become once more a secular prince. Even now he is the friend of all the Protestants, who grant him every thing because they do not fear him. He is only the enemy of Catholic Austria because her territory surrounds his own.

"Nevertheless," continued Napoleon, "it can not be doubted that, as Emperor, the species of incredulity which I felt was favorable to the nations which I had to govern. How could I have favored equally sects so opposed to one another, if I had been under the influence of one of them? How could I have preserved the independence of my thoughts and actions under the control of a confessor who would have governed me by the dread of hell? What power can not a wicked man, the most stupid of mankind, thus exercise over those by whom whole nations are governed? Is it not the sceneshifter at the Opera, who, from behind the scenes, moves Hercules at his will? Who can doubt that the last years of Louis XIV. would have been very different had he been directed by another confessor? I was so deeply impressed with the truth of these opinions, that I promised to do all in my power to bring up my son in the same religious persuasion which I myself entertained."

The Emperor concluded this conversation by requesting Immanuel Las Casas to bring him the New Testament. Opening to the Savior's Sermon upon the Mount, he read it from the commencement to the close, expressing himself struck with the highest admiration at the purity, the sublimity, and the beauty of the morality which it contained. As the Emperor read these sublime passages with deep emotion, all his companions partook of his impressions. The mystery of life is so profound and impenetrable, that no man who thinks can escape moments of skepticism. Faith and unbelief will often vibrate like the pendulum. It will be seen that succeeding years of grief and meditation dispelled all doubts from the Emperor's mind, and led him to a full and living faith in Christianity—a faith no longer fluctuating.*

June 9. It was a Sabbath morning; but there was no Sabbath bell and no church at St. Helena. The Emperor alluded to the creation of the Directory, and passed in review the portraits and character of the five directors.

"Barras," said he, "of a good family of Provence, was an officer in the regiment of the Isle of France. At the Revolution he was chosen deputy to the National Convention for the department of the Var. He had no talent for oratory, and no habits of business. After the 31st of May, he was, together with Freron, appointed commissioner to the army of Italy, and to Provence, which was then the seat of civil war. On his return to Paris he threw himself into the Thermidorian party. Threatened by Robespierre, as well as Tallien and the remainder of Danton's party, they united, and brought

---

* The Abbé Gregoire says, "One morning, when Napoleon was in the very crisis of his attempt to restore the Christian religion to France, I was called to Malmaison before sunrise. At that early hour the Emperor was walking in one of the alleys of the garden, earnestly discussing the subject of the restoration of Christianity with the renowned unbeliever, Senator Volney.

"'Yes, sir,' said the Emperor to the senator, 'let men say what they will, religion is necessary for a people, and especially a belief in God. And when I say for a *people*, sir, I do not pretend to exclude myself;' and he extended his arms with a kind of enthusiastic inspiration to the sun, which, precisely at that instant, was rising above the horizon: 'for *myself*,' he continued, in tones of deepest feeling, 'in view of such a spectacle, I yield myself to be moved, to be captivated, to be convinced.' And then, turning to the abbé, he continued, 'And you, sir, what do you say to this?' I could only reply," continues the abbé, "that such a spectacle was indeed calculated to give rise to the most serious and profound speculations."

about the events of the 9th Thermidor.* At the moment of the crisis, the convention named him to march against the *commune*, which had risen in favor of Robespierre. He succeeded. This event gave him great celebrity. After the downfall of Robespierre, all the Thermidorians became the leading men of France.

"At the critical period of the 12th Vendemiaire,† it was determined, in order to get rid at once of the three commissioners to the army of the interior, to unite in the person of Barras the power of commissioner and commander of that army; but the circumstances in which he was placed were too much for him; they were above his powers. Barras had no experience in war; he had quitted the service when only a captain; he had no knowledge of military affairs. The events of Thermidor and of Vendemiaire brought him into the Directory. He did not possess the qualifications required to fill that situation, but he acted better than was expected from him by those who knew him.

"He put his establishment on a splendid footing, kept a pack of hounds, and his expenses were considerable. When he went out of the Directory, on the 18th Brumaire,‡ he had still a large fortune, and he did not attempt to conceal it. That fortune was not large enough to have contributed in the least to the derangement of the finances, but the manner in which it had been acquired, by favoring the contractors, impaired the morality of the nation.

"Barras was tall. He spoke sometimes, in moments of agitation, and his voice filled the house. His intellectual capacity did not allow him to go beyond a few sentences, but the animation with which he spoke would have produced the impression that he was a man of resolution. This, however, he was not; and he had no opinion of his own upon any part of the administration of public affairs.

"In Fructidor§ he formed with Rewbel and La Reveillere Lapaux the majority against Carnot and Barthelemy. After that event, he became to all appearance the most considerable man of the Directory, but, in reality, it was Rewbel who possessed the greatest influence. Barras always appeared in public the warm friend of Napoleon. At the time of the 30th Prairial, he had the art to conciliate to himself the preponderating party in the Assembly, and he did not share the disgrace of his colleagues.

* "9th *Thermidor*" (July 17th, 1794). This was the day of the overthrow of the Jacobins, with Robespierre at the head, and of the sanguinary revolutionary tribunal, by a new party which rose in the convention, and which was named, from the *month* of its triumph, *Thermidorians*. This revolution released Josephine from the prison and the guillotine.

† "*Vendemiaire* 12th," Oct. 4th, 1795, when Napoleon established the power of the Directory by quelling the insurgent sections.

‡ "18th *Brumaire*," Nov. 9th, 1799, when Napoleon overthrew the Directory and was elected consul.

§ *In Fructidor* (18th Fructidor, Sept. 4th, 1797). On this day occurred one of those *coups d'état* for which Paris has ever been renowned. The Republican party assembled vast masses of troops, and obtained a decisive, though bloodless victory over the Royalists. The Republicans collected the reins of power into their own hands. It was an illegal act; but legality and revolution are almost necessarily antagonistic terms. When law is powerless, any strong arm may repress violence. "The Directory," says Thiers, "by the 18th of Fructidor, prevented civil war, and substituted in its stead a stroke of policy, executed with energy, but with all the calmness and moderation possible in times of revolution."

"La Reveillere Lapaux, born at Angers, belonged to the lower ranks of the middling class of society. He was short, and his exterior was as unprepossessing as can well be imagined. In his person he was a true Æsop. He wrote tolerably well, but his intelligence was confined, and he had neither habits of business nor knowledge of mankind. He was alternately governed, according to circumstances, by Carnot or Rewbel. The *Jardin des Plantes*, and the Theophilanthropy, a new religion of which he had the folly to become the founder, occupied all his time. In other respects, he was a patriot warm and sincere, an honest man, and a citizen full of probity and of learning. He was poor when he became a member of the Directory, and poor when he left it. Nature had not qualified him to occupy any higher station than than of an inferior magistrate.

"After my return from the army of Italy, I found myself, without knowing why, the object of the particular assiduity, the marked attentions and flatteries of the Director Reveillere, who asked me one day to dine with him, strictly *en famille*, in order, he said, that we might be more at liberty to converse together. I accepted the invitation, and found, as he had promised, nobody present but the director, his wife, and his daughter, who, by-the-way, were three paragons of ugliness. After the dessert the two ladies retired, and the conversation took a serious turn. La Reveillere descanted at length upon the disadvantages of our religion, upon the necessity, however, of having one, and extolled and enumerated the advantages of the religion which he wanted to establish, the Theophilanthropy. I was beginning to find the conversation rather long and heavy, when, on a sudden, La Reveillere, rubbing his hands with an air of satisfaction, said to me, affectedly and with an arch look,

" ' How valuable the acquisition of a man like you would be to us! What advantage, what weight would be derived from your name! and how glorious that circumstance would be to you! Now what do you think of it?'

" I was far from expecting such a proposal, but replied that I did not think myself worthy of such an honor; and my principles being, when treading an obscure path, to follow the track of those who had preceded me in it, I was resolved to act, on the article of religion, as my father and mother had done. This positive answer convinced the high-priest that nothing was to be done. He did not insist, but from that moment there was an end of all his attention and flatteries to me.

"Rewbel, born in Alsace, was one of the best lawyers in the town of Colmar. He possessed that kind of intelligence which denotes a man skilled in the practice of the bar; his influence was always felt in deliberations. He was easily inspired with prejudices; did not believe much in the existence of virtue; and his patriotism was tinged with a degree of enthusiasm. It is problematical whether he did or did not amass a fortune during the time he was in the Directory. He was surrounded by contractors, it is true, but, with his turn of mind, it is possible that he only amused himself by conversing with men of activity and enterprise, and that he enjoyed their flatteries without making them pay for the complaisance he showed them. He bore a particular hatred to the Germanic system. He displayed great energy in the assemblies, both before and after the period of his being a magistrate, and was fond of a life of application and activity. He had been a member f the Constituent Assembly and of the Convention. By the latter he was appointed commissioner at Mentz, where he gave no proofs of firmness or of military talent. He contributed to the surrender of the town, which might have held out longer. He, like all lawyers, had imbibed from his profession a prejudice against the army.

"Carnot, born in Burgundy, had entered very young the corps of engineers, and showed himself an advocate of the system of Montalembert. He was considered by his companions an eccentric character, and was already a knight of the Order of St. Louis when the Revolution began, the principles of which he warmly espoused. He became a member of the Convention, and was one of the Committee of Public Safety with Robespierre, Barrère, Couthon, St. Juste, Billaud Varennes, and Collot d'Herbois, &c. He showed himself particularly inveterate against the nobility, and found himself, in consequence, frequently engaged in quarrels with Robespierre, who, toward the close of his life, had taken a great many nobles under his protection.

"Carnot was laborious, sincere on every occasion, but unaccustomed to intrigue, and easily deceived. He was attached to Jourdan as commissioner from the Convention at the time Jourdan was employed in relieving the town of Mentz, which was besieged, and he rendered some services on the occasion. At the Committee of Public Safety he directed the operations of the war, and was found useful, but he had neither experience nor practice in the affairs of war. He showed, on every occasion, great strength of mind.

"After the events of Thermidor, when the Convention caused all the members of the Committee of Public Safety to be arrested with the exception of himself, Carnot insisted upon sharing their fate. This conduct was the more noble, inasmuch as public opinion had pronounced itself violently against the committee. He was named member of the Directory after Vendemiaire, but after the 9th Thermidor his mind was deeply affected by the reproaches of public opinion, which accused the committee of all the blood which had flowed on the scaffold. He felt the necessity of gaining esteem; and believing that he took the lead, he suffered himself to be led by some of those who directed the party from abroad. His merit was then extolled to the skies, but he did not deserve the praises of the enemies of France. He found himself placed in a critical situation, and fell in Fructidor.

"After the 18th Brumaire, Carnot was recalled by the First Consul, and placed in the department of war. He had several quarrels with the minister of the finances, and Dufresnes, the director of the treasury, in which, it is but fair to say, that he was always in the wrong. At last he left the department, persuaded that it could no longer go on for want of money.

"When a member of the Tribunate, he spoke and voted against the establishment of the Empire; but his conduct, open and manly, gave no uneasiness to the administration. At a later period he was appointed chief inspector of reviews, and received from the Emperor, on his retiring from the service, a pension of four thousand dollars. As long as things went on prosperously, the Emperor heard nothing of him; but after the campaign of Russia, at the time of the disasters of France, Carnot asked to be employed. He was appointed to command the town of Antwerp, and he behaved well at his post. On his return in 1815, the Emperor, after a little hesitation, appointed him to be minister of the interior, and had no cause to repent of having done so. He found him faithful, laborious, full of probity, and always sincere. In the month of June, Carnot was named one of the commission of the provisional government, but, being unfit for the place, he was duped.

"Le Tourneur de la Manche was born in Normandy. He had been an officer of engineers before the Revolution. It is difficult to explain how he came to be appointed to the Directory. It can only be from one of those unaccountable caprices of which large assemblies so often give an example. He was a man of narrow capacity, little learning, and of a weak mind. There were in the Convention five hundred deputies that were better qualified for the situation. He was, however, a man of strict probity, and left the Directory without any fortune.

"Le Tourneur made himself the talk and the laughing-stock of Paris. It was said that he came from his department to take possession at the Directory in a cart, with his housekeeper, his kitchen utensils, and his poultry. The wags of the capital marked him, and he was overwhelmed with ridicule. He was made, for instance, to return from the *Jardin des Plantes*, where he had run immediately on his arrival in Paris, and to give an account of the rare things he had found there; and on being asked whether he had seen Lacepede,* to express his surprise at having passed it unobserved, affirming that the camelopard was the only animal that had been pointed out to him.

"The Directory was hardly established before it began to lower itself in the public estimation by caprices, bad morals, and false measures. The faults and absurdities which it committed daily completed its discredit, and it was lost in reputation almost at the very moment of its formation. Intoxicated with their elevation, the Directors thought it became them to adopt a certain air, and sought to acquire the appearance and manners of *bon ton*. In order the better to succeed, they formed each to himself a little court, where they received and welcomed the higher classes, hitherto in disgrace, and who were naturally their enemies, and from which they excluded the greatest part of their old acquaintances and former companions as thenceforward too vulgar. All those who, during the Revolution, had shown more energy than the members of the Directory, or who had trodden in the same path with them, became odious to them, and were immediately removed; and the Directory thus rendered itself ridiculous to one party, and alienated from itself the affections of the other. These five little courts exacted a greater degree of servility in proportion as they were inferior and ridiculous; but numbers of men were found who could not bring themselves to bend and submit to formalities which the recollection of recent circumstances, the nature of the government, and the character of the governors rendered inadmissible.

* A distinguished professor of natural history.

"However, all the Directory could do to gain over the saloons of Paris proved of no avail. It did not succeed in acquiring any influence over them, and the Bourbon party was gaining ground. The Directory no sooner perceived this than they hastily retraced their steps; but it was too late to recover the good-will of the Republicans, whom they had estranged from themselves by their conduct. This led to a system of wavering which looked like caprice; no course was laid down to steer by, no object was kept in view, no unity prevailed. The reign of terror and of royalty were equally objected to; but, in the mean time, the road which was to lead to the goal was left untried. The Directory thought to put an end to this state of uncertainty, and avoid these perpetual waverings, by striking at one blow the two extreme parties, whether they had deserved it or not. If, therefore, a Royalist who had conspired or disturbed the public tranquillity was arrested by their orders, they caused a Republican, innocent or guilty, to be arrested at the same moment. This system was nicknamed *The Political See-saw*, but the injustice and fraud which characterized it entirely discredited the government. Every heart was closed. The government became one of lead. Every true and generous feeling was against the Directory.

"Men of business, jobbers, and intriguers, by possessing themselves of the springs of government, acquired the greatest influence. All places were given to worthless individuals, to *protegés*, or to relations; corruption crept into every branch of the administration. This was soon perceived, and those who had it in their power to waste the public money could act without fear. The foreign relations, the armies, the finances, the department of the interior, all felt the pernicious effects of a system so defective. This state of things soon gathered a storm on the political horizon, and led, by rapid strides, to the crisis of Fructidor.

"At that period the measures of the Directory were weak, capricious, and uncertain. Emigrants returned to France, and newspapers, paid by foreigners, dared openly to stigmatize the most deserving of our patriots. The fury of the enemies of our national glory exasperated the soldiers of the army of Italy, which declared itself loudly against them, while the councils, in their turn, acting the parts of real counter-revolutionists, spoke of nothing but priests, bells, and emigrants. All the officers of the army who had distinguished themselves more or less in the departments, in the battalions of volunteers, or even in the regiments of the line, feeling themselves thus attacked in their dearest interests, inflamed more and more the anger of their soldiers. The minds of all parties were in a state of effervescence. In a moment of such violent agitation, what measures could the general of the army of Italy adopt? He had the choice of three.

"1. To side with the preponderating party in the councils. But it was too late. The army had pronounced itself; and the leaders of that party, the orators of the council, by attacking incessantly both the general and his army, had not left him the possibility of adopting that resolution.

"2. To embrace the party of the Directory and of the Republic. That was the plainest course, that which duty pointed out, which the army inclined to, and that in which he was already engaged; for all the writers who had remained faithful to the Revolution had declared themselves, of their own accord, the ardent defenders and warm advocates of the army and its commanders.

"3. To overpower both factions by stepping forward boldly, and appearing openly in the contest as regulator of the republic. But, notwithstanding the strength which Napoleon felt he derived from the support of the army, although his character was highly esteemed in France, he did not think that the spirit of the times and public opinion were such as to allow him to take so daring a step; and besides, if this third measure had been that to which he secretly inclined, he could not have adopted it immediately, and without having previously sided with one of the two parties which appeared at that moment in the political lists. It was absolutely necessary, even in order to form a third party, to side first either with the councils or with the Directory.

"Thus, of the three measures to be adopted, the third, in its execution, merged into the two first, and he was entirely debarred from adopting the first of these two by the new formation of the councils, and by the attacks already made upon him by them.

"These considerations and conclusions," the Emperor continued, "were the natural result of a deep meditation upon the then existing state of affairs in France. The general had, therefore, nothing to do but to let events take their course, and second the impulse of his troops; and this view of the subject produced the proclamation to the army of Italy, and the far-famed order of the day of its general.

"'Soldiers!' he said, 'I know that your hearts are full of grief at the calamities of our country; but if it were possible that foreign armies should triumph, we would fly from the summit of the Alps with the rapidity of the eagle to defend once more that cause which has already cost us so much blood!'

"These words decided the question. The soldiers, in ecstasy, were for marching at once upon Paris. The noise of the event spread immediately to the capital, and produced a most powerful sensation. The Directory, which every body considered as lost, which the moment before was tottering alone and abandoned, found itself at once supported by public opinion. It immediately assumed the attitude and followed the course of a triumphant party, and defeated all its enemies.

"The general of the army of Italy had sent Augereau to convey to the Directory his proclamation to his soldiers, because he was a Parisian, and strongly pronounced in favor of the prevailing notions of the day.

"Nevertheless, the politicians of the day made the following surmises: 'What would Napoleon have done if the councils had triumphed—if that faction, instead of being overthrown, had, on the contrary, overthrown the Directory?' In that case, it appears that he was determined to march upon Lyons and Mirbel with fifteen thousand men, where he would have been joined by all the Republicans of Burgundy. The victorious council would not have been more than three or four days without coming to some violent rupture and division, for it is known that, if numbers of these councils were unanimous in their proceedings against the Directory, they were far from being so as to the farther course they meant to pursue. The leaders, such as Pichegru, Imbert Colomès, and others sold to foreign powers, exerted all their influence to restore royalty and bring about a counter-revolution, while Carnot and others sought to produce results quite opposite to these. France would therefore have become immediately a prey to confusion and anarchy, and in that case, all factions would have seen with satisfaction Napoleon appear as a rallying-point, an anchor of safety, capable of saving them, at the same time, from the terrors of royalty and from the terrors of demagogues. Napoleon would then naturally have repaired to Paris, and found himself at the head of affairs by the unanimous wish and consent of all parties. The majority of the councils was strong and positive, it is true, but it was only against the directors. It would divide *ad infinitum* as soon as they were overturned.

"The choice of three new directors having openly exposed the true intention of the measures of the counter-revolution, the greatest number of the citizens, in their alarm, were ready to fly to Napoleon with the national oriflamme* unfurled; for the true counter-revolutionists were, after all, few in number, and their pretensions were too ridiculous and absurd. Every thing would have given way before Napoleon.

"Had they called him Cæsar or Cromwell, still he proceeded supported by a religion and a party whose ideas were settled and popular. He was master of his soldiers, the coffers of the army were full, and he was in possession of every other means calculated to insure their constancy and their fidelity. If the question were now to be decided whether Napoleon, in the secret of his own mind, would or would not have wished affairs to take this turn, we should give our opinion in the affirmative; and we are led to believe, from the following fact, that his wishes and his hopes were in favor of the triumph of the majority of the councils. At the moment of the crisis between the two factions, a secret decree, signed by the three members composing the party of the Directory, asked him for three millions of francs to resist the attack of the councils; but Napoleon, under various pretenses, did not send them, although it would have been easy for him to do so. Yet it was well known that his disposition did not allow him to hesitate in money matters.

"Therefore," continued the Emperor, "when the struggle was over, and the Directory took pleasure in acknowledging openly that it owed its existence to Napoleon, it still entertained some vague suspicions that Napoleon had only espoused its party in the hope of seeing it overthrown and of taking its place. Be that as it may, after the 18th Fructidor, the enthusiasm of the army was at its height, and the triumph of Napoleon complete. But the Directory, notwithstanding its apparent gratitude, surrounded Napoleon from that moment with numerous agents, who watched over his motions, and endeavored to penetrate the secrets of his thoughts."

* The oriflamme was a flag which was carried before the kings of France.

CHAPTER XVI.
1816, June. Continued.

English Diplomacy—Lord Whitworth—Chatham—Castlereagh—Cornwallis—Fox—Lacretelle's History of the Convention—Puns—Public Characters—Bailli—La Fayette—Monge—Grégoire—St. Domingo—Dictations on the Convention.

June 10. The course of conversation led the Emperor to say, "Nothing is so dangerous and so treacherous as official conversations with diplomatic agents of Great Britain. The English ministers never represent an affair as from their nation to another, but as from themselves to their own nation. They care little what their adversaries have said or say. They boldly put forth what their diplomatic agents have said, or what they make them say, on the grounds that, those agents having a public and acknowledged character, faith must be placed in their reports. It is in pursuance of this principle that the English ministers published at the time, under the name of Lord Whitworth, a long conversation between me and Whitworth, the account of which was entirely false.

"This proved for me a lesson which altered my method forever. From this moment I never treated officially of political matters but through the intervention of my minister for foreign affairs. He, at any rate, could give a positive and formal denial, which the sovereign could not do. It is utterly false that any thing occurred in the course of our personal interview which was not in conformity with the common rules of decorum. Lord Whitworth himself, after our conference, being in company with other embassadors, expressed himself perfectly satisfied, and added that he had no doubt all things would be satisfactorily settled. But what was the surprise of those same embassadors when they read, a short time after, in the English newspapers, the report of Lord Whitworth, in which he charged me with having behaved in the interview with unbecoming violence! We had some warm friends among these embassadors, and some of them went so far as to express their surprise to the English diplomatist, observing to him that his report was very different from what he had said to them immediately after the conference. Lord Whitworth made the best excuse he could, but persisted in maintaining the assertions of the official document.

"The fact is," continued the Emperor, "that every political agent of Great Britain is in the habit of making two reports on the same subject—one public and false, for the ministerial archives, the other confidential and true, for the ministers themselves, and for them alone; and when the responsibility of ministers is at stake, they produce the first of these documents, which, although false, answers every purpose, and serves to exonerate them. And thus it is that the best institutions become vicious when they are no longer founded on morality, and when their agents are only actuated by selfishness.

pride, and insolence. Absolute power has no need of disguise; it is silent. Responsible governments, when obliged to speak, have recourse to artifice, and lie with effrontery.

"It is, however, a circumstance worthy of remark, that in my great struggle with England, the government of that country has constantly contrived to attach so much odium to my person and actions, and that they have so impudently exclaimed against my despotism, my selfishness, my ambition, and my perfidy, when they alone were guilty of all they dared to lay to my charge. A very strong prejudice must have been excited against me. I must have been, indeed, very much to be feared, since people could suffer themselves to be thus deceived. I can understand it from kings and cabinets: their existence was at stake; but from the people!!

"The British ministers spoke incessantly of my duplicity; but could any thing be compared to their Machiavelism, their selfishness, during the existence of disorders and convulsions which were kept alive by them?

"They sacrificed unfortunate Austria in 1805 merely to escape the invasion with which I threatened them.

"They sacrificed her again in 1809, to be more at liberty to act in the Peninsula.

"They sacrificed Prussia in 1816, in hopes of recovering Hanover.

"They did not assist Russia in 1807, because they preferred to go and seize upon distant colonies, and because they were attempting to take possession of Egypt.

"They gave to the world the infamous spectacle of bombarding Copenhagen in full peace, and lying in ambush to steal the Danish fleet. They had already, once before, exhibited a similar spectacle, by seizing, like highway robbers, also in full peace, four Spanish frigates laden with rich treasures.

"Lastly, during the war in the Spanish Peninsula, where they endeavored to prolong the existence of anarchy and confusion, their principal care was, to traffic with the wants and the blood of the Spanish nation, by obliging it to purchase their services and their supplies at the expense of gold and concessions.

"While all Europe, through their intrigues and their subsidies, was bathed in blood, they were only intent upon providing for their own safety, gaining advantages for their trade, and obtaining the sovereignty of the sea and the monopoly of the world. As for myself, I had never done any thing of the kind; and, until the unfortunate business with Spain, which, after all, is not to be compared with the affair of Copenhagen, I can say that my morality is unimpeachable. My actions had, perhaps, been dictatorial and peremptory, but never disgraced by perfidy. Who can be surprised, after all this, if in 1814, although England had really been the deliverer of Europe, not a single Englishman could show himself on the Continent without meeting, at every step, with maledictions, hatred, and execrations? Who can ask how this happened? Every tree bears its own fruit. We reap only what we have sown. And such was necessarily the infallible result of the misdeeds of the

English government, the tyranny and the insolence of the ministers in London, and of their agents all over the globe.

"For the last fifty years the administrations of Great Britain have gradually declined in consideration and in public estimation. Formerly they were disputed by great national parties, characterized by grand and distinct systems; but now we see only the bickerings of one and the same oligarchy, having constantly the same object in view, and whose discordant members adjust their differences by compromise and concessions. They have turned the cabinet of St. James into a ship.

"The policy of Lord Chatham was marked by acts of injustice, no doubt, but at least he proclaimed them with boldness and energy. They had a certain air of grandeur. Pitt introduced into the cabinet a system of hypocrisy and dissimulation. Lord Castlereagh, the self-styled heir of Pitt, has brought into it the extreme of every kind of turpitude and immorality. Chatham gloried in being a merchant. Lord Castlereagh, to the serious injury of his nation, has indulged himself in the satisfaction of acting the fine gentleman. He has sacrificed his country to fraternize with the great people of the Continent, and from that moment has united in his person the vices of the saloon with the cupidity of the counting-house, the duplicity and obsequiousness of the courtier with the haughtiness and insolence of the upstart. The poor English Constitution is in imminent danger. What a difference between such men and the Foxes, Sheridans, and Greys! those great geniuses—those noble characters of the opposition, who have been the objects of the ridicule of a victorious oligarchy!

"Lord Cornwallis is the first Englishman that gave me, in good earnest, a favorable opinion of his nation; after him, Fox; and I might add to these, if it were necessary, our present admiral (Malcolm).

"Cornwallis was, in every sense of the word, a worthy, good, and honest man. At the time of the treaty of Amiens, the terms having been agreed upon, he had promised to sign the next day at a certain hour. Something of consequence detained him at home, but he pledged his word. The evening of that same day, a courier arrived from London proscribing certain articles of the treaty; but he answered that he had signed, and immediately came and actually signed. We understood each other perfectly well. I had placed a regiment at his disposal, and he took pleasure in seeing its maneuvers. I have preserved an agreeable recollection of him in every respect, and it is certain that a request from him would have had more weight with me, perhaps, than one from a crowned head. His family appears to have guessed this to be the case. Some requests have been made to me in its name, which have all been granted.

"Fox came to France immediately after the peace of Amiens. He was employed in writing a history of the Stuarts, and asked my permission to search our diplomatical archives. I gave orders that every thing should be placed at his disposal. I received him often. Fame had informed me of his talents, and I soon found that he possessed a noble character, a good heart, liberal, generous, and enlightened views. I considered him an ornament to mankind, and was very much attached to him. We often conversed together upon various topics without the least prejudice. When I wished to engage in a little controversy, I turned the conversation upon the subject of the *machine infernale*, and told him that his ministers had attempted to murder me. He would then oppose my opinion with warmth, and invariably ended by saying, in his bad French, 'First Consul, pray take that out of your head.' But he was not convinced of the truth of the cause he undertook to advocate, and there is every reason to believe he argued more in defense of his country than of the morality of its ministers."

The Emperor closed the conversation by saying,

"Half a dozen such men as Fox and Cornwallis would be sufficient to establish the moral character of a nation. With such men I should always have agreed. We should soon have settled our differences, and not only France would have been at peace with a nation at bottom most worthy of esteem, but we should have done great things together."

June 11. It was a tempestuous day of wind and rain. The Emperor read the History of the Convention by Lacretelle.

"It is," he said, "certainly not ill written, but it is ill digested, and makes no impression on the memory. The whole is a smooth surface, without a single asperity to arrest attention. The author did not thoroughly examine his subject. He does not do justice to many celebrated characters. He does not give an adequate coloring to the crimes of many others."

The torrents of rain which were falling prevented the Emperor from walking out. In the afternoon, he paced the floor of the dining-room for a long time, in conversation with Las Casas. The latter said to the Emperor,

"I have been informed that there are four thousand oxen in the island. The annual consumption consists of five hundred. Of this number, one hundred and fifty are appropriated to us, fifty to the colony, and three hundred to the shipping. The subsistence and consumption of these oxen constitute a great portion of the public interest in the island. A single beast can not be killed without a previous order of the governor. The owner of one of the houses or huts of the island, speaking on this subject, said,

"'It is reported that you complain up at Longwood, and consider yourselves unhappy, but we are at a loss to make it out, for it is said that you have beef every day, while we can not have it but three or four times a year, and even then we pay for it fifteen or twenty pence a pound.'"

"The Emperor laughed heartily at the story, and observed, 'You ought to have assured him that it cost *us* several *crowns*.'"

Las Casas remarks, "This was the only pun I had till then heard from the Emperor's mouth. But the person to whom I made the remark said he had heard of his having made a similar one, and on the same subject, in the Isle of Elba. A mason, employed in some buildings which were to be constructed by the Emperor's order, had fallen and hurt himself. The Emperor, wishing to encourage him, said,

"'You will soon be well again. I have had a much worse fall than yours. But look at me; I am on my legs and in good health.'"

R

June 12. For three days the rain had fallen in torrents. To-day a gleam of sunshine induced the Emperor to take an airing in his carriage. He had just finished reading the History of the Constituent Assembly by Rabaut de St. Etienne. He expressed very nearly the same opinion of this writer as of Lacretelle. He then spoke of several public characters.

"Bailli," said he, "was far from being a bad man, but was by no means a skillful politician. La Fayette was another such man, and not at all formed for the eminent character which he wished to represent. His political good-nature was such as to render him the constant dupe of men and things. All was lost on my return from Waterloo by his insurrection of the Chambers. Who could have persuaded him that I had arrived merely for the purpose of dissolving them—I, whose only safety was centred in them?"

"It was, however, sire," said Las Casas, "the same La Fayette who, treating afterward with the Allies, was filled with indignation at their proposal of delivering up your majesty, and eagerly asked if it were to the prisoner of Olmutz they dared to address themselves."

"But, sir," replied the Emperor, "you run from one subject to another, or, rather, you concur with instead of opposing my opinion. I have not attacked the sentiments or intentions of M. de La Fayette; I have only complained of their fatal results."

In continuation of the conversation, the Emperor remarked,

"Nothing is more common than to find men of that epoch quite the reverse in character of that which their words and actions seemed to establish. *Monges,* for instance, might be considered a terrible man. When war was resolved upon, he declared from the tribune of the Jacobins that he would give his two daughters in marriage to the two first soldiers who might be wounded by the enemy. This he was at liberty to do, in the strict sense of the gift, as far as it respected himself; but he maintained that others should be compelled to follow his example, and that all the nobility should be put to death. Yet Monges was one of the mildest and weakest men living, and would not allow a chicken to be killed if he were obliged to do it himself, or to see it done. This furious Republican, as he believed himself, cherished, however, a kind of worship for me, which he pushed to adoration.

"*Grégoire,* whose animosity to the clergy, whom he wished to bring back to their original simplicity, was so great that he might have passed for a champion of irreligion, may be mentioned as another instance; yet Grégoire, when the Revolutionists were denying their God and abolishing the priesthood, was very nearly being massacred in mounting the tribune for the purpose of boldly declaring his religious sentiments, and protesting that he would die a priest. At the very moment when the work of destruction was going on in all the churches against the altars, Grégoire erected one in his own apartment, and said mass there every day. This man's lot, however, is decidedly cast. If he be driven from France, he must take refuge in St. Domingo. The friend, the advocate, the eulogist of the negroes, will be a god or a saint among them."

The subject of St. Domingo was next introduced. Las Casas had been familiar with the colony in its most flourishing state. The Emperor put many questions to him, and, after his inquiries were over, observed, "After the Restoration, the French government had sent out emissaries and proposals which were laughed at by the negroes. As to myself, on my return from the Isle of Elba I would have settled all differences with them. I would have recognized their independence, contented myself with some factories like those on the coast of Africa, endeavored to draw them closer to the mother country, and to establish a kind of family commerce with them, which might, in my opinion, have been easily accomplished.

"I have to reproach myself with the attempt which was made upon the colony during the consulship. The design of reducing it by force was a great error. I ought to have been satisfied with governing it through the medium of Toussaint. Peace with England was not sufficiently consolidated, and the territorial wealth I should have acquired by its reduction would but have served to enrich our enemies. I have the greater reason to reproach myself with the attempt, because I had foreseen its failure, and it was executed against my inclination. I yielded solely to the opinion of the Council of State and of my ministers, hurried along as they were by the clamors of the colonists, who formed a considerable party at Paris, and were, besides, nearly all Royalists, or in the pay of the English faction.

"Toussaint was not a man destitute of merit, but he certainly was not so highly gifted as was attempted in his time to describe him. His character, besides, was ill calculated to inspire real confidence. He had given us serious causes of complaint. It would have been necessary to have been always distrustful of his sincerity. He was chiefly guided by an officer of engineers. That officer had come to France before Leclerc's expedition, and conferences were, for a long time, held with him. He exerted himself very much to prevent the attempt, and described with real precision all its difficulties, without pretending, however, that it was impossible.

"The Bourbons may possibly succeed in reducing St. Domingo by force, but it is not the result of arms which it is necessary to calculate here; it is rather the result of commerce and of grand political views. Three or four hundred millions of capital swept away from France to a remote country, an indefinite period for reaping the fruits of such a sacrifice, the very great certainty of seeing them engrossed by the English, or swallowed up by Revolution—these are the points for consideration. The colonial system which we have witnessed is closed for us, as well as the whole Continent of Europe. We must give it up, and henceforth confine ourselves to the free navigation of the seas, and the complete liberty of universal barter."

"The History of the Convention," says Las Casas, "of which Napoleon had already expressed his disapprobation, again presented itself to his thoughts. He was far from being satisfied with Lacretelle. 'Sentences in abundance,' he repeated, 'and but little coloring; no depth. He is an academician, but in no respect a historian.' He made me call my son, and dictated the following note, of which I give a literal copy, however imperfect it may be, for he never read it a second time."

"The Convention.

" The Convention, called together by a law of the Legislative Assembly to form a new Constitution for France, decreed the Republic; not that the most enlightened did not think the republican system incompatible with the existing state of manners in France, but because the monarchy could not be continued without placing the Duke of Orleans on the throne, which would have alienated a great part of the nation.

" An executive power, consisting of five ministers, was established by the Convention for conducting the affairs of the Republic. Two parties contended for the ascendency in the National Convention—that of the *Girondists*,* composed of men who had influenced the Legislative Assembly, and that of the *Mountain*,† formed by the commune of Paris, which had directed the atrocities of the 10th of August and of the 2d of September, and commanded the population of the capital.

" Vergniaud, Brissot, Condorcet, Gaudet, and Roland were the leaders of the Girondists. Danton, Robespierre, Marat, Collot d'Herbois, and Billaud Varennes headed the Mountain. These two parties were alike indebted for their rise to the principles of the Revolution. Their conductors sprang out of the popular societies which they had successively rendered subservient to their views.

"The party of the Girondists was more powerful in talents, and was eminently popular in the great provincial towns, particularly at Bordeaux, Montpellier, Marseilles, Caen, and Lyons. The party of the Mountain possessed more energy and enthusiasm, and was no less popular in the capital and among the clubs of the departments.

"The Girondist party, which in the Legislative Assembly had been the most ardent for the Revolution, became, in the Convention, the most moderate, because it had to contend there with a faction much more violent than itself, which had not found its way into the Assembly. The Girondists called their adversaries the faction of September, and constantly reproached them with the horrible massacre of which they were guilty. They accused them of being hostile to every kind of national assembly, and of endeavoring to transfer the government of France to the commune of Paris. But by these means the Girondists only excited against themselves the Jacobins of all the departments. On the other hand, the Mountain stigmatized the Girondists by the name of Federalists, and charged them with the design of establishing a federative system in France similar to that of Switzerland. They also accused them of endeavoring to stir up the provinces against the capital, and thus held them up to the detestation of the people of Paris, which could maintain its splendor only by the union and unity of the whole of the territory. When the Girondists inveighed against the Mountain for the massacres of

* The Girondists were moderate Republicans. The party was so called because the leaders were deputies from the department of the Gironde.
† The Jacobin party was often called the Mountain, or the Mountaineers, from the elevated seats which they occupied in the Convention.

the 2d of September, the latter reproached the former with having, during the Legislative Assembly, rashly and without cause, declared war against all Europe.

"The Girondists at first appeared to have the upper hand in the Convention, and they directed that Marat should be brought to trial, and that proceedings should be instituted against the assassins of September. But Marat, supported by the Jacobins, was acquitted by the Revolutionary Tribunal, and returned in triumph to the bosom of the Assembly.

"The trial of the king had been another apple of discord. The two parties seemed to proceed in unison, and voted, it is true, for his death; but the greater part of the Girondists also voted for an appeal to the people. And here it is difficult to account for their conduct during that crisis. If they wished to save the king, they were at liberty to do so; they had only to vote for deportation, exile, or the adjournment of the question; but to sentence him to death, and make his fate depend upon the will of the people, was in the highest degree absurd and impolitic. They seemed to be desirous that, after the extinction of the monarchy, France should be torn to pieces by civil war.

"The general opinion since the commencement of the Revolution, that the most audacious and unreasonable faction would always predominate, was from that moment verified. The Girondists, however, maintained the conflict with courage, and very often had majorities in the Assembly during all the months of March, April, and May; but the Mountain had recourse, in these circumstances, to an expedient which it had constantly employed. On the 31st of May the fate of the Girondists was decided by an insurrection of the sections of Paris. Twenty-seven were arrested, brought before the Revolutionary Tribunal, and sentenced to death. Seventy-three were thrown into prison, and from that period the triumphant Mountain had no obstacle to surmount in the Convention. Several Girondist deputies took refuge, however, at Caen, and there raised the standard of insurrection. Lyons, Marseilles, Bordeaux, Montpellier, and several towns of Brittany, embraced the cause of this party, and also took up arms against the Convention.

"All these efforts were of no avail against the capital, and the Mountain remained in tranquil possession of the national tribune. A circumstance altogether singular contributed to confirm the preponderance of Paris; it was the assignats,[*] then the only resource for supplying the treasury. Not a single tax was then paid. The provinces learned with considerable emotion the events of the 31st of May, and the death of the most celebrated characters of the Girondist party. The armies were not agitated by these results. They took no share in the insurrection of some of the provinces, and remained all attached to the Convention and to the dominant party at Paris.

"When the partial insurrection of certain towns in favor of the Girondists was known, all the armies had already taken the oath, and testified their adhesion to the Mountain; besides, in the eyes of Frenchmen, Paris was France.

[*] "The assignats," paper money issued by the Convention. A forced circulation was given to this paper, but it eventually became of no value.

The 31st of May deprived France of men of great talents, zealously attached to liberty and the principles of the Revolution. The catastrophe might afflict the well disposed, but could not surprise them. It was impossible for an assembly, which had extricated France from the critical situation to which she was reduced, to carry on public business with two parties so inveterately and irreconcilably opposed. It was necessary for the safety of the republic that one should extinguish the other, and there can be no doubt that, had the Girondists obtained the victory, they would have consigned their adversaries to the scaffold."

The Emperor, who had dictated, in his usual way, from memory alone, without any research, whether he was little satisfied with the task he had executed, or for some other reason, stopped here, for the purpose, as he said, of recommencing a new dictation on the same subject.

CHAPTER XVII.
1816, June. Continued.

The War and Royal Family of Spain—Errors—Ferdinand at Valençay—Historical Sketch of the Events—The Moniteurs—The Liberty of the Press—The Conference at Tilsit—Anecdotes of the Emperor of Russia—Of the King and Queen of Prussia—Anecdote of Savary—The Emperor's Magnanimity.

June 14. The Emperor had been quite ill all night, and was unable to leave his room. He spent the day alone, and breakfasted and dined in his chamber. After dinner, in the evening, he sent for Las Casas.

"The Emperor began the conversation," says Las Casas, "of which the constant subject was the Spanish war. It has been seen, in the notice which I have already taken of it, that the Emperor took upon himself the whole blame of the measure. I wish to avoid repetitions as much as possible, and shall therefore allude to those topics only which appeared new to me."

"The old king and queen," said the Emperor, "at the

THE EMPEROR AT BREAKFAST

moment of the event, were the objects of the hatred and contempt of their subjects. The Prince of Asturias conspired against them, forced them to abdicate, and at once united in his own person the love and hopes of the nation. That nation was, however, ripe for great changes, and demanded them with energy. I enjoyed vast popularity in the country, and it was in that state of things that all these personages met at Bayonne, the old king calling upon me for vengeance against his son, and the young prince soliciting my protection against his father, and imploring a wife at my hands. I resolved to convert this singular occasion to my advantage, with the view of freeing myself from that branch of the Bourbons, of continuing in my own dynasty the family system of Louis XIV., and of binding Spain to the destinies of France. Ferdinand was sent to Valençay, the old king to Marseilles, as he wished, and my brother Joseph went to reign at Madrid with a liberal Constitution, adopted by a junta of the Spanish nation, which had come to receive it at Bayonne.

"It seems to me," continued he, "that Europe, and even France, has never had a just idea of Ferdinand's situation at Valençay. There is a strange misunderstanding in the world with respect to the treatment he experienced, and still more so with respect to his wishes and personal opinions as to that situation. The fact is, that he was scarcely guarded at Valençay, and that he did not wish to escape. If any plots were contrived to favor his evasion, he was the first to make them known. An Irishman (Baron de Colli) gained access to his person, and offered, in the name of George III., to carry him off; but Ferdinand, far from embracing the offer, instantly communicated it to the proper authority.

"His applications to me for a wife at my hands were incessant. He spontaneously wrote to me letters of congratulation upon every event that occurred in my favor. He had addressed proclamations to the Spaniards recommending their submission; he had recognized Joseph. All these were circumstances which might, indeed, have been considered as forced upon him; but he requested from me the insignia of his grand order; he tendered to me the services of his brother, Don Carlos, to take the command of the Spanish regiments which were marching to Russia, proceedings to which he was in no respect obliged. To sum up all, he earnestly solicited my permission to visit my court at Paris; and if I did not lend myself to a spectacle which would have astonished Europe by displaying the full consolidation of my power, it was because the important circumstances which called me abroad, and my frequent absence from the capital, deprived me of the proper opportunity.

"Toward the beginning of a new year, at one of the levees, I happened to be next to the chamberlain, Count d'Arberg, who had been doing duty at Valençay near the persons of the princes of Spain. When I approached, I inquired if these princes conducted themselves with propriety, and added, 'You have brought me a very pretty letter; but, between ourselves, it was you that wrote it for them.' D'Arberg assured me that he was altogether unacquainted even with the nature of its contents. 'Well,' I added, 'a son could not write more cordially to his father.'

"When our situation in Spain," continued the Emperor, "turned out dangerous, I more than once proposed to Ferdinand to return and reign over his people; that we should openly carry on war against each other, and that the contest should be decided by the fate of arms.

"'No,' answered the prince, who seems to have been well advised, and never deviated from that way of thinking. 'My country is agitated by political disturbances. I should but multiply its embarrassments. I might become their victim, and lose my head upon the scaffold. I remain. But if you will choose a wife for me—if you will grant me your protection and the support of your arms, I shall set out, and prove a faithful ally.'

"At a later period, during our disasters, and toward the end of 1813, I yielded to that proposal, and Ferdinand's marriage with Joseph's eldest daughter was decided. But circumstances were then no longer the same, and Ferdinand was desirous that the marriage should be deferred.

"'You can no longer,' he observed, 'support me with your arms, and I ought not to make my wife a title of exclusion in the eyes of my people.' He left me," continued the Emperor, "as it seemed, with every intention of good faith, for he remained faithful to the principles which he avowed on his departure until the events of Fontainebleau. Had the affairs of 1814 turned out differently, I should unquestionably have accomplished his marriage with Joseph's daughter.

"The impolicy of my conduct was irrevocably decided by the results; but, independently of that kind of proof, depending upon consequences, I have to reproach myself with serious faults in the execution of my plans. One of the greatest was that of treating the dethronement of the dynasty of the Bourbons as a matter of importance, and of maintaining, as the basis of my system for a new sovereign, precisely the man who, by his qualities and character, was certain to produce its failure.

"During the assembly at Bayonne, Ferdinand's former preceptor and his principal counselor (Escoiquiz), at once perceiving the vast projects I entertained, said to me,

"'You wish to create for yourself a kind of Herculean labor when you have but child's play in hand. You wish to rid yourself of the Bourbons of Spain. Why should you be apprehensive of them? They have ceased to exist. They are no longer French. You have nothing to fear from them. They are altogether aliens with respect to your nation and your manners. You have here Madam de Montmorency, and some *new* ladies of your court. The Spanish princes are not more acquainted with the one than with the other, and view them all with equal indifference.'

"I unfortunately formed a different resolution. I took the liberty of telling him I had been assured by some Spaniards that, if the national pride had been respected, and the Spanish junta held at Madrid instead of Bayonne, or even if Charles IV. had been sent off and Ferdinand retained, the revolution would have been popular, and affairs would have taken another turn. I entertained no doubt of this; the enterprise was imprudently undertaken, and many circumstances might have been better conducted.

"Charles IV.," continued he, "was, however, too stale for the Spaniards; Ferdinand should have been considered in the same light. The plan most worthy of me, and the best suited to my project, would have been a kind of mediation, like that of Switzerland. I ought to have given a liberal Constitution to the Spanish nation, and charged Ferdinand with its execution. If he acted with good faith, Spain must have prospered and harmonized with our new manners; the great object would have been obtained, and France would have acquired an intimate ally and an addition of power truly formidable. Had Ferdinand, on the contrary, proved faithless to his new engagements, the Spaniards themselves would not have failed to dismiss him, and would have applied to me for a ruler in his place. At all events," concluded the Emperor, "that unfortunate war of Spain was a real affliction, and the first cause of the calamities of France.

"After my conferences at Erfurth with Alexander, England ought to have been compelled to make peace by the force of arms or of reason. She had lost the esteem of the Continent. Her attack upon Copenhagen had disgusted the public mind, while I distinguished myself at that moment by every contrary advantage, when that disastrous affair of Spain presented itself to effect a sudden change against me, and reinstate England in the public estimation. She was enabled, from that moment, to continue the war. The trade with South America was thrown open to her. She formed an army for herself in the Peninsula, and next became the victorious agent, the main point of all the plots which were hatched on the Continent. All this effected my ruin.

"I was then assailed with imputations, for which, however, I had given no cause. History will do me justice. I was charged in that affair with perfidy, with laying snares, and with bad faith; and yet I was completely innocent. Never, whatever may have been said to the contrary, have I broken any engagement, or violated my promise, either with regard to Spain or any other power.

"The world will one day be convinced that, in the principal transactions relative to Spain, I was completely a stranger to all the domestic intrigues of its court; that I broke no promise made either to Charles IV. or to Ferdinand VII.; that I violated no engagement with the father or the son; that I made use of no falsehoods to entice them both to Bayonne, but that they both strove which should be first to show himself there. When I saw them at my feet, and was enabled to form a correct opinion of their total incapacity, I beheld with compassion the fate of a great people. I eagerly seized the singular opportunity held out to me by Fortune for regenerating Spain, rescuing her from the yoke of England, and intimately uniting her with our system. It was, in my conception, laying the fundamental basis of the tranquillity and security of Europe. But I was far from employing for that purpose, as it has been reported, any base and paltry stratagems. If I erred, it was, on the contrary, by daring openness and extraordinary energy. Bayonne was not the scene of premeditated ambush, but of a vast master-stroke of state policy. I could have preserved myself from these imputations by a little hypocrisy, or by giving up the Prince of Peace to the fury of the people. But the idea appeared horrible to me, and struck me as if I was to receive the price of blood. Besides, it must also be acknowledged that Murat did me a great deal of mischief in the whole affair.

INTERVIEW WITH THE SPANISH PRINCES.

"Be that as it may, I disdained having recourse to crooked and commonplace expedients. I found myself so powerful, I dared to strike from a situation too exalted. I wished to act like Providence, which, of its own accord, applies remedies to the wretchedness of mankind by means occasionally violent, but for which it is unaccountable to human judgment.

"I candidly confess, however, that I engaged very inconsiderately in the whole affair. Its immorality must have shown itself too openly, its injustice too glaringly, and the transactions, taken altogether, present a disgusting aspect, more particularly since my failure; for the outrage is no longer seen but in its hideous nakedness, stripped of all loftiness in idea, and of the numerous benefits which it was my intention to confer. Posterity, however, would have extolled it had I succeeded, and perhaps with reason, on account of its vast and happy results. Such is our lot and such our judgment in this world! But I once more declare that in no instance was there any breach of faith, any perfidy or falsehood, and, what is more, there was no occasion for them.

"The court and the reigning family," continued the Emperor, " were split into two parties. The one was that of the monarch, blindly governed by his favorite, the Prince of Peace, who had constituted himself the real king. The other was that of the heir-presumptive, headed by his preceptor Escoiquiz, who aspired to the government. These two parties were equally desirous of my support, and made me the most flattering promises. I was, no doubt, determined to derive every possible advantage from their situation.

" The favorite, in order to continue in office, as well as to shelter himself from the vengeance of the son in case of the father's death, offered me, in the name of Charles IV., to effect in concert the conquest of Portugal, reserving as an asylum for himself the sovereignty of Algarva.

" On the other hand, the Prince of the Asturias (Ferdinand) wrote to me privately, without his father's knowledge, soliciting a wife of my choice, and imploring my protection.

" I concluded an agreement with the former, and returned no answer to the latter. My troops were already admitted into the Peninsula, when the son took advantage of a commotion to make his father abdicate, and to reign in his place.

" It has been foolishly imputed to me that I took part in all these intrigues; but so far was I from having any knowledge of them, that the last event, in particular, disconcerted all my projects with the father, in consequence of which my troops were already in the heart of Spain. The two parties were aware, from that moment, that I might and ought to be the arbiter between them. The dethroned monarch and the son had recourse to me, the one for the purpose of obtaining vengeance, and the other for the purpose of being recognized. They both hastened to plead their cause before me, and they were urged on by their respective counselors, those very persons who absolutely governed them, and who saw no means of preserving their own lives but by throwing themselves into my arms.

" The Prince of Peace, who had been very nearly massacred, easily persuaded Charles IV. and his queen to undertake the journey, as they had themselves been in danger of falling victims to the fury of the multitude.

" On his part, the preceptor Escoiquiz, the real author of all the calamities of Spain, alarmed at seeing Charles IV. protest against his abdication, and in dread of the scaffold unless his pupil triumphed, exerted every means to influence the young king. This canon, who had, besides, a very high opinion of his own talents, did not despair of making an impression on my decisions by his arguments, and of inducing me to acknowledge Ferdinand, making me a tender, on his own account, of his services to govern altogether under my control as effectually as the Prince of Peace could under the name of Charles IV. And it must be owned that, had I listened to several of his reasons and adopted some of his ideas, I should have been much better off.

" When I had them all assembled at Bayonne, I felt a confidence in my political system to which I never before had the presumption to aspire. I had not made my combinations, but I took advantage of the moment. I here found the Gordian knot before me, and I cut it. I proposed to Charles IV. and the queen to resign the crown of Spain to me, and to live quietly in France. They agreed, I could say almost with joy, to the proposal, so inveterately were they exasperated against their son, and so earnestly did they and their favorite wish to enjoy for the future tranquillity and safety. The Prince of Asturias made no extraordinary resistance to the plan, but neither violence nor threats were employed against him; and if he was influenced by fear, which I am very willing to believe, that could only be his concern.

"There you have, in very few words, the complete historical sketch of the affair of Spain; whatever may be said or written on it must amount to that; and you see that there could be no occasion for me to have had recourse to paltry tricks, to falsehoods, to breaches of faith, or violation of engagements. In order to establish my guilt, it would have been necessary to show my inclination to degrade myself gratuitously. But of that propensity I have never given an instance."

TORTURE-ROOM OF THE SPANISH INQUISITION.

June 13. The Emperor was reading, as Las Casas entered his apartment, back numbers of the Moniteur.

"These Moniteurs," said Napoleon, "so terrible to many reputations, are uniformly favorable to me. It is with official documents that men of sense and talent will now write history. Now these documents are full of the spirit of my government, and to them I make an earnest and solemn appeal. I made the Moniteur the soul and the life-blood of my government, and it was the intermediate instrument of my communications with public opinion, both abroad and at home. Every government has since followed my example, more or less, in that respect.

"Whatever serious fault might be committed by any one of the high functionaries employed in the interior, immediately an inquiry was set on foot by the three councilors of state. They made their report to me, in which they ascertained the facts and discussed the principles. For my own part, I had nothing more to do than to write at the bottom, '*Dispatched for execution, according to the laws of the Republic or of the Empire.*' My interference was at an end, the public result accomplished, and popular opinion did justice to the transaction. It was the most formidable and dreadful of my tribunals.

"Did any question arise abroad respecting certain grand political combinations, or some delicate points of diplomacy? The objects were indirectly hinted at in the Moniteur. They instantly attracted universal attention, and became the topics of general investigation. The conduct was at once the orderly signal for the adherents of the throne, and an appeal for all parties to public opinion. The Moniteur has been reproached for the acrimony and virulence of its notes against the enemy; but, before we condemn these notes, we are bound to take into consideration the benefits they may have produced, the anxiety with which they have occasionally perplexed the enemy, the terror with which they struck a hesitating cabinet, the stimulus which they gave to our allies, and the confidence and intrepidity with which they inspired our troops."

The conversation then turned upon the liberty of the press. The subject was for some time discussed with much animation by the companions of the Emperor, he listening attentively to their remarks.

"Nothing," said one, "can resist the influence of a free press. It is capable of overthrowing every government, of agitating every society, of destroying every reputation."

"It is only," said another, "its prohibition which is dangerous. If it be restricted, it becomes a mine which must explode; but, if left to itself, it is merely an unbent bow, that can inflict no wound."

"The liberty of the press," said the Emperor, "is no longer a question open for consideration. There are institutions now, and the liberty of the press is one of them, upon the excellence of which we are no longer called to decide, but solely to determine upon the possibility of withholding them from the overbearing influence of public opinion. Its prohibition under a representative government is a gross anachronism, a downright absurdity. I therefore, on my return from Elba, abandoned the press to all its excesses, and I am confident that the press in no respect contributed to my downfall. When it was proposed in the council, in my presence, to discuss the means of sheltering the authority of the state from its attacks, I rather jocosely remarked, 'Gentlemen, it is probably yourselves you wish to protect, for, with respect to me, I shall henceforth continue a stranger to all such proceedings.' The press has exhausted itself upon me during my absence, and I now heartily defy it to produce any thing new or provoking against me."

June 15. Napoleon breakfasted in his bath. A little sliding table was put over the bath, upon which the dishes were placed. Conversing with Dr. O'Meara upon the manner of living in France and England, the Emperor inquired,

"Which eats the most, the Frenchman or the Englishman?"

"I think the Frenchman," said Dr. O'Meara.

"I do not think so," the Emperor added. "The French eat but two meals a day."

"Though they nominally," said Dr. O'Meara, "make but two meals, they really have four. They take something at nine in the morning, at eleven, at four, and at seven or eight in the evening."

"I," the Emperor replied, "never eat more than twice daily. You English always eat four or five times a day. Your cooking is more healthy than ours. Your soup is, however, very bad; nothing but bread, pepper, and water. You drink an enormous quantity of wine. Pointkowski, who dines sometimes in camp with the officers of the 53d, says that they drink by the hour; that after the cloth is removed they pay so much an hour, and drink as much as they like, which sometimes lasts until four o'clock in the morning."

"So far from the truth is this," said Dr. O'Meara, "that some of the officers do not drink wine more than twice a week, and that on days in which strangers are permitted to be invited. There is a third of a bottle put on for each member who drinks wine, and when that is exhausted another third is put on, and so on. Members only pay in proportion to what they drink."

"The Emperor seemed surprised," says O'Meara, "and observed how easily a stranger, having only an imperfect knowledge of the language, was led to give a wrong interpretation to the customs and actions of other nations."

It was a magnificent day, and the Emperor rode out in his calash. From one of the heights, a large ship was observed approaching the island. This led the Emperor to speak of his numerous friends in Europe who would be glad to share his exile. He then spoke of the motives which might have influenced those who were with him.

"Bertrand," said he, "is henceforth identified with my fate. It is an historical fact. Gourgaud was my first officer of ordnance. He is my own work. He is my child. Montholon is Semonville's son, a brother-in-law to Joubert, a child of the Revolution and of camps. But you, my friend," said he to Las Casas, "you, my good friend, let us know by what extraordinary chance you find yourself here?"

"Sire," Las Casas replied, "by the influence of my happy stars, and for the honor of the emigrants."

June 16. The day was again very fine, and the Emperor, in cheerful spirits, walked for a long time in the garden, conversing with great familiarity and animation upon the scenes through which he had passed. The celebrated interview at Tilsit was the subject upon which his thoughts chanced to turn.

"Had the Queen of Prussia," said he, "arrived at the commencement of the negotiations, she might have exercised considerable influence with respect to the result. Happily, she arrived when they were sufficiently advanced to enable me to decide upon their conclusion four-and-twenty hours afterward. The king, it was thought, had prevented her early appearance in consequence of a rising jealousy against a great personage, which was confidently stated not to have been destitute of some slight foundation.

"The moment of her arrival I made her a visit. The Queen of Prussia had been very beautiful, but she was beginning to lose the charms of her youth. She received me like Mademoiselle Duchénais in the character of Chimene, thrown back into a grand attitude calling aloud for justice. It was altogether a theatrical scene. The representation was truly tragic. For a moment I was unable to speak, and thought that the only way of extricating myself was to bring back the business to the tone of regular comedy, which I attempted by presenting her with a chair, and gently forcing her to be seated. She did not, however, discontinue the most pathetic expressions.

"'Prussia,' she exclaimed, 'has been blindfolded with respect to her power. She has dared to contend with a hero; to oppose herself to the destinies of France; to neglect his auspicious friendship. She has been deservedly punished for it. The glory of the great Frederick, his memory and his inheritance, have puffed up the pride of Prussia, and have caused her ruin.'

"She solicited, supplicated, implored. Magdeburg in particular was the object of her efforts and wishes. I kept my ground as well as I could. Fortunately, her husband made his appearance. The queen reproved, with an expressive look, the unseasonable interruption, and showed some pettishness. In fact, the king attempted to take part in the conversation, spoiled the whole affair, and I was set at liberty.

"I entertained the queen at dinner. She played off all her wit against me—she had a great deal; all her manners, which were very fascinating; all her coquetry—she was not without charms; but I was determined not to yield. I found it necessary, however, to keep a great command over myself, that I might continue exempt from all kind of engagement and every expression which might be taken in a doubtful sense, and the more so because I was carefully watched, and peculiarly by Alexander. An instant before dinner I took a very beautiful rose from a flower-stand and presented it to the queen. She at first expressed by the motion of her hand a kind of prepared refusal, but, suddenly recollecting herself, she said, '*Yes, but at least with Magdeburg.*' I replied, 'But I must observe to your majesty that it is I who present, and you who are about to receive it.' The dinner and the remainder of the time passed over in that manner.

"The queen was seated at table between the two Emperors, who rivaled each other in gallantry. She was placed near Alexander's best ear—with one ear he can scarcely hear. The evening came, and, the queen having retired, I resolved to bring matters to a point. I sent for M. de Talleyrand and

Prince Kourakin, talked large to them, and, uttering some hard words, observed that, after all, a woman and gallantry ought not to alter a system conceived for the destiny of a great people, and that I insisted upon the immediate conclusion of the negotiations and signing of the treaty. It took place according to my orders. Thus the Queen of Prussia's conversation advanced the treaty by a week or fortnight.

"The queen was preparing to renew her attacks the next day, and was indignant when she heard that the treaty was signed. She wept a great deal, and resolved not to see the Emperor Napoleon any more. She would not accept a second invitation to dinner. Alexander was himself obliged to prevail on her. She complained most bitterly, and maintained that Napoleon had broken his word. But Alexander had been always present. He had even been a dangerous witness, ready to give evidence of the slightest action or word on the part of Napoleon in her favor. 'He has made you no promise,' was his observation to her; 'if you can prove the contrary, I here pledge myself, as between man and man, to make him keep his promise, and he will do so, I am convinced.'

" 'But he has given me to understand—' said she.

" 'No,' Alexander replied; 'and you have nothing to reproach him with.'

"She came up at length. Having no longer any occasion to be on my guard, I redoubled my attentions. She played off, for a few moments, the airs of an offended coquette, and when dinner was over, and she was about to retire, I presented my hand and conducted her to the middle of the staircase, where I stopped. She squeezed my hand, and said, with a kind of tenderness,

" 'Is it possible that, after having been so near to the hero of the century and of history, he will not leave me the power and the satisfaction of being enabled to assure him that he has attached me to him for life ?'

" 'Madam,' I replied, 'I am to be pitied; it is the result of my unhappy star.'

"I then took leave of her. When she reached the carriage, she threw herself into it in tears, sent for Duroc, whom she highly esteemed, renewed all her complaints to him, and said, pointing to the palace, 'There is a place in which I have been cruelly deceived.'

"The Queen of Prussia," continued the Emperor, "was unquestionably gifted with many happy resources. She possessed a great deal of information, and had many excellent capabilities. It was she who really reigned for more than fifteen years. She also, in spite of my dexterity and all my exertions, took the lead in conversation, and constantly maintained the ascendency. She touched, perhaps too often, upon her favorite topic; but she did so, however, with great plausibility, and without giving the slightest cause of uneasiness. It must be confessed that she had an important object in view, and that the time was short and precious.

"I learn that the politicians of the present day find great fault with my treaty of Tilsit. They have discovered that I had, by that means, placed Europe at the mercy of the Russians. But if I had succeeded at Moscow

1816, June.] RESIDENCE AT LONGWOOD. **273**

—and it is now known how very near I was to success—they would, no doubt, have admired us for having, on the contrary, by that treaty, placed the Russians at the mercy of Europe. I entertained great designs with respect to the Germans, but I failed, and therefore was wrong. This is according to every rule of justice.

THE THREE SOVEREIGNS AT TILSIT.

"Had it been my wish, Alexander would certainly have given me his sister in marriage. His politics would have dictated the match, even had his inclination been against it. He was petrified when he heard of the marriage with Austria, and exclaimed, 'This consigns me to my native forests.' If he seemed at first to shift about, it was because some time was necessary to enable him to come to a decision. His sister was very young, and the consent of his mother was requisite. This was settled by Paul's will, and the Empress-mother was one of my greatest enemies. She was also the dupe of all the absurdities, all the ridiculous stories which had been circulated on my personal account. 'How can I,' she exclaimed, 'marry my daughter to a man who is unfit to be any one's husband?'* 'Mother,' said Alexander, 'can you be so credulous as to believe the calumnies of London and the insinuations of the saloons of Paris?'

"If Alexander's affection for me was sincere, it was alienated from me by

* The purity of Napoleon's morals was so singular in those days of general corruption, that those who could not deny this purity accused him of being *physically impotent.*

S

the force of intrigue. Certain persons—Metternich, or others at the instigation of Talleyrand—lost no seasonable opportunity of mentioning instances of my turning him into ridicule, and they assured him that, at Tilsit and Erfurth, he no sooner turned his back than I took my opportunity of laughing at his expense. Alexander is very susceptible, and they must have easily soured his mind. It is certain that he made bitter complaints of it at Vienna during the Congress, and yet nothing was more false. He pleased me, and I loved him. Alexander is in possession of all the graces, and equal, in elegance of manners, to the most polished and amiable ornaments of our Parisian drawing-rooms. The King of Prussia was always awkward and unlucky; Alexander was at times so tired of his companion, who seemed lost in his own sorrows or in some other cause, that we mutually agreed to break up our common meeting to get rid of him. We separated immediately after dinner, under the pretense of some particular business; but Alexander and I met shortly afterward to take tea with one another, and we then continued in conversation until midnight, and even beyond it.

"I sent Savary, immediately after the treaty of Tilsit, to Alexander at St. Petersburg. He was loaded with favors. The efforts and liberality of Alexander were inexhaustible to render himself agreeable to his new ally. Savary was, on his return from Russia, appointed minister of police in Paris. In 1814, just after the restoration of the Bourbons, some one said to him at the Tuileries, in a manner quite careless and unreserved,

"'Now that all is over, you may as well tell us every thing. Pray who was your agent at Hartwell?'

"This, as every one knows, was the residence of Louis XVIII. in England. Savary, surprised at the indelicacy of the question, replied with dignity,

"'M. le Comte, the Emperor considered the asylum of kings as an inviolable sanctuary. It was a principle which he impressed upon his police, and we adhered to it. We have since learned that the same conduct was not observed with respect to him; but you, sir, should entertain less doubt than any other person. When I arrived at St. Petersburg you were then on the side of the king. The Emperor Alexander, in the first warmth of his reconciliation, acquainted me with every thing that respected you, and asked me whether it was the wish of my government that you should be ordered to leave his dominions. I had received no instructions on that head. I wrote for them to the Emperor. His answer was, by the return of courier, that he was satisfied with the sincere friendship of Alexander; that he would never interfere with his private arrangements; that he entertained no personal hatred against the Bourbons; and that, if he believed it possible for them to accept it, he would offer them an asylum in France, and any royal residence which might be agreeable to them. If you were then ignorant of these instructions, you will no doubt find them among the papers of the foreign office.'"

CHAPTER XVIII.
1816, June. Continued.

Arrival of the Commissioners—Etiquette established by Napoleon—Mode of dictating—The Return of the Monks—Departure of the *Northumberland*—Remarks on the History of the Russian Campaign—Lord Holland—Arrival of Books—Ideas on Political Economy—Annoyance by the Rats—Lord Castlereagh—French Heiresses—Allusion by Napoleon to his own History—Summary of three Months.

June 17. Two ships arrived from England, bringing the bill of the British Parliament respecting the detention of the Emperor, and also bringing the commissioners of Russia, Austria, and France, appointed by the Allies to watch their dreaded captive. Admiral Sir Pulteney Malcolm came to replace Sir George Cockburn in the command of the naval station of St. Helena and the Cape of Good Hope. In the course of the day, the Emperor, speaking of the etiquette which he had introduced, said,

"I found it a very difficult thing to give myself up to my own inclinations. I started into public notice from the multitude. Necessity compelled me to form a state of external importance, to model a certain system of solemnity—in a word, to establish an etiquette. I should otherwise have been every day liable to be slapped on the shoulder. In France we are naturally inclined to a misplaced familiarity, and I had to guard myself against those who had at once, without any preparatory study, become men of education. We become courtiers very easily. We are very obsequious in the outset, and addicted to flattery and adulation; but, unless it be repressed, a certain familiarity soon takes place, which might, with great facility, be carried as far as insolence. It is well known that our kings were not exempt from this inconvenience."

"The Emperor," says Las Casas, "was a scrupulous observer of decorum. He was very sensible to all the little attentions he received, and though it was a sort of system with him to suffer no manifestation of gratitude to escape him, yet the expression of his eye or the tone of his voice sufficiently denoted what he felt. Unlike those whose lips overflow with the expression of the sentiments which their hearts never feel, Napoleon seemed to make it a rule to repress or disguise the kind emotion by which he was frequently inspired.

"I usually sat beside my son while he wrote to the Emperor's dictation. The Emperor always walked about the room when dictating, and he frequently stood for a moment behind my chair to look over the writing, so that he might know where to take up the thread of his dictation. When in this situation, how many times has my head been inclosed between his arms, and even slightly pressed to his bosom! Then, immediately checking himself, he seemed to have been merely leaning over my shoulders, or playfully bearing all his weight upon me, as if to try my strength.

THE EMPEROR DICTATING.

"The Emperor was very fond of my son, and I have often seen him bestow a manual caress on him, and then, as it were, to do away with the effect of his motion, he would immediately accompany it by some words uttered in a loud and somewhat sharp tone of voice. One day, as he was entering the drawing-room, in a moment of good-humor and forgetfulness, I saw him take Madam Bertrand's hand and affectionately raise it to his lips; but, suddenly recollecting himself, he turned away in a manner that would have had a very awkward effect had not Madam Bertrand, with that exquisite grace for which she is so peculiarly distinguished, removed all embarrassment by impressing a kiss on the hand that had been extended to her."

June 18. Dr. O'Meara called, and mentioned that the commissioners from Russia, France, and Austria had arrived.

"Have you seen any of them?" inquired the Emperor.

"Yes, sire, I saw the French commissioner."

"What sort of a man is he?"

"He is an old emigrant," the doctor replied, "the Marquis of Montchenu, extremely fond of talking. While I was standing in the midst of a group of officers on the terrace opposite the admiral's house, he came out, and addressing himself to me, said, in French,

"'If you, or any of you, speak French, for the love of God make it known to me, for I do not speak a word of English! I have arrived here to finish my days among the rocks, and I can not speak a word of the language.'"

SCENERY AT ST. HELENA.

"Chatterbox! simpleton!" exclaimed the Emperor. "What folly it is to send these commissioners out here! Without charge or responsibility, they will have nothing to do but to walk about the streets and creep up the rocks. The Prussian government has displayed more judgment, and saved its money."

The Emperor spent most of the day alone, reading the European journals which had just arrived. Just before dinner he sent for Las Casas, and in conversation remarked,

"France still remains in a state of agitation and uncertainty. One only care seems to engross the Bourbons, that of disinterring the dead. Any remains found, real or supposed, are to them a great affair. It is by the creation of monks that they expect to gain those new triumphs which are henceforth to ennoble the nation. It is certain that they wish to do every thing in their power to bring poor France again under the dominion of the priests, and this more from hypocrisy than from devotion, so fully are they convinced that their throne and priestcraft are natural allies, indispensable to enchain and to degrade the people. Oh nations! with all your wisdom, what are every where your destinies? You are the sport of passions and caprice, as a ship is driven by the winds. Now we hear only of priests, convents, and sermons; all my barracks are to be transformed into monasteries, and perhaps there will be a conscription of abbés to replace our conscription of soldiers."

After dinner he resumed reading the journals, commenting upon them to his companions as he read.

"Present circumstances, the necessities of the moment, and sympathies of old date, concur in favoring the return of the monks to France. This is a characteristic circumstance in France, as in the territories of the Pope. As for the Pope, it is his special affair, and is calculated to restore his power. Would any one believe that while he was a prisoner at Fontainebleau, and while the question of his own political existence was under consideration, he argued with me seriously on the existence of the monks, and endeavored to induce me to re-establish them. This was truly like the court of Rome."

Las Casas alluded to the fact that this day was the anniversary of the battle of Waterloo. The remark produced a very visible impression upon the Emperor. After a moment of silent thought, he exclaimed, in the most affecting tones of emotion and anguish,

THE RETREAT FROM WATERLOO.

"Incomprehensible day! Concurrence of unheard-of fatalities! Grouchy! Ney! Derlon! was there treachery or misfortune? Alas! poor France!"

Here he covered his eyes with his hands, and for a moment there was entire silence. Then he continued,

"All was not lost until the moment when all had succeeded. Singular campaign, in which three times in less than a week I saw the certain triumph of France, and the establishment of her destinies, escape from my hands. Had it not been for the desertion of a traitor, I should have annihilated the enemy at the opening of the campaign. I should have destroyed him at

Ligny if my left had done its duty. I should have destroyed him again at Waterloo if my right had not failed me. Singular defeat, by which, notwithstanding the most fatal catastrophe, the glory of the conquered has not suffered, nor the fame of the conqueror been increased! The memory of the one will survive his destruction, the memory of the other will perhaps be buried in his triumph!"

June 19. The *Northumberland*, which brought the Emperor to St. Helena, this day sailed on its return to Europe. The departure of the ship revived the most melancholy recollections in the bosoms of the exiles. The Emperor passed a sleepless night, and was suffering from a violent headache. At three o'clock Sir Hudson Lowe called to present Sir Pulteney Malcolm. The Emperor, though quite unwell, received the new admiral with much courtesy, and conversed with him with frankness and cheerfulness. After they had withdrawn, the Emperor said to his friends,

"I am much pleased with Admiral Malcolm. His look, his attitude, his language, are those of an honest man. I really felt pleasure in seeing and conversing with him. If he commanded here in the place of that execrable Sicilian constable, we should be at peace. Nay, I really believe that, if we were the most distrustful of guests, we should gain confidence in him, his appearance announces so clearly that his heart is good and that he is an honest man."

Before and after dinner the Emperor amused himself with a work on the Russian campaign, written by a former aid-de-camp of the Viceroy Eugene. He had heard it described as an odious production, but, accustomed as he was to every form of abuse, he did not find the publication so bad as he had expected.

"An historian," said he, "would select from it only what is good. He would take the facts and omit the declamation, which is only calculated to please imbeciles. The author of this work proves that the Russians burned Moscow and Smolensko. He describes the French as having been victorious in every engagement. The facts that are to be found in this work have evidently been described for the purpose of being published during my reign, in the period of my power. The declamatory passages have been interpolated since my fall. The author could not easily pervert the groundwork of his subject, though he has interspersed it with abusive remarks, after the fashion of the day. As to the disasters of the retreat, I left him nothing to say more than other libelists. My twenty-ninth bulletin plunged them into despair. In their rage they accused me of exaggeration. They were provoked to a pitch of madness. I thus deprived them of an excellent subject. I carried off their prey."

In allusion to these efforts of the partisans of the Bourbons to cast dishonor upon France under the Empire, he said,

"It is a circumstance unexampled in history to see a nation strive to depreciate her own glory—to see her own sons thus intent on destroying her trophies; but, from the bosom of France, avengers will doubtless rise up. Posterity will brand with disgrace the madness of the present day. Can these be Frenchmen who speak and write in this strain? Are their hearts dead to every spark of patriotism? But no, they can not be Frenchmen! They speak our language, it is true; they were born on the same soil with us, but they are not animated by the feelings and principles of Frenchmen."

June 21. The Emperor was walking in the garden accompanied by all his suite. Dr. O'Meara joined them. The Emperor said to him,

"I have seen the new admiral. *There* is a man with a countenance really open, intelligent, frank, and sincere. There is the face of an Englishman. His countenance bespeaks his heart, and I am sure that he is a good man. I never yet beheld a person of whom I so immediately formed a good opinion as of that fine, soldier-like old man. He carries his head erect, and speaks out openly and boldly what he thinks, without being afraid to look you in the face at the time. His physiognomy would make every person desirous of a further acquaintance, and render the most suspicious confident in him."

Some allusion was made to the fact, very gratifying to the Emperor, that Lord Holland, and the Duke of Sussex, brother of George IV., had filed their *protest* in the House of Lords against the illegal imprisonment of Napoleon.*

"When passions," said he, "are calmed, the conduct of these two peers will be handed down to posterity with as much honor as that of the proposers of the measure will be loaded with ignominy."

He asked several questions concerning the reduction of the English army, and observed,

"It is absurd in the English government to endeavor to establish the nation as a great military power, without having a population sufficiently numerous to afford the requisite number of soldiers to enable them to vie with the great, or even the second-rate Continental powers, while they neglect and seem to undervalue the navy, which is the real force and bulwark of England. They will yet discover their error."

* *Protest of Lord Holland.*

"To consign to distant exile and imprisonment a foreign captive chief, who, after the abdication of his authority, relying on British generosity, had surrendered himself to us in preference to his other enemies, is unworthy of the magnanimity of a great country. And the treaties by which, after his captivity, we have bound ourselves to detain him in custody, at the will of sovereigns to whom he had never surrendered himself, appear to me repugnant to the principles of equity, and utterly uncalled for by expedience or necessity.

"(Signed) VASSALL HOLLAND."

At the third reading of the bill, his royal highness the Duke of Sussex entered his protest for the same reasons.

The conversation then turned upon the possibility of the exiles ever seeing France again.

"My dear friends," said the Emperor, in tones of the most touching emotion and affection, "you will return."

"Not without you, sire!" all exclaimed, with one voice.

This led to an analysis of the probable chances of leaving St. Helena, and it was the general impression that this could only take place through the intervention of England.

"But how," said the Emperor, "can this intervention ever be brought about? The impression is made—it has taken too deep root—they will everlastingly fear me. Pitt told them, 'There can be no safety for you with a man who has a whole invasion in his own head.'"

"But," said Las Casas, "suppose new interests should rise up in England—suppose a truly constitutional and liberal ministry should be established, would the English government find no advantage in fixing, through you, sire, liberal principles in France, and thereby propagating them throughout Europe?"

"Certainly," replied the Emperor, "I admit all this."

"Well, then," continued Las Casas, "would not this constitutional administration find a guarantee in these liberal principles and in your own interests?"

"I admit this also," the Emperor replied; "I can suppose Lord Holland, as prime minister of England, writing to me at Paris, 'If you do so and so, I shall be ruined.' Or I can imagine the Princess Charlotte of Wales, whom we will suppose to have removed me hence, saying to me, 'If you act thus, I shall be hated, and shall be looked upon as the scourge of my country.' At these words I should stop short. They would arrest me in my career more effectually than armies.

"And, after all, what is there to fear? That I should wage war? I am now too old for that. Is it feared that I should resume my pursuit of glory? I have enjoyed glory even to satiety, and it may be said to be a thing which I have rendered henceforth at once common and difficult. Is it supposed that I would recommence my conquests? I did not persevere in them through mania. They were the result of a great plan, and I may even say that I was urged to them by necessity. They were reasonable at the moment when I pursued them, but they would now be impossible; they were practicable once, but now it would be madness to attempt them; and, besides, the convulsions and misfortunes to which France has been subjected will henceforth give rise to so many difficulties that to remove them will be a sufficient source of glory without seeking for any other."

The Emperor returned to his room, and requested Las Casas to accompany him. He alluded to the Historical Atlas of Las Casas, a work of great celebrity, which the Emperor had examined at St. Helena, and which he greatly admired.

"How happened it," said Napoleon, "that none of your friends should have given me a correct idea of it? I never saw it until I was on board the

Northumberland. Such is the misfortune of sovereigns, for certainly no one entertained better intentions than myself. Since I have become acquainted with the value of your charts, I regret not having established a kind of normal school, in which the students would have been uniformly instructed by the help of the Historical Atlas. Why did you not call my attention to it? I knew nothing of your work; if I had, it would have been a powerful circumstance in your favor. I was not aware that you had, like myself, attended the military school at Paris. That would have been another claim to my notice. You had been an emigrant; you would, therefore, never have enjoyed my full confidence. I knew that you had been much attached to the Bourbons; you would, therefore, never have been initiated in the great secrets of my government."

"But, sire," said Las Casas, "your majesty permitted me to approach your person. You made me a councilor of state, and intrusted me with various missions."

"That," the Emperor added, "was because I conceived you to be an honest man; and, besides, I am not of a distrustful disposition."

"Sire," said Las Casas, "I experienced deep mortification at finding that your majesty never addressed a word to me at your court circles and levees, and yet you never failed to speak of me to my wife when I happened to be absent."

"If I spoke of you when absent," the Emperor replied, "it was because I always made it a rule to speak to ladies about their husbands when the latter were sent out on missions. If I neglected you when present, it was because I attached too little value to you. It is a great fault to keep in the background at court. To my eyes you were a mere blank."

"Sire," continued Las Casas, "my situation was the more painful, since my friends were constantly congratulating me upon the favors I received at court. It was asserted that I had been created maritime prefect of Brest, Toulon, or Antwerp, or that I had received an important trust connected with the education of the King of Rome."

"Well," said the Emperor, "now that you call the matter to my recollection, some of the reports are not entirely destitute of foundation. I certainly did entertain the idea of employing you in the education of the King of Rome; I also intended to appoint you maritime prefect of Toulon. In this instance, your friend the minister turned my attention from you. You belonged to the old navy, he observed; your prejudices and those of the new officers must inevitably clash. This appeared to me a decided objection to your appointment. I think, also, that I entertained some other ideas respecting your advancement; but I must again repeat, that you neglected your own interests; you retreated when you ought to have marched forward. Need I tell you that, with the best intentions on my part the chance against procuring an appointment to an important post was as great as that against winning a prize in a lottery? An idea occurred to me, and I formed my decision; but, if that decision were not immediately carried into effect, it escaped my recollection, for I had so much business on my hands— But I interrupt you."

"Sire," continued Las Casas, "being ignorant of your majesty's good intentions with respect to me, I was placed in a situation truly ridiculous, amid the numerous congratulations I received. I never asked your majesty for more than one thing, and that was the situation of Master of Requests, which was immediately granted to me."

"It is curious," said the Emperor, "how my memory revives, now that I am speaking on this subject. You addressed several written communications to me; you transmitted to me some plans respecting the Adriatic Sea, with which I was much pleased; you also presented some other things to my notice."

"Sire," said Las Casas, "you probably allude to the ideas respecting the system of maritime warfare to be adopted against England, accompanied by an explanatory map."

"Yes, I recollect; the map lay for several days on the desk in my closet. I expressed a wish to see you, but you were absent on a mission."

"Sire," Las Casas continued, "about the same time I had the honor to address to you a plan for transforming the Champ de Mars into a naumachy. I purposed that the basin should be dug sufficiently deep to admit the launching of small corvettes, which might have been rigged, manned, and worked by the pupils of the naval school."

"Ah!" exclaimed the Emperor, "I was not aware of the extent of your plan. This design would have pleased me. It might have produced immense results. From this plan there was but a step to that of rendering the Seine navigable, and cutting a canal from Paris to the sea. This could not have been regarded as too stupendous an enterprise. More was done by the Romans in ancient times, and more has already been effected by the Chinese of the present day. It would have afforded a pastime to the army in time of peace. I had conceived many plans of the same kind, but our enemies kept me chained to war. Of what glory have they robbed me!"

June 22. Several boxes of books arrived. The Emperor, in his eagerness, helped, with hammer and chisel, in opening the boxes in the topographical cabinet. He expressed unfeigned delight in finding a file of the Moniteur, and began immediately to peruse them.

June 23. The Emperor had been so overjoyed at the receipt of his new books, that he had passed the whole night in reading and dictating notes to Marchand. He said to O'Meara, pointing to several books he had thrown on the floor, according to his custom, after having read them,

"What a pleasure I have enjoyed! I can read forty pages of French in the time that it would require me to comprehend two of English."

The conversation naturally turned on the subject of memory. "A head without memory," said the Emperor, "is like a garrison without fortifications. Mine is a useful kind of memory. It is not general and absolute, but relative, faithful, and only retentive of what is necessary."

"My memory," Las Casas observed, "is like my sight. It becomes confused by the distance of places and objects as I remove from one situation to another."

"For my part," said the Emperor, "my memory is like my heart. It preserves a faithful impression of all that has ever been dear to me."

After dinner he called for the Historical Atlas of Las Casas, and, while examining it, began to converse on trade.

"The principles of political economists," said he, "are correct in theory, though erroneous in their application. The political constitutions of different states must render these principles defective. Local circumstances continually call for deviations from their uniformity. Duties, which are so severely condemned by political economists, should not, it is true, be an object to the treasury. They should be the guarantee and protection of a nation, and should correspond with the nature and the objects of its trade. Holland, without productions, without manufactures, having only a commerce of transit and commission, ought not to know either impediments or barriers. France, on the contrary, rich in productions, in manufactures of every kind, ought incessantly to be on the guard against the importations of a rival who might still continue superior to her, and also against the cupidity, egotism, and indifference of mere commission merchants.

"I have been careful not to fall into the error of modern sympathizers, who imagine that all the wisdom of nations is centred in themselves. Experience is the true wisdom of nations. And what does all the reasoning of political economists amount to? They incessantly extol the prosperity of England, and hold her up as our model. But the Custom-house system is more burdensome and arbitary in England than in any other country. They also condemn prohibitions. Yet it is England which has set the example of prohibitions, and they are, in fact, necessary for certain objects. Duties can not adequately supply the place of prohibitions. Means will always be found to defeat the object of the legislator. In France, we are still far in arrears in these delicate matters. They are still unperceived, or not understood by the mass of society. Yet what advances have we not made! what correctness of ideas has been introduced by my gradual classification of agriculture, manufactures, and trade! objects so distinct in themselves, and which present so great and positive a graduation.

"1. Agriculture; the soul, the first basis of the Empire.

"2. Manufactures; the comfort and happiness of the population.

"3. Foreign commerce; the superabundance, the proper employ of the two others.

"Agriculture was continually improving during the whole course of the Revolution. Foreigners thought it ruined in France. In 1814, however, the English were compelled to admit that we had little or nothing to learn from them.

"Manufactures and internal trade made immense progress during my reign. The application of chemistry to manufactures caused them to advance with giant strides. I gave an impulse, the effect of which extended throughout Europe.

"Foreign commerce, which, in its results, is infinitely inferior to agriculture, is an object of subordinate importance in my mind. Foreign commerce is made for agriculture and home manufactures, and not the two latter for the former. The interests of these three fundamental bases are diverging and frequently conflicting. I always promoted them in their natural gradation, but I could not and I ought not to have ranked them all on an equality. Time will unfold what I have done, the national resources which I have created, and the emancipation from the English which I brought about. We have now the secret of the commercial treaty of 1783. France still exclaims against its author, but the English demanded it on pain of resuming the war. They wished to do the same after the treaty of Amiens; but I was then all-powerful—I was a hundred cubits high. I replied that if they were in possession of the heights of Montmartre, I would still refuse to sign the treaty. These words we echoed through Europe.

"The English will now impose some such treaty on France, at least if popular clamor and the opposition of the mass of the nation do not force them to draw back. This thraldom would be an additional disgrace in the eyes of that nation, which is now beginning to acquire a just perception of her own interests.

"When I came to the head of the government, the American ships, which were permitted to enter our ports on the score of their neutrality, brought us raw materials, and had the impertinence to sail from France without freight, for the purpose of taking in cargoes of English goods in London. They, moreover, had the additional impertinence of making their payments, when they had any to make, by giving bills on persons in London. Hence the vast profit reaped by the English manufacturers and brokers entirely to our prejudice. I made a law that no American should import goods to any amount without immediately exporting their exact equivalent. A loud outcry was raised against this. It was said that I had ruined trade. But what was the consequence? Notwithstanding the closing of my ports, and in spite of the English, who ruled the seas, the Americans returned and submitted to my regulations. What might I not have done under more favorable circumstances?

"Thus I naturalized in France the manufacture of cotton, which includes, 1. *Spun cotton;* we did not previously spin it ourselves; the English supplied us with it as a sort of favor. 2. *The web;* we did not yet make it; it came to us from abroad. 3. *The printing;* this was the only part of the manufacture which we performed ourselves. I wished to naturalize the two first branches, and I proposed to the Council of State that their importation should be prohibited. This excited great alarm. I sent for Oberkamp, and conversed with him a long time. I learned from him that this prohibition would doubtless produce a shock, but that, after a year or two of perseverance, it would prove a triumph whence we should derive immense advantages. Then I issued my decree in spite of all. This was a true piece of statesmanship (*coup d'état*).

"I at first confined myself merely to prohibiting the web; then I extended the prohibition to spun cotton; and we now possess within ourselves the three branches of the cotton manufacture, to the great benefit of our population, and to the injury and regret of the English, which proves that in civil government, as in war, decision of character is often indispensable to success. I offered two hundred thousand dollars as a reward for the discovery of a method of spinning flax like cotton; and this discovery would undoubtedly have been made but for our unfortunate circumstances. I should then have prohibited cotton if I could not have naturalized it on the Continent.

"The encouragement of the production of silk was an object that equally claimed my attention. As Emperor of France and King of Italy, I calculated on receiving an annual revenue of fourteen millions of dollars from the production of silk. The system of commercial licenses was no doubt mischievous. Heaven forbid that I should have laid it down as a principle. It was the invention of the English. With me it was only a momentary resource. Even the Continental system, in its extent and rigor, was by me regarded merely as a measure occasioned by the war and temporary circumstances. The difficulties, and even the total stagnation of foreign commerce during my reign, arose out of the force of events and the accidents of the time. One brief interval of peace would immediately have restored it to its natural level."

June 26. Speaking of the campaigns of Italy, Las Casas said to the Emperor, "The rapid successes of your daily victories must have been a source of great delight."

"By no means," the Emperor replied; "those who were at a distance might have supposed so, for they knew only of our success; they knew nothing of our situation. If those victories could have procured me pleasure, I should have enjoyed repose; but I had always the aspect of danger before me, and the victory of to-day was speedily forgotten through the obligation of gaining another to-morrow."

June 27. Las Casas records, "We had nearly gone without our breakfast. An incursion made by the rats, who had entered our kitchen from several points during the night, had deprived us of every thing eatable. We are much infested by these animals. They are of enormous size, and very daring and mischievous. It took them very little time to penetrate our walls and floors. Attracted by the smell of the victuals, they would make their way into our drawing-room while we were at dinner. We were several times obliged to give them battle after the dessert. One evening, when the Emperor wished to retire, and his hat was handed to him, a rat of the largest size jumped out of it."

During the day the Emperor was reading an English review, in which it was stated that Lord Castlereagh had asserted at a public meeting that Napoleon, ever since his fall, had not hesitated to declare that, as long as he had reigned, he would have continued to make war upon England, having never had any object but her destruction.

The Emperor was indignant at the base calumny. "Lord Castlereagh," said he, with much feeling, "must be very familiar with falsehood, and must place great dependence on the credulity of his auditors. Can their own good sense allow them to believe that I could ever make such a foolish speech, even if I had such intentions?"

It was again stated, in the same review, that Lord Castlereagh had said in Parliament that the reason why the French army was so much attached to Bonaparte was that he made a kind of conscription of all the heiresses of the empire, and distributed them among her generals.

"Here again," the Emperor exclaimed, with warmth, "Lord Castlereagh utters a willful falsehood. He came among us. He had an opportunity of seeing our manners and laws, and of knowing the truth. He must be certain that such a thing was quite impossible, entirely beyond my power. What does he take our nation for? The French were never capable of submitting to such tyranny. I have, no doubt, made a great number of matches, and I would gladly have made thousands more. It was one of the most effectual methods of amalgamating and uniting irreconcilable factions. If I had had more time to myself, I should have taken great pains to extend these unions to the provinces, and even to the confederation of the Rhine, in order to strengthen the connection of those distant portions of the empire with France; but in such proceedings I only exerted my influence, and never my authority. Lord Castlereagh disregards such distinctions. It is important to his policy to render me odious. He is not scrupulous about the means. He does not shrink from any calumny. He has every advantage over me. I am in chains. He has taken all precautions for keeping my mouth shut, and preventing the possibility of my making any reply, and I am a thousand leagues from the scene of action. His position is commanding. Nothing stands in his way. But certainly this conduct is the *ne plus ultra* of impudence, baseness, and cowardice."

June 28. Sir Hudson Lowe called upon General Bertrand, and stated that it had been expected in London that the permission which had been offered to the members of the Emperor's household to return to Europe would have induced many of them to leave. The government, he said, had never intended to allow the Emperor more than a table for four persons daily, at the most, and for company to dine once a week.*

June 30. The Emperor sent for Las Casas to breakfast with him. He was sick, exceedingly depressed in spirits, and quite unable to converse. Chance having led to the mention of London, the Emperor said, languidly,

"You must have seen at London the court, the king, the Prince of Wales,

---

* Earl Bathurst wrote to Sir Hudson Lowe, "I think it necessary that you should lose no time in regulating, and, if necessary, abridging the expenditure of Bonaparte's table and household, so that the annual cost may not exceed £8000, including wines and extraordinaries of every kind. In case of his remonstrating against the retrenchments which this regulation may occasion, you are at liberty to allow him the full extent of the indulgences he may require, in regard to table and so forth, provided he will produce the funds necessary to cover the expense beyond the £8000 a year. That he can command the pecuniary means I apprehend that there is no doubt; and he must pay the salaries and wages of such of his followers and servants as may persevere in remaining with him; but I hope you will persuade most of them to accept the release we have offered.

"(Signed), BATHURST."

Sir Henry Bunbury also wrote, at the same time, to the governor, "By an intercepted letter to Bonaparte, which Sir George Cockburn sent home, it is clear that the ex-Emperor has large sums of money in different parts. *We have been unable hitherto to obtain any clew to this matter; it is very desirable to discover both the treasure and the agents!*"—See *Letters and Journals of Sir Hudson Lowe,* vol. i., p. 170.

Mr. Pitt, Mr. Fox, and other great personages who figured at that time. Tell me what you know of them. What did people think of them? Give me an historical sketch."

The Emperor listened, occasionally asking a question, while Las Casas gave a long and a very interesting account of the events of his emigration. At its conclusion Napoleon remarked,

"It has been said of me that scarcely had I attained power when I exercised a despotic and arbitrary sway. But it was rather a dictatorship; and the circumstances of the times will be a sufficient excuse for me. I have also been reproached with having suffered myself to be intoxicated with pride at my alliance with the house of Austria, and having thought myself more truly a sovereign after my marriage—in fact, of having considered myself, from that time, as Alexander, become the son of a god.

"But can all this be just? Did I really fall into such errors? A young, handsome, agreeable woman fell to my lot. Was it inadmissible for me to testify some satisfaction? Could I not devote a few moments to her without incurring blame? Was I not to be allowed to surrender myself to a few hours of happiness? Was I required to use my wife ill from the very first night, like your Prince of Wales? Or was I, like the sultan we have read of, to have her head struck off in order to escape the reproaches of the multitude? No, my only fault in that alliance was that of carrying too plebe-

NAPOLEON CHOSEN CORPORAL.

ian a heart within me. How often have I said that the heart of a statesman ought to be in his head! Mine, unfortunately, in this instance, remained in its place, subject to family feelings, and this marriage ruined me, because I believed, above all things, in the religion, the piety, the morality, and the honor of Francis. He has cruelly deceived me. I am willing to believe that he was himself deceived, and I forgive him with all my heart. But will history spare him? If, however——"

Here Napoleon remained for a moment in silent meditation, his forehead resting upon his hand. Then rising from his chair, he remarked, "But what a romance is my life! Open the door. Let us walk out."

The attachment of the soldiers to Napoleon was very peculiarly strong and tender. They usually called him "The Little Corporal." This title was conferred upon him by the soldiers after one of his signal victories in the First Italian Campaign.

At one time Napoleon was alone at night taking the round of his outposts, when he came to a point where a sentinel was stationed, who refused to allow him to pass. The faithful young soldier was a new recruit, and he did not recognize Napoleon.

"I am a general officer," said Napoleon, "and am in the discharge of my duties."

"I can not help that," said the sentinel. "I have orders to let no one pass; and if you were the Little Corporal himself, you should not go by."

Napoleon was compelled to turn back; but the next day he sent for the faithful soldier, and rewarded him for his fidelity.

THE SENTINEL AND THE LITTLE CORPORAL.

T

Mrs. Abell, then Miss Betsy Balcombe, thus describes a visit which she made about this time to Longwood:

"Before terminating our visit, Napoleon took us over the garden and grounds which surrounded his house. Nothing could exceed the dreariness of the view which presented itself from them. A spectator unaccustomed to the savage and gigantic scenery of St. Helena could not fail to be impressed with its singularity. On the opposite side the eye rested on a dismal and rugged-looking mountain, whose stupendous side was here and there diversified by patches of wild samphire, prickly pears, and aloes, serving to break but slightly the uniform sterility of the iron-colored rocks, the whole range of which exhibited little more than huge apertures of caverns and overhanging cliffs, which, in the early years of the colonization of the island, afforded shelter to herds of wild goats. I remember hearing Madam Bertrand tell my mother that one of Napoleon's favorite pastimes was to watch the clouds as they rolled over the highest point of that gigantic mountain, and, as the mists wreathed themselves into fantastic draperies around its summit, sometimes obscuring the valleys from sight, and occasionally stretching themselves out far to sea, his imagination would take wing, and indulge itself in shaping out the future from those vapory nothings."

Las Casas gives the following summary of April, May, and June:

"1. A new governor arrives, who turns out to be a man of either very narrow views or very bad intentions—a corporal with his watchword instead of a general with his instructions.

"2. A declaration is required from every one of the captives that he submits to all the restrictions that may be imposed on Napoleon, and this in the hope of detaching them from his person.

"3. An official communication is made to us of the convention of the allied sovereigns, who, without further ceremony, proclaim and consecrate the banishment of Napoleon.

"4. We receive the bill of the British Parliament which converts into a law the act of oppression of the English ministers toward the person of Napoleon.

"5. Commissioners come, in the name of their sovereigns, to watch over the fetters and contemplate the sufferings of the victims. Thus our horizon grows darker and darker, our chains are shortened, all hopes of amelioration vanish, and the most gloomy prospects are all that the future presents.

"The Emperor's health is visibly affected. Contrary to his natural temperament, he very frequently feels indisposed. On one occasion he was confined to his room for six days in succession. A secret melancholy, which endeavors to conceal itself from every eye, begins to take possession of him. The latent seeds of disease appear already to be lurking in his system. He contracts every day the circle, already so confined, of his movements and his diversions. He gives up riding on horseback. He no longer invites any Englishmen to dinner. He even abandons his daily occupations. The dictations, in which he had hitherto seemed to take pleasure, are at a stand. The greatest part of his days are passed in turning over some books in his own apartment, or in conversing with us either publicly or in private; and in the evening, after his dinner, he reads to us some plays of our great poets, or any other work which chance or the choice of the moment brings to his hand.

"Yet the serenity of his mind, the equanimity of his disposition toward us, are not in the least impaired. On the contrary, we seem more united—like one family. He is more ours, and we belong more to him. His conversations offer a greater degree of confidence, effusion, and interest."

CHAPTER XIX.
1816, July.

Pillage in War—Character of the French Soldier—Anecdotes of Brumaire—Sièyes—Grand Elector—Cambacères—New Vexations—Little Tristam—Difficulty of judging Men—Junot: his Wife—Bernadotte—Lannes—Murat: his Character and Death.

July 1. The son of Las Casas was slightly injured by being thrown from his horse. The Emperor kindly called to visit the little sufferer, whose foot was badly sprained. He then went into the garden, and breakfasted under a tree with Las Casas. The conversation turned upon pillage by armies, and the horrors occasioned by it.

"Pavia," said the Emperor, "is the only place I have ever given up to pillage. I had promised it to the soldiers for twenty-four hours; but, after three hours, I could bear it no longer, and I put an end to it. I had but twelve hundred men; the cries of the populace which reached my ears prevailed. If there had been twenty thousand soldiers, their numbers would have drowned the complaints of the people, and I should have heard nothing of it. Happily, however, policy and morality are equally opposed to the system of pillage. I have meditated much on this subject, and have often been urged to gratify my soldiers in this manner, but nothing is so certain to disorganize and completely ruin an army. A soldier loses all discipline as soon as he gets an opportunity to pillage; and if by pillage he enriches himself, he immediately becomes a bad soldier, and will not fight. Besides, pillage is incompatible with our French manners. The hearts of our soldiers are not bad; when the first transport of fury is over, they come to themselves again. It would be impossible for French soldiers to pillage for twenty-four hours; many of them would employ the latter part of the time in repairing the mischief they had done in the beginning. They afterward reproach each other, in their quarters, with the excesses they have committed, and load with reprobation and contempt those whose conduct has been particularly odious."

HONOR TO UNFORTUNATE COURAGE.

The Emperor was very attentive not only to his own wounded, but also to the wounded of the enemy. After one of his most signal victories, as he was riding along with his staff, he met a wagon laden with wounded Austrians. He immediately stopped, took off his hat, and saying, "Honor to unfortunate courage," remained uncovered till the sad procession had passed along.

The Emperor took a rapid ride in the calash with Las Casas alone. The day was fine. He was in cheerful spirits, and very social. "He spoke much of my son," says Las Casas, "and of his future prospects, with a degree of interest and kindness which went to my heart. After dinner his companions collected around him, and the conversation turned on the overthrow of the Directory on the 18th Brumaire."

"My situation," said the Emperor, "on my return from Egypt was unprecedented. I found myself immediately applied to by all parties, and was intrusted with all their secrets. There were three which were particularly distinct: the *Manege*, or Jacobins, of which Bernadotte was one of the leaders; the *Moderates*, directed by Sièyes; and the *Rotten* party, with Barras at their head. The determination which I formed to ally myself with the *Moderates* exposed me to great danger. With the Jacobins I should have risked nothing. They offered to name me Dictator; but, after conquering with them, it would have been necessary, almost immediately, to conquer against them. A club can not endure a permanent chief; it wants one for every successive passion. Now to make use of a party one day in order to attack it the next, under whatever pretext it is done, is still a piece of treachery. It was inconsistent with my principles.

"It is certain that there never was a great revolution which caused less inconvenience, it was so generally desired. It was consequently crowned with universal applause. For my part, all my share in the plot for effecting this change was confined to the assembling the whole crowd of my visitors at the same hour in the morning, and marching at their head to seize on power. It was at the threshold of my door, from the top of my own steps, and without my friends having any previous knowledge of my intentions, that I led them to this conquest. It was amid the brilliant escort they formed, their lively joy and unanimous ardor, that I presented myself at the bar of the Ancients to thank them for the dictatorship with which they invested me.

"Metaphysicians have disputed, and will long dispute, whether we did not violate the laws, and whether we were not criminal; but these are mere abstractions, at best fit for books and tribunes, and which ought to disappear before imperious necessity. One might as well blame a sailor for waste and destruction when he cuts away his masts to avoid being overset. The fact is, had it not been for us, the country must have been lost. We saved it. The authors and chief agents of that memorable state transaction may and ought, instead of denials and justifications, to answer their accusers proudly, like the Roman: '*We protest that we have saved our country. Come with us and render thanks to the gods.*'

"Surely all those who at that time took a part in the political turmoil have the less cause to complain, since every thing conspired to render a change inevitable. All desired it, and each one endeavored to effect it for his own party. I secured the change by the aid of the *Moderates*. The sudden termination of anarchy, the immediate return of order, of union, of strength, and of glory, were the results. Would the triumph of either of the other parties have been more favorable? We may surely say no! Nevertheless, it is very natural that they should have been dissatisfied, and that they should have raised loud cries of remonstrance. It belongs to future times and to disinterested men to give an impartial judgment upon that great affair.

"Moreover, contemplate two facts which will aid one in forming an estimate of the true condition of the republic at the time of *Brumaire*. After that day there was not sufficient money in the treasury to send out a courier; and when the consul wished to ascertain the precise force of the army, he was compelled to apply to persons at those distant places. 'You ought,' said he, 'to have on file a list of those in the army.'

"'Of what advantage would it be?' was the reply. 'There are so many changes that the soldiers can not be counted.'

"'But at least you ought to know the amount of pay which is due—'

"'We do not pay them.'

"'But the food—'

"'We do not feed them.'

"'But the clothing—'

"'We do not clothe them.'

"When we were about to fix on a Constitution," continued the Emperor, "Sièyes treated us with a very entertaining scene. Circumstances and public opinion had made him a sort of oracle in these matters. He accordingly unfolded his various propositions in the committees of the two councils with great mystery, importance, and method. They were all adopted, good, imperfect, or bad. Finally, he crowned the work by displaying the summit, which had been expected with lively and anxious impatience. He proposed a Grand Elector, who was to reside at Versailles, to enjoy twelve hundred thousand dollars a year, to represent the national dignity, and to have no other duty than the nomination of two consuls, one for peace and the other for war, entirely independent in their functions. Moreover, if this Elector should make a bad choice, the Senate was to *absorb* him himself. This was the technical expression, meaning to remove him by replacing him, as a punishment, in the crowd of private citizens.

"For want of experience in assemblies, and also through a degree of circumspection which the circumstances of the moment required, I had taken little or no share in what had preceded, but now, at this decisive point, I began to laugh in Sièyes's face, and to cut up all his metaphysical nonsense without mercy. Sièyes did not like to defend himself, nor did he know how to do it. He made the attempt, however, by saying,

"'After all, a king is nothing more.'

"'But,' Napoleon replied, 'you take the abuse for the principle; the shadow for the body; and how can you imagine, M. Sièyes, that a man of any talent or the least honor will resign himself to act the part of a pig fattening on a few millions?'

"After this sally, which made those who were present laugh immoderately, Sièyes remained overwhelmed. It was no longer in his power to resume the subject of his Grand Elector. A First Consul was determined on, who was to have the supreme decision and nomination of all offices, with two accessory consuls, who were to have deliberative voices only. It was, in fact, from that moment a unity of power. The First Consul was precisely the President of America, veiled under the forms which the irritable spirit of the times rendered necessary. My reign began in reality from that day.

"I regretted in some measure that Sièyes had not been nominated one of the consuls. Sièyes, who at first refused the appointment, afterward regretted it himself, but not until it was too late. He had fallen into a mistake respecting the nature of these consuls. He was fearful of mortification, and of having the First Consul to contend with at every step, which would have been the case had all the consuls been equal. We should then have all been enemies. But the Constitution having made them subordinate, there was no room for the struggles of obstinacy, no cause for enmity, but a thousand reasons for a genuine unanimity. Sièyes discovered this, but too late. He might have been very useful in council, better, perhaps, than the others, because he had occasionally novel and most luminous ideas, but in other respects he was wholly unfit to govern.

"After all, in order to govern, it is necessary to be a military man. One can only rule in boots and spurs. Sièyes, without being fearful, was always in fear. His police spies disturbed his rest. At the Luxembourg, during the provisional consulate, he often awakened me and harassed me about the new plots he every moment heard of from his private police.

"'Have they corrupted our guard?' I would say to him.

"'No!'

"'Then go to bed. In war, my dear sir, as in love, we must come to close quarters to conclude matters. It will be time enough to be alarmed when our six hundred men are attacked.'

"For the permanent government I had chosen, in Cambacères and Lebrun, two distinguished characters. Both were prudent, moderate, and able, but they were of completely opposite principles. The one was the advocate of abuses, prejudices, old institutions, and the revival of honors and distinctions. The other was cold, austere, insensible, contending against all these ideas, yielding to them without illusion, and naturally falling into ideology. Sièyes might have contributed to give a different color, another characteristic, to the imperial administration."

"But this variation," said Las Casas, "would have been injurious. Your majesty's choice was much approved of at the time. It was said that the men selected were not liable to be objected to by Europe. They greatly contributed to conciliate public opinion in France, which ran wholly against Sièyes. There was an anecdote, eagerly repeated at the time, which shows all the ill-will that was borne toward him. It was said that, while he was talking with the Emperor at the Tuileries about Louis XVI., he suffered the word *tyrant* to escape him.

"'M. Abbé,' the Emperor was said to have replied, 'if Louis XVI. had been a tyrant, you would now be saying mass, and I should not be here.'

"The Emperor smiled at this anecdote," says Las Casas, "without confirming or denying it. It will hereafter appear that it was false."

July 6–8. Las Casas complains bitterly of the merciless vexations of Sir Hudson Lowe. "He has just," he writes, "withheld from us some letters from Europe, although they came open and in the most ostensible manner, merely because they had not passed through the hands of the secretary of state, without considering that a want of formality can easily be rectified in England, but that it is irremediable at the distance of six thousand miles. It is not many days since, the Countess Bertrand having written to town, he had the note seized, and sent it back to her as having been written without his permission. He accompanied this insult with an official letter, by which he prohibited us for the future from all written or even verbal communication with the inhabitants, without submitting it to his approbation. To one of his communications, in which he said that, if the restrictions imposed on us seemed too hard, we might relieve ourselves from them by going away, the Emperor dictated the following addition to the answer we had already written: 'Having been honored by him during his prosperity, we consider it our chief pleasure to serve him now that he can do nothing for us. If there are persons to whom this conduct is incomprehensible, so much the worse for them.'"

July 11. The governor had issued a proclamation ordering that all letters and notes addressed by the residents at Longwood to any of the inhabitants of the island, on any occasion whatever, should be sent to him within twenty-four hours. He also forbade the inhabitants to visit General Bertrand and his wife, who resided at the entrance of Longwood. This blockade was at one time so vigorous, that some medicine sent by the doctor for a very sick person could not be delivered. It was only by way of accommodation that the officer at last ventured to pass the medicine over the wall, having first torn from the bottle the directions of the physician, which were written in a language which he did not understand, and which, he apprehended, might contain some dangerous intelligence.

Madam Montholon had been for several weeks confined to her room. The Emperor frequently visited her, and conversed for half an hour at her bedside. To-day he met little Tristam Montholon, a bright and playful child seven or eight years of age. The Emperor placed him between his knees and taught him some fables. Tristam confessed to the Emperor that he did not work every day.

"Do you not eat every day?" said the Emperor.

"Yes, sire."

"Well, then, you ought to work every day; no one should eat who does not work."

"Oh! if that be the case, I will work every day," said the child, quickly.

"Such is the influence of the stomach," said the Emperor, tapping that of little Tristam; "it is hunger that makes the world move. Come, my little man, if you are a good boy we will make a page of you."

1816, July.]   RESIDENCE AT LONGWOOD.   297

THE EMPEROR AND LITTLE TRISTAM.

In the afternoon the Emperor was reading. He came to a passage where the author observed that the face often gave a false idea of the character. The Emperor paused, laid down the book, and said, in tones of conviction,

"This is most true; and it is also true that no study will enable us to avoid this deception. How many proofs of this kind have I had! For instance, I had a person about me: his countenance was undoubtedly good, but, after all, he had a mischievous eye; I ought to have guessed something from that. We had known each other from infancy. I had long placed entire confidence in this individual, who had talents and resources; I even thought he was attached and faithful to me; but he was much too covetous—he was too fond of money. When I was dictating to him, and he sometimes had to write *millions*, it was never without a peculiar change of countenance, a licking of his lips, and a restlessness in his chair, which several times induced me to ask what ailed him. This vice was too glaring to allow me to retain this person about me. But, considering his other qualities, I ought, perhaps, to have contented myself with removing him into a different situation."

July 12. The Emperor was sick and much dejected. Dr. O'Meara called, in behalf of the governor, to inquire whether General Bonaparte would prefer to have the house at Longwood enlarged and repaired, or to have a new house erected in another part of the island.

"In this wretched place," replied the Emperor, "I wish for nothing from him. I hate this Longwood. The sight of it makes me melancholy. Let him put me in some place where there is shade, verdure, and water. Here, it either blows a furious wind, loaded with rain and fog, which afflicts my soul, or, if that is wanting, the sun broils my brain, through the want of shade, when I go out. Let him put me on the Plantation House side of the island if he really wishes to do any thing for me. But what is the use of his coming up here, proposing things and doing nothing? There is Bertrand's house, not the least advanced since his arrival. The admiral, at least, sent his carpenter here, who made the work go on."

"The governor," said O'Meara, "has desired me to say that he did not like to undertake any thing without first knowing that it would meet with your approval; but that, if you will propose a plan for the house, he will immediately order every workman on the island to set about it. The governor fears that making additions to the present building will annoy you by the noise of the workmen."

"Certainly it would," replied the Emperor; "I do not wish him to do any thing to this house, or on this dismal place. Let him build a house on the other side of the island, where there is shade, verdure, and water, and where I may be sheltered from this bleak wind. If it is determined to build a new house for my use, I would wish to have it erected on the estate of Colonel Smith, or at Rosemary Hall. But his proposals are all a delusion. Nothing advances since he came. Look at those windows! I was obliged to order a pair of sheets to be put up as curtains, as the others were so dirty that I could not approach them, and none could be obtained to replace them. He is a bad man, and worse than the island. Observe his conduct to that poor lady, Madam Bertrand! He has deprived her of the little liberty she had, and has prevented people from coming to visit and to chat an hour with her, which was some little solace to a lady who had always been accustomed to see company."

"The governor has said," O'Meara replied, "that it was in consequence of Madam Bertrand having sent a note to the French commissioner, Marquis Montchenu, without having caused it to pass through the governor's hands."

"Trash!" the Emperor replied. "By the regulations in existence when he arrived, it was permitted to send notes to residents, and no communication was made to them of an alteration having taken place. Besides, could not she and her husband have gone to town to see Montchenu? Weak men are always timorous and suspicious. This man is fit to be the head of a police gang, but not a governor."

Dr. O'Meara reported to Sir Hudson Lowe the situations the Emperor had suggested for the new house, but the governor refused to accept either of them, saying that General Bonaparte could not be so easily watched in either of those places.

July 13. The conversation turned upon Junot, the Duke of Abrantes. "Of the considerable fortunes," said Napoleon, "which the Emperor bestowed, that of Junot was one of the most extravagant. The sums conferred upon him almost exceeded belief, and yet he was always in debt. He squandered treasures without credit to himself, without discernment or taste, and too frequently in gross debauchery. Being fond of Junot, and actuated by a sort of feeling derived from the similarity of birth-place, he being also originally from Corsica, I one day sent for Madam Junot to give her some paternal admonitions on the subject of the extravagance of her husband's expenditure, the profusion of diamonds which she herself had inconsiderately displayed after her return from Portugal, and her intimate connections with a certain foreigner, which might give umbrage in a political point of view. But she rejected this advice, dictated alone by concern for her interest. She grew angry, and behaved like a child. Nothing then remained for me to do but to abandon her to her fate. She fancied herself a princess of the family of the Commines, and Junot had been made to believe it when he was induced to marry her. Her family was from Corsica, and resided in the neighborhood of mine. They were under great obligations to my mother, not merely for her benevolence toward them, but for services of a more positive nature."

July 14. The subject of dress came up at the dinner-table.

"None," said Las Casas, "had carried the ridiculous in that point farther than Murat. His dress was for the most part so singular and fantastic, that the public called him King Franconi."*

The Emperor laughed very heartily at this, and said, "Certain costumes and manners did indeed sometimes give to Murat the air of a quack operator or a mountebank."

"Bernadotte and Lannes," added Las Casas, "also took infinite pains with their dress."

"I am surprised to hear this," said the Emperor. "Poor Lannes! How sincerely I regretted his loss! He passed the night which preceded the battle of Essling in Vienna, and not alone. He appeared on the field without having taken any food, and fought the whole day. The physician said that this triple concurrence of circumstances caused his death. He required a great deal of strength after the wound to enable him to bear it, and, unfortunately, nature was almost exhausted before.

"It is generally observed that there are certain wounds to which death seems preferable, but this is seldom the case, I assure you. It is at the moment we are about to part with existence that we cling to it with all our might. Lannes, the most courageous of men, deprived of both his legs, would not hear of death. He had, unfortunately, overheard the two surgeons who attended him whisper to each other, as they thought without being overheard, that it was impossible he could recover. He was irritated to that degree that he declared that the surgeons deserved to be hanged for behaving so brutally toward a marshal. Every moment the unfortunate Lannes called for the Emperor. He twined himself around me with all he had left of life. He would hear of no one but me; he thought but of me. It was a kind of instinct. Undoubtedly he loved his wife and children better than me, yet he did not speak of them. It was he who protected them, while I, on the contrary, was his protector. I was, for him, something vague and undefined —a superior being—his providence, which he implored."

"Rumor, in the saloons," said Las Casas, "has spoken a different language. It was reported that Lannes died like a maniac, vociferating imprecations against the Emperor, at whom he seemed enraged. It was said that he had always had an aversion to the Emperor, and had often manifested it to him with insolence."

* Director of a theatre in Paris.

" What an absurdity!" the Emperor replied. " Lannes, on the contrary, adored me. He was assuredly one of the men on whom I could most implicitly rely. It is very true that, in the impetuosity of his disposition, he has sometimes suffered some hasty expressions against me to escape his lips, but he would probably have broken the head of any person who chanced to hear them."

Reverting to Murat, Las Casas remarked that he had greatly influenced the unfortunate events of 1814.

" He determined them," said the Emperor. " He is one of the principal causes of our being here. But the fault is originally mine. There were several men whom I had made too great. I had raised them above the sphere of their intelligence. I was reading, some days ago, Murat's proclamation on abandoning the viceroy, which I had not seen before. It is difficult to conceive any thing disgraced by a greater degree of turpitude. He says in that document that the moment has come to choose between two banners—that of crime or that of virtue. It is my banner which he calls the banner of crime! And it is Murat, my creation, the husband of my sister, the man who owed every thing to me, who would have been nothing without me, who exists by me, and is known through me alone, who writes this! It is impossible to desert the cause of misfortune with more unfeeling brutality, and to run with more unblushing baseness to hail a new destiny.

" From that moment Madam* refused to have any farther intimacy with either Murat or his wife. To all their entreaties she invariably answered that she held traitors and treachery in abhorrence. As soon as she was at Rome, after the disasters of 1814, Murat hastened to send her eight magnificent horses out of his own stables at Naples, but Madam would not accept them. She resisted in like manner every effort of her daughter Caroline, who constantly repeated that, after all, the fault was not hers; that she had no share in it; that she could not command her husband. But Madam answered, like Clytemnestra,

" ' If you could not command him, you ought, at least, to have opposed him. But what struggles have you made? what blood has flown? At the expense of your own life you ought to have defended your own brother, your benefactor, your master, against the sanguinary attempts of your husband.'

" On my return from Elba," continued the Emperor, " Murat's head was turned on hearing that I had landed in France. The first intelligence he received of this event informed him that I was at Lyons. He was accustomed to my great returns of fortune; he had, more than once, seen me placed in most extraordinary circumstances. On this occasion he thought me already master of all Europe, and determined to wrest Italy from me; for that was his object, the aim of all his hopes. It was in vain that some men of the greatest influence among the nations which he attempted to excite to rebellion threw themselves at his feet, and assured him that he was mistaken; that the Italians had a king on whom alone they had bestowed their love and their esteem. Nothing could stop him. He lost himself, and contrib-

* Napoleon's mother.

uted to lose us a second time; for Austria, supposing that he was acting at my instigation, would not believe my professions, and mistrusted me. Murat's unfortunate end corresponds with his conduct. He was endowed with extraordinary courage and but little intelligence: the too great disproportion between these two qualifications explains the man entirely. It was difficult, even impossible, to be more courageous than Murat and Lannes; but Murat had remained courageous, and nothing more. The mind of Lannes, on the contrary, had risen to a level with his courage—he had become a giant. However, the execution of Murat is nevertheless terrible; it is an event in the history of the morals of Europe—an infraction of the rules of public decorum: a king has caused another king, acknowledged by all the others, to be shot. What a spell he has broken!"

PORTRAIT OF MURAT.

CHAPTER XX.
1816, July. Continued.

The Works of Cherbourg—Designs of the Emperor—Audience given to the Governor—Faubourg St. Germain—Aristocracy—Democracy—The Emperor's Intention to marry a French woman—Difficulties in reforming Society—Etiquette at Longwood.

July 15. About ten o'clock in the morning, the Emperor knocked at the door of Las Casas's apartment, and invited him to take a walk. They directed their steps toward some gum-wood trees, where the Emperor had ordered the calash to be in waiting. Upon their return, the Emperor retired to his room and spent the day alone, breakfasting and dining in his chamber.

After dinner he sent for Las Casas again. The Emperor had been reading journals of the past all day. Conversation turned upon the immense marine works which he had commenced at Cherbourg. The plan of constructing an artificial harbor there had been conceived during the reign of Louis XVI., and he had visited Cherbourg with some French engineers.

Cherbourg is situated on the French coast, at the bottom of a bay formed by the Isle Pelée on the right, and the point Querqueville on the left. It is opposite Portsmouth, and about sixty miles from that celebrated naval depôt of England. For a long distance the two coasts of France and England here run parallel to each other.

"Nature," said Napoleon, "has done every thing for our rivals, nothing for us. Their shores are safe and free from obstruction. They abound in good soundings, in the means of shelter, in harbors, and excellent ports. Ours are, on the contrary, filled with rocks, their water is shallow, and they are every day choking up. We have not, in these parts, a single real port of large dimensions, and it might be said that the English are, at the same moment, both at home and on our coast, since it is not necessary for their squadrons, at anchor in Portsmouth, to put to sea to molest us. A few light vessels are sufficient to convey intelligence of our movements, and in an instant, without trouble or danger, they are enabled to seize upon their prey.

"If, on the contrary, our squadrons are daring enough to appear in the British Channel, which ought, in reality, to be called the French Sea only, they are exposed to perpetual danger. Their total destruction may be effected by the hurricanes or the enemy's superiority, because in both these cases there is no shelter for them. This is what happened at the famous battle of La Hoyne, where Tourville might have been enabled to unite the glory of a skillful retreat with that of a hard-fought and so unequal a contest, had there been a port for him to take shelter in.

"In that state of things, men of great sagacity, and attached to the good of their country, prevailed upon government, by dint of projects and memorials, to seek, by the assistance of art, for those resources of which we had been deprived by nature. After a great deal of hesitation, the Bay of Cherbourg was selected, and was to be suited to the design by means of an immense dike projecting into the sea. In that way we were to acquire, even close to the enemy, an artificial road, whence our ships might be enabled, in all times and weather, to attack his, and where they might escape from their pursuit.

"It was," said the Emperor, "a magnificent and glorious undertaking, very difficult with respect to the execution and to the finances of that period. The dike was to be formed by immense cones, constructed empty in the port, and towed afterward to the spot, where they were sunk by the weight of the stones with which they were filled. There certainly was great ingenuity in the invention. Louis XVI. honored these operations with his presence. His departure from Versailles was a great event. In those times a king never left his residence; his excursions did not extend beyond the limits of a hunting party; they did not hurry about as at present; and I really believe that I contributed not a little to the rapidity of their movements.

"However, as it was absolutely necessary that things should be impressed with the character of the age, the eternal rivalry between the land and sea, that question which can never be decided, continued to be carried on. It might be said, in that respect, that there were two kings in France, or that he who reigned had two interests, and ought to have two wills, which proved rather that he had none at all. Here the sea was the only subject for consideration, yet the question was decided in favor of the land, not by superiority of argument, but by priority of right. Where the fate of the Empire was at stake, a point of precedence was substituted, and thus the grand object, the magnificent enterprise, failed of success. The land party established itself at the Isle Pelée and at Fort Querqueville. It was employed there merely to lend an auxiliary hand to the construction of the dike, which was itself the chief object; but, instead of that, it began by establishing its own predominance, and afterward compelled the dike to become the instrument of its convenience, and subservient to its plans and discretion. What was the result? The harbor which was forming, and which ought to contain the mass of our navy, whether designed to strike at the heart of the enemy's power, or to take occasional shelter, could only accommodate fifteen sail, at most, while we wanted anchorage for more than a hundred, which might have been effected without more labor and with little more expense, had the work been carried more forward into the sea, merely beyond the limits which the land party had appropriated to itself.

"Another blunder, highly characteristic and scarcely conceivable, took place: all the principal measures for completing the harbor were fixed upon; the dike commenced; one of the channels, that to the eastward, finished, and the other, to the westward, on the point of being formed, without an exact and precise knowledge of all the soundings. This oversight was so great, that the channel already formed, that to the eastward, five hundred fathoms broad, having been extended too closely to the fort, did not, without inconvenience, admit of vessels at low water, and that the other, which was about to be constructed to the westward, would have been impracticable, or, at least, very dangerous, but for the individual zeal of one officer, M. de Chavagnac, who made that important discovery in time, and caused the works on the left extremity of the dike to be stopped at the distance of twelve hundred fathoms from Querqueville Fort, by which it was to be defended. This seems to me, and is in fact, too great a distance.

"The system adopted in the works of the dike, which is more than a league from the shore, and more than nineteen hundred fathoms long by ninety feet broad, was also liable to numerous changes, suggested, however, by experience. The cones, which, according to the established principle, ought to have touched each other in their bases, were separated in that respect, either by accident or with a view of economy. They were damaged by storms, eaten by worms, or they rotted with age. They were at length altogether neglected with the exception of stones thrown at random into the sea, and when it was observed that these were scattered by the rolling of the waves, recourse was had to enormous blocks, which finally answered every expectation.

"The works were continued without interruption under Louis XVI. An increased degree of activity was imparted to them by our legislative assemblies, but, in consequence of the commotions which soon followed, they were completely abandoned, and at the time of the Consulate there was not a trace of that famous dike to be seen. Every thing had been destroyed for several feet under low-water level by the original imperfection of the plan, by the length of time, and the violence of the waves. The moment, however, I took the helm of affairs, one of my first employments was to turn my attention to so important a point. I ordered commissions of inquiry. I had the subject discussed in my presence. I made myself acquainted with the local circumstances, and I decided that the dike should be run up with all possible means and expedition, and that two solid fortifications should, in the course of time, be constructed at the two extremities, but measures should be immediately taken for the establishment of a considerable provisional battery. I had then to encounter, on all sides, the inconveniences, the objections, the particular views, and the fondness which attaches itself to individual opinions. Several maintained that the thing could not be done. I continued steady; I insisted, I commanded, and the thing was done.

"In less than two years a real island was seen to rise, as it were by magic, from the sea, on which was erected a battery of large calibre. Until that moment our labors had almost constantly been the sport of the English. They had, they said, been convinced, from their origin, that they would be fruitless. They had foretold that the cones would destroy themselves; that the small stones would be swept away by the waves; and, above all, they relied upon our lassitude and inconstancy. But here things were completely altered, and they made a show of molesting our operations. They were, however, too late. I was already prepared for them. The western channel naturally continued very wide, and the two extreme fortifications, which defended each its peculiar passage, being incapable of maintaining a cross fire, it was probable that an enterprising enemy might be enabled to force the western channel, come to anchor within the dike, and there renew the defeat of Aboukir. But I had already guarded against this with my central provisional battery. However, as I am for permanent establishments, I ordered within the dike, in the centre, by way of support, and which, in its turn, might serve as an envelope, an enormous elliptical pier to be constructed, commanding the central battery, and mounted itself in two casemated tiers, bomb-proof, with fifty pieces of large calibre, and twenty mortars of an extensive range, as well as barracks, powder magazine, and cisterns. I have the satisfaction of having left this noble work in a finished state.

"Having provided for the defensive, my only business was to prepare offensive measures, which consisted in the means of collecting the mass of our fleets at Cherbourg. The harbor, however, could contain but fifteen sail. For the purpose of increasing the number, I caused a new port to be dug. The Romans never undertook a more important, a more difficult task, or one which promised a more lasting duration. It was sunk into the granite to the depth of fifty feet, and I caused the opening of it to be celebrated by the presence of Maria Louisa, while I myself was on the fields of battle in Saxony. By this means I procured anchorage for twenty-five sail more. Still, that number was not sufficient, and I therefore relied upon very different means of augmenting my naval strength. I was resolved to renew the wonders of Egypt at Cherbourg. I had already erected my pyramid in the sea. I would have also had my Lake Mœris. My great object was to be enabled to concentrate all our maritime force, and in time it would have been immense, and adequate to strike a fatal blow against the enemy.

"I was preparing my scene of action in such a way that the two nations, in their totality, might have been enabled to grapple with each other man to man, and the issue could not be doubtful, for we should have been more than forty millions of French against fifteen of English. I should have wound up the war with a battle of Actium; and, afterward, what did I want of England? Her destruction? Certainly not. I merely wanted the end of an intolerable usurpation, the enjoyment of imprescriptible and sacred rights, the deliverance, the liberty of the seas, the independence, the honor of flags. I was speaking in the name of all and for all, and I should have succeeded by concession or by force. I had on my side power, indisputable right, and the wishes of nations."

July 16. The Emperor rode out in the morning, in the calash, with Las Casas and Dr. O'Meara. On his return, he invited them to breakfast with him in the garden. He conversed at great length on the endless vexations of the governor. O'Meara remarked that Madam Sturmer, the wife of one of the commissioners, was very desirous of seeing the Emperor, but that the commissioners believed that he would not receive them.

"Who told them so?" inquired the Emperor. "I am willing to receive them whenever they ask through General Bertrand. I shall receive them as private characters. I never refuse to see any person when asked in a proper way, and especially I should be always happy to see a lady.

"It appears that your ministers," he continued, "have sent out a great many articles of dress for us, and other things which it was supposed might be wanted. Now, if this governor were possessed of the feelings of a gentleman, he would have sent a list of them to Bertrand, stating that the English government had sent a supply of certain articles, which it was thought we might want, and that, if we stood in need of them, we might order such as we pleased; but instead of acting in the manner pointed out by the rules of politeness, this jailer converts into an insult what probably your government intended as a civility. He selects such things as he himself pleases, and sends them up in a contemptuous manner, without consulting us, as if he were sending alms to a set of beggars, or clothing to convicts. Truly he has the heart of an executioner; for no one but an executioner would unnecessarily increase the miseries of people situated like us, already too unhappy. His hands soil every thing that passes through them."

About two o'clock a message was brought to the Emperor to ascertain whether he was willing to receive the governor. The Emperor admitted him to a long audience, and afterward gave to Las Casas the following account of the interview:

"I ran over," said the Emperor, "without falling into a passion, all the objects under discussion. I recapitulated all our grievances, enumerated all our wrongs, addressed myself by turns to his understanding, his imagination,

U

his feelings, and his heart. I put it in his power to repair all the mischief he had done, to recommence upon a plan altogether new; but in vain, for that man is without fibres; nothing is to be expected of him."

The governor assured the Emperor that, when the arrest of M. de Montholon's servant took place, he did not know he was in our service, and he added that he had not read Madam Bertrand's sealed letter.

"Your letter to Count Bertrand," replied the Emperor, "is altogether repugnant to our manners and in direct opposition to our prepossessions. If I were but a simple general and private individual, and had received such a letter from you, I would have called you out. A man so well known and respected in Europe as the grand marshal is not to be insulted under the penalty of social reprobation. You do not take a correct view of your situation with regard to us. All your actions here come within the province of history, and even the conversation which passes at this moment belongs to history. You injure every day by your conduct your own government and your own nation, and in time you may feel the consequences of it. Your government will disclaim your conduct in the end, and a stain will attach itself to your name which will disgrace your children. Will you allow me to tell you what we think of you? We think you capable of every thing—*yes, of every thing;* and while you retain your hatred, we shall retain our opinion. I shall still wait for some time, because I like to act upon certainties; and I shall then have to complain, not that the worst proceeding of the ministers was to send me to St. Helena, but that they gave you the command of it. You are a greater calamity to us than all the wretchedness of this horrible rock.

"With respect to the commissioners of the allied powers, whom the governor wished to present to me, I informed him that I rejected them in their official capacity, but that I would readily receive them as private individuals. I assured him that I had no dislike to any one of them, not even to the French commissioner, M. Montchenu, who might be a very worthy man, who had been my subject for ten years, and who, having been an emigrant, was probably indebted to me for the happiness of returning to France; that, besides, after all, he was a Frenchman; that that title was indelible in my eyes, and that there was no opinion which could destroy it in my estimation.

"With regard to the new buildings at Longwood, which were the great object of the governor's visit, I replied that I did not wish for them; that I preferred my present inconvenient residence to a better one situated at a great distance, and at the expense of a great deal of noise and the trouble of moving; that the buildings which he had just mentioned to me would require years to be completed, and that before that time either we should not be worth the cost incurred for our maintenance, or Providence would deliver him from us."

July 17. Napoleon walked in the garden with Dr. O'Meara. He spoke of the new house which the English government had sent out, and said,

"If I expected to remain long in St. Helena, I should wish to have it erected at the Plantation House side; but I am of opinion that, as soon as the affairs of France are settled, and things remain quiet, the English government will allow me to return to Europe, and finish my days in England. I do not believe that they are foolish enough to be at the expense of eight millions annually to keep me here when I am no longer to be feared. I am, therefore, not very anxious about the house.

"As to escape, even if we were inclined to try it, there are ninety-eight chances out of a hundred against one succeeding. Notwithstanding which, this jailer imposes as many restrictions as if I had nothing more to do than to step into a boat and be off. It is true, that while one lives there is always a chance. Although chained, inclosed in a cell, and every human precaution taken, there is still a chance of escape, and the only effectual way to prevent it is to put me to death. It is only the dead who never come back. Then all uneasiness on the part of the European powers and Lord Castlereagh will cease. No more expense, no more squadrons to watch me, or poor soldiers fatigued to death with pickets and guards, or harassed carrying loads up those rocks."

July 18. The Emperor was very unwell, and spent three hours in the bath. He read two volumes while in the bath. About four o'clock he sent for Las Casas. Gradually the Emperor became animated in conversation, and in reply to some amusing anecdotes related by Las Casas respecting the Faubourg St. Germain, the abode of the ancient nobility, to which class Las Casas belonged, he said,

"I see plainly that my plan with respect to your Faubourg St. Germain was ill managed. I did too much or too little. I did enough to dissatisfy the opposite party, and not enough to connect the other with me altogether. Although some of them were fond of money, the multitude would have been content with the rattles and sound, with which I could have satiated them, without any injury, in the main, to our new principles. My dear Las Casas, I did too much and not enough, and yet I was earnestly occupied with the business. Unfortunately, I was the only one seriously engaged in the undertaking. All who were about me thwarted instead of promoting it, and yet there were but two grand measures to be taken with regard to you—that of annihilating, or that of melting you down in the great mass of society. The former could not enter my head, and the latter was not an easy task, but I did not consider it beyond my strength; and, in fact, although I had no support, and was even counteracted in my views, I nearly realized them at length. Had I remained, the thing would have been accomplished.

"This will appear astonishing to him who knows how to appreciate the heart of man and the state of society. I do not think that history can furnish any case of a similar kind, or that so important a result, obtained in so short a space of time, can be found. I should have carried that fusion into effect, and cemented that union by every sacrifice. It would have rendered us invincible. The opposite conduct has ruined us, and may for a long time protract the misfortunes, perhaps the last gasps of unhappy France. I once more repeat that I did too much or too little. I ought to have attached the emigrants to me upon their return. I might have easily become an object of adoration with the aristocracy. An establishment of that nature was necessary for me. It is the real, the only support of monarchy, its guide, its lever, its point of resistance. Without it, the state is but a vessel without a rudder, a real balloon in the air. But the essence of aristocracy, its talismanic charm, consists in antiquity, in age, and these were the only things I could not create. The intermediate means were wanting. M. de Breteuil, who had insinuated himself into my favor, encouraged me. On the contrary, M. de Talleyrand, who certainly was not a favorite with the emigrants, discouraged me by every possible means. Reasonable democracy contents itself with securing equality for all, to seek and to obtain. The real line of conduct would have been to employ the remains of aristocracy together with the forms and design of democracy. Above all, it was necessary to collect the ancient names, those celebrated in our history. This is the only mode of giving an instantaneous air of old age to the most modern institutions.

"I entertained upon that subject ideas which were altogether peculiar to myself. Had any difficulties been started by Austria and Russia, I would have married a French woman. I would have selected one of the most illustrious names of the monarchy. That was ever my original thought, my real inclination. My ministers were unable to prevent me but by their earnest appeals to political views. Had I been surrounded by the Montmorencies, the Nesles, and the Clissons, I should, by adopting their daughters, have united them with foreign sovereigns. My pride and my delight would have been to extend these noble French stocks, had they taken part with, or given themselves up to us altogether. They, and those belonging to me, thought that I was influenced by prejudice alone, when I was acting in conformity with the most profound combinations. Be that as it will, your friends have lost more in me than they are aware of. They are destitute of soul, of the feeling of true glory. By what unhappy propensity have they preferred wallowing in the mire of the Allies to the noble task of following me to the top of Mount Simplon, and from its summit commanding the respect and admiration of the rest of Europe! Senseless men!

"I had, however, a project in my portfolio which would have rallied around me a great number of that description of persons, and which would have been but just. Time alone was wanting to mature it. It was, that every descendant of ancient marshals or ministers should be considered at all times capable of getting himself declared a duke by presenting the requisite endowment. All the sons of generals and governors of provinces were to be qualified to assume the title of count upon the same principle, and so on in gradation. This would have advanced some, raised the hopes of others, excited the emulation of all, and hurt the pride of none; grand but altogether harmless rattles, and belonging, besides, to my system and my combinations.

"Old and corrupt are not governed like ancient and virtuous nations. For one individual at present who would sacrifice himself for the public good, there are thousands and millions who are insensible to every thing but their own interests, enjoyments, and vanity. To pretend to regenerate a people in an instant, or as if one were traveling fast, would be an act of madness. The genius of the workman ought to consist in knowing how to employ the materials he has at hand, and that is one of the causes of the resumption of all the monarchical forms, of the re-establishment of titles, of classes, and of the insignia of orders. The secret of the legislator should consist in knowing how to derive advantage even from the caprice and irregularities of those whom he pretends to rule. And, after every consideration, all these gewgaws were attended with few inconveniences, and not destitute of some benefits. At the point of civilization to which we have now attained, they are calculated to attract the respect of multitudes, provided, always, that the person decorated with them preserves respect for himself. They may satisfy the vanity of the weak without alarming strong and powerful minds in the slightest degree."

It was now a late hour of the night, and the Emperor said to Las Casas, in parting, "There is another pleasant evening spent."

July 19. Under this date Las Casas speaks of the etiquette observed by the French gentlemen in their intercourse with the Emperor.

"The Emperor behaved to us in the kindest manner, and with a paternal familiarity. We were, on our part, the most attentive and respectful of courtiers; we uniformly endeavored to anticipate his wishes; we carefully watched all his wants, and he had scarcely time to make a sign with his hand before we were in motion.

"None of us entered his apartment without being sent for, and if any thing of importance was to be communicated to him, he was previously made acquainted with it. If he walked separately with any of us, no other presumed to intrude. In the beginning we constantly remained uncovered near his person, which appeared strange to the English, who had been ordered to put on their hats after the first salute. This contrast appeared so ridiculous to the Emperor that he commanded us, once for all, to behave like them. Nobody, except the two ladies, took a seat in his presence, unless desired to do so. He was never spoken to but at his own summons, and when the conversation became general, which was always and in all cases under his control and guidance. Such was the etiquette of Longwood, which entirely was, as it must be evident, that of our recollections and feelings."

CHAPTER XXI.
1816, July.   Continued.

Establishments for Mendicity—Illyria—Prisoners of State—Freedom of the French People—Egypt—The Desert—Anecdotes—Paternal Advice—Remarkable Conversations—Cagliostro, Mesmer, Gall, Lavater, Madam de Balbi—Conversation with the Admiral—Commissioners—Santini—Nuns—Convents—Monks—The French Clergy.

July 20. The Emperor was reading an English work on the poor-rate, the immense sums raised, and the vast number of individuals maintained at the expense of the parishes. He was amazed at the development of poverty and misery, and was apprehensive that he could not have read the work correctly.

"The thing," said he, "seems altogether impossible. I can not conceive by what vices and defects so many poor could be found in a country so opulent, so industrious, and so abundant in resources for labor as England. I am still less capable of comprehending by what prodigy the proprietors, overloaded with a horrible ordinary and extraordinary taxation, are also enabled to provide for the wants of such a multitude. But we have nothing in France to be compared to it in the proportion of a hundredth or a thousandth degree. Have you not told me," said he to Las Casas, " that I sent you into the departments on a particular mission with regard to mendicity? Let us see, what is the number of our beggars? What did they cost? How many poor-houses did I establish? What was the number they held? What effect had they in removing mendicity?"

Las Casas replied, "It is impossible for me to enter into correct statements from mere recollection. I have, however, the official report itself among the few papers which I have preserved."

"Go instantly and look for it," said the Emperor. "Things are not profitable unless seasonably applied, and I shall soon run over it *with my thumb*, as Abbé de Pradt ingeniously said, although, to deal candidly with you, I am not, at present, over-desirous to devote my attention to such objects. They put me in mind of mustard after dinner.

"Well," said he, after looking at the report for a few minutes, "this has no resemblance whatever to England. Our organization, however, had failed. I suspected as much, and it was on that account I intrusted you with the mission. Your report would have been in perfect conformity with my views. You took up the consideration ingenuously, and like an honest man, without the fear of exciting the displeasure of the minister by depriving him of a great many appointments. I am pleased with a great number of your details. Why did not you come and converse with me about them yourself? You would have satisfied me, and I should have known how to value your services."

"Sire," said Las Casas, "as things were then situated, it would have been impossible for me. We were then involved in the confusion and embarrassment caused by our misfortunes."

"Your observation is perfectly correct," replied the Emperor. "You establish an unquestionable position. In the flourishing state to which I had raised the empire, no hands could any where be found destitute of employment. It was laziness and vice alone that could produce mendicants. You think that their complete annihilation was possible. I think so too. I am confident of it.

"Your levy in mass, to construct a vast single prison in each department, was equally adapted to the tranquillity of society and the well-being of those confined in it. Your idea of constructing monuments to last for centuries would have attracted my attention. That gigantic undertaking, its utility, its importance, the permanence of its results, all these points belonged to my system. With respect to your university for the people, I am very apprehensive that it would have been but a beautiful chimera of philanthropy, worthy of the unsophisticated Abbé de Saint Pierre. There is, however, some merit in the aggregate of those conceptions, but an energy of character, and an unbending perseverance, for which we are not generally distinguished, would be requisite to produce any good result.

"As for the rest, I every day collect ideas from you in this place of which I did not imagine you capable; but it was not at all my fault. You were near me; why did you not open your mind to me? I did not possess the gift of divination. Had you been minister, those ideas, however fantastical they might have at first appeared to me, would not have been the less attended to, because there is, in my opinion, no conception altogether unsusceptible of some positive good; and a wrong notion, when properly controlled and regulated, often leads to a right conclusion. I should have handed you over to commissioners who would have analyzed your plans. You would have defended them by your arguments, and after a thorough knowledge of the subject, I alone should have finally decided according to my own judgment. Such was my way of acting and my intention. I gave an impulse to industry. I put it into a state of complete activity throughout Europe. I was desirous of doing as much for all the faculties of the mind, but time was not allowed me. I could not bring my plans to maturity in full gallop, and, unfortunately, I but too often wasted them upon a sandy foundation, and consigned them to unproductive hands. But what were the other missions with which I intrusted you? Have you the reports?"

"Yes, sire," replied Las Casas; "one was in Holland, another in Illyria."

"Get the reports," said the Emperor; "but never mind; come back; spare me the trouble of reading such matters! They are henceforth, in reality, altogether useless. In obtaining possession of Illyria, it was never my intention to retain it. I never entertained the idea of destroying Austria. Her existence was, on the contrary, indispensably requisite for the execution of my plans. But Illyria was, in our hands, a vanguard to the heart of Austria, calculated to keep a check upon her, a sentinel at the gates of Vienna, to keep her steady to our interests. Besides, I was desirous of introducing and establishing in that country our doctrines, our system of government, and our codes. It was an additional step to the regeneration of Europe. I had merely taken it as a pledge, and intended to exchange it for Gallicia at the restoration of Poland, which I hurried on against my own opinion. I had, however, more than one project with regard to Illyria, for I frequently fluctuated in my designs, and had few ideas that were fixed on solid grounds. This arose rather from adapting myself to circumstances than from giving an impulse and direction to them, and I was every instant compelled to shift about. The consequence was, that for the greater part of the time I came to no absolute decision, and was occupied merely with projects. My predominant idea, particularly after my marriage, was to give Illyria up to Austria as an indemnity for Gallicia on the re-establishment of Poland, at whatever cost, as a separate kingdom. Not that I cared upon whose head, whether on that of a friend, an enemy, or an ally, the crown was placed, provided the thing was effected. It was all the same to me. I have, my dear Las Casas, formed vast and numerous projects, all unquestionably for the advancement of reason and the welfare of the human race. I was dreaded as a thunderbolt. I was charged with having a hand of iron; but, the moment that hand had struck the last blow, every thing would have been softened down for the happiness of all. How many millions would have poured their benedictions on me, both then and in future times!

"But how numerous, it must be confessed, the fatal misfortunes which were accumulated and combined to effect my overthrow at the end of my career! My unhappy marriage, the perfidies which resulted from it; that villainous affair of Spain, from which I could not disengage myself; that fatal war with Russia, which occurred through a misunderstanding; that horrible rigor of the elements, which devoured a whole army, and then the whole universe against me! Is it not wonderful that I was still able to make so long a resistance, and that I was more than once on the point of surmounting every danger, and emerging from that chaos more powerful than ever? Oh, destiny of man! What is human wisdom, human foresight!"

"It is an observation," said Las Casas, "which made an immediate and striking impression upon me during my mission in those countries, that, all other things fairly averaged, mendicity is much more rare in those parts which are poor and barren, and much more common in those which are fruitful and abundant. It is also infinitely more difficult to effect its destruction in places where the clergy have superior wealth and power. In Belgium, for instance, mendicants were seen to derive honor from their trade, and boast of having followed it for several generations. These claims belonged peculiarly to them, and that country was accordingly the rendezvous of mendicity."

"But I am not surprised at it," resumed the Emperor. "The difficulty of this important consideration consists entirely in discriminating accurately between the *poor* man who commands our respect and the *mendicant* who ought to excite our indignation. Besides, our religious oddities confound these two classes so completely that they seem to make a merit, a kind of virtue, of mendicity, and to encourage it by the promise of heavenly rewards. The mendicants are, in reality, neither more nor less than monks *au petit pied;* and that such is the fact is evident from the mendicant monks being so classed in the vocabulary. How was it possible for such ideas not to produce confusion in the mind and disorder in society? A great number of saints have been canonized whose only apparent merit was mendicity. They seem to have been transplanted to heaven for that which, considered as a matter of sound police, ought to have subjected them to castigation and confinement in this world. This would not, however, have prevented them from being worthy of heaven. But go on."

"What struck me also," said Las Casas, "very forcibly in La Vendée and the adjacent country was, that insanity had increased there perhaps tenfold more than in any other part of the empire, and that individuals were detained in the mendicity establishments and other places of confinement who were treated as vagabonds, or likely to become so, and who, having been taken up in their childhood, had no knowledge of their parents or origin. Some of them had wounds on their persons, but were ignorant how they had been inflicted. They were marks which had, no doubt, been inflicted upon them in their infancy. The opportunity of employing these individuals, who had not acquired a single social idea, has been suffered to pass by; they are now unfit for any purpose."

"Ah!" exclaimed the Emperor, "this is civil war and its hideous train, its inevitable consequences and its certain fruits! If some leaders make fortunes and extricate themselves from danger, the dregs of the population are always trodden under foot, and become the victims of every calamity! In order to proceed regularly in your mission, it was incumbent upon you to ascertain, in the first place, whether your information was well grounded, and to hear the evidence against the persons accused. And, then, it must be frankly admitted that abuses are inherent in every human establishment. You see that almost every thing of which you complained was committed by the very persons who were expressly intrusted with the means of prevention. Can a remedy be provided when it is impossible to, see what passes every where? There is something like a kind of net-work, which, extended on flat grounds, envelops the lower classes. A mesh must be broken, and discovered by a fortunate observer like you, before any thing of the matter is known in the upper regions. Accordingly, one of my dreams would have been, when the grand events of war were completely terminated, and I returned to the interior in tranquillity and at ease, to look out for half a dozen or a dozen of real good philanthropists—of those worthy men who live but to do good. I should have distributed them through the empire, which they would have secretly inspected for the purpose of making their report to me. They would have been the *spies of virtue!* They would have addressed themselves directly to me, and would have been my confessors, my spiritual directors, and my decisions with them would have been my good works in secret. My grand occupation, when at full leisure and at the height of my power, would have been the amelioration of every class of society.

"I should have descended to the details of individual comfort, and, had I found no motive for that conduct in my natural disposition, I should have been actuated by the spirit of calculation; for, after the acquisition of so much glory, what other means would have been left to me to make any addition to it? It was because I was well aware that that swarm of abuses necessarily existed, because I wished for the preservation of my subjects, and was desirous of throwing every impediment in the way of subordinate and intermediate tyranny, that I conceived my system of state prisons adapted to any crisis that might occur."

"Yes, sire," replied Las Casas; "but it was far from being well received in our saloons, and did not a little contribute to make you unpopular. An outcry was raised against the *new bastiles*, against the renewal of *lettres de cachet*."

"I know it very well," said the Emperor. "The outcry was echoed by all Europe, and rendered me odious. And yet observe how powerful the influence of words envenomed by perfidy! The whole of the discontent was principally occasioned by the preposterous title of my decree, which escaped me from distraction or some other cause; for, in the main, I contend that the law itself was an eminent service, and rendered individual liberty more complete and certain in France than in any other country of Europe. Considering the crisis from which we had emerged, the factions by which we had been divided, and the plots which had been laid and were still contriving, imprisonment became indispensable. It was, in fact, a benefit, for it superseded the scaffold. But I was desirous of sanctioning it by legal enactments, and of placing it beyond the reach of caprice, of arbitrary power, of hatred, and of vengeance.

"Nobody, according to my law, could be imprisoned and detained as a prisoner of state without the decision of my privy council, which consisted of sixteen persons; the first, the most independent, and most distinguished characters of the state. What unworthy feeling would have dared to expose itself to the detection of such a tribunal? Had I not voluntarily deprived myself of the power of consigning individuals to prison? None could be detained beyond a year without a fresh decision of the privy council, and four votes out of sixteen were sufficient to effect his release. Two councilors of state were bound to attend to the statements of the prisoners, and became from that moment their zealous advocates with the privy council. These prisoners were also under the protection of the committee of individual liberty appointed by the Senate, which was the object of public derision merely because it made no parade of its labors and their results. Its services, however, were great; for it would argue a defective knowledge of mankind to suppose that senators, who had nothing to expect from ministers, and who were their equals in rank, would not make use of their prerogative to oppose and attack them whenever the importance of the case called for their interference. It must also be considered that I had assigned the superintendence of the prisoners and the police of the prisons to the tribunals, which, from that instant, paralyzed the exercise of every kind of arbitrary authority belonging to the other branches of administration and their numerous subordinate agents. After such precautions, I do not hesitate to maintain that civil liberty was as effectually secured by that law in France as it possibly could be. The public misconceived, or pretended to misconceive, that truth, for it is necessary for us Frenchmen to murmur at every thing and on every occasion.

"The fact is, that, at the time of my downfall, the state prisons scarcely contained two hundred and fifty individuals, and I found nine thousand in them when I became consul. It will appear from the list of those who are imprisoned, and upon examination into the causes and motives of their confinement, that almost every one of them deserved death, and would have been sentenced to it by regular process of law, and it consequently follows that their imprisonment was, on my part, a benefit conferred upon them. Why is there nothing published against me on this subject at present? Where are the serious grievances to be found with which I am reproached? There are none in reality. If some of the prisoners afterward made a merit of their sufferings with the king on account of their exertions in his favor, did they not, by that proceeding, pronounce their own sentence and attest my justice? For what may seem a virtuous action in the king's eye was incontestably a crime under me; and it was only because I was repugnant to the shedding of blood on account of political crimes, and because such trials would have but tended to the continuance of commotion and perplexity in the heart of the country, that I commuted the punishment to simple detention.

"I repeat it, the French were, at my era, the freest people of all Europe, without excepting even the English; for in England, if any extreme danger causes the suspension of the *Habeas Corpus Act*, every individual may be sent to prison at the mere will of ministers who are not called upon to justify their motives or give an explanation of their conduct. My law was very differently restricted. And then, at last, if, in spite of my good intention, and notwithstanding my utmost care, all that you have just said, and, no doubt, many other things, were well founded, it must not still be considered so easy a task as it is thought to create a beneficial establishment for a nation. It is a remarkable circumstance that the countries which have been separated from us have regretted the loss of the laws with which I governed them. This is a homage paid to their superiority. The real, the only mode of passing sentence upon me with regard to their defects would be to show the existence of a better code in any other country. New times are drawing near, it will be seen."

July 21. The Emperor spent the morning dictating the campaign of Egypt. At three o'clock he took a walk with Las Casas to the bottom of the wood, where the calash was appointed to meet them to take them back. At dinner the Emperor was very animated in conversation.

"The campaign of Egypt," said he, "will be as interesting as an episode of romance. The position which I occupied in the middle of Syria, with twelve thousand men only, was, it must be admitted, an audacious measure. I was at the distance of five hundred leagues from Desaix, who formed the other extremity of my army. It has been related by Sydney Smith that I lost eighteen thousand men before St. Jean d'Acre, although my army consisted but of twelve thousand. Had I been master of the sea, I should have been master of the East; and the thing was so practicable, that it failed only through the stupidity or bad conduct of some officers of the navy.

THE MARCH THROUGH THE DESERT.

"Volney, who traveled in Egypt before the Revolution, had stated his opinion that that country could not be occupied without three great wars— against England, the Grand Seignior, and the inhabitants. The latter, in particular, seemed difficult and terrible to him. He was altogether mistaken in that respect, for it gave us no trouble. We had even succeeded in making friends of the inhabitants in the course of a short time, and in connecting their cause with ours. A handful of Frenchmen had then been sufficient to conquer that fine country, which they ought never to have lost. We had actually accomplished prodigies in war and in politics. Our undertaking was altogether different from the Crusades, for the Crusaders were innumerable, and hurried on by fanaticism. My army, on the contrary, was very small, and the soldiers were so little inclined to the enterprise, that they were frequently tempted to carry off the colors and return. I had, however, succeeded in familiarizing them with the country, which supplied every thing in abundance, and at so cheap a rate, that I was at one time on the point of placing them on half pay, for the purpose of laying by the other half for them. I had acquired such an ascendency over them, that I had it in my power, by a simple order of the day, to convert them to Mohammedanism. They would have treated it as a joke. The population would have been gratified, and the Christians of the East themselves would have considered themselves gainers, and approved of it, as they knew that we could do nothing better for them and for ourselves.

"The English were struck with consternation at seeing us in possession of Egypt. We exposed to Europe the certain means of wresting India from them. They have not yet dismissed their apprehensions, and they are in the right. If forty or fifty thousand European families ever succeed in establishing their industry, laws, and government in Egypt, India will be more effectually lost to the English by the commanding influence of circumstances than by the force of arms.

RUINS OF EGYPT.

"The desert," continued the Emperor, "always had a peculiar influence on my feelings. I have never crossed it without being subject to a certain emotion. It seemed to me the image of immensity. It showed no boundaries, and had neither beginning nor end: it was an ocean on terra firma.

"When I was in Syria," said the Emperor, "it was a settled opinion at Cairo that I never would be seen there again; and I recollect the thieving and impudence of a little Chinese who was one of my servants. He was a little deformed dwarf whom Josephine once took a fancy to at Paris. He was the only Chinese in France, and was generally placed behind her carriage. She took him to Italy, but as he was in the constant habit of pilfering, she wished to get rid of him. With that view, I put him on board my Egyptian expedition. Egypt was a lift to him half way on his journey. This little monster was intrusted with the care of my cellar; but I had no sooner crossed the desert, than he sold, at a very low price, two thousand bottles of delicious claret. His only object was to make money, and he was convinced that I should never come back. He was not at all disconcerted at my return, but came eagerly to meet me, and acquainted me, like a faithful servant, as he said, with the loss of my wine. The robbery was so glaring that he was himself compelled to confess it. I was much urged to have him hanged, but I refused, because, in every sense of justice, I ought to have done as much to those in embroidered clothes who had knowingly bought and drank the wine. I contented myself with discharging him and sending him to Suez, where he was at liberty to do what he pleased."

July 22. About ten o'clock the Emperor knocked at the door of Las Casas's apartment, and took him out to walk. All the exiles breakfasted together under some gnarled and almost verdureless gum-trees in the garden. It was a clear and brilliant day, and the heat was intense, but a gentle breeze swept over the cliffs, and all were in cheerful spirits. The Emperor looked around upon his devoted companions with paternal affection, and, alluding to some misunderstanding which had recently occurred between some of them, said,

" You are bound, when you are one day restored to the world, to consider yourselves as *brothers* on my account. My memory will dictate this conduct to you. Be so, then, from this moment."

" He next described to us," says Las Casas, " how we might be of mutual advantage to each other, and the sufferings we had it in our power to alleviate. It was all at once a family and a moral lesson, alike distinguished for excellent sentiment and practical rules of conduct. It ought to have been written in letters of gold. It lasted nearly an hour and a quarter, and will, I think, never be forgotten by any of us. For myself, not only the principles and the words, but the tone, the expression, the action, and, above all, the entire affection with which he delivered them, will never be effaced from my mind."

At the dinner-table conversation turned on dreams and presentiments. The Emperor, with his inexhaustible mental fertility, as usual, took the lead.

" All these quackeries," said he, " and as many others, such as those of Cagliostro, Mesmer, Gall, and Lavater, are destroyed by this simple answer, '*All that may exist, but it does not exist.*'

" Man is fond of the marvelous. It has for him irresistible fascinations. He is ever ready to abandon that which is near at hand, to run after that which is fabricated for him. He voluntarily lends himself to his own delusions. The truth is, that every thing about us is a wonder. There is nothing which can be properly called a phenomenon. Every thing in nature is a phenomenon. The wood that is put in the fire-place, and warms me, is a phenomenon. That candle there, which gives me light, is a phenomenon. All the first causes, my understanding, my faculties, are phenomena, for they all exist, and we can not define them. I take leave of you here, and lo! I am at Paris, entering my box at the Opera. I bow to the audience, I hear the acclamations, I see the performers, I listen to the music; but if I can bound over the distance from St. Helena, why should I not bound over the distance of centuries? Why should I not see the future as well as the past? Why should the one be more extraordinary, more wonderful than the other? The only reason is, that it does not exist. This is the argument which will always annihilate, without the possibility of reply, all visionary wonders. All these quacks deal in very ingenious speculations; their reasoning may be just and seductive, but their conclusions are false, because they are unsupported by facts.

"Mesmer and Mesmerism have never recovered from the blow dealt at them by Bailly's report in the name of the Academy of Sciences. Mesmer produced effects upon a person by magnetizing him before his face, yet the same person, magnetized behind without his knowing it, experienced no effect whatever. It was, therefore, on his part, an error of imagination, a debility of the senses. It was the act of the somnambule, who at night runs along the roof without danger, because he is not afraid, but who would break his neck in the day, because his senses would confound him.

"I once attacked the quack Puységur on his somnambulism at one of my public audiences. He wished to assume a very lofty tone. I brought him down to his proper level with only these words: 'If your doctrine is so instructive, let it tell us something new. Mankind will, no doubt, make a very considerable progress in the next two hundred years: let it specify any single improvement which is to take place within that period! Let it tell me what I shall do within the following week! Let it ascertain the numbers of the lottery which will be drawn to-morrow!'

"I behaved in the same manner to Gall, and contributed very much to the discredit of his theory. Corvisart was his principal follower. He and all who resemble him have a great attachment to materialism, which is calculated to strengthen their theory and influence. But nature is not so barren. Were she so clumsy as to make herself known by external forms, we should go to work more promptly, and acquire a greater degree of knowledge. Her secrets are more subtile, more delicate, more evanescent, and have hitherto escaped the most minute researches. We find a great genius in a little hunchback, and a man with a fine, commanding person turns out to be a stupid fellow. A big head with a large brain is sometimes destitute of a single idea, while a small brain is found to possess a vast understanding. And observe the imbecility of Gall! He attributes to certain protuberances propensities and crimes which are not inherent in nature, which arise solely from society and the compact of mankind. What becomes of the protuberance denoting thievery where there is no property to steal? of that indicating drunkenness where there are no fermented liquors? and of that characterizing ambition where there is no social establishment?

"The same remarks apply to that egregious charlatan, Lavater, with his physical and moral relations. Our credulity lies in the defect of our nature. It is inherent in us to wish for the acquisition of positive ideas, when we ought, on the contrary, to be carefully on our guard against them. We scarcely look at a man's features before we undertake to ascertain his character. We should be wise enough to repel the idea, and to neutralize those deceitful appearances. I was robbed by a person who had gray eyes; and from that moment am I never to look at gray eyes without the idea, the fear of being robbed? It was a weapon that wounded me, and of that I am apprehensive wherever I see it; but was it the gray eyes that robbed me? Reason and experience—and I have been enabled to derive great benefit from both—prove that all those external signs are so many falsehoods. We cannot be too strictly on our guard against them; and the only true way of appreciating and gaining a thorough knowledge of mankind is by trying them, and associating with them. After all, we sometimes meet with countenances so hideous, it must allowed, that the most powerful understanding is confounded, and condemns them in spite of itself."

July 24. Admiral Malcolm kindly sent up a lieutenant and a party of seamen to pitch a tent, formed of a lower studding-sail. This was quite a comfort to the Emperor, as he was very fond of being in the open air, and no shade was afforded by the straggling, gnarly, storm-withered gum-trees of Longwood. It was a damp day, and the Emperor, being unable to go out, amused himself for a short time at a billiard-table which his companions had just laid down. Sitting in his chamber before dinner with a few of his friends, conversation turned upon the emigrants, and the name of Madam de Balbi was mentioned.

The Emperor asked, "But is not this Madam de Balbi a very dangerous woman?"

"Certainly not," replied Las Casas; "she is, on the contrary, one of the best women in the world, with a great deal of wit and an excellent judgment."

"If that is the case," said the Emperor, "she must have much cause to complain of me. This is the painful consequence of false representations. She was pointed out as a very dangerous character."

"Yes, sire," Las Casas added, "you made her very unhappy. Madam de Balbi placed all her happiness in the charms of society, and you banished her from Paris. I met with her in one of my missions, confined within her province, and pining away with vexation. Yet she expressed no resentment against your majesty, and spoke of you with great moderation."

"Well, then," said the Emperor, "why did you not come to me and set me right?"

"Ah! sire," Las Casas answered, "your character was then so little known to us compared with what I know it to be at present, that I should not have dared to take it upon myself; but I will mention an anecdote of Madam de Balbi when at London, during the high tide of our emigration, which will make you better acquainted with her than any thing I could say. At the time when you were declared Consul, a person just arrived from Paris was invited to a small party at her house. He engrossed the attention of the company, in consequence of all the particulars he had to communicate respecting a place which interested us so very materially. He was asked several questions respecting the Consul. 'He can not,' said he, 'live long: he is *so yellow as to inspire delight.*' These were his words. He grew more animated by degrees, and gave as a toast, 'The death of the First Consul!' 'Oh, horrible!' was the instantaneous exclamation of Madam de Balbi. 'What, drink to the death of a human being! For shame! I will give a much better toast—*The king's health!*' "

"Well," said the Emperor, "I repeat that she was very ill used by me, in consequence of the representations which were made to me. She had been described as a person fond of political intrigues, and remarkable for the bitterness of her sarcasms. And this puts me in mind of an expression which is perhaps wrongly attributed to her, but which struck me, however, solely on account of its wit. I was assured that a distinguished personage, who was very much attached to her, was seized with a fit of jealousy, for which she clearly proved she had given no cause. He persisted, however, and observed that she ought to know that the wife of Cæsar should be free from suspicion. Madam de Balbi replied that the remark contained two important mistakes, for it was known to all the world that she was not his wife, and that he was not Cæsar."

July 25. The Emperor received letters from his mother, his sister Pauline, and his brother Lucien; also several European journals up to the 12th of May. He was much shocked in reading that his friend and companion, General Bertrand, was condemned by the Bourbons, for his fidelity to the Emperor, to death. For a moment he seemed quite lost in astonishment, and then recollecting himself, said,

"By the laws of France, a man accused of a capital offense may be tried and condemned to death *by outlawry*, but the sentence can not be executed. The individual must be tried again and be actually present. I am distressed, however, on account of the effect which this sentence must produce on Madam Bertrand. In revolutions every thing is forgotten. The benefits you confer to-day are forgotten to-morrow. The side once changed, gratitude, friendship, parentage, every tie vanishes, and all that is sought for is self-interest."

About three o'clock Admiral Malcolm called, and requested to be presented to the Emperor. He brought with him some French journals to aid the captive to beguile the weary days of imprisonment. The Emperor received him with frankness and cordiality, and conversed with him upon various topics for nearly three hours. Sir Hudson Lowe was evidently much piqued at the kind relations existing between the Emperor and the admiral. In an official document to Earl Bathurst, he says, "Sir Pulteney Malcolm has had long conversations with Bonaparte, and *appears* much in his good graces."

In reference to this interview, Las Casas says, "The admiral gave great pleasure to the Emperor, who treated him from the first with a great deal of freedom and good-nature, as if he had been an old acquaintance. The admiral was entirely of the Emperor's opinion with regard to a great number of subjects. He admitted that it was extremely difficult to escape from St. Helena, and that he could see no inconvenience in allowing the Emperor to visit freely all parts of the island. He considered it absurd that Plantation House had not been given up to the Emperor, and felt, but only since his arrival, he confessed, that the title of *general* might be offensive. He thought that Governor Lowe had good intentions, but did not know how to act. Ministers had, in his opinion, been embarrassed with respect to the Emperor, but entertained no hatred against him. They did not know how to dispose of him. Had he remained in England, he had been, and was still, a terror to the Continent, and he would have been too dangerous and efficient an instrument in the hands of the opposition. He was apprehensive, however, that all these circumstances would detain us here a long time; and he expressed his confidence that it was the intention of the ministers, with the exception of the necessary precautions to prevent his escape, that Napoleon should be treated with every possible indulgence at St. Helena. All this was said in a manner so courteous, that the Emperor discussed the business with him with as little warmth as if the matter was one in which he had no personal interest whatever."

At one moment the Emperor produced a sensible effect upon the admiral, when, alluding to the commissioners, he pointed out the impossibility of receiving them in their official capacity.

"After all, sir," said Napoleon, "you and I are men. I appeal to you: is it possible that the Emperor of Austria, whose daughter I married, who implored that union on his knees, who retains my wife and my son, should send me his commissioner without a line to myself, without the smallest scrap of a bulletin with respect to my son's health? Can I receive him with consistency? Can I have any thing to communicate to him? I may say the same thing of the commissioner sent by Alexander, who gloried in calling himself my friend, with whom, indeed, I carried on political wars, but had no personal quarrel. It is a fine thing to be a sovereign, but we are not, on that account, the less entitled to be treated as men. I lay claim to no other character at present. Can they all be destitute of feeling? Be assured, sir, that when I object to the title of *General*, I am not offended. I decline it merely because it would be an acknowledgment that I have not been Emperor, and in this respect I advocate the honor of others more than my own. I advocate the honor of those with whom I have been, in that rank, connected by treaties, by family and political alliances. The only one of these commissioners whom I might perhaps receive would be that of Louis XVIII., who owes me nothing. That commissioner was a long time my subject. He acted merely in conformity to circumstances, independent of his option, and I should accordingly receive him to-morrow, were I not apprehensive of the misrepresentations that would take place, and of the false coloring that would be given to the circumstance."

July 28. Sir Hudson Lowe had now adopted the extraordinary and exasperating measure of carefully examining all the European journals, and sending to the Emperor only those which he was willing that his prisoner should see. If a paper was filled with abuse, it was at once sent to Longwood. If an article appeared in any journal defending the Emperor, it was detained. Sir Hudson Lowe had the insolence to defend this atrocity under the pretense of humanity. He said that these friendly articles might excite expectations in the bosom of the Emperor which would be only doomed to disappointment.

Mr. Hobhouse, afterward Lord Broughton, sent to the Emperor a very friendly work, in two volumes, written by himself, entitled "The Substance of some Letters written by an Englishman resident at Paris during the last Reign of Napoleon." These letters did some little justice to the abused and calumniated victim of combined despotisms. The governor refused to deliver these volumes for the assigned reason that the author had written in one of them, "*Imperatori Napoleon.*" Alluding to this fact in conversation with O'Meara, the Emperor said,

"This galley-slave would not allow the book to be sent to me because it had 'the Emperor Napoleon' written upon it—because he thought that it would give me some pleasure to see that all men were not like him, and that I was esteemed by some of his nation. I could not have believed that a man could be so base and vile."

In allusion to this subject, the governor subsequently said to Dr. O'Meara, as additional reasons for not delivering the volume, "I could not send the book to Longwood, as it had not been forwarded through the channel of the Secretary of State. Moreover, Lord Castlereagh was extremely ill spoken of, and I had no idea of allowing General Bonaparte to read a book in which a British minister was treated in such a manner, or even to let him know that such a book could be published in England."

July 29. At the dinner-table to-day the Emperor astonished all his companions by turning, with a stern look, to one of the servants in waiting, and exclaiming,

"So, then, assassin, you resolved to kill the governor! Wretch! if such a thought ever again enters your head, you will have to do with me. You will see how I shall treat you."

Then turning to the gentlemen at the table, he said,

"Gentlemen, it is Santini, there, who determined to kill the governor. That rascal was about to involve us in a sad embarrassment. I found it necessary to exert all my authority, all my indignation, to restrain him. It was only by imperial, by pontifical authority that I finally succeeded in making the scoundrel desist altogether from his project. Observe for a moment the fatal consequences he was about to produce. I should also have passed for the murderer, the assassin of the governor; and, in reality, it would have been very difficult to destroy such an impression in the minds of a great number of people."

Santini was a Corsican, of intense passions, and devoted to the Emperor with fervor almost supernatural. Enraged by the affronts he saw heaped upon his master by the governor, he formed the project of shooting the petty despot, and of then putting an end to his own existence. He revealed the plan to his countryman Cypriani, saying that he was determined thus to rid the world of a monster. Cypriani, not being able to dissuade him from his atrocious enterprise, revealed his design to the Emperor.

- *July* 31. The weather to-day was dark, wet, and dismal, so that the Emperor found great difficulty in going to Madam de Montholon's saloon. After dinner he read, first, La Mère Coupable, and next, the Mélanie of La Harpe, which he thought wretchedly conceived and very badly executed.

"It is," said he, "a turgid declamation, in perfect conformity with the taste of the times, founded in fashionable calumnies and absurd falsehoods. When La Harpe wrote that piece, a father certainly had not the power of forcing his daughter to take the veil. The laws would never have allowed it. This play, which was performed at the beginning of the Revolution, was solely indebted for its success to the momentary caprice of public opinion. Now that the inducement is over, it would be a wretched performance! La Harpe's characters are all unnatural. He should not have attacked defective institutions with defective weapons.

"La Harpe has so completely failed in his object with regard to my own impressions, that all my feelings are in favor of the father, while I am shocked at the daughter's conduct. I have never seen the performance without being tempted to start from my seat and call out to the daughter, 'You have but to say No, and we will all take your part. You will find a protector in every citizen.' When I was on service with my regiments, I often witnessed the ceremony of taking the veil. It was a ceremony very much attended by the officers, and which raised our indignation, particularly when the victims were handsome. We ran in crowds to it, and our attention was alive to the slightest incident. Had they but said no, we should have carried them off, sword in hand. It is consequently false that violence is used. The only means employed are the arts of seduction. Those upon whom they are practiced are kept not unlike recruits. They are exposed to the blandishments and exhortations of the nuns, the abbess, the spiritual director, and the bishop; to the examination of the civil officer, and, finally, to public view. Thus every thing seems to concur in prevailing upon them to make the sacrifice.

"I am an enemy," he continued, "to convents in general, as useless, and productive of degrading inactivity. In another point of view, certain reasons may be pleaded in their favor. The best *mezzo termine*, and I have adopted it, is, in my opinion, that of tolerating them, of obliging the members to become useful, and of recognizing annual vows alone. I have not been allowed time enough to complete my institutions. It was my intention to enlarge the establishments of Saint Denis and Ecouen, for the purpose of giving an asylum to the widows of soldiers, or women advanced in years. And then it must be allowed that there are characters and imaginations of all kinds. Compulsion ought not to be used with regard to persons of an eccentric turn, provided their oddities are harmless; and an empire like France may, and has a right to, have houses for madmen called *Trappistes*. With respect to the latter, if any one ever thought of inflicting upon others the discipline which they practice, it would be justly considered a most abominable tyranny, and it might, notwithstanding, constitute the delight of him who exercised it upon himself. This is man! these his fanatical pursuits, or his folly! I have tolerated the monks of Mount Cenis, but these, at least, were useful, very useful, and might be even called heroical.

" I have nothing to say against the ancient bishops. They have shown themselves grateful for what I did for religion. All these ancient bishops possessed my confidence, and none of them deceived me. It is not a little singular that those of whom I had the greatest cause to complain were precisely those whom I had chosen myself. So very true is it that the holy unction, in approximating us to heaven, does not deliver us from the infirmities of earth, from its irregularities, its turpitudes."

The conversation then turned upon the want of priests in France. They had been ordained at a very early age—at twenty-one, and even at sixteen. The Emperor had wished to wait for more mature years. "It is very well," replied the bishops and the Pope; "your reasons are just; but, if you wait for that period, you will find none to ordain."

" I have no doubt," the Emperor continued, " that after me other principles will be adopted. A conscription of priests and nuns will perhaps be seen in France, as a military conscription was seen in my time. My barracks will probably be turned into convents and seminaries. Thus the world runs on. Poor people! In spite of all your knowledge, all your wisdom, you continue, like simple individuals, the slaves of fashionable caprice."

The conversation was thus continued until nearly one o'clock in the morning. The Emperor, as he retired, said, " It is a real victory over tediousness, and a great relief for the want of sleep."

CHAPTER XXII.
1816, August.

Maria Antoinette—Manners of Versailles—The Father of a Family—Napoleon's Sentimental Journey—Spirit of the Times—The 10th of August—Piedmont—Canals of France—Plans for Paris —Versailles—Fontainebleau—History of Europe—Turkey—The Regency—Gustavus IV.—Bernadotte—Paul—Projects on India—War with Russia—Talleyrand—Madam de Staël.

August 1. Another dark and dismal day enveloped in mist and gloom the storm-scathed rock. The Emperor was oppressed with melancholy. Speaking of the court of Louis XVI., he said,

" Louis XVI. would have been the model of a good man in private life, but he was a wretched king. The queen would, no doubt, have been at all times the ornament of every circle; but her levity, her inconsistencies, and her want of capacity contributed not a little to promote and accelerate the catastrophe. She deranged the manners of Versailles. Its ancient gravity and strict etiquette were transformed into the free-and-easy prettinesses and absolute tittle-tattle of a private party. No man of sense and importance could avoid the jests of the young courtiers, whose natural disposition for raillery was sharpened by the applauses of a young and beautiful sovereign."

After dinner the Emperor read to the assembled exiles in his room *The Father of a Family*. He censured the work severely. "All it contains," said he, "is false and ridiculous. Why reason with a madman in the height of a raging fever? He stands in need of remedies and of a decisive mode of treatment. Who does not know that the only safeguard against love is flight? When Mentor wishes to secure Telemachus, he plunges him into the sea. When Ulysses endeavors to preserve himself from the Syrens he gets himself tied fast, after having stopped the ears of his companions with wax."

August 3. The Emperor improved a tolerably pleasant morning in taking a walk with Las Casas. During his walk he conversed a great deal about a journey which he took to Burgundy in the beginning of the Revolution. This he calls his *Sentimental Journey* to Nuitz.

"I supped there," said he, "with my comrade *Gassendi*, at that time captain in the same regiment, who was advantageously married to the daughter of a physician of the place. I soon remarked the difference of political opinion between the father and son-in-law. Gassendi was, of course, an aristocrat, and the physician a flaming patriot. The latter found in me a powerful auxiliary, and was so delighted, that the following day, at dawn, he paid me a visit of acknowledgment and sympathy.

"The appearance of a young officer of artillery, with good logical reasoning and a ready tongue, was," continued the Emperor, "a precious and rare accession to the place. It was easy for me to perceive that I had made an impression in my favor. It was Sunday, and hats were taken off to me from the bottom of the street. My triumph, however, was not without a check. I went to sup at the house of a Madam Maret or Muret, where another of my comrades seemed to be comfortably established. Here the aristocracy of the canton were accustomed to meet, although the mistress was but the wife of a wine-merchant; but she had great property and the most polished manners—she was the duchess of the place. All the gentlefolks were to be found there. I was caught in a real wasp's nest, and it was necessary for me to fight my way out again.

"The contest was unequal. In the very heat of the action the mayor was announced. I believed him to be an assistant sent to me by Heaven in the critical moment, but he was the worst of all my opponents. I see the villainous fellow now before me, in his fine Sunday clothes, fat and bloated, in a large crimson coat. He was a miserable animal. I was happily preserved by the generosity of the mistress of the house, perhaps by a secret sympathy of opinion. She unceasingly parried with her wit the blows which were dealt at me, and was a protecting shield on which the enemy's weapons struck in vain. She guarded me from every kind of wound, and I have always retained a pleasing recollection of the services I received from her in that species of skirmish.

"The same diversity of opinions was then to be met with in every part of France. In the saloons, in the streets, on the highways, in the taverns, every one was ready to take part in the contest, and nothing was easier than for a person to form an erroneous estimate of the influence of parties and opinion, according to the local situation in which he was placed. Thus a patriot might easily be deceived when in the saloons, or among an assembly of officers where the majority was decidedly against him; but the instant he was in the street or among the soldiers, he found himself in the midst of the entire nation. The sentiments of the day succeeded even in making proselytes among the officers themselves, particularly after the celebrated oath '*to the nation, the law, and the king.*'

"Until that time, had I received an order to point my cannon against the people, I have no doubt that custom, prejudice, education, and the name of the king would have induced me to obey; but the national oath once taken, this would have ceased, and I should have acknowledged the nation only. My natural propensities thenceforth harmonized with my duties, and happily accorded with all the metaphysics of the Assembly. The patriotic officers, however, it must be allowed, constituted but the smaller number; but with the aid of soldiers, they led the regiment and imposed the law. The comrades of the opposite party, and the principals themselves, had recourse to us in every moment of the crisis. I remember, for instance, having rescued from the fury of the populace a brother officer, whose crime consisted in singing from the windows of our dining-saloon the celebrated romance of 'O Richard! O mon Roi!' I had little notion then that that air would one day be also proscribed in the same manner on my account. Just so, on the 10th of August, when I saw the palace of the Tuileries carried by force, and the person of the king seized upon, I was certainly very far from thinking that I should replace him, and that that palace would be my place of residence.

"I was, during that horrible epoch at Paris, in lodgings in the Rue du Mail, Place des Victoires. On hearing the sound of the tocsin, and the news which were circulated of the assault upon the Tuileries, I ran to the Carrousel, to the house of *Fauvelet*, the brother of Bourienne, who kept a furniture warehouse. He had been my comrade at the military school of Brienne. It was from that house, which, by-the-by, I was never afterward able to find in consequence of the great alterations effected there, that I saw all the particulars of the attack. Before I reached the Carrousel, I had been met by a group of hideous-looking men, carrying a head at the end of a pike. Seeing me tolerably well dressed, with the appearance of a gentleman, they called upon me to shout *Vive la Nation!* which, as it may be easily believed, I did without hesitation. The palace was attacked by the vilest rabble. The king had unquestionably for his defense as many troops as the Convention afterward had on the 13th Vendemiaire, and the enemies of the latter were much more disciplined and formidable. The greater part of the National Guard showed themselves favorable to the king; this justice is due to them."

"I actually belonged," said Count Bertrand, "to one of the battalions that evinced the most determined devotion. I was several times on the point of being massacred as I returned alone to my residence. The National Guard of Paris has constantly displayed the virtues of its class, the love of order, devotedness to authority, the dread of plunder, and the detestation of anarchy."

THE ATTACK UPON THE TUILERIES.

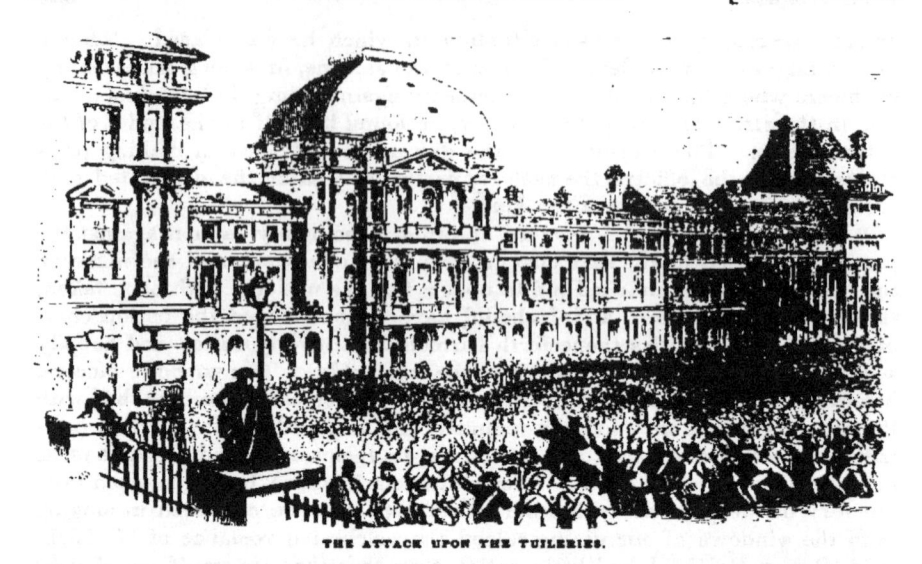

"The palace being forced," continued the Emperor, "and the king received within the bosom of the Assembly, I ventured to penetrate into the garden. Never since has any of my fields of battle given me the idea of so many dead bodies as I was impressed with by the heaps of Swiss, whether the smallness of the place seemed to increase the number, or that it was the result of the first impression I experienced of that nature. I saw well-dressed women commit the grossest indecencies on the dead bodies of the Swiss. I went through all the coffee-houses in the neighborhood of the Assembly. The irritation was every where extreme; fury was in every heart, and showed itself in every countenance, although the persons thus inflamed were far from belonging to the class of the populace. And all these places must necessarily have been frequented daily by the same visitors; for, although I had nothing particular in my dress, or perhaps it was because my face was more calm, it was easy for me to perceive that I excited many hostile and distrustful looks, as some one unknown or suspected."

August 4. The weather was much improved, and the Emperor rode out in his calash. Conversation ran upon all topics. Speaking of Piedmont, he said,

"In fact, the Piedmontese do not like to be a small state. Their king was a real feudal lord, whom it was necessary to pay court to, or to dread. He had more power and authority than I, who, as Emperor of the French, was but a supreme magistrate, bound to see the laws executed, and incompetent to dispense with them. Had I it in my power to prevent the arrest of a courtier for debt? Could I have put a stop to the regular action of the laws, no matter upon whom they operated?"

He afterward spoke of the canals which he had ordered to be constructed in France, and remarked, "I hope sufficient progress was made in the canal from Strasburg to Lyons, which I caused to be commenced, to induce others to finish it. I think that out of thirty millions of francs, twenty-four must have been already expended. Communications are now established in the interior from Bordeaux to Lyons and Paris. I had constructed a great number of canals, and projected a great many more."

"A proposal for one very useful canal was submitted to you, sire," observed Las Casas, "but measures were taken to deceive you, for the purpose of preventing your acceptance of the offer."

"Without doubt," replied the Emperor, "the plan must have appeared advantageous only on paper. But I suppose it would have been necessary to advance money, which was drawn from me with difficulty."

"No, sire, the refusal was but the effect of intrigue. Your majesty was deceived."

"It was impossible, with respect to such a subject," said the Emperor; "you speak without sufficient information."

"But I am confident of it, sire," continued Las Casas. "I was acquainted with the plan, the offers, and the subscribers. My relations had put down their names for considerable sums. The intended object was the union of the Meuse with the Marne. The extent of the canal would have been less than seven leagues."

"But you do not tell us all," observed the Emperor. "It was perhaps required that I should grant away immense national forests in the environs, which I should not have agreed to."

"No, sire, the whole was an intrigue of your board of bridges and roads."

"But even then it was necessary for them to allege some reasons, some appearance of public interest. What reasons did they assign?"

"Sire, that the profits would have been too considerable."

"But, in that case, the plan ought to have been submitted to me in person, and I would have carried it into execution. I repeat that you are not justified by facts. You are speaking now to a man upon the very subject which constantly engaged his attention. The board of bridges and roads were, on their part, never happier than when they were employed. There never was an individual who proposed the construction of a bridge that was not taken at his word. If he asked a toll for twenty-five years, I was disposed to grant him one for thirty. If it cost me nothing, it was a matter of indifference whether it would prove useful. It was always a capital with which I enriched the soil. Instead of rejecting proposals for canals, I eagerly courted them. But, my dear sir, there are no two things that resemble each other so little as the conversation of a saloon and the consideration of an administrative council. The projector is always right in a saloon. His projects would be magnificent and infallible if he were listened to, and if he can, by some little contrivance, but connect the refusal under which he suffers with some bottle of wine, with some intrigue carried on by a wife or mistress, the romance is complete, and that is what you probably heard. But an administrative council is not to be managed so, because it comes to no decision but on facts and accurate measurement. What is the canal you mentioned? I can not be unacquainted with it."

"Sire, from the Meuse to the Marne, a distance of seven leagues only."

"Very well, my dear sir; it is from the Meuse to the Aisne, you mean to say, and it would have been less than seven leagues. I shall soon recollect all about it. There is, however, but one difficulty to overcome, and that is, that at this very instant it is doubtful whether the project be practicable. There, as in other places, Hippocrates says *yes*, and Galen says *no*. Tarbé maintained that it was impossible, and denied that there was a sufficiency of water at the points of separation. I repeat that you are speaking to him who, of all others, is the most attentive to these objects, more especially in the environs of Paris. It was the subject of my perpetual dreams to render Paris the real capital of Europe. I sometimes wished it, for instance, to become a city with a population of two, three, or four millions—in a word something fabulous, colossal, unexampled till our days, and with public establishments suitable to its population."

Las Casas observed, "Ah! sire, if Heaven had allowed you to reign sixty years, as it did Louis XIV., you would have left many grand monuments."

"Had Heaven but granted me twenty years, and a little more leisure," said the Emperor, with vivacity, "ancient Paris would have been sought for in vain. Not a trace of it would have been left; and I should have changed the face of France. Archimedes promised every thing provided he was supplied with a resting-place for his lever. I should have done as much wherever I could have found a point of support for my energy, my perseverance, and my budgets. A world might be created with budgets. I should have displayed the difference between a constitutional emperor and a king of France. The kings of France have never possessed any administrative or municipal institution. They have merely shown themselves great lords, who ruined their men of business. The nation itself has nothing in its character but what is transitory and perishable. Every thing is done for the gratification of the moment and of caprice, nothing for duration. That is our motto, and it is exemplified by our manners in France. Every one passes his life in doing and undoing—nothing is ever left behind. Is it not unbecoming that Paris should not possess even a French theatre, or an Opera-house, in any respect worthy of its high claims?

"I have often set myself against the feasts which the city of Paris wished to give me. They consisted of dinners, balls, artificial fire-works, at an expense of two or three hundred thousand dollars, the preparations for which obstructed the public for several days, and which afterward cost as much to take away as they had in their construction. I proved that, with these idle expenses, they might have erected lasting and magnificent monuments.

"One must have gone through as much as I have in order to be acquainted with all the difficulty of doing good. If the business related to chimneys, partitions, and furniture for some individuals in the imperial palaces, the work was quick and effectual; but if it was necessary to lengthen the garden of the Tuileries, to render some quarters wholesome, to clean some sewers, and to accomplish a task beneficial to the public, in which no particular person had a direct interest, I found it requisite to exert all the energy of my character, to write six, ten letters a day, and to get into a downright passion. It was in this way that I paid out as much as thirty millions in sewers, for which nobody will ever thank me. I pulled down a property of seventeen millions in houses in front of the Tuileries for the purpose of forming the Carrousel and throwing open the Louvre. What I did is immense. What I had resolved to do, and what I projected, were much more so."

"Your labors, sire," replied Las Casas, "were not limited either to Paris or to France. Almost every town in Italy supplies instances of your creative powers. Every where one travels, at the foot as well as at the top of the Alps, on the sands of Holland, on the banks of the Rhine, Napoleon, always Napoleon, is to be seen."

"At one time," remarked the Emperor, "I had determined on draining the Pontine Marshes. Cæsar was about to undertake it when he perished. But to return to France. The kings had too many country houses and useless objects. Any impartial historian will be justified in blaming Louis XIV. for his excessive and idle expenditure at Versailles, involved as he was in wars, taxes, and calamities. He exhausted himself for the purpose of forming, after all, but a bastard town. The advantages of an administrative town, that is to say, calculated for the union of the different branches of administration, seem to me truly problematical. The capital is not a fit residence at all times for the sovereign; but, in another point of view, Versailles was not suitable to the great, the ministers, and the courtiers. Fontainebleau is the real abode for kings, the house for centuries. It is not, perhaps, strictly speaking, an architectural palace, but it is, unquestionably, well planned and perfectly suitable. It is certainly the most commodious and the most happily situated in Europe for the sovereign. It is also the most suitable political and military situation.

"I reproach myself for the sums I expended on Versailles, but it was necessary to prevent it from falling into ruins. It was proposed, during the Revolution, to take away the middle, and thus to separate the two sides. It would have been of essential service to me, for nothing is so expensive or so truly useless as this multitude of palaces; and if, notwithstanding, I undertook that of the King of Rome, it was because I had views peculiar to myself, and besides, in reality, I never thought of doing more than preparing the ground. There I should have stopped. My errors, in disbursements of this kind, could not, after all, be very great. They were, thanks to my budgets, observed and necessarily corrected every year, and could never exceed a small part of the expense occasioned by the original fault.

"I experienced every difficulty in making my system of budgets intelligible, and in carrying it into execution. Whenever a plan, to the amount of thirty millions, which suited me was proposed, 'Granted' was my answer, but to be wound up in twenty years, that is to say, at fifteen hundred thousand francs a year [$300,000]. So far, all went on smoothly. But what am I to get, I added, for my first year? for, if my expenditure is divided into parts, it is, however, my determination to have the result, the work entire and complete. In this manner, I wished at first for a recess, an apartment, no matter what, but something perfect, for my fifteen hundred thousand francs. The architects seemed resolved not to comprehend my meaning. It narrowed their expansive views and their grand effects. They would at once have willingly erected a whole façade, which must have remained for a long time useless, and thus involved me in immense disbursements, which, if interrupted, would have swallowed up every thing.

"It was in that manner which was peculiar to myself, and in spite of so many political and military obstacles, that I executed so many undertakings. I had added forty millions [$8,000,000] to the crown effects, of which four millions [$800,000], at least, consisted of silver plate. How many palaces have I not repaired! Perhaps too many. I return to that subject. Thanks to my mode of acting, I was enabled to inhabit Fontainebleau within one year after the repairs were begun, and it cost me no more than five or six hundred thousand francs [$120,000]. If I have since expended six millions on it [$1,200,000], that was merely the result of six years. It would have cost me much more in the course of time. My principal object was to make the expense light and imperceptible, and to give durability to the work.

"During my visits to Fontainebleau, from twelve to fifteen hundred persons were invited and lodged with every convenience. Upward of three thousand might be entertained at dinner, and this cost the sovereign very little, in consequence of the admirable order and regularity established by Duroc. More than twenty or twenty-five princes, dignitaries, or ministers were obliged to keep their households there.

"I disapproved of the building of Versailles; but, in my notions respecting Paris, and they were occasionally gigantic, I thought of making it useful, and of converting it, in the course of time, into a kind of faubourg, an adjacent site, a point of view from the grand capital. I had conceived a plan, of which I had a description sketched out, for the more effectually appropriating it to that end. It was my intention to expel from its beautiful thickets those nymphs, the productions of a wretched taste, and those ornaments *à la Turcaret*, and to replace them by panoramas, in masonry, of all the capitals into which we had entered victorious, and of all the celebrated battles which had rendered our arms so illustrious. It would have been a collection of so many eternal monuments of our triumphs and our national glory, placed at the gate of the capital of Europe, which necessarily could not fail of being visited by the rest of the world."

August 5. "Sir Hudson Lowe came to Longwood," says Dr. O'Meara, "and, calling me aside in a mysterious manner, asked if I thought that General Bonaparte would take it well if he invited him to a ball at Plantation House on the Prince Regent's birth-day? I replied that, under all circumstances, I thought it most probable that he would look upon it as an insult, especially if made to *General Bonaparte.* His excellency remarked that he would avoid that by asking him in person."

The Emperor, however, declined seeing the governor, and, to avoid his intrusion, remained in the bath until Sir Hudson Lowe had left Longwood. While in the bath he read two volumes of Ottoman history. Conversing upon this subject with Las Casas, he said,

"I have conceived the idea, and regret that I have been unable to execute it, of having all the histories of Europe, since Louis XIV., composed on the very documents belonging to our foreign affairs, which contained the official reports of all the embassadors. My reign would have been a perfect epoch for that object. The superiority of France, its independence and regeneration, enabled the actual government to make such a publication without inconvenience. It would have resembled the publication of ancient history. Nothing could have been more valuable.

"I once wrote to Sultan Selim III., 'Sultan, come forth from thy seraglio, place thyself at the head of thy troops, and renew the glorious days of thy monarchy.' Selim, the Louis XVI. of the Turks, who was very much attached and very favorable to us, contented himself with answering that the advice was excellent for the first princes of his dynasty, but that the manners of those times were very different, and that such a conduct would at present be unseasonable and altogether uproductive.

"Nobody knows," added the Emperor, "how to calculate with certainty the energy of the sudden burst which might be produced by a sultan of Constantinople, who was capable of placing himself at the head of his people, of infusing new spirits into them, and of exciting that fanatical multitude to action. For my own part, if I had been able to unite the Mamelukes with my French, I should have considered myself the master of the world. With that chosen handful, and the rabble recruited on the spot, to be expended in the hour of need, I know nothing that could have resisted me. Algiers trembled at it. The Dey of Algiers said one day to the French consul, 'But, should your sultan ever take it into his head to pay us a visit, what safety could we hope for, for he has defeated the Mamelukes?' The Mamelukes were, in fact, objects of veneration and terror throughout the East. They were looked upon as invincible until our time."

The Emperor, while waiting for dinner, was reclining upon his couch in the midst of his friends. He took up a book which was lying by his side. It was the History of the Regency.

"This," exclaimed the Emperor, "was one of the most abominable eras of our annals. It is indeed deplorable that it has been described with the levity of the age, and not with the severity of history. It has been strewed with the flowers of fashionable life, and set off with the coloring of the graces, instead of having been treated with exact justice. The regency was, in reality, the reign of the depravity of the heart, of the libertinism of the mind, and of the most radical immorality of every species. It was such that I believe in all the horrors and abominations with which the manners of the Regent were reproached in the bosom of his own family. The epoch of the Regent witnessed the overthrow of every kind of property, and the destruction of public morals. Nothing was held sacred, either in manners or in principles. The Regent was personally overwhelmed with infamy."

August 6. The tent, which had been delayed and damaged by the bad weather, was now completed. It was quite an important contribution to the comfort of the Emperor. He went out to visit it, very kindly thanked the seamen for their labor, and invited the English officer who had superintended the work to breakfast with him and his friends beneath its refreshing shade.

August 7. The Emperor again breakfasted in his tent, and then employed many hours in reviewing the chapters on the Campaign of Italy. He then took a ride, with some of his friends, in his calash. Upon his return to his apartment, he made the following interesting and remarkable observations:

NAPOLEON DESCENDING THE ALPS.

"Gustavus IV.," said the Emperor, "on his appearance in the world, announced himself as a hero, but he terminated his career merely as a madman. He distinguished himself in his early days by some very remarkable traits. While yet under age, he was seen to insult Catharine by the refusal of her granddaughter, at the moment, even, when that great empress, seated on her throne and surrounded by her court, waited only for him to celebrate the marriage ceremony.

"At a later period he insulted Alexander in no less marked a manner, by refusing, after Paul's catastrophe, one of the new emperor's officers entrance into his territory, and by answering to the official complaints addressed to him on this subject that Alexander ought not to be displeased; that he who still wept for the assassination of his father should shut the entrance of his states against one of those accused by the public voice of having immolated his own.

"On my accession to the sovereignty he declared himself my great antagonist. It might have been supposed that nothing short of renewing the exploits of the great Gustavus Adolphus would have satisfied him. He ran over the whole of Germany for the purpose of stirring up enemies against me. At the time of the catastrophe of the Duke d'Enghien he swore he would exact vengeance in person, and at a later period he insolently sent back the black eagle to the King of Prussia because the latter had accepted my Legion of Honor.

"His fatal moment at length arrived. A conspiracy of no common kind tore him from the throne and transported him out of his states. The unanimity evinced against him is no doubt a proof of the wrongs he had committed. I am ready to admit that he was inexcusable and even mad, but it is, notwithstanding, extraordinary and unexampled that a single sword was not drawn in his defense in that crisis, whether from affection, from gratitude, from virtuous feeling, or even from mere simplicity, if it must be so, and truly it is a circumstance which does little honor to the atmosphere of kings.

"After the battle of Leipsic, I was informed, on the part of Gustavus, that he had no doubt been my enemy a long time, but for a long time I was, of all others, the sovereign of whom he had the least to complain, and, for a long time also, his only sentiments with regard to me had been those of admiration and sympathy; that his actual misfortunes permitted him to express his feelings without restraint; that he offered to be my aid-de-camp, and requested an asylum in France. I was affected, but I soon reflected that, if I received him, my dignity would be pledged to make exertions in his favor.

"Besides, I no longer ruled the world, and then common minds would not fail to discover in the interest I took for him an impotent hatred against Bernadotte; finally, Gustavus had been dethroned by the voice of the people, and it was the voice of the people by which I had been elevated. In taking up the cause, I should have been guilty of inconsistency in my own conduct, and have acted upon discordant principles. In short, I dreaded lest I should render affairs more complicated than they were, and silenced my feelings of generosity. I caused him to be answered that I appreciated what he offered me, and that I was sensible of it; but that the political interest of France did not allow me to indulge in my private feelings, and that it even imposed upon me the painful task of refusing, for the moment, the asylum which he asked; that he would, however, greatly deceive himself if he supposed me to entertain any other sentiments than those of extreme good-will and sincere wishes for his happiness.

"Some time after the expulsion of Gustavus, while the succession to the crown was vacant, the Swedes, desirous of recommending themselves to me and securing the protection of France, asked me to give them a king. My attention was for an instant turned to the Viceroy Eugene, but it would have been necessary for him to change his religion, which I deemed beneath my dignity, and that of all those who belonged to me; besides, I did not think the political result sufficiently important to excuse an action so contrary to our manners. I attached, however, too much value to the idea of seeing the throne of Sweden in possession of a Frenchman. In my situation, it was a puerile sentiment. The real king, according to my political system and the true interests of France, was the King of Denmark, because I should then have governed Sweden by the influence of my simple contact with the Danish provinces. Bernadotte was elected, and he was indebted for his elevation to his wife, the sister-in-law of my brother Joseph, who then reigned in Madrid. Bernadotte, affecting great dependence upon me, came to ask for my approbation, protesting, with too visible an anxiety, that he would not accept the crown unless it was agreeable to me.

"I, the elected monarch of the people, had to answer that I could not set myself against the elections of other people. It was what I told Bernadotte, whose whole attitude betrayed the anxiety excited by the expectation of my answer. I added that he had only to take advantage of the good-will of which he had been the object; that I wished to be considered as having had no weight in his election, but that it had my approbation and my best wishes. I felt, however, a secret instinct, shall I say it, which made the thing disagreeable and painful. Bernadotte was, in fact, the serpent which I nourished in my bosom. He had scarcely left us when he clung to the system of our enemies, and we were obliged to watch and dread him. At a later period he was one of the great active causes of our calamities. It was he who gave to our enemies the key of our political system, and communicated the tactics of our armies. It was he who pointed out to them the way to the sacred soil. In vain would he excuse himself by saying that, in accepting the crown of Sweden, he was thenceforth bound to be a Swede only. Pitiful excuse! valid only with those of the populace and the vulgar that are ambitious. In taking a wife, one does not renounce his mother, still less is he bound to transfix her bosom and tear out her entrails. It is said that he afterward repented—that is to say, when it was no longer time, and when the mischief was done. The fact is, that in finding himself once more among us, he perceived that opinion exacted justice of him. He felt himself struck with death. Then the film fell from his eyes, for no one knows to what dreams his presumption and his vanity might have incited him in his blindness."

"It seems to me," said Las Casas, "a very fantastical and extraordinary matter of chance, that the soldier Bernadotte, elevated to a crown for which Protestantism was a necessary qualification, was actually born a Protestant, and that his son, destined to reign over the Scandinavians, presented himself in the midst of them with the national name of *Oscar*."

"My dear Las Casas," replied the Emperor, "it is because that chance, so often cited, of which the ancients made a deity, which astonishes us every day and strikes us every instant, does not, after all, appear so singular, so capricious, so extraordinary, but in consequence of our ignorance of the secret and altogether natural causes by which it is produced. And yet this single combination is sufficient to create the marvelous and give birth to mysteries! Here, for instance, with respect to the first point, that of having been born a Protestant, let not the honor of that circumstance be assigned to chance; blot that out. With regard to the second, the name of Oscar, it was I who was his godfather, and when I gave him the name I was raving mad with Ossian. It presented itself, of course, very naturally. You now see how simple that is which so greatly astonished you."

Speaking of Paul of Russia, the Emperor said,

"He had been promised Malta the moment it was taken possession of by the English. Malta reduced, the English ministers denied that they had promised it to him. It is confidently stated that, on the reading of this shameful falsehood, Paul felt so indignant, that, seizing the dispatch in full council, he run his sword through it, and ordered it to be sent back in that condition by way of answer. If this be a folly, it must be allowed that it is the folly of a noble soul. It is the indignation of virtue, which was incapable until then of suspecting such baseness.

"At the same time, the English ministers, treating with us for the exchange of prisoners, refused to include the Russian prisoners taken in Holland, who were in the actual service and fought for the sole cause of the English. I had hit upon the bent of Paul's character. I seized time by the forelock. I collected these Russians. I clothed them, and sent them back without any expense. From that instant that generous heart was altogether devoted to me; and as I had no interest in opposition to Russia, and should never have spoken or acted but with justice, there is no doubt but that I should have been enabled, for the future, to dispose of the cabinet of St. Petersburg. Our enemies were sensible of the danger, and it has been thought that this good-will of Paul proved fatal to him. It might well have been the case, for there are cabinets with whom nothing is sacred."

The Emperor had remarked that Bernadotte had scarcely ascended the throne of Sweden ere he began to adopt measures inimical to the interests of France. The following extracts from a frank and noble letter from Napoleon to Bernadotte, dated Tuileries, August 8, 1811, throw clear light upon the generous and comprehensive policy of the Emperor in the celebrated Continental system:

"The right of blockade which England has arrogated to herself is as injurious to the commerce of Sweden, and as hostile to the interests of her flag, as it is injurious to the commerce of the French empire and to the dignity of its power. I will even assert that the domineering pretensions of England are still more offensive with regard to Sweden, for your commerce is more maritime than Continental. The real strength of the kingdom of Sweden consists as much in the existence of its navy as in the existence of its army.

"The development of the forces of France is altogether Continental. I have been enabled to create within my states an internal trade, which diffuses subsistence and money from the extremities to the centre of the empire, by the impulse given to agricultural and manufacturing industry, and by the rigorous prohibition of foreign productions. This state of things is such that it is impossible for me to decide whether French commerce would have much to gain by peace with England. The maintenance of the decree of Berlin is, therefore, more in the interests of Sweden and of Europe than in the particular interests of France.

"Such are the reasons which my ostensible policy may set up against the ostensible policy of England. The secret reasons which influence England are the following : She does not desire peace ; she has rejected all the overtures which I have caused to be made to her ; her commerce and her territory are enlarged by war ; she is apprehensive of restitutions ; she will not consolidate the new system by a treaty ; she does not wish that France should be powerful.

"I wish for peace. I wish for it in its perfect state, because peace alone can give solidity to new interests, and to states created by conquest. I think that, on this point, your royal highness ought not to differ in opinion from me. I have a great number of ships. I have no seamen. I can not carry on the contest with England for the purpose of compelling her to make peace. Nothing but the Continental system can prove successful. In this respect I experience no obstacle on the part of Russia and Prussia. Their commerce can only be a gainer by the prohibitive system.

"Your cabinet is composed of enlightened men. There is dignity and patriotism in the Swedish nation. The influence of your royal highness in the government is generally approved. You will experience few impediments in withdrawing your people from a mercantile submission to a foreign nation. Do not suffer yourself to be caught by the too tempting baits which England may hold out to you. The future will prove that, whatever may be the revolutions which time must produce, the sovereigns of Europe will establish prohibitive laws which will leave them masters in their own dominions, &c.

"(Signed), NAPOLEON."

August 10. The Emperor was quite unwell. He spent the morning upon his sofa, reading. At three o'clock he walked out with Las Casas, ordering the calash to meet them at an appointed spot. In the morning he had been reading the history of Catharine of Russia.

"She was," said he, "a commanding woman. She was worthy of having a beard upon her chin. The catastrophes of Peter and of Paul were seraglio revolutions, the work of janizaries. These palace soldiers are terrible, and dangerous in proportion as the sovereign is absolute. My Imperial Guard might also have become fatal under any one but myself.

"Paul and I were on the best terms together. At the time of his murder, I had concerted a plan with him for an expedition to India, and I should certainly have prevailed upon him to carry it into execution. Paul wrote to me very often, and at great length. His first communication, written with his own hand, was curious and original.

"'I do not,' he wrote, 'discuss the merits of the rights of man ; but when a nation places at its head a man of distinguished merit and worthy of esteem, it has a government, and France has henceforth one in my eyes.'"

The Emperor, on his return, found Admiral Malcolm and his lady at the house. With great affability and kindness, he took them both into his carriage, and made another tour of the short ride to which he was limited. He then walked for some time with Lady Malcolm, conversing with her in the most frank and cheerful manner.

Sir Hudson Lowe had called while the Emperor was breakfasting in his tent in the morning, but he did not succeed in obtaining an interview.

August 11. The Emperor breakfasted in his tent. It was a pleasant Sabbath morning. "If we were in a Christian country," said he, "we should have mass this morning, and that would employ a portion of the day. I have been always fond of the sound of the church bells in the country. We ought to choose a priest from among ourselves—the curate of St. Helena."

"But how ordain him," one inquired, "without a bishop?"

"And am I not one?" inquired the Emperor. "Have I not been anointed with the same oil, consecrated in the same manner? Were not Clovis and his successors anointed at the time with the formula *Rex Christique sacerdos?* Were they not, in fact, real bishops? Was not the subsequent suppression of that formula caused by the jealousy and policy of the bishops and popes?"

August 13. The Emperor, early in the morning, took a long walk with Las Casas. There was in the vicinity of Longwood a valley, where there was a spring of cool water and a few trees. Its peculiar silence and solitude,

VALLEY AT ST. HELENA.

being mostly surrounded by craggy peaks, and commanding a view of the ocean, made it a favorite resort of the Emperor. Upon his deathbed he requested that he might be buried in this valley, beneath some weeping-willows, should the English government refuse to allow his remains to be removed to his native land.

Napoleon had been, during the morning, reading from recently-received files of the Moniteur the debates in the French Chambers. His emotions were intensely excited, and, as he walked along, he gave utterance to his feelings in glowing yet saddened tones.

" He reverted sadly," says Las Casas, " to the numerous fatalities which had hastened his overthrow; to the perfidious security caused by his marriage with Austria; to the infatuation of the Turks, who made peace with Russia precisely at the moment when they ought to have made war; to the treachery of Bernadotte; to the unseasonable rigor of a Russian winter; to the diplomatic talent of M. Narbonne, who, by discovering the designs of Austria, compelled her to take active measures. He alluded to the victories of Lutzen and Bautzen, which, by bringing back the King of Saxony to Dresden, put Napoleon in possession of the hostile signatures of Austria, and deprived her of all further subterfuge. 'What an unhappy concurrence!' he exclaimed; 'and yet, the day after the battle of Dresden, Francis had already sent a person to treat. It was necessary that Vandamme's disaster should happen at a given moment, to second, as it were, the decree of Fate.' "

" Talleyrand," continued the Emperor, " strongly urged me to make peace on my return from Leipsic. I must do him that justice. He found fault with my speech to the Senate, but warmly approved of that which I made to the Legislative Body. He uniformly maintained that I deceived myself with respect to the energy of the nation; that it would not co-operate with mine, and that it was requisite for me to arrange my affairs by every possible sacrifice. It appears that he was then sincere. I never, from my own experience, found Talleyrand eloquent or persuasive. He dwelt a great deal and a long time on the same idea. Perhaps, also, as our acquaintance was of old date, he behaved in a peculiar manner to me. He was, however, so skillful in his evasions and ramblings, that, after conversations which lasted several hours, he has gone away frequently avoiding the explanations and objects I expected to obtain from him on his coming in."

Returning from this walk, the Emperor breakfasted with his friends in the tent. He then read to them several chapters of the Corinne of Madam de Staël. At last, in disgust, he laid the book aside, saying,

" I can not get through it. Madam de Staël has drawn so complete a likeness of herself in her heroine, that she has succeeded in convincing me that it is herself. I see her, I hear her, I feel her, I wish to avoid her, and I throw away the book. I had a better impression of this work on my memory than what I feel at present. Perhaps it is because, at the time, I read it with my thumb, as M. l'Abbé de Pradt ingeniously says, and not without some truth. I shall, however, persevere. I am determined to see the end of it. I still think that it can not be destitute of some interest. Yet I can not forgive Madam de Staël for having undervalued the French in her romance. The family of Madam de Staël is unquestionably a very singular one. Her father, her mother, and herself, all three on their knees, regaling each other with reciprocal incense, for the better edification and mystification of the public. Madam de Staël may, notwithstanding, exult in surpassing her noble parents when she presumed to write that her sentiments for her father were such that she detected herself in being jealous of her mother.

"Madam de Staël," he continued, "was ardent in her passions, vehement and extravagant in her expressions. This is what was read by the police while she was under its superintendence. 'I am far from you' (she was probably writing to her husband); 'come instantly; I command, I insist upon it. I am on my knees; my daughter is beside me; I beseech you, come; if you hesitate, I shall kill her first, and then myself: you alone will be guilty of our destruction.' She had combined all her efforts and all her means to make an impression on the general of the army of Italy. Without any knowledge of him," continued the Emperor, "she wrote to him when far off, she tormented him when present. If she was to be believed, the union of genius with an insignificant little Creole, incapable of appreciating or comprehending him, was a monstrosity. Unfortunately, the general's only answer was indifference, which women never forgive, and which, indeed," he remarked, with a smile, "is hardly to be forgiven.

"On his arrival at Paris he was followed with the same eagerness, but he maintained, on his part, the same reserve, the same silence. Madam de Staël, resolved, however, to extract some words from him, and to struggle with the conqueror of Italy, attacked him, face to face, at the grand entertainment given by M. de Talleyrand, minister of foreign affairs, to the victorious general. She challenged him, in the midst of a numerous circle, to tell her who was the greatest woman in the world, dead or living. 'She who has had most children,' answered Napoleon, with great simplicity. Madam de Staël was at first a little disconcerted, and endeavored to recover herself by observing that it was reported that he was not very fond of children. 'Pardon me, madam,' again replied Napoleon, 'I am very fond of my wife.'

"I might, no doubt, have excited the enthusiasm of the Genevese Corinne to its highest pitch, but I dreaded her political perfidy and her proverbial intemperance. I was, perhaps, in the wrong. The heroine had been too eager in her pursuit, and too often discouraged, not to become a violent enemy. She instigated the person who was then under her influence, and he did not enter upon the business in a very honorable manner. On the appointment of the Tribunate, he employed the most pressing solicitations with me to be nominated a member. At eleven o'clock at night he was on his knees; but at midnight, when the favor was granted, he was already erect, and almost in an insulting attitude. The first meeting of the Tribunes was a splendid occasion for his invective against me. At night, Madam de Staël's hotel was illuminated. She crowned her Benjamin in the middle of a brilliant assembly, and proclaimed him a second Mirabeau. This farce, which was ridiculous enough, was followed by more dangerous plans. At the time of the Concordat, against which Madam de Staël was violently inflamed, she united at once against me the aristocrats and the Republicans. 'You have,' she exclaimed, 'but a single moment left. To-morrow the tyrant will have forty thousand priests at his disposal.'

"Madam de Staël, having at length tired out my patience, was sent into exile. Her father had seriously offended me before, at the time of the campaign of Marengo. I wished to see him on my way, and he struck me merely as a dull, bloated pedant. Shortly afterward, no doubt with the hope of appearing again in public life by my help, he published a pamphlet, in which he proved that France could neither be a republic nor a monarchy. What it might be was not sufficiently evident from his book. In it he called the First Consul *the necessary man.* Lebrun replied to him in a letter of four pages, in his admirable style, and with all his powers of sarcasm. He asked him whether he had not done sufficient mischief to France, and whether his pretensions to govern her again were not exhausted by his experiment of the Constituent Assembly.

"Madam de Staël, in her disgrace, carried on hostilities with the one hand and supplicated with the other. She was informed, on my part, that I left her the universe for the theatre of her achievements; that I resigned the rest of the world to her, and only reserved Paris for myself, which I forbade her to approach. But Paris was precisely the object of her wishes. No matter; I was invariably inflexible. She occasionally renewed her attempts. Under the empire, she wished to be lady of the palace. Yes or no might certainly be pronounced; but by what means could Madam de Staël be kept quiet in a palace?"

"After dinner," says Las Casas, "the Emperor read the Horatii, and was frequently interrupted by our bursts of admiration. Never did Corneille appear grander, more noble, more nervous to us than on our rock."

CHAPTER XXIII.
1816, August. Continued.

Avoiding the Governor—The Emperor's Birth-day—Present from Lord Holland—Remarks on Religion—Angry Interview with the Governor—Regrets of the Emperor—Libels—General Sarrazin—The Hypocrite—Threats of Sir Hudson Lowe.

August 14. The Emperor breakfasted in his tent, and remained there with his companions, revising his dictations upon the Campaign of Italy. It was announced to him that the governor was approaching Longwood. He immediately retired from the tent to his chamber to avoid an interview.

"I am determined," said he, "to have no more to do with Sir Hudson Lowe. Harsh remarks escape me, which affect my character and my dignity. Nothing should fall from my lips but what is kind and complimentary."

The governor expressed an earnest desire to see his prisoner, but the Emperor retired to his bath, and avoided the pain of an audience. After the governor had returned to Plantation House, the Emperor, suffering from a severe headache, decided to ride out on horseback. He had not mounted his horse for eight weeks.

"The limits are so circumscribed," he said to Dr. O'Meara, who had persuaded him to ride out, "that I can not ride more than an hour; but, in order to do me any good, I should ride very hard for three or four hours. Here has been, this morning, that Sicilian constable. I should have remained in the tent an hour longer if I had not been informed of his arrival. My mind recoils from seeing him. He is perpetually unquiet, and appears always in a passion with somebody, or uneasy, as if something tormented his conscience, and that he was anxious to run away from himself. A man to be well fitted for the governor of St. Helena ought to be a person of great politeness, and, at the same time, of great firmness; one who could gloss over a refusal, and lessen the miseries of the persons detained, instead of eternally putting them in mind that they were considered as prisoners. Instead of such, they have sent out a man not known, who has never had command, who has neither regularity nor system, who can not make himself obeyed, who has no breeding nor civility, and who seems to have always associated with thieves."

At dinner, some one remarked that it was the eve of the 15th of August, the Emperor's birth-day. Napoleon remarked, "Many healths will be drunk to-morrow in Europe to St. Helena. There are certainly some friendly sentiments, some kind wishes which will traverse the ocean."

August 15. The Emperor's companions had arranged to wait upon him in a body at eleven o'clock, with their affectionate greetings on his birth-day; but the Emperor anticipated them by calling at their rooms at nine o'clock, and in cheerful spirits inviting them all to breakfast with him in the large and beautiful tent, which he found to be so valuable an acquisition. He said that he wished to pass the whole day with them. They accordingly continued together in walking, riding, conversation, reading, and other congenial pursuits. In the evening, the servants, including the English, had a grand supper and a dance. "To the astonishment of the French," says Dr. O'Meara, "not a single Englishman got drunk."

August 16. At a very early hour in the morning the Emperor went to his tent, where he met Las Casas and his son. He dictated to them until two o'clock, they breakfasting with him. As he was busily engaged in his work, it was announced that the governor was approaching. The Emperor, to avoid him, immediately retired to his chamber, exclaiming, "The wretch, I believe, envies me the very air I breathe!"

The governor, not being able to see the Emperor without palpable intrusion, held a long conversation with Montholon and O'Meara upon the object of his visit. He complained bitterly of the expenses of Longwood, and urged that common salt, instead of table salt, should be made use of at the table of the servants.

Lord Holland, who, with his lady, cherished a very high respect for the outraged Emperor, sent to him one of Leslie's pneumatic machines for making ice. Admiral Malcolm took great pleasure in delivering it to the Emperor. The machine was put up in one of the rooms, and the Emperor, with the admiral and several of the gentlemen of Longwood, witnessed the successful experiment of freezing water beneath the sun of the tropics. Napoleon and the admiral then took a friendly walk together, engaging in conversation upon a great variety of topics.

August 17. Though the wind blew a gale, accompanied by occasional showers, the Emperor breakfasted in his tent. The wetness, however, soon obliged him to retire to his room. He read to his friends *Zaire* and *Œdipus*. The conversation then turned upon priests and religion. This led the Emperor to the following remarkable observations:

"Man, entering into life, asks himself, From whence do I come? What am I? Whither am I to go? These are so many mysterious questions which urge us on to religion. We eagerly embrace it; we are attracted by our natural propensity; but, as we advance in knowledge, our course is stopped. Instruction and history are the two great enemies of religion, deformed by human imperfection. Why, we ask ourselves, is the religion of Paris neither that of London nor of Berlin? Why is that of Petersburg different from that of Constantinople? Why is the latter different from that of Persia, of the Ganges, and of China? Why is the religion of ancient times different from that of our days? Then reason is sadly staggered; it exclaims, O religions! religions! the children of man! We very properly believe in God, because every thing around us proclaims him, and the most enlightened minds have believed in him—not only Bossuet, whose profession it was, but also Newton and Leibnitz, who had nothing to do with it. But we know not what to think of the doctrine that is taught us, and we find ourselves like the watch, which goes without knowing the watchmaker that made it. And observe a little the stupidity of those who educate us. They should keep away from us the idea of paganism and idolatry, because their absurdity excites the first exercise of our reason, and prepares us for a resistance to passive belief. They bring us up, notwithstanding, in the midst of the Greeks and Romans, with their myriads of divinities. Such, for my own part, has literally been the progress of my understanding. I felt the necessity of belief. I did believe, but my belief was shocked and undecided the moment I acquired knowledge and began to reason, and that happened to me at so early an age as thirteen. Perhaps I shall again believe implicitly. God grant I may. I shall certainly make no resistance, and I do not ask a greater blessing. It must, in my mind, be a great and real happiness.

"In violent agitations, however, and in the casual suggestions of immorality itself, the absence of that religious faith has never, I assert, influenced me in any respect. And I never doubted the existence of God; for, if my reason was inadequate to comprehend it, my mind was not the less disposed to adopt it. My nerves were in sympathy with that sentiment.

"When I seized on the helm of affairs, I had already fixed ideas of all the primary elements by which society is bound together. I had weighed all the importance of religion. I was convinced, and I determined to re-establish it; but the resistance I had to overcome in restoring Catholicism would scarcely be credited. I should have been more willingly followed had I hoisted the standard of Protestantism. This reluctance was carried so far, that in the Council of State, where I found great difficulty in getting the Concordat adopted, several yielded only while forming a plan to extricate themselves from it. 'Well,' they said to one another, 'let us turn Protestants, and that will not affect us.'

"It is unquestionable that, in the disorder to which I succeeded, on the ruins where I was placed, I was at liberty to choose between Catholicism and Protestantism. And it may also be said, with truth, that the general disposition at the moment was quite in favor of the latter; but, besides my real adherence to the religion in which I was born, I had the most important motives to influence my decision. What should I have gained by proclaiming Protestantism? I should have created two great parties very nearly equal in France, when I wished for the existence of none at all. I should have revived the fury of religious disputes, when their total annihilation was called for by the light of the century and my own feelings. These two parties would have destroyed France by their mutual distractions, and rendered her the slave of Europe, when I had the ambition to make her the mistress of it. By the help of Catholicism, I attained, much more effectually, all the grand results I had in view. In the interior, at home, the smaller number was swallowed up by the greater, and I relied upon my treating the former with such an equality that there would be shortly no motive for marking the difference. Abroad, the Pope was bound to me by Catholicism, and with my influence, and our forces in Italy, I did not despair, sooner or later, by some means or another, of obtaining for myself the direction of that Pope, and from that time, what an influence! What a lever of opinion on the rest of the world!

"Francis I. was really in a state to adopt Protestantism at its birth, and declare himself the head of it in Europe. Charles V., his rival, was the zealous champion of Rome, because he considered that measure as an additional means to assist him in his project of enslaving Europe. Was not that circumstance alone sufficient to point out to Francis the necessity of taking care of his independence? But he abandoned the greater to run after the lesser advantage. He persevered in pursuing his imprudent designs on Italy, and, with the intention of paying court to the Pope, he burned Protestants at Paris. Had Francis I. embraced Lutheranism, which is favorable to royal supremacy, he would have preserved France from the dreadful religious convulsions brought on at later periods by the Calvinists, whose efforts, altogether Republican, were on the point of subverting the throne and dissolving our noble monarchy. Unfortunately, Francis I. was ignorant of all that, for he could not allege his scruples for an excuse—he who entered into an alliance with the Turks, and brought them into the midst of us. It was precisely because he was incapable of extending his views so far. The folly of the time! The extent of feudal intellect! Francis I., after all, was but a hero for tilts and tournaments, and a gallant for the drawing-room; one of those pigmy great men.

"De Voisin, the Bishop of Nantes," said the Emperor, "made me a real Catholic by the efficacy of his arguments, by the excellence of his morals, and by his enlightened toleration. Maria Louisa, whose confessor he was, consulted him once on the obligation of abstaining from meat on Fridays.

"'At what table do you dine?' asked the bishop.

"'At the Emperor's.'

"'Do you give all the orders there?'

"'No.'

"'You can not, then, make any alteration in it; would he do it himself?'

"'I am inclined to think not.'

"'Be obedient, then, and do not provoke a subject for scandal. Your first duty is to obey, and make him respected; you will not be in want of other means to amend your life, and to suffer privations in the eyes of God.'

"He also behaved in the same way with respect to a public communion which some persons put into Maria Louisa's head to celebrate on Easter day. She would not consent without the advice of her prudent confessor, who dissuaded her from it by similar arguments. What a difference had she been worked upon by a fanatic! What quarrels, what disagreements might he not have caused between us! What mischief might he not have done in the circumstances in which I was placed!

"The Bishop of Nantes had lived with Diderot in the midst of unbelievers, and had uniformly conducted himself with consistency. He was ready with an answer to every one, and, above all, he had the good sense to abandon every thing that was not maintainable, and to strip religion of every thing which he might not be capable of defending. He was asked,

"'Has not an animal, which moves, combines, and thinks, a soul?'

"'Why not?' was his answer.

"'But whither does it go? for it is not equal to ours.'

"'What is that to you? It dwells, perhaps, in limbo.'

"He used to retreat within the last intrenchments, even within the fortress itself, and there he reserved excellent means of defending himself. He argued better than the Pope, whom he often confounded. He was the firmest pillar, among the bishops, of the Gallican liberties. He was my oracle, my luminary; in religious matters he possessed my unbounded confidence; for, in my quarrels with the Pope, it was my first care, whatever intriguers and marplots in cassocks may say, not to touch upon any dogmatic point. I was so steady in this conduct, that the instant this good and venerable Bishop of Nantes said to me, 'Take care! there you are grappling with a dogma,' I immediately turned off from the course I was taking to return to it by other ways, without amusing myself by entering into dissertations with him, or by seeking even to comprehend his meaning; and as I had not let him into my secret, how amazed must he not have been at the circuits I made! How whimsical, obstinate, capricious, and incoherent must I not have appeared to him! It was because I had an object in view, and he was unacquainted with it.

"The popes could not forgive our liberties of the Gallican Church. The four famous propositions of Bossuet, in particular, provoked their resentment. It was a real hostile manifesto, in their opinion, and they accordingly considered us at least as much out of the pale of the Church as the Protestants. They thought us as guilty as them, perhaps more so, and if they did not overwhelm us with their ostensive thunders, it was because they dreaded the consequences—our separation. The example of England was before them. They did not wish to cut off their right arm with their own hand, but they were constantly on the watch for a favorable opportunity; they trusted to time for it. No doubt they are on the point of believing that it has now actually happened. They will be again disappointed, however, by the light of the century and the manners of the times.

"Some time before my coronation, the Pope wished to see me, and made it a point to visit me himself. He had made many concessions. He had come to Paris for the purpose of crowning me; he consented not to place the crown on my head;* he dispensed with the ceremony of the public communion. He had, therefore, in his opinion, many compensations to expect in return. He had, accordingly, at first dreamed of Romagna and the Legations, and he began to suspect that he should be obliged to give up all that. He then lowered his pretensions to a very trifling favor, as he called it—my signature to an ancient document—a worn-out rag—which he held from Louis XIV. 'Do me that favor,' said he; 'in fact, it signifies nothing.' 'Cheerfully, most holy father, and the thing is done, if it be feasible.' It was, however, a declaration, in which Louis XIV., at the close of his life, seduced by Madam Maintenon, or prevailed upon by his confessors, expressed his disapprobation of the celebrated Articles of 1682, the foundations of the liberties of the Gallican Church. I replied that I had not, for my own part, any personal objection, but that it was requisite for me, as a matter of form, to speak to the bishops about it; on which the Pope repeatedly observed that such a communication was by no means necessary, and that the thing did not deserve to make so much noise. 'I shall never,' he remarked, 'show the signature; it shall be kept as secret as that of Louis XIV.' 'But if it signifies nothing,' said I, 'what use is there for my signature? And if any signification can be drawn from it, I am bound, by a sense of propriety, to consult my doctors.'"

"The Bishop of Nantes and the other bishops, who were really French, came to me in great haste. They were furious, and watched me as they would have watched Louis XIV. on his deathbed to prevent him from turning Protestant. The Sulpicians were called in; they were Jesuits on a small scale; they strove to find out my intention, and were ready to do whatever I wished. The Pope had dispensed with the public communion in my favor, and it is by his determination in that respect that I form my opinion of the sincerity of his religious belief. He had held a congregation of cardinals for the purpose of settling the ceremonial. The greater number warmly insisted on my taking the communion in public, asserting the great

* It will be remembered that Napoleon took the crown and placed it on his own head, and then crowned Josephine.

THE CORONATION.

influence of the example on the people, and the necessity of my holding it out. The Pope, on the contrary, fearful lest I should fulfill that duty as if I were going through one of the articles of M. de Ségur's programme, looked upon it as a sacrilege, and was inflexible in opposing it.

"'Napoleon,' said he, 'is not, perhaps, a believer; the time will come, no doubt, in which his faith will be established, and, in the mean time, let us not burden his conscience or our own.'"

"In his Christian charity, for he really is a worthy, mild, and excellent man, he never once despaired of seeing me a penitent at his tribunal. He has often let his hopes and thoughts on that subject escape him. We sometimes conversed about it in a pleasant and friendly manner.

" 'It will happen to you sooner or later,' said he, 'with an innocent tenderness of expression. 'You will be converted by me or by others, and you will then feel how great the content, the satisfaction of your own heart.'

"In the mean time, my influence over him was such, that I drew from him, by the mere power of my conversation, that famous Concordat of Fontainebleau, in which he renounced the temporal sovereignty—an act, on account of which he has since shown that he dreaded the judgment of posterity, or, rather, the reprobation of his successors. He had no sooner signed than he felt the stings of repentance. He was to have dined the following day with me in public, but at night he was, or pretended to be, ill. The truth is, that, immediately after I left him, he again fell into the hands of his habitual advisers, who drew a terrible picture of the error he had committed. Had we been left by ourselves, I might have done what I pleased with him. I should have governed the religious with the same facility that I did the political world. He was, in truth, a lamb, a good man in every respect—a man of real worth, whom I esteem and love greatly, and who, on his part, I am convinced, is not altogether destitute of interest with regard to me."*

"You will not see him make any severe complaints against me, nor prefer, in particular, any direct or personal accusation against me more than the other sovereigns. There may, perhaps, be some vague and vulgar declamations against ambition and bad faith, but nothing positive and direct, because statesmen are well aware that, when the hour of libels is past, no one would be allowed to prefer a public accusation without corroborative proofs, and they have none of these to produce; such will be the province of history. On the other hand, there will, at most, be some wretched chroniclers shallow enough to take the ravings of clubs or intrigues for authentic facts, or some writers of memoirs, who, deceived by the errors of the moment, will be dead before they are enabled to correct their mistakes.

"When the real particulars of my disputes with the Pope shall be made public, the world will be surprised at the extent of my patience, for it is known that I was not of a very enduring temper. When he left me after my coronation, he felt a secret disgust at not having obtained the compensations he thought he had deserved. But, however grateful I might have been in other respects, I could not, after all, make a traffic of the interests of the empire by way of acquitting my own obligations, and I was too proud to exhibit a seeming acknowledgment that I had purchased his kindnesses. He had hardly set his foot on the soil of Italy when the intriguers and mischiefmakers, the enemies of France, took advantage of the disposition he was in to govern his conduct, and from that instant every thing was hostile on his part. He no longer was the gentle, the peaceful *Chiaramonti*, that worthy bishop

---

* "I am acquainted with Pope Pius VII. During his journey to Paris in 1804, and since then, even till his death, I have not ceased to receive from that venerable pontiff proofs not only of kindness, but even of confidence and affection. Since the year 1814 I have resided at Rome. I have had frequent occasions to see the Pope, and I can affirm that, in the greater number of my interviews with his holiness, he has assured me that he had been treated by the Emperor with all the personal regard which he could desire."—*Réponse à Sir Walter Scott, sur son Histoire de Napoléon, par Louis Bonaparte, frère de l'Empereur*

of Imola, who had, at so early a period, shown himself worthy of the enlightened state of the century. His signature was thenceforth affixed to acts only which characterized the Gregories and Bonifaces more than him. Rome became the focus of all the plots hatched against us. I strove in vain to bring him back by the force of reason, but I found it impossible to ascertain his sentiments. Our wrongs became so serious, and the insults offered to us were so ostensible, that I was imperiously called upon to act in my turn. I therefore seized upon his fortresses, I took possession of some provinces, and I finished by occupying Rome itself, at the same time declaring and strictly observing that I held him sacred in his spiritual capacity, which was far from being satisfactory to him.

"A crisis, however, presented itself. It was believed that Fortune had abandoned me at Essling, and measures were in immediate readiness for exciting the population of that great capital to insurrection. The officer who commanded there thought that he could escape the danger only by getting rid of the Pope, whom he sent forward on his journey to France. That measure was carried into effect without my orders, and was even in direct opposition to my views. I dispatched orders for stopping the Pope wherever he might be met with, and he was kept at Savona, where he was treated with every possible care and attention; for I wished to make myself feared, but not to ill-treat him; to bend him to my views, not to degrade him. I entertained very different projects. This removal served only to inflame the spirit of resentment and intrigue. Until then, the quarrel had been but temporal. The Pope's advisers, in the hope of re-establishing their affairs, involved it in all the jumble of spirituality. I then found it necessary to carry on the contest with him on that head. I had my council of conscience, my ecclesiastical councils, and I invested my imperial courts with the power of deciding in cases of appeal from abuses, for my soldiers could be of no further use in all this. I felt it necessary to fight the Pope with his own weapons. To his men of erudition, to his sophists, his civilians, and his scribes, it was incumbent on me to oppose mine.

"An English plot was laid to carry him off from Savona. It was of service to me. I caused him to be removed to Fontainebleau; but that was to be the period of his sufferings and the regeneration of his splendor. All my grand views were accomplished in disguise and mystery. I had brought things to such a point as to render the development infallible, without any execration, and in a way altogether natural. It was accordingly consecrated by the Pope in the famous Concordat of Fontainebleau, in spite even of my disasters at Moscow. What, then, would have been the result, had I returned victorious and triumphant? I should have consequently obtained the separation, which was so desirable, of the spiritual from the temporal, which is so injurious to his holiness, and the commixture of which produces disorder in society, in the name and by the hands of him who ought himself to be the centre of harmony; and from that time I intended to exalt the Pope beyond measure, to surround him with grandeur and honors. I should have succeeded in suppressing all his anxiety for the loss of his temporal power; I should have made an idol of him; he would have remained near my person. Paris would have become the capital of Christendom, and I should have governed the religious as well as the political world. It was an additional means of binding tighter all the federative parts of the empire, and of preserving the tranquillity of every thing placed without it. I should have had my religious as well as my legislative sessions; my councils would have constituted the representation of Christianity, and the Popes would have only been the presidents. I should have called together and dissolved those assemblies, approved and published their discussions, as Constantine and Charlemagne had done; and if that supremacy had escaped the Emperors, it was because they had committed the fault of letting the spiritual heads reside at a remote distance from them, who took advantage of the weakness of the princes, or of the critical events, to shake off their dependence, and enslave them in their turn.

"But to accomplish that object, I had found it requisite to maneuver with a great deal of dexterity; above all, to conceal my real way of thinking, to give a direction altogether different to general opinion, and to feed the public with vulgar trifles for the purpose of more effectually concealing the importance and depth of my secret design. I accordingly experienced a kind of satisfaction in finding myself accused of barbarity toward the Pope, and of tyranny in religious matters. Foreigners, in particular, promoted my wishes in this respect, by filling their wretched libels with invectives against my pitiful ambition, which, according to them, had driven me to devour the miserable patrimony of St. Peter. But I was perfectly aware that public opinion would again declare itself in my favor at home, and that no means could exist abroad for disconcerting my plan. What measures would not have been employed for its prevention, had it been anticipated at a seasonable period! for how vast its future ascendency over all Catholic countries, and how great its influence even upon those that are not so, by the co-operation of the members of that religion who are spread throughout these countries!

"This deliverance from the court of Rome, this legal union, the control of religion in the hands of the sovereign, had been the constant object of my meditations and my wishes for a long time. England, Russia, the northern crowns, and part of Germany, are in possession of it. Venice and Naples have enjoyed it. No government can be carried on without it; a nation is, otherwise, affected in its tranquillity, its dignity, and its independence every instant. But the task of obtaining it was very difficult. At every step I was alive to the danger. I was induced to think that, once engaged in it, I should be abandoned by the nation. I more than once sounded and strove to elicit public opinion, but in vain; and I have been enabled to convince myself that I never should have had the national co-operation."

August 18. A stormy night was succeeded by a dull and melancholy day. About three o'clock in the afternoon the weather cleared up a little, and the Emperor walked out with Las Casas and Madam Montholon. As they were engaged in very cheerful conversation, the approach of the governor was announced. The Emperor was in feeble health; his nerves were irritated; his pride of character was stung to the quick by outrages and insults, and he could not endure the sight of his detested jailer. Knowing that he could not, under the circumstances, command his passions, and that he did but wound his own self-respect by giving vent to his unavailing indignation, he was anxious to avoid an interview. He accordingly hastily retired, with his friends, to a small grove at some distance from the house.

In a few moments Count Montholon came and acquainted the Emperor that the governor and the admiral were at the house, and earnestly requested the honor of speaking to him on business of importance. He consequently returned to the garden, where he received them. Admiral Malcolm generously attempted the part of mediator, and endeavored favorably to explain the intentions of the governor. The Emperor, addressing himself to the admiral, observed,

"The faults of Sir Hudson Lowe proceed from his habits of life. He has never had the command of any but foreign deserters—of Piedmontese, Corsicans, and Sicilians, all renegades and traitors to their country—the dregs and scum of Europe. If he had commanded Englishmen, if he were one himself, he would show respect to those who have a right to be honored."

Sir Hudson Lowe remarked that General Bertrand had insulted him. "It is obvious, after this," the governor continued, "that I can have no further communication with General Bertrand. I wish, in consequence, to learn with whom it is your desire I should in future communicate on questions in regard to your affairs. General Bonaparte," continues Sir Hudson, in his official account of the interview, "made no reply for so considerable a time that I thought that he did not mean to speak at all."

At length the Emperor, still disdaining to address the governor, and directing his remarks to the admiral, exclaimed, in suppressed tones of indignation,

"General Bertrand is a man who has commanded armies, and *he* treats him as if he were a corporal. General Bertrand is a man well known throughout Europe, and *he* has no right to insult him. He treats us all as if we were deserters from the royal Corsican or some Italian regiment. He has insulted Marshal Bertrand, and he deserved what the marshal said in reply. There are two kinds of people employed by governments—those whom they honor and those whom they dishonor. *He* is one of the latter. The situation they have given him is that of an executioner. There is a moral courage as necessary as courage in the field of battle. M. Lowe does not exercise it here in regard to us, in dreaming only of our escape, rather than in employing the only real, prudent, reasonable, and sensible means for preventing it. Though my body is in the hands of evil-minded men, my soul is as lofty and independent as when at the head of four hundred thousand men, or when, on the throne, I disposed of kingdoms."

The governor defended himself as best he could, and introduced the subject of the expenses of Longwood, and the necessity either of a reduction or that the Emperor should pay from his own funds all excess over forty thousand dollars a year.

"All these details," the Emperor exclaimed, replying to the governor, but addressing himself to the admiral, "are very painful to me. They are mean. You might place me on the burning pile of Montezuma or Guatimozin without extracting from me the gold, which I do not possess. Besides, who asks you for any thing? Who entreats you to feed me? When you discontinue your supply of provisions, those brave soldiers whom you see there," pointing to the camp of the 53d, "will take pity on me. I shall go and place myself at the grenadiers' table, and they will not, I am confident, drive away the first, the oldest soldier of Europe.

"Sir Hudson Lowe," the Emperor continued, "knows not how to treat men of honor. He has insulted General Bertrand, and put him under arrest in his own house. He has rendered my situation forty times worse than it was before his arrival. I can not even write a polite note to my Lady Malcolm without his seeing it. Not even a lady can call on me without his permission. I can not see the officers of the 53d regiment. He refused to deliver a book sent to me by a member of Parliament. He has no feeling. Even the soldiers of the 53d look upon me with compassion, and weep as they pass me."

Here the governor interrupted with denials and explanations. "I detained the book," said the governor, "because it was addressed to the *Emperor*."

"And who," replied the Emperor, with indignant emotion, "gave *you* the right of disputing that title? In a few years your Lord Castlereagh, your Lord Bathurst, and all the others, you who speak to me, will be buried in the dust of oblivion; or, if your names be remembered, it will be only on account of the indignity with which you have treated me; but the Emperor Napoleon shall doubtless continue forever the subject, the ornament of history, and the star of civilized nations. Your libels are of no avail against me. You have expended millions on them. What have they produced? Truth pierces through the clouds; it shines like the sun, and, like it, is imperishable."

"He was continuing in this strain," says Sir Hudson Lowe, "when I interrupted him with saying, with a tone indicative of the sentiments which I felt, 'You make me smile, sir. Your misconception of my character and the rudeness of your manners excite my pity. I wish you good-day.' And I left him without any other salutation. The admiral quitted him immediately afterward with a salute of the hat."

After this interview the Emperor was much mortified in reflecting upon his own violence and want of self-control. His friends were sufficiently near to observe the party, but not to overhear what was said. The Emperor, in giving an account of the interview to them, severely condemned himself.

"I repeatedly," said he, "during this conversation, seriously offended Sir Hudson Lowe. I must also do him the justice to acknowledge that he did not precisely show, in a single instance, any want of respect. He contented himself with muttering between his teeth sentences which were not audible. The only failure, perhaps, on the part of the governor, and which was trifling compared with the treatment he received, was the abrupt way in which he retired.

"After all, I must reproach myself with that scene. I must see this officer no more. He makes me fly into a violent passion. It is beneath my dignity. Expressions escape me which would have been unpardonable at the Tuileries. If they can at all be excused here, it is because I am in his hands and subject to his power."

August 19. The weather continued most dismal. A tornado swept over the gloomy rock, which was deluged with floods of rain. The Emperor, not being able to go out, called at the apartment of Las Casas. As he was leaving the room, he struck his ankle against a projecting nail, which tore his stocking and scratched his skin. Playfully the Emperor remarked,

"You owe me a pair of stockings. A polite man does not expose his visitors to such dangers in his apartments. You are lodged too much like a seaman. It is true that it is not your fault. I thought myself careless about these matters, but you actually surpass me."

About ten o'clock it cleared up for a moment, and the Emperor walked into the garden. As he approached the spot which was the scene of the painful interview with the governor the previous day, he again reverted to it, reproaching himself with the violence of his expressions.

"I am sorry," said he, "that I lost my temper so much. During the whole time I was on the throne of France, I never was in such a passion. I never made use of such language to any one before. I have lowered myself by it. It would have been more worthy of me, finer and greater, to have expressed all these things with composure. They would, besides, have been more impressive. I recollect, in particular, a name which escaped me against M. Lowe, *an officer's scribe*, which must have shocked him, and the more so because it described the truth, and that, we know, is always offensive.

"I have myself experienced that feeling in the island of Elba. When I ran over the most infamous libels, they did not affect me even in the slightest manner. When I read that I had strangled, poisoned, ravished, that I had massacred my sick, that my carriage had been driven over my wounded, I smiled out of commiseration; but when there was a slight approach to truth, the effect was no longer the same. I felt the necessity of defending myself. I accumulated reasons for my justification; and even then, it never happened that I was left without some traces of a secret torment. My dear Las Casas, this is man."

The Emperor had received from Sir Hudson Lowe the treaty of the 2d of August, 1815, in which the four great powers of Europe combined to oppress one single man. To this document he dictated an exceedingly powerful and eloquent protest. In this protest, alluding to the insulting declaration by the English ministers that he was a usurper, and that popular suffrage could not confer upon him the dignity of Emperor, he referred to the negotiations at Paris and at Chatillon, in which the English government had acknowledged the imperial title. He, however, in this protest, made no reference to the treaty of Fontainebleau at the time of his second abdication, in which his lawful sovereignty was still more emphatically admitted. Las Casas ventured to allude to this apparently inadvertent omission.

"It was," the Emperor replied quickly, "done on purpose. I have nothing to do with that treaty. I am ashamed of it. I disclaim it. It was discussed for me by others, and I was betrayed. If I had then been willing to enter into a reasonable treaty, I should have obtained either the kingdom of Italy, Tuscany, or Corsica. My decision was the result of a fault inherent in my character, a caprice on my part, a real constitutional excess. I was seized with disgust of every thing around me. I took pleasure in bidding defiance to Fortune. I cast my eye on a spot of land where I might be uncomfortable, and where I could take adyantage of the mistakes which might be made; I fixed on the island of Elba. It was the act of a soul of rock. I am, no doubt, my dear Las Casas, of a very singular disposition; but we should not be extraordinary were we not of a peculiar mould. I am a piece of rock launched into space. You will not, perhaps, easily believe me, but I do not regret my departed grandeur. You see me slightly affected by what I have lost."

Notwithstanding the storm, the Emperor ordered breakfast in his tent. The water did not penetrate the canvas, but the squalls of wind and rain whistled fiercely around, sweeping sheets of mist sublimely through the valley. The Emperor gazed for a time upon the sombre yet imposing spectacle, and about two o'clock retired to his room.

After dinner the Emperor read to his assembled friends *The Hypocrite*, by Molière. Laying down the book, he said,

"The whole of *The Hypocrite* is unquestionably finished with the hand of a master. It is one of the *chefs d'œuvre* of an inimitable writer. The piece is, however, of such a character, that I am not surprised that its representation should have been the subject of much discussion at Versailles, and of a great deal of hesitation on the part of Louis XIV. If I have a right to be astonished at any thing, it is at his allowing it to be performed. It presents, in my view, religion under colors so odious; a certain scene presents a situation so decisive, so exceedingly immodest, that, for my own part, I do not hesitate to say, that if the comedy had been written in my time, I would not have allowed it to be represented."

August 22. Sir Hudson Lowe sent for Dr. O'Meara to call upon him at Plantation House. At the close of a long conversation, in which he complained bitterly of his intractable prisoner, he said,

"General Bonaparte had better reflect on his situation, for it is in my power to render him much more uncomfortable than he is. He is a prisoner of war, and I have a right to treat him according to his conduct. I'll build him up. Tell General Bonaparte that he had better take care what he does. He has been the cause of the loss of the lives of millions of men, and may be again if he gets loose. I consider Ali Pacha to be a much more respectable scoundrel than Bonaparte."

CHAPTER XXIV.
1816, August. Continued.

Protest against the Treaty of 2d August, 1815—Remarks on Russia—The Burning of Moscow—Projects of Napoleon had he returned victorious—Decrees of Berlin and Milan—Political Defense—Remarks to Captain Poppleton.

August 23. The day was dark, wet, and gloomy. The Emperor, seriously indisposed, spent the hours alone in his room, reading. About half past three he sent for Las Casas. After dinner he read to his companions, though often interrupted by a cough, the tales of Marmontel. At ten o'clock, weary and sad, he retired. During the day he sent to Sir Hudson Lowe his protest against the treaty of the 2d of August. It was dictated by the Emperor to Count Montholon. The document is one of so much importance that we give it entire.

"*To General Sir Hudson Lowe.*
"Longwood, August 23, 1816.

"SIR,—I have received a copy of the treaty of the 2d of August, 1815, concluded between his Britannic majesty, the Emperor of Austria, and the Emperor of Russia, and the King of Prussia, inclosed in your letter of July 23d.*

* *Treaty of the 2d of August*, 1815.

"Napoleon Bonaparte being in the power of the allied sovereigns, their majesties the King of the United Kingdom of Great Britain and Ireland, the Emperor of Austria, the Emperor of Russia, and the King of Prussia, have determined, by virtue of the stipulations of the treaty of the 26th of March, 1815, on the measures best calculated to render it impossible for him, by any new enterprise, to disturb the peace of Europe.

"*Art.* 1. Napoleon Bonaparte is regarded by the powers who have signed the treaty of the 26th of March last as their prisoner.

"*Art.* 2. His safe-keeping is intrusted to the British government. The choice of the place, and of the measures best calculated to insure the object of these stipulations, is reserved to his Britannic majesty.

"*Art.* 3. The imperial courts of Austria and Russia, and the royal court of Prussia, shall appoint commissioners to reside in the place which his Britannic majesty shall determine on as the residence of Napoleon Bonaparte, and who, without being responsible for his safe custody, shall assure themselves of his presence.

"*Art.* 4. His most Christian majesty is invited, in the name of the four courts above named, in like manner to send a French commissioner to the place of Napoleon Bonaparte's detention.

"*Art.* 5. His majesty the King of the United Kingdom of Great Britain and Ireland binds himself to fulfill the engagements assigned to him by the present convention.

"*Art.* 6. The present convention shall be ratified, and the ratifications exchanged within a few days, or sooner, if possible.

"In ratification of which, the respective plenipotentiaries have affixed their hands and seals.
"Given at Paris, the 2d of August, 1815.

"(Signed), PRINCE METTERNICH,
ABERDEEN,
"[A true copy.] PRINCE HARDENBERG,
COUNT NESSELRODE.

"HUDSON LOWE, Governor of the island of St. Helena, and
"Commissioner of his Britannic majesty."

"The Emperor Napoleon protests against the contents of this treaty. He is not the prisoner of the English government. After having resigned his crowns into the hands of representatives for the advantage of the Constitution adopted by the French people, and in favor of his son, he retired freely, and of his own will, to England, to live there as a private individual, under the protection of British laws. The violation of laws can never constitute a right. In point of fact, the Emperor is in the power of England, but neither *de facto* nor *de jure* has he been, nor is he, in the power of Austria, Russia, or Prussia, even according to the laws and customs of England, which never included the Russians, the Austrians, the Prussians, the Spaniards, or Portuguese in any exchange of prisoners, even while allied with those powers and carrying on war conjointly with them. The treaty of the 2d of August, agreed to fifteen days after the Emperor Napoleon's arrival in England, can have no effect in law; it merely presents the spectacle of the four greatest powers of Europe entering into a coalition for the oppression of a single individual—a coalition in direct opposition to the feelings of all nations, as it is to the doctrines of sound morality.

"The Emperors of Austria and of Russia, and the King of Prussia, having, neither in fact nor in law, any authority over the person of the Emperor Napoleon, could not legally make any arrangement respecting him. If the Emperor Napoleon had fallen into the power of the Emperor of Austria, that prince would have remembered the relation which the laws of religion and nature have established between father and son—a relation which can never be disregarded with impunity. He would have remembered that Napoleon had four times restored to him his crown—at Leoben in 1797, and at Luneville in 1801, when his armies were at the walls of Vienna; at Presburg in 1806, and at Vienna in 1809, when his armies were masters of the capital and of three fourths of the empire. That prince would have remembered the protestations of friendship which he had made to him at the bivouac in Moravia in 1806, and at the interview at Dresden in 1812.

"If the person of the Emperor Napoleon had fallen into the power of the Emperor Alexander, he would have remembered the bonds of friendship contracted at Tilsit, at Erfurt, and during twelve years of daily intercourse. He would have remembered the conduct of the Emperor Napoleon the day after the battle of Austerlitz, when he might have made him prisoner with the wreck of his army, but contented himself with his parole, and allowed him to retreat. He would have remembered the personal danger to which the Emperor Napoleon exposed himself in his endeavors to extinguish the fire of Moscow, and to preserve his capital. Certainly this prince would not have violated the duties of friendship and gratitude toward a friend in misfortune.

"If the person of the Emperor had ever fallen into the power of the King of Prussia, that sovereign would not have forgotten that it had been in the power of the Emperor, after the battle of Friedland, to have placed another prince on the throne of Berlin. He would not have forgotten, before a disarmed enemy, the protestations of friendship, and the sentiments he expressed toward him at Dresden in 1812.

"Thus we see by Articles 2 and 5 of the said treaty of the 2d of August, that these princes, not being able to influence in any degree the fate of the Emperor, refer to what his Britannic majesty, who takes upon him to fulfill all their obligations, may determine on the subject. These princes have reproached the Emperor for having preferred the protection of England to theirs. The false ideas which the Emperor entertained respecting the liberality of the English laws, and in reference to the influence which the opinion of a generous and free people ought to have upon its government, determined him to prefer the protection of its laws to those of his father-in-law or of his old friend. The Emperor Napoleon always had it in his power to secure his personal freedom by means of a diplomatic treaty, either by putting himself at the head of the army of the Loire, or by taking the command of the army of the Gironde, then commanded by General Clausel. But as he sought merely for retreat and the protection of free laws, whether English or American, all stipulations appeared to him unnecessary. He believed that the English people would be more bound by his frank, noble, and generous proceeding than it would have been by any treaty whatever. He has been deceived. But this error will always cause a true Briton to blush, either in the present generation or in those to come, and will be a lasting proof of the want of honor displayed by the English government.

"Austrian and Russian commissioners have arrived at St. Helena. If their mission is intended to fulfill a part of the duties which the Emperors of Austria and Russia have contracted in consequence of the treaty of the 2d of August, and to take care that, in a little island surrounded by the ocean, the agents of the English government should not treat with disrespect a prince connected with them by the bonds of relationship and by several other ties, this proceeding is worthy of the character of these two sovereigns. But you, sir, have taken upon you to assert that these commissioners have neither the right nor the power to have an opinion on any thing which may take place on this rock.

"The English ministry has caused the Emperor Napoleon to be sent to St. Helena, two thousand leagues from Europe. This rock, situated under the tropic, at five hundred leagues from any continent, is exposed to the dreadful heat of these latitudes. It is covered with clouds and fogs three fourths of the year. It is, at the same time, the driest and the most humid climate in the world. It is hatred alone which has presided over the choice of this residence, detrimental as it is, and must be, to the health of the Emperor, as well as over the instructions dispatched by the English government to the officers commanding at St. Helena. They were ordered to address the Emperor as general, wishing to oblige him to acknowledge that he had never reigned in France; and it was this that determined him not to assume an *incognito*, as he had decided upon doing when he quitted France. When chief magistrate of the Republic, under the title of First Consul, he concluded the preliminaries of the treaty of London and the treaty of Amiens with the King of Great Britain. He received as embassadors Lord Cornwallis, Mr. Merry, and Lord Whitworth, who signed the treaty as such at his court.

He accredited, as embassadors at the court of Great Britain, Count Otto and General Andreossy, who resided as such at the court of Windsor. When, after an exchange of notes between the ministers of foreign affairs of the two monarchies, Lord Lauderdale came to Paris as plenipotentiary from the King of England, he treated with the plenipotentiaries of the Emperor Napoleon, and remained for several months at the court of the Tuileries. When, afterward, at Chatillon, Lord Castlereagh signed the ultimatum which the allied powers laid before the Emperor Napoleon, he recognized in this act the fourth dynasty.

"This ultimatum was more advantageous than the treaty of Paris, but it was required by it that France should give up Belgium and the left bank of the Rhine, which was contrary to the arrangements of Frankfort and to the proclamations of the allied powers, and also to the oath which the Emperor had sworn at his coronation, to maintain the integrity of the empire. The Emperor thought, then, that these natural limits were necessary to the protection of France, as well as to the balance of power in Europe. He considered that the French nation, in the circumstances in which it was then placed, ought rather to run the risk of a war than to depart from them. France would have obtained its claims, and with them have preserved its honor, if treason had not aided the Allies.

"The treaty of the 2d of August and the bill passed by the British Parliament call the Emperor Napoleon Bonaparte, and give him no title but that of general. The title of *General Bonaparte* is, no doubt, an eminently glorious one. The Emperor was only General Bonaparte at Lodi, at Castiglione, at Rivoli, at Arcola, at Leoben, at the Pyramids, at Aboukir; but for seventeen years he has borne the names of First Consul and Emperor. This would, in effect, amount to acknowledging that he had neither been first magistrate of the republic nor sovereign of the fourth dynasty. Those who consider nations as flocks of sheep, which, by divine right, are the property of some family, belong neither to the century nor to the spirit of English legislation, which has several times changed the order of its dynasty, because great changes which had occurred in public opinion, and in which the reigning princes had not participated, had rendered them unfit to provide for the happiness of the majority of the nation; for kings are but hereditary magistrates, who exist merely for the happiness of the nations, not nations for the satisfaction of kings.

"It is this same spirit of hatred which has decreed that the Emperor Napoleon is not to be allowed to write or receive any letter which has not been opened and read by the English officers at St. Helena. By this means he has been prevented from receiving any account of his mother, his wife, his son, or his brothers; and when he wished to free himself from the inconvenience of his letters being read by subaltern officers, and endeavored for this purpose to send a sealed letter to the Prince Regent, he received for answer that only unsealed letters could be received—that such were the instructions of the ministry. This measure must give strange ideas of the spirit of the administration by which it was dictated; it would not have been acknowledged at Algiers. Letters arrived for general officers in the service of the Emperor; they were opened, and sent to you. You detained them because they did not pass through the English ministry. They were obliged to perform a journey of four thousand leagues, and these officers had the pain of knowing that there were, on this rock, accounts of their wives, their mothers, and their children, and that they would be obliged to wait six months before receiving them. The heart revolts.

"We have not been allowed to subscribe to the 'Morning Chronicle,' to the 'Morning Post,' or to some French newspapers. Occasionally, some copies of 'The Times' have been sent to Longwood. In consequence of the request made on board the *Northumberland*, some books have been sent us; but all those relating to the affairs of the last few years were carefully kept away. At a later period, we wished to enter into correspondence with a London bookseller, to obtain directly such books as we might require; this was prevented. An English author, having written an account of a journey in France, sent you a copy of his work, which he had printed in London, to present it to the Emperor. You did not do so, because it had not come through the medium of the English government. It is said, also, that several books, forwarded by their authors for the Emperor, have not been given to him, because the address on some was to 'the Emperor Napoleon,' on others to 'Napoleon the Great.' The English ministry has no right to inflict all these vexations. The law of the British Parliament, although unjust, considers the Emperor Napoleon as a prisoner of war, and prisoners of war have never been prevented from subscribing to newspapers, or from receiving books. Such a prohibition is as yet only known in the dungeons of the Inquisition.

"The island of St. Helena is ten leagues in circumference. It is inaccessible on every side. Vessels guard the coast, and sentries are placed along the shore within sight of one another, thus rendering any communication with the sea impossible. There is but one little town, Jamestown, where vessels touch or get ready for sea. To prevent any individual from escaping from the island, it would be sufficient to blockade the coast by sea and land. By preventing the Emperor from enjoying the liberty of the interior of the island, only one object can be gained, that of depriving him of an opportunity of enjoying a ride or walk of eight or ten miles, the privation of which exercise, according to medical men, will tend to shorten his life.

"The Emperor has been settled at Longwood, which is exposed to every wind, is on a barren soil, uninhabited, without water, and susceptible of no cultivation. There is a space of about two thousand or three thousand yards without any cultivation. At a distance of some six hundred yards a camp has been established. Another has been placed at about the same distance on the opposite side; so that, under all the heat of the tropics, on whichever side you turn your eyes, you only see camps. Admiral Malcolm, perceiving of what use a tent would be to the Emperor, caused one to be erected by his sailors about twenty paces from the house. This is the only spot where there is any shade. The Emperor feels himself here compelled to remark that he has had every reason to be satisfied with the spirit which animates both officers and men of the 53d, as he also was with the crew of the *Northumberland*.

"The house at Longwood was built to serve as a barn for the Company's farm. At a later period, the deputy governor of the island had some rooms built there. It served him as a country-house, but was in no respect suitable for a dwelling. The Emperor has been settled there a year. During the whole time, workmen have been employed in and about the house, and he has constantly been subject to the inconvenience and unhealthiness of living in a house in course of building or repair. The room in which he sleeps is too small to contain a bed of an ordinary size. But any additional building would cause the inconvenience of workmen to be prolonged. And yet in this miserable island there are some beautiful spots, with fine trees, gardens, and tolerable houses—among others, Plantation House. But the positive instructions of the ministry forbid you to give up this house, which would have spared you a considerable expense, employed in building at Longwood cabins covered with pitched paper, which are already out of repair. You have prohibited all correspondence between us and the inhabitants of the island. You have, in fact, isolated the house of Longwood. You have even perverted our intercourse with the officers of the garrison. You seem, then, to have taken pains to deprive us of all the resources which even this miserable country offers, and we are just as we should be on the uncultivated and uninhabited rock of Ascension. In the four months during which you have been here, sir, you have rendered the Emperor's situation much worse. Count Bertrand has already had occasion to remark to you that you were violating even the laws of your Legislature—that you were trampling under foot the right of general officers when prisoners of war. You replied that you only recognized the letter of your instructions, and that they were worse still than your conduct appeared to us.

"(Signed), GENERAL COUNT MONTHOLON.

"P.S.—I had already signed this letter, sir, when I received yours of the 17th, in which you inclose an estimate concerning an annual sum of £20,000 [$100,000], which you consider necessary for the expenses of the establishment at Longwood, after all the reductions which you have thought it necessary to make. The discussion of this estimate can not concern us in any respect. The table of the Emperor is scarcely furnished with what is strictly necessary; all the provisions are of bad quality, and four times as dear as at Paris. You require from the Emperor a sum of £12,000 [$60,000] for all these expenses. I have already had the honor of informing you that the Emperor has no funds at his disposal; that, during the last year, he has neither written nor received any letter, and that he is completely ignorant of every thing which has taken place, or which might have taken place, in Europe. Violently carried off to this rock, at a distance of two thousand leagues from Europe, without being able to receive or write any letters, he is entirely at the discretion of English agents. The Emperor has always desired, and still desires, to bear all his own expenses of every kind, and he will do so as soon as you make it possible, by removing the prohibition to the merchants of the island with reference to conveying his correspondence, and as soon as he is certain of its being submitted to no examination from you or any of your agents. As soon as the necessities of the Emperor become known in Europe, those who take an interest in him will send him the necessary funds.

"The letter of Lord Bathurst, which you have communicated to me, gives rise to strange ideas. Were your ministers ignorant that the sight of a great man struggling with adversity is a most sublime sight? Were they ignorant that Napoleon at St. Helena, in the midst of persecutions of all kinds, which he meets with never-changing serenity, is greater, more sacred, more venerable than upon the first throne in the world, where he was so long the arbiter of kings? Those who fail in respect to Napoleon in such a situation merely debase their own character and the nation which they represent.

"(Signed), GENERAL COUNT MONTHOLON."

August 24. The Emperor passed a night of sleeplessness and of suffering. He coughed much and was quite feverish. At two o'clock, as the weather was mild, he walked out, but found himself so feeble that he was soon compelled to return. At eight o'clock he dined in his bath. A small table was placed by the side of it for Las Casas to dine. He had been, during the day, examining Russia, and the Russian possessions in America, in the celebrated Historical Atlas of Las Casas. In conversation with his intelligent companion, he reverted to this subject.

"Did Peter the Great," asked he, "act with wisdom in founding a capital at Petersburg at so vast an expense? Would not the results have been greater had he expended all his money at Moscow? What was his object, and did he accomplish it?"

"If Peter had remained at Moscow," replied Las Casas, "his nation would have continued Muscovite, a people altogether Asiatic. It was necessary that it should be displaced for its reform and alteration. He therefore selected a position on the frontiers; he connected himself with European society; he established his power in the Baltic, where he could prevent the Poles and the Swedes from forming alliances against him."

"I am not altogether satisfied," said the Emperor, "with these reasons. However it may be, Moscow has disappeared, and who can compute the wealth that has been swallowed up there? Let us contemplate Paris with the accumulation of centuries, of works, and of industry. Had its capital increased but a million of francs a year for the fourteen hundred years it has existed, what sums! Let us connect with that the warehouses, the furniture, the union of sciences and the arts, the complete establishments of trade and commerce, and this is the picture of Moscow, and yet all that vanished in an instant! What a catastrophe! Does not the bare idea of it make one shudder? I do not think it could be re-established at the expense of two thousand millions.

"Never, with all the powers of poetry, have all the fictions of the burning of Troy equaled the reality of that of Moscow. The city was of wood, the wind was violent, all the pumps had been carried off. It was literally an ocean of fire. Nothing had been saved from it, our march was so rapid, our entrance so sudden. We found even diamonds on the women's toilets, they had fled so precipitately. They wrote to us a short time afterward that they had sought to escape from the first bursts of a dangerous soldiery. They recommended their property to the generosity of the conquerors, and would not fail to reappear in the course of a few days to solicit their kindnesses and testify their gratitude.

CONFLAGRATION OF MOSCOW.

"The population was far from having plotted that atrocity. Even they themselves had delivered up to us three or four hundred criminals, escaped from prison, who had executed it."

"Sire," said Las Casas, "may I ask, if Moscow had not been burned, did not your majesty intend to establish your quarters there?"

"Certainly," answered the Emperor, "and I should then have exhibited the singular spectacle of an army wintering in the midst of a hostile nation, pressing upon it from all points. It would have been the ship caught in the ice. You would have been, in France, without any intelligence from me for several months. You would have remained quiet: you would have acted wisely. Cambacères would have conducted affairs in my name as usual, and all would have been as orderly as if I had been present. The winter in Russia would have weighed on every one heavily, the torpor would have been general, but the spring would have revived all the world. All would have been at once in motion, and it is well known that the French are as active as any others. On the first appearance of fine weather, I should have marched against the enemy, I should have beaten them, I should have been master of their empire. Alexander, be assured, would not have suffered me to proceed so far. He would have agreed to all the conditions which I might have dictated, and France would then have begun to enjoy all her advantages. And truly my success depended upon a mere trifle; for I had undertaken the expedition to fight against armed men, not against Nature in the violence of her wrath. I defeated armies, but I could not conquer the flames, the frost, stupefaction, and death! I was forced to yield to Fate. And, after all, how unfortunate for France—indeed, for all Europe!

"Peace concluded at Moscow would have fulfilled and wound up my hostile expeditions. It would have been, with respect to the grand cause, the end of casualties and the commencement of security. A new horizon, new undertakings, would have unfolded themselves, adapted to the well-being and prosperity of all. The foundation of the European system would have been laid, and my only remaining task would have been its organization. Satisfied on these grand points, and every where at peace, I should have also had my Congress and my Holy Alliance. These are plans which were stolen from me. In that Assembly of all the sovereigns, we should have discussed our interests in a family way, and settled our accounts with the people as a clerk does with his master.

"The cause of the age was victorious, the Revolution accomplished. The only point in question was to reconcile it with what it had not destroyed. But that task belonged to me. I had for a long time been making preparations for it, at the expense, perhaps, of my popularity. No matter. I became the arch of the old and new alliance, the natural mediator between the ancient and modern order of things. I maintained the principles and possessed the confidence of the one, I had identified myself with the other. I belonged to them both; I should have acted conscientiously in favor of each. My glory would have consisted in my equity.

"Powerful as we were, all that we might have conceded would have appeared grand. It would have gained us the gratitude of the people. At present, what they may extract will never seem enough to them, and they will be uniformly distrustful and discontented.

"I wished to establish the same principles, the same system every where. A Europeon code, a court of European appeal, with full powers to redress all wrong decisions, as ours redresses at home those of our tribunals, money of the same value, but with different coins, the same weights, the same measures, the same laws. Europe would soon, in that manner, have really been but the same people, and every one who traveled would have every where found himself in one common country. I should have required that all the rivers should be navigable in common; that the seas should be thrown open; that the great standing armies should in future be reduced to the single establishment of a guard for the sovereign. On my return to France, in the bosom of my country, at once great, powerful, magnificent, at peace and glorious, I would have proclaimed the immutability of boundaries, all future wars *purely defensive*, all new aggrandizement *anti-national.* I would have associated my son with the empire. My dictatorship would have terminated, and his constitutional reign commenced. Paris would have been the capital of the world, and the French the envy of nations. My leisure and my old age would have been consecrated, in company with the Empress, and during the royal apprenticeship of my son, in visiting, with my own carriage, every corner of the empire, in receiving complaints, in redressing wrongs, in founding monuments, and in doing good every where and by every means. These, my dear Las Casas, were among my dreams."

August 25. It was a lovely morning, and the Emperor breakfasted in his tent with all his companions. After dinner, the turn of the conversation led to a review of the maritime dispute with England.

"Her pretensions to blockade on paper," the Emperor observed, "produced my famous Berlin decree. The British Council, in a fit of passion, issued its Orders; it established a right of toll on the seas. I instantly replied by the celebrated Milan decrees, which denationalized every flag that yielded obedience to the English acts. It was then that the war became in England truly personal. Every one connected with trade was enraged against me. England was exasperated at a struggle and energy of which she had no example. She had uniformly found those who had preceded me more complaisant.

"I influenced the Americans to make war against the English by discovering the way of connecting their interests with their rights, for people fight much more readily for the former than for the latter. I am at present expecting the attempt, on the part of the English, on the sovereignty of the seas, for the establishment of the right of universal toll. It is one of the principal resources left them for discharging their debts, for extricating themselves from the abyss into which they are plunged—in a word, of getting rid of their embarrassments. If they have among them an enterprising genius, a man of strong intellect, they will certainly undertake something of the kind. Nobody is powerful enough to oppose it, and they set up their claim with a species of justice. They may plead in its justification that it was for the safety of Europe they involved themselves in difficulties; that they succeeded, and that they are entitled to some compensation. And then the only ships of war in Europe are theirs. They reign, in fact, at present, over the seas. There is an end to the existence of public rights when the balance is broken. The English may now be omnipotent, if they will but confine themselves to their navy; but they will endanger their superiority, complicate their affairs, and insensibly lose their importance if they persevere in keeping soldiers on the Continent."

August 26. Early in the morning the Emperor repaired to his tent to dictate. He breakfasted there with his companions, and then continued his labors till two o'clock. Dr. O'Meara called.

"Have you seen," inquired the Emperor, "the protest written by Count Montholon to Sir Hudson Lowe, and do you think this governor will send it to England?"

"I have seen it," said O'Meara, "and I have no doubt he will send it.

The governor told me that he had offered not only to send your letters home, but to get them published in the newspapers."

"It is a falsehood," replied the Emperor. "He said that he would send letters to Europe and have them published *provided he approved of their contents*. Besides, even if he wished to do so, his government would not permit it. Suppose, for example, I sent him an address to the French people?

"I do not think," continued the Emperor, "that the government will allow a letter, which covers them with so much disgrace, to be published. The people of England wish to know why I call myself Emperor, after having abdicated. I have explained it in that letter. It was my intention to have lived in England as a private person, incognito. But as they have sent me here, and want to make it appear that I was never chief magistrate or Emperor of France, I still retain the title."

Additional sentinels were now stationed around the house, and a ditch, about ten feet deep, was dug, which encircled the premises. The Emperor could not walk out in the evening, after the blaze of a tropical sun had disappeared, and when only walking was pleasant, without exposing himself to insult and arrest.

August 27. The Emperor spent the whole morning dictating. The wind was so rough that he could not ride out. On rising from the dinner-table, he adverted to his protest against the treaty of the 2d of August.

"I intend," said he, "to draw up another protest, on a more extended and important scale, against the bill that has been passed in the British Parliament. I shall prove that that bill is not a law, but a violation of every existing law. The English Parliament have done, not what was just, but what was deemed to be expedient. It has imitated Themistocles without hearing Aristides."

The Emperor then arraigned himself before all the nations in Europe, and proved that each would necessarily acquit him. He took a review of the different acts of his reign, and justified them all.

"The French and the Italians," said he, "lament my absence. I carry with me the gratitude of the Poles, and even the late and bitter regrets of the Spaniards. Europe will soon deplore the loss of the equilibrium, to the maintenance of which my French empire was absolutely necessary. The Continent is now in the most perilous situation, being continually exposed to the risk of being overrun by Cossacks and Tartars; and the English will deplore their victory of Waterloo. Things will be carried to such a length, that posterity, together with every well-disposed person among our contemporaries, will regret that I did not succeed in all my enterprises."

Look at Europe now. Its condition is awful! The agitated masses, frantic with oppression, are struggling to break those chains which were newly riveted at Waterloo. If the masses triumph, unskilled in government, with impetuous and distracted councils, there is, in all probability, anarchy and untold woe. If the despots triumph, they must bind still heavier fetters upon the exasperated multitudes. This position of affairs is England's inexpiable crime. Had Napoleon not been crushed, Continental Europe would now have been blessed with constitutional monarchies, sacredly protecting the rights of contented peoples. "The victory at Waterloo," said Napoleon, truly, "was the triumph of the cause of kings against that of the people, of privileges against equality, of the oligarchs against the Liberals, and of the principles of the Holy Alliance against those of the sovereignty of the people."

In conversation with Dr. O'Meara, the political measures adopted by the Bourbons were alluded to.

"The Bourbons," said the Emperor, "wish to introduce the old system of nobility into the army. Instead of allowing the sons of peasants and laborers to be eligible to be made generals, as they were in my time, they wish to confine it entirely to the old nobility, to *emigrants*, like the imbecile Montchenu. When you have seen him, you have seen all the old nobility of France before the Revolution. Such were all the race; and such they have returned, ignorant, vain, and arrogant as they left it. They have learned nothing, they have forgotten nothing. They were the cause of the Revolution and of so much bloodshed. And now, after twenty-five years of exile and disgrace, they return, loaded with the same vices and crimes for which they were expatriated, to produce another Revolution. They are a curse to the nation. It is of such as them that the Bourbons wish to make generals. I made most of mine from the people.

"Wherever I found talent and courage, I rewarded it. My principle was *a career open to talents*, without asking whether there were any quarters of nobility to show. It is true that I sometimes promoted a few of the old nobility, from a principle of policy and justice. The people now see the revival of feudal times. They see that it will soon be impossible for their progeny to rise in the army. Every true Frenchman reflects with anguish that a family for so many years odious to France has been forced upon them over a bridge of foreign bayonets."

Napoleon practically made himself one of the people, and in his campaigns

THE EMPEROR'S BIVOUAC.

shared all the hardships of the soldiers. He often refused to sleep in ceiled houses, that he might share with them their bivouac in the open air.

August 30. The Emperor rose at three o'clock in the morning, and wrote till six, when he again retired to bed. Just before dinner, he sent Count Bertrand to request Captain Poppleton, the English orderly officer at Longwood, to call at his room.

"I believe, Captain Poppleton," said the Emperor, "that you are the senior captain of the 53d regiment."

"I am," he replied.

"I have an esteem for the officers and men of the 53d," continued the Emperor. "They are brave men, and do their duty. I have been informed that it is said in camp that I do not wish to see the officers. Will you be so good as to tell them that whoever asserted this told a falsehood? I never said or thought so. I shall be always happy to see them."

"The information you have received is, I think," said Captain Poppleton, "incorrect. The officers of the 53d are acquainted with the good opinion which you have previously expressed, and which is highly gratifying to them. They also cherish the greatest respect for you."

Napoleon smiled and said, "I love a brave soldier, who has undergone the baptism of fire, to whatever nation he may belong."

CHAPTER XXV.
1816, September.

Faded Dresses—The Campaign of Saxony—Reflections—The Massacres of the Third of September—Remarks on Revolutions—Unhappy Fate of Louis XVI.—Letters of Madam de Maintenon—Errors of the English Ministers—The Debt of England—The Emperor's Court at the Tuileries—The Emperor's Munificence—Guards of the Eagle—Lucien's Charlemagne.

September 1. The weather was very dull and dispiriting, and the Emperor remained in his own room till three o'clock. He then walked out to the wood, where the calash was appointed to meet him. A shower suddenly came on, and he sought shelter beneath the scanty foliage of a gum-tree. He was quite wet before the calash came. As he was returning home with all speed, he saw the governor approaching. He immediately ordered the coachman to turn, observing that, of two evils, he would choose the least. Notwithstanding the wind and the rain, he took a circuitous route home, and thus avoided the governor.

During dinner the Emperor playfully alluded to the worn and faded dresses of the ladies. "Your garments," said he, "will soon resemble the gay trappings of those old misers who purchase their wardrobe from the dealers in second-hand clothes. They no longer display the freshness and elegance that characterized the millinery of Leroi, Despaux, and Herbault."

The ladies craved the Emperor's indulgence for St. Helena; and one of the gentlemen spoke of the Emperor's supposed fastidiousness with regard to female dress at the Tuileries.

Napoleon smilingly replied, "The idea of my scrupulous taste in dress was a mere invention of the ladies of the court, who made it a pretense or an excuse for their extravagance." He then added, in reference to the threadbare aspect of all their clothing, "I have told Marchand that I shall wear every day the hunting-coat I now have on, until it shall be past the possibility of being worn any longer."

"It was already," says Las Casas, "very far gone."

The Emperor was quite low-spirited, played a few games of chess, and early retired to bed.

September 2. The Emperor went out to his tent, but the wind blew so violently that he was soon compelled to return to his dreary chamber. He went into his library, and, after trying in vain to get interested in several books, he took up one relating to his last campaigns. After perusing it for a time, he threw it down as Las Casas entered, saying,

"It is a downright rhapsody—a mere tissue of contradictions and absurdities. The memorable campaign of Saxony will be regarded as the triumph of courage in the youth of France; of intrigue and cunning in English diplomacy; of intelligence on the part of the Russians, and of effrontery in the Austrian cabinet. It will mark the period of the disorganization of political societies; the great separation of subjects from their sovereigns; finally, the decay of the first military virtues, fidelity, loyalty, and honor. It will be in vain to write and comment, to invent falsehoods and suppositions; we must always arrive at the odious and mortifying result. Time will develop both its truth and its consequences.

"But it is a remarkable circumstance in this case, that all discredit is equally removed from sovereign, soldiers, and people. It was entirely the work of a few military intriguers and headlong politicians, who, under the specious pretext of shaking off the foreign yoke and recovering the national independence, purposely sold their own rulers to envious rival cabinets. The results soon became manifest. The King of Saxony forfeited half his possessions. The King of Bavaria was compelled to make valuable restitutions. What did the traitors care for that? They enjoyed their rewards and their wealth, and those who had proved themselves most upright and innocent were visited with the severest punishment. The King of Saxony, the most honest man who ever wielded a sceptre, was stripped of half his provinces. The King of Denmark, so faithful to all his engagements, was deprived of his crown. This, however, was affirmed to be the restoration and the triumph of morality! Such is the distributive justice of this world!

"To the honor of human nature, and even to the honor of kings, I must once more declare, that never was more virtue manifested than amid the baseness which marked this period. I never for a moment had cause to complain individually of the princes, our allies. The good King of Saxony continued faithful to the last. The King of Bavaria loyally avowed to me that he was no longer his own master. The generosity of the King of Wurtemberg was particularly remarkable. The Prince of Baden yielded only to force, and at the very last extremity. I must render them the justice to acknowledge that all gave me due notice of the storm that was gathering, in order that I might adopt the necessary precautions. But how odious, on the other hand, was the conduct of subaltern agents! Can military parade obliterate the infamy of the Saxons, who returned to our ranks for the purpose of destroying us? Their treachery became proverbial among the troops, who still use the term *Saxonner* to designate a soldier who assassinates another. To crown all, it was a Frenchman (Bernadotte)—a man for whom French blood had purchased a crown—a nursling of France, who gave the finishing stroke to our disasters. Great God!

"But, in the situation in which I was placed, the circumstance which served to fill up the measure of my distress was that I beheld the decisive hour approach. The star grew dim. I felt the reins slip from my hands, and yet I could do nothing. Only a sudden turn of fortune could save us. To treat for, or to conclude any compact, would have been to yield like an imbecile to the enemy. I was convinced of this, and the event proved that I was not mistaken. We had, therefore, no alternative but to fight, and every day, by some fatality or other, our chances diminished. Treason began to penetrate our ranks. Great numbers of our troops sank under the effects of fatigue and discouragement. They were no longer the same men who figured at the commencement of the Revolution, or who had distinguished themselves in the brilliant moments of my success. I have been informed that some presumed to allege in their defense that at first they fought for the Republic and for their country, while afterward they fought only for a single man, for his individual interests, and his ambition.

"Unworthy subterfuge! Ask the young and brave soldiers, and the officers of intermediate rank in the French army, whether such a calculation ever entered their thoughts—whether they ever saw before them any thing but the enemy, or behind them any thing save the honor, glory, and triumph of France? These men never fought better than at the period alluded to. Why dissemble? Why not make a candid avowal? The truth is, that most of the officers of high rank had gained every object of their ambition. They were sated with wealth and honors. They had drunk of the cup of pleasure, and they henceforth wished for repose, which they would have purchased at any price. The sacred flame was extinguished; they were willing to sink to the level of the marshals of Louis XV.

"How was I perplexed to find myself the only one to judge of the extent of our danger, and to adopt means to avert it! I was harassed on the one hand by the coalesced powers, who threatened our very existence, and on the other hand by the spirit of my own subjects, who, in their blindness, seemed to make common cause with them. I was harassed by our foreign enemies, who were laboring for my destruction, and by the importunities of my people, and even my ministers, who urged me to throw myself on the mercy of foreigners; and I was obliged to maintain a good appearance in this embarrassing situation, to reply haughtily to some, and sharply to rebuff others who created difficulties in my rear, encouraged the mistaken course of public opinion instead of seeking to give it a proper direction, and suffered me to be tormented by demands for peace when they ought to have proved that the only means of obtaining it was to urge me ostensibly to war.

"However, my determination was fixed. I awaited the result of events, firmly resolved to enter into no concessions or treaties which could present only a temporary reparation, and would inevitably have been attended by fatal consequences. Any middle course must have been dangerous. There was no safety except in victory, which would have preserved my power, or in some catastrophe which would have brought back my allies. In what a situation was I placed! I saw that France, her destinies, her principles, depended on me alone."

"Sire," said Las Casas, "this was the opinion generally entertained, and yet some parties reproached you for it, exclaiming with bitterness, 'Why would he connect every thing with himself personally?'"

"That was a vulgar accusation," resumed the Emperor, warmly. "My situation was not one of my own choosing, nor did it arise out of any fault of mine. It was produced entirely by the nature and force of circumstances, by the conflict of two opposite orders of things. Would the individuals who held this language, if indeed they were sincere, have preferred to go back to the period preceding Brumaire, when our internal dissolution was complete, foreign invasion certain, and the destruction of France inevitable? From the moment when we decided on the concentration of power which could alone save us, when we determined on the unity of doctrines and resources which rendered us a mighty nation, the destinies of France depended solely on the character, the measures, and the principles of him who had been invested with this accidental dictatorship. From that moment the public interest, *the state, was myself*.

"These words, which I addressed to men who were capable of understanding them, were strongly censured by the narrow-minded and ill-disposed; but the enemy felt the full force of them, and therefore his first object was to effect my overthrow. The same outcry was raised against other words which I uttered in the sincerity of my heart—when I said that *France stood more in need of me than I stood in need of her*. This solid truth was declared to be merely excess of vanity. But, my dear Las Casas, you now see that I can relinquish every thing, and as to what I endure here, my suffering can not be long. My life is limited; but the existence of France—" Here the Emperor for a moment paused, silent through excess of emotion. He then resumed,

"The circumstances in which we were placed were extraordinary and unprecedented. It would be vain to seek for any parallel to them. I was myself the keystone of an edifice totally new! Its stability depended on each of my battles! Had I been conquered at Marengo, France would have encountered all the disasters of 1814 and 1815 without those prodigies of glory which succeeded, and which will be immortal. It was the same at Austerlitz and Jena, and again at Eylau and elsewhere.

"The vulgar failed not to blame my ambition as the cause of all these wars; but they were not of my choosing. They were produced by the na-

EYLAU AFTER THE BATTLE.

ture and force of events. They arose out of that conflict between the past and the future, that constant and permanent coalition of our enemies, which obliged us to subdue under pain of being subdued."

September 3. It was a cheerless day of wind and rain. The Emperor was sitting in his chamber, before a large fire, conversing with Count Montholon and others of his friends, when some one chanced to remark that it was the third of September.

It was during this period of terrible strife that Napoleon, surrounded by innumerable foes, passed a night in the wagoner's shop, meditating upon the inexpressible difficulties of his position. Nobly he resolved to endure every conceivable calamity rather than dishonor France and himself by acceding to those disgraceful terms which his haughty foes demanded.

"To-day," said the Emperor, "is the anniversary of a hideous remem-

THE EMPEROR IN THE WAGONER'S SHOP

brance; of the massacres of September, the St. Bartholomew of the French Revolution. The atrocities of the third of September were not committed under the sanction of government, which, on the contrary, used its endeavors to punish the crime. The massacres were committed by the mob of Paris, and were the result of fanaticism rather than of absolute brutality. The Septembriseurs did not pillage, they only wished to murder. They even hanged one of their own party for having appropriated a watch which belonged to one of their victims.

"This dreadful event arose out of the force of circumstances and the spirit of the moment. We must acknowledge that there has been no political change unattended by popular fury as soon as the masses enter into action. The Prussian army had arrived within one hundred miles of Paris. The famous manifesto of the Duke of Brunswick was placarded on all the walls of the city. The people had persuaded themselves that the death of all the Royalists in Paris was indispensable to the safety of the Revolution. They ran to the prisons and intoxicated themselves with blood, shouting *Vive la Revolution!* Their energy had an electric effect from the fear with which it inspired one party, and the example which it gave to the other. One hundred thousand volunteers joined the army, and the Revolution was saved.

"I might have preserved my crown by turning loose the masses of the people against the advocates of the restoration. You well recollect, Montholon, when, at the head of your *faubouriens*, you wished to punish the treachery of Fouché, and proclaim my dictatorship. I did not choose to do so. My whole soul revolted at the thought of being king of another mob. As a general rule, no social revolution can take place without terror. Every revolution is in principle a revolt, which time and success ennoble and render legal, but of which terror has been one of the inevitable phases. How indeed can we say to those who possess fortune and public situations, '*Begone, and leave us your fortunes and your situations*,' without first intimidating them, and rendering any defense impossible. In France, this point was effected by the lantern and the guillotine.

"The Reign of Terror began, in fact, on the night of the fourth of August, when privileges, nobility, titles, and feudal rights were abolished, and all these remains of the old monarchy were thrown to the people. Then only did the people understand the Revolution, and they wished to preserve it even at the expense of blood. Till then, many of the peasants believed that, without a king and tithes to the clergy, the harvest could not be good. Barrère said truly, 'The people coin money upon the Place of Louis XVI.,' alluding to the guillotine, which enriched the national treasury by the death of the nobles, whose wealth became the property of the nation.

"A revolution, whatever some may think, is one of the greatest calamities with which divine anger can punish a nation. It is the scourge of the generation which brings it about, and all the advantages it secures can not compensate for the misery with which it is attended. It subverts every thing, and, at its commencement, brings misery to all and happiness to none. True social happiness consists in the harmonious and peaceful possession of the relative enjoyments of each class of people. In regular and tranquil times, every individual has his share of felicity. The cobbler in his stall is as content as the king on his throne. The soldier is not less happy than the general. The best-conducted revolutions bring universal destruction in their train. This is the immediate effect. The advantages they produce are reserved for future ages. I gave millions every year to the poor. I made immense sacrifices to promote and assist industry, and yet France has more poor now than in 1787.

"Our revolution was a national convulsion, as irresistible in its effects as an eruption of Vesuvius. When the mysterious fusion which takes place in the entrails of the earth is at such a crisis that an explosion follows, the eruption bursts forth. The unperceived workings of the discontent of the people follow exactly the same course. In France, the sufferings of the people, the moral combinations which produce a revolution, had arrived at maturity, and the explosion accordingly took place."

"Do you think," said Las Casas, "that it would have been possible to suppress the Revolution at its birth?"

"I do not think so," the Emperor replied. "Still, it is possible that the storm might have been averted by some great Machiavelian act—by striking with one hand the great ringleaders, and with the other making concessions to the nation, granting freely the reformation required by the age. And yet, after all, this would only have been to guide and direct the Revolution. Besides, the education of Louis XVI., as well as his personal convictions, made him regard as belonging lawfully to him all that of which the nation wished to deprive him, and which he would have been obliged to give up voluntarily to put an end to the revolutionary movement.

"At the time when the States were convoked, it was out of the power of man to prevent the Revolution. Thus I understood it in my youth, and my opinion has not been changed by what I have learned and seen of royalty. A revolution can neither be made nor prevented. One or several of its children can direct it by dint of victories. Its enemies may repress it for a moment by force of arms, but the fire of revolution glimmers under the ashes, and sooner or later the flame kindles again and devours all before it.

"The Bourbons are greatly deceived if they believe themselves firmly seated on the throne of Hugh Capet. I do not know whether I shall ever again see Paris, but what I do know is, that the French people will one day break the sceptre which the enemies of France have confided to Louis XVIII. My son will reign if the popular masses are permitted to act without control. The crown will belong to the Duke of Orleans if those who are called Liberals gain the victory over the people. But, sooner or later, the people will discover that they have been deceived; that the white are always white, the blue always blue, and that there is no guarantee for their true interests except under the reign of my dynasty, because it is the work of their creation.

"I did not usurp the crown. I picked it up from the gutter; the people placed it on my head. I was king of the people as the Bourbons are kings of the nobles, under whatever color they may disguise the banner of their ancestors. When, full of confidence in the sympathy of the nation, I returned from Elba, my advisers insisted that I ought to take notice of some chiefs of the royal party. I constantly refused, answering to those who gave me this advice, 'If I have remained in the hearts of the mass of the people, I have nothing to do with the Royalists; if not, what will some, more or less, avail me to struggle against the opinion of the nation?'"

The clock struck eleven. "Gentlemen," said the Emperor, "we have had enough of politics for this evening."

September 5. Sir Hudson Lowe sent Major Gorrequer to Longwood to inform Count Montholon that the expenses must be reduced.

"When the British government," said the major, "fixed forty thousand dollars as the maximum of the expense of General Bonaparte's establishment, they contemplated a great reduction of the persons composing it by the general officers and others returning to Europe. As this reduction has not taken place, the governor is willing to allow sixty thousand dollars a year for all expenses. Nothing more than this can be allowed. Any additional expense General Bonaparte must pay himself by bills drawn upon some banker in Europe."

While Sir Hudson Lowe was ordering that the expenditures at Longwood should be reduced to sixty thousand dollars a year, he at the same time transmitted a calculation to Lord Bathurst to prove that the existing establishment could not be supported for less than about seventy-five thousand dollars, even with the most rigid economy.

"The Emperor," Count Montholon replied, "is ready to pay all the expenses of the establishment if any mercantile or banking-house in St. Helena, London, or Paris, chosen by the British government itself, can serve as intermediators, through whom the Emperor can send sealed letters and receive sealed answers. On the one side, the Emperor will pledge his honor that the letters shall relate solely to pecuniary matters, and the correspondence shall be held equally sacred on the other part."

"No sealed letters," said the major, "can be suffered to leave Longwood. The reductions will commence on the 15th of the present month. After that date but five thousand dollars a month will be allowed."

The expenses of the establishment at Longwood, even with all the privations and discomforts to which the exiles were exposed, amounted to one hundred thousand dollars a year. It was now demanded that the Emperor should either pay forty thousand dollars each year, or send away from the island many of those friends whose devotion alone cheered his weary hours. The English government, which had already emptied Napoleon's trunks, seemed very anxious to ascertain where he had any treasure deposited in Europe.

"It is clear," said Sir Henry Bunbury, in a letter to Sir Hudson Lowe, "that the ex-Emperor has large sums of money in different parts, and that his agents have lodged money on his account in the principal towns of America as well as in England, with the hope of his being able to get at one or other of their deposits. We have been unable hitherto to obtain any clue to this matter. It is very desirable to discover both the treasure and the agents."

Under such circumstances, it was indeed absurd, nay, savage, to endeavor to torture the Emperor to draw for funds through Sir Hudson Lowe.

September 6. It was a dark and stormy day. The Emperor retired with Las Casas to the library, and entered into a long and confidential conversation.

"We have now," said he, "been in captivity more than a year; and how many mortifications have I to encounter! A victim to the persecutions of Fate and man, I am assailed on every side and at all hands. My whole body is covered with wounds. Even you, my faithful friends and consolers, help to increase my anguish. Your jealousies and your contentions afflict me sorely."

"Sire," Las Casas replied, "these things should remain unnoticed by your majesty. In all that concerns you, our jealousy is merely emulation. All our dissension ceases on the expression of your slightest wish. We live only for you."

At the dinner-table, speaking of Madam de Maintenon, whose letters he had been reading during the day, the Emperor said,

"I am charmed with her style, her grace, and the purity of her language.

1816, September.] RESIDENCE AT LONGWOOD. 377

If I am violently offended with what is bad, I am, at the same time, exquisitely sensible to what is good. I think I prefer Madam de Maintenon's Letters to those of Madam de Sevigny. They communicate more. Madam de Sevigny will certainly always remain the true model of the epistolary style. She has a thousand charms and graces. But there is this defect in her writings, that one may read a great deal of them without retaining any impression of what one has read. They are like a dish of egg snow-balls, of which a man may eat till he is tired without overcharging his stomach."

September 7. Governor Lowe rode up to Longwood with General Meade, who had just arrived at St. Helena, and with a numerous suite, and pointed out the precautions adopted to secure the prisoner. The insulted and outraged Emperor passed the day in his chamber, reading. He was perusing a work upon the state of England. As Las Casas entered, the policy of England became the topic of conversation.

"The colonial system," said the Emperor, "is now at an end for all—for England, who possesses every colony, and for the other powers, who possess none. The empire of the seas now belongs indisputably to England; and why should she, in a new situation, wish to continue the old system? Why does she not adopt plans that would be more profitable to her? She must look forward to a sort of emancipation of her colonies. In course of time, many will doubtless escape from her dominion, and she should therefore avail herself of the present moment to obtain new securities and more advantageous connections.

"Why does she not propose that the majority of her colonies shall purchase their emancipation by taking upon themselves a portion of the general debt, which would thus become specially theirs? The mother country would by this means relieve herself of her burdens, and would, nevertheless, preserve all her advantages. She would retain as pledges the faith of treaties, reciprocal interests, similitude of language, and the force of habit. She might, moreover, reserve, by way of guarantee, a single fortified point, a harbor for her ships, after the manner of the factories on the coast of Africa. What would she lose? Nothing; and she would spare herself the trouble and expense of an administration which too often serves only to render her odious. Her ministers, it is true, would have fewer places to give away, but the nation would certainly be no loser.

"I doubt not that, with a thorough knowledge of the subject, some useful result might be derived from the ideas which I have just thrown out, however erroneous they may be in their first hasty conception. Even with regard to India, great advantages might be obtained by the adoption of new systems. The English who are here assure me that England derives nothing from India in the balance of trade; the expenses swallow up, and even exceed, the profits. It is, therefore, merely a source of individual advantage, and of a few private fortunes of colossal magnitude; but these are so much food for ministerial patronage, and therefore good care is taken not to meddle with them.

"These nabobs, as they are styled on their return to England, are useful recruits to the aristocracy. It signifies not that they bear the disgrace of having acquired fortunes by rapine or plunder, or that they exercise a baneful influence on public morals by exciting in others the wish to gain the same wealth by the same means. The present ministers are not so scrupulous as to bestow a thought on such matters. These men give them their votes, and the more corrupt they are, the more easily are they controlled. In this state of things, where is the hope of reform? On the least proposition of amendment, what an outcry is raised! The English aristocracy is daily taking a stride in advance, but as soon as there is any proposal for retrograding, were it only for the space of an inch, a general explosion takes place. If the minutest details be touched, the whole edifice begins to totter. This is very natural. If you attempt to deprive a glutton of his mouthful, he will defend himself like a hero."

At another time the Emperor said, "The national debt is the worm that preys on England; it is the chain of all her difficulties. It occasions the enormity of taxation, and this, in its turn, raises the price of provisions. Hence the distress of the people, the high price of labor and of manufactured articles, which are not disposed of with equal advantage in the Continental markets. England then ought, at all hazards, to contend against this devouring monster. She should assail it on all sides, and at once subdue it *negatively* and *positively*, that is to say, by the reduction of her expenditure and the increase of her capital.

"Can she not reduce the interest of her debt, the high salaries, the sinecures, and the various expenses attending her army establishment, and renounce the latter in order to confine herself to her navy? In short, many things might be done which I can not now enter into. With regard to the increase of her capital, can she not enrich herself with the ecclesiastical property, which is immense, and which she would acquire by a salutary reform, and by the extinction of titular dignities, which would give offense to no one? But if a word be uttered on this subject, the whole aristocracy is in commotion, and succeeds in putting down the opposition; for in England it is the aristocracy that governs and for which the government acts. They repeat the favorite adage that if the least stone of the old foundation be touched, the whole fabric will fall to the ground. This is devoutly re-echoed by the multitude; consequently, reform is stopped, and abuses are suffered to increase and multiply.

"It is but just to acknowledge that, in spite of a compound of odious, mean, and antiquated details, the English Constitution presents the singular phenomenon of a grand and happy result; and the advantages arising out of it secure the attachment of the multitude, who are fearful of losing any of the blessings they enjoy. But is it to the objectionable nature of the details that this result must be attributed? On the contrary, it would shine with increased lustre if the grand and beautiful machine were freed from its mischievous appendages.

"England presents an example of the dangerous effects of the borrowing system. I would never listen to any hints for the adoption of that system in France. I was always a firm opposer of it. It was said at the time that I contracted no loans for want of credit, and because I could find no one willing to lend; but this was false. Those who know any thing of mankind and the spirit of stock-jobbing, will be convinced that loans may always be raised by holding out the chance of gain and the attraction of speculation. But this was no part of my system, and by a special law I fixed the amount of the public debt at what had generally been supposed to be conducive to the general prosperity, namely, at eighty millions [$16,000,000] for France in her utmost extent and after the union with Holland, which in itself produced an augmentation of twenty millions [$4,000,000]. This sum was reasonable and proper. A greater one would have been attended by mischievous consequences. What was the result of this system? What resources have I left behind me? France, after so many gigantic efforts and terrible disasters, is now more prosperous than ever. Her finances are the first in Europe. To whom and to what are these advantages to be attributed?

"So far was I from wishing to swallow up the future, that I had resolved to leave a treasury behind me. I had even formed one, the funds of which I lent to different banking-houses, embarrassed families, and the individuals who were about my person. I should not only have carefully preserved the sinking fund, but I calculated on having, in course of time, surpluses which would have been constantly increasing, and which might have been actively applied for the furtherance of public works and improvements. I should have had the fund of the empire for general works, the fund of the departments for local works, and the fund of the communes for municipal works."

In another conversation the Emperor remarked, "England is said to traffic in every thing; why, then, does she not sell liberty, for which she might get a high price without any fear of exhausting her own stock; for modern liberty is essentially moral, and does not betray its engagements. For example, what would not the poor Spaniards give her to free them from the yoke to which they have been again subjected? I am confident they would willingly pay any price to recover their freedom. It was I who inspired them with this sentiment, and the error into which I fell might be turned to good account by another government. As to the Italians, I have planted in their breasts principles that never can be rooted out. What can England do better than to promote and assist the noble impulses of modern regeneration?

"Sooner or later this regeneration must be accomplished. Sovereigns and old aristocratic institutions may exert their efforts to oppose it, but in vain. They are dooming themselves to the punishment of Sisyphus. But, sooner or later, some arm will tire of resistance, and then the whole system will fall to nothing. Would it not be better to yield with a good grace? This was my intention. Why does England refuse to avail herself of the glory and advantage she ought to derive from this course of proceeding? Every thing passes away in England as well as elsewhere. Castlereagh's administration will pass away, and that which may succeed it, and which is doomed to inherit the fruit of so many errors, may become great by only discontinuing the system that has hitherto been pursued.

"He who may happen to be placed at the head of the English cabinet has merely to allow things to take their course, and to obey the winds that blow. By becoming the leader of liberal principles, instead of leaguing with absolute power, like Castlereagh, he will render himself the object of universal benediction, and England will forget her wrongs. Fox was capable of so acting, but Pitt was not. The reason is, that in Fox the heart warmed the genius, while in Pitt the genius withered the heart.

"But it may be asked why I, all-powerful as I was, did not pursue the course I have traced out? how, since I can speak so well, I could have acted so ill? I reply to those who make this inquiry with sincerity, that there is no comparison between my situation and that of the English government. England may work on a soil which extends to the very bowels of the earth, while I could labor only on a sandy surface. England reigns over an established order of things, while I had to take upon myself the great charge, the immense difficulty of consolidating and establishing. I purified a revolution in spite of hostile factions. I combined together all the scattered benefits that could be preserved, but I was obliged to protect them with a nervous arm against the attacks of all parties. In this situation, it may truly be said that the public interest, *the state, was myself.*

"Foreign nations, in arms, assailed our principles, and, in the name of these very principles, I was assailed by enemies at home. Had I relaxed in the least degree, we should soon have been brought back to the time of the Directory. I should have been the object, and France the infallible victim, of a *counter Brumaire.* We are in our nature so restless and inconsiderate, if twenty revolutions were to ensue, we should have twenty constitutions. This is one of the subjects that are studied most and observed the least. We have much need to grow older in this great and glorious path, for here our great men have all shown themselves to be mere children. Heaven grant that the present generation may profit by the faults that have been committed hitherto, and prove as wise as it is enthusiastic!"

"To-day," writes Las Casas, "the governor commenced his grand reductions, and it was thought proper to deprive us of eight English domestics, who had formerly been granted to us. To the servants this was a subject of deep regret. It was gratifying to us to observe that we won the regard of all who were permitted to approach us. We are now absolutely in want of daily necessaries, to supply which the Emperor proposes to dispose of his plate. This is his only resource."

At night the Emperor, suffering from a violent headache, sent for Dr. O'Meara. "He was sitting," says O'Meara, "in his bed-room, with only a wood fire burning, the flames of which, alternately blazing and sinking, gave at moments a most singular and melancholy expression to his countenance, as he sat opposite it, with his hands crossed upon his knees, probably reflecting upon his forlorn condition."

The Emperor was silent for a moment after his physician entered, and then said, in pensive tones,

"Doctor, have you any opiate which will give sleep to the sleepless?"

But this is beyond your art. I have been trying in vain to procure a little rest. I can not comprehend the conduct of your ministers. They go to the expense of three hundred thousand dollars in sending out furniture, wood, and building materials for my use, and, at the same time, send orders to put me nearly on rations, and oblige me to discharge my servants, and make reductions incompatible with the decency and comfort of the house. Then we have aid-de-camps making stipulations about a bottle of wine and two or three pounds of meat with as much gravity and consequence as if they were treating about the distribution of kingdoms. I see contradictions that I can not reconcile; on the one hand, enormous and useless expenditure; on the other, unparalleled meanness and littleness.

"Why do they not allow me to provide myself with every thing instead of disgracing the character of the nation? They will not furnish my followers with what they have been accustomed to, nor will they allow me to provide for them by sending sealed letters through a mercantile house even of their own selection; for no man in France would answer a letter of mine when he knew that it would be read by the English ministers, and that he would consequently be denounced to the Bourbons, and his property and person exposed to certain destruction.

"Moreover, your ministers have not given a specimen of good faith in seizing upon the trifling sums of money that I had in the *Bellerophon*. This gives reason to suppose that they would do the same again, if they knew where any of my property was placed. It must be to deceive the English nation. The English people, seeing all this furniture sent out, and so much parade and show in the preparations made in England, conclude that I am well treated here. If they knew the truth, and the dishonor which it reflects upon them, they would not suffer it.

"But who," the Emperor continued, "was that general officer who was with the governor to-day?"

"It was General Meade," said Dr. O'Meara, "who, with Mrs. Meade, arrived a few days ago. I was under his command in Egypt, where he was severely wounded."

"What sort of a man is he?"

"He bears a very excellent character."

"That governor," continued the Emperor, "was seen stopping him frequently, and pointing in different directions. I suppose he has been filling his head with falsehood about me, and has told him that I hate the sight of every Englishman, as was told to the officers of the 53d. I shall order a letter to be written to tell him that I will see him."

After O'Meara had retired, the Emperor again endeavored to obtain some sleep, but finding all his efforts in vain, about midnight he sent for Las Casas, and for two hours engaged with him in confidential conversation.

September 8. The Emperor had no sleep through the night, and at an early hour in the morning, depressed and languid, breakfasted with his friends in the tent. It was a pleasant day, and he rode out in the calash. The conversation turned upon the Emperor's court at the Tuileries.

"It is more difficult," said Napoleon, "than is generally supposed, to speak to every one in a crowded assemblage, and yet say *nothing* to any one; to seem to know a multitude of people, nine tenths of whom are utter strangers to you. Now that I am reduced to the level of a mere private individual, and can reflect philosophically upon the time when I was called to execute the designs of Providence, without, however, ceasing to be a man, I can see how much the fate of those I governed really depended upon chance, and how often favor and credit were purely accidental. Intrigue is so dexterous and merit often so maladroit; these extremes approximate so closely to each other, that, with the best intentions in the world, I find that my benefits were distributed like prizes in a lottery? And yet, could I have done better? Was I faulty in my intentions or remiss in my exertions? Have other sovereigns done better than I did? It is only thus that I can be judged. The fault was in the nature of my situation and in the force of things."

"A vessel which had come from the Cape," says Las Casas, "sailed for Europe this day. Several English military officers, who were passengers on board this ship, had not been permitted to wait upon the Emperor, in spite of their repeated solicitations. This was a new instance of the governor's malevolence. These officers were men of distinction, and their report, on their return home, might have had some influence. The governor, in defiance of all truth, informed them that Napoleon had determined to see no one."

The Emperor consequently requested Count Montholon to write a note to General Meade, inviting him to call at Longwood. A verbal message was also, at the same time, sent to Lady Meade, that, though the Emperor could not, in courtesy, invite a lady to come and see him, still he should be most happy to see her. According to the regulations, this note was presented open to Sir Hudson Lowe by the English orderly officer at Longwood, Captain Poppleton. The governor handed the note to General Meade. In reply, General Meade stated in a note to Count Montholon that there were restrictions in the way, which would render it necessary for him to apply to the governor for permission, and that the vessel was ready to sail, and he could not detain her.

September 9. The Emperor, suffering from chills and fever, and severe colic, sent for Dr. O'Meara. Alluding to the note of apology from General Meade to Count Montholon, expressing his inability to accept the invitation which had been given the day before, Napoleon said,

"I am convinced that, in reality, he was prevented by the governor. When you see him, you may say that I think that he prevented General Meade from coming to see me."

At an early hour Las Casas called. The Emperor, sleepless, appetiteless, dejected, and in pain, was lying upon the sofa, with a fire burning on the hearth. He gradually became animated as in conversation he retraced the eventful and marvelous past. Speaking of the large sums he had conferred upon those about him, he said,

"It would be difficult to estimate all that I bestowed in that way. I might, on more than one occasion, have been accused of profuseness, and I am grieved to see that it has been of little use in any respect. There must certainly have been some fatality on my part, or some essential defect in the individuals whom I favored. What a difficulty was I placed in! It can not be believed that my extravagance was caused by personal vanity. To act the part of an Asiatic monarch was not a thing to my taste. I was not actuated either by vanity or caprice; every thing was with me a matter of calculation. Though certain individuals might be favorites with me, yet I did not wish to lavish my bounty on them merely because I liked them. I wished to found through them great families, who might form rallying-points in great national crises. The great officers of my household, as well as all my ministers, independently of their enormous salaries, often received from me handsome gratifications, sometimes complete services of plate.

"What was my object in this profuseness? I required that they should maintain elegant establishments, give grand dinners and brilliant balls. And why did I wish this? In order to amalgamate parties, to form new unions, to smooth down old asperities, and to give a character to French society and manners. If I conceived good ideas, they miscarried in the execution. None of my chief courtiers ever kept up a suitable establishment. If they gave dinners, they only invited their party friends, and when I attended their expensive balls, whom did I find there? All the court of the Tuileries—not a new face, not one of those who were offended at the new system—those sullen malcontents, whom a little honey would have brought back to the hive. They could not enter into my views, or did not wish to do so. In vain I expressed displeasure, entreated, and commanded: things still went on in the same way. I could not be every where at once, and they knew that. And yet it was affirmed that I ruled with a rod of iron. How, then, must things go under gentle sovereigns?"

September 10. Dr. O'Meara had an interview with Sir Hudson Lowe.

"Has General Bonaparte," inquired the governor, "made any observations relative to General Meade's not having accepted the offer made to him?"

"He says," O'Meara replied, "that he is convinced that you prevented him from accepting it, and desired me to say to you that such was his opinion."

The countenance of this vulgar man turned pale with rage. "He is a d——d lying rascal, a d——d black-hearted villain. I wished General Meade to accept it, and told him to do so." Walking about in an agitated manner, he continued, "None but a black-hearted villain would have entertained such an idea." Then, mounting his horse, he rode away; he had not, however, proceeded more than a hundred steps, before he wheeled round, and came back, and said, in emphatic tones of anger, "Tell General Bonaparte that the assertion that I prevented General Meade from going to see him is an infamous lie, and the person who said it is a great liar. Tell him my exact words."

"It is unnecessary for me to say," continues Dr. O'Meara, "that I did not deliver this message in the manner in which I was directed to convey it."

September 12. Two of the inmates of Longwood had rode to town a few days before, to call upon the French and Russian commissioners. An English officer was ordered to follow them, and keep them constantly in sight. In consequence of some misunderstanding, they received treatment which they considered a gross insult. Speaking of this misunderstanding, the Emperor said,

"What I complain of is the disingenuous manner in which they act in order to prevent any of the French from going to town. Why do they not say at once manfully, 'You can not go to town,' and then nobody will ask, instead of converting officers into spies and gendarmes by making them follow the French and listen to their conversation? But their design is to throw so many impediments in the way, and to render it so disagreeable to us as to amount to a prohibition, without giving any direct orders. Thus this governor will be enabled to say that we have the liberty of the town, but that we do not choose to avail ourselves of it."

The Emperor continued seriously sick. His narrow camp bed, so small that he could hardly turn himself in it, was poorly adapted for hours of restlessness and pain. He ordered his camp bed to be carried into his cabinet and placed beside a sofa, so as to increase his comforts in the tossings of sleepless nights. To such privations was the Emperor driven from the saloons of the Tuileries.

September 13. The Emperor, though apparently no better, having eaten nothing for three days, and drinking only a little warm lemonade, rose from his bed, declaring that he would indulge in sickness no longer. He repaired to the drawing-room, and for two or three hours dictated to one of his suite. General Bertrand entering, Napoleon asked him how he thought he looked. "Only a little yellow," the general replied. The Emperor burst into a laugh, and rising, good-humoredly pursued the general into the saloon to catch him by the ear, exclaiming,

"Rather yellow, indeed! Do you intend to insult me, grand marshal? Do you mean to say that I am bilious, morose, atrabilarious, passionate, unjust, tyrannical? Let me catch hold of your ear, and I will take my revenge."

Dinner hour arrived. The Emperor took some slight refreshment in his own room, and then returned to the dining-room while his friends were at the table. Observing their scanty fare, for Sir Hudson Lowe was determined to starve them into terms, he said, "I really pity you." He immediately gave orders that a portion of his plate should be sold every month to supply what was necessary for the table.

CHAPTER XXVI.
1816, September. Continued.

Scarcity of Food—The Emperor's Freedom from Animosity—The Bourbons—On Impossibilities—Statistical Calculations—Sale of Plate—Fresh Vexations—Debt of St. Domingo—Plans of Administration—On Sensibility—Holland and King Louis—The Emperor's Family—Business Habits of the Emperor—Treasures of Napoleon.

September 14. The Emperor was in much better health, and spent much of the day dictating. "At dinner," says Las Casas, " we had literally hardly any thing to eat. The Emperor ordered some additional provisions to be purchased and paid for out of the sale of his plate."

In the evening he sent for Las Casas, and said to him, " I am not inclined to sleep, and I sent for you to help me keep my vigil. Let us have a little chat together."

The conversation turned, as usual, upon the wonderful drama of the past.

"They may explain this as they will," said the Emperor, "but I assure you I never entertained any direct or personal hatred of those whose power I subverted. To me it was merely a political contest. I was astonished to find my heart free of animosity, and, I may add, animated by good-will toward my enemies. You saw how I released the Duke d'Angoulême; and I would have done the same by the king, and even have granted him an asylum of his own choosing. The triumph of the cause in no way depended on his person, and I respected his age and his misfortunes. Perhaps, also, I felt grateful for a certain degree of consideration which he, in particular, had observed toward me. It is true that, at the moment to which I am now alluding, he had, I believe, outlawed me, and set a price on my head; but I looked upon all this as belonging to the *manifesto style*. The same kind of denunciations were also issued by the Austrian government, without, however, giving me much uneasiness, though I must confess that my dear father-in-law was rather too severe on the husband of his beloved daughter."

A few weeks before this, an English officer, who was presented to the Emperor, speaking of the return from Elba, said,

"That astonishing event presented to the eyes of Europe the contrast of all that was most feeble and most sublime—the Bourbons abandoning a monarchy and flying on the approach of a single man, who, by his own individual efforts, boldly undertook the conquest of an empire."

"Sir," said the Emperor, "you are mistaken. You have taken a wrong view of the matter. The Bourbons were not wanting in courage. They did all they could. The Count d'Artois flew to Lyons. The Duchess d'Angoulême proved herself an Amazon in Bordeaux; and the Duke d'Angoulême offered as much resistance as he could. If, in spite of all this, they could attain no satisfactory object, the fault must not be attributed to them, but to

B B

the force of circumstances. The Bourbons, individually, could do no more than they really did. The contagion had spread in every direction."

September 16. "In the morning," says Las Casas, "my servant came to tell me that there was neither coffee, sugar, milk, nor bread for breakfast. Yesterday, some hours before dinner, feeling hungry, I asked for a mouthful of bread, and was told there was none for me. Thus we are denied the very necessaries of life. The fact will scarcely be credited, and yet I have stated nothing but the truth."

It was a fine day, and the Emperor, though tottering with weakness, walked out into the garden. As he was walking about, Madam Montholon drove away a dog that had come near her.

"You do not like dogs, madam?" inquired the Emperor.

"No, sire," she replied.

"If you do not like dogs," the Emperor playfully rejoined, "you do not like fidelity, you do not like those who are attached to you, and therefore you are not faithful."

"But—but—" said Madam Montholon, in embarrassment.

"But—but—" repeated the Emperor, "where is the error of my logic? Refute my arguments if you can."

One of the Emperor's suite had, a few days before, proposed making some chemical experiments. The Emperor inquired whether he had obtained success. "No, sire," was the reply; "I could not procure the necessary apparatus."

"A true child of the Seine," exclaimed the Emperor; "an absolute Parisian cockney! Do you think you are still at the Tuileries? True industry does not consist in executing by known and given means. The proof of art and genius is to accomplish an object in spite of difficulties, and to find little or no *impossibility*. But what do you complain of? The want of a pestle, when the spar of any chair might answer the same purpose? The want of a mortar? Any thing is a mortar that you choose to make use of. This table is a mortar—any pot or kettle is a mortar! Do you think that you are still in the Rue St. Honore, amid all the shops in Paris?"

"This reminds me," said General Bertrand, "of something which occurred the first time I had the honor of being presented to your majesty. I was about to leave the army of Italy to proceed on a mission to Constantinople, when you gave me a commission relative to the department of engineers. On my return, I came up with you at a short distance from head-quarters, and I informed you that I had found the thing impossible. On this, your majesty, whom I had addressed with great diffidence, said, with the most familiar air,

"'But let us see how you set to work, sir. That which you found impossible may not be so to me.'

"Accordingly, when I mentioned the means by which I proposed to execute what your majesty wished, you immediately substituted others. In a few moments I was perfectly convinced of the superiority of your majesty's plans. And this circumstance furnished me with sentiments and recollections which have since proved very useful to me."

September 18. The record of this day illustrates the peculiar intellectual activity of the Emperor, and the wide range of his thoughts. His sallow and wasted cheeks proclaimed his failing health, and he was so feeble that the promenade of a few moments exhausted him. It was a fine day. The Emperor took a short walk in the garden, and then breakfasted with all his companions in the tent. He then rode for an hour in his calash, and on his return engaged in his studies. He dictated, in turns, to Las Casas and to General Bertrand. Las Casas aided him, in the library, in searching for documents which would give information respecting the interior of Africa. After dinner he was engaged, with the pen in his hand, in investigating the comparative production of the soils of Egypt and France. He found the production of France to be greatly inferior to that of Egypt. This investigation gave rise to other corresponding questions, such as, What was the probable possible population of Egypt in ancient times? What might have been the population of the Israelites, if, during the short period they remained in captivity, they had increased to the degree mentioned in Scripture? The Emperor also made many ingenious, novel, and striking remarks upon the probabilities of human life, suggested by *Puchet's Statistical Estimates of France*.

Las Casas was requested to investigate the question of the population of the Israelites compared with the Mosaic account. This calculation interested the Emperor exceedingly. He scrutinized it with great acumen, and found that it confirmed the Scripture narrative. During dinner he exercised himself in the English language by questioning young Las Casas in that language upon points of history and geometry. After dinner he took up the Odyssey, and read with comments to his companions. Such was the employment of a sick day with the Emperor Napoleon. Such was the character of the man whom the nobles of England tore from France, and chained, to die in protracted torments, upon the rock of St. Helena. The crime is too great for human nature to pardon.

Dr. O'Meara records, "Major Gorrequer, in the course of conversation with me relative to the provisioning of Longwood, said that Sir Hudson Lowe had observed that any soldiers who would attend at Longwood as servants of General Bonaparte were unworthy of rations."

September 19. The Emperor spent the morning collecting from modern authors information on the sources of the Nile. He took a short ride in the calash, and on his return examined a large basket of plate which was broken up, and which was to be sent to town and sold the next day. A very natural pride made the Emperor unwilling that the pieces of this beautiful service, the tokens of his power and of his fall, should be hawked about Europe as curiosities. Though five hundred dollars were offered for a single plate, he ordered the arms to be erased, and the pieces to be broken up into masses of silver, so as to leave no trace of the plate having belonged to him. The dish covers were topped with small eagles of solid silver. The Emperor characteristically would not have the eagles injured. They were cut off and carefully laid aside. The grief of the servants in applying the hammer to these objects of their veneration, associated as they were with their homage to the Emperor, was sincere and deep. It seemed to them like sacrilege. Many of them shed tears on the occasion.

September 20. It was a lovely morning, and at eight o'clock the Emperor walked out into the garden. He breakfasted in his tent, and then dictated to General Gourgaud the relation of the battle of Marengo. At three o'clock he called into the room of Las Casas, and finding him revising the account of the battle of Arcola, wished to read it again. The perusal of this account awakened his ideas relative to what he called *that beautiful spot, Italy.*

He requested Las Casas and his son to follow him into the drawing-room, where he dictated to them for several hours. He caused his immense map of Italy, which covered the greater part of the drawing-room, to be spread open on the floor. Having laid himself down upon it, he went over it on his hands and his knees with a compass and a pencil in his hand, comparing and measuring the distances with a long piece of string.

"It is thus," said the Emperor, laughing, "that a country should be measured in order to form a correct idea of it, and to lay down a good plan for a campaign."

THE EMPEROR DICTATING.

"We have experienced to-day," Las Casas records, "a fresh and inconceivable vexation from the governor. He has forbidden us to sell our plate, when broken up, to any other person than the one he should point out.

What can have been his intention in committing this new act of injustice?" The purchaser of the plate was also forbidden to pay the money to any of the suite of General Bonaparte, but was ordered to deposit it with Mr. Balcombe, the English agent for the supply of Longwood.

September 21. Admiral Malcolm, who was about to sail from St. Helena to the Cape of Good Hope, called to take leave of his friends at Longwood. He was much esteemed by them all, and he had a long and very friendly interview with the Emperor.

After dinner the conversation turned upon what the Emperor termed the celebrated debt of St. Domingo. It gave rise to the following curious details:

" The administrator of St. Domingo," said the Emperor, " took it into his head one day to draw from the Cape, without authority, the sum of sixty millions [$12,000,000] in bills on the treasury of Paris, which bills were all payable the same day. France was not then, and had, perhaps, never been, rich enough to meet such a demand. Besides, where and by what means had the administration of St. Domingo acquired so much credit? The First Consul could not command any thing like it in Paris. It was as much as M. Necker could have done at the time of his greatest popularity. When these bills appeared in Paris, where they arrived before the letters of advice, I was applied to from the treasury to point out what was to be done. 'Wait for the letters of advice,' said I, 'in order to learn the nature of the transaction. The treasury is like a capitalist; it possesses the same rights, and should follow the same course. These bills are not accepted; they are, consequently, not payable.'

" The necessary information and the vouchers arrived. These bills stated value received, but the receipts of the officers in charge of the chests, into whose hands the money had been paid, were only for one tenth, one fifth, one third the amount of the respective bills. The treasury, therefore, would only acknowledge and refund the sum really and *bona fide* paid, and the bills, in their tenor, were declared to be false. This raised a great clamor, and produced a terrible agitation among the merchants. A deputation waited upon me, and I opened the business at once.

" ' Do you take me for a child ?' said I. ' Do you think that I will thus sport with the purest blood of the people, or that I am so indifferent a guardian of the public interest? What I refuse to give up does not affect me personally, does not trench upon my civil list; but it is public property, of which I am the guardian, and which is the more sacred in my eyes on that account.'

" I then addressed myself directly to the two persons at the head of the deputation, saying, ' You, gentlemen, who are merchants, bankers, men of business, give me a positive answer. If one of your agents abroad were to draw upon you for very large sums, contrary to your expectations and to your interests, would you accept, would you pay his bills ?' They were obliged to admit that they would not.

" ' Then,' said I, ' you, who are simple proprietors, and, in the right of your majority, responsible to yourselves only, would wish to possess a right which you refuse to allow me, proprietor in the name of all, and who am, in that quality, always a minor, and subject to revision! No, gentlemen, I shall act in the name and for the benefit of all. The actual amount received for your bills shall be repaid you, and no more. I do not ask the merchants to take the bills of my agents. It is an honor, a mark of credit to which I do not aspire. If the merchants do take them, it must be at their own risk. I only acknowledge and consider as sacred the acceptance of my minister of the treasury.'

"Upon this they expostulated again, and a great deal of idle talk ensued. They would be obliged, they said, to declare themselves bankrupts; they had received these bills for ready money. Their agents abroad had committed the error of taking them through respect for, and confidence in the government. 'Very well,' said I, 'become bankrupts.' But they did not. They had not received these bills for ready money, and their agents had not committed any error. They left me, convinced in their own minds of the validity of my reasons; nevertheless, they filled Paris with their clamors and with falsehoods in misrepresenting the affair altogether. This transaction and its details explain many other transactions which have been much spoken of in Paris under the imperial administration. The commercial world declared that this proceeding was unexampled; that such a violation of credit was a thing hitherto unheard of. I replied that I would set that question at rest by quoting precedents, and recalled to their minds the bills of Louis XIV., the liquidations of the regent, the company of the Mississippi, the liquidations of the wars of 1763 and 1782, and proved to them that what they contended to be a thing unexampled had been the constant practice of the monarchy."

The conversation turned to the different branches of the administration, and the Emperor defended the institution of the post of inspector of reviews.

"It is only through them," said he, "that the actual number of men present can be ascertained; through them alone has this advantage been obtained; and it is one of immense importance in the active operations of war. And these inspectors are not less useful in an administrative point of view; for, whatever trifling abuses may exist in the details, and however numerous these abuses may be, it is on a general principle that such things should be considered. In order to estimate fairly the utility of this institution, it should be asked what other abuses would have taken place if it had not existed. For myself I must say, that, checking the expenditure by trying how much the total number of troops ought to have cost according to their fixed rates of pay, I have always found the sum paid by the treasury to fall short of my estimate. What result more beneficial could be required?

"The administration of the navy," continued the Emperor, "was the most regular and honest. It had become a *chef d'œuvre*. In that consisted the great merit of Decrés. France is too large to have only one minister for the administration of the war department. It was a task beyond the powers of one man. Paris has been made the centre of all decisions, contracts, supplies, and organizations, while the correspondence of the minister has been subdivided among a number of persons equal to the number of regiments and corps. The contrary ought to have been the case; the correspondences should have been centred, and the resources subdivided, by raising them on the spot where they were required. I had long meditated a plan to establish in France twenty or twenty-five military districts, which would have composed so many armies. There would have been that number of accountants; these would have been twenty under ministers, for which it would have been necessary to find twenty honest men. The minister would have had only twenty correspondents. He would have centred the whole, and conducted the business with celerity and dispatch.

Messrs. Gaudin and Mollien were of opinion that it was necessary that public functionaries, into whose hands the public money was received, public financiers and contractors, should have very large fortunes, that they should have it in their power to make considerable profits, and openly avow them in such a manner as to retain a degree of consideration which they might be careful not to endanger, and a reputation of honor which they might wish not to compromise. In this way, credit, support, and service could be obtained from them in case of need.

"Another set of men, Defermonts, Lacuée, and Marbois, thought, on the contrary, that it was impossible to be too exact, too saving, and too strict. I was inclined to be of the opinion of the first, considering the views of the last to be narrow, and such as were applicable to a regiment, but not to an army; to the expenses of a private household, but not to the expenditures of a great empire. I called them the Puritans and the Jansenists of the professions.

"The minister of the treasury and the secretary of state were two of the institutions on which I most congratulated myself, and from which I derived the greatest assistance. The minister of the treasury concentrated all the resources and controlled all the expenses of the empire. From the secretary of state all acts emanated. He was the minister of ministers, imparting life to all intermediate acts, the grand notary of the empire, signing and authenticating all documents. Through the first, I knew at every moment the state of my affairs; and through the second, I made known my decisions and my will in all directions and every where. With my minister of the treasury and my secretary of state alone, and a half dozen clerks, I would have undertaken to govern the empire from the remotest parts of Illyria, or from the banks of the Niemen, with as much facility as in my capital."

September 23. The conversation turned upon sensibility. The Emperor alluded to one of his companions, who never mentioned the name of his mother but with tears in his eyes.

"Is this not peculiar to him?" said the Emperor. "Is this a general feeling? Do you experience the same thing, or am I unnatural in that respect? I certainly love my mother with all my heart. There is nothing which I would not do for her; yet, if I were to hear of her death, I do not think that my grief would manifest itself by a single tear; but I would not affirm that this would be the case were I to lose a friend, or my wife, or my son. Is this distinction founded on nature? What can be the cause of it? Is it that my reason has prepared me beforehand to expect the death of my mother as being in the natural course of events, whereas the loss of my wife, or of my son, is an unexpected occurrence, a hardship inflicted by Fate which I endeavor to struggle against? Perhaps, also, this distinction merely proceeds from our natural disposition to egotism. I belong to my mother, but my wife and my son belong to me."

Las Casas testifies to the intensity of Napoleon's affection for his wife and his child. He loved to talk of them in his hours of retirement. "Not a day passed," says Las Casas, "in which his wife did not form a part of his private conversations. There is no circumstance, no minute particularity relating to her, which he has not repeated to me a hundred times."

September 24. The conversation to-day, turning upon Holland and King Louis, became very interesting.

"Louis is not devoid of intelligence," said the Emperor, "and has a good heart, but even with these qualifications a man may commit many errors and do a great deal of mischief. Louis is naturally inclined to be capricious and fantastical, and the works of Rousseau have contributed to increase this disposition. Seeking to obtain a reputation for sensibility and beneficence, incapable by himself of enlarged views, and competent only to local details, Louis acted like a prefect rather than a king. No sooner had he arrived in Holland, than, fancying that nothing could be finer than to have it said that he was thenceforth a true Dutchman, he attached himself entirely to the party favorable to the English, promoted smuggling, and thus connived with our enemies. It became necessary from that moment to watch over him, and even to threaten to wage war against him. Then, seeking refuge against the weakness of his disposition in the most stubborn obstinacy, and mistaking a public scandal for an act of glory, he fled from his throne, declaiming against me and my insatiable ambition, my intolerable tyranny. What, then, remained for me to do? Was I to abandon Holland to our enemies? Ought I to have given it another king? In that case, could I have expected more from him than from my own brother? Did not all the kings that I created act nearly in the same manner? I therefore united Holland to the empire; and this act produced a most unfavorable impression in Europe, and contributed not a little to lay the foundation of our misfortunes.

"Louis had been delighted to take Lucien as his model. Lucien had acted in nearly the same manner. If, at a later period, he has repented, and has even nobly made amends for his errors, this conduct, which did honor to his character, did not produce any favorable change in our affairs. On my return from Elba in 1815, Louis wrote a long letter to me from Rome, and sent an embassador to me. It was his treaty, he said, the conditions upon which he would return to me. I answered that I would not make any treaty with him; that he was my brother, and that, if he came back, he would be well received. Will it be believed that one of his conditions was that he should be at liberty to divorce Hortense! I severely rebuked the negotiator for having dared to be the bearer of so absurd a proposal, and for having believed that such a measure could ever be made the subject of a negotiation. I reminded Louis that our family compact positively forbade it, and represented to him that it was no less forbidden by the laws of policy and morality, and by public opinion.

"I farther assured him that, actuated by all these motives, if his children were to lose their estate through his fault, I should feel more interested for them than for him, although he was my brother. Perhaps an excuse might be found for the caprice of Louis's disposition in the deplorable state of his health, the age at which it became deranged, and the horrible circumstances which produced that derangement, and which must have had a considerable influence upon his mind. He was on the point of death on the occasion, and has ever since been subject to the most cruel infirmities. He is almost paralytic on one side.

"It is certain that I have derived little assistance from my own family, and that they have greatly injured me and the great cause for which I fought. The energy of my disposition has often been extolled, but I have been very yielding with my own family; this they knew; after the first moment of anger was over, they always carried their point by perseverance and obstinacy. I became tired of the contest, and they did with me just as they pleased. These are great errors which I have committed. If, instead of this, each of them had given a common impulse to the different bodies which I have placed under their direction, we should have marched on to the poles.

PORTRAIT OF JOSEPH BONAPARTE, THE BROTHER OF NAPOLEON.

Every thing would have given way before us. We should have changed the face of the world. Europe would now enjoy the advantages of a new system, and we should have received the benedictions of mankind.

"I have not been so fortunate as Genghis Khan with his four sons, each of whom rivaled the other in zeal for his service. No sooner had I made a man a king than he thought himself king *by the grace of God*, so contagious is the use of the expression. He was then no longer a lieutenant on whom I could rely, but another enemy whom I was obliged to guard against. His efforts were not directed toward seconding me, but toward rendering himself independent. They all immediately imagined that they were adored and preferred to me. From that moment I was in their way, I endangered their existence. Legitimate monarchs would not have behaved differently, would not have thought themselves more firmly established. Weak-minded men! who may have been enlightened when I fell, since the enemy has not even done them the honor to demand the surrender of their dignities, or even to allude to it. If they are now put under personal restraint, if they are subject to vexation, it must proceed on the part of the conqueror from a wish to impose the weight of power, or from the base motive of gratifying his vengeance. If the members of my family excite a great interest among mankind, it is because they belong to me and to the common cause, but assuredly there is not the least danger of any movement being produced by any of them.

"Notwithstanding the philosophy of several of them, for some of them have said, after the fashion of the *Chambellans* of the Faubourg St. Germain, that they were *forced* to reign, their fall must have been sensibly felt by them, for they had soon accommodated themselves to the pleasures and comforts of their station. They have all really been kings, thanks to my labors; all have enjoyed the advantages of royalty. I alone have known its cares. I have all the time carried the world on my shoulders, and this occupation is rather fatiguing.

"It will perhaps be asked why I persisted in erecting states and kingdoms? But the manners and the situation of Europe required it. Every time that another country was annexed to France, the act, added to the universal alarm which already prevailed, excited loud murmurs, and diminished the chances of peace. Then why, will it be further said, did I indulge in the vanity of placing every member of my family on a throne? for the generality of people will have thought me actuated by vanity alone. Why did I not rather fix my choice on some private individuals possessing greater abilities? To this I reply, that it is not with thrones as with the functions of a prefect. Talents and abilities are so common in the present age among the multitude, that one must be cautious to avoid awakening the idea of competition. In the agitation of our situation, and with our modern institutions, it was proper to think rather of consolidating and concentrating the hereditary right of succession, in order to avoid innumerable feuds, factions, and misfortunes.

"The principal defect in my person and my elevation, consistently with the plan of universal harmony which I meditated for the repose and happiness of all, was that I had risen at once from the multitude. I felt that I stood insulated and alone, and I cast anchors around me on all sides. Where could I more naturally look for support than among my own relations? Could I expect more from strangers? And it must be admitted that, if the members of my family have had the folly to break through these secred ties, the morality of the people, superior to their blind infatuation, fulfilled, in part, my object. With them their subjects thought themselves more quiet, more united as in one family.

"Acts of that importance were not to be considered lightly. They were involved in considerations of the highest order. They were connected with the tranquillity of mankind, the possibility of ameliorating its condition. If, notwithstanding all these measures, taken with the best intentions, it seems that no permanent good has been effected, we must admit the truth of this great maxim, that to govern is very difficult for those who wish to do it conscientiously."

September 27. "The Emperor," says Las Casas, "for some days past has been remarkably assiduous in his application. All our mornings have been spent in making researches respecting Egypt in the works of the ancient authors. We have looked over Herodotus, Pliny, and Strabo together, without any other intermission than that which we required to eat our breakfast. The weather was bad, and the Emperor dictated every day, and the whole day. At dinner, the Emperor remarked that his health was much better."

"But, sire," said Las Casas, "you do not go out of the house, and are occupied eight, ten, or twelve hours of the day."

"That is the very reason," replied the Emperor, "of my being better. Occupation is my element; I am born and made for it. I have found the limits beyond which I could not exercise the power of motion; I have seen the extent to which I could use my eyes, but I have never known any bounds to my capability of application. I nearly killed poor Méneval. I was obliged to relieve him from the duties of his situation, and place him, for the recovery of his health, near the person of Maria Louisa, where his post was a mere sinecure. If I were in Europe, and had leisure, my pleasure would be to write history. The researches in which I have been lately engaged have proved to me the very indifferent manner in which history has been written every where, beyond any thing I could ever have suspected.

"We have no good history, and we can not have any. The other nations of Europe are nearly in the same predicament as ourselves. Monks and privileged individuals, men friendly to abuses, and inimical to information and learning, have monopolized this branch of writing. They have told us what they thought proper, or, rather, that which favored their interests, gratified their passions, or agreed with their views. I had formed a plan for remedying the evil as much as possible. I intended, for instance, to appoint commissioners from the Institute, or learned men whom public opinion might have pointed out to me, to revise, criticise, and republish our historical annals. I wished also to add commentaries to the classic authors which are put into the hands of our youth, to explain them with reference to our modern institutions. With a good programme, competition, and rewards, this end would have been accomplished. Every thing can be obtained by such means.

"It was my intention to have caused the history of the last reigns of our kings to be written from the original documents taken from the archives of our foreign affairs. There were also several manuscripts, ancient and modern, in the imperial library, which I intended to have caused to be printed, classifying and embodying them under their different heads, so as to form codes of doctrines on science, morality, literature, and fine arts. In order to check the production of the immense number of inferior works with which the public is inundated, without, however, trenching upon the liberty of the press, what objection could there be to the formation of a tribunal of opinion, composed of members of the Institute, of members of the University, and of persons appointed by the government, who would examine all works with reference to these three points of view, science, morality, and politics? who would have criticised them, and defined the degree of merit possessed by each? This tribunal would have been the light of the public. It would have operated as a warranty in favor of works of real merit, would have insured their success, and thus produced emulation; and it would also have discouraged the publication of inferior productions."

Las Casas here records the following habits of the Emperor when upon the throne.

"The Emperor was almost always in his closet. It might be said that he spent the whole day and part of the night in it. He usually went to bed at ten or eleven o'clock, and got up again about twelve, to work a few hours more. He himself read all the letters which were addressed to him. To some he answered by writing a few words in the margin, and to others he dictated an answer. Those that were of great importance were always put by and read a second time, and were never answered until some time had elapsed. He often said '*To-morrow; night is a good adviser.*' Indeed, he has frequently remarked that he worked much more at night than during the day; not that thoughts of business prevented him from sleeping, but because he slept at intervals, according as he wanted rest, and a little sufficed him. It often happened to the Emperor, during the course of his campaigns, to be roused suddenly upon some emergency of business. He would then immediately get up, and it would have been impossible to guess, from the appearance of his eyes, that he had just been sleeping. It has sometimes happened that he has been called up as much as ten times in the same night, and each time he was always found to have fallen asleep again, not having as yet taken his supply of rest."

September 29. During dinner, somebody mentioned a pool which stands in the garden, where a lamb had been drowned.

"Is it possible," said the Emperor to one of his household, "that you have not yet had this pool filled up? How guilty you would be, and what would not be your grief, if your son were to be drowned in it, as might easily happen?"

"Sire," replied the person thus accused, "I often intended to have it done, but it was impossible to get workmen."

"That is not an excuse," said the Emperor. "If *my* son were here, I should go and fill it up with my own hands."

September 30. "Whenever the Emperor took up a subject," says Las Casas, "if he was in the least animated, his language was fit to be printed. He has often, when an idea struck him forcibly, dictated to any one of us who happened to be in his way pages which, at the first throw, were of the finest diction. On one occasion, when the English ministerial newspaper spoke of the large treasures which Napoleon must possess, and which he no doubt concealed, the Emperor dictated as follows:

"'You wish to know the treasures of Napoleon. They are immense, it is true, but they are all exposed to light. They are the noble harbors of Antwerp and Flushing, which are capable of containing the largest fleets, and of protecting them against the ice from the sea; the hydraulic works of Dunkirk, Havre, and Nice; the immense harbor of Cherbourg; the maritime works at Venice; the beautiful roads from Antwerp to Amsterdam, from Mentz to Metz, from Bordeaux to Bayonne; the passes of the Simplon, of Mount Cenis, of Mount Geneve, of the Corniche, which open a communication through the Alps in four different directions, and which exceed in grandeur, in boldness, and in skill of execution all the works of the Romans. In these alone you will find eight hundred millions [$160,000,000].

"'The treasures of Napoleon may be found in the roads from the Pyrenees to the Alps, from Parma to Spezia, from Savona to Piedmont; in the bridges of Jena, Austerlitz, Des Arts, Sevres, Tours, Rouanne, Lyons, Turin; in the bridges of Isere, of the Durance, of Bordeaux and Rouen; in the canal which connects the Rhine with the Rhone by the Doubs, and thus unites the North Sea with the Mediterranean; in the canal which connects the Scheldt with the Somme, and thus joins Paris and Amsterdam; in the canal which unites the Rance to the Vilaine; the canal of Arles, that of Pavia, and that of the Rhine; in the draining of the marshes of Burgoine, of the Contentin, of Rochefort; in the rebuilding of the greater number of the churches destroyed during the Revolution, the building of others, and the institution of numerous establishments of industry for the suppression of mendicity; in the building of the Louvre, the construction of public warehouses, of the bank, of the canal of the Ourcq, and the distribution of water in the city of Paris; in the numerous drains, the quays, the embellishments, and the monuments of that large capital; in the works for the embellishment of Rome, the re-establishment of the manufactures of Lyons, the creation of many hundred manufactories of cotton for spinning and for weaving, which employ several millions of workmen; in the funds accumulated to establish upward of four hundred manufactories of sugar from beet-roots for the consumption of part of France, and which would have furnished sugar at the same price as it can be obtained from the West Indies, if they had continued to receive encouragement only four years longer; in the substitution of woad for indigo, which would, at last, have been brought to a state of perfection in France, and obtained as good and cheap as the indigo from the colonies; in numerous manufactories for all kinds of objects of art; in fifty millions [$10,000,000] expended in repairing and beautifying the palaces belonging to the crown; in sixty millions [$12,000,000] in furniture for the palaces belonging to the crown in France, Holland, Turin, and at Rome; in sixty millions in diamonds for the crown, all purchased with Napoleon's money—the *Regent* (the only diamond that was left belonging to the former diamonds of the crown) withdrawn from the hands of the Jews at Berlin, in whose hands it had been left as a pledge for three millions [$600,000]; in the Napoleon Museum, valued at upward of four hundred millions [$80,000,000], filled with objects legitimately acquired either by money or treaties of peace known to the whole world, by virtue of which the master-pieces it contains were given in lieu of territory or of contributions; in several millions amassed to be applied to the encouragement of agriculture, which is the paramount consideration for the interest of France; in the introduction of Merino sheep, &c. These form a treasure of several thousand millions, which will endure for ages. These are the monuments that will confute calumny.

" 'History will say that all these things were accomplished in the midst of perpetual wars, without having recourse to any loan, and while the national debt was even diminishing every day, and that nearly fifty millions of taxes were remitted. Very large sums still remain in his private treasure. They were guaranteed to him by the treaty of Fontainebleau as the result of the savings effected on the civil list and of his other private revenues. These sums were divided, and did not go entirely into the public treasury, nor altogether into the treasury of France.'"

On another occasion the Emperor read in an English newspaper that Lord Castlereagh had said, in an assembly in Ireland, that Napoleon had declared at St. Helena that he never would have made peace with England but to deceive her, take her by surprise, and destroy her; and that if the French army was attached to the Emperor, it was because he was in the habit of giving the daughters of the richest families in marriage to his soldiers.

The Emperor was moved with indignation by a libel so atrocious, and immediately dictated the following reply:

"These calumnies, uttered against a man who is so barbarously oppressed, and who is not allowed to make his voice heard in answer to them, will be disbelieved by all persons well educated and susceptible of feeling. When Napoleon was seated on the first throne in the world, then, no doubt, his enemies had a right to say whatever they pleased. His actions were public, and were a sufficient answer to them. At any rate, his conduct belonged to public opinion and history; but to utter new and base calumnies against him at the present moment, is an act of the utmost meanness and cowardice, and which will not answer the end proposed. Millions of libels have been and are still published every day, but they are without effect. Sixty millions of men, of the most polished nations in the world, raise their voices to confute them; and fifty thousand Englishmen, who are now traveling on the Continent, will, on their return home, publish the truth to the inhabitants of the three kingdoms of Great Britain, who will blush at having been so grossly deceived.

"As for the bill, by virtue of which Napoleon has been dragged to this rock, it is an act of proscription similar to those of Sylla, and still more atrocious. The Romans unrelentingly pursued Hannibal to the utmost extremities of Bythinia, and Flaminius obtained from King Prusias the death of that great man; yet at Rome Flaminius was accused of having acted thus in order to satisfy his personal hatred. It was in vain that he urged in his defense that Hannibal, yet in the vigor of life, might still become a dangerous enemy, and that his death was necessary. A thousand voices were raised, and answered that acts of injustice and ungenerous deeds can never be useful to a great nation; and that upon such pretenses as those now set forth, murder, poisoning, and every species of crime might be justified. The following generation reproached their ancestors with this base act. They would have given any thing to have the stain effaced from their history. And since the re-establishment of letters among nations, every succeeding age has added its imprecations to those pronounced by Hannibal at the moment when he drank the fatal cup. He cursed Rome, who, while her fleets and legions covered Europe, Asia, and Africa, satiated her vengeance against one man, alone and unprotected, because she feared or pretended to fear him.

"The Romans, however, never violated the rights of hospitality. Sylla found an asylum in the house of Marius. Flaminius did not, before he banished Hannibal, receive him on board his ship, and declare that he had orders to treat him favorably. The Roman fleet did not convey him to the port of Ostia. And Hannibal, instead of placing himself under the Romans, preferred trusting his person to a king of Asia. At the moment when he was banished, he was not under the protection of the Roman flag; he was under the banners of a king who was an enemy of Rome.

"If in future ages a king of England should be one day brought before the awful tribunal of his nation, his defenders will urge in his favor the sacred character of a king, the respect due to the throne, to all crowned heads, and to the anointed of the Lord! But his accusers will have a right to answer thus:

"'One of the ancestors of this king whom you defend banished a man who was his guest, in time of peace. Afraid to put him to death in the presence of a nation governed by positive laws, and by regular and public forms, he caused his victim to be exposed on the most insalubrious point of a rock, situated in another hemisphere, in the midst of the ocean, where this guest perished after a long agony, a prey to the climate, to want, to insults of every kind! Yet that guest was also a great sovereign, raised to the throne on the shields of thirty-six millions of citizens. He was master of almost every capital of Europe. The greatest kings composed his court. He was generous toward all. He was, during twenty years, the arbitrator of nations. His family was allied to every reigning family, even to that of England. He was twice the anointed of the Lord—twice consecrated by the august ceremonies of religion.'"

"The Emperor," says Las Casas, "always dictated without the least preparation. I never saw him, on any occasion, make any research respecting our history or that of any other nation, and yet no man ever quoted history more faithfully, more *apropos*, or more frequently. One might have supposed that he knew history by quotations only, and that these quotations occurred to him as by inspiration. And here I must be allowed to mention a fact which has often struck me, and which I never could satisfactorily account for to myself; but it is so very remarkable, and I have witnessed it so often, that I can not pass it in silence. It is, that Napoleon seems to possess a stock of information on several points, which remains with him, as it were, in reserve, to burst forth with splendor on remarkable occasions, and which, in his moments of carelessness, appears to be not only slumbering, but almost unknown to him altogether.

"With respect to history, for instance, how often has it happened to him to ask me whether St. Louis had reigned before or after Philippe le Bel, and other questions of the same kind. But if the occasion offered, when his moment came, then he would quote without hesitation, and with the most minute details. And when it has sometimes happened to me to be in doubt, and to go and verify, I have always found him to be right, and almost scrupulously exact. I have never been able to detect him in error."

CHAPTER XXVII.
1816, October.

Fatalism—The Governor seeks another Interview—New Demands and Restrictions—Remarks to Dr. O'Meara—Laws—Communication from Sir Thomas Reade—Reduction of Expenses—Influence of Public Opinion—The Emperor's Son—The Sacred Cause of Washington and of Napoleon—Great Grief of the Emperor.

October 1. Among the numerous subjects of conversation, fatalism was mentioned. The Emperor made many remarkable observations upon this subject.

"Pray," said he, "am I not supposed to be given to the belief in fatalism?"

"Yes, sire, at least by many people," replied Las Casas.

"Well, well, let them say on," said he. "But what are men? How much easier it is to occupy their attention, and to strike their imaginations by absurdities than by rational ideas! But can a man of sound sense listen for one moment to such a doctrine? Either fatalism admits the existence of free will, or it rejects it. If it admits it, how can that result be fixed in advance, which a simple determination, a step, a word, may alter or modify, ad infinitum? If fatalism, on the contrary, rejects the existence of free will, it is quite another question. In that case, a child need only be thrown into its cradle as soon as it is born; there is no necessity for bestowing the least care upon it; for, if it be irrevocably determined that it is to live, it will grow though no food should be given to it.

"You see that such a doctrine can not be maintained. Fatalism is but a word without meaning. The Turks themselves, the patrons of fatalism, are not convinced of the doctrine, or medicine would not exist in Turkey. A man residing on a third floor would not take the trouble to go down by the longer way of the stairs; he would immediately throw himself out of the window. You see to what a string of absurdities that will lead."

"About three o'clock," says Las Casas, "the Emperor was told that the governor wished to communicate to him some instructions which he had just received from London. The Emperor replied that he was unwell; that the instructions might be sent to him, or communicated to some one of his suite; but the governor insisted on being admitted, saying that he wished to communicate directly with the Emperor. He added that he had also a few words to say to us in private after having spoken to *the General*. The Emperor again refused; upon which the governor retired, saying that he begged that he might be informed when he *could* see *the General*. This period may be distant indeed; the Emperor, with whom I was at that moment, having said to me that he was determined never to receive him again."

In the afternoon Dr. O'Meara called with a message from Sir Hudson Lowe.

"I expect nothing," said the Emperor, "from the present ministry but ill treatment. The more they want to lessen me, the more will I exalt myself. It was my intention to have assumed the name of Colonel Muiron, who was killed by my side at Arcola, covering me with his body, and to have lived as a private person in England, in some part of the country where I might have lived retired, without ever desiring to mix in the grand world. I would have never gone to London, nor have dined out. Probably I should have seen very few persons. Perhaps I might have formed a friendship with some of the literary and scientific men. I would have rode out every day, and then have returned to my books."

"As long," said O'Meara, "as you retain the title of majesty, the English ministers will have a pretext for keeping you in St. Helena."

"They force me to it," the Emperor replied. "I wanted to assume an incognito on my arrival here, which was proposed to the Admiral Cockburn, but they will not permit it. They insist on calling me *General Bonaparte*. I have no reason to be ashamed of that title; but I will not take it from them. If the republic had not a legal existence, it had no more right to constitute me general than chief magistrate. If Admiral Cockburn had remained, perhaps matters might have been arranged. He had some heart, and, to do him justice, was incapable of a mean action. Do you think he will do us an injury on his arrival in England?"

"I do not think," Dr. O'Meara replied, "that he will render you any service, particularly in consequence of the manner in which he was treated when he last came up to see you. But he will not tell any falsehoods. He will strictly adhere to the truth, and give his opinion about you, which is not very favorable."

"Why so?" inquired the Emperor; "we were very well together on board ship. What can he say of me? that I want to escape, and mount the throne of France again?"

"It is, in my opinion, very probable," answered the doctor, "that he will both think and say so."

"Bah!" exclaimed the Emperor: "if I were in England now, and a deputation from France were to come and offer me the throne, I would not accept of it, unless I knew such to be the unanimous wish of the nation. Otherwise I should have to turn executioner, and cut off the heads of thousands to keep myself upon it: oceans of blood must flow to maintain me there. I have made noise enough in the world already, perhaps too much, and am now getting old, and want retirement. These were the motives which induced me to abdicate the last time."

"When you were Emperor," O'Meara added, "you caused Sir George Cockburn's brother to be arrested when envoy at Hamburg, and conveyed to France, where he was detained for some years."

The Emperor appeared surprised, and, after endeavoring for some time to recall the circumstance, said, "Are you sure that the person so arrested was Sir George Cockburn's brother?"

"I am perfectly sure," O'Meara replied, "as the admiral has told me of the circumstance himself."

"It is likely enough," the Emperor added; "but I do not recollect the name. I suppose, however, that it must have been at the time when I caused all the English I could find on the Continent to be detained, because your government had seized upon all the French ships, sailors, and passengers they could lay their hands upon, in harbor or at sea, before the declaration of war. I, in my turn, seized upon all the English that I could find on land, in order to show them that, if they were all-powerful at sea, and could do what they liked there, I was equally so by land, and had as good a right to seize people on my element as they had on theirs. *Now* I can comprehend the reason why your ministers selected him. I am surprised, however, that he never told me any thing about it. A man of delicacy would not have accepted the task of conducting me here under similar circumstances. But you will see that, in a short time, the English will cease to hate me. So many of them have been and are in France, where they will hear the truth, that they will produce a revolution of opinion in England. I will leave it to them to justify me, and I have no doubt about the results.

"Do you know what the governor wanted," inquired the Emperor, "or why he wished to see me?"

"Perhaps," O'Meara replied, "he had some communication from Lord Bathurst, which he did not like to deliver to any other person."

"It will be better for us not to meet," said the Emperor. "It is probably some stupidity of Lord Bathurst, which he will make worse by his ungracious manner of communicating. I am sure that it is nothing good. Lord Bathurst is a bad man, his communications are bad, and the governor is worse than all. Nothing good can arise from an interview. The last time I saw him, he laid his hand on his sabre two or three times in a violent manner; therefore go to him, and inform him that, if he has any thing to communicate, he had better send it to General Bertrand, or Bertrand will call at his house. Assure him that he may rely on Bertrand's making a faithful report. Or, let him send Colonel Reade to me to explain what he has to say. I will receive and hear him, because he will be only the bearer of orders, not the giver of them; therefore, if he comes on a bad mission, I shall not be angry, as he will only obey the orders of a superior."

"I endeavored," says O'Meara, "to induce him to meet the governor, in order, if possible, to make up the differences between them."

"To meet him," the Emperor replied, "would be the worst mode of attempting it. I am confident that it is some stupidity of Lord Bathurst, which he would make worse and convert into an insult by his brutal mode of communicating it. You know I never got into a passion with the admiral, because, even when he had something to communicate, he did it with some feeling; but this man treats us as if we were so many deserters."

"Sir Thomas Reade," said O'Meara, "is incapable of explaining in French or Italian the purport of any communication. If he should commit what he has to say to paper, would you read it or allow it to be read to you?"

"Certainly," the Emperor replied. "Let him do this, or send it to General Bertrand. As to me, perhaps I shall not see the governor for six months. Let him break open the doors or level the house, I am not subject to the English laws, because they do not protect me. I am sure that he has nothing pleasant to communicate, or he would not be so anxious to do it personally. Nothing but insults or bad news ever came from Lord Bathurst. I wish they would give orders to have me dispatched. I do not like to commit suicide. It is a thing I have always disapproved of. I have made a vow to drain the cup to the last draught, but I should be more rejoiced if they would send directions to put me to death."

October 2. Napoleon suffered much pain from the toothache, and was kept awake most of the night. In the morning he sent for Doctor O'Meara.

"Go to the governor," said he, "and inform him that, in consequence of indisposition, pain, and want of sleep, I find myself unfit to listen calmly to communications or to enter into discussions; therefore I wish that the governor would communicate to Count Bertrand whatever he has to say. If he can not communicate it to Count Bertrand, or to any other resident of Longwood, I shall have no objection to receive it from Colonel Reade."

He then added, in conversation with O'Meara, "If that man were to bring me word that a frigate had arrived for the purpose of taking me to England, I should conceive it to be bad news, because he was the bearer of it. With such a temper of mind, you must see how improper it would be that an interview should take place. He came up here yesterday surrounded with his staff, as if he were going in state to assist at an execution instead of asking privately to see me. Three times has he gone away in a passion, therefore it will be better that no more interviews should take place between us, as no good can arise from it; and, as he represents his nation here, I do not like to insult or make severe remarks to him, similar to those I was obliged to express before."

To the courteous message which Doctor O'Meara delivered, the governor returned an answer, in which he requested the doctor to inform General Bonaparte that he expected an apology both from General Bertrand and from General Bonaparte for the intemperate language used in their last interview; that the governor wished to communicate a message to General Bonaparte in the presence of some of his own staff and of a French officer; but if General Bonaparte refused to see the governor, he would communicate through Sir Thomas Reade the *general purport* of what he had to say, leaving some points for future discussion. O'Meara faithfully communicated the message. "Napoleon," said he, "smiled contemptuously at the idea of *his* apologizing to Sir Hudson Lowe."

October 3. "Saw Napoleon in the morning," Dr. O'Meara writes. "After I had inquired into the state of his health, he entered upon the business of yesterday."

"As this governor," said Napoleon, "declares that he will not communicate the whole to Reade, but intends to reserve some future points for discussion, I shall not see him, for I only agree to see Reade in order to avoid the sight of the other; and by reserving the points he speaks of, he might come up again to-morrow or next day, and demand another interview. If he wants to communicate, let him send his adjutant general to Bertrand, or to Montholon, or to Las Casas, or Gourgaud, or to you; or send for one of them, and explain it himself; or let him communicate the *whole* to Reade, or to Sir George Bingham, or somebody else; and then I will see the person so chosen. If he still insists on seeing me, I will write myself in answer, 'The Emperor Napoleon will not see you, because the last three times you were with him you insulted him, and he does not wish more communication with you.'

"I well know that, if we have another interview, there will be disputes and abuse. He, for his own sake, ought not to desire one, after the language which I applied to him the last time. I told him, before the admiral, when he said that he only did his duty, that so did the hangman, but that one was not obliged to see that hangman until the moment of execution. Shameful scenes! I do not wish to renew them. I know that my blood will be heated. I will tell him that no power on earth obliges a prisoner to see and debate with his executioner, for his conduct has made him such to me. He pretends that he acts according to his instructions.

"A government two thousand leagues distant can do no more than point out the general manner in which things must be conducted, and must leave a great discretionary power, which he distorts and turns in the worst possible manner, in order to torment me. A proof that he is worse than his government is, that they have sent out several things to make me comfortable; but he does nothing but torment, insult, and render my existence as miserable as possible. To complete the business, he writes letters full of smoothness and sweetness, professing every regard, which he afterward sends home, to make the world believe that he is our best friend. I want to avoid another scene with him.

"I never, in the height of my power, made use of such language to any man as I was compelled to apply to him. It would have been unpardonable at the Tuileries. He has a bad mission, and fulfills it badly. I do not think that he is aware how much we hate and despise him. I should like him to know it. He suspects every body; even his own staff are not free from it. You see that he will not confide to Reade. Why does he not go to Montholon or Las Casas if he does not like Bertrand?"

"Sir Hudson Lowe has said," O'Meara replied, "that he can not repose confidence in the fidelity of either of them in reporting the purport of his conversation."

"Oh," said Napoleon, "he is offended with Montholon about that letter, written in August last, and with Las Casas because he not only writes the truth to a lady in London, but tells it every where here."

"The governor," O'Meara replied, "has accused Count Las Casas of having written many falsehoods respecting what has passed here."

"Las Casas," the Emperor replied, "would not be blockhead enough to write falsehoods when he was obliged to send the letters containing them through his hands. He only writes the truth, which that jailer does not wish to be known. I am sure that he wants to tell me that some of my generals are to be removed, and wishes to throw the odium of sending them away upon me, by leaving the choice to me. They would send you away too if they were not afraid you would do some mischief in England by telling what you have seen. Their design, I believe, is to send every body away who might be inclined to make my life less disagreeable. Truly they have chosen a pretty representative for Bathurst. I would sooner have an interview with the corporal of the guard than with that *galeriano*. How different it was with the admiral! We used to converse together sociably on different subjects like friends; but this man is only fit to oppress and insult those whom misfortune has placed in his power."

After breakfast the Emperor walked for a short time in the garden with his companions. He spoke of the mysterious communication which the governor had to make, and all formed conjectures upon the subject. The air was cold and damp, and the Emperor soon returned to his room. He turned over the pages of an English book on jurisprudence, and the criminal codes of France and England. In the course of a conversation upon this subject, the Emperor remarked,

"Laws which in theory are a model of clearness, become too often a chaos in their application, because men, with their passions, spoil every thing they touch. Men can only avoid being exposed to the arbitrary acts of the judge by submitting to the despotism of the law. I had at first fancied that it would be possible to reduce all laws to simple geometrical demonstrations, so that every man who could read, and connect two ideas together, would be able to decide for himself; but I became convinced almost immediately that this idea was absurd. However, I should have wished to start from some fixed point, and follow one road known to all, have no other laws but those inserted in the code, and proclaim, once for all, that all laws that were not in the code were null and void; but it is not easy to obtain simplicity from practical lawyers. They first prove to you that simplicity is impossible, that it is a mere chimera, and endeavor next to demonstrate that it is incompatible with the stability and the existence of power. Power, they say, is exposed alone to the unexpected machinations of all. It must therefore have, in the moment of need, arms kept in reserve for unforeseen cases, so that, with some old edicts of Chilperic or Pharamond brought forward for the occasion, nobody can say that he is secure from being hanged in due form and according to law.

" So long as the subjects of discussion in the Council of State were referable to the Code, I felt very strong, but when they diverged from it I was quite in the dark, and Merlin was then my resource; he was my light. Without possessing much brilliancy, Merlin is very learned, wise, upright, and honest, a veteran of the good old cause. He was very much attached to me. No sooner had the Code made its appearance, than it was almost immediately followed by commentaries, explanations, elucidations, and interpretations. I usually exclaimed, on seeing this, Gentlemen, we have cleaned the stable of Augeas, do not let us fill it up again."

The day was oppressively hot, and the Emperor was depressed, harassed, and exhausted with the sleeplessness of the night; but, with characteristic firmness, at one o'clock he sent for Las Casas, as he wished to take his usual English lesson. Wearied nature, however, rebelled, and two or three times during the lesson he fell asleep. He afterward took a drive in his calash. On his return he found General Bertrand, who reported to him the interview he had just held with Sir Hudson Lowe relative to the signature and the removals.

"After dinner," says Las Casas, " the Emperor amused himself by solving some problems in geometry and algebra. This, he said, reminded him of his youthful days. It surprised us all to find that the subjects were still so fresh in his recollection."

October 4. Sir Thomas Reade came to Longwood to make the much-talked-of communication. He was admitted to an audience, and read the following paper to the Emperor:

"The French who wish to remain with General Bonaparte must sign the simple form, which will be given to them, of their willingness to submit to whatever restrictions may be imposed upon General Bonaparte, without making any remarks of their own upon it. Those who refuse will be sent off directly to the Cape of Good Hope. The establishment is to be reduced in number four persons. Those who remain are to consider themselves amenable to the laws in the same manner as if they were British subjects, especially to those which have been framed for the safe custody of General Bonaparte. The aiding of him to escape is declared felony. Any of them abusing, reflecting upon, or behaving ill to the governor or the government they are under, will be forthwith sent to the Cape, where no facilities will be furnished for their conveyance to Europe."*

---

* The following was the inclosed form of declaration: " I, the undersigned, do hereby declare that it is my desire to remain on the island of St. Helena, and to participate in the restrictions im-

The English government, at the same time, made a demand upon the Emperor for seven thousand dollars paid for books which had been sent to Longwood. Lord Bathurst knew very well that the Emperor had no money at St. Helena, for he had already rifled his trunks; but he wished to ascertain where the Emperor's money was deposited in Europe. The torture was applied to compel him to draw.

Sir Thomas Reade then called upon Count Bertrand, and informed him that the governor wished to see him and the other officers of General Bonaparte's suite, either collectively, or in any other manner which might best suit their convenience. These gentlemen were then informed of the paper which they must sign, or be sent from the island. The whole household at Longwood were by these proceedings plunged into dismay. Four of the Emperor's companions were to be torn from him, and all the rest were to be sent away, leaving the Emperor to journey sadly to the grave, friendless and alone, unless they would sign a paper which, under the peculiar circumstances, subjected them to deep humiliation. Such torture, inflicted upon these helpless exiles by the proud and powerful British government, in combination with the allied despotisms of Europe, must forever excite the indignation of every generous mind.

The Emperor alone appeared calm. He had received Sir Thomas Reade with studied civility, and had patiently listened to the atrocious document. His soul was nerved for the endurance of any outrage, and, concealing the anguish which consumed him, he calmly asked,

"What four persons are to leave me?"

"I can not tell," Sir Thomas Reade replied.

"Are they to be officers?" he again inquired.

"I can not tell," was again the cold and mechanical answer.

The Emperor soon retired to the solitude of his room. The conflicting emotions of indignation and anguish which agitated him through the sleepless night are known only to God.

October 5. At an early hour in the morning, Las Casas, before he had risen, heard some one tap at his door. In a moment the bed-curtains were drawn aside, and, to his astonishment, he saw the Emperor standing before him. Napoleon, unable to sleep, had risen at this early hour, and had called for Las Casas, his most serious and congenial companion, to accompany him on a walk. He conversed for a long time upon the events of the preceding day. He then returned to his room for a bath. Soon after, seeing Doctor O'Meara in the garden, he went out and called to him. They walked for some time together in friendly conversation.

"There was nothing," said the Emperor, "in the intelligence which the governor pretended he could only communicate to myself which might not have been made known through Bertrand or any one else; but he thought that he had an opportunity of insulting and grieving me, which he eagerly embraced. He came up here with his staff, just as if he were going to announce a wed-

posed upon Napoleon Bonaparte personally." If the person was married, the words "with my wife and family" were added.

ding, with exultation and joy painted upon his countenance at the idea of having it in his power to afflict me. He thought to plant a dagger in my heart, and could not deny himself the pleasure of witnessing and enjoying it personally. Never has he given a greater proof of a bad mind than in thus wishing to stab to the heart one whom misfortunes had placed in his power."

Doctor O'Meara urged the Emperor to be careful, and not irritate the governor, lest he should suffer more severely; suggesting that, if Sir Hudson Lowe were conciliated, he might send away four domestics instead of officers.

"We are in the power of a despot," said the Emperor, "and there is for us no remedy. They will send away the rest by degrees. It is as well for them to go now as after a little time. What advantage shall I gain by having them here until the arrival of the next ship from England, or until that *animal* finds out some pretext to send them away? I would rather they were all gone than to have four or five persons trembling about me, having the dread of being forced on board ship constantly hanging over their heads; for, by that communication of yesterday, they are placed entirely at his discretion. Let him send every body away, plant sentinels at the doors and windows, and send up nothing but bread and water, I regard it not. My mind is free. I am just as independent as when I commanded an army of six hundred thousand men, as I told him the other day. This heart is as free as when I gave laws to Europe. He wants them to sign restrictions without knowing what they are.

"No honest man would sign an obligation without first knowing what it was. But he wants them to sign whatever he likes to impose hereafter, and then, with falsehood always at command, he will assert that he has changed nothing. He is angry with Las Casas because he wrote to his friends that he was badly lodged and badly treated. Was there ever heard of such tyranny? He treats people in the most barbarous manner, heaps insults and injuries upon them, and then wants to deprive them of the liberty of complaint. I do not think that Lord Liverpool, or *even* Lord Castlereagh, would allow me to be treated in the way I am. I believe that this governor only writes to Lord Bathurst, to whom he tells what he likes."

October 6. The Emperor, while he was dressing, and waiting for the grand marshal to take his turn in writing, amused himself by conversing upon different subjects. He spoke of the influence of opinion. He traced its secret progress, its uncertainty, and the caprice of its decisions. He then adverted to the natural delicacy of the French, which, he said, was exquisite in matters of decorum, to the laudable susceptibility of French manners, and to the graceful action and gentleness which authority must employ if an attempt be made to interfere with the national feeling.

"In conformity with my system," observed he, "of amalgamating all kinds of merit, and of rendering one and the same reward universal, I had an idea of presenting the cross of the Legion of Honor to Talma, but I refrained from doing this in consideration of our capricious manners and absurd prejudices. I wished to make a first experiment in an affair that was out of date and unimportant, and I accordingly gave the iron crown to Crescentini. The decoration was foreign, and so was the individual on whom it was conferred. This circumstance was less likely to attract public notice, or to render my conduct the subject of discussion; at worst, it could only give rise to a few malicious jokes. Such is the influence of public opinion. I distributed sceptres at will, and thousands readily bowed beneath their sway; and yet I could not give away a ribbon without the chance of incurring disapprobation, for I believe my experiment with regard to Crescentini was a failure."*

At the dinner-table, the Emperor said that he had worked that day twelve hours.

October 9. Sir Hudson Lowe sought an interview with Dr. O'Meara, and informed him that it was his duty to report to the governor all the private conversation which had passed between him and General Bonaparte. O'Meara declined playing thus the part of a spy, under the guise of being the Emperor's physician.

"If there were any plot for escape," said the doctor, "I should conceive it my duty to give notice of it; but I can not think of telling every thing that passes between us, unless ordered to do so."

"But one of the means," said the governor, "which General Bonaparte has of escaping, is vilifying me. Abusing and lessening the character of the ministry is a vile way of endeavoring to escape from the island."

After a sharp conference, Dr. O'Meara remarked, "If you are not satisfied with the manner in which matters stand, I am ready to resign the situation I hold. I am determined not to give up my rights as a British officer."

"We will renew the subject," the governor replied, "some other day."

Sir Hudson Lowe then went and put under arrest Captain Piontkowski, a Polish officer of the Emperor's household. This was the first of the four who was to be sent from Longwood. All the rest were in dismay, no one knowing who would be next arrested. The Emperor, in calm and silent dignity, awaited his destiny. In that dreary prison, he was in danger of being left, bereft of every friend, till anguish should terminate his days. His only refuge was to devote himself as entirely as possible to his intellectual pursuits. In mathematical investigations, in scientific research, in the treasures of literature, and in dictating his campaigns, the Emperor endeavored to forget insult and outrage. About noon Las Casas called at his room. The Emperor was sitting alone, silent and dejected.

The conversation led him to allude to Austria, to the wrongs he had received from that power, to the blind policy of her cabinet, and to the danger of her situation. "She now stands," said he, "in the most imminent peril, advancing to meet the embraces of a Colossus in her front, while she can not recede a single step, because an abyss is yawning on her flanks and rear."

This turn of conversation naturally led the Emperor to speak of his son,

* Talma was a distinguished tragedian, of much intelligence and great moral worth. Crescentini was a celebrated singer. Napoleon wished to reward distinction in all the walks of life, and conferred upon these celebrities the cross of the Legion of Honor. Many of Napoleon's generals and statesmen murmured loudly at this. They could not appreciate the capacious views of the Emperor, and wished that these public honors should be conferred only upon political, literary, or military renown.

who was virtually a prisoner in the palace of Schoenbrun. "What education will they give him?" said he. "What sort of principles will they ingraft in his youthful mind? On the other hand, if he should prove weak in intellect! if he should bear any resemblance to the legitimates! if they should inspire him with hatred of his father! these thoughts fill me with horror. And where is the antidote to all this? Henceforth there can be no medium of communication, no faithful tradition between him and me. At best, my memoirs, or perhaps your journal, may fall into his hands. But to subdue the false precepts imbibed in early life, to counteract the errors of a bad education, requires a certain capacity, a certain strength of mind and decision of judgment which falls not to the share of every one."

These thoughts overwhelmed the parental heart of the Emperor, and he seemed deeply affected. After a few moments of silent meditation, he said suddenly, and with emphasis, "Let us talk of something else."

But the gloom which darkened his spirit was too dense to be dispelled by a sudden volition. For some time a profound silence was maintained. The Emperor, then rousing himself, requested Las Casas to take the pen, and for two hours he dictated a glowing narrative of the eventful past. General Bertrand then came in and relieved Las Casas, and the Emperor continued his dictation. But the sorrows of this dismal day were not yet ended. While the Emperor was thus employed, an official document was presented from the governor. Sir Hudson Lowe sent to his writhing captive a package of papers, formally reiterating his demands, and imposing new restrictions. The substance of these documents was as follows:

1. Four persons are to be removed from the Emperor's household. 2. All who remain must consent to every restriction imposed upon Napoleon Bonaparte. 3. Any attempt or connivance at his escape will be punished with death. 4. Any one who treats the governor disrespectfully will be sent from St. Helena, and will be set ashore at the Cape of Good Hope, without being provided with the means of returning to Europe.

Another document contained a summary of the severe restrictions which the governor had decided to enforce upon Napoleon, and upon all the companions of his captivity. These restrictions, needless and merciless, were as follows:

1. The limits of their jail-yard were hereafter to consist of the inclosed ground at Longwood, and the road, about a mile in length, to Hut's Gate. This deprived the inmates of Longwood of the pleasure of calling at the hospitable house of Secretary General Brooks, and also cut them off from the favorite resort of a fountain overshadowed by eight or ten oak-trees.

2. Sentinels were to be stationed along these lines, and no one was to approach Longwood without permission of the governor. This arrangement placed the captives in close and solitary confinement.

3. If the Emperor wished to prolong his ride beyond the assigned limits, he could do so by giving notice to the orderly officer, who was to accompany him, and never to allow him, for one moment, to escape his sight.

4. General Bonaparte was forbidden to enter into any conversation, except

the interchange of salutations, with any individuals he might happen to meet, even within his accustomed limits, except in the presence of an English officer.

5. Those persons who might receive the governor's permission to visit General Bonaparte were forbidden to communicate with any individual whatever of his suite, unless a permission to that effect had been specially expressed.

6. At sunset, the garden of Longwood alone was to be the extent of their boundaries. Sentinels were to be posted round it. During the night, sentinels were to be stationed close to the house. All admission was then prohibited until the sentinels should be withdrawn in the morning.

7. All letters to and from Longwood were to be delivered open to Sir Hudson Lowe, that he might peruse their contents.

These documents were read to the Emperor by Count Montholon. He listened to them calmly, and soon after met his companions at the dinner-table. The contents of these papers from the governor, of course, engrossed their conversation. The Emperor was thoughtful and sad, and made but few remarks himself, as he listened to the observations of the others. Some one of the gentlemen spoke in terms of ridicule and contempt of the threat of leaving obnoxious persons at the Cape of Good Hope without furnishing them with the means of returning to Europe. The Emperor remarked,

"Of course, this threat appears to you very extraordinary and ridiculous, but no doubt it was perfectly natural to Lord Bathurst. I dare say he could not imagine a more terrible punishment. It is a true shop-keeper's idea."

In the attempt to dispel painful thoughts, the Emperor in the evening read to his assembled friends the drama of Adelaide Duguesclin, which contains a glowing eulogy upon the Bourbons. After reading it, he said,

"During the time of my power, an order was given for suppressing the performance of this drama, under the idea that it would be offensive to me. This circumstance accidentally came to my knowledge, and I ordered the piece to be revived. Many things of the same kind took place. People often acted very unwisely under the idea that they were serving or pleasing me."

The Emperor, woe-worn and weary, exposed to blows which he could not parry, and to insults which he could not resent, soon retired to the solitude and the sleeplessness of his pillow.

It was well known that the Emperor would never consent to the indignity of riding, like a handcuffed criminal, with a guard by his side. Within the boundaries to which he was now restricted, there was not a single spot where he could enjoy the sight of trees or water. He could not venture out after sunset without exposing himself to the insult of being challenged by a sentinel. A drunken sentinel at one time attempted to shoot him. His friends, men of lofty character, and accustomed to homage and respect, were arrested and taken to the guard-house for the night if they accidentally delayed their return to the house for a few moments after the sun had set. This insult had not unfrequently happened.

What was the crime which Napoleon had committed which drew down upon him so merciless an infliction? It was precisely the same crime of which George Washington had been guilty. The Americans renounced George III., and chose George Washington for their chief magistrate. Washington accepted their suffrage, and, aided by the width of the Atlantic Ocean and by the alliance of France, in a long and bloody conflict maintained the right of popular suffrage and the independence of his country. And every generous heart blesses him.

France, imitating the example of the United States, renounced Louis XVI., and chose Napoleon for its sovereign. Napoleon accepted the office. All the despots of Europe combined to crush him. Long did Napoleon hold them at bay, with almost superhuman energy, courage, and sagacity. But at last, overwhelmed by numbers, with nearly two millions of bayonets pressing upon him, he was vanquished. And then his unrelenting foes punished him with cruelty a thousand fold more dreadful than that of the scaffold or the stake. But his glorious labors, and the magnanimity with which he endured his sufferings, have won for him the love, the enthusiastic love of the *people* of all lands. There are a few ignoble spirits who still venture to malign this great champion of popular rights, but they are very few, and henceforth utterly powerless.

Mysterious is the justice of God. He visits upon the children the iniquities of their fathers. Napoleon would have wisely introduced to France and to all Europe constitutional governments, sustaining popular supremacy and equal rights beneath the ægis of invincible law. But now the great battle between aristocracy and democracy is again to be fought. The apocalyptic vials of woe are apparently to be opened, till the blood shall come up to the horses' bridles. Is despotism to be triumphant? Is unenlightened and maddened democracy to run riot? Humanity ponders the question, and is appalled.

October 13. At breakfast the Emperor said, "I have given orders for drawing up some notes relative to the new restrictions of the governor, to prevent condemnation being passed on us without a sort of responsibility being attached to those who pass the sentence." He then proceeded to calculate the lots of plate which remained to be sold, and the period during which they would serve to maintain his establishment. The basket of plate which had now been sold brought twelve hundred dollars. This would help them for about six weeks. The money was deposited in the hands of the English agent for the supply of Longwood. Las Casas repeated offers of pecuniary assistance which he had before made, saying, "It is hard, sire, that you should be reduced to the necessity of disposing of your plate."

"My dear Las Casas," replied the Emperor, "under whatever circumstances I may be placed, those articles of luxury are never of any importance to me; and as far as regards others, that is to say, as far as regards the public, simplicity will always be my best ornament. I can, as a last resort, claim the assistance of Prince Eugene, and I am even inclined to write to him for the loans which will be necessary for my subsistence when the plate shall be exhausted. I intend to commission Eugene to forward to me some important books, which I wish should be sent from London, together with a small quantity of choice wine, which it is necessary I should take as a medicine. This commission for wine will make our enemies in Europe say that we think of nothing here but eating and drinking. I shall feel no hesitation in addressing myself, on this subject, to Eugene, who owes to me every thing he possesses. It would be insulting the character of the prince to doubt his readiness to serve me, particularly as I have a legal claim upon him for about ten or twelve millions."

In the course of the day Dr. O'Meara called in to see the Emperor. He found him feverish, and suffering from the headache.

"Truly," said Napoleon, "it requires great resolution and strength of mind to support such an existence as mine, in this horrible abode. Every day fresh stabs of the dagger from this executioner! It appears to be his only amusement. Daily he imagines modes of annoying, insulting, and making me undergo fresh privations. He wants to shorten my life by daily irritations. By his last restrictions I am not permitted to speak to any one I may meet. To people under sentence of death, this is not denied. It is a piece of tyranny unheard of except in the instance of the man with the iron mask.

"In the tribunals of the Inquisition a man is heard in his own defense, but I have been condemned unheard, and without a trial, in violation of all laws, divine and human; detained as a prisoner of war in time of peace; separated from my wife and child; violently transported here, where arbitrary and hitherto unknown restrictions are imposed upon me, extending even to the privation of speech. I am sure that none of the ministers, except Lord Bathurst, would give their consent to this last act of tyranny. His great desire of secrecy shows that he is afraid of his conduct being made known even to the ministers themselves.

"They profess, in England, to supply my wants. This man comes out, reduces every thing, obliges me to sell my plate to obtain the necessaries of life, imposes arbitrary restrictions, insults me and my followers, denies me the faculty of speech, and then has the impudence to write that he has changed nothing. He says that, if strangers come to visit me, they can not speak to any of my suite, and wishes that they should be presented by him. If my *son* came to the island, and it were required that he should be presented by him, I would not see him. You know that it was more a trouble than a pleasure for me to receive many of the strangers who arrived, some of whom merely came to gaze at me as at a *curious beast;* but still it was consoling to have the right to see them if I pleased."

October 14. All the inmates of Longwood sent to the governor the acknowledgment of their willingness to submit to whatever restrictions might be imposed upon the *Emperor Napoleon*, simply substituting those words instead of *Napoleon Bonaparte.*

In reference to this procedure, Las Casas said that the gentlemen of the Emperor's suite had met together to deliberate. "The point in question," he says, "was of the most serious and difficult nature. We were required to subject ourselves to new restrictions, and to place ourselves entirely in the power of the governor, who shamefully abused his authority. The Emperor, indignant at the mortifications to which we were exposed on his account, insisted that we should no longer submit to them. He urged us to quit him, to return to Europe, and to bear witness that we had seen him buried alive. "But how could we, for a moment, endure this thought? Death was preferable to separation from him whom we served, admired, and loved; to whom we became daily more and more attached through his personal qualities, and the miseries which injustice and hatred had accumulated upon him."

With such feelings, they all signed the demands of the British ministers as expressed by the governor, with the simple alteration mentioned above.

The Emperor bore up strongly against these irremediable outrages. Las Casas, at one o'clock, went into his room. He found him reading a work upon the government of France. He appeared much fatigued and dispirited. In conversation, speaking of several individuals, he alluded to one as a very base and immoral character. Las Casas, who knew this person, defended him with much warmth. The Emperor interrupted him, saying,

"I give full credit to what you say, but I had heard a different account of him; and though I generally made it a rule to hear things of this kind with suspicion, yet you see that I could not always avoid retaining some impression of what I heard. Was this my fault? When I had no particular motive for inquiry, how could I arrive at the knowledge of facts? This is the inevitable consequence of civil commotions. There are always two reputations between two parties. What absurdities—what ridiculous stories are related of the individuals who figured in our Revolution! The saloons of Paris are full of them. I have borne my full share of this kind of scandal. After me, who can have any right to complain?"

CHAPTER XXVIII.
1816, October. Continued.

The Declaration to be signed—Perplexity and Dismay—The Emperor proposes an Incognito—Remarks of the Emperor upon this Subject—Savary—Fouché—Sièyes—Conversation with Sièyes. —Anecdotes of the Emperor—Enthusiasm of the Parisian Populace—New Vexations—Four removed from Longwood.

October 15. The governor sent back the declaration which the inmates of Longwood had signed, threatening to send them immediately to Africa unless they signed the paper which styled the Emperor *Napoleon Bonaparte.* General Bertrand and Las Casas immediately called upon the Emperor. He was in his narrow and comfortless chamber, and was much annoyed by this new source of irritation. As he slowly and thoughtfully paced the floor, he said,

"The insults which are daily heaped upon those who have devoted themselves to me, insults which there is every probability will be multiplied to a still greater extent, present a spectacle which I can not and must not longer endure. Gentlemen, you must leave me. I can not see you submit to the restrictions which are about to be imposed on you, and which will doubtless soon be augmented. I will remain here alone. Return to Europe, and make known the horrible treatment to which I am exposed; bear witness that you saw me sink into a premature grave. I will not allow any one of you to sign this declaration in the form that is required. I forbid it. It shall never be said that hands which I had the power to command were employed in recording my degradation. If obstacles are raised respecting a mere foolish formality, others will be started to-morrow for an equally trivial cause. It is determined to remove you in detail, but I would rather see you removed altogether and at once. Perhaps this sacrifice may produce a result."

With these words he dismissed the gentlemen. In a few moments he sent for Las Casas. He was walking up and down through the whole length of his two little rooms. There was a peculiar softness and even tenderness in the tone of his voice.

"Well, my dear Las Casas," said he, "I am going to turn hermit."

"Sire," replied Las Casas, "are you not one already? What resources does our society present to you? We can only offer you prayers and wishes. The arguments which you just now addressed to us admit of no reply. Your determination is in unison with your character; it will astonish no one; but its execution is beyond our power. The thought of leaving you here alone exceeds in horror all that our imagination can picture."

"Such, however, is my fate," replied the Emperor, "and I am ready to meet it; but yet I have sufficient strength to resist to the last. They will end my life, that is certain."

After breakfast the French gentlemen called upon the governor with the earnest entreaty that he would not compel them to dishonor their Emperor. The governor was unrelenting. He declared that, as an Englishman, he could not recognize Napoleon as entitled to the designation of Emperor, and that they must immediately sign the paper he had presented, or be sent from the island. As Napoleon was dressing for dinner, Las Casas, Bertrand, Montholon, and Gourgaud had another interview with him. The wind was boisterous, but they walked out toward the wood. The Emperor reviewed the conduct of the governor. He concluded by saying,

"If to-day you agree to sign the declaration in order to avoid being separated from me, to-morrow another ground of expulsion will be brought forward. I should prefer that your removal should be effected forcibly and at once, rather than tranquilly and in detail. But, after all," said he, assuming a tone of pleasantry, "I can hardly believe that the governor wishes to reduce his subjects to one only. And what sort of a subject would that one be? An absolute porcupine, on which he would find it impossible to lay a finger."

As they were walking, two strangers approached near to them. The Emperor was informed that they were to sail the next day for Europe, and that they would probably see Lord Bathurst. They were presented to the Emperor, and he thus addressed them:

"Tell Lord Bathurst," said Napoleon, "that his instructions with respect to my treatment here are most odious, and that his agent executes them with scrupulous fidelity. If he wishes to get rid of me he should have dispatched me at a blow, instead of thus killing me by inches. This conduct is truly barbarous. There is nothing English in it; and I can only attribute it to some personal hatred. I have too much respect for the Prince Regent, the majority of the ministers, and the English nation, to suppose that they are responsible for my treatment. Be this as it may, their power extends only to the body. The soul is beyond their reach. It will soar to heaven even from the dungeon."

At the dinner-table the Emperor was silent and ate but little. He concluded the evening by reading to his companions a portion of Don Quixote. As all for a moment forgot their griefs, and joined the Emperor in laughing at some comic passages, he remarked, "We certainly show a great deal of courage, since we can laugh at such trifles under our present circumstances." He paused for a moment, rapt in thought. Then rising, he said, in peculiarly affectionate tones, "Adieu, my friends," and retired to the solitude of his chamber.

At the dinner-table Las Casas received a letter from the governor, which he did not open until after the Emperor had retired. It was eleven o'clock at night. To his consternation, he read that, in consequence of the refusal of the French officers to sign the declaration with the words *Napoleon Bonaparte*, they and the domestics must all depart for the Cape of Good Hope *instantly*, in a ship which was ready for their reception. The agitation and dismay excited by this announcement were intense. These generous men were willing to go to the scaffold or to the stake from their love for the Emperor. This moral torture brought them to the cruel terms. After the reading of the letter, there was a moment of profound silence. General Gourgaud then arose, and almost convulsively exclaimed, "I am going to sign." The rest followed his example. The paper containing their signatures was immediately, at that late hour, forwarded to the governor, and at midnight Sir Hudson Lowe, in the luxury of Plantation House, exulted in having obtained his pound of flesh. Santini alone declined his signature. He refused to sign any paper in which his master was not designated *l'Empereur*.

October 16. At half past six o'clock the Emperor sent for O'Meara. "I have sent for you," said he, "that you may communicate to the governor my real sentiments on certain subjects upon which the governor has conversed recently with Count Bertrand. I have retained the title of the Emperor Napoleon in opposition to General Bonaparte, which the English ministry wished to give me. Whenever I am addressed as General Bonaparte, I feel as if it were a slap in the face, because, if the French nation have a right to give me one title, they have an equal right to give me another. They may call me *Monsieur Napoleon;* but as that name is too well known, and might, perhaps, recall recollections which it might be desirable should be forgotten, and besides, as it is a name not consonant with the forms of society, it would, perhaps, be better to drop it. In that case, I would prefer to be called Colonel

Meuron, or Baron Duroc. As colonel is a title denoting military rank, perhaps it might give umbrage, and therefore probably it would be better to adopt that of Baron Duroc, which is the lowest feudal rank. If the governor acquiesces in either of these names, it shall be adopted. It will remove many difficulties which this title has thrown in the way, and will facilitate communication. It will be the first step, as to the propriety of which we both agree. I made this same proposition to Admiral Cockburn, who promised to refer it to the British government. But I have heard nothing more of the matter."

That O'Meara might make no mistake in reporting these sentiments, the Emperor gave him the following paper, containing his proposal to assume an incognito. This paper was not to be presented as a document, but merely to guide O'Meara in his communication.

Proposal made by the Emperor to assume the Incognito.

"It occurs to me that, in the conversation which has taken place between General Lowe and several of those gentlemen, things have been stated relative to my position which are not conformable to my ideas.

"I abdicated into the hands of the representatives of the nation, and for the benefit of my son. I went with confidence to England, with intentions to live there, or in America, in the most profound retreat; and, under the name of a colonel killed at my side, resolved to remain a stranger to every political occurrence, of whatever nature it might be.

"Arrived on board of the *Northumberland*, I was informed that I was a prisoner of war; that I was to be transported beyond the line; and that I was to be called *General* Bonaparte. This obliged me to retain ostensibly the title of the Emperor Napoleon, in opposition to the name of General Bonaparte, which it was wished should be forced upon me.

"Seven or eight months ago, Count Montholon proposed to remedy these little difficulties, which were rising every moment, by adopting an ordinary name. The admiral thought it to be his duty to write on the subject to London. There the matter at present rests.

"A name is now given me" (Napoleon Bonaparte) "which has the advantage of not prejudging the past, but it is not in unison with the forms of society. I am always disposed to take a name which enters into ordinary usage, and I reiterate that, when it shall be judged proper to discontinue this cruel abode, I am willing to remain a stranger to politics, whatever event may occur in the world. Such is my determination, and no other declaration on this subject has my sanction."

Dr. O'Meara, instead of making the communication to the governor, presented to him the paper. The governor remarked that it was a very important document, and that he would lose no time in forwarding it to the *British government!* As it was six thousand miles to England, a response might be anticipated in the course of eight or ten months. He also informed Dr. O'Meara that he must have no official communication whatever with any official persons in England about Bonaparte, and insisted that he should not mention a word to them of the proposal which the Emperor had just made; that none of the ministers except Lord Bathurst ought to know any thing about what passed at St. Helena.

When O'Meara made a report of his interview to the Emperor, Napoleon wished him to recall the paper, as it was intended merely as a memorandum, and not as a public document.*

"If Sir Hudson Lowe," said the Emperor, "will make known to General Bertrand, or even to me, that he authorizes the change of name, and will address me accordingly, I will write a letter declaring that I will adopt one of the names which have been proposed, and will sign it and send it to the governor. One half of the vexations which I have experienced here have arisen from that title. I abdicated the throne of France, but not the title of Emperor. I do not call myself Napoleon, Emperor of France, but the Emperor Napoleon. Sovereigns generally retain their titles. Thus Charles of Spain retains the title of king and majesty after having abdicated in favor of his son. If I were in England I would not call myself Emperor; but they want to make it appear that the French nation had not a right to make me its sovereign. If they had not a right to make me Emperor, they were equally incapable of making me general.

"A man, when he is at the head of a few, during the disturbances of a country, is called a chief of rebels; but when he succeeds, effects great actions, and exalts his country and himself, from being styled chief of rebels, he is called general, sovereign. It is only success which makes him such. Had he been unfortunate, he would be still chief of rebels, and would, perhaps, perish on a scaffold. Your nation called Washington a leader of rebels, and refused to acknowledge either him or the Constitution of his country; but his successes obliged them to change and acknowledge both. It is success which makes the great man. It would appear truly ridiculous in me, were it not that your ministers force me to it, to call myself Emperor, situated as I am here, and would remind one of those poor wretches in Bethlehem, in London, who imagine themselves kings amid their chains and straw."

The Emperor then spoke in most affectionate terms of Counts Bertrand, Montholon, and Las Casas, for their devoted attachment to his person.

"They had," said he, "an excellent pretext to go, first by refusing to sign Napoleon Bonaparte, and next because I ordered them not to sign. But no; they would have signed the *tyrant Bonaparte*, or any other opprobrious name, in order to remain with me in misery here, rather than return to Europe, where they might live in splendor. The more your government tries to degrade me, so much more respect they will pay to me. They pride them-

---

* "The only reply," says Dr. O'Meara, " which his majesty's ministers condescended to make to this proposal, was contained in a scurrilous article in the Quarterly Review, No. XXXII., which Sir Hudson Lowe took care should be sent to Longwood as soon as it had reached the island. I think that I am justified in attributing the article alluded to to some ministerial person, as the transaction was known only to officers in their employment and to the establishment at Longwood, and it is evident that the persons composing the latter could not have been the authors of it."

selves in paying me more respect now than when I was in the height of my glory."

In continuation of the conversation, O'Meara inquired which he thought had been the best minister of police, Savary or Fouché, adding that both of them had a bad reputation in England.

"Savary," said the Emperor, "is not a bad man; on the contrary, he is a man of a good heart, and a brave soldier. You have seen him weep. He loves me with the affection of a son. The English who have been in France will soon undeceive your nation.

"Fouché is a miscreant of all colors—a priest, a Terrorist, and one who took an active part in many bloody scenes in the Revolution. He is a man who can worm all your secrets out of you with an air of calmness and of unconcern. He is very rich, but his riches were badly acquired. There was a tax upon gambling-houses in Paris, but, as it was an infamous way of gaining money, I did not like to profit by it, and therefore ordered that the amount of the tax should be appropriated to a hospital for the poor. It amounted to some millions; but Fouché, who had the collecting of the impost, put many of them into his own pocket, and it was impossible for me to discover the real yearly sum total."

O'Meara observed that it had excited considerable surprise that, during the height of his glory, he had never given a dukedom in France to any person, although he had created many dukes and princes elsewhere.

The Emperor replied, "Because it would have produced great discontent among the people. If, for example, I had made one of my marshals Duke of Bourgogne instead of giving him a title derived from one of my victories, it would have excited the greatest alarm in Bourgogne, as they would have conceived that some feudal rights and territory were attached to the title, which the duke would claim; and the nation hated the old nobility so much, that the creation of any rank resembling them would have given universal discontent, which I, powerful as I was, dared not venture upon. I instituted the new nobility to *écraser* the old, and to satisfy the people, as the greatest part of those I created had sprung from themselves, and every private soldier had a right to look up to the title of duke. I believe that I acted wrong in doing even this, as it lessened that system of equality which pleased the people so much; but, if I had created dukes with a French title, it would have been considered as a revival of the old feudal privileges, with which the nation had been cursed so long."

October 16. The Emperor remained alone in his cabinet until noon. He then sent for Las Casas. He made no allusion to the decision of his friends to sign the obnoxious paper. For some reason, the subject was studiously avoided. The turn of conversation introduced some anecdotes of former times, of which Sièyes was the subject. "While Sièyes was chaplain to the Princess of Orleans," said the Emperor, "being one day engaged in performing mass, something unexpectedly caused the princess to withdraw during the service. The abbé, looking up, and seeing only the valets present, immediately closed his book, observing that he was not engaged to perform mass to the rabble."

Las Casas repeated an anecdote of the Faubourg St. Germain, in which Sièyes was described as having used the epithet *tyrant* in speaking of Louis XVI., to which Napoleon was said to have replied, "Monsieur Abbé, if he had been a tyrant I should not be here, and you would still be performing mass."

"I might have thought so," said the Emperor, "but I should certainly not have been foolish enough to say so. This is one of the absurd stories invented in the drawing-rooms of Paris. I never committed blunders of that kind. My object was to extinguish, and not to feed the flame. The torrent of hostility was already too forcibly directed against certain leaders of the Revolution. I found it necessary to support and countenance them, and I did so. Some one having procured, I know not where, a bust of Sièyes in his ecclesiastical character, it was publicly exhibited, and occasioned a universal uproar. Sièyes, in a furious passion, set out to make a complaint to me, but I had already given the necessary reprimand, and the bust was again consigned to obscurity.

"My great principle," continued the Emperor, "was to guard against reaction, and to bury the past in oblivion. I never condemned any opinion, nor proscribed any act. I was surrounded by the men who had voted for the death of Louis XVI. They were in the ministry and in the Council of State. I did not approve of their doctrines; but what had I to do with them? What right had I to constitute myself their judge? Some had been actuated by conviction, others by weakness and terror, and all by the delirium and fury of the moment. The fatality of the Greek tragedy was exemplified in the life of Louis XVI."

"It was reported in the Faubourg St. Germain," said Las Casas, "that Sièyes had been detected in a conspiracy against you in the affair of M. Clement de Ris, and that you pardoned him on condition of his entirely withdrawing himself from any participation in public affairs."

"This is another idle story for which there is not the slightest foundation," replied the Emperor. "Sièyes was always attached to me, and I never had any cause to complain of him. He was probably vexed to find that I opposed his metaphysical ideas, but he was at length convinced that it was necessary for France to have a ruler, and he preferred me to any other. Sièyes was, after all, an honest and a very clever man. He did much for the Revolution.

"At one of the first public festivals that took place during the Consulate," continued the Emperor, "as I was viewing the illuminations in company with Sièyes, I asked him what he thought of the state of affairs. He replied in a cold and even disheartening tone. 'And yet,' said I, 'I had this morning very satisfactory proofs of the spirit of the people.'

"'It is seldom,' replied he, 'that the people show their real spirit when the man who is possessed of power presents himself to their gaze. I can assure you they are far from being satisfied.'

"'Then you do not think the present government firmly established?' said I.

"'No.'

"'And when do you suppose we shall be settled?'

"'When I see the dukes and marquises of the old court in your antechamber,' he replied.

"Sièyes little dreamed that this would so soon be the case. He was short-sighted, and could not see very far before him. I thought, as he did, that all could not end with the Republic, but I foresaw the establishment of the empire. Accordingly, two or three years afterward, the circumstance I have just related being still fresh in my recollection, I said to Sièyes at one of my grand audiences,

"'Well, you are now *pêle-mêle* with all the old dukes and marquises; do you think all is settled now?'

"'Oh yes,' replied Sièyes, bowing profoundly, 'you have accomplished miracles, which were never before equaled, and which I never could have foreseen.'"

NAPOLEON INCOGNITO.

"During the Consulate, and even during the Empire," continues Las Casas, " Napoleon used, at public festivals, to go out late at night *incognito* for the purpose of seeing the shows, and hearing the sentiments of the people. He once went out in this way accompanied by Maria Louisa, and they both walked, arm in arm, on the Boulevards, highly amused at seeing their majesties, the Emperor and Empress, and all the grandees of the court, represented in the magic lanterns."

" During the Consulate," said Napoleon, " I was once standing in front of the Hotel de la Marine, viewing a public illumination. Beside me was a lady, who, to all appearance, had formerly moved in a distinguished sphere, accompanied by her daughter, a very pretty girl, to whom she was pointing out all the persons of note as they passed to and fro in the apartments. Calling her daughter's attention to a certain individual, she said,

" 'Remind me to go and pay my respects to him some day. We ought to do so, for he has rendered us great service.'

" 'But, mother,' replied the young lady, 'I did not know that we were expected to show gratitude to such people. I thought they were too happy in being able to oblige persons of our quality.'

" Certainly," said the Emperor, as he related this anecdote, " La Bruyère would have turned this incident to good account."

Napoleon frequently went out early in the morning, traversing the streets of the capital, and conversing familiarly with the laboring people in the markets and the faubourgs. In the Council of State he often advised the Prefect of Police to adopt this plan, that he might ascertain with certainty the true state of public sentiment. This he called his *Calif system of police*.

On his return from the disasters of Leipsic he appeared frequently in the midst of the crowds in the market-place. One day, a woman of enormous obesity, with whom he had been holding a little dialogue, told him bluntly that he ought to make peace.

" Good woman," said the Emperor, " sell your herbs, and leave me to settle my affairs. Let every one attend to his own calling."

The by-standers supported the Emperor with shouts of applause.

On another occasion, in these days of gathering disaster and gloom, the Emperor had collected around him an immense concourse of people in the Faubourg St. Antoine, which was occupied by the most humble of the Parisian populace.

" Are affairs," some one inquired, " really as bad as they are represented to be ?"

" Certainly," the Emperor replied, " I can not say that things are going on very well."

" But what will be the end of this ?"

" Heaven only knows," the Emperor answered.

" Will the enemy enter France ?"

" Very possibly," said the Emperor. " And he may even march to Paris if you do not assist me. I have not a million of arms. I can not do all by my own individual efforts."

THE EMPEROR AND THE MARKET-WOMAN.

"We will support you," exclaimed a number of voices.

"Then I shall beat the enemy and preserve the glory of France," the Emperor replied.

"But what must we do?" was the inquiry.

"You must enlist and fight," said the Emperor.

"We will," said one of the crowd; "but we must make a few conditions. We will not pass the frontiers."

"You shall not be required to do so," said the Emperor.

The air instantly resounded with acclamations. Registers were immediately opened, and two thousand men enlisted in the course of the day. Napoleon returned to the Tuileries. As he entered the *Place Carrousel* surrounded by the multitude, whose acclamations rent the air, it was supposed that an insurrection had broken out, and the gates were about to be closed.

After the Emperor's return from Elba he made a similar visit to the Faubourg St. Antoine, and was conducted in a similar way back to the Tuileries. In passing through the Faubourg St. Germain, where were the palaces of the old nobility, who were in favor of the Bourbons, the multitude halted before some of the principal mansions, and manifested their hostile feelings by words and gestures. In alluding to this event, the Emperor said,

"I had scarcely ever been placed in so delicate a situation. How many evils might have ensued had a single stone been thrown by the mob! Had a single imprudent word, or even an equivocal look, escaped me, the whole faubourg might have been destroyed. And I am convinced that its preservation was to be attributed wholly to my presence of mind, and the respect which the multitude entertained for me."

The day was tempestuous, and a violent gale, sweeping over the bleak rock, rendered it impossible for the Emperor to enjoy his accustomed walk. His appetite failed, and at an early hour he retired to his bed, saying that he was afraid that he should not sleep, his sensations were so extraordinary.

October 17. The Emperor was but little refreshed by the repose of the night. He awoke languid and dejected, and at noon, immediately after breakfast, he sent for Las Casas. A strange lethargy still oppressed him. He endeavored to converse a little, and then read a few pages of the Vicar of Wakefield in English. Still complaining of drowsiness, he retired to his chamber for a nap. He did not rise again until dinner was ready. After dinner he endeavored to read Don Quixote; but the strange lethargy still continuing, he laid down the book and retired. After he had gone to bed he sent for Las Casas, and conversed with him for nearly an hour.

October 18. The weather was dismal in the extreme; still, the Emperor, though indisposed and very low-spirited, employed most of the day in his narrow and comfortless cabinet, dictating to General Bertrand. At five o'clock, all the individuals of his suite were invited to his apartment.

"The state of the weather," says Las Casas, "joined to the vexations to which we are exposed, concur in producing torments almost beyond endurance. The weather has an effect on the nerves, and the persecutions that are heaped upon us are still worse to bear. Every word uttered by the governor increases our misery. To-day he had signified his intention of removing four of our establishment, which has been the cause of general lamentation among the household. The individuals singled out for removal regret their separation from their companions, while those who are to remain are tormented by the fear of speedily sharing the same fate. We compared Sir Hudson Lowe to Scylla devouring the four companions of Ulysses. The governor has informed me that he also intends removing my servant, who is an inhabitant of the island, and with whom I am very well satisfied. He is doubtless afraid that the man will become too much attached to me. He proposes to send me a servant of his own choosing, a favor for which I feel very grateful, though I have no intention of availing myself of the kind offer."

The individuals whom the governor had selected to send away were Captain Piontkowski, Rousseau, Santini, and Archambaud, who was the Emperor's driver. A careful driver was very necessary over the rough and craggy roads of St. Helena. Archambaud had also a brother with the Emperor, and, on that account, was additionally reluctant to leave. For these reasons, Count Montholon, acting in behalf of the Emperor, urged the selection of some other servant instead of Archambaud. But the governor was inexorable. "By taking away my driver," said the Emperor, "he wishes to prevent me from taking a little carriage exercise."

"At dinner," says Las Casas, "the Emperor ate but little. During the dessert, however, his spirits revived somewhat, and we began to converse on the events of his early life. This is a subject on which he delights to dwell, and which always affords him a source of new and lively interest. He said that he loved to carry himself back to that happy age when all is gayety and enjoyment, that happy period of hope and rising ambition, when the world first opens before us, and the mind fondly cherishes every romantic dream. He spoke of his regiment, and the pleasures he had enjoyed when he first mingled with society. He reverted to the circumstances that first called him into notice, the sudden ascendency which he acquired by his first successes, and the ambition with which they inspired him."

"And yet," said the Emperor, "I was far from entertaining a high opinion of myself. It was not till after the battle of Lodi that I conceived those lofty notions of ambition, which were confirmed in Egypt, after the victory of the Pyramids and the possession of Cairo. Then I willingly resigned myself to every brilliant dream."

In such converse the Emperor became animated and cheerful, and did not retire until midnight.

CHAPTER XXIX.
1816, October. Continued.

Intellectual Employments—Sale of Plate—Madam de Staël—Baron Larrey—Remarks on the peculiar Situation of the Emperor—Expenses at St. Helena—Marshal Jourdan—The Russian War—The Chamber of Sickness—Lord Exmouth's Expedition—The Debt of England—Wellington and Waterloo—Sailors—Heartlessness of the Governor—Affecting Scene—Immorality—Want of Water—Playfulness of the Emperor—Thoughts on Italy.

October 19. The four individuals taken from the Emperor's household were to-day embarked for the Cape of Good Hope. The Emperor settled upon each of them an annual pension. Their persons and baggage were carefully examined lest they should take any communications to Europe. "Piontkowski," says O'Meara, "was stripped to the skin."

The Emperor remained in his room all the day, endeavoring, by reading and dictation, to forget the indignities heaped upon him. He uttered not a word of repining. His noble spirit endured in silence. In the evening, for a short time, he read aloud to his companions from the Arabian Nights; but he soon grew weary, laid aside his book, and retired.

October 20. Count Bertrand and family moved from Hut's Gate, which was about three miles distant, to rooms which were now prepared for them at Longwood. The Emperor passed the whole day in his room, in intense intellectual occupation.

October 21. Another dismal day of rain, and mist, and howling wind darkened over the unhappy captives. As the Emperor was dressing in the morning, he said to Las Casas,

"I am determined to apply once more regularly to my occupations, which have been interrupted by the late ill treatment from our horrible governor."

"The governor will only give," Las Casas records, "for the Emperor's plate, a sum which is more than a fifth less than the plate is valued at in Paris; and yet he will neither allow any competition for the sale of it in the island, nor of its being taken to London." The English ministers seemed determined to extort from the Emperor the knowledge of the places where he had funds deposited in Europe.

Napoleon went into his library. In the course of conversation Madam de Staël was mentioned.

"Her house," he said, "had become quite an arsenal against me. People went there to be armed knights. She endeavored to raise enemies against me, and fought against me herself. She was at once Armida and Clorinda. It can not be denied that Madam de Staël is a very distinguished woman, endowed with great talents, and possessing a considerable share of wit. She will go down to posterity. It was more than once hinted to me, in order to soften me in her favor, that she was an adversary to be feared, and might become a useful ally. It might, no doubt, have proved advantageous to me if she had spoken in my praise instead of reviling me as she did, for her position and abilities gave her absolute sway over the saloons, and their influence in Paris is well known.

"Notwithstanding all that she has said against me, and all she will say yet, I am certainly far from saying or thinking she had a bad heart. The fact is, that she and I have waged a little war against each other, and that is all."

Then taking a review of the numerous writers who have declaimed against him, he said, "I am destined to be their food, but I have little fear of becoming their victim. They will bite against granite. My history is made up of facts, and words alone can not destroy them. In order to fight against me successfully, somebody should appear in the lists armed with the weight and authority of facts on his side. If such a man as the great Frederick, or any other man of his cast, were to take to writing against me, then it would be a different thing. It would then, perhaps, be time for me to begin to be moved, but as for all other writers, whatever be their talent, their efforts will be vain. My fame will survive, and when they wish to be admired they will sound my praise."

Dr. O'Meara dined this day at Plantation House with the commissioners of the Allies. They complained bitterly that they had not yet seen Napoleon, and that they would be objects of ridicule in Europe as soon as it should be known that they had been so many months in St. Helena without ever once even seeing the individual to ascertain whose presence was the sole object of their mission. But the Emperor very properly refused to see them in their official capacity as spies appointed over him by his proud oppressors, and Sir Hudson Lowe was determined that they should not be presented in any other way. The commissioners complained severely of St. Helena, saying that it was "the worst abode in the world."

October 23. The weather still continued dark, wet, and stormy. The Emperor could take no exercise, and was suffering much from the severity of the climate. One of his cheeks was badly swollen, and he suffered much pain. He said to Dr. O'Meara,

"There is either a furious wind with fog, which gives me a swelled face when I go out, or, when that is wanting, there is a sun which scorches my brains for want of shade. They continue me purposely in the worst part of the island. When I was at the Briers, I had at least the advantage of a shady walk and of a mild climate. But here they will arrive at the end they seek more speedily."

In conversation with Las Casas, the Emperor spoke of the celebrated surgeon, Baron Larrey.

"Larrey," said he, "left the impression on my mind of a true, honest man. To science he united in the highest degree the virtue of active philanthropy. He looked upon all the wounded as belonging to his family. Every consideration gave way before the care which he bestowed upon the hospitals. In our first campaigns under the Republic, a most fortunate revolution took place in the surgical department, which has since spread to all the armies of Europe, and to Larrey it is, in great measure, that mankind is indebted for it. The surgeon now shares the dangers of the soldier. It is in

BARON LARREY.

the midst of the fire that he devotes his cares to him. Larrey possesses all my esteem and my gratitude."

The Emperor, in his will, remembered this great and good man, coupling with his name the following magnificent expression of his esteem: "*He was the most virtuous man I have ever known.*"

October 24. The Emperor, sick, dejected, and in pain, kept his room all the day and until ten o'clock at night, seeing no one, and partaking of no refreshment except a little soup. (He had employed eighteen hours of the day reading.) Two hours before midnight he sent for Las Casas, and entered upon the subject of their pecuniary resources. It had again become necessary to dispose of some more plate. Las Casas reiterated, and with urgency, an offer he had previously made of four thousand Louis [$20,000] which he had in the English funds. The Emperor now consented to accept them. He could repay Las Casas upon the return of the count to Europe.

"Mine," said the Emperor, "is a singular situation. I have no doubt that if a communication were allowed with me, and that my relatives, or even many strangers, could suspect that I am in want, I should soon be amply provided with every thing that I require. But ought I to be a burden to my friends, and expose them to the undue advantage which the English ministers might take of their good-will. I have applied to these ministers for a few books, and they have sent them to me with all the inattention and neglect of a careless agent. They claim from me nearly ten thousand dollars for what I might certainly have procured for less than two thousand. Would it not be the same with every thing else? If I accept what you offer, it must be strictly applied to our immediate wants; for, after all, we must live, and we really can not live upon what they give us.) The small addition of one hundred Louis [$500] per month would just be sufficient, and that is the sum which you must ask for, and appropriate accordingly."*

October 25. It was a fine day. The Emperor was very feeble, and, accompanied by Las Casas, took a short walk. He had not been out of his room for ten days. While walking, the younger Archambaud came up with the calash, driving four-in-hand. The Emperor declined getting in, as he did not think it safe to trust to so inexperienced a driver on roads so rough and perilous; but Archambaud said that, since his brother's departure, he had regularly practiced driving, and was sure that he could be trusted. The Emperor took a short ride, and called upon General Bertrand at his new residence. The evening was employed in reading the Medea of Longepierre. The Emperor ordered the celebrated Greek tragedy of Euripides on the same subject to be brought, and compared the two.

On returning to his chamber, he threw himself upon the sofa, and, happening to cast his eye on a list of the French marshals, he passed them all in review. He dwelt for a long time on Marshal Jourdan.

---

* A London paper of this date gives the following as the exorbitant price of provisions at St Helena: "Turkeys, seven and a half dollars each; geese, ten dollars; fowls, and these very bad, four and a half dollars a pair; potatoes, four dollars a bushel; butter, one dollar and a quarter a pound; cheese, seventy-five cents a pound; East India produce very high, as also European goods."

"I certainly," said he, "used that man very ill, and it was, of course, natural to expect that he would dislike me; but I have learned with pleasure that, since my fall, he invariably acted in the best manner. He has thus afforded an example of that praiseworthy elevation of mind which distinguishes men one from another. Jourdan is a true patriot, and that is an answer to many things which have been said of him."

Then speaking of the Russian war, he said,

"The Russian war should have been the most popular of any in modern times. It was a war of good sense and true interests; a war for the repose and security of all. It was purely pacific and preservative, entirely European and Continental. Its success would have established a balance of power, and would have introduced new combinations, by which the dangers of the time present would have been succeeded by future tranquillity. In this case, ambition had no share in my views. In raising Poland, which was the keystone of the whole arch, I would have permitted a king of Prussia, an archduke of Austria, or any other, to occupy the throne. I had no wish to obtain any new acquisition, and I reserved to myself the glory of doing good, and the blessings of posterity.

"Yet this undertaking failed and proved my ruin, though I never acted more disinterestedly, and never better merited success. As if popular opinion had been seized with contagion in a moment, a general outcry, a general sentiment arose against me. I was proclaimed to be the destroyer of kings —I, who had created them! I was denounced as the subverter of the rights of nations—I, who was about to risk all to secure them! And people and kings, those irreconcilable enemies, leagued together and conspired against me! All the acts of my past life were now forgotten. I said truly that popular favor would return to me with victory; but victory escaped me, and I was ruined. Such is mankind, and such is my history. But both people and kings will have cause to regret me, and my memory will be sufficiently avenged for the injustice committed upon me. That is certain."

October 26. The Emperor was very unwell, and desired Las Casas to attend him. He found Napoleon in his chamber, with a handkerchief bound around his head. He was seated in an arm-chair before a large fire which he had ordered to be kindled.

"What," said he, "is the severest disorder, the most acute pain, to which human nature is subject?"

"The pain of the present moment always appears to be most severe," replied Las Casas.

"Then it is the toothache," said the Emperor. His right cheek was much swollen and inflamed. Las Casas was alone in attendance upon him, and alternately warmed a flannel and a napkin, which he kept constantly applied to the part affected, and the Emperor said he felt greatly relieved by it. He was also affected with a severe nervous cough, and occasionally a yawning and shivering, which denoted approaching fever.

"What a miserable thing is man!" said he; "the smallest fibre in his body, assailed by disease, is sufficient to derange his whole system! On the other hand, in spite of all the maladies to which he is subject, it is sometimes necessary to employ the executioner to put an end to him. What a curious machine is this earthly clothing! And perhaps I may be confined in it for thirty years longer!"

He attributed his toothache to his late drive, as he had felt singularly affected by being out in the open air. "Nature is always the best counselor," said he. "I went out in spite of my inclination, and only in obedience to reason." He then spent the remainder of the day in his chamber, occasionally suffering severely from toothache. At intervals, when the pain abated, he walked up and down, between his chamber and the sofa, and conversed on different subjects. Alluding to an individual who had behaved very ill to him in 1814, he said,

"Probably you will suppose he fled on my return; but no such thing; on the contrary, I was beset by him. He very coolly acknowledged that he had felt a transient attachment for the Bourbons, for which, however, he assured me he had been heartily punished. But this, he said, had served only to revive the natural affection which all so justly entertained for me. I spurned him from me, and I have good reason to believe that he is now at the feet of the royal family, relating all sorts of horrors about me. Man is always and every where alike."

Dr. O'Meara called to visit his sick and suffering patient. The conversation turned upon Lord Exmouth's expedition to punish the pirates of the Barbary coast, and O'Meara inquired of the Emperor his opinion respecting the probability of success.

"I think that the expedition will succeed," said Napoleon, "especially if the fleet takes and destroys as many of the Algerine ships as it can, and then anchors opposite the town, and does not allow a single ship or vessel, not even a fishing-boat, to enter or go out. Continue that for a short time, and the Dey will submit, or else the populace will revolt and murder him, and afterward agree to any terms you like. But no treaty will be kept by them. It is a disgrace to the powers of Europe to allow so many nests of robbers to exist. Even the Neapolitans could put a stop to it, instead of allowing themselves to be robbed. They have upward of fifty thousand seamen in the kingdoms of Naples and Sicily, and with their navy they might easily prevent a single Barbary ship from stirring out."

O'Meara observed that the Neapolitans were so great cowards at sea, that the Algerines had the utmost contempt for them.

"They are cowards by land as well as by sea," replied the Emperor, "but that might be remedied by proper officers and discipline. At Amiens I proposed to your government to unite with me either to entirely destroy those nests of pirates or at least to destroy their ships and fortresses, and make them cultivate their country and abandon piracy. But your ministers would not consent to it, owing to a mean jealousy of the Americans, with whom the barbarians were at war. I wanted to annihilate them, though it did not concern me much, as they generally respected my flag, and carried on a large trade with Marseilles."

O'Meara asked if he thought it would be advisable for Lord Exmouth to disembark his marines and seamen, and attack the town of Algiers. "Oh no," replied he; "if he has but a small force, he will get half his men killed by the rabble in the houses and batteries; and it is not worth sending a large one, unless you are determined to destroy their power altogether."

After this, the conversation turned upon the national debt, and the great weight of taxes in England. Napoleon professed himself doubtful that the English could now continue to manufacture goods so as to be able to sell them at the same price as those made in France, in consequence of the actual necessaries of life being so much dearer in England than in France. He professed his disbelief that the nation could support the immense weight of taxes, the dearness of provisions, and the extravagance of a bad administration.

"When I was in France," continued he, "with four times the extent of territory, and four times the population, I never could have raised one half of your taxes. How the English people bear it, I can not conceive. The French would not have suffered one fourth of them. Notwithstanding your great successes, which are, indeed, almost incredible, and to which accident, and perhaps destiny, have much contributed, I do not think that you are yet out of the scrape. Though you have the world at command, I do not believe that you will ever be able to get over your debt. Your great commerce has kept you up. But that will fail when you shall no longer be able to undersell the manufacturers of other nations, who are rapidly improving. A few years will show if I am right.

"The worst thing England has ever done," continued he, "was that of endeavoring to make herself a great military nation. In attempting that, England must always be the slave of Russia, Austria, or Prussia, or at least subservient to some of them, because you have not a population sufficiently numerous to combat on the Continent with France, or with any of the powers I have named, and must consequently hire men from some of them; whereas, at sea, you are so superior—your sailors are so much better, that you can always command the others, with safety to yourselves, and with little comparative expense. Your soldiers have not the requisite qualities for a military nation. They are not equal in address, activity, or intelligence to the French. When they get from under the fear of the lash, they obey nobody. In a retreat they can not be managed. And if they meet with wine, they are so many demons, and adieu to subordination. I saw the retreat of Moore, and I never witnessed any thing like it. It was impossible to collect, or to make them do any thing. Nearly all were drunk. Your officers depend for promotion upon interest or money. Your soldiers are brave, nobody can deny it; but it was bad policy to encourage the military mania instead of sticking to your marine, which is the real force of your country, and one which, while you preserve it, will always render you powerful. In order to have good soldiers, a nation must *always be at war*.

"If you had lost the battle of Waterloo," continued he, "what a state would England have been in! The flower of your youth would have been destroyed, for not a man, not even Lord Wellington, would have escaped."

O'Meara observed that Lord Wellington had determined never to leave the field alive.

Napoleon replied, " He could not retreat. He would have been destroyed with his army if, instead of the Prussians, Grouchy had come up."

O'Meara asked if he had not believed for some time that the Prussians who had shown themselves were a part of Grouchy's corps.

" Certainly," he replied; " and I can now scarcely comprehend why it was a Prussian division and not that of Grouchy."

O'Meara then took the liberty of asking whether, if neither Grouchy nor the Prussians had arrived, it would not have been a drawn battle.

" The English army," Napoleon answered, " would have been destroyed. They were defeated at midday. But accident, or, more likely, destiny, decided that Lord Wellington should gain it. I could scarcely believe that he would have given me battle, because, if he had retreated to Antwerp, as he ought to have done, I must have been overwhelmed by the armies of three or four hundred thousand men that were coming against me. By giving me battle there was a chance for me. It was the greatest folly to disunite the English and Prussian armies. They ought to have been united, and I can not conceive the reason of their separation. It was folly in Wellington to give me battle in a place where, if defeated, all must have been lost, for he could not retreat. There was a wood in his rear, and but one road to gain it. He would have been destroyed.

" Moreover, he allowed himself to be surprised by me. This was a great fault. He ought to have been encamped from the beginning of June, as he must have known that I intended to attack him. He might have lost every thing. But he has been fortunate; his destiny has prevailed, and every thing he did will meet with applause. My intentions were to attack and to destroy the English. This, I knew, would produce an immediate change of ministry. The indignation against them for having caused the loss of forty thousand of the flower of the English army would have excited such a popular commotion that they would have been turned out. The people would have said, ' What is it to us who is on the throne of France—Louis or Napoleon? Are we to sacrifice all our blood in endeavors to place on the throne a detested family? No; we have suffered enough. It is no affair of ours. Let them settle it among themselves.' They would have made peace. The Saxons, Bavarians, Belgians, Wurtembergers, would have joined me. The coalition was nothing without England. The Russians would have made peace, and I should have been quietly seated on the throne. Peace would have been permanent, as what could France do after the treaty of Paris? What was to be feared from her?

" These," continued he, " were my reasons for attacking the English. I had beaten the Prussians. Before twelve o'clock I had succeeded. I may say every thing was mine, but accident and destiny decided it otherwise. Doubtless the English fought most bravely; nobody can deny it. But they must have been destroyed. Pitt and his politics nearly ruined England by keeping up a Continental war with France."

O'Meara remarked that it was asserted by many able politicians in England that, if England had not carried on that war, she would have been ruined, and ultimately have become a province of France.

"It is not true," said Napoleon. "England being at war with France, gave the latter a pretense and an opportunity of extending her conquest under me to the length she did, until I became emperor of nearly all the world, which could not have happened if there had been no war."

The conversation then turned upon the occupation of Malta. "Two days," said the Emperor, "before Lord Whitworth left Paris, an offer was made to the minister and to others about me of thirty millions of francs [$6,000,000], and to acknowledge me as King of France, provided I would give up Malta to you. The war, however, would have broken out, had Malta been out of the question."

Some conversation then took place relative to English seamen. Napoleon observed that the English seamen were as much superior to the French as the latter were to the Spaniards. O'Meara said that he thought the French would never make good seamen, on account of their impatience and volatility of temper. That especially they would never submit without complaining, as the English had done at Toulon, to blockade ports for years together, suffering from the combined effects of bad weather, and of privations of every kind.

"I do not agree with you there, Sir Doctor," said the Emperor, "but I do not think that they will ever make as good seamen as yours. The sea is yours. Your seamen are as much superior to ours as the Dutch were once to yours. I think, however, that the Americans are better seamen than yours, because they are less numerous."

O'Meara observed that the Americans had a considerable number of English seamen in their service who passed for Americans, which was remarkable, as, independent of other circumstances, the American discipline on board of men-of-war was much more severe than the English; and that, if the Americans had a large navy, they would find it impossible to have so many able seamen in each ship as they had at present. When O'Meara observed that the American discipline was more severe than theirs, the Emperor smiled and said, "That is difficult to believe."

October 27. The Emperor passed the whole day upon the sofa, or sitting in his arm-chair before the fire. He suffered much pain in his head and teeth. Las Casas applied warm flannel and napkins to his cheek, from which he experienced much relief. The Emperor seemed very grateful to Las Casas for his kind nursing. He several times placed his hand upon his secretary's shoulder, saying, "My dear Las Casas, my hospitable brother, you relieve me very much." Soothed by these remedies and exhausted by a sleepless night, he fell into a doze, but in a few moments a violent return of pain and severe chills awoke him. He continued in this state until late in the evening, taking no refreshment except a little toast and water, which he prepared himself, and in which he put some sugar and orange-flowers.

Dr. O'Meara called. The Emperor, in these hours of pain and languor, thought of the friends from whom he was so cruelly torn. The memory of his beloved Josephine came rushing upon him, and he spoke of her in terms of glowing affection. O'Meara was deeply moved by the sufferings of his illustrious patient, and, calling upon Sir Hudson Lowe, informed him that the Emperor attributed his indisposition to the bleak and exposed situation of Longwood, and that he earnestly desired to be removed either to the Briers or to the other side of the island. This merciless man heartlessly replied,

"The fact is that General Bonaparte wants to get Plantation House; but the East India Company will not consent to have so fine a plantation given to a set of Frenchmen to destroy the trees and ruin the gardens."

At eight o'clock in the evening O'Meara called again, and urged the Emperor to take some medicine. Napoleon mildly yet firmly declined.

"I have never," said he, "taken any medicine since my childhood. I know my own constitution, and am convinced that even a very small dose would produce violent effects. Moreover, its effects will be contrary to the efforts of nature. I will trust to diet."

At nine o'clock, after the Emperor had retired, he desired that all his suite might come to his chamber. They assembled affectionately in his narrow room, the gentlemen and the ladies, around his bedside. It was, indeed, a scene for the painter. These loving friends, not one of whom was allied to the Emperor by blood, had followed him six thousand miles, to the ocean's most dreary rock, to share his prison and his fate. They took the place which wife, child, mother, brothers, sisters, were most anxious to occupy, but from which they were unrelentingly excluded by the most despotic cruelty. The dilapidated hut in which they were assembled stood alone, amid the blackened crags, eighteen hundred feet above the level of the surrounding sea. It was dark night, and the ocean breeze wailed dismally around their lonely abode. The flickering blaze of the fire upon the hearth alone lighted the room. The Emperor, pale, emaciate, but calm and placid, was pillowed upon his bed. In softened tones of voice he conversed with those who loved him so well. His words, which they drank in eagerly, reflected his lofty character. The conversation chanced to turn upon purity of the lips and of life.

"Immorality," remarked the Emperor, "is, beyond a doubt, the worst of all faults in a sovereign, because he introduces it as a fashion among his subjects, by whom it is practiced for the sake of pleasing him. It strengthens every vice, blights every virtue, and infects all society like a pestilence. In short, it is a nation's scourge. Public morality, on the contrary, is the natural complement of the laws. It is a whole code in itself. The Revolution, in spite of all its horrors, has nevertheless been the true cause of the regeneration of morals in France. I do not hesitate to affirm that my government will mark the memorable epoch of the return of morality. We advanced at full sail, but, doubtless, the catastrophes which have ensued will, in a great measure, turn all back; for, amid so many vicissitudes and disorders, it is difficult to resist the various temptations that arise, the allurements of intrigue and cupidity, and the suggestions of venality.

"However, the rising impulse of improvement may be impeded and repressed, but not destroyed. Public morality belongs especially to the dominion of reason and information, of which it is the natural result, and reason and information can not again be retrograde. The scandalous turpitude of former ages, the adultery and libertinism of the Regency, and the profligacy of the reign which succeeded it, can not again be revived, unless the circumstances under which they existed should again return, and that is impossible. Before such a change can take place, the upper classes of society must again degenerate to a state of absolute idleness, so as to have no other occupation than licentiousness; the spirit of industry, which now animates and elevates the minds of people in the middle ranks, must be destroyed; and, finally, the lower classes must replunge into that state of subjection and degradation which once reduced them to the level of mere beasts of burden. Now all this is henceforth impossible. Public morals are, therefore, on the rise. It may safely be predicted that they will gradually improve all over the world."

After half an hour of such conversation, they all retired, and the Emperor, by his own wish, was left alone, sick, sleepless, and in pain.

October 28. "When I arose in the morning," says Las Casas, "I felt ill, and wished to bathe my feet, but no water could be procured for that purpose. I mention this circumstance to afford an idea, if possible, of our real situation at Longwood. Water has always been very scarce here; but there is now less than ever, and we consider ourselves singularly fortunate when we are able to procure a bath for the Emperor. We are no better provided with other things necessary in medical treatment. Yesterday the doctor was mentioning, in the Emperor's presence, drugs, instruments, and remedies of various kinds; but, as he enumerated each article, he added, 'Unfortunately, there is none to be procured on the island.' 'Then,' said the Emperor, 'when they sent us here, they took it for granted that we should always be well.' Indeed, we are in want of the veriest trifles and necessaries. As a substitute for a warming-pan, the Emperor has been obliged to have holes bored in one of the large silver dishes used for keeping the meat warm at table, which is now filled with coals, and used for the purpose of warming his bed. For some time past he has felt very much in want of spirits of wine, by means of which he might have been enabled to warm his drink."

The Emperor's face was much swollen, and the pain had abated. Calm and patient, he sat before the fire through the day, reading, and occasionally conversing with his friends.

October 29. The Emperor still continued quite ill, and was unwilling to take any medicine, notwithstanding the urgent entreaties of Dr. O'Meara. He sent for Las Casas about five o'clock in the afternoon. The Emperor was reading, and bathing his feet in hot water, as Las Casas entered. Observing some confectionery upon the bureau, Napoleon requested Las Casas to hand it to him. Seeing that Las Casas hesitated and felt embarrassed as to how he should present them, he said,

"Take them in your hand. There is no need of ceremony or form between us now; we must henceforth be messmates."

"I have already mentioned," says Las Casas, "that in his moments of good-humored familiarity, the Emperor was accustomed to salute me with all sorts of titles, such as, 'Good-morning, monseigneur! How is your excellency?' &c. One evening, when I was about entering the drawing-room, the usher opened the door for me, and, at the same moment, the door of the Emperor's apartment also opened, and he came out. We both met together. In a fit of abstraction, he stopped me, and, taking me by the ear, said, playfully, 'Well, where is *your majesty* going?' But the words had no sooner been uttered than he immediately let go my ear, and, assuming a grave expression of countenance, began to talk on some serious topic. The Emperor was evidently sorry for having suffered the expression *your majesty* to escape him. He seemed to think that, though other titles might be used in jest, yet the case was very different with the one he had just employed, both on account of its own peculiar nature, and the circumstances in which we were placed. Be this as it may, the reader may form what conjecture he pleases. I merely relate the fact."

October 30. The Emperor was no better to-day, and his periodical attack of fever returned at the usual hour. Las Casas alluded in conversation to the unpopularity of which the Emperor had lately been the object, and expressed surprise that he had not attempted to countermine the libels that were published against him, and to recover popular favor.

"I had higher objects in view," replied the Emperor, "than to concern myself about flattering and courting a petty multitude, a few insignificant coteries and sects. I should have returned victorious from Moscow, and then not only these people, but all France, and all the world, would have admired and blessed me. I might then have withdrawn myself mysteriously from the world, and popular credulity would have revived the fable of Romulus. It would have been said that I had been carried up to heaven to take my place among the gods."

Dr. O'Meara again saw Sir Hudson Lowe, informed him of the suffering condition of his patient, and of his desire to be removed from the bleak exposure of Longwood to the more sheltered residence at the Briers.

"If General Bonaparte," said the governor, "wishes to make himself comfortable, and to get reconciled to the island, he ought to draw for some of those vast sums of money which he possesses, and lay it out in purchasing a house and grounds."

At seven o'clock, the Emperor, finding himself very weak, retired to his bed. He drew the bed-curtains to shut out the light, and again gathered all his suite around him. After a little desultory conversation, he took a fancy to have Robinson Crusoe read to him. Each of the gentlemen read by turns for an hour or two. He then took leave of all except General Gourgaud, who remained a little time longer conversing with the Emperor.

October 31. Fair weather had now returned. The day was delightful. The Emperor had kept his chamber for six days, and, tired of the monotony of the scene, he determined to disobey the doctor's orders, and went out. He was extremely feeble, and, finding himself quite unable to walk, ordered the calash. He was silent and low-spirited, and suffered much pain from soreness of the mouth. After his return he sent for Las Casas. He felt very weak and drowsy. Las Casas prevailed on him to eat a little, and he also took a glass of wine, which, he said, somewhat revived him. He then entered into conversation.

"As soon as I set foot in Italy," said he, "I wrought a change in the manners, sentiments, and language of our Revolution. I did not shoot the emigrants. I protected the priests, and abolished those institutions and festivals which were calculated to disgrace us. In so doing, I was not guided by caprice, but by reason and equity, those two bases of superior policy. For example, if the anniversary of the king's death had always been celebrated, you emigrants would never have had an opportunity for rallying.

"I was the first person who applied to France the title of the *Great Nation*, and certainly she justified the distinction in the eyes of the prostrate world; and she will yet deserve and retain that proud title, if her national character should again rise to a level with her physical advantages and her moral resources."

Again, speaking of one of his companions, to whom he was much attached, he said, "His character resembles that of the *cow*—gentle and placid in all things except where his children are concerned. If any one meddle with them, his horns are immediately thrust forward, and he may be roused to a pitch of fury."

Speaking of another individual, who had passed his thirtieth year, and who, he happened to say, was too young, he observed, "And yet, at that age, I had made all my conquests, and I ruled the world. I had laid the revolutionary storm, amalgamated hostile parties, rallied a nation, established a government and an empire—in short, I wanted only the title of Emperor. It must be confessed, I have been the spoiled child of Fortune. From my first entrance into life I was accustomed to exercise command; and circumstances, and the force of my own character, were such that, as soon as I became possessed of power, I acknowledged no master and obeyed no laws except those of my own creating."

CHAPTER XXX.
1816, November.

Rupture of the Treaty of Amiens—Treatment of Prisoners—Exchange of Prisoners—Plan of employing Prisoners of War—Magnificent Views in reference to Antwerp—Reason for refusing the Terms offered at Chatillon—Confidence of the Emperor respecting the Verdict of Posterity—Disinthrallment of the Jews—Marriages—Freemasons—Illuminati—The Jesuits—The Affair of Mallet—The Emperor's Family—The Historical Atlas—Anecdotes.

November 1. The day was fine, and about two o'clock the Emperor walked out into the garden. Finding himself very much fatigued, he called at Madam Bertrand's to rest. His languor and exhaustion were so extreme that he sat there for an hour, in an arm-chair, without uttering a word. He then returned to his chamber, threw himself upon his sofa, and fell asleep.

At six o'clock he sent for Las Casas. He was still very feeble, but experienced some benefit from the bath. He conversed upon the situation of the French prisoners in England.

"The sudden rupture of the treaty of Amiens," said the Emperor, "on such false pretenses, and with so much bad faith on the part of the English ministry, greatly irritated me. I conceived that I had been trifled with. The seizure of several French merchant ships, even before war had been declared, roused my indignation to the utmost.

"To my urgent remonstrance, they coolly replied that it was a practice they had always observed, and here they spoke the truth; but the time was gone by when France could tamely submit to such injustice and humiliation. I had become the defender of her rights and glory, and I was resolved to let our enemies know with whom they had to deal. Unfortunately, owing to the reciprocal situation of the two countries, I could only avenge one act of violence by another still g͏͏ter. It was a painful thing to be compelled to make reprisals on innocent men, but I had no alternative.

"On reading the ironical and insolent reply that was returned to my complaints, I that very night issued an order for arresting, in every part of France, and in every territory occupied by the French, all Englishmen, of every rank whatever, and detaining them as prisoners, by way of reprisal for the unjust seizure of our ships. Most of these Englishmen were men of rank and fortune, who were traveling for pleasure; but the more extraordinary the measure, the greater the injustice, the better it suited my purpose. A general outcry was raised. The English appealed to me; but I referred them to their own government, on whose conduct their fate alone depended. Several of these individuals proposed raising a subscription to pay for the ships that had been seized, in the hope of thereby obtaining permission to return home. I, however, informed them that I did not want money, but merely to obtain justice and redress for injury. Could it have been believed that the

English government, as crafty and tenacious with respect to its maritime rights as the court of Rome is in its religious pretensions, suffered a numerous and distinguished class of Englishmen to be unjustly detained for ten years, rather than authentically renounce for the future an odious system of maritime plunder!

"When I was first raised to the head of the consular government, I had had a misunderstanding with the English cabinet on the subject of prisoners of war; but I now carried my point. The Directory had been weak enough to agree to an arrangement extremely injurious to France, and entirely to the advantage of England. The English maintained their prisoners in France, and we had to maintain ours in England. We had but few English prisoners, and the French prisoners in England were exceedingly numerous. Provisions were to be had for almost nothing in France, and they were exorbitantly dear in England. Thus the English had very trifling expenses to pay, while we, on the other hand, had to send enormous sums into a foreign country at a time when we could but ill afford it. This arrangement, moreover, required an exchange of agents between the respective countries. The English commissioner proved to be neither more nor less than a spy on the French government. He was the agent and contriver of all the intrigues that were carried on in France by the emigrants abroad.

"No sooner was I made acquainted with this state of things, than I erased the abuse by a stroke of the pen. The English government was informed that, thenceforward, each country must maintain the prisoners it should make, unless an exchange were agreed upon. A terrible outcry was raised, and a threat was held out that the French prisoners should be suffered to die of starvation. I doubted not that the English ministers were sufficiently obstinate and inhuman to wish to put this threat into execution, but I knew that any cruelty exercised toward the prisoners would be repugnant to the feelings of the nation. The English government yielded the point. The situation of our unfortunate prisoners was indeed neither better nor worse than it previously had been, but in other respects we gained great advantages, and got rid of an arrangement which had placed us under a sort of tribute.

"During the whole war I incessantly made proposals for an exchange of prisoners. The English government, under some pretense or other, constantly refused to accede, on the supposition that it would be advantageous to me. I have nothing to say against this. In war, policy must take precedence of feeling. But why exercise unnecessary cruelty? And this is what the English ministers unquestionably did, when they found the number of prisoners increasing. Then commenced for our unfortunate countrymen the odious system of confinement in the hulks—a species of torture which the ancients would have added to the horrors of the infernal regions, had their imaginations been capable of conceiving it. I readily admit there might be exaggeration on the part of the accusers. But was the truth spoken by those who defended themselves? We know what kind of a thing a report to Parliament is. We can form a correct idea of it when we read the calumnies and falsehoods that are uttered in Parliament, with such cool effrontery, by the base men who have blushed not to become our executioners. Confinement on board hulks is a thing that needs no explanation. The fact speaks for itself. When it is considered that men unaccustomed to live on shipboard were crowded together in little unwholesome cabins, too small to afford them room to move—that, by way of indulgence, they were permitted, twice during the twenty-four hours, to breathe pestilential exhalations at ebb-tide, and that this misery was prolonged for the space of ten or twelve years, the blood curdles at such an odious picture of inhumanity.

"On this point I blame myself for not having made reprisals. It would have been well had I thrown into similar confinement, not the poor sailors and soldiers, whose complaints would never have been attended to, but all the English nobility and persons of fortune who were then in France. I should have permitted them to maintain a free correspondence with their friends and families, and their complaints would soon have assailed the ears of the English ministers, and checked their odious measures. Certain parties in Paris, who were ever the best allies of the enemy, would, of course, have called me a tiger and a cannibal. But no matter. I should have discharged my duty to the French people, who had made me their protector and defender. In this instance my decision of character failed me. Were the French prisoners confined in the hulks at the time you were in England?"

"I can not positively say," replied Las Casas, "but I am inclined to think not. I recollect that it was proposed to convey the French prisoners to some small islands between England and Ireland, and to leave them to themselves, in a state of complete seclusion, with a few light vessels cruising about to guard them. To this plan it was objected that, in case of a descent of the enemy, his grand object would be to land on these islands, distribute arms among the prisoners, and thus recruit an army immediately. Perhaps this idea might have led to the use of the hulks, for the prisoners were rapidly increasing in numbers, and it was not thought safe to keep them on shore among the people, as the latter showed a strong disposition to fraternize with the French."

"Well," said Napoleon, "I can very readily conceive that there might be good grounds for rejecting the plan you have just mentioned. Safety and self-preservation before all things. But the confinement in the hulks is a stain on the English character for humanity, an irritating sting that will never be removed from the hearts of the French prisoners. On the subject of prisoners of war, the English ministers invariably acted with their habitual bad faith, and with the machiavelism that distinguishes the school of the present day. Being absolutely determined to avoid an exchange, which they did not wish to incur the blame of having refused, they invented and multiplied pretenses beyond calculation.

"In the first place," continued the Emperor, "that I should presume to regard as prisoners persons merely detained, was affirmed to be an atrocious violation of the laws of civilized nations, and a principle which the English government would never avow, on any consideration whatever. It happened that some of the individuals detained, who were at large on parole, escaped, and were received triumphantly in England. On the other hand, some Frenchmen effected their escape to France. I expressed my disapprobation of their conduct, and proposed that the individuals of either country who had broken their parole should be mutually sent back again. But I received for answer that persons detained were not to be accounted prisoners; that they had merely availed themselves of the lawful privilege of escaping oppression; that they had done right, and had been received accordingly. After this I thought myself justified in inducing the French to escape; and the English ministers filled their journals with the most insolent abuse, declaring me to be a man who scrupled not to violate moral principle, faith, and law.

"When at length they determined to treat for an exchange of prisoners, or, perhaps I ought rather to say, to trifle with me on this point, they sent a commissioner to France. All the great difficulties were waived, and, with a fine parade of sentiment, conditions were proposed for the sake of humanity. They consented to include persons detained in the list of prisoners, and to admit under that head the Hanoverian troops, who were my prisoners, but who were at large on parole. This latter point had been a standing obstacle, because, it was insinuated, the Hanoverians were not English.

"Thus far matters had proceeded smoothly, and there was every probability of their being brought to a conclusion; but I knew with whom I had to deal, and I guessed the intentions that were really entertained. There were infinitely more French prisoners in England than English prisoners in France; and I was well aware that, the English being once safely landed at home, some pretense would be found for breaking off the exchange, and the rest of my poor Frenchmen might have remained on board the hulks for life. I declared that I would accede to no partial exchange; that I would be satisfied only with a full and complete one; and, to facilitate matters, I made the following proposal: I admitted that there were fewer English prisoners in France than French prisoners in England, but I observed that there were among my prisoners Spaniards, Portuguese, and other *allies of the English*, who had been taken under their banners, and fighting in the same cause. With this addition I could, on my part, produce a far more considerable number of prisoners than there were in England. I therefore offered to surrender up all in return for all. This proposition at first occasioned some embarrassment. It was discussed and rejected; but, as soon as they had devised a scheme by which they thought they could secure the object they had in view, they acceded to my proposition.

"But I kept a watchful eye on them. I knew that if we began by merely exchanging Frenchmen for Englishmen, as soon as the latter should be secured, pretenses would be found for breaking off the business, and the old evasions would be resumed; for the English prisoners in France did not amount to one third of the French in England. To obviate any misunderstanding on either side, I therefore proposed that we should exchange by transports of only three thousand at a time; that three thousand Frenchmen should be returned to me, and that I would send back one thousand English, and two thousand Hanoverians, Spaniards, Portuguese, and others. Thus, if any misunderstanding arose and put a stop to the exchange, we should still stand in the same relative proportion as before, without having practiced any deception upon each other; but if, on the contrary, the affair should proceed uninterruptedly to a conclusion, I promised to surrender up gratuitously all the prisoners that might ultimately remain in my hands.

"My conjectures respecting the real designs of the English government proved to be correct. These conditions, which were really so reasonable, and the principle which had already been adopted, were rejected, and the whole business broken off. Whether the English ministers really sympathized in the situation of their countrymen, or whether they were convinced of my firm determination not to be duped, I know not, but it would appear that they were at length inclined to come to a conclusion when I subsequently introduced the subject by an indirect channel. However, our disasters in Russia at once revived their hopes and defeated my intentions.

"The treatment of prisoners of war in France was as generous and liberal as it possibly could be, and I think no nation could justly convey a reproach to us on that subject. We have in our favor the testimony and the sentiments of the prisoners themselves; for, with the exception of those who were ardently attached to their local laws, or, in other words, to notions of liberty, and these were exclusively the English and Spaniards, all the rest, namely, the Austrians, Prussians, and Russians, were willing to remain with us. They left us with regret, and returned to us with pleasure. This disposition on the part of the English and Spaniards has oftener than once influenced the obstinacy of their efforts or their resistance.

"It was my intention to have introduced into Europe a change with respect to the treatment of prisoners. I intended to enroll them in regiments, and to make them labor, under military discipline, at public works and monuments. They should have received whatever money they earned, and would thus have been secured against the misery of absolute idleness, and the disorders arising from it. They would have been well fed and clothed, and would have wanted for nothing, without being a burden on the state. All parties would have been benefited by this plan. But my idea did not meet the approval of the Council of State, which in this instance was swayed by the mistaken philanthropy that leads to so many errors in the world. It was said that it would be unjust and cruel to compel men to labor. It was feared lest our enemies should make reprisals. It was affirmed that a prisoner was sufficiently unfortunate in the loss of his liberty, without being placed under restraint as to the employment of his time.

"But here was the abuse of which I complained, and which I wished to correct. 'A prisoner,' said I, 'must and should expect to be placed under lawful constraint, and that which I would impose upon him is for his own advantage as well as that of others. I do not require that he should be subject to greater misery or fatigue, but to less danger than he is exposed to in his present situation. You are afraid lest the enemy should make reprisals, and treat French prisoners in the same manner. Heaven grant it should be so! I wish for nothing better. I should then behold my sailors and soldiers occupied in wholesome labor, in the fields or public roads, instead of seeing them buried alive on board those odious hulks. They would return home healthy, industrious, and inured to labor, and in every country they would leave behind them some compensation for the fatal ravages of war.' By way of concession, the Council of State agreed to the organization of a few corps of prisoners as voluntary laborers, or something of the sort, but this was by no means the fulfillment of the scheme I had in view."

November 2. The Emperor did not leave his chamber. He was very unwell, restless, and feverish, with occasional chills. He sat most of the day in his arm-chair before the fire. Las Casas was with him. Sometimes he conversed, and at others endeavored to sleep.

"I have done much for Antwerp," said he, "but it was little in comparison with what I proposed to do. I intended to have rendered it a fatal point of attack to the enemy by sea, and to have made it a certain resource by land, and a point of national security in case of great disasters. I would have rendered Antwerp capable of receiving a whole army in its defeat, and holding out against a close siege for the space of a year, during which time a nation would be enabled to rally in a mass for its deliverance, and to resume the offensive. Five or six places of this kind were to constitute the new system of defense which I intended to have established. Antwerp was as yet merely a commercial town. The military town was to have been constructed on the opposite bank of the river. For this purpose, ground had been purchased at a low rate, and it was to have been sold again at a high profit for the purpose of building, so that by this speculation the expenses attending the enterprise would have been considerably diminished. The winter docks would have been capable of admitting three-deck ships with all their guns on board, and covered dry docks were to have been constructed for laying up vessels in time of peace.

"The scheme I had formed would have rendered Antwerp a stupendous and colossean bulwark. It would have been a whole province in itself. This scheme was one of the causes of my exile to St. Helena. The demand for the cession of Antwerp was one of the circumstances which led me to reject the conditions of peace proposed at Chatillon. At that period I had doubtless many resources and chances, but still, how much may be said in favor of the resolution I adopted! I did right in refusing to sign the ultimatum, and I fully explained my reasons for that refusal. Therefore, even here, on this rock, amid all my misery, I have nothing to repent of. I am aware that few will understand me; but, in spite of the fatal turn of events; even the common mass of mankind must now be convinced that duty and honor left me no other alternative.

"If the Allies had thus far succeeded in degrading me, would they have stopped there? Were their offers of reconciliation and peace sincere? I knew them too well to put faith in their professions. Would they not have availed themselves of the immense advantages afforded them by the treaty to finish by intrigue what they had commenced by force of arms? Then where would have been the safety, independence, and future welfare of France? Where would have been my honor, my vows? Would not the Allies have ruined me in the estimation of the people as effectually as they ruined me on the field of battle? They would have found public opinion too ready to receive the impression which it would have been their aim to give to it. How would France have reproached me for suffering foreigners to parcel out the territory that had been intrusted to my care! How many faults would have been attributed to me by the unjust and the unfortunate! Could the French people, full of the recollections of their glory, have patiently endured the burdens that would have inevitably been imposed on them? Hence would have arisen fresh commotions, anarchy, and desolation. I preferred risking the last chances of battle, determining to abdicate in case of necessity."

"I acknowledge the justness of your observations, sire," replied Las Casas. "You have lost the throne, it is true, but voluntarily, and because you preferred to renounce it rather than compromise our welfare and your own honor. History will appreciate this sublime sacrifice. Power and life are transitory, but glory endures and is immortal."

"But, after all," said the Emperor, "the historian will perhaps find it difficult to do me justice, since the world is so overwhelmed with libels and falsehoods; my actions have been so darkened and misunderstood."

"Doubt can only exist during life, sire," replied Las Casas. "Injustice will be confined solely to your contemporaries. As you have already remarked, the clouds will disperse in proportion as your memory advances in posterity; and though the first catastrophe might have proved fatal to your memory, owing to the outcry that was then raised against you, yet the prodigies of your return, the acts of your brief government, and your exile to St. Helena, now leave you crowned with glory in the eyes of nations and of futurity."

"That is very true," replied the Emperor, with an air of satisfaction; "and my fate may be said to be the very opposite of others. A fall usually has the effect of lowering a man's character; but my fall, on the contrary, has elevated me prodigiously. Every succeeding day divests me of some portion of my tyrant's skin."

During the day the Emperor held a long conversation with Dr. O'Meara. The doctor inquired of the Emperor his reasons for encouraging the Jews so much.

"I wanted," he replied, "to make them leave off usury, and become like other men. There were a great many Jews in the countries I reigned over. By removing their disabilities, and by putting them upon an equality with Catholics, Protestants, and others, I hoped to make them become good citizens, and conduct themselves like the rest of the community. I believe that I should have succeeded in the end. My reasoning with them was, that as their rabbis explained to them that they ought not to practice usury against their own tribes, but were allowed to practice it with Christians and others; therefore, as I had restored them to all their privileges, and made them equal to my other subjects, they must consider me, like Solomon or Herod, to be the head of their nation, and my subjects as brethren of a tribe similar to theirs; that, consequently, they were not permitted to deal usuriously with them or me, but to treat us as if we were of the tribe of Judah; that, enjoying similar privileges to my other subjects, they were, in like manner, to pay taxes, and submit to the laws of conscription, and to other laws. By this I gained many soldiers. Besides, I should have drawn great wealth to France, as the Jews are very numerous, and would have flocked to a country where they enjoyed such superior privileges.

"Moreover, I wanted to establish a universal liberty of conscience. My system was to have no predominant religion, but to allow perfect liberty of conscience and of thought—to make all men equal, whether Protestants, Catholics, Mohammedans, Deists, or others, so that their religion should have no influence in getting them employments under government; in fact, that it should neither be the means of serving nor of injuring them, and that no objections should be made to a man's getting a situation on the score of religion, provided he were fit for it in other respects.

"I made every thing independent of religion. All the tribunals were so. Marriages were independent of the priests; even the burying-grounds were not left at their disposal, as they could not refuse interment to the body of any person of whatsoever religion. My intention was to render every thing belonging to the state and the Constitution purely civil, without reference to any religion. I wished to deprive the priests of all influence and power in civil affairs, and to oblige them to confine themselves to their own spiritual matters, and meddle with nothing else."

"I asked," says Dr. O'Meara, "if uncles and nieces had not a right to marry in France."

"He replied, 'Yes, but they must obtain a special permission.'

"I asked if the permission were to be granted by the Pope.

"'By the Pope!' said he, catching me by the ear, and smiling; 'no; I tell you that neither the Pope nor any of his priests had power to grant any thing—by the sovereign.'"

O'Meara asked some questions relative to the freemasons, and his opinions concerning them.

"A set of imbeciles," said the Emperor, "who meet to make merry, *à faire bonne chère*, and perform some ridiculous fooleries. However, they do some good actions. They assisted in the Revolution, and latterly to diminish the power of the Pope and the influence of the clergy. When the sentiments of a people are against the government, every society has a tendency to do mischief to it."

O'Meara then asked if the freemasons on the Continent had any connection with the Illuminati.

"No," he replied; "that is a society altogether different, and in Germany is of a very dangerous nature."

O'Meara asked if he had not encouraged the freemasons.

"Rather so," he said, "for they fought against the Pope."

O'Meara then asked if the Emperor would ever have permitted the re-establishment of the Jesuits in France.

"Never," said he; "it is the most dangerous of societies, and has done more mischief than all the others. Their doctrine is, that their general is the sovereign of sovereigns, and master of the world; that all orders from him, however contrary to the laws, or however wicked, must be obeyed. Every act, however atrocious, committed by them pursuant to orders from their general at Rome, becomes, in their eyes, meritorious. No, no; I would never have allowed a society to exist in my dominions under the orders of a foreign general at Rome. In fact, I would not allow any friars. There were priests sufficient for those who wanted them, without having monasteries filled with a rabble who did nothing but gormandize, pray, and commit crimes."

O'Meara observed that it was to be feared the priests and the Jesuits would soon have great influence in France.

"Very likely," Napoleon replied. "The Bourbons are fanatics, and would willingly bring back both the Jesuits and the Inquisition. In reigns before mine, the Protestants were as badly treated as the Jews. They could not purchase land. I put them upon a level with the Catholics. They will now be trampled upon by the Bourbons, to whom they and every thing else liberal will always be objects of suspicion. The Emperor Alexander may allow them to enter his empire, because it is his policy to draw into his barbarous country men of information, whatsoever their sect may be, and, moreover, they are not to be much feared in Russia, because the religion is different."

November 3. The Emperor was extremely weak and depressed in spirits. Some anecdotes of Paris society were related, which he found quite amusing, and he became somewhat animated.

"The saloons of Paris," said he, "might be truly styled the infernal regions. They keep up a constant system of slander and calumny. They might with justice engage the constant attention of all the tribunals of correctional police in the capital."

He said a great deal respecting the inaptitude of the French to close a revolution or to adhere to any fixed order of things.

"The affair of Mallet," said he, jokingly, "might be called a miniature or caricature of my own return from the Isle of Elba. Mallet's absurd plot might have been truly regarded as a trick. A prisoner of state, an obscure individual, effected his own liberation, and, in his turn, imprisoned the prefect, and even the minister of police, those keepers of dungeons and detectors of plots, who suffered themselves to be caught in the snare like so many sheep. A prefect of Paris, the born sponsor of his department, and, moreover, a very devoted subject, readily lent himself to every plan for assembling a government that had no existence. Ministers appointed by the conspirators were engaged in making their round of visits, when those who nominated them were again safely lodged in prison. Finally, the inhabitants of the capital learned, in the morning, the sort of political debauch that had taken place during the night, without having been in the least disturbed by it.

"Such an extravagant attempt," continued the Emperor, "could never have produced any result. Even had it succeeded, it must have fallen of itself in the space of a few hours, and the victorious conspirators would have thought only of escaping from amid their success. I was, therefore, far less incensed at the attempt of the criminal than at the facility with which those who appeared most attached to me had been prevailed on to become his accomplices. On my arrival, each candidly related to me the details that concerned himself, which served to criminate all. They frankly avowed that they had been caught, and had for a moment placed full faith in my overthrow. They did not deny that, in the delirium of the moment, they had entered into the designs of the conspirators, and they rejoiced with me at their happy escape. Not one of them mentioned the slightest resistance or the least effort made to defend and perpetuate the existing government. This seemed never to have entered their heads. So accustomed were they to changes and revolutions, that all were perfectly resigned to the establishment of a new order of things. All, therefore, changed countenance, and manifested the utmost embarrassment when, in a resolute tone of voice, I said,

"'Well, gentlemen, it appears you thought my reign at an end. To that I have nothing to say. But where were your oaths to the King of Rome? What became of your principles and doctrines? You make me tremble for the future.'

"I found it necessary," the Emperor continued, "to make an example, were it only for the sake of putting weak men on their guard for the future, and judgment fell upon poor Frochot, the Prefect of the Police, who, I am sure, loved me well. Yet, at the mere request of one of these mountebank conspirators, instead of the resistance which his duty required—instead of manifesting a firm determination to perish at his post rather than yield, he very contentedly issued orders for preparing a place for the sitting of the new government! Indeed, the readiness with which the French people accommodate themselves to change is calculated to prolong vicissitudes, which no other nation but themselves could endure. Thus individuals of every party seem to be well convinced that all is not yet settled; and Europe shares this opinion, which is founded no less on our natural inconstancy and volatility than on the mass of events that have risen up during the last thirty years."

November 4. Speaking of the wonders of his life and the vicissitudes of his fortune, the Emperor remarked, "I ought to have died at Moscow, because at that time my military glory had experienced no reverse, and my political career was unexampled in the history of the world."

Observing that the countenance of Las Casas was not exactly expressive of assent, he said, "This is not your opinion? You do not think I ought to have closed my career at Moscow?"

"No, sire," was the reply, "for in that case history would have been deprived of the return from Elba—of the most generous and most heroic act that ever man performed—of the grandest and most sublime event that the world ever witnessed."

"Well," replied the Emperor, "there may be some truth in that. But what say you to Waterloo? Ought I not to have perished there?"

"Sire, if I have obtained pardon for Moscow," said Las Casas, "I do not see why I should not ask it for Waterloo. The future is beyond the will and the power of man. It is in the hands of God alone."

The Emperor then spoke of the different members of his family, the little assistance he had received from them, and the many embarrassments they had occasioned him. He particularly alluded to the mistaken notion they had conceived, that, being once placed at the head of a people, they should become identified with them, so as to prefer their sectional interests to those of the common country.

"This idea," said he, "might have originated in honorable feeling, but it was most erroneous and mischievous in its application. In their mistaken notions of independence, the members of my family sometimes seemed to consider their power as detached, forgetting that they were merely parts of a great whole, whose views and interests they should have aided instead of opposing; but, after all, they were very young and inexperienced, and were surrounded by snares, flatterers, and intriguers, with secret and evil designs. And yet, if we judge from analogy, what family, in similar circumstances, would have acted better? Every one is not qualified to be a statesman. That requires a combination of powers that does not often fall to the lot of one. In this respect, all my brothers were singularly situated; they possessed at once too much and too little talent. They felt themselves too strong to resign themselves blindly to a guiding counselor, and yet too weak to be left entirely to themselves; but, take them all in all, I have certainly good reason to be proud of my family.

"Joseph would have been an ornament to society in any country, and Lucien would have been an honor to any political assembly."

"Jerome, as he advanced in life, would have developed every qualification requisite in a sovereign."

"Louis would have been distinguished in any rank or condition in life."

"My sister Eliza was endowed with masculine powers of mind; she must have proved herself a philosopher in her adverse fortune."

"Caroline possessed great talents and capacity."

"Pauline, perhaps the most beautiful woman of her age, has been, and will continue to the end of her life, the most amiable creature in the world."

"As to my mother, she deserves all kind of veneration."

"How seldom is so numerous a family entitled to so much praise! Add to this that, setting aside the jarring of political opinions, we sincerely loved each other. For my part, I never ceased to cherish fraternal affection for them all, and I am convinced that in their hearts they felt the same sentiments toward me, and that, in case of need, they would have given me proof of it."

In the evening, after the Emperor had retired, all his suite assembled around his bed. He was cheerful and social, and entertained them with his rich and varied conversation for more than an hour.

November 5. The Emperor continued confined to his room. About two o'clock he sent for Las Casas. The Emperor had the celebrated Historical

PORTRAIT OF PAULINE, THE SISTER OF NAPOLEON.

Atlas of Las Casas in his hand, which he was earnestly studying. He remarked on the irregular distribution of land and sea. He paused for a time on the continent of Asia, and from the vast Pacific Ocean passed to the more contracted limits of the Atlantic. He started many questions relative to the variable and the trade winds, the monsoons of the Indian Ocean, the calm of the Pacific, and the hurricanes of the Antilles. He appeared much pleased with the scientific accuracy of the map, and said to Las Casas,

"Tables are of the highest use in assisting the mind to draw comparisons. They awaken and excite ideas. You have fallen on an excellent plan in thus making your tables of history and geography embrace all the remarkable circumstances and phenomena connected with these sciences."

During the course of the day Las Casas had some conversation with an English seaman, who had been a prisoner of war in France, and who had thus become an enthusiastic admirer of the Emperor. He related several anecdotes of events which had occurred under his observation, and which strikingly illustrated the character of Napoleon.

"We were treated," said the English seaman, "in the best possible manner. At Verdun, the depôt of the English prisoners of war, we enjoyed the

F F

same privileges as the inhabitants. Verdun is a very pleasant town, and we found provisions and wine exceedingly cheap. We were allowed to walk several miles beyond the town without asking permission. In short, we were so well protected against all sorts of vexations, that the general under whose command we were placed, having been guilty of some irregularities in his treatment of us, was ordered to Paris by the special command of Napoleon, and, from fear of the punishment which awaited him, he committed suicide.

" It once happened that we received orders to confine ourselves to our lodgings, and we were informed that we should not be allowed to quit them for several days. The reason assigned for this measure was that the Emperor intended to pass through Verdun, and that it was not thought safe to allow him to be surrounded by so many of the enemy's prisoners. Besides the disappointment of our curiosity, for we very much desired to see Napoleon, this order wounded our feelings exceedingly. Is it possible, we thought, that they distrust brave English seamen—that they confound us with assassins? But on the day of Napoleon's arrival, we were, to our surprise, informed that we were again at liberty, and that the Emperor very much disapproved of the order that had been given for our confinement. We eagerly thronged to see the Emperor, and he passed by us, unattended by any escort, with an air of perfect security, and even with an expression of kindness which quite delighted us. Our acclamations were no less sincere than those of the French themselves."

Among the prisoners in France there was an English gentleman by the name of Manning, who had been traveling for the sake of scientific investigation. He thought that he might possibly obtain his liberty by addressing a petition to Napoleon praying for permission to visit the interior of Africa. His friends laughed at his simplicity. But he turned the laugh against them, when, at the expiration of a few weeks, he informed them of the success of his application. This same Mr. Manning, as will hereafter be seen, after a peregrination of several years, touched at St. Helena on his return to Europe. He there found his benefactor, the Emperor of France, in sickness, poverty, and imprisonment.

CHAPTER XXXI.
1816, November. Continued.

Remarks on Russia—Contrast between Pitt and Fox—Monopolies—Wants of the French Navy—Remarks on the Imperial Government—Troubles in La Vendée—Remarks on Tragedy—Anecdotes—Remarks on Religion; on Instinct—Blucher—The Treatment of Soldiers—The Neapolitans—On Peace with England—Sir Sydney Smith—The Regeneration of Spain—Sir Hudson Lowe—Duplicity of the English Government.

November 6. The Emperor was much better, and received several visitors about the middle of the day. In the evening, in conversation with his friends, he resumed his geographical observations.

" He dwelt," says Las Casas, " particularly on Asia; on the situation of

Russia, and the facility with which the latter power might make an attempt on India, or even on China, and the alarm which she might therefore justly excite in the English. He calculated the number of troops which Russia might employ, their probable points of departure, the route they would be likely to pursue, and the wealth they would obtain in such an enterprise. On all these subjects he made the most curious and valuable remarks. I very much regret my inability to record them here, for my notes, in this instance, afford me only slight hints, and I can not trust to the accuracy of my memory in filling up the details."

"Russia," said the Emperor, "has a vast superiority over the rest of Europe in regard to the immense powers she can call up for the purpose of invasion, together with the physical advantages of her situation, under the pole, and backed by eternal bulwarks of ice, which, in case of need, will render her inaccessible. Russia can only be attacked during one third or one fourth of the year, while she can, throughout the whole twelve months, maintain attacks upon us. Her assailants must encounter the rigors and privations of a frigid climate and a barren soil, while her troops, pouring down upon us, would enjoy the fertility and charms of our southern region. To these physical circumstances may be added the advantage of an immense population, brave, hardy, devoted, and passive, including those numerous uncivilized hordes to whom privation and wandering are the natural state of existence.

"Who can avoid shuddering at the thought of such a vast mass, unassailable either on the flanks or in the rear, descending upon us with impunity—if triumphant, overwhelming every thing in its course; or, if defeated, retiring amid the cold and desolation, that may be called its forces of reserve, and possessing every facility of issuing forth again at a future opportunity! Is not this the head of the hydra, the Antæus of the fable, which can only be subdued by seizing it bodily, and stifling it in the embrace? But where is the Hercules to be found? France alone could think of such an achievement, and it must be confessed we made but an awkward attempt of it.

"Should there arise an Emperor of Russia, valiant, impetuous, and intelligent—in a word, a Czar with a beard on his chin" [this he pronounced very emphatically], "Europe is his own. He may commence his operations on the German territory, at one hundred leagues from the two capitals, Berlin and Vienna, whose sovereigns are his only obstacles. He secures the alliance of the one by force, and, with his aid, subdues the other by a single stroke. He then finds himself in the heart of Germany, amid the princes of the second rank, most of whom are either his relations or dependents. In the mean while, he may, should he think it necessary, throw a few firebrands across the Alps on the soil of Italy, ripe for explosion, and he may then march triumphantly to Paris to proclaim himself the new liberator. I know, if I were in such a situation, I would undertake to reach Calais in a given time and, by regular marching stations, there to become the master and arbiter of Europe."

Then, after a few moments' silence, he added, "Perhaps, my dear Las Casas, you may be tempted to say, as the minister of Pyrrhus said to his master, '*And after all, to what purpose?*' My answer is, to establish a new state of society, and to avert great misfortunes. This is a blessing which Europe expects and solicits. The old system is ended, and the new one is not consolidated, and will not be so until after long and furious convulsions."

The Emperor was again silent. After measuring with a pair of compasses the distances on the map, he said,

"Constantinople is, from its situation, calculated to be the centre and seat of universal dominion."

The names of Pitt and Fox were afterward mentioned. "Pitt," said the Emperor, "was the master of European policy. He held in his hand the moral fate of nations, but he made an ill use of his power. He kindled the fire of discord throughout the universe; and his name, like that of Erostratus, will be inscribed in history amid flames, lamentations,

THE EMPEROR CONTEMPLATING CONSTANTINOPLE.

and tears. The first sparks of our Revolution, then the resistance that was opposed to the national will, and, finally, the horrid crimes that ensued, all were his work. Twenty-five years of universal conflagration; the numerous coalitions that added fuel to the flame; the revolution and devastation of Europe; the bloodshed of nations; the frightful debt of England, by which all these horrors were maintained; the pestilential system of loans, by which the people of Europe are oppressed; the general discontent that now prevails—all must be attributed to Pitt. Posterity will brand him as a scourge; and the man so lauded in his own time will hereafter be regarded as the genius of evil. Not that I consider him to have been willfully atrocious, or doubt his having entertained the conviction that he was acting right. But St. Bartholomew had also its conscientious advocates. The Pope and cardinals celebrated it by a *Te Deum;* and we have no reason to doubt their having done so in sincerity. Such is the weakness of human reason and judgment!

"But that for which posterity will, above all, execrate the memory of Pitt, is the hateful school that he has left behind him; its insolent machiavelism, its profound immorality, its cold egotism, and its utter disregard of justice and human happiness. Whether it be the effect of admiration and gratitude, or the result of mere instinct and sympathy, Pitt is, and will continue to be, the idol of the European aristocracy. There was, indeed, a touch of the Sylla in his character. His system has kept the popular cause in check, and brought about the triumph of the patricians.

"As to Fox, one must not look for his model among the ancients. He is himself a model, and his principles will sooner or later rule the world. Certainly the death of Fox was one of the fatalities of my career. Had his life been prolonged, affairs would have taken a totally different turn. The cause of the people would have triumphed, and we should have established a new order of things in Europe."

Conversing with respect to the East India Company, "A company," said the Emperor, "places great advantages in the hands of a few individuals, who may attend very well to their own interests, while they neglect those of the mass. Thus every company soon degenerates into an oligarchy. It is always the friend of power, to which it is ready to lend every assistance. In this point of view, companies were exclusively suited to old times and old systems. Unrestricted commerce, on the contrary, is favorable to the interests of all classes. It excites the imagination and rouses the activity of a people. It is identical with equality, and naturally leads to independence. In this respect, it is most in unison with our modern system. After the treaty of Amiens, by which France regained her Indian possessions, I had this grand question discussed before me at great length. I heard both statesmen and commercial men, and my final opinion was in favor of free competition and against companies.

"Formerly only one kind of property was known, that which consisted in landed possessions. Afterward a second kind rose up, that of industry or manufactures, which is now in opposition to the first. Then arose a third, that which is derived from burdens levied on the people, and which, distributed by the neutral and impartial hands of government, might obviate the evils of monopoly on the part of the two others, intervene between them, and prevent them from coming into conflict.

"It is because men will not acknowledge this great revolution in property, because they persist in closing their eyes to these truths, that so many acts of folly are now committed, and that nations are exposed to so many disorders. The world has sustained a great shock, and it now seeks to return to a settled state. The whole cause of the universal agitation that at present prevails may be explained in a few words: the ship's cargo has been shifted, her ballast has been removed from the stem to the stern; hence are produced those violent oscillations which may occasion a wreck in the first storm, if obstinate efforts are made to work the vessel according to the usual method, and without obtaining a new balance."

Las Casas spoke of the wisdom and genius of M. de Suffren, who performed prodigies in India by overleaping all rules in naval tactics and trusting to his own genius.

"Oh!" exclaimed the Emperor, "why did not Suffren live till my time, or why did I not light on a man of his stamp! I would have made him our Nelson. I was constantly seeking for a man qualified to raise the character of the French navy, but I could never find one. There is in the navy a peculiarity, a technicality that impeded my conceptions. If I proposed a new idea, immediately Gantheaume, and the whole marine department, were up against me. 'Sire, that can not be.' 'Why not?' 'Sire, the winds do not admit of it.' Then objections were started respecting calms and currents, and I was obliged to stop short. How is it possible to maintain a discussion with those whose language we do not comprehend?

"How often, in the Council of State, have I reproached naval officers with taking an undue advantage of this circumstance! To hear them talk, one might have been led to suppose that it was necessary to be born in the navy to know any thing about it. Yet I have often told them that, had it been in my power to have performed a voyage to India with them, I should, on my return, have been as familiar with their profession as with the field of battle; but they could not credit this. They always repeated that no man could be a good sailor unless he was brought up to it from his cradle; and they at length prevailed on me to adopt a plan about which I long hesitated, namely, the enrollment of several thousand children from six to eight years of age.

"My resistance was vain. I was compelled to yield to the unanimous voice, while I assured those who urged me to this measure that I left all the responsibility with them. What was the result? It excited clamor and discontent on the part of the public, who turned the whole affair into ridicule, styling it the massacre of the innocents. Subsequently, De Winter, Verhuel, all the great naval commanders of the North, and others, assured me that from eighteen to twenty (the age for the conscription) was early enough to begin to learn the duties of a sailor. The Danes and Swedes employ their soldiers in the navy. With the Russians the fleet is but a portion of the army, which affords the invaluable advantage of keeping up a standing army, and for a twofold object.

"I had myself," added he, "planned something of the kind when I created my crews for men of war. But what obstacles had I to encounter, what prejudices to subdue, what perseverance was I obliged to exert, before I could succeed in clothing the sailors in uniform, forming them into regiments, and drilling them by military exercise! I was told that I should ruin all; and yet, can there be a greater advantage than for one country to possess both an army and a navy? The men, thus disciplined, were not worse sailors than the rest, while, at the same time, they were the best soldiers. They were, in case of need, prepared to serve as sailors, soldiers, pontooners, or artillerymen. If, instead of being thus opposed by obstacles, I had found in the navy a man capable of entering into my views and promoting my ideas, what importance might we not have obtained! But, during my reign, I never found a naval officer who could depart from the old routine, and strike out a new course. I was much attached to the navy. I admired the courage and patriotism of our seamen, but I never found, between them and me, an intermediate agent who could have brought them into operation in the way I wished."

November 7. Speaking of his imperial system, "It has been the means," said Napoleon, "of creating the most compact government, establishing the most rapid circulation in all its parts, and calling forth the most nervous efforts that have ever been witnessed; and nothing short of this would have enabled us to triumph over such numerous difficulties, and to achieve so many wonders. The organization of the prefectures, their operations, and the results they produced, were admirable. One and the same impulse was simultaneously communicated to more than forty millions of men, and by the help of those centres of local activity, the movement was no less rapid and energetic at the extremities than in the heart itself. Foreigners who visited France, and who were capable of observing and discerning, were filled with astonishment. To this uniformity of action over an immense extent of territory must be attributed those prodigious efforts and immense results which were acknowledged to have been hitherto inconceivable.

"The prefects, with their local authority and resources, were themselves emperors on a small scale. As their whole power proceeded from the main spring, of which they were the communicating channels; as their influence was not personal, but was derived from their temporary functions; as they had no connection with the district over which their jurisdiction extended, they presented all the advantages of the great absolute agents of the old system, without any of their disadvantages. It was necessary to create this power, for the force of circumstances had placed me in the situation of a dictator. It was requisite that all the filaments issuing from me should be in harmony with the first cause, or my system would have failed in its result. The net-work which I spread over the French territory required a violent tension and prodigious power of elasticity in order to make the terrible blows that were constantly leveled at us rebound to distant points. Thus most of the springs of my machinery were merely institutions connected with dictatorship and measures for warlike defense.

"When the moment should have arrived for slackening the reins, all my connecting filaments would have relaxed sympathetically, and we should then have proceeded to our peace establishments and local institutions. If we yet possessed none of these, it was because circumstances did not admit of them. Our immediate fall would have been the infallible consequence had we been provided with them at the outset. It must not be supposed that the nation was all at once prepared to make a proper use of her liberty. Both with respect to education and character, the bulk of the people were imbued with too many of the prejudices of past times. We were daily improving, but we had much yet to acquire. At the time of the revolutionary explosion, the patriots, generally speaking, were such by nature and by instinct. With them patriotism was an innate sentiment, a passion, a phrensy. Hence the effervescence, the extravagance, the fury that marked the period. But it is vain to attempt to naturalize and mature the modern system by blows or jumps. It must be implanted with education, and must take root with reason and conviction. This will infallibly take place in course of time, because modern principles are founded on natural truths.

"But the men of our time were eager for the possession of power, which they exercised with a domineering spirit, to say no worse; while, on the other hand, they were ready to become the slaves of those who were above them. We have always wavered between these two extremes. In the course of my journeys, I was often obliged to say to the high officers who were about my person, 'Pray let the prefect speak for himself.' If I went to some subdivision of a department, I then found it necessary to say to the prefect, 'Let the sub-prefect or the mayor make his reply.' So eager were all to eclipse each other, and so little did they perceive the advantage that might arise from direct communication with me. If I sent my great officers or ministers to preside at the electoral colleges, I always advised them not to get nominated as candidates for the Senate, as their seats were secured to them by other means, and I wished that they should resign the honor of the nomination to the principal individuals of the provinces; but they never conformed to my wishes.

"I granted enormous salaries to prefects and others; but, with regard to my liberality on this head, it is necessary to distinguish between what was systematic and what was incidental. The latter forced me to grant lucrative appointments; the former would ultimately have enabled me to obtain gratuitous services. At the first outset, when the object was to conciliate individuals, and to re-establish some kind of society and morality, liberal salaries, absolute fortunes were indispensable. But the result being obtained, and, in course of time, the natural order of things restored, my intention would have been to render almost all high public duties gratuitous. I would have discarded those needy individuals, who can not be their own masters, and whose urgent wants engender political immorality. I would have wrought such a change in opinion that public posts should have been sought after for the mere honor of filling them. The functions of magistrate or justice of the peace would have been discharged by men of fortune, who, being guided solely by duty, philanthropy, and honorable ambition, would have afforded the surest pledge of independence. It is this that constitutes the dignity and majesty of a nation, that exalts her character, and establishes public morals. Such a change had become indispensable in France, and the dislike of getting into place might have been considered the forerunner of our return to political morality.

"I have been informed that the mania of place-hunting has crossed the sea, and that the contagion has been communicated to our neighbors. The English of former days were as much superior to this kind of meanness as the people of the United States now are. The love of place is the greatest injury to public morals. A man who solicits a public post feels his independence sold beforehand. In England, the greatest families, the whole peerage, disdain not to hunt after places. Their excuse is, that the enormous burdens of taxation deprive them of the means of living without additions to their income. Pitiful pretense! It is because their principles are more decayed than their fortunes. When people of a certain rank stoop to solicit public posts for the sake of emolument, there is an end to all independence and dignity of national character.

"In France, the shocks and commotions of our revolutions might have afforded an apology for such conduct. All had been unsettled, and all felt the necessity of re-establishing themselves. To promote this object with the least possible offense to delicacy of feeling, I was induced to attach considerable emolument and high honor to all public posts; but, in course of time, I intended to work a change by the mere force of opinion. And this was by no means impossible. Every thing must yield to the influence of power when it is directed to objects truly just, honorable, and great.

"I was preparing a happy reign for my son. For his sake I was rearing in the new school the numerous class of auditors of the Council of State. Their education being completed, they would, on attaining the proper age, have filled all the public posts in the empire, thus confirmed in modern principles, and improved by the example of their predecessors. They would all have been twelve or fifteen years older than my son, who would by this means have been placed between two generations and all their advantages—maturity, experience, and prudence above him, youth, promptitude, and activity below him."

"Sire," said Las Casas, "I can not refrain from expressing my astonishment that you should never have thrown out a hint of the grand and important objects you had in contemplation."

"What would have been the benefit of promulgating my intentions?" replied the Emperor. "I should have been styled a quack, accused of insinuation and subtilty, and have fallen into discredit. Situated as I was, deprived of hereditary authority, and of the illusion called legitimacy, I was compelled to avoid entering the lists with my opponents. I was obliged to be bold, imperious, and decisive. You have told me that in your faubourg they used to say, '*Why is he not legitimate?*' If I had been so, I certainly could not have done more than I did, but my conduct might have appeared more amiable."

November 8. The Emperor dictated to one of his suite, the exertion of which seemed to have roused his spirits so much that he was in a very social mood. The troubles of La Vendée, and the men who were distinguished in them, formed the principal topics of discourse. Charette was the only individual to whom the Emperor attached particular importance. Pacing the floor of his narrow chamber, he said,

"I have read a history of La Vendée, and, if the details and portraits were correct, Charette was the only great character, the true hero of that remarkable episode of our Revolution, which, if it presented great misfortunes, at least did not sacrifice our glory. In the wars of La Vendée, Frenchmen destroyed each other, but they did not degrade themselves. They received aid from foreigners, but they did not stoop to the disgrace of marching under their banners, and receiving daily pay for merely executing their commands. Yes, Charette impressed me with the idea of a great character."

"Charette," said Las Casas, "very much astonished those who had been acquainted with him by his brilliant exploits. It is true that, when he began to rise into celebrity, we recollected a circumstance which certainly indicated decision of character. When he was first called into service, during the American war, and while yet a mere youth, he sailed out of Brest on board a cutter during the winter. The cutter lost her mast, and, to a vessel of that description, such an accident was equivalent to certain destruction. The weather was very stormy. Death seemed inevitable; and the sailors, throwing themselves on their knees, lost all presence of mind, and refused to make any effort to save themselves. Charette, notwithstanding his extreme youth, killed one of the men in order to compel the rest to make the necessary exertions. This dreadful example had the desired effect, and the vessel was saved."

"You see," said the Emperor, "true decision of character always develops itself under critical circumstances. Here was the spark that distinguished the hero of La Vendée. Men's dispositions are often misunderstood. There are sleepers whose waking is terrible. Kleber was an habitual slumberer, but, at the needful moment, he never failed to awake like a lion."

"The vessel of Charette," said Las Casas, "at one time, during a long, dark night in December, was entangled among ridges, and, being deprived of her mast and all nautical aid, she sailed on at hazard, and the crew had resigned themselves to the will of fate, when they unexpectedly heard the ringing of a bell. They sounded, and, finding but little depth of water, they cast anchor. What was their surprise and joy, at daybreak, on finding themselves at the mouth of the River Landerneau! The bell they had heard was that of the neighboring parish church. The vessel had been carried through the narrow inlet of the port, miraculously escaping the numerous sandbanks about the entrance of Brest, and had found a calm station at the mouth of the river."

"This," said the Emperor, "shows the difference between the blindfold efforts of man and the certain course of nature. That at which you express so much surprise must necessarily have happened. It is very probable that, with the full power of exerting the utmost skill, the confusion and errors of the moment would have occasioned the wreck of the vessel; whereas, in spite of so many adverse chances, nature saved her. She was borne onward by the tide, the force of the current carried her precisely through the middle of each channel, so that she could not possibly have been lost.

"I was withdrawn from the army of the Alps," continued the Emperor, "for the purpose of being transferred to La Vendée, but I preferred resigning my commission to entering a service where I conceived I should only be concurring in mischief without the probability of obtaining any personal benefit. One of the first acts of my Consulate was to quell the troubles in La Vendée. I did much for that unfortunate department, the inhabitants of which were very grateful to me; and when I passed through it, even the priests appeared sincerely favorable to me. Thus the late insurrections did not present the same character as the first. Their prominent feature was not blind fanaticism, but merely passive obedience to a ruling aristocracy. Lamarque, whom I sent there at the height of the crisis, performed wonders, and even surpassed my hopes."

"The Emperor," says Las Casas, "dined with us to-day for the first time since his illness, that is to say, for the space of sixteen days. Our dinner was therefore a sort of fête. But we could not help remarking, with regret, the change in the Emperor's countenance, which presented obvious traces of the ill effects of his long confinement. After dinner we resumed our readings, which we had so long suspended. The Emperor read the Agamemnon. We were particularly struck with the graduation of terror which characterizes the productions of this father of tragedy. Agamemnon being ended, the Emperor asked for the Œdipus of Sophocles, which also interested us exceedingly; and the Emperor expressed his regret at not having had it performed at St. Cloud. Talma has always opposed the idea, but the Emperor was sorry that he had relinquished it."

"Not," said he, "that I wished to correct our drama by antique models. Heaven forbid! But I merely wished to have opportunity of judging how far ancient composition would have harmonized with modern notions. Voltaire's Œdipus contains the finest scene in the French drama. As to its faults, they must not be attributed to the poet, but to the manners of the age and the great actresses of the day, to whose laws a dramatic writer is forced to submit. I am surprised that the Romans should have no tragedies; but then tragedy in dramatic representation would have been ill calculated to rouse the feelings of the Romans, since they performed real tragedy in their circuses. The combats of the gladiators—the sight of men consigned to the fury of wild beasts—were far more terrible than all our dramatic horrors put together. These, in fact, were the only tragedies suited to the iron nerves of the Romans."

Under this date Dr. O'Meara makes the following record:

"Napoleon asked me many anatomical and physiological questions, and observed that he had studied anatomy himself for a few days, but had been sickened by the sight of some bodies that were opened, and abandoned any further progress in that science. After some development of his ideas touching the soul, I made a few remarks upon the Poles who had served in his army, who, I observed, were greatly attached to his person.

"'Ah!' replied the Emperor, 'they *were* much attached to me. The present viceroy of Poland was with me in my campaigns in Egypt. I made him a general. Most of my old Polish guard are now, through policy, employed by Alexander. They are a brave nation, and make good soldiers. In the cold which prevails in the northern countries, the Pole is better than the Frenchman.'

"I asked him if, in less rigorous climates, the Poles were as good soldiers as the French.

"'Oh no, no,' he replied; 'in other places the Frenchman is superior. The commandant at Dantzic informed me that, during the severity of the winter, when the thermometer sunk eighteen degrees, it was impossible to make the French soldiers keep their posts as sentinels, while the Poles suffered nothing. Poniatowsky,' continued he, 'was a noble character, full of honor and bravery. It was my intention to have made him King of Poland, had I succeeded in Russia.'

"I asked to what he principally attributed his failure in that expedition.

"'To the cold, the premature cold, and the burning of Moscow,' replied Napoleon. 'I was a few days too late. I had made a calculation of the weather for fifty years before, and the extreme cold had never commenced until about the 20th of December—twenty days later than it began this time. While I was at Moscow, the cold was at three of the thermometer, and was such as the French could with pleasure bear; but on the march, the thermometer sunk eighteen degrees, and consequently nearly all the horses perished. In one night I lost thirty thousand. The artillery, of which I had five hundred pieces, was in a great measure obliged to be abandoned. Neither ammunition nor provisions could be carried. We could not, through the want of horses, make a *reconnaissance*, or send out an advance of men on horseback to discover the way.

"'The soldiers lost their spirits and their senses, and fell into confusion. The most trifling circumstance alarmed them. Four or five men were sufficient to terrify a whole battalion. Instead of keeping together, they wandered about in search of fire. Parties, when sent out on duty in advance, abandoned their posts, and went to seek the means of warming themselves in the houses. They separated in all directions, became helpless, and fell an easy prey to the enemy. Others lay down, fell asleep, a little blood came from their nostrils, and, sleeping, they died. In this manner thousands perished. The Poles saved some of their artillery, but the French, and the soldiers of the other nations, were no longer the same men. In particular, the cavalry suffered. Out of forty thousand, I do not think that three thousand were saved.

"'Had it not been for that fire at Moscow, I should have succeeded. I would have wintered there. There were in that city about forty thousand citizens who were in a manner slaves, for you must know that the Russian nobility keep their vassals in a sort of slavery. I would have proclaimed liberty to all the slaves in Russia, and abolished vassalage and nobility. This would have procured me the union of an immense and a powerful party. I would either have made peace at Moscow, or else I would have marched the next year to Petersburg. Alexander was assured of it, and sent his diamonds, valuables, and ships to England. Had it not been for that fire, I should have succeeded in every thing. Two days before, I beat them in a great action at Moskwa; I attacked the Russian army of two hundred and fifty thousand strong, intrenched up to their necks, with ninety thousand, and totally defeated them. Seventy thousand Russians lay upon the field.

"'They had the impudence to say that they had gained the battle, although I marched into Moscow two days after. I was in the midst of a fine city, provisioned for a year; for in Russia they always lay in provisions for several months before the frost sets in. Stores of all kinds were in plenty.

The houses of the inhabitants were well provided, and many had even left their servants to attend upon us. In most of them there was a note left by the proprietor, begging of the French officers who took possession to be careful of their furniture and other effects; that they had left every article necessary for our wants, and hoped to return in a few days, when the Emperor Alexander had accommodated matters, at which time they would be happy to see us. Many ladies remained behind. They knew that I had been in Berlin and Vienna with my armies, and that no injury had been done to the inhabitants; and, moreover, they expected a speedy peace. We were in hopes of enjoying ourselves in winter-quarters, with every prospect of success in the spring.

" 'Two days after our arrival, a fire was discovered, which at first was not supposed to be alarming, but to have been caused by the soldiers kindling their fires too near to the houses, which were chiefly of wood. I was angry at this, and issued very strict orders on the subject to the commandants of regiments and others. The next day it had increased, but still not so as to give serious alarm. However, afraid that it might gain upon us, I went out on horseback, and gave every direction to extinguish it. The next morning a violent wind arose, and the fire spread with the greatest rapidity. Some hundred miscreants, hired for that purpose, dispersed themselves in different parts of the town, and with matches, which they concealed under their cloaks, set fire to as many houses to windward as they could, which was easily done, in consequence of the combustible materials of which they were built. This, together with the violence of the wind, rendered every effort to extinguish the fire ineffectual. I myself narrowly escaped with life.

" 'In order to show an example, I ventured into the midst of the flames, and had my hair and eyebrows singed, and my clothes burned off my back; but it was in vain, as they had destroyed most of the pumps, of which there were above a thousand; out of all these, I believe that we could only find one that was serviceable. Besides, the wretches that had been hired by Rostopchin ran about in every quarter, disseminating fire with their matches, in which they were but too much assisted by the wind.

" 'This terrible conflagration ruined every thing. I was prepared for all but this. It was unforeseen, for who would have thought that a nation would have set its capital on fire? The inhabitants themselves, however, did all they could to extinguish it, and several of them perished in their endeavors. They also brought before us numbers of the incendiaries with their matches, as amid such a populace we never could have discovered them ourselves. I caused about two hundred of these wretches to be shot.

" 'Had it not been for this fatal fire, I possessed every thing my army wanted: excellent winter-quarters; stores of all kinds were in plenty; and the next year would have decided it. Alexander would have made peace, or I would have been in Petersburg.'

"I asked if he thought that he could entirely subdue Russia.

" 'No,' replied Napoleon; 'but I would have caused Russia to make such a peace as suited the interests of France. I was five days too late in quitting Moscow. Several of the generals were burned out of their beds. I myself remained in the Kremlin until surrounded by flames. The fire advanced, seized the Chinese and India warehouses, and several stores of oil and spirits, which burst forth in flames and overwhelmed every thing. I then retired to a country-house of the Emperor Alexander, distant about a league from Moscow, and you may figure to yourself the intensity of the fire when I tell you that you could scarcely bear your hands upon the walls or the windows on the side next to Moscow, in consequence of their heated state. It was the spectacle of a sea and billows of fire, a sky and clouds of flame; mountains of red rolling flames, like immense waves of the sea, alternately bursting forth and elevating themselves to skies of fire, and then sinking into the ocean of flame below. Oh, it was the most grand, the most sublime, and the most terrific sight the world ever beheld! *Allons, docteur.*"*

November 9. To-day the Emperor felt himself infinitely better. He was surrounded by all his suite, and began to talk of the prodigies of his early career. "They must," said he, "have produced a great impression in the world."

"So great an impression," said Las Casas, "that some were induced to regard them as supernatural. At the time of the explosion of the infernal machine, a person who had just heard the news called at a house in a certain quarter of the capital, and hastily entering the drawing-room, in which a party was assembled, he informed the company that Napoleon was no more; and after giving an account of the event that had just taken place, he concluded by saying, 'He is fairly blown up.'

"'He blown up!' exclaimed an old Austrian officer, who had eagerly listened to all that was said, and who had been witness to many of the dangers

THE INFERNAL MACHINE.

* This was Napoleon's general expression when he wished the doctor to retire.

which the young general of the army of Italy had so miraculously escaped; 'he blown up! Ah! you know a great deal about it. I venture to say that he is, at this very moment, as well as any of us. I know him and all his tricks of old.'"

The name of Madam Regnault having been mentioned, some one remarked that she had evinced much attachment for the Emperor during his stay at the Isle of Elba.

"How! She?" exclaimed the Emperor, with mingled surprise and satisfaction.

"Yes, sire."

"Poor lady!" said he, in a tone of deep regret; "and yet how ill I treated her! Well, this at least repays me for the ingratitude of those sycophants on whom I lavished so many favors." Then, after a few moments' silence, he said, "It is very certain that one can never know people's characters and sentiments until after great trials."

At dinner the Emperor was very good-humored and cheerful. He congratulated himself on having got through his late illness without paying tribute to the doctor.

"At this," said he, "the doctor has been very much vexed. He would have been content with ever so little. He only asked for compliance with form, like a priest in confession." The Emperor laughed, and added, "Out of complaisance, I made trial of a gargle, but its strong acidity disagreed with me. Mild medicines are best suited to my constitution. Gentle remedies, whether physical or moral, are the only ones that take effect on me."

In conversation with Dr. O'Meara, the subject of religion was introduced.

"There are so many different religions," said the Emperor, "or modifications of them, that it is difficult to know which to choose. If one religion had existed from the beginning of the world, I would think that the true one. As it is, I am of opinion that every person ought to continue in the religion in which he was brought up—in that of his fathers. What are you?"

"A Protestant," O'Meara replied.

"Was your father so?"

"Yes, sire."

"Then continue in that belief. In France I received Catholics and Protestants alike at my levee. I paid their ministers alike. I gave the Protestants a fine church at Paris, which had formerly belonged to the Jesuits. In order to prevent any religious quarrels in places where there were both Catholic and Protestant churches, I prohibited them from tolling the bells to summon the people to worship in their respective churches unless the ministers of the one and the other made a specific request for permission to do so, and stating that it was at the desire and request of the members of each religion. Permission was then given for a year, and if, at the expiration of that year, the demand was not renewed by both parties again, it was not continued. By these means I prevented the squabbles which had previously existed, as the Catholic priests found that they could not have their own bells tolled unless the Protestants had a similar privilege.

"There is a link between animals and the Deity. Man," added he, "is merely a more perfect animal than the rest. He reasons better. But how do we know that animals have not a language of their own? My opinion is that it is presumption in us to say no, because we do not understand them. A horse has memory, knowledge, and love. He knows his master from the servants, though the latter are more constantly with him. I had a horse myself who knew me from any other person, and manifested, by capering and proudly marching, with his head erect, when I was on his back, his knowledge that he bore a person superior to the others by whom he was surrounded. Neither would he allow any other person to mount him except one groom, who constantly took care of him, and, when ridden by him, his motions were far different, and such as seemed to say that he was conscious he bore an inferior. When I lost my way, I was accustomed to throw the reins down his neck, and he always discovered it in places where I, with all my observation and boasted superior knowledge, could not. Who can deny the sagacity of dogs? There is a link between all animals. Plants are so many animals who eat and drink, and there are gradations up to man, who is only the most perfect of them all. The same spirit animates them all in a greater or a lesser degree."

O'Meara asked some questions about Blucher.

"Blucher," said he, "is a very brave soldier. He is like a bull who shuts his eyes, and, seeing no danger, rushes on. He committed a thousand faults, and, had it not been for circumstances, I could repeatedly have made him and the greatest part of his army prisoners. He is stubborn and indefatigable, afraid of nothing, and very much attached to his country; but, as a general, he is without talent. I recollect that, when I was in Prussia, he dined at my table after he had surrendered, and he was then considered to be an ordinary character."

Speaking about the English soldiers, he observed, "The English soldier is brave, nobody more so, and the officers generally men of honor, but I do not think them yet capable of executing grand maneuvers. I think that if I were at the head of them, I could make them do any thing. However, I know them not enough yet to speak decidedly. I had a conversation with Bingham about it; and, although he is of a different opinion, I would alter your system. Instead of the lash, I would lead them by the stimulus of honor. I would instill a degree of emulation into their minds. I would promote every deserving soldier, as I did in France. After an action, I assembled the officers and soldiers, and asked, 'Who have acquitted themselves best? *Quels sont les braves?*' and promoted such of them as were capable of reading and writing. Those who were not, I ordered to study five hours a day until they had learned a sufficiency, and then promoted them.

"What might not be expected from the English army, if every soldier hoped to be made a general if he behaved well? Bingham says, however, that the greatest part of your soldiers are brutes, and must be driven by the stick; but surely the English soldiers must be possessed of sentiments sufficient to put them at least upon a level with the soldiers of other nations, where the degrading system of the lash is not used.

"Whatever debases man can not be serviceable. Bingham says that none but the dregs of the people voluntarily enter as soldiers. This disgraceful punishment is the cause of it. I would remove it, and make even the situation of a private soldier be considered as conferring honor upon the individual who bore it. I would act as I did in France. I would encourage young men of education, the sons of merchants, gentlemen, and others, to enter as private soldiers, and promote them according to their merits. I would substitute confinement, bread and water, the contempt of his comrades, and such other punishments, for the lash. When a soldier has been debased and dishonored by stripes, he cares but little for the glory or the honor of his country.

"What honor can a man possibly have who is flogged before his comrades? He loses all feeling, and would as soon fight against as for his country, if he were better paid by the opposite party. When the Austrians had possession of Italy, they in vain attempted to make soldiers of the Italians. They either deserted as fast as they raised them, or else, when compelled to advance against an enemy, they ran away on the first fire. It was impossible to keep together a single regiment. When I got Italy, and began to raise soldiers, the Austrians laughed at me, and said that it was in vain; that they had been trying for a long time, and that it was not in the nature of the Italians to fight or to make good soldiers. Notwithstanding this, I raised many thousands of Italians, who fought with a bravery equal to the French,

NAPOLEON AT MONTEREAU.

and did not desert me even in my adversity. What was the cause? I abolished flogging and the stick, which the Austrians had adopted. I promoted those among the soldiers who had talents, and made many of them generals. I substituted honor and emulation for terror and the lash."

The soldiers considered the Emperor as their *comrade*. He mingled with them freely, addressed them in terms of friendly familiarity, and bore his full proportion of hardship and toil. In one of his last conflicts, at Montereau, he dismounted from his horse, and with his own hand directed a gun in several discharges.

"The Neapolitans," continued the Emperor, "are the most vile rabble in the world. Murat ruined me by advancing against the Austrians with them. When old Ferdinand heard of it, he laughed, and said, in his jargon, that they would serve Murat as they had done him before, when Championet dispersed a hundred thousand of them, like so many sheep, with ten thousand Frenchmen. I had forbidden Murat to act; for, after I returned from Elba, there was an understanding between the Emperor of Austria and me, that if I gave him up Italy, he would not join the coalition against me. This I had promised, and would have fulfilled it; but that *imbecile*, in spite of the direction I had given him to remain quiet, advanced with his rabble into Italy, where he was blown away like a puff.

"The Emperor of Austria, seeing this, concluded directly that it was by my orders, and that I deceived him, and being conscious that he had betrayed me himself before, supposed that I did not intend to keep faith with him, and determined to endeavor to crush me with all his forces. Twice Murat betrayed and ruined me. Before, when he forsook me, he joined the Allies with sixty thousand men, and obliged me to leave thirty thousand in Italy when I wanted them so much elsewhere. At that time his army was well officered by French. Had it not been for this rash step of Murat's, the Russians would have retreated, as their intentions were not to have advanced if Austria did not join the coalition; so that you would have been left to yourselves, and have gladly made a peace.

"I had always been willing," continued Napoleon, "to conclude a peace with England. Let your ministers say what they like, I was always ready to make a peace. At the time that Fox died there was every prospect of effecting one. If Lord Lauderdale had been sincere at first, it would also have been concluded. Before the campaign in Prussia, I caused it to be signified to him that he had better persuade his countrymen to make peace, as I would be master of Prussia in two months; for this reason, that although Russia and Prussia united might be able to oppose me, yet that Prussia alone could not; that the Russians were three months' march distant; and that, as I had intelligence that their plan of campaign was to defend Berlin, instead of retiring, in order to obtain the support of the Russians, I would destroy their army and take Berlin before the Russians came up, whom alone I would easily defeat afterward. I therefore advised him to take advantage of my offer of peace before Prussia, who was your best friend on the Continent, was destroyed. After this communication I believe that Lord Lauderdale was sincere, and that he wrote to your ministers recommending peace; but they would not agree to it, thinking that the King of Prussia was at the head of a hundred thousand men, that I might be defeated, and that a defeat would be my ruin. This was possible. A battle sometimes decides every thing, and sometimes the most trifling circumstance decides the fate of a battle. The event, however, proved that I was right; after Jena, Prussia was mine. After Tilsit and at Erfurth," continued he, "a letter containing proposals of peace to England, and signed by the Emperor and myself, was sent to your ministers, but they would not accept of them."

He spoke of Sir Sydney Smith. "Sydney Smith," said he, "is a brave officer. He displayed considerable ability in the treaty for the evacuation of Egypt by the French. He took advantage of the discontent which he found to prevail among the French troops at being so long away from France, and other circumstances. He also manifested great honor in sending immediately to Kleber the refusal of Lord Keith to ratify the treaty, which saved the French army; if he had kept it a secret for seven or eight days longer, Cairo would have been given up to the Turks, and the French army necessarily obliged to surrender to the English. He also showed great humanity and honor in all his proceedings toward the French who fell into his hands."

O'Meara asked if Sir Sydney had not displayed great talent and bravery at Acre.

"Yes," Napoleon replied. "The chief cause of the failure there was that he took all my battering train, which was on board of several small vessels. Had it not been for that, I would have taken Acre in spite of him. He behaved very bravely, and was well seconded by Philippeaux, a Frenchman of talent, who had studied with me as an engineer. There was a Major Douglas, also, who behaved very gallantly. The acquisition of five or six hundred seamen as cannoneers was a great advantage to the Turks, whose spirits they revived, and whom they showed how to defend the fortress. But he committed a great fault in making sorties, which cost the lives of two or three hundred brave fellows, without the possibility of success, for it was impossible he could succeed against the number of the French who were before Acre.

"I would lay a wager that he lost half of his crew in them. He dispersed proclamations among my troops, which certainly shook some of them, and I, in consequence, published an order stating that he was *mad*, and forbidding all communication with him. Some days after, he sent, by means of a flag of truce, a lieutenant or a midshipman with a letter containing a challenge to me to meet him at some place he pointed out, in order to fight a duel. I laughed at this, and sent him back an intimation that when he brought Marlborough to fight me, I would meet him. Notwithstanding this, I like the character of the man."

O'Meara remarked that the invasion of Spain had been a measure very destructive to the Emperor.

Napoleon replied, "If the government I established had remained, it would have been the best thing that ever happened for Spain. I would have regenerated the Spaniards. I would have made them a great nation. Instead of a feeble, imbecile, and superstitious race of Bourbons, I would have given them a new dynasty, that would have no claim on the nation except by the good it would have rendered unto it. For an hereditary race of asses, they would have had a monarch with ability to revive the nation, sunk under the yoke of superstition and ignorance. Perhaps it is better for France that I did not succeed, as Spain would have been a formidable rival. I would have destroyed superstition and priestcraft, and abolished the Inquisition and the monasteries of those lazy beasts of friars. I would, at least, have rendered the priests harmless. The guerrillas, who fought so bravely against me, now lament their success. When I was last in Paris, I had letters from Mina and many other leaders of the guerrillas, craving assistance to expel their *friar* from the throne."

Napoleon afterward made some observations relative to the governor, whose suspicious and mysterious conduct he contrasted with the open and undisguised manner in which Sir George Cockburn conducted himself.

"Though the admiral was severe and rough," said he, "yet he was incapable of a mean action. He had no atrocities in contemplation, and therefore made no mystery or secrecy of his conduct. Never have I suspected him of any sinister design. Although I might not like him, yet I could not despise him. I despise the other. As a jailer, the admiral was kind and humane, and we ought to be grateful to him; as our host, we have reason to be dissatisfied, and to complain of him. This jailer deprives life of every inducement to me. Were it not that it would be an act of cowardice, and that it would please your ministers, I would get rid of it. *Tengo la vita per la gloria.* There is more courage in supporting an existence like mine than in abandoning it. This governor has a double correspondence with your ministers, similar to that which all your embassadors maintain; one written so as to deceive the world, should they ever be called upon to publish it, and the other giving a true account, for themselves alone."

O'Meara observed that he believed all embassadors and other official persons, in all countries, wrote two accounts, one for the public, and the other containing matters which it might not be right to divulge.

"True, Sir Doctor," replied Napoleon, taking his ear in a good-humored manner, "but there is not so Machiavelian a ministry in the world as your own. *Cela tient à votre système.* That, and the liberty of your press, obliges your ministers to render some account to the nation, and therefore they want to be able to deceive the public in many instances. But as it is also necessary for them to know the truth *themselves*, they have a double correspondence; one official and false, calculated to gull the nation when published, or called for by the Parliament; the other private and true, to be kept locked up in their own possession, and not deposited in the archives. In this way they manage to make every thing appear as they wish to John Bull. Now this system of falsehood is not necessary in a country where there is no obligation to publish or to render an account. If the sovereign does not like to make known any transaction officially, he keeps it to himself, and gives no explanation; therefore there is no need of causing varnished accounts to be written in order to deceive the people. For these reasons, there are more falsifications in your official documents than in those of any other nation."

CHAPTER XXXII.
1816, November. Continued.

Dumouriez—Leopold—The Tuileries—Monarchies and Republics—Hostility of the English Ministry—Designs of the Emperor—The Reorganization of Italy—Causes of the Emperor's Downfall—Bernadotte—Wounds of the Emperor—Devotion of his Soldiers—The Return from Elba—Plans after Waterloo—Talleyrand—The Sword of Frederick—The Second Marriage—Anecdote—Dismissal of the Servant of Las Casas—Causes of Success—Alexander the Great—Cæsar—Hannibal—Frederick the Great—The Conscription—Lawyers—The Clergy.

November 10. During dinner the Emperor spoke of the campaign of Dumouriez in Champagne, which he had just been reading. He thought little of the Duke of Brunswick, who, with a plan of offensive operations, had advanced only eighteen leagues in forty days. But he very much blamed Dumouriez, whose position, he said, was far too hazardous.

"For me, this is saying a great deal," added he, "for I consider myself to have been the most venturous man in war that perhaps ever lived; yet I should certainly have been afraid to keep the position that Dumouriez retained, so numerous were the dangers it presented. I could only explain his maneuver on the supposition that he could not venture to retire. He would probably have encountered greater risks in retreating than in staying where he was. Wellington was placed in the same situation at Waterloo. The French are the bravest troops in the world. They will fight in whatever position they may be attacked, but they can not retreat before a victorious enemy. If they experience the least check, they lose all presence of mind and discipline; they slip through your fingers, as it were. Dumouriez, I suppose, calculated on this, or perhaps he might have been influenced by some secret negotiation of which we are ignorant."

The newspapers which were read mentioned the marriage of Prince Leopold of Saxe-Coburg to Princess Charlotte of Wales.

"Prince Leopold," said the Emperor, "once had a chance of becoming my aid-de-camp. He solicited the appointment, and I do not know what prevented him from obtaining it. However, it was lucky for him that his application proved unsuccessful. Had it been otherwise, his present marriage would never have taken place. Who can pretend to say what is fortunate or unfortunate in the events of human life?"

Referring again to Prince Leopold's petition to become his aid-de-camp, the Emperor remarked,

"A crowd of German princes solicited the same favor. When I established the Confederation of the Rhine, the sovereigns who were included in it took it for granted that I intended to revive in my person the etiquette and forms of the Holy Roman Empire; and all, even kings themselves, were eager to join my retinue. One wished to be appointed my cup-bearer, and another my grand butler. At this period the princes of Germany literally invaded the Tuileries; they crowded the saloons, and modestly mingled with the officers of my household. It was the same with Italians, Spaniards, and Portuguese. All the most exalted individuals in Europe were assembled at the Tuileries. The fact is, that during my reign Paris was in itself a nation, and the first in the world!"

November 11. The Emperor did not leave his chamber for the day. Las Casas spent nearly the whole day with him in continued conversation. Speaking of the elements of society, the Emperor said,

"Democracy may be furious, but it has some heart—it can be moved. As to aristocracy, it is always cold and unforgiving."

At another time he said, "All human institutions present two opposite points of view—all have their advantages and disadvantages; for example, both republican and monarchical government may be defended and opposed. Doubtless it is easy to prove in theory that both are equally good, and very good, but this is not quite so easy in application. The extreme boundary of the government of the many is anarchy; of a single one, it is despotism. A just medium between both is unquestionably the best, were it in the power of wisdom steadily to pursue such a course. These truths have been repeated, until they have become absolutely commonplace, without producing any result that is good. On this subject many volumes have been written, and many will still be written, without effect."

The Emperor at another moment said, "Despotism is not absolute, but merely relative. A man can not with impunity absorb all power in himself. If a sultan strike off the heads of his subjects according to the whim of the moment, he incurs the risk of losing his own by the same sort of caprice. Excess will always incline either to one side or the other. What the sea gains by encroachment in one direction, it loses elsewhere. When I was in Egypt, a conqueror, an absolute ruler and master, dictating laws to the people by mere orders of the day, I could not have presumed to search the houses, and it would have been out of my power to have prevented the inhabitants from speaking freely in their coffee-houses, where liberty and independence prevailed even in a greater degree than in Paris. The people yielded like slaves in all other places; but they were resolved to enjoy full liberty in their coffee-houses, which were absolutely the citadels of freedom, the bazars of public opinion. Here they loudly declaimed and passed judgment on the measures of the day. It would have been impossible to close their mouths. If I happened to enter these places, all bowed before me, it is true, but this was a mark of esteem to me personally. No such homage was shown to my lieutenants.

"France, when subject to the opposing influences of many, was on the point of falling beneath the blows of combined Europe. But she placed the helm in the hands of one, and immediately the First Consul laid down the law to Europe. Such is the power of unity and concentration. These are facts which must be convincing to the meanest understanding.

"It is curious to observe that the old cabinets of Europe were unable to conceive the importance of this change, and they continued to treat with unity and concentration, in the same manner that they had done with the multitude and dispersion. It is no less remarkable that the Emperor Paul, who was looked upon as a fool, was the first to appreciate this difference; while the English ministers, reputed to be so skillful and experienced, were the very last. 'I set aside the abstractions of your Revolution,' Paul wrote to me, 'I confine myself to a fact: in my eyes you are a government, and I address myself to you, because we can understand each other, and I can treat with you.'

"With regard to the English ministry, I was ever obliged to conquer and force peace, and absolutely to detach England from the rest of Europe, before I could get them to listen to me; and even when they opened negotiations with me, they followed all the traces of the old routine. They tried to divert my attention by delays, protocols, forms, ceremonies, precedents, and I know not what, but I felt myself so powerful that I could afford to laugh at all this.

"A new state of things required a new line of conduct, but the English ministers seemed to have no idea of the age, or of the men and things belonging to it. My manner quite disconcerted them. I commenced in diplomacy as I had already commenced in arms. 'These are my propositions,' said I to the English ministry. 'We are masters of Holland and Switzerland, but I am ready to resign both in return for the restitutions that you may make to us or our allies. We are also masters of Italy, of which I will surrender one portion and retain the other, for the purpose of guaranteeing the existence of all. These are my bases: you are free to build round them as much as you please. I care not for that; but the object and result must remain as I have specified. I will not yield a hair's breadth of my determination. My object is not to purchase concessions from you, but to enter into reasonable, honorable, and lasting engagements. This is the circle I have traced out. It appears to me that you have formed no notion of our respective situations or resources. I fear not your refusal, your efforts, nor any difficulties you may throw in my way. I have a strong arm, and I only want a weight to lift.'

"This unusual language produced the desired effect. In the negotiations of Amiens they had intended merely to divert us, but they now began to treat seriously. Not knowing at what point I was vulnerable, they offered to make me King of France. This was a good idea! *King by the grace of foreigners, when I was already sovereign by the will of the people!*

"Such was the ascendency I had acquired, that, even while the negotiations were pending, I got myself elected president of the Italian republic; and this circumstance, which, in the ordinary course of European diplomacy, would naturally have created so many obstacles, occasioned no interruption of the proceedings. Matters were brought to a conclusion, and I gained my point by plain dealing better than if I had fallen into all the usual diplomatic subtleties. Many libelous pamphlets, and manifestoes of no better character, accused me of perfidy and of breach of faith in my negotiations;

but I never merited these charges, which, on the contrary, might always have been justly applied to the other cabinets of Europe.

"At Amiens, I sincerely thought the fate of France, and Europe, and my own destiny were permanently fixed; I hoped that war was at an end. However, the English cabinet again kindled the flame. England is alone responsible for all the miseries by which Europe has since been assailed. For my own part, I intended to have devoted myself wholly to the internal interests of France, and I am confident I should have wrought miracles. I should have lost nothing in the scale of glory, and I should have achieved the moral conquest of Europe, which I was afterward on the point of accomplishing by force of arms. Of how much glory was I thus deprived!

"My enemies always spoke of my love of war, but was I not constantly engaged in self-defense? After every victory I gained, did I not immediately make proposals of peace? The fact is, I never was master of my own actions. I never was entirely myself. I might have conceived many plans, but I never had it in my power to execute any. I held the helm with a vigorous hand, but the fury of the waves was greater than any force I could exert in resisting them. I prudently yielded, rather than incur the risk of sinking through stubborn opposition. (I never was truly my own master, but was always controlled by the force of circumstances.) Thus, at the commencement of my rise, during the Consulate, my sincere friends and warm partisans frequently asked me, with the best intentions, and as a guide for their own conduct, *what point I was aiming at;* and I always answered that I did not know. They were surprised, probably dissatisfied, and yet I spoke the truth. Subsequently, during the Empire, when there was less familiarity, many faces seemed to put the same question to me, and I might still have given the same reply. I was not master of my actions, because I was not foolish enough to attempt to twist events into conformity with my system; on the contrary, I moulded my system according to the unforeseen succession of events. This often appeared like unsteadiness and inconsistency, and of these faults I was sometimes unjustly accused."

After alluding to some other subjects, the Emperor said, "One of my great plans was the rejoining, the concentration of those same geographical nations which have been disunited and parceled out by revolution and policy. There are dispersed in Europe upward of thirty millions of French, fifteen millions of Spaniards, fifteen millions of Italians, and thirty millions of Germans, and it was my intention to incorporate these several people each into one nation. It would have been a noble thing to have advanced into posterity with such a train, and attended by the blessings of future ages. I felt myself worthy of this glory!

"After this summary simplification, it would have been possible to indulge the chimera of the *beau idéal* of civilization. In this state of things, there would have been some chance of establishing in every country a unity of codes, of principles, of opinions, of sentiments, views, and interests. Then, perhaps, by the help of the universal diffusion of knowledge, one might have thought of attempting, in the great European family, the application of the

American Congress or the Amphictyons of Greece. What a perspective of power, grandeur, happiness, and prosperity would thus have appeared!

"The concentration of thirty or forty millions of Frenchmen was completed and perfected. That of fifteen millions of Spaniards was nearly accomplished. Because I did not subdue the Spaniards, it will henceforth be agreed that they were invincible, for nothing is more common than to convert accident into principle. But the fact is that they were actually conquered, and at the very moment when they escaped me, the Cortes of Cadiz were secretly in treaty with me. They were not delivered either by their own resistance or the efforts of the English, but by the reverses which I sustained at distant points, and, above all, by the error I committed in transferring my whole forces to the distance of a thousand leagues from them. Had it not been for this, the Spanish government would shortly have been consolidated, the public mind would have been tranquillized, and hostile parties would have been rallied together. Three or four years would have restored the Spaniards to profound peace and brilliant prosperity. They would have become a compact nation, and I should have well deserved their gratitude, for I should have saved them from the tyranny by which they are now oppressed, and the terrible agitations that await them.

"With regard to the fifteen millions of Italians, their concentration was already far advanced; it only wanted maturity. The people were daily becoming more firmly established in the unity of principles and legislation, and also in the unity of thought and feeling—that certain and infallible cement of human concentration. The union of Piedmont to France, and the junction of Parma, Tuscany, and Rome, were, in my mind, only temporary measures, intended merely to guarantee and promote the national education of the Italians. You may judge of the correctness of my views and of the influence of common laws. The portions of Italy that were united to France, though that union might have been regarded as the insult of invasion on our part, were, in spite of their Italian patriotism, the very places that continued most attached to us. Now that they are restored to themselves, they conceive that they have been invaded and disinherited, and so they certainly have been!*

"All the south of Europe, therefore, would soon have been rendered compact in point of locality, views, opinions, sentiments, and interests. In this state of things, what would have been the weight of all the nations of the

---

* The Emperor, in dictating his memoirs to Count Montholon, more fully unfolded his majestic designs in the following language:

"It was Napoleon's desire to raise up the Italian nation, and to reunite the Venetians, Milanese, Piedmontese, Genoese, Tuscans, Parmesans, Modenese, Romans, Neapolitans, Sicilians, and Sardinians in one independent nation, bounded by the Alps and the Adriatic, Ionian and Mediterranean Seas. Such was the immortal trophy he was raising to his glory. This great and powerful kingdom would have been, by land, a check to the house of Austria; while at sea its fleets, combined with those of Toulon, would have ruled the Mediterranean, and protected the old course of trade to India by the Red Sea and Suez. Rome, the capital of this state, was the Eternal City; covered by the three barriers of the Alps, the Po, and the Apennines; nearer than any other to the three great islands. But Napoleon had many obstacles to surmount. He said at the Council of Lyons, 'It will take me twenty years to establish the Italian nation.'"

North? What human efforts could have broken through so strong a barrier? The concentration of the Germans must have been effected more gradually, and therefore I had done no more than simplify their monstrous complication. Not that they were unprepared for concentralization; on the contrary, they were too well prepared for it, and they might have blindly risen in reaction against us before they had comprehended our designs. How happens it that no German prince has yet formed a just notion of the spirit of his nation, and turned it to good account? Certainly, if Heaven had made me a prince of Germany amid the critical events of our times, I should infallibly have governed the thirty millions of Germans combined; and from what I know of them, I think I may venture to affirm that, if they had once elected and proclaimed me, they would not have forsaken me, and I should never have been at St. Helena."

Then, after some melancholy details and comparisons, resuming the previous subject, he said,

"At all events, this concentration will be brought about, sooner or later, by the very force of events. The impulse is given, and I think that, since my fall, and the destruction of my system, no grand equilibrium can possibly be established in Europe except by the concentration and confederation of the principal nations. The sovereign who, in the first great conflict, shall sincerely embrace the cause of the people, will find himself at the head of all Europe, and may attempt whatever he pleases.

"It will perhaps be asked why I did not suffer these ideas to transpire? why I did not submit them to public discussion, since they would, doubtless, have become popular, and popularity would have been an immense re-enforcement to me? My answer is, that malevolence is ever more active than good intention; that at the present day the power of wit overrules good sense, and obscures the clearest points at will; and to have submitted these important points to public discussion would have been to consign them to the mercy of party spirit, passion, intrigue, and gossiping, while the infallible result would have been discredit and opposition. I conceived, therefore, that secrecy was the most advisable course. I surrounded myself with that halo of mystery which pleases and interests the multitude, gives birth to speculations which occupy the public mind, and finally affords opportunities for those sudden and brilliant disclosures which exercise such important influence. It was this very principle that accelerated my unfortunate march to Moscow. Had I been more deliberate, I might have averted every evil; but I could not delay and afford time for comment. With my career already traced out, with my ideas formed for the future, it was necessary that my movement and my success should seem, as it were, supernatural.

"I will name another occasion on which accident was taken for principle. I failed in my expedition against the Russians, and they therefore consider themselves invincible. But can any thing be more erroneous? Ask men of sense and reflection among them. Ask Alexander himself, and let him recollect the opinions he entertained at the time. Was I defeated by the efforts of the Russians? No; my failure must be attributed to pure accident, to absolute fatality. First, a capital was burned to the ground by foreign intriguers, in defiance of its inhabitants. Second, the frost set in with such unusual suddenness and severity that it was regarded as a kind of phenomenon. To these disasters must be added a mass of false reports, silly intrigues, treachery, and stupidity, and many things that will, perhaps, one day come to light, which will excuse or justify the two great errors I committed in diplomacy and war, namely, to have undertaken such an enterprise, leaving on my flanks, which soon became my rear, two cabinets of which I was not master, and two allied armies, who, on the least check, would become my enemies. But to come to a conclusion, and to annul with a word every charge that can be brought against me, I may say that this famous war, this bold enterprise, were perfectly involuntary on my part. I did not wish to give battle, neither did Alexander; but, being once in presence, circumstances urged us on, and Fate accomplished the rest."

After a few moments' silence, and as if waking from a reverie, the Emperor added, "A Frenchman (Bernadotte) had in his hands the fate of the world! If he had possessed judgment and spirit equal to the exalted situation in which he was placed, if he had been a good Swede, as he pretended he was, he might have restored the glory and power of his adopted country, have retaken Finland, and arrived at St. Petersburg before I reached Moscow. But he was swayed by personal considerations, silly vanity, and all sorts of mean passions. His head was turned when he saw that he, an old Jacobin, was courted and flattered by Legitimates—when he found himself face to face, holding political and friendly conferences with an emperor of all the Russias, who took great pains to cajole him. It is affirmed that hints were even thrown out to him of the possibility of his obtaining the hand of one of the sisters of the Russian Emperor by divorcing his wife; and in a letter addressed to him by a French prince, the writer remarked, with complacency, that Bearn was the cradle of both their houses. *The house of Bernadotte,* forsooth!

"Dazzled by his rise of fortune, he sacrificed both his adopted and his mother country, his true power, the cause of the people, and the welfare of Europe! For this he will pay dearly. No sooner had he accomplished all that was expected of him, than he began to feel what awaited him. It is said that he has repented of his conduct, but he has not yet expiated it. He is now the only upstart sovereign in Europe. The scandal can not remain unpunished. It would be too dangerous an example."

Dr. O'Meara records: "Napoleon showed me the marks of two wounds, one a very deep cicatrix above the left knee, which he said he had received in his first campaign of Italy, and was of so serious a nature that the surgeons were in doubt whether it might not be ultimately necessary to amputate. He observed that, when he was wounded, it was always kept a secret, in order not to discourage the soldiers. The other was on the toe, and had been received at Eckmühl.

"'At the siege of Acre,' continued the Emperor, 'a shell thrown by Sydney Smith fell at my feet. Two soldiers, who were close by, seized and closely embraced me, one in front and the other on one side, and made a rampart of their bodies for me against the effect of the shell, which exploded, and overwhelmed us with sand. We sunk into the hole formed by its

THE BOMB-SHELL.

bursting; one of them was wounded. I made them both officers. One has since lost a leg at Moscow, and commanded at Vincennes when I left Paris. When he was summoned by the Russians, he replied that, as soon as they sent him back the leg he had lost at Moscow, he would surrender the fortress.

"'Many times in my life,' continued he, 'have I been saved by my soldiers and officers throwing themselves before me when I was in the most imminent danger. At Arcola, when I was advancing, Colonel Muiron, my aid-de-camp, threw himself before me, covered me with his body, and received the wound which was destined for me. He fell at my feet, and his blood spouted up in my face. He gave his life to preserve mine. Never yet, I believe, has there been such devotion shown by soldiers as mine have manifested for me. In all my misfortunes, never has the soldier, even when expiring, been wanting to me; never has man been served more faithfully by his troops. With the last drop of blood gushing out of their veins, they exclaimed *Vive l'Empereur!*'"

O'Meara asked, if he had gained the battle of Waterloo, whether he would have agreed to the treaty of Paris.

Napoleon replied, "I would certainly have ratified it. I would not have made such a peace myself. Sooner than agree to much better terms, I abdicated before; but finding it already made, I would have kept it, because France had need of repose."

November 12. The conversation turned upon the Emperor's return from Elba, and his second fall at Waterloo.

"It is very certain," said the Emperor, "that during the events of 1815 I relinquished the anticipation of ultimate success. I lost my first confidence. Perhaps I found that I was wearing beyond the time of life at which Fortune usually proves favorable, or perhaps, in my own eyes, in my own imagination, the spell that had hung over my miraculous career was broken; but, at all events, I felt that something was wanting. Kind Fortune no longer followed my footsteps, and took pleasure in lavishing her smiles upon me. She was now succeeded by rigid Fate, who took ample revenge for the few favors I obtained, as it were by force. It is a remarkable fact, that every advantage I obtained at this period was immediately succeeded by a reverse.

"I marched through France, and arrived in the capital amid the enthusiasm and universal acclamations of the people. But no sooner had I reached Paris, than, by a sort of magic, and without any adequate motive, all around me retracted and grew cold. I had adduced plausible reasons for obtaining a sincere reconciliation with Austria, whither I had dispatched agents more or less acknowledged; but Murat was there with his fatal enterprise. It was concluded at Vienna that he was acting under my orders, and, measuring me by their own scale, they regarded my whole conduct as a complication of artifice, and determined to overreach me by counter-intrigue.

"The opening of my campaign was well managed, and proved successful. I should have surprised the enemy in detail but that a deserter from among our generals gave him timely notice of our plans. I gained the brilliant victory of Ligni, but my lieutenant robbed me of its fruits. Finally, I triumphed even at Waterloo, and was immediately hurled into the abyss. Yet I must confess that all these strokes of Fate distressed me more than they surprised me. I felt the presentiment of an unfortunate result. Not that this in any way influenced my determinations and measures, but the foreboding certainly haunted my mind."

The Emperor's first thought after the battle of Waterloo was to return to Paris. "At my command," said he, "the whole population would have risen. I should suddenly have found my forces recruited by the addition of one or two hundred thousand men. But the Allies, on retiring, might have burned the capital, and this disaster would have been accounted my work. It is true, the burning of Paris might have proved, in reality, the salvation of France, as the burning of Moscow was the salvation of Russia; but such sacrifices can only be made by the parties interested."

The second thought was to proceed to Italy, to form a junction with the viceroy. "But this," said Napoleon, "would have been a desperate course, without the chance of obtaining an adequate result. It would have removed the theatre of conflict to too remote a point. Public enthusiasm would have had time to subside, and we should no longer have been fighting in France, on whose sacred soil alone we could hope to work prodigies that had become indispensable."

He very much regretted having yielded in 1814, when in his position at

St. Dizier and Doulevant, to the various representations and suggestions by which he was assailed, and which induced him, against his inclination, to make a countermarch upon Paris.

"Here I wanted firmness," said he. "I should have followed up my intention of advancing to the Rhine, collecting re-enforcements from all the garrisons on my way, and exciting the rise of the peasantry; by this means I should soon have possessed an immense army. Murat would immediately have rejoined me; and he and the viceroy would have made me master of Vienna, if the Allies had presumed to deprive me of Paris. But no; the enemy would have shrunk from the dangers with which he would have been surrounded. The allied sovereigns would have regarded it as a favor to have been permitted to retire. The storm that assailed us would have subsided. Peace would have been concluded and sincerely maintained, for all were exhausted, all had wounds to heal!

"Abroad, war could no longer have been thought of; and at home, such a result must have had the effect of destroying all illusion, frustrating every evil design, and permanently blending the opinions, views, and interests of all parties. I should once more have seated myself triumphantly on the throne, surrounded by my invincible bands. The heroic and faithful portion of the people would have regulated those who had wavered, and the men who had shown themselves so eager for repose might have enjoyed it. A new generation of chiefs would have remoulded our character. Every effort would have been directed to the internal welfare of the country, and France would have been happy."

"The departure of the Empress from Paris," observed Las Casas, "produced a fatal effect on the public mind. The young King of Rome, contrary to custom, obstinately refused to quit the palace. He wept bitterly, and it was found necessary to carry him away by force. It was universally reported that the Empress wished to remain, and that the council was inclined to second her wishes, until precise orders were received from the Emperor, directing her to quit Paris in case of urgent danger on the part of the enemy."

"Yes," said the Emperor; "and those orders were very necessary. The Empress was young and totally inexperienced. Had she been capable of personal decision, my directions would have been quite the contrary. Paris then would have been her proper post; but I foresaw the intrigues of which she would be the object, and I wished to prevent at Paris what subsequently occurred at Orleans. There, the men who were planning the regency, in the expectation of ruling under the Empress, prevented her from joining me. What fatal consequences were thus produced! Would to heaven that I had also dispatched timely orders directing her to quit Orleans!"

The Emperor was in his bath when he received Dr. O'Meara. He was very social, and in reply to a question respecting his opinion of Talleyrand, he said,

"Talleyrand is the most vile of agitators, a base flatterer. He is a corrupt man, who has betrayed all parties and persons. Wary and circumspect, always a traitor, but always in conspiracy with Fortune. Talleyrand treats his enemies as if they were one day to become his friends, and his friends as if they were to become his enemies. He is a man of talent, but venal in every thing. Nothing could be done with him but by means of bribery. The Kings of Wurtemberg and Bavaria made so many complaints of his rapacity and extortion that I took his portfolio from him. Besides, I found that he had divulged to some intriguers a most important secret which I had confided to him alone.

"He hates the Bourbons in his heart. When I returned from Elba, Talleyrand wrote to me from Vienna, offering his services, and to betray the Bourbons, provided I would pardon and restore him to favor. He argued upon a part of my proclamation, in which I said there were circumstances which it was impossible to resist, which he quoted. But I considered that there were a few I was obliged to except, and refused, as it would have excited indignation if I had not punished somebody."

November 13. This morning, Las Casas, being in the Emperor's apartment, examined the large watch of Frederick the Great, which hung beside the chimney-piece. This led the Emperor to say, "I have been the possessor of glorious and valuable relics. I had the sword of Frederick the Great, and the Spaniards presented to me, at the Tuileries, the sword of Francis I. This was a high compliment, and must have cost them something of a sacrifice. The Turks and Persians have also sent me arms which were said to have belonged to Genghis Khan, Tamerlane, Shah Nadir, and I know not whom else; but I attached importance, not to the fact, but to the intention."

"I wonder, sire," said Las Casas, "that you had not endeavored to keep the sword of Frederick."

"Why, I had my own," replied Napoleon, smiling, and gently pinching Las Casas's ear.

Afterward, alluding to his second marriage, "I had intended," said he, "to make choice of a French woman, and it would have been well if I had done so. Such a union would have been eminently national. France was sufficiently great, and her monarch sufficiently powerful, to set aside every consideration of foreign policy. Besides, among sovereigns, the ties of blood are always made to yield to political interests: hence what scandalous violations of moral feeling are frequently exhibited to the world. Another objection that may be urged against marriages of this kind is the admission of a foreign princess into state secrets, which she may be tempted to betray; and if a sovereign place trust in his connections abroad, he may find that he has set his feet on an abyss covered with flowers. It is absurd to suppose that such alliances can guarantee or insure any advantage."

Many of the most distinguished statesmen of France were very sanguine that the Emperor's second marriage would secure peace for the country. Others, less informed about the real state of affairs, and who thought it was in the Emperor's power to make peace whenever he should wish to do so, thought that Napoleon would be enticed by the enjoyments of his new bridal to seek repose. A few days after the announcement of the intended alliance, the Emperor, in a moment of good-humored familiarity, said to the Duke of Decrés,

"Well, it appears that people are very much pleased with my intended marriage."

"Yes, sire," was the reply.

"I suppose they expect that the lion will slumber," added the Emperor.

"To say the truth, sire," the duke replied, "we are somewhat inclined to form that expectation."

"Well," resumed Napoleon, after a moment's silence, "it is a mistake. And it is not the fault of the lion either. Slumber would be as sweet to him as to any other; but do you not see that, while I am, to all appearances, *incessantly attacking*, I am nevertheless always engaged in *self-defense ?*"

The correctness of this assertion no one will now dispute.

To-day the governor sent word to Las Casas that he intended to remove Las Casas's servant, and give him another, which the governor would select. The count, preferring not to have a spy of Sir Hudson Lowe in attendance upon him, very properly replied,

"The governor has it in his power to send away my servant if he pleases, but he may spare himself the trouble of sending me one of his choosing. I am daily learning better and better how to dispense with the comforts of life. I can, if necessary, serve myself. This additional privation will be but slightly felt amid the sufferings to which we are daily subjected."

"I rendered an account of the affair to the Emperor," says Las Casas, "who applauded my determination of not admitting a spy among us."

"But," said he, in the most engaging manner, "as this sacrifice has been made for the interests of us all, it is not proper that you alone should be the sufferer. Send to Gentilini, my footman, and let him wait on you. He will be happy to earn a few Napoleons in addition to his wages; besides, tell him it is by my desire."

The Emperor then sent for Gentilini himself, and repeated the order with his own mouth, as Gentilini had some scruples about the propriety of a servant of the Emperor waiting upon a private person. He feared that he should thus appear wanting in respect to his illustrious master.

November 14. The Emperor spent the whole day in his room, dictating to Count Montholon a chapter on maritime rights. This chapter will be found in his memoirs as published by the count. It is a masterly state paper, and no man will now undertake to controvert the conclusions which he there establishes. The principles which he there avows, and which he contended for through life, have now become the faith of all nations, if we except a feeble and lingering remonstrance which England, so long the intolerant despot of the seas, occasionally ventures to utter.

At six o'clock the Emperor sent for Las Casas. He read and corrected some valuable notes which he had dictated to General Bertrand on ancient and modern warfare, and on the different plans of composing and regulating armies. In the conversation which ensued, he said,

"No series of great actions is the mere work of chance and fortune. It is always the result of reflection and genius. Great men rarely fail in the most perilous undertakings. Look at Alexander, Cæsar, Hannibal, and the great Gustavus; they always succeeded. Were they great men merely because they were fortunate? No; but because, being great men, they possessed the power of commanding fortune. When we come to inquire into the causes of their success, we are astonished to find that they did every thing to obtain it.

"Alexander, when scarcely beyond the age of boyhood, with a mere handful of brave troops, conquered a quarter of the globe. But was this achievement the result of a mere accidental irruption, a sort of unexpected deluge? No; all was profoundly calculated, boldly executed, and prudently managed. Alexander proved himself at once a distinguished warrior, politician, and legislator. Unfortunately, on attaining the zenith of glory and success, his head was turned and his heart corrupted. He commenced his career with the mind of Trajan, but he closed it with the heart of Nero and the manners of Heliogabalus.

"Cæsar, the reverse of Alexander, commenced his career at an advanced period. His youth was passed in indolence and vice, but he ultimately evinced the most active and elevated mind. He is one of the most amiable characters in history. Cæsar overcame the Gauls and the laws of his country; but his great warlike achievements must not be attributed merely to chance and fortune.

"Hannibal is, perhaps, the most surprising character of any, from the intrepidity, confidence, and grandeur evinced in all his enterprises. At the age of twenty-six he conceived what is scarcely conceivable, and executed what must have been looked upon as impossible. Renouncing all communication with his country, he marched through hostile or unknown nations, which he was obliged to attack and subdue; he crossed the Pyrenees and the Alps, which were presumed to be impassable, and descended upon Italy, sacrificing the half of his army for the mere acquisition of his field of battle, the mere right of fighting.

"He occupied and governed Italy for the space of sixteen years, being several times within a hair's breadth of possessing himself of Rome, and only relinquished his prey when his enemies, profiting by the lesson he had set them, marched to attack the Carthaginian territory. Can it be supposed that Hannibal's glorious career and achievements were the mere result of chance and fortune's favors? Certainly Hannibal must have been endowed with great vigor of mind, and he must have also possessed a vast consciousness of his own skill in the art of war, when, being interrogated by his youthful conqueror, he hesitated not to place himself, though subdued, next in rank to Alexander and Pyrrhus, whom he esteemed as the first of warriors.

"All the great captains of antiquity, and those who, in modern times, have successfully retraced their footsteps, performed vast achievements only by conforming with the rules and principles of art, that is to say, by correct combinations, and by justly comparing the relation between means and consequences, efforts and obstacles. They succeeded only by the strict observance of these rules, whatever may have been the boldness of their enterprises, or the extent of the advantages gained. They invariably practiced war as a science. Thus they have become our great models, and it is only by closely imitating them that we can hope to come near them.

"My greatest successes have been ascribed merely to good fortune, and my reverses will no doubt be imputed to my faults; but if I should write an account of my campaigns, it will be seen that, in both cases, my reason and my faculties were exercised in conformity with principles.

"With Condé, science seemed to be instinctive, Nature having created him with maturity of intellect. Turenne, on the contrary, perfected his talent by dint of study and acquirements."

"Turenne," said Las Casas, "formed no pupils, while Condé left many distinguished ones behind him."

"That," replied Napoleon, "was the mere caprice of chance; the contrary ought to have happened. But it is not always in the master's power to form good pupils. Nature must lend her aid; the seed must be sown in fertile soil.

"Frederick the Great," he continued, "was in all respects a superexcellent tactician, and possessed the art of rendering his troops absolute machines. How often men's characters prove to be totally different from what their early actions indicate! Do they themselves know what they really are? Frederick, at the commencement of his career, took to flight in the very face of victory; and certainly the whole of his subsequent history proves him to have been the most intrepid, most tenacious, and coolest of men."

After dinner, the conversation still continued upon the art of war. "There can be no perfect army," said the Emperor, "until, in imitation of the Roman plan, the soldier shall receive his supply of corn, grind it in his handmill, and bake his bread himself. We could not hope to possess an army until we abolish our monstrous train of civil attendants and commissary officers. I contemplated all these changes, but they never could have been put in practice except during profound peace. An army, in a state of war, would infallibly have rebelled against such innovations. By the adoption of the ancient plan, an army might march to the farther extremity of the world; but it would require time to bring about such a transition; it could not be accomplished by a mere order of the day. I long entertained the idea of such a change, but, however great might have been my power, I should never have attempted to introduce it by force. There is no subordination with empty stomachs. Such an object could only have been effected in time of peace, and by insensible degrees. I should have accomplished it by creating new military manners."

The Emperor constantly insisted on subjecting the whole nation to the laws of the conscription. "I am inexorable," said he, one day, in the Council of State, "on the subject of exemption. It would be criminal. How could I acquit my conscience with having exposed the life of one man for the advantage of another? I do not even think that I would exempt my own son. The conscription is the root of a nation, its moral purification, the real foundation of its habits. By means of the conscription, the nation is classed according to its real interests for defense abroad and tranquillity at home. Organized, built up in this way, the French people may defy the world, and may with justice renew the saying of the proud Gauls, '*If the sky should fall, we will keep it up with our lances.*'"

According to Napoleon's plans, the conscription, instead of impeding education, was to have been the means of promoting it. He intended to have established in every regiment a school for the prosecution of studies, and labors of every kind, in polite education, the liberal arts, and mechanics.

"Nothing," he remarked, "would have been so easy. The principle being once adopted, we should have seen each regiment supplied with all that was necessary out of its own ranks. And what advantages would have accrued to the mass of society by the dispersion of these young men, with their acquired knowledge, even had it been merely elementary, and the habits necessarily produced by it!"

In the course of conversation, the Emperor spoke of the evil arising from lawsuits. "They are," said he, "an absolute leprosy, a social cancer. My Code had singularly diminished lawsuits by placing numerous causes within the decision of every individual. But there still remained much for the legislator to accomplish. Not that he could hope to prevent men from quarreling—that they have done in all ages—but he might have prevented a third party in society from living upon the quarrels of the two others, and even stirring up disputes to promote their own interest. It was, therefore, my intention to establish the rule, that lawyers should never receive fees except when they gained cases. Thus what litigations would have been prevented! On the first examination of a cause, a lawyer would have rejected it had it been at all doubtful. There would have been little fear that a man, living by his labor, would have undertaken to conduct a lawsuit from mere motives of vanity; and if he had, he would himself have been the only sufferer in case of failure. But my idea was opposed by a multitude of objections, and as I had no time to lose, I postponed the further consideration of the subject. Yet I am still convinced that the scheme might, with certain modifications, have been turned to the best account."

When speaking of the clergy, the Emperor remarked that he intended to have rendered curates a more useful set of men.

"The more they are enlightened," said he, "the less will they be inclined to abuse their ministry. I wished them to acquire a knowledge of agriculture, and the elements of medicine and law. Thus dogmatism and controversy, the battle-horse and armor of fools and fanatics, would gradually have become more and more rare in the pulpit, from whence would have been promulgated the doctrines of pure morality, always pleasing, eloquent, and persuasive. As men usually love to discourse on what they know, the curates would have instructed the peasantry in their agricultural labors, counseled them against chicanery, and given advice to the sick. Such pastors would have been real blessings to their flocks; and as they would have been allowed a liberal stipend, they would have enjoyed high consideration; they would have respected themselves, and been respected by all. They would have possessed the power of feudal lords, and they might, without danger, have exercised all their influence. A curate would have been a natural justice of peace, a true moral chief, to whom the direction of the population might have been safely intrusted, because he would himself have been dependent on the government for his appointment and salary. If to all this be added the study and privation necessary for the calling, and supposing the individuals to be possessed of good qualities of heart and mind, it must be confessed that pastors, thus constituted, would have produced a revolution in society highly advantageous to the cause of morality."

It was one of Napoleon's favorite plans to establish a *European Institution* and European prizes to stimulate the learned societies of every country. He also wished to establish throughout Europe uniformity of coins, weights, measures, and of legislation. "Why," said he, "might not my Napoleon Code have served as the groundwork for a European Code, and my Imperial University have been the basis of a European University. Thus the whole population of Europe would have become one and the same family. And every man, while he traveled abroad, would still have found himself at home."

CHAPTER XXXIII.
1816, November. Continued.

Longwood invested—Dramatic Readings—Lord Liverpool—Lord Sidmouth—Lord Bathurst—Lord Castlereagh—The Division of Europe—Remarks on Wellington and Waterloo—Character of the French Ministers—Duroc—Marmont—Gaming—Memorable Remarks—A Hereditary Nobility—Truth of History—The Bourbon Conspiracy—Pichegru—Moreau.

November 15. About three o'clock in the afternoon the Emperor sent for Las Casas, and took a short walk. He, however, was quite exhausted, and calling at General Bertrand's, sat for some time languidly in an arm-chair. Though cheerful, he was pale and emaciate, and was evidently fast sinking beneath his cruel privations.

"As we passed through the wood," says Las Casas, "the Emperor saw the fortifications with which we are about to be surrounded. He could not forbear smiling at these useless and absurd preparations. He remarked that the ground in our neighborhood had been entirely disfigured by the removal of the kind of turf with which it was covered, and which had been carried away for the purpose of raising banks. In fact, for the last two months the governor has been incessantly digging ditches, constructing parapets, and planting palisadoes. He has quite blockaded us in Longwood, and the stable, at present, presents every appearance of a redoubt. We are at a loss to guess where will be the advantage equivalent to the expense and labor bestowed on these works, which excite, by turns, the ill humor and ridicule of the soldiers and Chinese who are employed upon them, and who call Longwood *Fort Hudson*, and the stable *Fort Lowe*. We are assured that Sir Hudson often starts out of his sleep to devise new measures of security."

THE EMPEROR EXAMINING THE FORTIFICATIONS.

"Surely," said the Emperor, "this seems something like madness. Why can not the man sleep tranquilly and let us alone? Has he not sense enough to perceive that the security of our local situation here is sufficient to remove all his panic terrors?"

After dinner the Emperor ordered the works of Racine to be brought from the library, and read to his friends some of the finest passages of Iphigenia, Mithridates, and Bajazet.

"Though Racine," said he, "has produced chefs d'œuvres in themselves, yet he has diffused over them a perpetual air of insipidity. Love is eternally introduced, with its tones of languor and its tiresome accompaniments; but these faults must not be attributed entirely to Racine, but to the manners of the age in which he wrote. Love was then, and even at a later period, the whole business of life with every one. This is always the case when society is in a state of idleness. As for us, our thoughts have been cruelly turned to other subjects by the great events of the Revolution."

November 16. Las Casas found the Emperor amusing himself by looking over an English publication, a kind of political almanac. Alluding to the members of the English ministry who were mentioned in the work, he said to Las Casas,

"Do you know any of them? What was the general opinion of them when you were in England?"

"Sire," replied Las Casas, "it is so long since I left England that nearly all who are now distinguished in the ministry were then only commencing their career. At that time, none of them had come forward to the scene."

"Lord Liverpool," said the Emperor, "appears to me to be the most worthy man among them. I have heard a great deal of good of him. He seems to have some feeling of propriety and decorum. I have no objection to a man being my enemy; every one has his own business and his own duties to perform, but I have certainly a right to be indignant at unworthy conduct and measures. Lord Sidmouth, I am told, too, is a worthy man enough, but he possesses no great share of understanding. He is one of those honest blockheads who, with the utmost sincerity, concur in all sorts of mischief."

"Sire," said Las Casas, "in my time Lord Sidmouth, under the name of Addington, was a member of the House of Commons, and was a man generally esteemed. He was said to be the creature of Mr. Pitt, who was understood to have appointed Addington as his successor, in order to insure to himself the means of returning to the ministry whenever he should think fit. The public were certainly greatly astonished to see Mr. Addington succeed Pitt, as the post was considered to be far beyond his talents. One of the English opposition papers, alluding to Mr. Addington, quoted the remark made by a philosopher—Locke, I believe—who says that the mind of a child is a blank sheet of paper on which Nature has yet written nothing; and the journal in question humorously observed, that when Nature wrote upon the blank sheet of the Doctor—the nickname then given to Mr. Addington—it must be confessed she left plenty of margin."

"Well," resumed Napoleon, "what do you know of that sad fellow into whose keeping we have been delivered up—that Lord Bathurst?"

"Absolutely nothing, sire, either of his origin, his person, or his character."

"For my part," said the Emperor, with some degree of warmth, "I have no opportunity of knowing him except by his conduct toward me; and, in judging from that, I hold him to be the most vile, the most base, the most mean-spirited of men. The brutality of his orders, the coarseness of his language, the choice of his agents, all authorize me to make this declaration. An executioner, such as he has sent here, is not easily found. Such a selection could not be made at random. He must have been sought for, tried, judged, and instructed. Certainly this, in my opinion, is sufficient to justify the moral condemnation of the man who could stoop to so base a course. By the arm which he moves, it is easy to guess what must be his heart!

"Lord Castlereagh," continued the Emperor, "governs every thing, and rules even the prince himself by dint of impudence and intrigue. Supported by a majority of his own creating, he is always ready to contend, with the utmost effrontery, against reason, law, justice, and truth. No falsehood staggers him: he stops at nothing, well knowing that he can always command votes to applaud and legalize whatever he does. He has completely sacrificed his country, and is daily degrading her by acting in opposition to her policy, doctrines, and interests. In short, he has entirely delivered her up to the Continent. The situation of England is becoming worse and worse. Heaven knows how she will extricate herself!

"Lord Castlereagh is, I am informed," continued the Emperor, "looked upon, even in England, as a man politically immoral. He commenced his career by an act of political apostasy, which, though common enough in his country, nevertheless always leaves an indelible stain. He entered upon public life as an advocate of the people, and he has finally become the engine of power and despotism. If all that is said of him be correct, he must be execrated by his countrymen, the Irish, whom he has betrayed, and by the English, who may justly regard him as the destroyer of their domestic liberties and foreign interests.

"He has had the impudence to bring forward in Parliament, as authentic facts, statements which he knew to be false, and which probably he himself fabricated; and yet, on the authority of these documents, Murat's dethronement was decided. Lord Castlereagh makes it his business to belie himself daily, in Parliament and in public meetings, by putting into my mouth language calculated to prejudice me in the eyes of the English, though he is well aware that he is making false assertions. This conduct is base, since he himself withholds from me the power of refuting him.

"He is the pupil of Pitt, of whom he probably thinks himself the equal, though he is merely the ape of that distinguished statesman. He has incessantly pursued the plans and plots of his master against France. But even here, pertinacity and obstinacy were, perhaps, his only good qualities. But Pitt had grand views. With him his country's interest took place of every consideration. He possessed talent and ingenuity, and from England he moved the lever by which he ruled and influenced the Continental sovereigns at will. Castlereagh, on the contrary, substituting intrigue for ingenuity, and subsidies for genius, is regardless of his country's interest, and has incessantly employed the credit and influence of the Continental sovereigns merely to confirm and perpetuate his own power. However, such is the course of things in this world, that Pitt, with all his talent, constantly failed, while Castlereagh has been completely successful. Oh, blindness of Fortune!

"Castlereagh has proved himself entirely the man of the Continent. When master of Europe, he satisfied all the monarchs of the Continent, and only forgot his own country. His conduct has been so prejudicial to the national interests, so incompatible with the doctrines of his country, and altogether presents so much the appearance of inconsistency, that it is difficult to conceive how so wise a people as the English can allow themselves to be governed by such a fool!

"He adopts legitimacy as the basis of his creed, and wishes to establish it as a political dogma, while that principle would sap the very foundation of the throne of his own sovereign. Besides, he acknowledges Bernadotte in opposition to the legitimate Gustavus IV., who sacrificed himself for England; and he acknowledges the usurper Ferdinand VII. to the detriment of his venerable father, Charles IV.

"He and the Allies establish, as another fundamental basis, the restoration of the old order of things, the redress of what they term past injuries, injustice, and degradation—in fine, the returning of political morality; yet he scrupled not to sacrifice the republics of Venice and Genoa by abandoning the former to Austria and annexing the latter to Piedmont. He enriched Russia by the possession of Poland. He robbed the King of Saxony for the advantage of Prussia, who can no longer afford any aid to England. He separated Norway from Denmark, while, had the latter power been left more independent of Russia, she might have surrendered to England the key of the Baltic; and Norway was transferred to Sweden, which, by the loss of Finland and the islands of the Baltic, has fallen entirely under the subjection of Russia. Finally, by a violation of the first principles of general policy, he neglected, in his all-powerful situation, to restore the independence of Poland, thereby exposing Constantinople, endangering the whole of Europe, and preparing a thousand troubles in Germany.

"I need say nothing of the monstrous inconsistency of a minister, the representative of a nation pre-eminently free, restoring Italy to the yoke of slavery, keeping Spain in a state of bondage, and exerting every effort to forge fetters for the whole Continent. Does he think that liberty is only proper for the English, and the rest of Europe not fit to enjoy it? But even supposing him to entertain this opinion, how does he explain his conduct with regard to his own countrymen, whom he is daily depriving of some of their rights? for example, the suspension of the Habeas Corpus Act, right or wrong; the enforcement of the Alien Bill, by which, will it be credited? the wife of an Englishman, should she happen to be a foreigner, may be driven from England at the will and pleasure of the minister; the endless dispersion of spies and informers, those exciting agents and infernal instigators, by whose aid criminals may always be created and victims multiplied. In short, he has established at home the system of cold violence, the iron yoke, which he exercises over foreign dependencies. No; Lord Castlereagh is not calculated to be the minister of a free people, or to command the respect of foreign nations. He is the vizier of the Continental sovereigns, at their instigation training his countrymen to slavery. He is the connecting link, the conductor by which English gold is dispersed over the Continent, and the despotic doctrines of other countries imported into England.

"He proves himself to be the partisan, the obsequious associate of the Holy Alliance, that mysterious coalition, of which I can not guess either the meaning or the object, which can afford neither utility nor advantage. Can it be directed against the Turks? It would then be for the English to oppose it. Can it really have for its object the maintenance of a general peace? That is a chimera by which it is impossible diplomatic cabinets can be duped. With them alliances can only be formed for the purpose of opposition or counterpoise. They can not all be allied together. I can not, therefore, comprehend this Holy Alliance, except by regarding it as a league of sovereigns against subjects. But in that case, what has Castlereagh to do with it? If it be so, ought he not, one day, to pay dearly for his conduct?

"I once had Lord Castlereagh in my power. He was intriguing at Chatillon, when, during one of our momentary successes, my troops passed beyond the seat of Congress, which was, by this means, surrounded. The prime minister of England maintained no public character, and was unprotected by the law of nations. He was aware of his embarrassing situation, and manifested the utmost uneasiness at thus finding himself in my power. I intimated to him that he might give himself no anxiety, as he was at perfect liberty. I did this on my own account, and not on his, for certainly I had no reason to expect any good from him. However, some time after this, he evinced his gratitude in a very peculiar way. When he saw me make choice of the Isle of Elba, he caused England to be proposed as my asylum, and employed all his eloquence and subtlety to induce me to make choice of that country as my place of residence. Now I may justly entertain suspicion of his offers, and, doubtless, he already meditated the horrible treatment which he is at this moment exercising toward me.

"It was a misfortune for England that her prime minister treated personally with the Continental sovereigns. It was a violation of the spirit of the British Constitution. The English at first felt their pride flattered at seeing their representative dictate laws to Europe, but they have now abundant cause to repent, since the result has proved that, on the contrary, he only stipulated for embarrassment, degradation, and loss. It is an undoubted fact that he might have obtained all, while from blindness, incapacity, or perfidy, he sacrificed every thing. When seated at the banquet of monarchs, he blushed to bargain for peace like a merchant, and determined to treat liberally like a lord. Thus he gained something in point of vanity, and, it may be presumed, *he* lost nothing in point of interest. His *country* alone suffered, and will continue to suffer.

"And the Continental sovereigns are likely to repent of having permitted their prime ministers to come into personal contact with each other. The result seems to have been, that these premiers have created among themselves a sort of secondary sovereignty, which they naturally guarantee to each other, and there is good reason to suppose it is accompanied by subsidies furnished with the knowledge of their respective sovereigns. This business may be very easily managed. Nothing can be more simple, and, at the same time, more ingenious. In fixing the secret-service money, it is very easy to mention that such a one on the Continent has been very useful, that he may still continue to be so, and, therefore, that it is proper to make an acknowledgment for his services. This individual, in his turn, may represent to his government that some man or other abroad has rendered important services, and even compromised his own interests, and that, consequently, he should not be forgotten. It was probably some such arrangements as these that occasioned a distinguished individual at Vienna to exclaim, in a moment of irritation, '*Such a one costs me as dear as my eyes.*' Doubtless these disgraceful schemes and transactions will one day come to light. We shall then see what enormous fortunes have thus been squandered and swallowed up. They will perhaps hereafter be recorded in new letters of Barillon; but nothing will be unfolded, no characters will be disgraced, because contemporaries will have anticipated all."

After this energetic effusion, in which Napoleon for the first time expressed himself with such warmth and bitterness against the individuals of whom he had personally cause to complain, he was silent a few minutes. Then resuming, he said,

"And Lord Castlereagh is artful enough to support himself entirely on Lord Wellington. Wellington has become his creature. Can it be possible that the modern Marlborough has linked himself in the train of a Castlereagh, and yoked his victories to the turpitude of a political mountebank? It is inconceivable! Can he endure the thought? Has not his mind risen to a level with his success?"

"I had remarked," says Las Casas, "that, in general, the Emperor disliked to speak of Lord Wellington. He seemed carefully to avoid pronouncing his opinion upon him, feeling, no doubt, the impropriety of publicly depreciating the general who had triumphed over him. On the present occasion, however, he yielded, without reserve, to the full expression of his feelings. The consciousness of the indignities that were heaped upon him seemed at this moment to rise forcibly in his mind. His gestures, his features, his tone of voice, were all expressive of the utmost indignation.

"'I have been told,' said he, 'that it is through Wellington that I am here, and I believe it. It is conduct well worthy of him, who, in defiance of a solemn capitulation, suffered Ney to perish—Ney, with whom he had so often been engaged on the field of battle. For my own part, it is very certain I gave him a terrible quarter of an hour. This usually constitutes a claim on noble minds. His was incapable of feeling. My fall, and the lot that might have been reserved for me, afforded him the opportunity of reaping higher glory than he has gained by all his victories. But he did not understand this. Well, at any rate, he ought to be heartily grateful to old Blucher. Had it not been for him, I know not where "his grace" might have been to-day; but I know that I, at least, should not have been at St. Helena. Wellington's troops were admirable, but his plans were despicable; or, I should rather say, he formed none at all. He had placed himself in a situation in which it was impossible he could form any; and, by a curious chance, this very circumstance saved him. If he could have commenced a retreat, he must infallibly have been lost. He certainly remained master of the battle-field, but was his success the result of skill? He has reaped the fruit of a brilliant victory, but did his genius prepare it for him? His glory is wholly negative. His faults were enormous. He, the European generalissimo, in whose hands so many interests were intrusted, and having before him an enemy so prompt and daring as myself, left his forces dispersed about, and slumbered in a capital until he was surprised. And yet, such is the power of fatality! in the course of three days, I three times saw the destiny of France and of Europe escape my grasp.

"'In the first place, but for the treason of a general, who deserted our ranks and betrayed my designs, I should have dispersed and destroyed all the enemy's detached parties before they could have combined themselves into army corps.

"'Next, had it not been for the unusual hesitations of Ney at Quatre Bras, I should have annihilated the whole English army.

"'Finally, on my right, the extraordinary maneuvers of Grouchy, instead of securing victory, completed my ruin, and hurled France into the abyss.

"'No,' continued Napoleon, 'Wellington possesses only a special kind of talent. Berthier also had his. In this he perhaps excels, but he has no ingenuity. Fortune has done more for him than he has done for her. How different from Marlborough, of whom he seems to consider himself the rival and equal! Marlborough, while he gained battles, ruled cabinets and guided statesmen. Wellington has only shown himself capable of following the views and plans of Castlereagh. Madam de Staël said of him that, when out of the field of battle, he had not two ideas. The saloons of Paris, so distinguished for delicacy and correctness of taste, at once decided that Madam de Staël was in the right, and the French plenipotentiary at Vienna confirmed that opinion. His victories, their result, and their influence, will rise in history, but his name will fall even during his lifetime.'"

Alluding to ministries in general, but particularly to collective ministries, the intrigues, the great and petty passions that agitate the men who compose them, the Emperor said,

"After all, they are only so many plagues. No one escapes the contagion. A man may be honest when he enters a ministry, but it seldom happens that he retires from one without having forfeited his purity of character. I may, perhaps, except only two—mine, and that of the United States. Mine, because my ministers were merely my men of business, and I alone stood responsible; and that of the United States, because there ministers are men of public credit, always upright, always vigilant, and always rigid.

"I believe that no sovereign was ever surrounded by more faithful servants than I was toward the close of my reign. And if I did not obtain due credit for the selection I had made, it was because the French are too apt to murmur incessantly. My two great dignitaries, Cambacérès and Lebrun, were distinguished men, and perfectly well disposed. Bassano and Caulaincourt were remarkable for sincerity and rectitude. Molé, whose name reflects honor on the French magistracy, is probably destined to act a part in future ministries.

"Montalivet was an honest man. The ministry of Decrés was pure and rigorous. Gaudin was distinguished for steady and well-directed labor. Mollien possessed vast perspicuity and promptitude; and all my councilors of state were prudent and assiduous. All these names will remain inseparably connected with mine. What country, what age, ever presented a better-composed or more moral ministry? Happy the nation that possesses such instruments, and knows how to turn them to good account! Though I was not given to praise, and though my approbation was in general purely negative, yet I nevertheless fully appreciated the value of those who served me, and who have everlasting claims on my gratitude. Their number is immense, and the most modest are not the least meritorious. I shall not attempt to name them, because many of them would have to complain of being omitted, and such omission might appear like ingratitude on my part."

November 17. The Emperor was quite unwell, and remained in his room all day. O'Meara, in conversation, mentioned to the Emperor that he had been informed he had saved Marshal Duroc's life during his first campaigns in Italy, when seized and condemned to death as an emigrant, which was asserted to have been the cause of the great attachment subsequently displayed by Duroc to him until the hour of his death.

Napoleon looked surprised, and replied, "No such thing. Who told you that tale?"

O'Meara replied that he had heard the Marquis Montchenu repeat it at a public dinner.

"There is not a word of truth in it," replied Napoleon. "I took Duroc out of the artillery train when he was a boy, and protected him until his death. But I suppose Montchenu said this because Duroc was of an old family, which in that booby's eyes is the only source of merit. He despises every body who has not as many hundred years of nobility to boast of as himself. It was such as Montchenu who were the chief cause of the Revolution. Before it, such a man as Bertrand, who is worth an army of Montchenus, could not even be a sub-lieutenant, while *vieux enfans* (old children) like him would be generals. God help the nation that is governed by such. In my time, most of the generals, of whose deeds France is so proud, sprung from that very class of plebeians so much despised by him."

In the evening the Emperor sent for Las Casas. Speaking of the generals of the army of Italy, he dwelt particularly on Marmont.

"I was very strongly attached," said the Emperor, "to Marmont. His defection proved a severe wound to my heart. From what I know of him, I am sure that he must occasionally suffer deeply from remorse. Never was defection more fatal or more decidedly avowed. It was recorded in the Moniteur, and by his own hand. It was the immediate cause of our disasters, the grave of our power, the cloud of our glory. And yet," he added, in a tone of affection, "I am convinced that his sentiments are better than his reputation. His heart is superior to his conduct. Of this he appears himself to be conscious. The newspapers inform us that, when soliciting vainly for the pardon of Lavalette, he exclaimed, with warmth, in reply to the obstacles urged by the monarch, '*Sire, have I not given you more than my life?*' We were, it is true," continued the Emperor, "betrayed by others, and in a manner still more vile; but no other act of apostasy was so solemnly recorded by official documents."

The conversation then turned to Paris, its immense population, and manners. "The Emperor," says Las Casas, "adverted to the many evils which, he said, must inevitably exist in all great capitals, where depravity of every kind is continually stimulated by want, passion, wit, and the facilities afforded by bustle and confusion. He often repeated that all capitals were so many Babylons. The Emperor said that he had endeavored to suppress many sources of immorality, and particularly the gaming-houses. He questioned me respecting the kind of gaming practiced in Paris. Observing that in my replies I always used the plural *we*, he interrupted me, inquiring,

"'Were you yourself a gamester?'

"'Alas! sire,' I replied, 'I unfortunately was; only, however, occasionally, and at long intervals. But still, when the fit seized me, it urged me to excess.'

"'I am very glad,' said the Emperor, 'that I knew nothing of it at the time, otherwise you would have been ruined in my esteem. This circumstance shows how little we knew of each other, and it also proves that you could not have made yourself many enemies, for there were charitable souls about me who would have taken care to inform me of your failing. My prejudice against gaming was well known. A gamester was sure to forfeit my confidence. I had not leisure to inquire whether I was right or wrong; but, whenever I heard that a man was addicted to gaming, I placed no more reliance in him.'"

November 19. Under this date Las Casas records the following memorable and characteristic remarks of the Emperor, made on different occasions.

Some one was speaking of the pains which the Bourbons had taken to obliterate from all the public monuments the emblems and devices of the Empire. The Emperor smiled, and said,

"They may be withdrawn from the public eye, but they can not be erased from the page of public history, or from the recollection of connoisseurs and artists. I acted differently. I respected all the vestiges of royalty that existed when I came into power. I even restored the *fleur de lis*, and other royal emblems, when chronological correctness required it."

How does it happen, it was one day asked, that misfortunes which are yet uncertain, often distress us more than miseries which have been already suffered?

"Because," the Emperor replied, "in the imagination, as in calculation, the power of what is unknown is *incommensurable*."

The Emperor had ordered particular attention to be devoted to improving and embellishing the markets of the capital. "The market-place," said he, "is the Louvre of the common people."

The great principle of Napoleon's reign was *equal rights for all men*. All conditions and all colors were under the same impartial law. In speaking upon this subject to a councilor of state, he said,

"I have not reigned all my life. Before I became a sovereign, I recollect having been a subject; and I can never forget how powerfully the sentiment of equality influences the mind and animates the heart. Let me charge you to respect *liberty*, and, above all, *equality*. With regard to liberty, it may be proper to restrain it in a case of extremity. Circumstances may demand and justify such a step, but Heaven forbid that we should ever infringe upon equality. It is the passion of the age, and I wish to continue to be the man of the age."

Speaking of himself one day at St. Helena, the Emperor said, "Nature seems to have calculated that I should have to endure great reverses, for she has given me a mind of marble. Thunder can not ruffle it. The shaft merely glides along."

On one occasion, in view of some new and intolerable vexation on the part of Sir Hudson Lowe, one of the Emperor's suite exclaimed, "Ah! sire, this must indeed increase your hatred of the English." The Emperor, shrugging his shoulders, said, in mingled tones of pleasantry and reproof,

"Prejudiced man! say, rather, that at most it may increase my hatred of this or that individual Englishman. But, since we are on this subject, let me tell you that a man, he who has the true feelings of a man, never cherishes hatred. His anger or ill-humor never goes beyond the irritation of the moment—the electric stroke. He who is formed to discharge high duties, and to exercise authority, never considers persons. His views are directed to things, their weight and consequences."

On another occasion, in serious and earnest utterance, he said, "I can not doubt but that my character will gain in proportion as it advances in posterity. Future historians will conceive themselves bound to avenge the injustice of contemporaries. Excess is always succeeded by reaction. Besides, I am of opinion that, when viewed from a distance, my character will appear in a more favorable light, by being relieved from many useless incumbrances. I shall hereafter be judged by general views, and not by petty details. Every thing will be in harmony, and all local irregularities will disappear. I can now, as hereafter, proudly submit every act of my private life to the most rigid scrutiny, confident that the severest judges will pronounce me free from crime."

Speaking of his high regard for the Germans, he said, "I levied many millions of imposts upon them, it is true. That was necessary. But I should never have insulted them, or treated them with contempt. I esteemed the Germans. They may hate me; that is natural enough. I was forced for ten years to fight over the dead bodies of their countrymen. They could not know my real designs, or give me credit for my ultimate intentions, which were calculated to render Germany a great nation."

One day mention was made of an individual who, though distinguished for his abilities, was rude and upolished in his language and manners. The Emperor remarked,

"*The fault is in his early education. His swaddling-clothes have been neither fine nor clean.*"

Speaking of the discontent which the incessant wars of the Empire occasionally incited in Paris, the Emperor said, "What did they expect me to do, after all I had accomplished?"

"Sire," Las Casas replied, "it was wished that your majesty would stop your horse."

"Stop my horse!" resumed Napoleon. "That was easily said. My arm was strong enough, it is true, to stop, with a single check, all the horses of the Continent, but I could not bridle the English fleet. There lay all the mischief. Had not the people sense enough to see this?"

In allusion to the nobility which he had created, he said, "I regret that this was so ill understood. It was one of my grandest and happiest ideas. I had in view three objects of the highest importance. 1. To reconcile France with Europe, and to restore harmony by seeming to adopt European customs. 2. By the same means to bring about a complete reconciliation and union between old and new France. 3. To banish feudal nobility, the only kind which is offensive, oppressive, and unnatural.

"By my plan, I should soon have succeeded in instituting positive and meritorious qualities for antiquated and odious prejudices. My national titles would have exactly restored that equality which feudal nobility proscribed. They were conferred as the reward of merit of every kind. For genealogical parchments I substituted noble actions; and for private interests, the interests of the country. Family pride would no longer have been founded on obscure and imaginary circumstances, but would have rested on the noblest pages of our history. Finally, I would have banished the odious pretension of blood—an absurd idea—a theory which has no real existence. We all know very well that there is but one race of men, and that one is not born with boots on his legs, and another with a pack-saddle on his back."

In conversation with Count Montholon, the Emperor, in the following language, more fully developed his plans in the establishment of an hereditary nobility. It is very difficult accurately to record conversation. With the most honest intentions, the Emperor was sometimes misunderstood, and sentiments were recorded which he would have modified. His general idea, however, in the admission of an order of nobles with titles, but with no exclusive privileges, is here made perfectly plain.

"My object was to destroy the whole feudal system, as organized by Charlemagne. With this view, I created a nobility from among the people, in order to swallow up the remains of the feudal nobility. The foundations of my ideas of fitness were abilities and personal worth, and I selected the son of a farmer or an artisan to make a duke or a marshal of France. I sought for true merit among all ranks of the great mass of the French people, and was anxious to organize a true and general system of equality. I was desirous that every Frenchman should be admissible to all the employments and dignities of the state, provided he was possessed of talents and character equal to the performance of the duties, whatever might be his family. In a word, I was eager to abolish, to the last trace, the privileges of the ancient nobility, and to establish a government which, at the same time that it held the reins of government with a firm hand, should still be a *popular government.* The oligarchs of every country in Europe soon perceived my design, and it was for this reason that war to the death was carried on against me by England. The noble families of London, as well as those of Vienna, think themselves prescriptively entitled to the occupation of all the important offices in the state, and the management and handling of the public money. Their birth is regarded by them as a substitute for talents and capacities; and it is enough for a man to be the son of his father to be fit to fulfill the duties of the most important employments and highest dignities of the state. They are somewhat like kings by divine right; the people are in their eyes merely milch cows, about whose real interests they feel no concern, provided the treasury is always full, and the crown resplendent with jewels.

"In short, in establishing an hereditary nobility, I had three objects in view:
"1st. To reconcile France with the rest of Europe.
"2d. To reconcile old with new France.
"3d. To put an end to all feudal institutions in Europe by reconnecting the idea of nobility with that of public services, and detaching it from all prescriptive or feudal notions.

"The whole of Europe was governed by nobles who were strongly opposed to the progress of the French Revolution, and who exercised an influence which proved a serious obstacle to the development of French principles. It was necessary to destroy this influence, and with that view to clothe the principal personages of the Empire with titles equal to theirs. The success was complete. From that time forward the nobility of Europe ceased to be opposed to France, and with secret joy witnessed the creation of a new nobility, which appeared inferior to the ancient merely because it was new. They did not foresee the consequences of the French system, which tended to depreciate and uproot the feudal nobility, or at least to compel its members to reconstitute themselves by a new title.

"The ancient nobility of France, on their restoration to their country and to a part of their estates, eagerly resumed all their titles; and, although not legally, yet in fact, considered themselves more than ever as a privileged class. Every attempt at fusion or amalgamation with the chiefs of the Revolution was attended with difficulties, which were at once completely removed by the creation of new titles. There were none of the ancient families which did not willingly form alliances with the new dukes; in fact, the Noailles, Corbelts, Louvois, and Fleurys, were new houses, creations of Louis XIV. and Louis XV. From their origin, the most ancient houses in France sought for their alliance, and in this way the families of the Revolution were consolidated, and old and new France reunited. It was particularly with this view that I conferred the first title on Marshal Lefebvre. The marshal had been a common soldier, and every one in Paris had known him as a sergeant in the French Guards.

"My plan was to reconstruct the ancient nobility of France. Every family which reckoned among the number of its ancestors a cardinal, a great officer of the crown, a marshal of France, chancellor, keeper of the seals, minister, &c., was entitled on that account to sue for the title of duke. You, Montholon, for example, would have been a duke, because you were descended from chancellors and keepers of the great seal of France. Every family which had had an archbishop, embassador, chief president, lieutenant general, or vice admiral, the title of count; every family which had had a bishop, major general, rear admiral, councilor of state, or president of Parliament, the title of baron. These titles would not have been encumbered with any other charge than an obligation on the part of the claimants to provide a fixed income for the eldest son, of $25,000 for a duke, 6000 for a count, and 2000 for a baron. This principle was to form a rule for the past and the present, and intended also as a standard for the future. From this plan there sprung up an historical nobility, which united the past, the present, and the future; and was founded, not upon any distinctions of blood, which constitute an imaginary nobility, inasmuch as there is only one race of men, but upon services done to the state. In the same manner, therefore, the son of a peasant might say to himself, 'I shall one day be a cardinal, marshal of France, or minister;' so might he on this principle say, 'I shall one day be a duke, count, or baron,' as he may now say, 'I shall follow commerce, and gain millions for my family.' A Montmorency would have been made a duke, not because he was a Montmorency, but because one of his ancestors had been constable of France, and rendered important services to the state. This changed the whole nature of the nobility, which had been hitherto feudal, and established on its ruins an historical nobility, founded upon the claims of its possessors to the love of their country or the respect of their sovereign. This idea, like that of the Legion of Honor, and the University, was in itself eminently liberal, well calculated, at the time, to consolidate social order and to annihilate the pride of the nobility. It at once destroyed the pretensions of the oligarchy, and maintained in all their integrity the dignity and legal rights of mankind. It was a creation, organizing a liberal idea, and completely characteristic of the new age. I never had recourse to precipitation in the execution of any of my projects, always believing I had time before me. I often said to my Council of State that I required twenty years for the accomplishment of my plans, but I have only had fifteen."

November 20. "It must be admitted, my dear Las Casas," said the Emperor, "it is most difficult to obtain certainties for the purposes of history. Fortunately, it is, in general, more a matter of mere curiosity than of real importance. There are so many kinds of truths! The truth which Fouché, or other intriguers of his stamp, will tell, for instance—even that which many very honest people may tell, will, in some cases, differ essentially from the truth which I may relate. The truth of history, so much sought for, to which every body eagerly appeals, is too often but an idle tale. At the time of the events, during the heat of conflicting passions, it can not exist; and if, at a later period, all parties are agreed respecting it, it is because those persons who were interested in the events, those who might be able to contradict what is asserted, are no more. What then is, generally speaking, the truth of history? A fable agreed upon. As it has been very ingeniously remarked, there are in these matters two essential points, very distinct from each other: the positive facts, and the moral intentions. With respect to the positive facts, it would seem that they ought to be incontrovertible. Yet you will not find two accounts agree together in relating the same facts. Some have remained contested points to this day, and will ever remain so. With regard to moral intentions, how shall we judge of them, even admitting the candor of those who relate events?

"And what will be the case if the narrators be not sincere, or if they should be actuated by interest or passions? I have given an order, but who was able to read my thoughts, my real intentions? Yet every one will take up that order, and measure it according to his own scale, or adapt it to his own plans or system. See the different colorings that will be given to it by the intriguer whose plan it disturbs or favors. See how he will distort it. The man who assumes importance, to whom the minister or the sovereign may have hinted something in confidence on the subject, will do the same thing, as will the numerous idlers of the palace, who, having nothing better to do than to listen under the windows, invent when they have not heard. And each person will be so certain of what he tells! and the inferior classes, who will have received their information from these privileged individuals, will be so certain, in their turn, of its correctness! And then, memoirs are digested, memoranda are written, witticisms and anecdotes are circulated, and of such materials history is composed!

"I have seen the plan of my own battle, the intention of my own orders, disputed with me, and opinion decide against me! Is not that the creature giving the lie to its creator? Nevertheless, my opponent, who contradicts me, will have his adherents. This it is which has prevented me from writing my own private memoirs, from disclosing my individual feelings, which would naturally have exhibited the shades of my private character. I could not condescend to write confessions after the manner of Jean Jacques Rousseau, which every body might have attacked, and therefore I have thought proper to confine the subjects of my dictations here to public acts. I am aware that even these relations may be contested; for where is the man in this world, whatever be his right, and the strength and power of that right, who may not be attacked and contradicted by an adverse party? But in the eyes of men who are wise and impartial, of those who reflect and are reasonable, my voice will have as much power as another's, and I have little dread of the final decision. So much light has been diffused in our day, that I rely upon the splendor that will remain after passions shall have subsided and clouds have passed away. But, in the mean time, how many errors will arise! People will often give me credit for a great deal of depth and sagacity on occasions which were, perhaps, most simple in themselves. I shall be suspected of plans which I never formed. It will be inquired whether I did or did not aspire to universal dominion. The question will be argued at length, Whether my arbitrary sway and my arbitrary acts were the result of my character or of my calculations? whether they were determined by my own inclination or by the force of circumstances? whether I was led into the wars in which I was engaged by my own taste or against my will? whether my insatiable ambition, which has been so much deprecated, was kindled by the thirst for dominion and glory, or by my love of order and my concern for the general welfare? for that ambition will deserve to be considered under all those different aspects.

"People will canvass the motives which guided me in the catastrophe of the Duke d'Enghien, and so on with respect to many other events. Sometimes they will distort what was perfectly straight, and refine what was quite natural. It was not for me to treat upon all those subjects here. It would have appeared as if I were pleading my cause, and that I disdain to do. If the rectitude and the sagacity of historians can enable them to form, from what I have dictated on general matters, a correct opinion and just notions respecting those things which I have not mentioned, so much the better. But along with the faint ray thus afforded, how many false lights will appear to them from the fables and falsehoods of the great intriguers (who all had their views, their plots, their private negotiations, which, being mixed up with the main objects, tend to render the whole an inextricable chaos), to the disclosures, *the portfolios*, and even the assertions of my ministers, who, with the best intentions, will have to state, not so much what really existed, as what they believe to have existed; for which of them ever possessed the entire general conception of my mind? Their share of it was, most frequently, one of the elements of a great whole, which they did not know. They will, therefore, only have seen that side of the prism which concerned themselves, and even then, how will they have seen it? Did it reach them entire? Was it not already broken?

"And yet probably every one of them, judging from what he has seen, will give the fantastical result of his own combinations as my true system. And here, again, we have the admitted fable which will be called history. Nor can it be otherwise. It is true that, as there are many, they will be far from agreeing together. However, in their positive assertions they would have the advantage over me, for I should very frequently have found it most difficult to affirm confidently what had been my whole idea on any given subject. It is well known that I did not strive to subject circumstances to my ideas, but that, in general, I suffered myself to be led by them. And who can calculate beforehand the chances of accidental circumstances or unexpected events? I have, therefore, often found it necessary to alter essentially my plan of proceeding, and have acted through life upon general *principles* rather than according to fixed *plans*. The mass of the general interests of mankind, what I considered to be the advantage of the greater number, such were the anchors on which I relied, but around which I most frequently floated at the caprice of chance."

In conversation upon the conspiracy of Georges and Pichegru, and the trial of the Duke d'Enghien, the Emperor remarked:

"War had some time since recommenced with England, when suddenly our coasts, our high roads, and the capital, were inundated with agents from the Bourbons. A great number of them were arrested, but their plans could not yet be discovered. They were of all ranks and descriptions. All the passions were roused. The agitation of the public became extreme. A storm was gathering. The crisis assumed the most alarming aspect. The agents of the police had exhausted all their means without being able to obtain any information. My own sagacity saved me. Having risen, on one occasion, in the night, to work, as I used frequently to do, chance, which governs the world, directed my eyes to one of the last reports of the police, containing the names of those persons who had already been arrested in consequence of this affair, to which no clue had yet been obtained. Among those names I observed that of a surgeon in the army. I immediately concluded that such a man must be an intriguer rather than a devoted fanatic, and I ordered every measure likely to extort a prompt confession to be immediately resorted to against him. The affair was immediately placed in the hands of a military commission. In the morning he was sentenced, and threatened with immediate execution if he did not speak. Half an hour afterward he had disclosed every thing, even to the most minute details. The nature and extent of the plot, which had been got up in London, was then known, and the intrigues of Moreau, and the presence of Pichegru in Paris, were discovered soon after."

With respect to the accusation relative to the death of Pichegru, who was said to have been strangled by order of the First Consul, Napoleon said that it was too absurd, and that it would be degrading to attempt to repel it.

"What advantage," asked he, "could accrue to me from his death? A man of my stamp does not act without some powerful motive. Have I ever been known to shed blood through caprice? Notwithstanding all the efforts that have been made to blacken my reputation and misrepresent my character, those who know me know that crime is foreign to my nature. There is not a private act that has occurred during the whole course of my administration of which I might not speak openly before a tribunal, not only without any disadvantage, but even with some credit to myself. The fact is, that Pichegru found himself placed in a hopeless situation. His high mind could not bear to contemplate the infamy of a public execution. He despaired of my clemency, or disdained to appeal to it, and put an end to his existence.

"Had I been disposed to crime," continued the Emperor, "it is not against Pichegru, who could do no harm, that I should have leveled the blow, but at Moreau, who had at that moment placed me in a most perilous situation. If the latter had unfortunately also killed himself while in prison, my justification would have been rendered much more difficult, on account of the great advantage it would have been to me to get rid of him. Those Frenchmen who were abroad, and the ultra-Royalists who were in France, have never known the true state of public opinion in France. Pichegru, having been once unmasked, and exposed as a traitor to the nation, no longer excited sympathy in any breast. This feeling went so far, that the circumstance of his being connected with Moreau was sufficient to effect the ruin of the latter, who saw himself abandoned by many of his adherents; for in the struggle of parties, the majority of the people cared more about the commonwealth than about individuals.

"I judged so correctly in this business, that when Real came to propose to me to arrest Moreau, I rejected the proposal without hesitation. Moreau is a man of too much importance, said I to him; he is too directly opposed to me; I have too great an interest in getting rid of him to expose myself thus to the conjectures of public opinion. But, replied Real, if Moreau conspires with Pichegru? The case is then different; prove that to me, show me that Pichegru is in Paris, and I will instantly sign the order for the apprehension of Moreau. Real had received indirect information of Pichegru's arrival, but had not yet been able to trace his steps. Hasten to his brother's, said I; if he has left his residence, it will be a strong indication that Pichegru is in Paris. If he is still in his lodgings, arrest him; his surprise will soon inform you of the truth. This brother had been a monk, and lived on a fourth floor in Paris. As soon as he found himself arrested, he asked, before any question was put to him, what fault he had committed, and whether it was imputed to him as a crime that he had received against his will a visit from his brother. He had been the first, he said, to represent to him the peril of his situation, and to advise him to go away again.

"This was quite enough. Moreau's arrest was ordered and carried into effect. Moreau appeared, at first, to be under no apprehension; but when he found, after he had been taken to prison, that he was arrested for having conspired, together with Pichegru and Georges, against the state, he was quite disconcerted and extremely agitated. As for the greater number of those who composed that party, the name of Pichegru seemed to them a triumph. They exclaimed on all sides that Pichegru was in London, and that in a few days this would be proved, for they either did not know that he was in Paris, or believed that it would be easy for him to escape thence. In the midst of this affair that of the Duke d'Enghien happened, and rendered the whole a strange complication."

The Emperor used to consider this last affair under two distinct aspects: with reference to the common law or the established rules of justice, and with reference to the law of nature or acts of violence. In the presence of strangers, he adopted a line of argument founded almost exclusively on the law of nature and state politics.

"If I had not had in my favor the laws of the country to punish the criminal, I should still have had the right of the law of nature, of legitimate self-defense. The duke and his party had constantly but one object in view, that of taking away my life. I was assailed on all sides and at every instant. Air-guns, infernal machines, plots, ambuscades of every kind, were resorted to for that purpose. At last I grew weary, and took an opportunity of striking them with terror in their turn in London. I succeeded, and from that moment there was an end of conspiracies. Who can blame me for having acted so? What! blows threatening my existence are aimed at me day after day, from a distance of one hundred and fifty leagues! no power on earth, no tribunal, can afford me redress, and I shall not be allowed to use the right of nature, and return war for war! What man, unbiased by party feeling, possessing the smallest share of judgment and justice, can take upon himself to condemn me? On what side will he not throw blame, odium, and criminal accusations? Blood for blood! such is the natural, inevitable, and infallible law of retaliation: woe to him who provokes it! Those who foment civil dissensions or excite political commotions expose themselves to become the victims of them.

"It would be a proof of imbecility or madness to imagine and pretend that a whole family should have the strange privilege to threaten my existence day after day, without giving me the right of retaliation. They could not reasonably pretend to be above the law to destroy others, and claim the benefit of it for their own preservation. The chances must be equal. I had never personally offended any of them. A great nation had chosen me to govern them. Almost all Europe had sanctioned their choice. My blood, after all, was not ditch water. It was time to place it on a par with theirs. And what if I had carried retaliation further? I might have done it. The disposal of their destiny, the heads of every one of them, from the highest to the lowest, were more than once offered to me, but I rejected the offer with indignation. Not that I thought it would be unjust for me to consent to it, in the situation to which they had reduced me, but I felt myself so powerful,

I thought myself so secure, that I should have considered it a base and gratuitous act of cowardice. My great maxim has always been, that, in war as well as in politics, every evil action, even if legal, can only be excused in case of absolute necessity. Whatever goes beyond that is criminal.

"It would have been ridiculous in those who violated so openly the law of nations to appeal to it themselves. The violation of the territory of Baden, of which so much has been said, is entirely foreign to the main point in question. The law of the inviolability of territory has not been devised for the benefit of the guilty, but merely for the protection of the independence of nations and the dignity of the sovereign. It was therefore for the Duke of Baden, and for him alone, to complain, and *he* did not. He yielded, no doubt, to violence, and to the sentiment of his political inferiority. But even then, what has that to do with the merits of the plots and outrages which I had to complain of, and of which I had every right to be revenged? The real authors of the dreadful catastrophe, the persons who alone were responsible for it, were those who had favored and excited from abroad the plots formed against the life of the First Consul."

CHAPTER XXXIV.
1816, November. Continued.

Secret Visit from the Servant of Las Casas—Arrest of Las Casas—His Imprisonment—Indignation of the Emperor—Fainting-fit of O'Meara.

November 21–24. The servant whom Sir Hudson Lowe had taken from Las Casas obtained a situation with a person who was about to sail for London. Favored by the darkness of the night, and his knowledge of the localities of the island, he scaled precipices and avoided sentinels, and at midnight succeeded in entering the room of his former master. He offered to secrete about his person, and take to Europe, any communication which Las Casas might intrust to him. After a short interview the servant left, in the darkness, promising to call again.

Las Casas records, "The next day I immediately communicated my good fortune to the Emperor, who appeared much pleased at the intelligence. I strenuously urged that we had already been here above a year without having taken one single step toward the prospect of better days. We were lost in the universe. Europe was ignorant of our real situation. It behooved us to make it known. Day after day the newspapers showed us the veil of imposture which had been thrown over us, and the impudent and disgusting falsehoods of which we were the object. It was for us, I urged, to publish the truth. It would find its way to the ears of the sovereigns, to whom it was perfectly unknown. It would become known to the people, whose sympathy would be our consolation, and whose indignation would at least revenge us upon our cruel persecutors. We immediately began to search among our records. The Emperor portioned them out, pointing out the share which each of us was to take, in order to transcribe them with greater dispatch. The day, however, passed without any thing being done on the subject.

"The next day, as soon as I saw the Emperor, I took the liberty of reminding him of our plans of the preceding day; but he now appeared to think less of the matter, and ended the conversation by saying, 'We must see.' This day passed like the preceding. I was on thorns. At night, as if to add to my impatience, my servant came again, and renewed the unreserved offer of his services. He left, promising that he would call the day after the next, which would be the eve of his sailing. The next day, as soon as I saw the Emperor, I communicated to him what I had heard from the servant, dwelling upon the circumstance of our having only twenty-four hours more; but the Emperor, with the utmost indifference, turned the conversation to some other topic. I was struck with surprise. I knew the Emperor's disposition, and I was perfectly satisfied that the indifference, the sort of absence of mind which he manifested at this moment, could not be the effect of chance, still less the result of caprice. But what, then, could his motives be? This idea haunted my mind the whole day, and rendered me melancholy and miserable. At night, the same sentiment which had agitated my breast during the day prevented me from sleeping. I painfully recalled every circumstance connected with this affair, when suddenly a new light broke in upon me.

"What do I require of the Emperor, thought I? that he should stoop to the execution of trifling details too much beneath him! No doubt disgust and secret dissatisfaction have occasioned the silence which has caused my uneasiness. Ought we to be useless to him? Can we not serve him without afflicting him? And then several of his former observations came across my mind. Had I not informed him of the affair? Had he not approved of it? What more could I expect? Henceforth it was for me to act, and I made up my mind in one instant. I resolved to proceed in the business without mentioning another word to him on the subject; and, in order that it might remain more secret, I determined to keep it entirely to myself."

Las Casas accordingly wrote a long letter to Napoleon's brother Lucien, giving a minute, but perfectly truthful and unexaggerated account of the Emperor's history since he left France, and of his situation and sufferings. The letter was intended for the mother, brothers, and sisters of Napoleon, that they might know the true condition of the beloved captive, and that they might exert their influence to mitigate his woes. It was a noble letter, and highly honorable to the head and the heart of the writer. Prince Lucien, with the mother of Napoleon, and most of the other members of the family, were at Rome. Las Casas accordingly inclosed his letter in an envelope addressed to a friend in England, Lady Clavering, to be forwarded by her to its destination. The servant called; the letters were sewed into the lining of his clothes, and he took his departure from Longwood. It was midnight. Las Casas went to bed with a light heart.

November 25. At four o'clock in the afternoon the Emperor sent for Las

Casas. "I have been busy with General Bertrand," said he, "all day upon the subject of fortifications, and the day has appeared to me very short." They walked out to the tent. Five oranges, with a knife and some sugar, were brought on a plate. They were a present from Lady Malcolm, who had kindly sent them to the Emperor from the Cape. The Emperor requested Las Casas to put one of the oranges into his pocket for his son. Seated on the trunk of a tree, he cut the others into slices, and with his own hand distributed them to Las Casas and to another gentleman of his suite who was present. The wind blew up cold, and the Emperor returned with his companions to his chamber. As he was pacing the floor, engaged in social conversation, his attention was suddenly arrested by the appearance of the governor, with a numerous staff, approaching Longwood. The Emperor looked from the window to observe their approach. In a few moments, word was brought that the governor wished to see Las Casas.

"Go, my dear friend," said the Emperor, " and see what that animal wants of you, and *come back soon.*"

THE GOVERNOR AND HIS AIDS.

"These," says Las Casas, " were for me the last words of Napoleon.

Alas! I have never seen him since. But his accent, the tone of his voice, still sound in my ears. How often since have I taken delight in allowing my imagination to dwell upon them! and what mingled sensations of pleasure and regret may be produced by a painful recollection!"

It seems that the servant had revealed his secret to his father, and his father had betrayed Las Casas to the governor. As Las Casas entered his room, he and his son were immediately arrested by Sir Thomas Reade. His room was guarded by dragoons. He was not permitted to bid adieu to the Emperor, but, with his son, was immediately hurried away from Longwood. "We were both of us," says Las Casas, "shut up in a wretched hovel. I was obliged to sleep on a miserable pallet, and to make room for my poor son by my side, lest he should have to lie on the floor. I considered his life to be at this moment in danger. He was threatened with an aneurism, and had been on the point of expiring in my arms a few days before. We were kept until eleven o'clock without food; and when, in order to supply the wants of my son, I went to the door, and to each of the windows, to ask the men who guarded them for a morsel of bread, they answered me only by presenting their bayonets."

ARREST OF LAS CASAS.

As Dr. O'Meara was riding to Longwood from town, he met the governor. Sir Hudson called out to him immediately with a triumphant air, "You will meet your friend Las Casas in custody." In a few moments the doctor met the count, conducted by two dragoons. The Emperor, from his window, had noticed most of these proceedings.

November 26. Las Casas was kept in close confinement in his room. His friends earnestly, but vainly, solicited permission to visit him in his prison. As a demonstration of respect and kindness, they came within sight of the hut where he was guarded, and made signs to him of sympathy. All his private papers were seized and examined, and all the valuable dictations of the Emperor, which were in Las Casas's possession. Napoleon was heavily afflicted. He sympathized deeply with his friend in sufferings, and also greatly deplored his own loss in being deprived of so congenial a companion. The Emperor, thus suddenly bereaved, concealed his grief in the solitude of his chamber. To O'Meara, who soon entered his apartments, the Emperor said,

"I am indeed grieved to lose him. Las Casas is the only one of the French who can speak English well, or who can explain it to my satisfaction. I can not now read the English newspapers. Las Casas was necessary to me. Ask the admiral to interest himself for that poor man. He will die under these afflictions, for he has no bodily strength, and his unfortunate son will finish his existence a little before him."

November 27. Las Casas and his son still remained in their solitary and wretched prison, secluded from all intercourse with Longwood and its unhappy inmates. The Emperor still remained a silent mourner in his room, enduring with dignity these tremendous blows of adverse fortune. O'Meara visited his illustrious patient. He found him deeply distressed about the treatment which Las Casas suffered, and the detention of his own papers.

"If there had been any plot in Las Casas's letter," said the Emperor, "the governor could have perceived it in ten minutes' perusal. In a few moments he could also see that the Campaigns of Italy contained nothing treasonable. It is contrary to all law to detain papers belonging to me. Perhaps he will come up here some day and say that he has received intimation that a plot to effect my escape is in agitation. What guarantee have I, that when I have nearly finished my history, he will not seize the whole of it? It is true that I can keep my manuscripts in my own room, and with a couple of brace of pistols I can dispatch the first who enters. I must burn the whole of what I have written. It served as an amusement to me in this dismal abode, and might, perhaps, have been interesting to the world; but with this Sicilian constable there is no guarantee nor security. He violates every law, and tramples under foot decency, politeness, and the common forms of society. He came up with a savage joy beaming from his eyes because he had an opportunity of insulting and tormenting us. While surrounding the house with his staff, he reminded me of the savages of the South Sea Islands dancing round the prisoners whom they were going to devour. Tell him," continued he, "what I said about his conduct."

For fear that O'Meara should forget, he repeated his expressions about the savages a second time, and made the doctor repeat it after him.

November 28. To-day Las Casas and his son were removed to a wretched hovel situated but a short distance from Longwood, but separated from it by precipitous crags and wild ravines which were almost impassable. A detachment of soldiers kept guard over them, while numerous sentinels watched all the approaches to their prison.

"All communications were strictly intercepted," says Las Casas; "we were placed in a state of the most absolute seclusion. On the summit of the hills which surrounded the hollow in which our house was situated there was a road on which we saw to-day General Gourgaud, accompanied by an English officer. We could observe his efforts to come as near to us as possible, and we received with feelings of joy and affection the signs and demonstrations of friendship which our companion addressed to us from that distance, and returned ours to him in the same manner. The kind and excellent Madam Bertrand sent us again some oranges. We were not allowed to write her to thank her, and were obliged to confine the expression of our gratitude to sending her some roses which we gathered in our prison."

November 29. The governor had seized Las Casas's journal, with his other papers, and had read with chagrin the record of his own doings. He knew that this memorial was intended for eventual publication, and he was greatly annoyed. As he eagerly examined it, in the presence of Las Casas, turning over the pages to see every thing which was said respecting himself, Las Casas said to him,

"If you find it often necessary to use forbearance, it is not my fault, but the fault of your own indiscretion. My journal is not yet known to any body. The Emperor himself has only read the first pages of it. You can, of course, do as you please about proceeding farther, but I protest against the abuse of authority which you will thus exercise."

The governor respected this protest, and the journal was sealed up.

EXAMINING THE PAPERS OF LAS CASAS.

The Emperor, hearing that the journal of Las Casas had been seized and examined by the governor, was curious to know what kind of record Las Casas had made of their prison life. He sent, accordingly, for one of the household, St. Denis, who had made a careful copy of the journal, and asked him the nature of it.

"It is," said St. Denis, "a journal of every thing remarkable that has taken place since the embarkation on board the *Bellerophon*, and contains diverse anecdotes of Sir George Cockburn and many other persons."

"How is Sir George Cockburn treated?" inquired the Emperor.

"So so," was the reply.

"Is it said that I called him a shark?"

"Yes, sire."

"What is said of Sir George Bingham and General Wilkes?"

"They are very well spoken of."

"Is any thing said about Admiral Malcolm? Does it say that I observed, 'Behold the countenance of a real Englishman?'"

"Yes, sire; he is very well treated."

"Is any thing said about the governor?"

"Yes, sire," replied St. Denis, smiling, "a great deal."

"Does it say that I said, 'He is an *ignoble* man, and that his face was the most ignoble I had ever seen?'"

"It does, sire," said St. Denis, "but the expressions are frequently *moderated*."

"Is the anecdote of the coffee-cup related?"

"I do not recollect it," was the reply.

"Is it said that I called him a Sicilian constable? (*sbirre Sicilien*.)"

"Yes, sire."

"That's his name (*c'est son nom*)," said the Emperor.

Shortly after, the Emperor had an interview with Dr. O'Meara. He said,

"This governor, if he had any delicacy, would not have continued to read a work in which his conduct was depicted in its true light. He must have been little satisfied with the comparisons made between Cockburn and him, especially where it is mentioned that I said the admiral was rough, but incapable of a mean action, but that his successor was capable of every thing that was oppressive and contemptible. I am glad, however, that he has read it, because he will see the real opinion that we have of him."

"While he was speaking," says O'Meara, "my vision became indistinct, every thing appeared to swim before my eyes, and I fell upon the floor in a fainting-fit.[*] When I recovered my senses and opened my eyes, the first object which presented itself to my view I shall never forget: it was the countenance of Napoleon bending over my face, and regarding me with an expression of great concern and anxiety. With one hand he was opening my shirt collar, and with the other holding a bottle *de vinaigre des quatre voleurs* to my nostrils. He had taken off my cravat, and dashed the contents of a bottle of *eau de Cologne* over my face.

"'When I saw you fall,' said he, 'I at first thought that your foot had slipped; but seeing you remain without motion, I apprehended that it was a fit of apoplexy; observing, however, that your face was the color of death,

---

[*] O'Meara was quite unwell, and had been, that morning, profusely bled by Dr M‘Lean, of the 53d regiment, in consequence of aggravated symptoms of a liver complaint, a disease extremely prevalent in the island.

your lips white and without motion, and no evident respiration or bloated countenance, I concluded directly that it was a fit of syncope, or that your soul had departed.'

"Marchand now came into the room, whom he ordered to give me some orange-flower water, which was a favorite remedy of his. When he saw me fall, in his haste he broke the bell-ribbon. He told me that he had lifted me up, placed me in a chair, torn off my cravat, dashed some *eau de Cologne* and water over my face, &c., and asked if he had done right. I informed him that he had done every thing proper, and as a surgeon would have done under similar circumstances, except that, instead of allowing me to remain in a recumbent posture, he had placed me in a chair. When I was leaving the room, I heard him tell Marchand, in an under voice, to follow me, for fear I should again faint."

CHAPTER XXXV.
1816, December.

Decision of Las Casas to return to Europe—Remarks of the Emperor upon the Conduct of the Governor—Remarks on Moreau, Desaix, Massena—Message to the Emperor from the Governor—Indignant Remarks of the Emperor—Character of Alexander—The Expedition to Copenhagen—The Call from Lady Lowe—Continued Imprisonment of Las Casas—Political Blunders of Lord Castlereagh—The Manufactures of France.

December 1. The new month dawned gloomily upon the Emperor. Las Casas was in close confinement, and greatly perplexed respecting his probable fate. His son was sick, and fast sinking, apparently, in the arms of death. The governor was probably no less embarrassed to know what to do with his prisoner. He could not wantonly detain him for months and years in solitary confinement at St. Helena, for in his papers there had not been found the slightest indication of any plot to assist in the escape of the Emperor. Should he send his prisoner to Europe, he would there reveal, to the millions who loved Napoleon with deathless fervor, all the awful secrets of his prison-house.

Eight days of imprisonment slowly passed away without the least apparent approach to any result. After meditating long and anxiously, Las Casas wrote a letter to the governor, appealing to the tribunals of England for justice and judgment, and demanding that he, with his papers, should immediately be sent there.

The Emperor also expressed to Dr. O'Meara the opinion that that would be the best course he could pursue.

"I hope," said he, "that Las Casas will return to England. Three or four months' stay in St. Helena will be of little utility either to him or to me. The next to be removed, under some pretext, will be Montholon, as they see that he is a most useful and consoling friend to me, and that he always endeavors to anticipate my wants. I am less unfortunate than they are. I see nobody. They are subject to daily insults and vexations. They can not speak, they can not write, they can not stir out, without submitting to degrading restrictions. I am sorry that, two months ago, they did not all go. I have sufficient force to resist alone against all this tyranny. It is only prolonging their agony to keep them here a few months longer. After they have been taken away, you will be sent off, and then the crime will be consummated.

"They are subject to every caprice which arbitrary power chooses to inflict, and are not protected by any laws. He is at once jailer, governor, accuser, judge, and sometimes executioner; for example, when he seized that East Indiaman, who was recommended by that brave man, Colonel Skelton, to General Montholon, as a good servant. He came up here and seized the man with his own hands, under my windows. He did justice to himself, certainly. The business of a constable becomes him much better than that of the representative of a great nation. A soldier is better off than they are, as, if he is accused, he must be tried according to known forms before he can be punished. In the worst dungeon in England, a prisoner is not denied printed papers and books. Except obliging me to see him, he has done every thing to annoy me."

December 3–4. The Emperor remained in his room, and was quite unwell. Dr. O'Meara records the following conversation as occurring in his sick-chamber:

"Moreau," said the Emperor, "was an excellent general of division, but not fit to command a large army. With a hundred thousand men, Moreau would divide his army in different positions, covering roads, and would not do more than if he had only thirty thousand. He did not know how to profit either by the number of his troops or by their position. Very calm and cool in the field, he was more collected and better able to command in the heat of an action than to make dispositions prior to it. He was often seen smoking his pipe in battle. Moreau was not naturally a man of a bad heart. He was a merry fellow, but he had but little character. He was led away by his wife and another intriguing Creole. His having joined Pichegru and Georges in the conspiracy, and subsequently having closed his life fighting against his country, will ever disgrace his memory. As a general, Moreau was infinitely inferior to Desaix, or to Kleber, or even to Soult.

"Of all the generals I ever had under me, Desaix and Kleber possessed the greatest talents, especially Desaix, as Kleber only loved glory inasmuch as it was the means of procuring him riches and pleasures, whereas Desaix loved glory for itself, and despised every thing else. Desaix was wholly rapt up in war and glory. To him riches and pleasure were valueless, nor did he give them a moment's thought. He was a little, black-looking man, about an inch shorter than I am, always badly dressed, sometimes even ragged, and despising comfort or convenience.

"When in Egypt, I made him a present of a complete field-equipage several times, but he always lost it. Wrapped up in a cloak, Desaix threw himself under a gun, and slept as contentedly as if he were in a palace. For him luxury had no charms. Upright and honest in all his proceedings, he was called by the Arabs *the just sultan.* He was intended by Nature for a great general. Kleber and Desaix were a loss irreparable to France. Had Kleber lived, your army in Egypt would have perished. Had that imbecile Menou attacked you on your landing with twenty thousand men, as he might have done, instead of the division Lanusse, your army would have been only a meal for them. You were seventeen or eighteen thousand strong, without cavalry.

"Massena," said he, "was a man of superior talent. He generally, however, made bad dispositions previous to a battle, and it was not until the dead fell around him that he began to act with that judgment which he ought to have displayed before. In the midst of the dying and the dead, of balls sweeping away those who encircled him, then Massena was himself—gave his orders, and made his dispositions with the greatest *sang froid* and judgment. This is true nobleness of blood. It was truly said of Massena that he never began to act with judgment until the battle was going against him. He was, however, a robber. He went halves along with the contractors and commissaries of the army. I signified to him often that, if he would discontinue his peculations, I would make him a present of eight hundred thousand or a million of francs, but he had acquired such a habit that he could not keep his hands from money. On this account he was hated by the soldiers, who mutinied against him three or four times. However, considering the circumstances of the times, he was precious; and, had not his bright parts been soiled with the vice of avarice, he would have been a great man."

Sir Hudson Lowe came up to Longwood, and observed to Dr. O'Meara that General Bonaparte had adopted a very bad mode of procedure, by in a manner declaring war against him (Sir Hudson), when he was the *only* person who had it in his power to render him a service or to make his situation comfortable. He then made some remarks upon "General Bonaparte's constantly confining himself to his room," and asked what O'Meara supposed would induce him to go out.

O'Meara replied, "An enlargement of his boundaries, taking off some of the restrictions, and giving him a house at the other side of the island. He has frequently complained that he could not walk out at Longwood without getting a pain in his head from the sun, as there was no shade; or, if the rays of the sun were obscured, his cheeks became inflamed; or a catarrh was produced by the sharp wind blowing over an elevated spot without shelter." O'Meara observed, also, that the allowance of provision was totally insufficient, as the French laid out seven or eight pounds a day in articles which were indispensable, and which he enumerated.

Sir Hudson Lowe answered, "With respect to this last, I have exceeded by one half what is allowed by the ministers, who are answerable to Parliament that the expenses of Longwood do not exceed eight thousand pounds per annum, and perhaps I may be obliged hereafter to pay the surplus out of my own salary. My instructions are much more rigid than those of my predecessor. The British government do not wish to render General Bonaparte's existence miserable, or to torture him. It is not so much himself they are afraid of; but turbulent and disaffected people in Europe will make use of his name and influence to excite rebellion and disturbances in France and elsewhere, in order to aggrandize themselves, and otherwise answer their own purposes. Las Casas is also very well treated, and wants for nothing."

This he desired O'Meara would communicate to General Bonaparte. The doctor communicated some of those remarks of the governor's to Napoleon, who replied,

"I do not believe that he acts according to his instructions; or if he does, he has disgraced himself by accepting a dishonorable employment. A government two thousand leagues off, and ignorant of the localities of the island, can never give orders in detail. They can only give general and discretionary ones. They have only directed him to adopt every measure he may think necessary to prevent my escape. Instead of that, I am treated in a manner dishonorable to humanity. To kill and bury a man is well understood, but this slow torture, this killing in detail, is much less humane than if they ordered me to be shot at once.

"I have often heard," continued he, "of the tyranny and oppressions practiced in your colonies, but I never thought that there could exist such violations of law and of justice as are practiced here. From what I have seen of you English, I think there is not a nation on earth more enslaved."

Here O'Meara begged him not to form his opinion of the English nation by a little colony, placed under peculiar circumstances, and subject to military law.

"I only speak of you," said the Emperor, "as I have seen you, and I find you to be the greatest slaves upon earth. All trembling with fear at the sight of that governor! There is Sir George Bingham, who is a well-disposed man, yet he is so much afraid that he will not come and see me, through fear that he might give umbrage to the governor. The rest of the officers run away at the sight of us."

O'Meara observed that it was not fear, but delicacy, which prevented Sir George Bingham from coming, and that, as to the other officers, they must obey the orders which they had received.

Napoleon replied, "If they were French officers, they would not be afraid of expressing their opinion as to the barbarity of the treatment pursued here; and a French general, second in command, would, if he saw his country dishonored in the manner yours is, write a complaint of it himself to his government. As to myself," continued he, "I would never make a complaint, if I did not know that, were an inquiry demanded by the nation, your ministers would say, 'He has never complained, and *therefore* he is conscious that he is well treated, and that there are no grounds for it.' Otherwise I should conceive it degrading to me to utter a word, though I am so disgusted with the conduct of this *sbirro* that I should, with the greatest pleasure, receive the intimation that orders had arrived to shoot me. I should esteem it a blessing."

O'Meara observed that Sir Hudson Lowe had professed himself very desirous to accommodate and arrange matters in an amicable manner.

Napoleon replied, " If he wishes to accommodate, let him put things upon the same footing they were during the time of Admiral Cockburn. Let no person be permitted to enter here for the purpose of seeing me without a letter from Bertrand. If he does not like to give Bertrand liberty to pass people in, let him make out a list himself of such persons in the island as he will allow to visit, and send it to Bertrand, and let the latter have the power to grant them permission to enter, and to write to them.

" When strangers arrive, in like manner let him make out a list of such as he will permit to see us, and, during their stay, let them be allowed to visit with Bertrand's pass. Perhaps I should see very few of them, as it is difficult to distinguish between those who come up to see me as they would a wild boar, and others who are actuated by motives of respect; but still I should like to have the privilege. It is for him to accommodate, if he likes. He has the power, I have none. I am not governor; I have no places to give away. Let him take off his prohibitions that I shall not quit the high road, or speak to a lady if I meet one. In a few words, let him behave well to me. If he does not choose to treat me like a man, let him not treat me worse than a galley-slave or a condemned criminal, as they are not prohibited to speak. Let him do this, and then I will say that he acted at first inconsiderately, through fear of my escaping, but that when he saw his error he was not ashamed to alter his treatment. Then I will say that I formed a hasty opinion of him—that I have been mistaken. You are a child, doctor; you have too good an opinion of mankind. This man is not sincere. I believe the opinion I first formed of him is correct; that he is a man whose natural badness is increased by suspicion and dread of the responsibility of the situation which he holds. He is a man crafty, abject, and entirely unfitted for his office.

" I would wager my life," continued he, " that if I sent for Sir George Bingham, or the admiral, to ride out with me, before I had gone out three times with either the one or the other, this governor would make some insinuations to them which would render me liable to be affronted by their refusing to accompany me any longer. He says that Las Casas is well treated, and wants for nothing, because he does not starve him. He is a man truly ignoble. He degrades his own species. He pays no attention to the moral wants which distinguish the man from the brute; he only looks to the physical and grosser ones. Just as if Las Casas were a horse or an ass, and that a bundle of hay was sufficient to entitle him to say he is happy; because his stomach was full, therefore all his wants were satisfied."

December 5. Dr. O'Meara had a long conversation with the Emperor in his bath. He asked his opinion of the Emperor Alexander, "*C'est un homme extrêmement faux—un Grec du bas empire,*"* replied Napoleon. He is plausible, a great dissimulator, very ambitious, and a man who studies to make himself popular. It is his foible to believe himself skilled in the art of war, and he likes nothing so well as to be complimented upon it, although every thing that originated with himself, relative to military operations, was

* He is a man extremely treacherous—a Greek of the Lower Empire.

ill-judged and absurd. At Tilsit, Alexander and the King of Prussia used frequently to occupy themselves in contriving dresses for dragoons; debating upon what button the crosses of the orders ought to be hung, and such other fooleries. They fancied themselves on an equality with the best generals in Europe, because they knew how many rows of buttons there were upon a dragoon's jacket. I could scarcely keep from laughing sometimes, when I heard them discussing these trivialities with as much gravity and earnestness as if they were planning an impending action between two hundred thousand men. However, I encouraged them in their arguments, as I saw it was their weak point."

Speaking of his own wonderful career, the Emperor said, "Nothing has been more simple than my elevation. It was not the result of intrigue or crime. It was owing to the peculiar circumstances of the times, and because I fought successfully against the enemies of my country. What is most extraordinary, and, I believe, unparalleled in history, is, that I rose from being a private person to the astonishing height of power I possessed without having committed a single crime to obtain it. If I were on my death-bed I could make the same declaration."

Speaking of the expedition to Copenhagen, he remarked, "That expedition showed great energy on the part of your ministers. But, setting aside the violation of the laws of nations which you committed, for, in fact, it was nothing but a robbery, I think that it was injurious to your interests, as it made the brave Danish nation irreconcilable enemies to you, and, in fact, shut you out of the north for three years. When I heard of it, I said, I am glad of it, as it will embroil England irrecoverably with the northern powers. The Danes being able to join me with sixteen sail of the line was of but little consequence. I had plenty of ships, and only wanted seamen, whom you did not take, and whom I obtained afterward; while by the expedition your ministers established their characters as faithless, and as persons with whom no engagements, no laws were binding."

Lady Lowe came up to Longwood, and paid a visit, for the first time, to Countesses Bertrand and Montholon.

December 6. Las Casas still remained in his prison, entirely uninformed respecting his future destiny. Dreary hours of monotony, of sickness, and of gloom oppressed the Emperor. The memory of his wife and of his beloved child, whom he was never to see again, weighed heavily upon him. When Dr. O'Meara called this day upon his patient, sinking by slow torture to the grave, Napoleon said,

"The visit of Lady Lowe yesterday appeared to me to be an artifice of her husband to throw dust in the eyes; to make people believe that, notwithstanding the arrest of Las Casas, the governor was very well received at Longwood, and had only done his duty; and that there was no foundation for the reports which had been spread of the ill treatment said to be inflicted upon the inhabitants of Longwood."

Dr. O'Meara remarked that Lady Lowe had been always desirous to call upon Countesses Bertrand and Montholon, and had embraced the first opportunity which presented itself after her accouchement.

Napoleon replied, "I am far from thinking that she participates in the designs of her husband, but she has badly chosen the time. At the moment when he treats Las Casas so barbarously and illegally, he sends her up. It is either an artifice of her husband's to blind the world, or else he mocks our misfortunes. Nothing is so insulting as to add irony to injury."

Dr. O'Meara observed that more probably it was a preliminary step of the governor's toward an accommodation.

"No," replied Napoleon, "that can not be. If he really wished to accommodate, the first step would be to take away some of his useless and oppressive restrictions. Yesterday, after his wife had been here, Madam Bertrand and family went out to walk. On their return, they were stopped and seized by the sentinels, who refused to let them in because it was six o'clock. Now, in the name of Heaven, if he had a mind to accommodate, would he continue to prevent us from walking at the only time of the day when, at this season, it is agreeable? Tell him," continued Napoleon, "candidly, the observations I have made, if he asks you what I thought of the visit."

December 7. Las Casas makes the following record: "Our situation still offers the same uniformity; no appearance of our approaching toward any result whatever. It is now almost a fortnight since the unfortunate event took place, and we are still in the same state of seclusion, exposed to the same restrictions, the same torments. We seldom receive any news of the Emperor, and then only through the governor himself. Our prison is situated precisely opposite to, and at no great distance from Longwood, from which we are only separated by precipices. Whenever we raise our eyes we see before us that object of our thoughts and wishes, and we are forever turning them toward it. We can follow the daily avocations of its inhabitants, which are so familiar to us, but we can not possibly distinguish any living object. This constant attraction constantly opposed, this proximity, and, at the same time, this great distance, this object of our wishes forever present, and, as it were, forever withdrawn from us, all this together forms something like the hell of the ancients.

"My son continues to be extremely ill. Dr. Baxter, senior medical officer of the island, and an inmate of Government House, came, with a degree of politeness of which I preserve the recollection with a sincere feeling of gratitude, to add his cares with those of Dr. O'Meara. They both have represented to Sir Hudson Lowe the critical state of my son, and warmly supported my request that he might be sent to Europe. Dr. O'Meara having, after a fresh crisis, renewed the subject alone, Sir Hudson Lowe put an end to his importunities by the following words, which Dr. O'Meara has since repeated to my son and myself:

"'Well, sir, after all, what matters the death of a child in a case of politics?'

"I hand over the naked phrase to every paternal heart and to all mothers."

December 8. The Emperor, while in his bath, received Dr. O'Meara. He regarded the doctor with very friendly feelings, and, though he could not converse with him, a foreigner and an English officer, confidingly respecting his conflicts and his griefs, he could freely communicate his thoughts upon all topics of general interest. He spoke quite at length upon the depressed condition of England, which he attributed to the incapacity of Lord Castlereagh. Then turning to France, he said,

"You will find that in a few years very little English merchandise will be sold on the Continent. I gave a new era to manufactories. The French already excel you in the manufacture of cloths and many other articles; the Hollanders in cambric and linen. I formed several thousand. I established the Polytechnic School, from which hundreds of able chemists went to the different manufactories. In each of them, I caused a person well skilled in chemistry to reside. In consequence, every thing proceeded upon certain and established principles, and they had a reason to give for every part of their operations, instead of the old, vague, and uncertain mode.

"Times are changed," continued Napoleon, "and you must no longer look to the Continent for the disposal of your manufactures. America, the Spanish and Portuguese Main, are the only vent for them. Recollect what I say to you. In a year or two, your people will complain, and say, 'We have gained every thing, but we are starving; we are worse than we were during the war.' Then perhaps your ministers will endeavor to effect what they ought to have done at first. You are not able to face even Prussia in the field, and your preponderance on the Continent was entirely owing to that naval sovereignty which perhaps you may lose by this military disease of your ministers."

CHAPTER XXXVI.
1816, December. Continued.

Letter from the Emperor to Las Casas—Arrival of Sir Thomas Strange—Brutality of Colonel Reade—Death of Moreau—Anecdote—Continued Imprisonment of Las Casas—Relentings of the Governor—Views of the Emperor respecting his Situation—Las Casas forbidden to take leave of the Emperor—Departure of Las Casas—His subsequent Persecutions.

December 10. The Emperor still kept his room. He was feeble and in low spirits. Sir Hudson Lowe returned two or three chapters of the Campaigns of Italy, but retained the rest. Napoleon requested Dr. O'Meara to inform the governor that he supposed he was getting them copied, and according as they were finished he would send them back.

The governor was very angry in the reception of this message, and said, at the close of a long and passionate conversation,

"General Bonaparte can not be permitted to run about the country. If the intentions of ministers were only to prevent his escape from the island, a company's governor would have answered as well as any other person. But there are other objects in view, and material ones, which I have been sent out to fulfill. There are several strong reasons for not allowing him to communicate in the island. Any man might secure his person by planting sentries about him; but much more is to be done. Tell General Bonaparte that it is very fortunate for him that he has so good a man as myself for governor over him. Others, with the instructions which I have, would put him in chains for his conduct."

December 11. The Emperor wrote the following letter to Las Casas:

"Longwood, December 11, 1816.

"MY DEAR COUNT LAS CASAS,—My heart is deeply sensible of what you are suffering. Torn from me seventeen or eighteen days ago, you are secretly imprisoned, and I can neither hear from you nor send news of myself; you have not been allowed to communicate with any one, either French or English, and are even deprived of a servant of your own choice.

"Your conduct at St. Helena has been, like your life, honorable and blameless; I have pleasure in telling you so.

"Your letter to your friend in London contains nothing reprehensible. You there poured out your heart into the bosom of friendship. This letter is like the eight or ten others which you sent open. The governor of this island, having had the indelicacy to scrutinize the expressions which you confided to friendship, reproached you with them; lastly, he threatened to send you from the island if your letters contained any more complaints. In acting thus, he violated the first duty of his post, the first article of his restrictions, and the first sentiment of honor. He thus authorized you to seek some means of opening your heart to your friends, and of acquainting them with the guilty conduct of the governor. But you are incapable of artifice; it was easy to surprise your confidence.

"A pretext was wanted for seizing your papers. A letter to your friend in London could not authorize a police visit to your apartment, for this letter contains no plot, no mystery; it is but the outpouring of an open and noble heart. The illegal and precipitate conduct pursued on this occasion bears the character of a mean and personal hatred.

"In the least civilized countries, exiles, prisoners, and even criminals, are under the protection of the laws or magistrates. The persons appointed to guard them have superiors, either in the administration or in the judicial order, who inspect their conduct. But here, on this rock, the same man who makes the most absurd regulations, executes them with violence, and transgresses all laws, and there is no one to restrain the excess of his caprice.

"Longwood is wrapped in a veil which he would fain make impenetrable, in order to hide criminal conduct. This peculiar care to conceal matters gives room to suspect the most odious intentions.

"False rumors have been spread, for the purpose of deceiving the officers, strangers, and inhabitants of this island, and even the foreign agents, who, they say, are kept here by Austria and Russia. The English government is certainly deceived, in the same manner, by cunning and false information.

"Your papers, among which it was well known that there were some belonging to me, were seized, without any formality, close to my apartment, and with expressions of ferocious joy. I was informed of this some few moments afterward. I looked through the window, and saw them taking you away. A numerous staff pranced about you. I imagined I saw some

South Sea Islanders dancing round the prisoners whom they were about to devour.

"Your services were necessary to me; you alone could read, speak, and understand English. How many nights have you watched over me during my illness! Nevertheless, I request you, and, in case of need, command you, to require the governor to send you to the Continent. He can not refuse, because he has no power over you except through the voluntary document which you signed. It would be a great consolation to me to know that you were on your way to more happy countries.

"When you arrive in Europe, whether you go to England or return to France, forget the misfortunes to which you have been subjected. Boast of the fidelity you showed me, and all the affection I bore you.

"If you should some day see my wife and my son, embrace them from me. For two years I have had no news from them, direct or indirect. A German botanist, who saw them a few days before his departure, in the garden of Schoenbrun, has been residing here for six months, but the barbarians will not allow him to come and tell me what he knows of them.

"And, lastly, be consoled, and console my friends. My body is, it is true, in the power of my enemies' hatred, and they neglect nothing which may gratify their vengeance. They are killing me by slow degrees, but Providence is too just to allow this to be much prolonged. The unhealthiness of this destroying climate, and the want of every thing which sustains and animates life, will soon—I feel it—put an end to an existence whose last moments will be the disgrace of the English character. Europe will one day point with horror at the hypocritical and wicked man whom true Englishmen will disown as a countryman.

"As all circumstances incline me to think that you will not be permitted to come and see me before your departure, receive my embraces, and the assurances of my esteem and friendship. Be happy!

"Yours affectionately,
"(Signed), NAPOLEON."

This letter, sealed, was sent to the governor, to be given by him to Las Casas; but Sir Hudson Lowe immediately returned it, with a note to General Bertrand, stating that no communications could be permitted between Longwood and Las Casas except such as were transmitted open. The Emperor was reclining upon his sofa at the moment when the letter was brought back to him with this new obstacle. He took the letter, broke the seal, and returned it, without even looking at the person who had brought back the letter to him. The governor then called upon Las Casas, and, after a long and awkward preamble, said,

"I hold in my hand a letter, which my situation gives me a right to withhold from you; but I know how dear to you is the hand that wrote it, and how much you value the sentiments which it expresses. I am, therefore, going to show it to you, notwithstanding the many personal motives I may have for not doing so."

"It was," says Las Casas, "a letter from the Emperor. I showed myself so much affected that the governor appeared to be moved by it, and consented to my request of being allowed to take a copy of what was merely personal in the letter. My son copied it in a hurry, so much we dreaded lest he should alter his mind; and when he left us, we recopied it in many ways and in many places. We even learned it by heart, so great was our fear that the night's reflections might occasion Sir Hudson Lowe to repent."

December 12. Sir Thomas Strange, judge of the Supreme Court in Calcutta, had called at St. Helena on his return from England. He was very anxious to see the Emperor. Sir Hudson Lowe requested Dr. O'Meara to endeavor to obtain for him an interview.

"I informed the Emperor," says Dr. O'Meara, "that Sir Thomas Strange, who had been chief judge in the East Indies, was desirous of paying his respects to him, and that his intended visit did not arise from curiosity, but was a mark of that attention which every person ought to show toward so great a man, and one who had filled so high a station in the world."

Napoleon replied, "I will see no person who does not first go to Bertrand. Persons sent direct by the governor I will not see, as it would have the appearance of obeying a command from him."

Count Bertrand now came in, and mentioned that the governor was at Longwood, and wanted to see Dr. O'Meara.

Napoleon then said, "If he asks you any questions about my thoughts, tell him that I intend writing a protest to the Prince Regent against his barbarous conduct; that his keeping Las Casas in custody, when there is nothing against him, is illegal; that he ought either to be sent back here, or sent off the island, or tried; that if he wishes to accommodate differences, as he informed you, let him alter his conduct, and put matters upon the footing they were during the time of Admiral Cockburn. As to the visit of the judge, whom he wishes me to see, tell him *that those who have gone down to the tomb receive no visits;* and take care that the judge be made acquainted with my answer."

When the governor received this answer, he was extremely angry, and Sir Thomas Reade replied,

"If I were governor, I'll be d—d if I would not make him feel that he was a prisoner."

"Why, you can not," said Dr. O'Meara, "do much more to him than you have already done, unless you put him in irons."

"Oh," answered Reade, "if he did not comply with what I wanted, I'll be d—d if I wouldn't take his books from him, which I'll advise the governor to do. He is a d—d outlaw and a prisoner, and the governor has a right to treat him with as much severity as he likes, and nobody has any business to interfere with him in the execution of his duty."

December 13. In an interview with Dr. O'Meara, the Emperor spoke of the probability of a revolution in France.

"Ere twenty years have elapsed, when I am dead and buried," said he, "you will witness another revolution in France. It is impossible that twenty-nine millions of Frenchmen can live contented under the yoke of sovereigns imposed upon them by foreigners, and against whom they have fought and bled for nearly thirty years. Can you blame the French for not being willing to submit to the yoke of such *animals* as Montchenu? You are very fond in England of making a comparison between the restoration of Charles the Second and that of Louis, but there is not the smallest similitude. Charles was recalled by the mass of the English nation to the throne which his successor afterward lost for a *mass;* but as to the Bourbons, there is not a village in France which has not lost thirty or forty of the flower of its youth in endeavoring to prevent their return. The sentiments of the nation are, '*We* have not brought back those wretches; no, those who have ravaged our country, burned our houses, and violated our wives and our daughters, have placed them on the throne by force.'"

O'Meara asked the Emperor some questions about the share that Moreau had in Georges' conspiracy.

"Moreau," said he, "confessed to his advocate that he had seen and con-

THE FALL OF MOREAU.

versed with Georges and Pichegru, and that, on his trial, he intended to avow it. Moreau, in an interview with the other two conspirators, insisted that the first step to be taken was to kill me; that when I was disposed of, he should have great power and influence with the army, but that, as long as I lived, he could do nothing.

"In the battle before Dresden," said Napoleon, "I ordered an attack to be made upon the Allies by both flanks of my army. While the maneuvers for this purpose were executing, the centre remained motionless. At the distance of about from this to the outer gate,* I observed a group of persons collected together on horseback. Concluding that they were endeavoring to observe my maneuvers, I resolved to disturb them, and called to a captain of artillery, who commanded a field battery of eighteen or twenty pieces, '*Jettez une douzaine de boulets à la fois dans ce groupe là, peut-être il y a quelques petits généraux.*' (Throw a dozen of bullets at once into that group; perhaps there are some little generals in it.) It was done instantly. One of the balls struck Moreau, carried off both his legs, and went through his horse. Many more, I believe, who were near him, were killed and wounded. A moment before, Alexander had been speaking to him."

It was during this campaign that Bessières, one of Napoleon's most valued and devoted friends, fell at his side.

DEATH OF BESSIÈRES.

December 15. Dr. O'Meara mentioned to the Emperor that Sir Hudson Lowe had inquired if the interference of Sir George Bingham as intermediator would probably be of any service in bringing about a reconciliation between the governor and his captives.

"Perhaps it might be of some service," said the Emperor; "but all he has to do is to conduct himself no longer as a jailer, but behave like a gentleman. If any person were to undertake the office of mediator, the most suitable would be the admiral, both because he is independent of Sir Hud-

* About five hundred yards.

son Lowe, and because he is a man with whom I can reason and argue. But when your ministry is insincere, wants to shuffle, or has nothing good to execute, a miscreant like Drake, or Sir Hudson Lowe, is sent out as embassador or governor. When it is the contrary, and it wishes to conciliate or treat, such a man as Lord Cornwallis is employed. A Cornwallis here would be of more avail than all the restrictions that could be imagined."

December 18. The governor was now evidently much embarrassed to know what to do with Las Casas. He was a dangerous man to send to Europe, to proclaim there all the secret outrages of Longwood. But Las Casas, after the solitary imprisonment of more than a month, had fully decided to insist upon this as his right.

"I can," said he to himself, "no longer be of any great service to the Emperor here, but I may, perhaps, be useful to him elsewhere. I will go to England, and appeal to the ministers. Whatever I say will evidently come from the heart. I will paint the truth, and they can not but be touched with the miseries I shall unfold to them. They will ameliorate the condition of the illustrious captive, and I will myself return and lay at his feet the consolation which my zeal will have procured."

He was confirmed in this opinion by a sentence in the Emperor's letter, indicating coincidence in the same judgment:

"I request you, and, in case of need, *command* you to require the governor to send you to the Continent."

But the more urgently Las Casas pressed this claim, the more reluctant the governor appeared to grant it; and now he told Las Casas plainly that he was willing that he should return to Longwood.

Dr. O'Meara, in his visit to the Emperor to-day, mentioned that the governor had offered to allow Las Casas to return to Longwood. After some conversation, the Emperor said,

"I can give no advice to Las Casas about it. If he comes back, I shall receive him with pleasure; if he goes away, I shall hear of it with pleasure. But, in the latter case, I should wish to see him once more before he leaves the island. Since the arrest of Las Casas, I have requested all my generals to go away. I shall be more independent without them, as then I should not labor under the fear of their suffering ill treatment by the governor, in order thereby to revenge himself upon me. I," continued he, "am not afraid that they will send *me* off the island."

December 20. The governor seemed very reluctant to have Las Casas go to England, and appears to have hoped that a threat to send him to the Cape of Good Hope would induce him to remain at Longwood. He accordingly wrote him to-day a communication, stating that he was to be sent to the Cape. With this communication he, however, sent another letter, saying, "In communicating to you the decision contained in the inclosed paper, I beg leave, at the same time, to acquaint you that I shall have no objection, as already verbally communicated to you, to your remaining on this island, if you should prefer remaining here to proceeding to the Cape of Good Hope, until I may receive instructions from the British government respecting you."

December 24. The son of Las Casas was very sick. For seven days he had not seen a physician. The affectionate and agonized father wrote an imploring letter to the governor, beseeching that they might be transferred to the town, even to the common jail if necessary, where his sick and apparently dying child might be within the reach of medical aid. The governor acceded to his request, and in the evening an orderly officer came and conducted the two prisoners, the father and the son, to the governor's castle at Jamestown.

"How anxiously," says Las Casas, "did we turn our eyes to Longwood at the moment of our departure! What were our thoughts and sensations as we proceeded along the road! What a wound was inflicted on my heart when, for the last time, I turned my look on Longwood, and saw it gradually disappear from my eyes!"

December 26. Several days passed away, and the governor continued to hold up his threat to send Las Casas, not to Europe, but to the Cape of Good Hope. At the same time, he seemed disposed to relent a little in his severe treatment of the Emperor. He was evidently alarmed, and very apprehensive of the communications which Las Casas might make to the public. He requested Dr. O'Meara to tell General Bonaparte that several of the restrictions should be removed, especially those relating to speaking; that the limits should be enlarged, and that liberty should be granted for him to receive visits nearly as in former times under the admiral. To this Napoleon replied:

"I desire no more than to have matters put, as nearly as possible, as they were under the admiral. I think it right and just, if the governor suspected either an inhabitant of the island, or a passenger, or any other individual, that he should not allow such persons to enter Longwood. But what I desire is that the majority of respectable passengers or inhabitants should be allowed to visit me, and not one or two who have been picked out and sent up by the governor or by his staff, as a keeper of galley-slaves would send a curious traveler to his galleys to see some extraordinary criminal."

Count Bertrand this day wrote a letter remonstrating against sending Las Casas to the Cape instead of to England, and intimating a strong desire on the part of Napoleon that Las Casas might be permitted to visit Longwood to take leave of the Emperor previous to his departure.

"Criminals," said the Emperor to Dr. O'Meara, "condemned to death, and on the point of being led out to execution, are allowed to bid adieu to their friends, without it being required that a third person should be present. Bertrand has written to the governor that he hopes he will not refuse his consent to a matter of so little consequence. If he refuses, Bertrand will go down to see Las Casas with an officer, which I could not consent to do. What can the governor be afraid of? that I would tell Las Casas to write to my wife? He will do that without direction. That I would tell him my sentiments and intentions? He knows them already. Does he think that Europe is a mine of gunpowder, and Las Casas the spark to blow it up?"

The governor, however, peremptorily refused to permit any interview unless it could take place in the presence of a British officer. To this indignity the Emperor was not disposed to submit.

Shortly afterward, Count Bertrand and Baron Gourgaud went to town, under guard of the English orderly officer, Captain Poppleton, to take leave of Count Las Casas.

"It is difficult," says Dr. O'Meara, "to reconcile the conduct pursued toward them there with the other measures practiced by Sir Hudson Lowe, and with the importance which he professed to attach to '*cutting off* all communication with Longwood.' At breakfast they were left to themselves, with the exception of Captain Poppleton, who understands French with difficulty, and not at all when spoken in the quick manner in which Frenchmen usually converse with each other. For some hours they remained together in the large room of the castle, which is about fifty feet by twenty, walking up one side, while Colonel Wynyard and Major Gorrequer, who were to watch them, remained on the opposite side of the room; so that, in fact, Las Casas might just as well have been permitted to come to Longwood, and thereby a refusal, which was considered as an insult, would have been spared to Napoleon."

December 29. To-day Las Casas and his son were sent on board a ship to be transported to the Cape of Good Hope, two thousand miles further from Europe. His journal, and every paper he had relating to the Emperor, were taken from him. After a passage of eighteen days they arrived at Jamestown. Here the British authorities, guided by letters from Sir Hudson Lowe, immediately arrested the sick and suffering exiles, and imprisoned them in the Castle. Las Casas wrote to the governor at the Cape, Lord Charles Somerset, demanding the cause of his imprisonment, and claiming a trial if any changes were brought against him. The governor coolly replied that he considered him a prisoner *on the report of Sir Hudson Lowe*, and that here he must remain until instructions arrived from England. For upward of seven months the father and son were here held in most cruel captivity. At last they were sent to England in a very small brig of two hundred tons.

After a passage of one hundred days, on the 15th of November, 1817, they arrived in the Downs; but the vengeance of Sir Hudson Lowe had preceded them. They were immediately arrested by the British ministry, prohibited from landing, sent on board an alien ship, and ordered immediately to leave England. The ministers did not wish the people of England to hear the voice of Las Casas. So great was the fear of Lord Bathurst that the English people might become acquainted with the atrocious crime which the ministry were so mercilessly perpetrating at Longwood! An accidental delay detained Las Casas and his son a few days at Dover, and there, under a guard, they were carefully shut up in an inn. Las Casas wrote to Lord Bathurst, Lord Sidmouth, and others, but in vain; the friend of Napoleon was an outlaw.

He was again put on board a packet, after all his papers had been taken from him, and sent to Ostend; but the malign eye of Lord Bathurst, vigilant through conscious guilt, followed him. He had hardly entered his room at an inn ere he was again arrested. He, however, succeeded in reaching Brussels, when he was again seized, placed in a carriage between a police-officer and a *gendarme*, and without an hour of rest, and without intermission, was transferred from town to town, from police to police, across the whole kingdom of the Netherlands. No notice whatever was taken of his demands, his protests, his supplication. Such was the *liberty* which the Allies had restored to Europe.

When he arrived on the frontiers of Prussia, he was placed in the hands of the Prussian police. The matter seemed to be perfectly understood by these allied governments. On arriving at Cologne, he was so ill that he could not be conveyed any farther, and he was allowed twenty-four hours for repose. Here he was overtaken by his devoted wife, who had been for many days, in intense anxiety, tracing and following the path of her husband and son. At last he arrived at Frankfort. Here he was permitted to remain, with shattered health and crushed heart, for fifteen months. Though under the careful watch of the police, he did every thing which mortal energy, inspired by deathless affection, could do, to secure some relief for the illustrious sufferer at Longwood. He wrote to all the relatives of the Emperor; again and again to the British ministers; to the Prince Regent; to the King of Prussia, and to the Emperors of Austria and of Russia; but there was no relenting in the hard hearts of the enemies of Napoleon.

The mother of Napoleon, heart-broken in view of the woes of her noble and beloved son, wrote the following touching letter to the allied sovereigns then assembled in Congress at Aix-la-Chapelle:

The Mother of Napoleon to the Allied Sovereigns.

"Sires,—A mother, afflicted beyond all expression, has long cherished the hope that the meeting of your imperial and royal majesties will afford some alleviation of her distress. The prolonged captivity of the Emperor Napoleon gives occasion for appealing to you. It is impossible but that your magnanimity, your power, and the recollection of past events should induce your imperial and royal majesties to interest yourselves for the deliverance of a prince who has had so great a share in your regard and even in your friendship.

"Would you suffer to perish in miserable exile a sovereign who, relying on the magnanimity of his enemy, threw himself into his power? My son might have demanded an asylum from the emperor, his father-in-law. He might have consigned himself to the generosity of the Emperor Alexander, of whom he was once the friend. He might have taken refuge with his Prussian majesty, who, in that case, would have no doubt recollected his old alliance. Should England punish him for the confidence he reposed in her?

"The Emperor Napoleon is no longer to be feared. He is infirm. And even if he were in the full enjoyment of his health, and had the means which Providence once placed in his hands, he abhors civil war.

"Sires, I am a mother. My son's life is dearer to me than my own. Pardon my grief, which prompts me to take the liberty of addressing this letter to your imperial and royal majesties. Do not render unavailing the entreaties of a mother who thus appeals against the long series of cruelties that has been exercised toward her son.

"In the name of Him who is in essence goodness, and of whom your imperial and royal majesties are the image, I entreat that you will interest yourselves to put a period to my son's misery, and to restore him to liberty. For this I implore God, and I implore you, who are his lieutenants upon earth. Reasons of state have their limits; and posterity, which gives immortality, adores, above all things, the generosity of conquerors.

"I am, &c., MADAME MÈRE."

The Allies did not condescend to pay any attention to this affecting appeal.

Lucien applied, with heartfelt earnestness, to the British government to be permitted to proceed to St. Helena, and reside there two years, with or without his wife and children, engaging not to occasion any augmentation of expense, and promising to submit to every restriction imposed on his brother, or that might be imposed on himself, either before his departure or after his return. His pleas were unavailing.

The Emperor's mother, brothers, and sisters, who now received the first authentic tidings respecting the condition of the illustrious sufferer, immediately decided to transmit to him annually thirty thousand dollars; but, by a singular fatality, it was a long time before the Emperor received any relief from this source.

All the despotisms of Europe seemed to be watching Las Casas with a jealous eye. All his efforts to recover his private papers and his journal were unavailing. It was not until after the death of the Emperor that he was enabled to recover his journal, and to publish his world-renowned memorial of St. Helena.

From this digression let us turn again to the tragedy enacting at Longwood.

December 31. The gloom of the prison was now settling more and more heavily over the unhappy Emperor. His most congenial friend, the one to whom he most willingly confided his thoughts, was torn from him. We have no longer the minute record of his long and dreary hours. He passed much of his time in reading, and in dictating his campaigns to Bertrand, Montholon, and Gourgaud. Dr. O'Meara daily visited his patient, and daily recorded his remarkable conversation. But Dr. O'Meara, however numerous might have been his excellences, was not a man to win the confiding affection of Napoleon. The Emperor respected his physician, and treated him ever with courtesy and kindness. But the soul of Napoleon and the soul of Dr. O'Meara could not freely and intimately blend.

Thus sadly terminated the year 1816.

CHAPTER XXXVII.
1817, January.

New-Year's Gifts—Representations of Chateaubriand and of Sir Robert Wilson—Annoyance from Rats—Secret Amours of Napoleon—The Invasion of England—Conduct of the Governor.

January 1. Dr. O'Meara was admitted to the Emperor in the drawing-room, and wished him a happy New-year. Napoleon smiled and said,

"I hope that the succeeding year will find me better situated. Perhaps I shall be dead, which will be much better. Worse than this can not be.".

He then, with his own hand, presented to Dr. O'Meara a snuff-box, saying,

"Here, doctor, is a present I make to you, for the attention which you have manifested toward me during my illness."

He also presented to the Countesses Bertrand and Montholon some beautiful vases of porcelain, which had been presented to him by the city of Paris. To Count Bertrand he gave a set of chess-men; to Montholon and Gourgaud, handsome ornaments. Each one of the children also received some elegant gift from him. It was a dark and dismal day, and the island was enveloped in fog which the eye in vain attempted to penetrate.

January 12. Dr. O'Meara saw Napoleon in his chamber. The conversation turned upon the representations which Chateaubriand and Sir Robert Wilson had made of the Emperor. O'Meara observed that some persons were surprised that Napoleon had never written, or caused to be written, an answer to Sir Robert Wilson's work, and to others containing similar assertions.

"It was unnecessary," the Emperor replied. "Such charges will fall to the ground of themselves. Sir Robert Wilson has already contradicted them by the answer which he has given in his interrogation, when tried in Paris, for having assisted Lavalette in his escape. And I am convinced that Wilson is now sorry for having published what he then had been led to believe was true. Moreover, the English who return from their travels in France will return undeceived as to my character, and will undeceive their countrymen."

Speaking of his intense application to the duties of the cabinet, the Emperor said,

"I have frequently labored in state affairs for fifteen hours without a moment's cessation, and without taking any nourishment. On one occasion I continued at my labors for three days and nights without lying down to sleep."

When Napoleon rose from the dinner-table to-day, as he took his hat from the sideboard, a large rat sprang out of it. The miserable hovel in which the Emperor was imprisoned was so dilapidated and rat-infested that there was no refuge from these repulsive vermin by day or by night.

January 14. The Emperor, notwithstanding his health was severely suffering, proposed to remain in the seclusion of his room rather than ride out under the guard of an English officer, or expose himself to the indignity of being stopped and turned back by a sentinel. Dr. O'Meara, anxious for his patient, whose strength was rapidly failing, made inquiries of Brigade Major Harrison, who was stationed at Hut's Gate, if any alteration had been made in the orders so as to allow Napoleon to pass the picket at that gate, and to go round by Miss Mason's and Woody Range unaccompanied by a British officer. Major Harrison replied that no change of orders to that effect had been given, and that, if he attempted to pass, he would be stopped by the sentinel.

January 21. Dr. O'Meara informed the Emperor that he had a book entitled " The Secret Amours of Napoleon Bonaparte." The Emperor smiled, and wished him to bring the book, saying, " It will, at least, make me laugh."

As the Emperor glanced his eye over the book, he often laughed heartily at the absurd stories, and remarked, in conclusion,

" There is not a single word of truth in these anecdotes. Even the names of the greatest number of the females are unknown to me."

January 26. The Emperor had not been out of his dilapidated and gloomy rooms for more than nine weeks. On the 17th of this month a son was born to Madam Bertrand. The Emperor had often inquired for her very affectionately, and to-day he paid her a visit. As he complimented her upon her beautiful child, the countess remarked,

" I have the honor to present to your majesty the first Frenchman who, since your arrival, has entered Longwood without Lord Bathurst's permission."

January 27. The Emperor was suffering much from headache and sleeplessness. He, however, entered into a long conversation with Dr. O'Meara. The doctor inquired if he really had intended to invade England.

" It was my firm intention to do so," said the Emperor, " and I should have headed the expedition myself. I had given orders for two fleets to proceed to the West Indies. Instead of remaining there, they were merely to show themselves among the islands, and return directly to Europe, raise the blockade of Ferrol, take the ships out, proceed to Brest, where there were about forty sail of the line, unite and sail to the Channel, where they would not have met with any thing strong enough to engage them, and clear it of all English men-of-war. By false intelligence, adroitly managed, I calculated that you would have sent squadrons to the East and West Indies and Mediterranean in search of my fleets. Before they could return, I would have had the command of the Channel for two months, as I should have had about seventy sail of the line, besides frigates.

" I would have hastened over my flotilla with two hundred thousand men, landed as near Chatham as possible, and proceeded direct to London, where I calculated to arrive in four days from the time of my landing. I would have proclaimed a republic (I was First Consul then), the abolition of the nobility and House of Peers, the distribution of the property of such of the latter as opposed me among my partisans, liberty, equality, and the sovereignty of the people. I would have allowed the House of Commons to remain, but would have introduced a great reform. I would have published a proclamation declaring that we came as friends to the English, and to free the nation from a corrupt and flagitious aristocracy, and restore a popular form of government—a democracy, all which would have been confirmed by the conduct of my army, as I would not have allowed the slightest outrage to be committed by my troops. Marauding or ill-treating the inhabitants, or the most trifling infringement of my orders, I would have punished with instant death. I think," continued he, "that with my promises, together with what I would actually have effected, I should have had the support of a great many. In a large city like London, where there are so many *canaille* and so many disaffected, I should have been joined by a formidable body. I would, at the same time, have excited an insurrection in Ireland."

O'Meara observed that his army would have been destroyed piecemeal; that he would have had a million of men in arms against him in a short time; and, moreover, that the English would have burned London rather than have suffered it to fall into his hands.

"No, no," said Napoleon, "I do not believe it. You are too rich and too fond of money. A nation will not so readily burn its capital. How often have the Parisians sworn to bury themselves under the ruins of their capital, rather than suffer it to fall into the hands of the enemies of France? and yet twice it has been taken. There is no knowing what would have happened, Mr. Doctor. Neither Mr. Pitt, nor you, nor I, could have foretold what would have been the result. The hope of a change for the better, and of a division of property, would have operated wonderfully among the people, especially that of London. The people of all rich nations are nearly alike. I would have made such promises as would have had a great effect. What resistance could an undisciplined army make against mine in a country like England, abounding in plains? I considered all you have said, but I calculated on the effect that would be produced by the possession of a great and rich capital, the bank and all your riches, the ships in the river and at Chatham.

"I expected that I should have had the command of the Channel for two months, by which I should have had supplies of troops; and when your fleet came back, they would have found their capital in the hands of an enemy, and their country overwhelmed by my armies. I would have abolished flogging, and promised your seamen every thing, which would have made a great impression upon their minds. The proclamations stating that we came only as friends, to relieve the English from an obnoxious and despotic aristocracy, whose object was to keep the nation eternally at war, in order to enrich themselves and their families with the blood of the people, together with the proclaiming a republic, the abolition of the monarchical government and the nobility, the declaration of the forfeiture of the property of such of the latter as should resist, and its division among the partisans of the Revolution, with a general equalization of property, would have gained me the support of the *canaille*, and of all the idle, the profligate, and the disaffected in the kingdom.

"If," continued the Emperor, "I were at the head of affairs in England, I would devise some means of paying off the national debt. I would appropriate to that purpose the whole of the Church livings except a tenth, always excepting those whose incomes were moderate, in a manner that the salary of the highest among the clergy should not exceed eight hundred or a thousand a year. What business have those priests with such enormous incomes? They should follow the directions of Jesus Christ, who ordered that, as pastors to the people, they should set an example of moderation, humanity, virtue, and poverty, instead of wallowing in riches, luxury, and sloth."

O'Meara made some observations upon the intolerance which had been manifested on some occasions by the Catholics.

"The inability," the Emperor replied, "to rise above a certain rank, and to be members of Parliament, and other persecutions, once removed from your Catholic brethren, you will find that they will be no longer intolerant or fanatical. Fanaticism is always the child of persecution. That intolerance which you complain of is also the result of your oppressive laws. Remove them once, and put them on a similar footing with the Protestants, and in a few years you will find the spirit of intolerance disappear. Do as I did in France with the Protestants."

January 30. Though the governor had again and again promised to refer the difficulties between himself and his illustrious prisoner to the mediation of Admiral Malcolm, he was ever finding pretexts to refuse to keep his promise. The Emperor could not enjoy a ride without being dogged by an English officer, to remind him constantly that he was a captive, and to report all his words. He was thus compelled, in self-respect, to shut himself up in the solitude of his room. His health failed, his spirits sank, and life became almost an intolerable burden. To-day he said, indignantly, to Dr. O'Meara,

"Tell the governor that, in consequence of his conduct in having accepted the proposed intermediation of the admiral, declaring that he would charge the admiral with it, and afterward doing nothing, I conceive him to be a man without word and without faith; that he has broken his word with me, broken a compact which is held sacred by robbers and Bedouin Arabs, but not by the agents of the British ministers. Tell him that when a man has lost his word, he has lost every thing which distinguishes the man from the brute. Tell him that he has forfeited that distinction, and that I hold him to be inferior to the robber of the desert. Independent," continued he, "of his conduct with respect to the admiral, he has broken his word about the limits. He charged you to inform me that we were permitted to ride any where through the old bounds, and specifically named the path by Miss Mason's. Now Gourgaud went a few days ago and asked the question from the major at Hut's Gate, who told him that he could not pass, and that no change had been made in the orders by the governor."

January 31. Dr. O'Meara had a long interview with the governor, endeavoring to induce him to mitigate some of his cruel restrictions. The governor closed the conversation by saying,

"I can not think of allowing General Bonaparte's officers to run about the country telling lies of me as Las Casas and Montholon have done. General Bonaparte would be much better if he had not such liars as Montholon, and such a blubbering, whining son of a b——h as Bertrand about him."

It is not strange that the Emperor's stomach refused a cup of coffee upon which the shadow of such a man had fallen.

The governor then added, "The restrictions imposed are not ordered by the ministers. No minute details are given. It is left to my judgment, and I take what measures I think proper, and do as I like. I am ordered to take particular care that he does not escape. The rest is left to myself."

CHAPTER XXXVIII.
1817, February.

Message from the Governor—Remarks of the Emperor upon his Treatment—Russia and the Emperor Paul—On the Invasion of India—Designs of Alexander—The Ambigu—The Return from Elba—Character of the French—Newspapers withheld from the Emperor—Vigilance with which the Emperor was guarded—Blunders of Lord Castlereagh—The Botanist who had seen Maria Louisa.

February 1. Dr. O'Meara, by request of Sir Hudson Lowe, informed the Emperor that the governor was very busy in ascertaining how far his instructions would enable him to comply with the wishes of General Bonaparte; "that when he has finished this business, he will have no objection to authorize the admiral, or any other person General Bonaparte may think proper, to act the part of an intermediator, although the intermediation of any person will have no influence whatever in inducing the governor to grant more or less than he would do of his own free will and judgment."

When this was given to the Emperor, he said,

"I maintain that his last restrictions are worse than any in force at Botany Bay, because even there it is not attempted to prohibit people from speaking. It is useless for him to endeavor to persuade us that we have not been ill treated by him. We are not simpletons or ordinary people. There is not a free-born man whose hair would not stand on end with horror on reading such an atrocious proceeding as that prohibition against speaking. His assertion that it was intended as civility is a mockery, and adds irony and insult to injury. I know well that, if he really intended to grant any thing, it is in his power to do so without a mediator. It was a mark of imbecility in him to have accepted the proposition; but, having once accepted it, he ought not to have broken his word. Sometimes I believe that he is an executioner who has come to assassinate me; but most probably he is a man of incapacity and without heart, who does not comprehend his office."

In the afternoon Dr. O'Meara saw the governor, and spoke to him of the deplorable condition of the health of Napoleon. He informed him that, on the bleak heights of Longwood, it was generally a matter of great difficulty, and often quite impossible, to obtain the necessary quantity of water for a bath. Sir Hudson Lowe brutally replied,

"I do not know what right General Bonaparte has to *stew himself in hot water* so many hours, and so often, when the 53d regiment can scarcely procure enough water to cook their victuals."

February 3. Dr. O'Meara, by request of Sir Hudson Lowe, informed the Emperor that, in prohibiting him from speaking to any whom he might meet, the governor intended an act of civility, as it would prevent the necessity of the interference of an English officer.

The Emperor replied,

"I would give two millions that those restrictions were signed by the English ministry, in order to show to Europe what base, tyrannical, and dishonorable arts they are capable of, and the manner in which they have fulfilled the promises they have made of treating me well. According to law, this governor has no right to impose any restrictions upon me. The bill, illegal and iniquitous as it is, says that I shall be subject to such restrictions as the ministers think fit and necessary, but it does not say that they shall have the power to delegate that authority to any other person. Therefore, every restriction laid upon me ought not only to be signed by a minister, but, properly speaking, by all the ministers assembled.

"It is possible," continued Napoleon, "that part of his bad treatment arises from his imbecility and his fear, for he is a man who has no elevation of character. He has a little cunning and much imbecility. It is an injury to his nation, and an indignity and insult to the Emperor of Austria, to the Emperor of Russia, and to all those sovereigns whom I have conquered and treated with.

"I had paid your nation," continued the Emperor, "a great compliment, and showed what a high sense I entertained of the English honor, by giving myself up to them, after so many years' war, in preference to my father-in-law or to my old friend. The English would have been my greatest friends had I remained in France. United, we could have conquered the world. The confidence which I placed in the English shows what an opinion I entertained of them, and what steps I would have taken to have rendered such a nation my friends. And I should have succeeded. There is nothing that I would not have sacrificed to have been in friendship with them. They were the only nation I esteemed.

"As to the Russians, Austrians, and others, I had no esteem for them. Now I am sorry to see that I erred in opinion; for, had I given myself up to the Emperor of Austria, he, however he might differ with me in politics, and think it necessary to dethrone me, would have embraced me closely as a friend, and have treated me with every kindness; so also would my old friend, the Emperor of Russia. The treatment of the Calabrese to Murat was humanity compared to what I endure, as the Calabrese soon finished Murat's misery; but here they torture me to death by pin-pricks. I think that your own nation will feel very little obliged to this governor for having conferred upon it a dishonor which will be recorded in history; for you are proud, and have the honor of your nation more at heart than even your money. Witness the thousands that your lords throw away annually in France and in other parts of the Continent, to raise and exalt the English name. Many of your nobility and others would voluntarily have subscribed thousands to have prevented the stigma which this *imbecille* has brought upon your nation."

February 7. Sir Hudson Lowe, in a long conversation with Dr. O'Meara, suggested that he might perhaps consent to an extension of the Emperor's limits by receiving a pledge that he would not enter any house unless accompanied by an English officer. "There is a great difference," said he, "between limits for exercise and limits for correspondence." O'Meara communicated this to the Emperor. After some further conversation with Dr. O'Meara, the Emperor said,

"Communicate to the governor that, if he will send a list to Count Bertrand of the houses within the limits which he is *unwilling that I should visit*, I will not enter them. If, on the other hand, he sends me a list of the houses *he will permit me to enter*, I can not accept it, for then I should seem to be visiting by his permission. Tell him this, although I am sure that it is some shuffling trick on his part, and will come to nothing.

"I think that it is owing to some small remains of the influence of *my star* that the English have treated me so ill; at least, that this man, whom they have sent out as governor, has conducted himself in such a brutal manner. At least posterity will avenge me."

February 10. Dr. O'Meara informed Napoleon that he had communicated his desires to Sir Hudson Lowe, who had promised to talk the matter over with Count Bertrand.

Napoleon replied, "You may depend upon it that it will end in nothing. It is merely to deceive *you*. He will act as he has done in that affair with the admiral."

February 12. Dr. O'Meara, anxious for his patient, again saw the governor relative to the enlargement of the Emperor's limits. The governor would by no means consent to allow the Emperor to enter such houses as he was not *prohibited from entering*. He said that the Emperor must have some deep design in this plan. Dr. O'Meara seemed much mortified at this result, and intimated to the governor that it would afford Napoleon a foundation for another charge of shuffling. Sir Hudson gave his ever-ready reply, "Tell General Bonaparte that he may consider himself very fortunate in having so good a man as myself to deal with."

When Dr. O'Meara communicated to the Emperor the result, he said,

"Do not bring me any more communications or propositions from Sir Hudson Lowe. He is a liar, a man of insinuations, like the petty tyrants of Italy. There is nothing English about him. He is rabid to tease and to torment."

February 14. O'Meara breakfasted with Napoleon. The Emperor spoke of Russia. "If Paul had lived," said he, "there would have been a peace with England in a short time, as you would not have been long able to contend with the united northern powers. I wrote to Paul to continue building ships, and to endeavor to unite the north against you; not to hazard any battles, as the English would gain them, but allow you to exhaust yourselves, and by all means to get a large fleet into the Mediterranean."

O'Meara inquired if he thought that Paul had been insane. "Latterly," said Napoleon, "I believe that he was. At first he was strongly prejudiced against the Revolution and every person concerned in it, but afterward I had rendered him reasonable, and had changed his opinions altogether. If Paul had lived, you would have lost India before now. An agreement was made between Paul and myself to invade it. I furnished the plan. I was to have sent thirty thousand good troops. He was to send a similar number of the best Russian soldiers, and forty thousand Cossacks. I was to subscribe ten millions for the purchase of camels and other requisites for crossing the desert. The King of Prussia was to have been applied to by both of us to grant a passage for my troops through his dominions, which would have been immediately granted. I had, at the same time, made a demand to the King of Persia for a passage through his country, which would also have been granted, although the negotiations were not entirely concluded, but would have succeeded, as the Persians were desirous of profiting by it themselves."

O'Meara asked if it were true that Alexander had intended to have seized upon Turkey.

Napoleon answered, "All his thoughts are directed to the conquest of Turkey. We have had many discussions about it; at first I was pleased with his proposals, because I thought it would enlighten the world to drive those brutes, the Turks, out of Europe. But when I reflected upon the consequences, and saw what a tremendous weight of power it would give to Russia, on account of the numbers of Greeks in the Turkish dominions who would naturally join the Russians, I refused to consent to it, especially as Alexander wanted to get Constantinople, which I would not allow, as it would have destroyed the equilibrium of power in Europe. I reflected that France would gain Egypt, Syria, and the islands, which would have been nothing in comparison with what Russia would have obtained. I considered that the barbarians of the north were already too powerful, and probably, in the course of time, would overwhelm all Europe, as I now think they will.

"Austria already trembles. Russia and Prussia united, Austria falls, and England can not prevent it. France, under the present family, is nothing, and the Austrians are so mean-spirited that they will be easily overpowered. They are a nation that may be ruled with blows. They will offer little resistance to the Russians, who are brave and patient. Russia is the more formidable, because she can never disarm. In Russia, once a soldier, always a soldier — barbarians, who, one may say, have no country, and to whom every country is better than the one which gave them birth. When I am dead and gone, my memory will be esteemed, and I shall be revered in consequence of having foreseen, and endeavored to put a stop to, that which will yet take place. It will be revered when the barbarians of the north will possess Europe, which would not have happened had it not been for you, sirs Englishmen."

Had Napoleon succeeded in his intention of re-establishing Poland and making the noble Poniatowski king, Europe would have been saved from many wars which must now probably be encountered.

DEATH OF PONIATOWSKI.

Napoleon expressed great anxiety relative to Count Montholon, as the governor had made some insinuations that his removal was in contemplation.

"I should feel," continued he, "the loss of Montholon most sensibly, as, independent of his attachment to me, he is most useful, and endeavors to anticipate all my wants. I know that it would grieve him much to leave me, though, in truth, it would render him a great service if he were removed from this desolate place, and restored to the bosom of his friends, as he is not proscribed, and has nothing to fear in France. Moreover, being of a noble family, he might readily find favor with the Bourbons, if he chose."

Sir Hudson Lowe now sent word to the Emperor that he could not allow him to enter any house whatever unaccompanied by an English officer.

February 17. A new magazine, The Ambigu, had been started in Europe, which was full of abuse of Napoleon. Sir Hudson Lowe gave several numbers to Dr. O'Meara, and wished him to hand them to the Emperor. The doctor informed the Emperor that he had the periodical, but that it was very abusive. Napoleon smiled and said,

"Children only care for abuse. Bring them to me." As his eye fell upon the name of the editor, he said, "Ah, Pelletier! He has been libeling me these twenty years; but I am very glad to get them." He afterward remarked to O'Meara, "I find the Ambigu very interesting, although it contains many falsehoods and absurdities. I have been reading the account of the battle of Waterloo contained in it, which is nearly correct. I have been considering who could have been the author. It must have been some person about me. Had it not been for the imbecility of Grouchy, I should have gained that day."

Speaking of his return from Elba, he said, "The enthusiasm was astonishing. I might have entered Paris at the head of four hundred thousand men, if I had liked. What is still more surprising, and, I believe, unparalleled in history, is that it was effected without any conspiracy. There was no plot, no understanding with any of the generals in France. Not one of them knew my intentions.

"There never was yet," continued Napoleon, " a king who was more the sovereign of the *people* than I was. If I were not possessed of the smallest talent, I could reign easier in France than Louis and the Bourbons, endowed with the greatest abilities. The mass of the French nation hate the old nobles and the priests. I have not sprung from the *ancienne noblesse*, nor have I ever too much encouraged the priests. The French nation have predominant in them vanity, levity, independence, and caprice, with an unconquerable passion for glory. They will as soon do without bread as without glory, and a proclamation will lead them. Unlike England, where the inhabitants of a whole county may be inflamed by, and will follow the opinion of two or three noble families, they must be themselves courted.

"Some young and ignorant peasants," continued Napoleon, "who were born since the Revolution, were conversing with some older and better-informed men about the Bourbons. 'Who are those Bourbons?' said one. 'What are they like?' 'Why,' replied one of the older men, 'they are like that old ruined chateau which you see near our village: like it, their time is past and gone; they are no longer of the age.'

"The Bourbons will find," added he, "that their caressing the marshals and generals will not answer. They must caress the *people*. To *them* they must address themselves. Unless they adopt some measures to render themselves popular, you will see a terrible explosion burst forth in France. The nation will never bear to live debased and humiliated as it is at present. When I hear of a nation living without bread, then I will believe that the French will exist without glory."

Napoleon then made some remarks upon Longwood, expressed his surprise that some person had not made a contract to bring a supply of water to it and to the camp, stipulating that he should be permitted to establish a garden in the valley, by means of which a sufficiency of vegetables might be produced at a cheap rate, not only for Longwood and the camp, but also for the ships.

"Here," continued he, "if water were brought by a conduit, Novarre, with the help of two or three Chinese, would produce a sufficiency of the vegetables which we so much want. How preferable would it be to dispose of the public money in conducting water to those poor soldiers in camp, than in digging ditches and throwing up fortifications around this house, just as if an army were coming to attack it! A man who has no regard for his soldiers ought never to have a command. The greatest necessity of the soldier is water."

"Sir Thomas Reade," says Dr. O'Meara, "made a long harangue this day upon the impropriety of allowing Bonaparte any newspapers unless such as had previously been inspected by the governor."

February 18. "Saw Sir Hudson Lowe," Dr. O'Meara records, "at Plantation House. Found him busied in examining some newspapers for Longwood, several of which he put aside as not being, in his opinion, proper to be sent to Napoleon, observing to me, at the same time, 'that, however strange it might appear, General Bonaparte ought to be obliged to him for not sending him newspapers indiscriminately, as the perusal of articles written in his own favor might excite hopes which, when not ultimately realized, could not fail to afflict him; that, moreover, the British government thought it improper to let him know every thing that appeared in the newspapers.'"

February 19. "Sir Thomas Reade," says Dr. O'Meara, "was very busy in circulating reports in the town that 'General Bonaparte was sulky and would see nobody; that the governor was too good, and that the villain ought to be put in chains.'"

February 20. Napoleon passed a sleepless night. Restless and languid, he rose at five o'clock and paced his solitary room. Soldiers, with loaded muskets and fixed bayonets, were stationed before his door and beneath his windows. One hundred and thirty-five sentinels surrounded the grounds by day and by night. A regiment of soldiers were intrenched within gun-shot of his door. All the forts of the island were thoroughly equipped and manned, as if there were danger that this one dreaded captive would seize the island. Ships of war cruised along the shores to prohibit any vessel from approaching. But even all these precautions were not deemed sufficient. A store-ship had now arrived, loaded with a heavy iron railing, that Longwood might henceforth be surrounded by an impassable picket.

When O'Meara called he found the Emperor alone, reclining upon his sofa, languid and depressed. He looked up, and with a faint voice saluted the doctor. In conversation he gradually became animated, and said, adverting to the commercial distress of England,

"Lord Castlereagh deserves the reprobation of the English nation for the little care which he took of their interests at the time of the general peace. The misfortunes which befell me gave such an ascendency to England that almost any demand made by her would have been granted, independent of the *right* which she had to claim a recompense for the vast expense which she had been at. An opportunity offered itself, which probably will never occur again, for England to recover and extricate herself from all her difficulties in a few years, and to relieve her from the immense load of debt which weighs her down.

"I see no other way now," continued he, "to extricate you from your difficulties than by reducing the interest of the national debt, confiscating the greatest part of the revenues of the clergy, all the sinecures, diminishing considerably the army, and establishing a system of reduction altogether. Let those who want priests pay them. Your sinking fund is a humbug. Impose a heavy tax upon absentees. It is too late now for you to make commercial treaties. What would *then* have been considered as only just and reasonable would now be thought far different. The opportunity is gone, and the nation is indebted to your *imbecilles* of ministers for all the calamities which will befall it, and which are solely to be attributed to their criminal neglect."

"I understand," said he, "that the botanist[*] is on the eve of departure without having seen me. In the most barbarous countries it would not be prohibited, even to a prisoner under sentence of death, to have the consolation of conversing with a person who had lately seen his wife and child. Even in that worst of courts, the Revolutionary Tribunal of France, such an instance of barbarity and of callousness to all feeling was never known; and your nation, which is so much cried up for liberality, permits such treatment. I am informed that this botanist has made application to see me, which was refused; and in my letter to Las Casas, which was read by the governor, I complained of it as a hardship, and thereby made application to see him. If I had asked it in any other manner, I should have exposed myself to the insult of a refusal from this wretch. It is the height of cruelty. He must indeed be a barbarian who would deny to a husband and a father the consolation of discoursing with a person who had lately seen, spoken to, and touched his wife, his child" [here Napoleon's voice faltered], "from whose embraces he is forever separated by the cruel policy of a few. The Anthropophagi of the South Seas would not practice it. Previous to devouring their victims, they would allow them the consolation of seeing and conversing with each other. The cruelties which are practiced here would be disavowed by cannibals."

Napoleon now walked up and down for some time, much agitated. Afterward he proceeded: "You see the manner in which he endeavors to impose upon the passengers going to England, that he may make them believe he is all goodness to me, and that it is all my own fault if I do not receive stran-

[*] "Napoleon had been informed," says O'Meara, "and I believe with truth, that this gentleman had seen and conversed with the Empress and her son a short time before he left Germany for St. Helena."

gers. His object now is to impress upon the minds of the public that I hate the sight of an Englishman. That is the reason he desired you to tell me that Las Casas had made me say that I abhorred the sight of the English uniform."

O'Meara observed that Sir Hudson Lowe had also told him that he conceived it to be an invention of Las Casas.

"It is an invention of his own," replied the Emperor, "in order to impose upon you. If I had hated the English, should I have given myself up to them, instead of going to the Emperor of Russia or of Austria? Is it possible that I could have given a greater proof of esteem for a nation than that which I have done for the English—unfortunately for myself?"

CHAPTER XXXIX.
1817, March.

False Assertion of Lord Castlereagh—O'Meara's previous Estimate of the Emperor—Napoleon's Confidence in the Verdict of Posterity—The Libels of Pelletier—The iron Railing—The Distress in England—Napoleon's Proposition to assume an Incognito—Warden's Book—Prince Regent—Montchenu—The Bookseller Palm—The New Testament—Conduct of the Governor—Talleyrand—Remarks on Egypt—Menou—The Secret Memoirs—Uniting the Nations.

March 2. Dr. O'Meara found the Emperor lying upon his sofa, low-spirited and pale, and suffering from sickness. He, however, declined medicine, and would receive only chicken-broth and barley-water. The Emperor had been reading an English journal, and remarked,

"In the papers they make me serve for all purposes, and say whatever suits their views. Lord Castlereagh, on his return to Ireland, publicly asserted a falsehood relative to what had been my intentions upon England, and put expressions into my mouth since my arrival here which I never made use of."

O'Meara observed that, in all probability, Lord Castlereagh had been informed that he had said so.

Napoleon replied, "It may be; but your ministers have little scruple in having recourse to falsehood when they think it will forward any object they have in view. It is always dishonorable and base to belie the unfortunate, and doubly so when in your power, and when you hold a padlock upon the mouth to prevent a reply."

March 3. "Saw Napoleon dressing," says O'Meara. "He was free from any complaint. Laughed and quizzed me about some young ladies, and asked me to give all the *little* news of the town. Appeared to be in better spirits than he had been for a long time. Had some further conversation relative to the governor's declaration that Count Las Casas had, in his journal, made Napoleon say that he abhorred the sight of the British uniform, and his excellency's assertion that Las Casas had endeavored to make him hate the English."

"I can not conceive," said Napoleon, "what object Las Casas could have in view by doing so. What could he gain by it? On the contrary, Las Casas always spoke well of the English; said that he had been ten years among them, and had been always well treated. It is an invention of this man's, whose whole superstructure is built upon falsehood. I said, certainly, that I did not like to see officers in uniform closely attending or watching me, because the uniform reminded me that I was considered as a prisoner, and gave rise to unpleasant reflections. If even *you* were to come into my apartment every day in your uniform, it would give me the idea of your being a *gendarme*. But this man has no delicacy of appreciation. The admiral had, and immediately understood the delicacy of it when it was mentioned to him."

While walking about the room, he said cheerfully to the doctor, "What sort of a man did you take me to be before you became my surgeon? What did you think of my character, and what I was capable of? Give me your real opinion frankly."

O'Meara replied, "I thought you to be a man whose stupendous talents were only to be equaled by your measureless ambition; and although I did not give credit to one tenth part of the libels which I had read against you, still I believed that you would not hesitate to commit a crime when you found it to be necessary, or thought it might be useful to you."

"This is just the answer that I expected," replied Napoleon, "and is, perhaps, the opinion of Lord Holland, and even of numbers of the French. I have risen to too great a pitch of human glory and elevation not to have excited the envy and jealousy of mankind. They will say, 'It is true that he has raised himself to the highest pinnacle of glory, but to attain it he has committed many crimes.' Now the fact is that I not only never committed any crimes, but I never even thought of doing so. I have always gone with the opinion of great masses and with events. I have always made little account of the opinion of individuals, of that of the public a great deal. Of what use, then, would crime have been to me? I am too much a fatalist, and have always despised mankind too much to have had recourse to crime to frustrate their attempts. I have always marched with the opinion of five or six millions of men. Of what use, then, would crime have been to me?

"In spite of all libels," continued he, "I have no fear whatever about my fame. Posterity will do me justice. The truth will be known, and the good that I have done, with the faults I have committed, will be compared. I am not uneasy for the result. Had I succeeded, I should have died with the reputation of the greatest man that ever existed. As it is, although I have failed, I shall be considered as an extraordinary man. My elevation was unparalleled, *because* unaccompanied by crime. I have fought fifty pitched battles, almost all of which I have gained. I have framed and carried into effect a code of laws that will bear my name to the most distant posterity. From nothing I raised myself to be the most powerful monarch in the world. Europe was at my feet. My ambition was great, I admit, but it was of a cold nature, and caused by events and the opinion of great bodies.

"I have always been of opinion that the sovereignty lay in the people. In fact, the imperial government was a kind of republic. Called to the head of it by the voice of the nation, my maxim was, *la carrière ouverte aux talens* (the career open to talents), without distinction of birth or fortune, and this system of equality is the reason that your oligarchy hate me so much.

"It is not," added Napoleon, "by what the Quarterly Review or Pichon says, or by what I could write myself, that posterity will judge of me. It is by the voice of so many millions of inhabitants who have been under my government. Those who consented to the union of Poland with Russia will be the execration of posterity, while my name will be pronounced with respect when the fine southern countries of Europe are a prey to the barbarians of the North. Perhaps my greatest fault was not having deprived the King of Prussia of his throne, which I might easily have done."

March 4. The Emperor was in good health and cheerful spirits. He returned to Dr. O'Meara the numbers of The Ambigu for 1816, and desired him to obtain the numbers for 1815. O'Meara made some inquiries respecting the editor, Pelletier.

"Pelletier," said the Emperor, "is a miscreant who would write for any body that would pay him. He made offers to me to change his style, and write for me in such a manner that the British government would not be aware that he was employed by me. One time, in particular, he sent to the police a manuscript copy of a book written against me, with an offer that it should not be printed provided he were paid a certain sum of money. This was made known to me. I ordered the police to answer that, if he paid the expenses of printing, the work should be published in Paris for him. He was not the only one who made offers of the kind to me when I was in power. Some of the editors of the English newspapers made similar advances, and declared that they could render me most essential services, but I *then* did not attach sufficient importance to their offers, and refused them.

"When I was on the throne," continued he, "there were thirty clerks employed in translating English newspapers, and in making extracts from English works of merit. Matters which appeared of importance were extracted from the newspapers, and daily submitted to me. But I never had it done in my presence, or endeavored to accompany the translator in his progress, as has been asserted."

Sir Hudson Lowe sent word to Longwood of his intention of putting an iron railing around the house, the gates to which he should cause to be locked at seven or eight o'clock in the evening, and the keys to be sent to Plantation House, where they should remain till daybreak the next morning. At the same time, it was pretended that this iron railing was merely an ornamental fence to keep out the cattle.

March 5. The *Tortoise* store-ship arrived from England. It brought papers containing extracts from a work published by Dr. Warden, surgeon on board the *Northumberland*, respecting the Emperor. When Dr. O'Meara called at Longwood, he found the Emperor reclining on his sofa in a very pensive attitude, his head resting upon one of his hands, and apparently sunk in deep melancholy. His morning-gown was on, a Madras handkerchief bound around his head, and his beard unshaved. In a desponding manner, Napoleon looked up and said,

"Is the ship from England? What news does it bring?"

O'Meara replied that it came directly from England, and that a book had been published respecting the Emperor by Warden, of the *Northumberland*, which had excited great interest.

"What is the nature of the work?" inquired the Emperor. "Is it for or against me? Is it well written? What is the subject?"

The Emperor then, with the assistance of O'Meara, read some extracts which were in the Observer. He perused very attentively an article which stated that the Empress Maria Louisa had fallen from her horse into the Po, and with difficulty had been saved from a watery grave. He appeared considerably affected by the perusal.

Subsequently he conversed about the tumults in England, and the distress of the poorer classes.

"Your ministers," said he, "are answerable for all the misery and the distress of England, by their having neglected to take advantage of favorable circumstances to secure to the country great commercial advantages. In consequence of my misfortunes in Russia, successes unparalleled in the history of the world attended her, and, by the force of circumstances, an opportunity was afforded her of rendering herself the most flourishing and powerful nation in the world. I have always considered England to be in a dangerous state, in an unnatural state of over-exertion, and that, if some unforeseen circumstance did not arise to succor her, she must sink under the pressure of the exertions she has made and the load of taxation. Such an opportunity *has occurred*, but your ministers, like blockheads, have not taken advantage of it, but preferred paying their court to those kings to consulting the interests of their country.

"It appears to me," continued he, "to be clearly the intention of your ministers to subject England to a military yoke, to put down by degrees the liberty which prevails there, and to render their own power unlimited. All those honors conferred upon the military, and the tenor of several other steps lately adopted, are only so many preliminaries toward it. I can discern their object. Assistance, if necessary, will probably be rendered by the other sovereigns of Europe, who are jealous, and can not bear the idea that England should be the only free nation in Europe. They will assist in putting you down."

O'Meara observed that the English would never submit to be made a nation of slaves.

The Emperor replied, "There is every appearance that the attempt will be made."

The *Tortoise* brought, also, dispatches from Lord Bathurst to Sir Hudson Lowe. In the official documents of Sir Hudson Lowe, published in defense of his conduct, it is said,

"The French officers had flattered themselves that Sir Hudson Lowe's conduct was condemned by the ministers. In a letter dated October, 1816, Lord Bathurst said, 'I am commanded to convey to you his royal highness' entire approbation of your conduct. On the subject of General Bonaparte's proposition (*to assume an incognito*), I probably shall not give you any instruction. It appears harsh to refuse it, and there may arise much embarrassment in formally acquiescing in it. You will not, therefore, encourage any renewal of the conversation. As the proposition was not made by authority, no official answer need be given.'"

The advocate of Sir Hudson Lowe, who edits these documents, adds, "The embarrassment here alluded to by Lord Bathurst seems to have been that which might arise from a recognition of Bonaparte's right to assume an *incognito*, which is the privilege of monarchs; for, as the British government firmly refused to acknowledge him as Emperor, they did not wish to sanction what appeared to be claimed as an incident of sovereignty."

These are the men who have accused Napoleon of childishness in refusing to submit humbly to the insult. In this conflict Napoleon was true to his own lofty character. The English ministry had previously adopted the same course with George Washington. Refusing to recognize the right of the people to choose him *general-in-chief*, they insultingly addressed him as "*George Washington, Esq.*, &c., &c., &c." Washington refused to receive any such letters, and returned them all unopened. Fortunately, he was not their captive. As he had many English prisoners in his hands, and as it was necessary for them to communicate with him, they were compelled to recognize popular rights, and address Washington as general-in-chief. Napoleon also, though in his tomb, has triumphed. The successors of Bathurst, Castlereagh, and Wellington are now compelled to say "the Emperor Napoleon." It would be indeed amusing to hear them now talk of *General Bonaparte!*

Some broken numbers of the London Times were sent up to the Emperor, and several of his companions received letters from their friends. Napoleon, by the inhuman restrictions imposed upon him, was debarred from all intercourse with his family. He was not allowed to send his letters open through the Prince Regent. It was demanded that all his letters, and the answers to them, should be inspected by the petty despot at Longwood, whom he thoroughly despised. Self-respect would not allow him to submit to this. Though crushed by woe, he was firm through more than five long years, till his heart, in anguish, ceased to beat.

The only tidings he obtained from his mother, his wife, his child, his brothers and sisters, during all these years of imprisonment, were from occasional items which he gleaned from the newspapers. His mind was much excited by the accident which Maria Louisa had encountered. With great eagerness he examined the broken numbers of the Times, to find some farther intelligence from those he loved so dearly. In the evening, in his intense solicitude, he sent again for Dr. O'Meara.

"I am convinced," said he, "that the governor has kept back some letters and newspapers. I have no doubt that Sir Hudson Lowe received a complete series of papers, and that he has kept back some, according to his usual brutal custom, because there might have been an article which would prove agreeable to me.

"At first," said he, "I thought that there might have been some bad news of my wife; but a moment's reflection taught me that, if so, this man would not have failed to send it directly, in order to afflict me. Perhaps there may be some news of my son. When you go to town to-morrow, endeavor to see a complete series of papers, and look attentively at them."

March 10. The Emperor had been reading Warden's book, and appeared in cheerful spirits. Dr. O'Meara asked the Emperor's opinion of the work.

He replied, "The foundation of it is true, but he has badly understood what was said to him, as in the work there are many mistakes, which must have arisen from bad explanation. Warden does not understand French. He has acted wrong in making me speak in the manner he has done; for, instead of having stated that it had been conveyed through an interpreter, he puts down almost every thing as if I had been speaking to him all the time, and as if he could have understood me; consequently, he has put into my mouth expressions unworthy of me, and not in my style. Any person who knows me will readily see that it is not my style.

"In fact, most of what he has received through interpretation, and that composes a large portion of the work, is more or less incorrect. He has said that Massena had stormed the village of Esling thirteen times, which, if the work is translated into French, will make every French officer acquainted with the battle laugh, as Massena was not at that particular spot during the whole of the action.*

"What he says about the prisoners that had been made at Jaffa is also incorrect, as they were marched on twelve leagues in the direction of Bagdat, and not to Nazareth. They were Maugrabins from near Algiers, and not natives of the country that he mentions. He is incorrect in stating that I proposed to give the sick opium. I did not propose it. It was first made by one of the medical officers. He is wrong in the explanation which he has given of the reason why I wished Wright to live. My principal reason was to be able to prove, as I told you before, by Wright's evidence, that * * * had caused assassins, hired by the Count d'Artois, to be landed in France, to murder me. This I thought I should have effected by Wright's own evidence at a trial in presence of the embassadors of the powers in friendship with me. Now there was something glorious in Wright's death. He preferred taking away his own life to compromising his government.

"Shortly after Marengo," continued Napoleon, "Louis wrote a letter to me, which was delivered by the Abbé Montesquieu, in which he said that I delayed for a long time to restore him to his throne; that the happiness of France could never be complete without him, neither could the glory of the country be complete without me; that one was as necessary to it as the other; and concluded by desiring me to choose whatever I thought proper,

---

* These remarks show how easily conversation may be misunderstood. Undoubtedly there are other remarks here attributed to the Emperor which do not precisely express the ideas he intended to convey, but the general flow of conversation is too decided and strong for any misunderstanding.

which would be granted under him, provided I restored to him his throne. I sent him back a very handsome answer, in which I stated that I was extremely sorry for the misfortunes of himself and his family; that I was ready to do every thing in my power to relieve them, and would interest myself about providing a suitable income for them, but that he might abandon the thought of ever returning to France as a sovereign, as that could not be effected without his having passed over the bodies of five hundred thousand Frenchmen.

"Warden has been incorrectly informed that Maret was privy to my return to France. He knew nothing about it, and such a statement may injure his relations in France. He has acted also unguardedly in asserting matters upon the authority of Count and Countess Bertrand, as it may cause them many enemies. He ought to have said, 'I have been told at Longwood.' As to his saying that the information came from me, I care not, as I *fear nobody*, but he ought to have been cautious about the others.

"Warden," added he, "is a man of good intentions, and the foundation of his work is true, but many of the circumstances are incorrectly stated, in consequence of misconception and bad interpretation. Gourgaud was very angry yesterday about what was said of him. I told him that he ought to take example by me, and observe with what patience I bore the libels on me with which the press was overwhelmed; that they had made me a poisoner, an assassin, a violator, a monster who was guilty of incest and of every horrid crime; that he ought to reflect upon this, and be silent.

"I see," continued he, "by some answers in the Times, that the Morning Chronicle appears to defend me. What harm could it possibly be to let me see that paper—to let me read something favorable of myself? It is very seldom that I now see any thing of the kind, but it is a cruelty to withhold so slender a consolation.

"You recollect I told you that the English would change their opinion of me, and that, from the great intercourse they had with France and Italy, they would soon discover that I was not the horrid character they had believed me to be; and also that the English travelers, in returning from the countries which had been under my dominion, would bring back with them sentiments quite different from those with which they had set out. This is now beginning to take place, and will increase every day. Those people will say,

"'We have been deceived. On the Continent we have heard none of those horrid stories; on the contrary, wherever there was a fine road or a noble bridge, and we asked who made this, the answer has been Napoleon or Bonaparte.' They will naturally say, at least this man encouraged the arts and the sciences during his reign, and endeavored to facilitate and to increase the commerce of the countries under him.

"Lord Castlereagh," continued he, "has been guilty of a base libel by having declared that I had said, since I came here, that, 'in peace or in war, I aimed at the destruction of England.' It is wholly false, and I shall make it a subject of complaint to his master, the Prince Regent, and expose to him the unworthy conduct of his minister—conduct degrading to the character of a man. It is always dishonorable and base publicly to insult and belie the unfortunate, especially when in your power, and at such a distance as to preclude the possibility of a reply.

"Your ministers," said he, "reason thus for sending me to St. Helena. This Bonaparte is a man of talent, and has always been an enemy to England. The Bourbons are a set of *imbecilles*, and it is better for the English to have *imbecilles* on the throne of France than persons of talent; for the former will not have the ability, though they may have the inclination, to do as much mischief to England as the latter. We must do every thing we can to keep down the French, who are our natural enemies; and the best mode of effecting it is to place a set of fools upon the throne, who will occupy themselves in restoring the old superstition, ignorance, and prejudices of the nation, and consequently weaken instead of strengthening it.

"They would have done better," continued he, " to have left me upon the throne. I would have given the English great commercial advantages, which the Bourbons dare not offer. Besides, it would have kept up the importance of the English on the Continent; for the other powers, being afraid of me, would have made sacrifices to keep on good terms with them, in order to have them on their side, well knowing that, without their aid, they could do nothing against me; whereas now, as they are not afraid of the Bourbons, they will set but little value upon the friendship of a power that they are jealous of and want to humble. Moreover, your ministers could always have held *me* up *in terrorem* to the people of England whenever they wanted to command the exertions of the nation."

A few moments afterward Napoleon observed, " It is true, as has been stated in the papers, that the Belgians are sorry that the English gained the battle of Waterloo. They considered themselves as Frenchmen, and, in truth, they were such. The greatest part of the nation loved me, and wished that I might succeed. The stories that your ministers have taken such pains to circulate respecting the nations that I had united to France having hated me and detested my tyranny, are all falsehoods. The Italians, Piedmontese, Belgians, and others are an example of what I say. You will receive hereafter the opinions of those English who have visited the Continent. You will find that what I tell you is correct, and that *millions* in Europe now *weep* for me. The Piedmontese preferred being as a province of France to being an independent kingdom under the King of Sardinia."

March 12. At eleven o'clock in the morning Dr. O'Meara saw the Emperor. He was in cheerful spirits, and very social. He spoke of the distress which the journals announced as existing in England, and of the disturbance among the workmen.

"The Prince Regent," said he, "must adopt some measures in order to pacify the people, such as reducing the taxes. It is impossible that a nation in cold blood will consent to pay, in time of peace, taxes nearly equal to the amount of those paid by them in war, when there is no longer that stimulus, that irritation of mind which made them consider such drainings of their purses absolutely necessary to prevent their country from being devoured by a foreign nation. England is in an unnatural state, and some change must take place."

O'Meara said that, although great distress existed in England, the disturbances were confined to the lower classes, and that it would end by a few of them being hanged.

Napoleon replied, "It may be so, Mr. Doctor, but you must consider that the lower classes, as you call them, are the bulk of the people. They, and not the nobles, *form the nation.* When the lower class gains the day, it ceases to be any longer the lower class; it is then called the nation. If it does not, why, then some are executed, and they are called rabble, rebels, robbers, &c. Thus goes the world."

March 14. The French commissioner, the Marquis Montchenu, was an excessively weak man, and excessively vain of his lofty lineage. He affected to look with much contempt upon any one who could not count some hundred years of nobility. O'Meara informed the Emperor that a letter had appeared in the French papers stating that Napoleon had invited the marquis to dine with him, but that Montchenu replied, "I have been sent to St. Helena to guard Bonaparte, not to dine with him."

"These gentlemen," said the Emperor, "are always the same. It is very likely that he has been silly (*bête*) enough to write it. Those old French nobles are capable of any folly. He is worthy of being one of the *high-born* of France."

"One of the papers states," continued O'Meara, "that Sir George Cockburn has represented Napoleon as an ordinary character, destitute of talent."

"Probably," Napoleon remarked, "and with reason, he does not suppose me to be a god, or to be endowed with supernatural talents, but I will venture to say that he gives me credit for possessing some. If he has really expressed the opinion attributed to him, it pays a poor compliment to the discernment of the greatest part of the world. I wish you would bring me the paper which contains the report of Sir George Cockburn. I am so accustomed to read libels, that I care but little what is said, or what calumnies are published about me.

"The people of England with difficulty will believe," added he, "that I not only read these libels without anger, but even laugh at them. From the violence of temper which has been attributed to me, I suppose they think that I must be worked up by rage to fits of madness. They are mistaken; they only excite my laughter. The truth only wounds."

O'Meara made inquiries respecting the affair of Palm, saying that it was the only sanguinary act attributed to Napoleon of which a satisfactory explanation had not been given.

Napoleon replied, "I never have been asked any explanation about it. All that I recollect is, that Palm was arrested by order of Davoust, I believe, tried, condemned, and shot, for having, while the country was in possession of the French, and under military occupation, not only excited rebellion among the inhabitants, and urged them to rise and massacre the soldiers, but also attempted to instigate the soldiers themselves to refuse obedience to their orders, and to mutiny against their generals. I believe that he met with a fair trial. I should like," continued he, " to read the principal libels which have been published against me in England, if I could have them in French. There is Pelletier," added he, laughing, "who *proves* that I was *myself* the contriver of the infernal machine."

March 18. The Emperor, closely imprisoned in his room, passed the long and monotonous hours in reading, dictating, and conversing with his friends. Dr. O'Meara, in his endeavor to conciliate Sir Hudson Lowe, went to the very utmost extreme of propriety in reporting to the governor every thing which was said or done by his illustrious patient. The Emperor evidently made an effort, whenever his English physician entered, to appear firm and cheerful. To-day he remarked,

" Your ministers will not be able to impose always upon the nation. Because they are afraid of me, and think that I have some talent, and because I have been always at war with them, and that I have made France greater than ever she was before, they fear that I might do so again; and as any thing for the advantage of France would be disadvantageous to them, they endeavor by all means to prevent it, by putting a set of *imbecilles* on the throne, under whom France must necessarily decay. In order to find an excuse for sending me here, and to give a color to their proceedings, they seek all means of blackening my character. Mark me, the English themselves will be the first to justify me, and to vindicate my character from the calumnies which their ministers have thrown upon it. Posterity will revenge me. Recollect my words, and recollect that this is not the first time that I have told you so.

" I am told," added he, " that there is twenty thousand pounds' [$100,000] worth of iron railing sent out. It is money thrown into the sea. Before this railing can be fixed up here I shall be under ground, for I am sure that I shall not hold out more than two years under the treatment that I experience.

" If my greatest enemies knew the way in which I am treated, they would compassionate me. Millions in Europe will weep for my lot when it is known, and known it will be, in spite of the endeavors of this governor to envelop every thing in secrecy and mystery. He shows how little he knows of England by thinking to effect this. He has nothing English about him, either within or without. He badly serves his government, who are desirous that as little as possible should be said about me, but he takes the most certain method of effecting the contrary."

" Sir Hudson Lowe," says O'Meara, " was very busy inspecting the ditches and other works he had ordered to be thrown up about Longwood House and the stables."

March 19. Napoleon, while in his bath, received the doctor. He was reading a French New Testament. O'Meara observed that many people would not believe that he would read such a book, as it had been asserted, and credited by some, that he was an unbeliever.

Napoleon smiled and replied, "Nevertheless, it is not true. I am far from being an Atheist. In spite of all the iniquities and frauds of the teachers of religion, who are eternally preaching up that their kingdom is not of this world, and yet seize every thing which they can lay their hands upon, from the time that I arrived at the head of the government, I did every thing in my power to re-establish religion. But I wished to render it the foundation and prop of morality and good principles, and not *à prendre l'essor* of the human laws. Man has need of something wonderful. It is better for him to seek it in religion than in Mademoiselle le Normand.* Moreover, religion is a great consolation and resource to those who possess it, and no man can pronounce what he will do in his last moments."

Napoleon then made some remarks upon the conduct of the governor, whom he declared to be a man totally unfit for his situation. "If he were a suitable man," said he, "he might make it pleasant and interesting. He might spend much of his time with me, and get great information with respect to past occurrences, with which no other person could be so well acquainted or so satisfactorily account for. Even unknown to myself, he would imperceptibly have opportunities of getting information from me which would be very desirable to his ministers, and which I am certain they have ordered him to obtain, and that he burns to know. If I had really any intention of effecting my escape from this place, instead of disagreeing with him, I would caress and flatter him, endeavor to be on the best terms, go to Plantation House, call on his wife, and try to make him believe that I was contented, and thereby lull his suspicions asleep."

March 16. Napoleon spoke at length about Talleyrand. "The triumph of Talleyrand," said he, "is the triumph of immorality. A priest united to another man's wife, and who has paid her husband a large sum of money to leave her with him. A man who has sold every thing, betrayed every body and every side. I forbade Madam Talleyrand the court, first, because she was a disreputable character, and because I found out that some Genoese merchants had paid her four hundred thousand francs in hopes of gaining some commercial favors by means of her husband. She was a very elegant woman, English or East Indian, but simple and grossly ignorant.

"I sometimes asked Denon, whose works I suppose you have read, to breakfast with me, as I took pleasure in his conversation, and conversed very freely with him. Now all the intriguers and speculators paid their court to Denon, with a view of inducing him to mention their projects or themselves in the course of his conversations with me, thinking that even being mentioned by such a man as Denon, for whom I had a great esteem, might materially serve them. Talleyrand, who was a great speculator, invited Denon to dinner. When he went home to his wife, he said,

"'My dear, I have invited Denon to dine. He is a great traveler, and you must say something handsome to him about his travels, as he may be useful to us with the Emperor.'

"His wife, being extremely ignorant, and probably never having read any

---

* A celebrated fortune-teller at Paris.

other book of travels than that of Robinson Crusoe, concluded that Denon could be nobody else than Robinson. Wishing to be very civil to him, she, before a large company, asked him divers questions about his man Friday! Denon, astonished, did not know what to think at first, but at length discovered, by her questions, that she really imagined him to be Robinson Crusoe. His astonishment and that of the company can not be described, nor the peals of laughter which it excited in Paris, as the story flew like wildfire through the city, and *even* Talleyrand *himself* was ashamed of it.

"It has been said," continued the Emperor, "that I turned Mohammedan in Egypt. Now it is not the case. I never followed any of the tenets of that religion. I never prayed in the mosques. I never abstained from wine, or was circumcised, neither did I ever profess it. I said merely that we were the friends of the Mussulmans, and that I respected Mohammed their prophet, which was true; I respect him now."

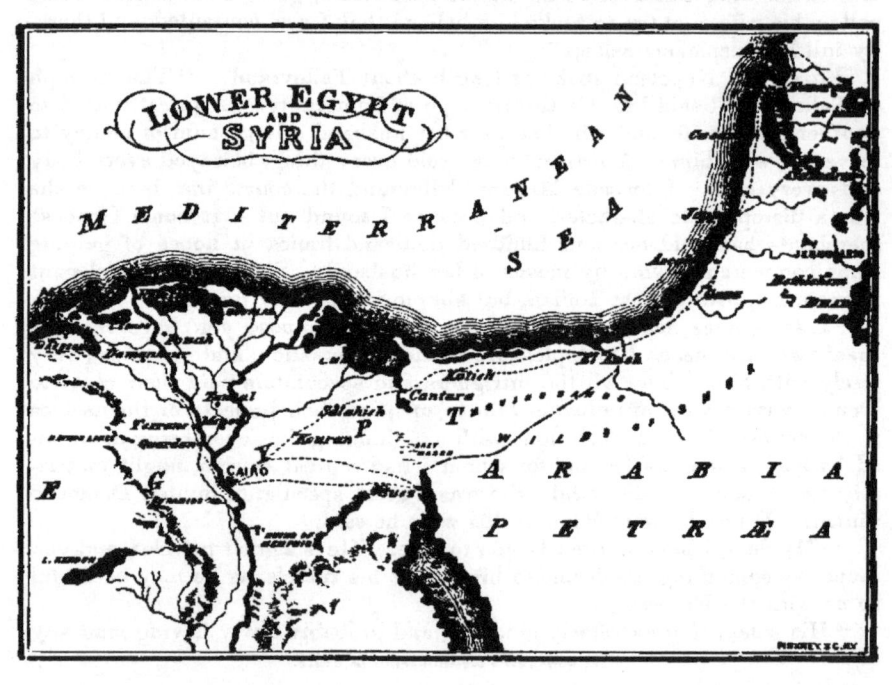

The Emperor then spoke about some of the plans that he had had in contemplation for making canals of communication in Egypt. "I intended," said he, "to have made two, one from the Red Sea to the Nile at Cairo, and the other to the Mediterranean. I had the Red Sea surveyed, and found that its waters were thirty feet higher than the Mediterranean when they were highest, but only twenty-four at the lowest. My plan was to have prevented any water from flowing into the canal unless at low water, and this, in the course of a distance of thirty leagues in its passage to the Mediterramean, would have been of little consequence. Besides, I would have had some sluices made. The Nile was seven feet lower than the Red Sea when at its lowest, but many feet higher during the inundation. The expense was calculated at eighteen millions of francs [$3,600,000], and two years' labor."

O'Meara asked if the Emperor had not saved Menou's life after the 13th of Vendemiaire.

He replied, "I certainly was the means of saving his life. The Convention ordered him to be tried, and he would have been guillotined. I was then commander-in-chief of Paris. Thinking it very unjust that Menou only should suffer, while three commissioners of the Convention, under whose orders he acted, were left untried and unpunished, but not venturing to say openly that he ought to be acquitted, for in those terrible times a man who told the truth lost his head, I had recourse to a stratagem. I invited the members who were trying him to breakfast, and turned the conversation upon Menou. I said that he had acted very wrong, and deserved to be condemned to death, but that first the commissioners of the Convention must be tried and condemned, as he had acted by their orders, and all must suffer. This had the desired effect. The members of the court said, 'We will not allow those civilians to bathe themselves in our blood, while they allow their own commissioners, who are more culpable, to escape with impunity.' Menou was immediately declared innocent."

O'Meara then asked how many men he supposed had lost their lives in the business of the 13th Vendemiaire.

He replied, "Very few, considering the circumstances. Of the people, there were about seventy or eighty killed, and between three and four hundred wounded; of the Conventionalists, about thirty killed, and two hundred and fifty wounded. The reason there were so few killed was, that, after the first two discharges, I made the troops load with powder only, which had the effect of frightening the Parisians, and answered as well as killing them would have done. I made the troops at first fire ball, because, to a rabble who are ignorant of the effect of fire-arms, it is the worst possible policy to fire powder only in the beginning; for the populace, after the first discharge, hearing a great noise, are a little frightened, but looking around them, and seeing nobody killed or wounded, pluck up their spirits, begin immediately to despise you, become doubly outrageous, and rush on without fear, and it is necessary to kill ten times the number that it would have been had ball been used at first.

"With a rabble every thing depends upon the first impressions made upon them. If they receive a discharge of firearms, and perceive the killed and wounded falling among them, a panic seizes them, they take to their heels instantly, and vanish in a moment. Therefore, when it is necessary to fire at all, it ought to be done with ball at first. It is a mistaken instance of humanity to use powder only at that moment, and, instead of saving the lives of men, ultimately causes an unnecessary waste of human blood."

March 25. O'Meara had loaned Napoleon several very atrocious libels against the Emperor. Napoleon remarked, "I have been reading all day yesterday 'The Secret Memoirs' of myself. These libels have done me more good than harm in France, because they irritated the nation both against the writers, and the Bourbons who paid them, by representing me as a monster, and by the improbable and scandalous falsehoods they contained against me and the government under me, which were degrading to them and the nation. Even Chateaubriand has done me good by his work.

"It appears from the books you lent me that at a very early age I poisoned a girl; that I poisoned others for the mere pleasure of poisoning; that I assassinated Desaix, Kleber, the Duke of Abrantes, and I know not how many others; that I went to the army of Italy, consisting of some thousand galley-slaves, who were extremely happy to see me, as being one of their fraternity. You English believed every thing bad of me, which belief was always encouraged by your ministers. Your ministry also, with the exception of Fox, who was sincere in his desire for peace, encouraged assassins against me." Here O'Meara made some observations in disbelief of the assertion, to which Napoleon replied,

"When they furnished ships to land, and money to support, men whose professed object was to assassinate me, was not that being privy to it?" O'Meara said that they had furnished ships and money to assist in accomplishing a revolution, but without having known that assassination formed part of their plans.

"Doctor," replied Napoleon, "you are a child. They knew it well. Fifty or sixty brigands, the most of them notorious for assassination, could have no other mode of effecting a revolution. They had republished in London, at the same time, a book called '*Killing no Murder*,' which had been originally printed in Cromwell's time, for the purpose of inculcating a belief that assassinating me was not only not a crime, but that it would be a praiseworthy and meritorious action."

Sir Pulteney and Lady Malcolm, Captains Stanfell and Festing, of the navy, came up and had an interview with Napoleon. When they came out, one of the gentlemen expressed his astonishment at finding Napoleon so different a person to what he was reported.

"Instead of being a rough, impatient, and imperious character," said he, "I found him to be mild, gentle in his manner, and one of the pleasantest men I ever saw. I shall *never* forget him, nor how different he is from the idea I had been led to form of him."

March 26. Napoleon conversed a good deal about the battle of Waterloo. "The plan of the battle," said he, "will not, in the eyes of the historian, reflect any credit on Lord Wellington as a general. In the first place, he ought not to have given battle with the armies divided; they ought to have been united and encamped before the 15th. In the next, the choice of ground was bad, because, if he had been beaten, he could not have retreated, as there was only one road leading to the forest in his rear. He also committed a fault which might have proved the destruction of all his army, without its ever having commenced the campaign or being drawn out in battle—he allowed himself to be surprised. On the 15th I was at Charleroi, and had beaten the Prussians without his knowing any thing about it. I had gained forty-eight hours of maneuvers upon him, which was a great object, and, if some of my generals had shown that vigor and genius which they had displayed in other times, I should have taken his army in cantonments without ever fighting a battle. But they were discouraged, and fancied that they saw an army of a hundred thousand men every where opposed to them.

"I had not time enough myself to attend to the *minutiæ* of the army. I accounted upon surprising and cutting them up in detail. I knew of Bulow's arrival at eleven o'clock, but I did not regard it; I had still eighty chances out of a hundred in my favor. Notwithstanding the great superiority of force against me, I was convinced that I should obtain the victory. I had about seventy thousand men, of whom fifteen thousand were cavalry. I had also two hundred and fifty pieces of cannon; but my troops were so good, that I esteemed them sufficient to beat a hundred and twenty thousand. Now Lord Wellington had under his command about ninety thousand, and two hundred and fifty pieces of cannon, and Bulow had thirty thousand, making a hundred and twenty thousand. Of all those troops, however, I only reckoned the English as being able to cope with my own; the others I thought little of. I believe that of English there were from thirty-five to forty thousand; these I esteemed to be as brave and as good as my own troops. The English army was well known latterly on the Continent; and, besides, your nation possesses courage and energy. As to the Prussians, Belgians, and others, half the number of my troops were sufficient to beat them. I only left thirty-four thousand men to take care of the Prussians.

"The chief causes of the loss of that battle were, first of all, Grouchy's great tardiness and neglect in executing his orders; next, the *grenadiers à cheval* and the cavalry under General Guyot, which I had in reserve, and which were never to leave me, engaged without orders and without my knowledge; so that after the last charge, when the troops were beaten, and the English cavalry advanced, I had not a single corps of cavalry in reserve to resist them, instead of one which I esteemed to be equal to double their own number. In consequence of this, the English attack succeeded, and all was lost. There was no means of rallying. The youngest general would not have committed the fault of leaving an army entirely without reserve, which, however, occurred here, whether in consequence of treason or not, I can not say. These were the two principal causes of the loss of the battle of Waterloo.

"If Lord Wellington had intrenched himself," continued he, "I would not have attacked him. As a general, his plan did not show talent. He certainly displayed great courage and obstinacy, but a little must be taken away even from that when you consider that he had no means of retreat, and that, had he made the attempt, not a man of his army would have escaped. First, to the firmness and bravery of his troops, for the English fought with the greatest obstinacy and courage, he is principally indebted for the victory, and not to his own conduct as a general; and next, to the arrival of Blucher, to whom the victory is more to be attributed than to Wellington, and more credit due as a general, because he, although beaten the day before, assembled his troops, and brought them into action in the evening. I believe, however," continued Napoleon, "that Wellington is a man of great firmness. The glory of such a victory is a great thing; but in the eye of the historian, his military reputation will gain nothing by it."

"Napoleon then spoke about the libels upon himself which I had collected for him. 'As yet,' said he, 'you have not procured me one that is worthy of an answer. Would you have me sit down and reply to Goldsmith, Pichon, or the Quarterly Review? They are so contemptible and so absurdly false, that they do not merit any other notice than to write false, false, in every page. The only truth I have seen in them is, that one day I met an officer—Rapp, I believe—in the field of battle, with his face covered with blood, and that I cried, *Oh, comme il est beau!* This is true enough; and of it they have made a crime. My admiration of the gallantry of a brave soldier is construed into a crime, and a proof of my delighting in blood; but posterity will do me that justice which is denied to me now. If I were that tyrant, that monster, would the people and the army have flown to join me with the enthusiasm they showed when I landed from Elba with a handful of men? Could I have marched to Paris, and have seated myself upon the throne, without a musket having been fired? Ask the French nation. Ask the Italian.'"

O'Meara mentioned that he had conceived that the Emperor had once expressed to him that his intentions had been to have united England to France, if he had found himself sufficiently powerful.

The Emperor promptly replied, "No, no; you must have misunderstood me. I said that I could *not* unite two nations so dissimilar. I intended, if I had succeeded in my projected descent, to have abolished the monarchy, and established a republic instead of the oligarchy by which you are governed. I would have separated Ireland from England, the former of which I would have made an independent republic. No, no; I would have left them to themselves after having sown the seeds of republicanism in their *morale*.

"As to annexing England and France, upon mature deliberation I conceived that it would have been impossible to have united nations so dissimilar in ideas, and that it would have been as difficult to effect as to have brought together India and Europe. After Amiens I was ready to conclude a *good peace* with England, that is to say, a peace which would establish the commercial relations of the two countries upon a similar and equal footing."

O'Meara observed that Lord Amherst was soon expected on his return from his embassy to China, and that it was likely that he would wish to see the Emperor.

"If he is to be presented by the governor," Napoleon replied, "or if the governor sends one of his staff with him, I will not receive him. If he comes with the admiral, I shall. Neither will I receive the new admiral if he comes with the governor. I would not receive my own son if he were to be presented by him."

CHAPTER XL.

1817, April and May.

On Aristocracy—Cornwallis—False Documents—Lord Whitworth—Commendation of the English Seamen—Habits of Writing—Pleasant Interview with Admiral Malcolm—Remarks on receiving Lord Amherst—The Princess of Wales—Prince Leopold—The Re-establishment of Poland—Deplorable State of Louis XVIII.—Lord Bathurst's Speech.

April 3. A midshipman who was on board the *Undaunted*, which conveyed Napoleon to Elba, happened to arrive at the island. He went up to Longwood, hoping to get a glimpse of the Emperor. Napoleon, who was walking in the garden, immediately recognized him, sent for him, told him that he had grown much since he had seen him, and conversed with him familiarly. O'Meara afterward remarked to the Emperor that the midshipman had said that the Emperor was much liked by the ship's company of the *Undaunted*.

"Yes," replied Napoleon, "I believe it was so. I used to go among them, speak to them kindly, and ask different questions. My freedom in this respect quite astonished them, as it was so different from that which they had been accustomed to receive from their own officers. You English are *aristocrats*. You keep a great distance between yourselves and the people."

O'Meara observed that, on board of a man-of-war, it was necessary to keep the seamen at a great distance, in order to maintain a proper respect for the officers.

"I do not think," replied the Emperor, "that it is necessary to keep up so much reserve as you practice. When the officers do not eat or drink, or make too many freedoms with the private soldiers, I see no necessity for any greater distinctions. Nature formed all men equal. It was always my custom to go among the soldiers and the common people, to converse with them, ask their little histories, and speak kindly to them. This I found to be of the greatest benefit to me. On the contrary, the generals and officers I treated with reserve, and kept them at a great distance."

April 6. Napoleon appeared in very good spirits. He mentioned Marquis Cornwallis in terms of great praise. "Cornwallis," said he, "was a man of probity, a generous and sincere character. He was the man who first gave me a good opinion of the English; his integrity, fidelity, frankness, and the nobleness of his sentiments, impressed me with a very favorable opinion of you. I recollect Cornwallis saying one day, 'There are certain qualities which may be bought, but a good character, sincerity, a proper pride, and calmness in the hour of danger, are not to be purchased.' These words made an impression upon me. I gave him a regiment of cavalry to amuse himself with at Amiens, which used to maneuver before him. The officers of it loved him much. I do not believe that he was a man of first-rate abilities, but he had talent, great probity, and sincerity. He never broke his word.

"At Amiens, the treaty was ready, and was to be signed by him at the Hotel de la Ville at nine o'clock. Something happened which prevented him from going, but he sent word to the French ministers that they might consider the treaty as having been signed, and that he would sign it the following day. A courier from England arrived at night with directions to him to refuse his consent to certain articles, and not to sign the treaty. Although Cornwallis had not signed it, and might easily have availed himself of this order, he was a man of such strict honor that he said he considered his promise to be equivalent to his signature, and wrote to his government that he had promised, and that, having once pledged his word, he would keep it; that, if they were not satisfied, they might refuse to ratify the treaty. *There* was a man of honor—a true Englishman. Such a man as Cornwallis ought to have been sent here, instead of a compound of falsehood, suspicion, and meanness. I was much grieved when I heard of his death. Some of his family occasionally wrote to me to request favors for some prisoners, which I always complied with."

Speaking of Lord Whitworth, the Emperor remarked,

"Lord Whitworth, in that famous interview which he had with me, during which I was by no means violent, said, on leaving the room, that he was well satisfied with me, and contented with the manner in which I had treated him, and hoped that all would go on well. This he said to some of the embassadors of the other powers. A few days afterward, when the English

INTERVIEW WITH LORD WHITWORTH.

newspapers arrived with his account of the interview, stating that I had been in such a rage, it excited the astonishment of every body, especially of those embassadors, who remonstrated with him, and said, 'My lord, how can this account be correct? You know that you allowed to us that you were well contented and satisfied with your reception, and stated your opinion that all would go on well.' He did not know what to answer, and said, 'But this account is also true.'"

Speaking of the British seamen, the Emperor said,

"I always had a high opinion of your seamen. When I was returning from Holland along with the Empress Maria Louisa, we stopped to rest at Givet. During the night a violent storm of wind and rain came on, which swelled the Meuse so much that the bridge of boats over it was carried away. I was very anxious to depart, and ordered all the boatmen of the place to be assembled, that I might be enabled to cross the river. They said that the waters were so high that it would be impossible to pass before two or three days. I questioned some of them, and soon discovered that they were fresh-water seamen. I then recollected that there were English prisoners in the caserns, and ordered that some of the oldest and best seamen among them should be brought before me to the banks of the river. The waters were very high, and the current rapid and dangerous. I asked them if they could join a number of boats so that I might pass over. They answered that it was possible, but hazardous. I desired them to set about it instantly. In the course of a few hours they succeeded in effecting what the other *imbeciles* had pronounced to be impossible, and I crossed before the evening was over. I ordered those who had worked at it to receive a sum of money each, a suit of clothes, and their liberty. Marchand was with me at the time."

April 30. For many weeks Napoleon had been endeavoring to beguile the weary hours by writing observations on the works of the great Frederick. The work was to consist of military observations and reflections, only with as much detail as would be necessary for the explanation of the operations commented on. It would probably comprise five or six octavo volumes. The Emperor frequently rose at three o'clock in the morning to engage in writing. In this work he did not employ an amanuensis, but used the pen himself.

"Formerly," said the Emperor, "I was frequently in the habit of writing only half or three quarters of each word, and running them into each other, which was not attended with much inconvenience, as the secretaries had become so well accustomed to it that they could read it with nearly as much facility as if it were written plainly. No person, however, except one well accustomed to my manner of writing, could read it. Latterly I have begun to write a little more legibly, in consequence of not being so much hurried as on former occasions."

May 6. The Emperor had recently had a long, and, as usual, a very pleasant interview with Admiral Malcolm. In giving an account of this interview to Dr. O'Meara, the Emperor remarked,

"The admiral held a long conversation with me a day or two ago. He praised the governor; said that I was mistaken in him; that he was an extremely well informed man, and had a good heart at bottom. He was very anxious that I should meet him, on an opportunity that soon would be afforded by the arrival of Lord Amherst, when he suggested that we might meet as if nothing had previously occurred. I told him that he did not know the governor; that, until he changed his conduct, I would not see him, unless by force. I observed that he might, without any discussion, alter his restrictions, and treat me as I would myself treat a person placed in a similar situation; in fact, in a word, put matters upon the same footing as he found them, or nearly so; but that it would answer no purpose for us to meet.

"I complain of the ill treatment I receive. He says, 'I comply with my instructions.' This is always his excuse. Now, although I am convinced that his instructions specify no more than that he should take every precaution to prevent my escape and otherwise to treat me well, and with as little possible expense as may be, yet I could not well tell him that he asserted a falsehood. All that I could reply would be by making a comparison (in doing which you must always exaggerate), by likening him to a hangman, who, while he puts a rope round your neck to dispatch you, only executes his orders, but that is not a reason that you should be obliged to make a companion of him, or receive him until the moment of execution. I could only say this, and tell him that if such were his orders, he had disgraced himself by accepting a dishonorable employment; that if they were not, he was still worse in being the contriver of such. As long as he treats me *à la Botany Bay*, so long will not I see him.

"I told the admiral," continued he, "that I hoped the Prince Regent would know of the treatment which I receive here. The admiral said that, if I thought myself aggrieved, I ought to complain, either to the Regent or to the ministers. I think it would be a degradation to me to complain to ministers who have treated me so ill, and who act from hatred.

"The admiral," continued Napoleon, "is very well informed about the history of the last few years; is really an Englishman, and defends his country whenever he can; but notwithstanding, he could not contradict several of the assertions I made to him, because they were incontrovertible facts. He returned frequently to the proposed interview with Lord Amherst, which he is most desirous should take place. I am convinced that no good would arise from it. I wish that he should know my sentiments on these matters."

O'Meara remarked that perhaps his refusing to see the embassador might be construed into an insult to the British government, and to the nation which he represented.

Napoleon replied, "It can not admit of such a construction. He is not sent as an embassador to St. Helena. He was embassador to the Emperor of China, and at St. Helena can only appear in his private capacity; consequently, there is no necessity for his being introduced by the governor. If he wants to see me, let him go to Bertrand, without being accompanied by any of the governor's people, then we will see about it. However, I think it would be better for both that it should not take place; for, if I receive him, I must put on an appearance of cheerfulness, and clothe my face with smiles, as it is contrary to my custom to receive any person otherwise; then, I must either be obliged to make complaints to a stranger of the barbarous treatment I receive here—which is lessening to the dignity and character of a man like me—or else I must furnish an opportunity to this governor to fill the embassador's head with falsehoods, and make him observe that I am so well treated that I have made no complaints, that I want for nothing, that I am treated with all possible respect, and enable him to write home a *bulletin* of falsehoods, with an appeal to the embassador in proof of the truth of them; so that it would place me in an awkward dilemma, and one which it would be better to avoid."

May 12. Napoleon received Dr. O'Meara while in his bath. In some conversation about the governor, he said, "If the governor, on his arrival here, had told Bertrand that, in consequence of orders from his government, he was under the necessity of imposing fresh restrictions, and had described the nature of them, directing that in future we should conform ourselves to them, instead of acting in the underhand manner he has done, I would have said, This is a man who does his duty clearly and openly, without tricks or shuffling. It is necessary that there should be in this world such men as jailers, scavengers, butchers, and hangmen; but still, one does not like to accept of any of those employments. If I were in the Tower of London I might possibly have a good opinion of the jailer for the manner in which he did his duty, but I would neither accept of his situation, nor make a companion of him."

After some conversation on the same subject, Napoleon said, "When I was at Elba, the Princess of Wales sent to inform me of her intention to visit me. I, however, on her own account, sent back an answer begging of her to defer it a little longer, that I might see how matters would turn out; adding, that in a few months I would have the pleasure of receiving her. I knew that at the time it could not fail to injure the princess, and therefore I put it off.

"Prince Leopold," continued he, "was one of the handsomest and finest young men in Paris at the time he was there. At a masquerade given by the Queen of Naples, Leopold made a conspicuous and elegant figure. The Princess Charlotte must doubtless be very contented and very fond of him. He was near being one of my aid-de-camps, to obtain which he had made interest and even applied; but by some means, very fortunately for himself, he did not succeed, as probably, if he had, he would not have been chosen to be a future king of England. Most of the young princes in Germany," continued he, "solicited to be my aids-de-camp, and Leopold was then about eighteen or nineteen years of age."

May 22. Speaking of Russia, the Emperor said, "The European nations will yet find that I had adopted the best possible policy at the time I intended to re-establish the kingdom of Poland, which will be the only effectual means of stopping the increasing power of Russia. It is putting a barrier, a dike to that formidable empire, which it is likely will yet overwhelm Europe. I do not think," said he to O'Meara, "that I shall live to see it, but you may. You are in the flower of your age, and may expect to live thirty-five years longer. I think that you will see that the Russians will either invade and take India, or enter Europe with four hundred thousand Cossacks and other inhabitants of the deserts, and two hundred thousand real Russians.

When Paul was so violent against you, he sent to me for a plan to invade India.

"If I had succeeded in my expedition to Russia, I would have obliged Alexander to accede to the Continental system against England, and thereby have compelled the latter to make peace. I would also have formed Poland into a separate and independent kingdom."

O'Meara asked what kind of a peace he would have granted England.

"A very good one," replied Napoleon. "I would only have insisted upon your discontinuing your vexations at sea. I was tired of war. I would have employed myself in the improving and adorning of France, in the education of my son, and in writing my history. At least the allied powers can not take from me hereafter the great public works which I have executed, the roads which I made over the Alps, and the seas which I have united. They can not place their feet to improve where mine have not been before. They can not take from me the code of laws which I formed, and which will go down to the latest posterity. Thank God, of these they can not deprive me."

O'Meara said that he had been seeking for the number of ships which had been seized by the English prior to the proclamation issued by him for the detention of the English in France, and could only discover that two luggers had been taken in Quiberon Bay.

"Two luggers!" exclaimed Napoleon; "why, there was property to the amount of seventy millions [$14,000,000], and I suppose above two hundred ships detained, before I issued the proclamation. But it is what England has always done. In the war of 1773, you did the same, and you gave as a reason that you had always done so. The great cause of dispute between you and us was, that I would not allow you to do what you liked at sea; or, at least, if so, that I would act as it pleased me by land. In short, I did not wish to receive laws from you, but rather to give them. Perhaps in this I pushed matters too far. Man is liable to err. When you blockaded France, I blockaded England; and it was not a paper blockade, as I obliged you to send your merchandise round by the Baltic, and occupy a little island in the North Sea, in order to smuggle. You said that you would shut me out from the seas, and I said that I would shut you out from the land. You succeeded; but, had it not been for accidents, you would not. Your country is nothing the better for it, through the imbecility of your ministers, who have aggrandized Russia instead of their native country.

"If," continued he, "Lord Castlereagh were to offer to place me again upon the throne of France on the same conditions that Louis fills it, I would prefer remaining where I am. There is no man more to be pitied than Louis XVIII. He is forced upon the nation as king, and instead of being allowed to ingratiate himself with the people, the Allies oblige him to have recourse to measures which must increase their hatred instead of conciliating their affections. Royalty is degraded by the steps they have made him adopt. They have rendered him so powerless and contemptible, that it reflects upon the throne of England itself. In place of making him respectable, they have covered him with mud.

"The French nation would never willingly consent to receive the Bourbons as kings, because the Allies wish it. They would desire me, because the Allies do not. But, putting me out of the question, the French are desirous to see the throne filled by one chosen by themselves, and for whom no enemies or foreign powers had interfered. Ask yourselves, you Englishmen, what your sentiments would be in a similar case? The wish of your ministers to re-establish despotic power and superstition in France can not be agreeable to the English. A free people, unless indeed a desire to humble and to injure prevails, can not wish to see another nation enslaved. Ill-treated as I have been, and deprived of every thing dear to me, I prefer my sojourn on this execrable rock to be seated on the throne of France like Louis, as I know that posterity will do me justice. Another year or two will probably finish my career in this world, but what I have done will never perish. Twelve hundred years hence my name will be mentioned with respect, while those of my oppressors will be unknown, or only known by being loaded with infamy and opprobrium.

"I am inclined," continued Napoleon, "to doubt very much what has been said of Cromwell. It has been asserted that he always wore armor, and continually changed his abode, through fear of assassination. Now both these assertions have been made of me, and both I know to be false, as were most likely those imputed to him.

"The conduct of your government in attempting to put down liberty and enslave the English, surprises me. For Russia, Prussia, and Austria to do so, I wonder not, as they do not merit the name of liberal or of free nations. In them, the will of the sovereign was always law; the slaves must obey; but that England should do so surprises me, unless, as I said to you on a former occasion, political motives, jealousy, *and a wish to humble and lessen those who have enriched themselves by trade prevail with your prince and among your oligarchy.*"

May 23. Doctor O'Meara makes the following record: "A message was sent for me to attend the governor at Plantation House. Found him in the library with Sir Thomas Reade. His excellency said that, 'the day before yesterday, some newspapers of a later date than any of his own had been received by Mr. Cole, the postmaster, some of which were lent to me in direct violation of the act of Parliament, which positively prohibited communication, verbal or written, with *General Bonaparte, or any of his family, or those about him*, without his (the governor's) knowledge; that he therefore wished to know from myself whether I had lent those papers, or any others, to General Bonaparte?'

"I replied that I had lent those and many others at various times to Napoleon, as I had been constantly in the habit of lending papers to him since I had been on the island; that Sir George Cockburn had, in more instances than one, given me newspapers to take to Longwood before having perused them himself.

"Sir Hudson Lowe replied that it was a violation of the act of Parliament.

"I replied that I was not included in the act of Parliament, as I had made an express stipulation that I should not be considered or treated as one of the French, and would immediately resign my situation if I were required to hold it upon such terms.

"His excellency said that 'he desired me to understand that, for the future, I was not to lend General Bonaparte *any newspaper, or be the bearer of any information—news or newspapers*—to him, without having previously obtained his sanction.'

"I observed that I felt it difficult to know how to act; for if, after the arrival of a ship, Napoleon asked me if there were any news, I could not possibly pretend ignorance.

"His excellency said that, 'as soon as a ship arrived, both Captain Poppleton and myself ought to be shut up in Longwood until the whole of the information or news brought was made known to him, and *then* I could obtain from him whatever news was proper to be communicated to General Bonaparte.'

"I replied that I would not remain an hour in my situation subject to such a restriction."

May 27. The conversation again turned upon Russia and the East.

"In the course of a few years," said the Emperor, "Russia will have Constantinople, the greatest part of Turkey, and all Greece. This I hold to be as certain as if it had already taken place. Almost all the cajoling and flattering which Alexander practiced toward me was to gain my consent to effect this object. I would not consent, foreseeing that the equilibrium of Europe would be destroyed. In the natural course of things, in a few years Turkey must fall to Russia. The greatest part of her population are Greeks, who you may say are Russians. The powers it would injure, and who could oppose it, are England, France, Prussia, and Austria. Now, as to Austria, it will be very easy for Russia to engage her assistance by giving her Servia, and other provinces bordering upon the Austrian dominions, reaching near to Constantinople. The only hypothesis that France and England may ever be allied with sincerity will be in order to prevent this. But even this alliance would not avail. France, England, and Prussia united can not prevent it. Russia and Austria can at any time effect it.

"Once mistress of Constantinople, Russia gets all the commerce of the Mediterranean, becomes a great naval power, and God knows what may happen. She quarrels with you, marches off to India an army of seventy thousand good soldiers, which to Russia is nothing, and a hundred thousand *canaille*, Cossacks and others, and England loses India. Above all the other powers, Russia is the most to be feared, especially by you. Her soldiers are braver than the Austrians, and she has the means of raising as many as she pleases. In bravery, the French and English soldiers are the only ones to be compared to them. All this I foresaw. I see into futurity farther than others, and I wanted to establish a barrier against those barbarians by re-establishing the kingdom of Poland, and putting Poniatowski at the head of it as king, but your *imbecilles* of ministers would not consent. A hundred years hence I shall be praised (*encensé*), and Europe, especially England, will lament that I did not succeed. When they see the finest countries in Europe overrun and a prey to those northern barbarians, they will say, 'Napoleon was right.'

"In my opinion, the only thing which can save England will be abstaining from meddling in Continental affairs, and by withdrawing her army from the Continent. Then you may insist upon whatever is necessary to your interests, without fear of reprisals being made upon your army. You are superior in maritime force to all the world united; and while you confine yourself to that arm, you will always be powerful, and be dreaded. You have the great advantage of declaring war when you like, and of carrying it on at a distance from your home. By means of your fleets, you can menace an attack upon the coasts of those powers who disagree with you, and interrupt their commerce without their being able materially to retaliate.

"By your present mode of proceeding you forfeit all those advantages. Your most powerful arm is given up, and you send an army to the Continent, where you are inferior to Bavaria in that species of force. You put me in mind of Francis the First, who had a formidable and beautiful artillery at the battle of Pavia; but he placed his cavalry before it, and thus masked the battery, which, could it have fired, would have insured him the victory. He was beaten, lost every thing, and made prisoner. So it is with you. You forsake your ships, which may be compared to Francis's batteries, and throw forty thousand men on the Continent, which Prussia, or any other power who chooses to prohibit your manufactures, will fall upon and cut to pieces, if you menace or make reprisals."

Napoleon then said to Dr. O'Meara, "If you are asked any questions by the embassador, Lord Amherst, about a reception at Longwood, you may say that I am not on good terms with the governor, and can not think of receiving him with that person; that, if he is desirous of being introduced, I will receive him presented by Count Bertrand or by the admiral. I have no doubt," continued the Emperor, "that this governor will tell him that I am very much dissatisfied with him for doing his duty, and that I am sulky; that, having been so long used to command myself, I have not philosophy enough to bear restraint; that I have been treated very well, and have made a very bad return for it. If the embassador asks you, you may say that I have my own way of receiving persons who wish to be introduced to me; that I do not wish to affront him, far from it, but that I can not see the governor."

May 28. A ship arrived from England, bringing the intelligence that Lord Holland had demanded an investigation in Parliament of the manner in which the Emperor was treated at St. Helena. This was a terrible annoyance to Sir Hudson Lowe. The journals which the ship brought reported the speech of Lord Bathurst, defending the course of the ministers. This speech contained statements so palpably and outrageously false, that Sir Hudson Lowe blushed to have the Emperor read it. He was well assured, however, that the news could not be concealed from the inmates of Longwood. He therefore said to Dr. O'Meara,

"If General Bonaparte asks you any questions relative to the motion made by Lord Holland in the House of Lords, you had better reply that the report of Lord Bathurst's speech, given in the newspapers, may be incorrect or unfaithful."

May 30. The Emperor received a copy of the London Times containing Lord Bathurst's speech. He immediately sent for Dr. O'Meara to come to his bed-room and aid him in translating it. To the utter amazement alike of the Emperor and of his physician, they read Lord Bathurst's assertion "that every change that had taken place had been for General Bonaparte's benefit; that the reason for contracting his limits had been his tampering with soldiers or inhabitants; and that the communication with officers and inhabitants was unrestricted and free." The Emperor, as these utterly false statements were read, calmly remarked,

"I am very glad to see that the English minister has justified his conduct, so atrocious toward me, to the Parliament, to his nation, and to Europe, with falsehood; a sad resource, which can not long continue. The reign of falsehood will not last forever."

"I felt greatly ashamed," says Dr. O'Meara, "and ready to sink into the earth, and stammered out the excuse that had been suggested to me by Sir Hudson Lowe."

In reference to the refusal of Sir Hudson Lowe to transmit a sealed letter from Napoleon to the Prince Regent, the Emperor said, "It is strange that a sovereign who, by the grace of God, is born lord and master of so many millions, can not receive a sealed letter! How can complaints be made to the sovereign of a corrupt or vile minister, if such be the rule? In time of war, if a minister betrays and sells his country, how can it be known to the king if the complaint must go through the hands of the persons complained of, at whose option it will be either to varnish and color it over as best suits his views, or suppress it altogether?"

The Emperor then spoke at length about the state of England. He observed, "It is necessary not to yield too much to the people, or to allow them to think that reforms are conceded through fear. Perhaps the suspension of the Habeas Corpus Act may, for a short time, be a proper step, as well as an army kept up to intimidate the populace; but I consider these to be only topical applications, which, if used without general remedies that should act upon the constitutional disease, might prove repellent and dangerous, by driving the complaint to nobler parts. England may be likened unto a patient requiring to have his system changed by a course of mercury. The only radical remedy is that which will affect the constitution, that is to say, relieve the misery which exists. This can only be effected by procuring a vent for your manufactures, and by reduction of expenditure—ministers setting the example themselves by giving up the sinecures, &c. This would contribute essentially to calm the public agitation. Had the ministers come forward like men at the opening of the session of Parliament, and thrown up their sinecures, this, with the example set by the Prince Regent, would have quieted all tumults and complaints. The people, in expectation of experiencing something radically beneficial from so good a beginning, would have united, and time would have been gained to adopt measures to relieve the general distress.

"You were greatly offended with me for having called you a *nation of shop-keepers*. Had I meant by this that you were a nation of cowards, you would have had reason to be displeased, even though it were ridiculous and contrary to historical facts. But no such thing was ever intended. I meant that you were a nation of merchants, and that all your great riches and your grand resources arose from commerce, which is true. What else constitutes the riches of England? It is not extent of territory, or a numerous population; it is not mines of gold, silver, or diamonds. Moreover, no man of sense ought to be ashamed of being called a shop-keeper; but your prince and your ministers appear to wish to change altogether the spirit of the English, and to render you another nation; to make you ashamed of your shops and your trade, which have made you what you are, and to sigh after nobility, titles, and crosses; in fact, to assimilate you with the French. What other object can there be in all those cordons, crosses, and honors which are so profusely showered? You are all nobility now instead of the plain old Englishmen. You are ashamed of yourselves, and want to be a nation of nobility and *gentlemen*.* Nothing is to be seen or heard of now in England but 'Sir John' and 'my lady.'

"All those things did very well with me in France, because they were conformable to the spirit of the nation; but believe me, it is contrary both to the spirit and interest of England. Stick to your ships, your commerce, and counting-houses, and leave cordons, crosses, and cavalry uniforms to the Continent, and you will prosper. Lord Castlereagh himself was ashamed of your being called a nation of merchants, and frequently said, in France, that it was a mistaken idea to suppose that England depended upon commerce, or was indebted to it for her riches; and added, that it was not by any means necessary to her. How I laughed when I heard of this false pride! He betrayed his country at the peace.

"I do not mean to say," continued he, laying his hand over his heart, "that he did it from here, but he betrayed it by neglecting its interests. He was, in fact, the commissioner of the allied sovereigns. Perhaps he wanted to convince them that you were not a nation of merchants by showing clearly that you would not make any advantageous bargain for yourselves; by magnanimously giving up every thing, that nations might cry, 'Oh! how nobly England has behaved!' Had he attended to the interests of his own country, had he stipulated for commercial treaties, for the independence of some maritime states and towns, for certain advantages to be secured to England, to indemnify her for the waste of blood and the enormous sacrifices she had made, why then they might have said, 'What a mercenary people! They are truly a nation of merchants. See what bargains they want to make!' and Lord Castlereagh would not have been so well received in the *drawing-rooms.*"

* This he said in English, as well as the words marked with commas, which follow.

O'Meara remarked, that in one of the Couriers sent him by the governor, he had observed a speech attributed to Sir Francis Burdett, accusing Napoleon of having established eight *bastiles* in France.

Napoleon replied, " In some respects it is true. I established a few prisons, but they were for certain persons who were under sentence of death. As I did not like to have the capital punishment executed, and could not send them to a Botany Bay, as you were masters of the sea and would have released them, I was obliged to keep them in prisons. But where is the country without jails ? Are there not some in England ?"

CHAPTER XLI.
1817, June.

The marble Bust—Present from Lady Holland and others—Grand Lama—Murat—Waterloo—The Delivery of the Bust—The Mother of Napoleon—Testimony of Mrs. Abell—Necessity for the second Abdication—Arrival of Lord Amherst.

June 6. The Emperor was informed that a marble bust of his son had been at Jamestown nine days, a present to him from Maria Louisa, and that Sir Hudson Lowe, in consequence of some alleged informality in the manner in which it had been forwarded, was refusing to deliver it, and even threatened to break it to pieces. We can only imagine the feelings of indignation which glowed in the bosom of the bereaved and insulted father. These were feelings which he would have communicated to his congenial friend Las Casas, but, from the peculiar position of Dr. O'Meara, the Emperor could not so freely unbosom to him his anguish. The bust was brought under the charge of Mr. Radwick, in an English vessel, the *Baring*, which arrived at St. Helena on the 28th of May. The captain of the vessel did not know that Mr. Radwick had the bust, and, as it had not been forwarded through the British ministers, Sir Hudson Lowe hesitated about delivering it. This rumor, of course, excited intense emotion at Longwood.

Mr. Manning, to whom we have alluded before as one of the *detained* in France whom Napoleon generously liberated that he might prosecute his travels, also arrived at the island, returning from an extensive tour through the East, where he had seen the Grand Lama. In gratitude to Napoleon, his kind benefactor, he had brought for him a few presents. Sir Hudson Lowe would not allow them to be delivered, and forbade Mr. Manning to inform the friends of the Emperor that he had such presents.

Lady Holland also, who, with her husband, Lord Holland, deeply sympathized with the Emperor in his sufferings and his wrongs, sent him some books, and some other articles, which might minister to his comfort. Thousands of the noblest hearts in England were indignant at the course pursued by the ministry. The only crime which Napoleon had committed was that he was the foe of aristocratic privilege, and the strong champion of *equal rights for all men*. Lord Holland in Parliament, as has just been mentioned, had demanded an investigation of the conduct of Sir Hudson Lowe;

but the ministry was too strong for the opposition. Any voice raised in behalf of Napoleon was instantly drowned in the clamor of the aristocracy; and yet there were some noble exceptions. Many persons of the highest rank blushed for the dishonor of their country.

June 7. Napoleon had heard of the arrival of the celebrated traveler from the East who had seen the Grand Lama. He was very desirous of seeing the man, though he had entirely forgotten the circumstance of his having been once *detained* in France.

"I am very curious," said the Emperor to O'Meara, "to get some information about this Grand Lama. I have never read any accounts about him that I could rely upon, and sometimes have doubted of his existence. When you go to town, I wish you would get acquainted with the traveler, and inquire what ceremonies were made use of, whether adoration was practiced, and inform yourself of every possible particular."

To-day, Mr. Manning, accompanied by Captain Balston, came up to Count Bertrand's. In the course of an hour, the Emperor called in with Count Montholon. In the conversation which ensued, Mr. Manning said,

"In the year 1805 I was one of the persons detained in France. I wrote a letter to your majesty, stating that I was traveling for the benefit of the world at large, which procured my release."

"What protection had you?" asked the Emperor. "Had you a letter from Sir Joseph Banks to me?"

"I had no protection whatever," Mr. Manning replied, "nor letter from Sir Joseph Banks, nor had I any friends to interest themselves in my behalf. I merely wrote a letter to your majesty stating my situation."

"Was it your simple letter which obtained your liberty?" asked Napoleon.

"It was my simple letter," he replied, "that induced you to grant it to me, for which I am very grateful, and beg to thank you."

Napoleon then questioned him with deep interest about his travels, following on the map the route he had pursued. The traveler gave a clear and concise reply to every question; said that he had seen the Grand Lama, whom he described as an intelligent boy about seven years old.

"How did you escape being taken as a spy?" inquired the Emperor.

"I hope," the eccentric man replied, "there is nothing in my countenance which would indicate my being a spy."

The Emperor smiled, and added, "How came it to pass that you, being *profane* according to their ideas, could gain admission to the presence of the Lama?"

"I honor and respect all religions," said Mr. Manning, "and thereby gained admission." Thus the conversation for a long time continued.

The Emperor's servant, Santini, who had been sent away from St. Helena by Sir Hudson Lowe, published in Europe a pamphlet giving an account of scenes at St. Helena. It was written by some other person from information which the unlettered servant could communicate, and was, of course, full of misconceptions and errors. O'Meara gave the Emperor a copy of the pamphlet. He read it, occasionally remarking, as he turned over the leaves, "true," "partly true," "false," "stuff."

June 10. O'Meara informed the Emperor that Colonel Macirone, aid-de-camp to Murat, had published some anecdotes of his late master.

"What does he say of me?" inquired Napoleon.

"He speaks ill of you," was the reply.

The Emperor smiled, and said, "Oh, that is nothing; I am well accustomed to that. But what does he say?"

"It is asserted," O'Meara replied, "that Murat had imputed the loss of the battle of Waterloo to the cavalry not having been properly employed, and had said that if he had commanded them, the French would have gained the victory."

"It is very probable," replied Napoleon. "I could not be every where; and Murat was the best cavalry officer in the world. He would have given more impetuosity to the charge. There wanted but very little, I assure you, to gain the day for me—to break two or three battalions, and in all probability Murat would have effected that. There were not, I believe, two such officers in the world as Murat for the cavalry, and Drouot for the artillery. Murat was a most singular character. Four-and-twenty years ago, when he was a captain, I made him my aid-de-camp, and subsequently raised him to be what he was. He loved—I may rather say, adored me. In my presence he was, as it were, struck with awe, and ready to fall at my feet. I acted wrong in having separated him from me, as without me he was nothing; with me, he was my right arm. Order Murat to attack and destroy four or five thousand men in such a direction, it was done in a moment; but leave him to himself, he was an *imbecille* without judgment. I can not conceive how so brave a man could be so characterless. He was nowhere brave unless before the enemy. *There* he was probably the bravest man in the world. His boiling courage carried him into the midst of the enemy, *couvert de pennes jusqu'au clocher*, and glittering with gold. How he escaped is a miracle, being as he was always a distinguished mark, and fired at by every body. Even the Cossacks admired him on account of his extraordinary bravery.

"He was a paladin, in fact, a Don Quixote in the field; but take him into the cabinet, he was a poltroon without judgment or decision. Murat and Ney were the bravest men I ever witnessed. Murat, however, was a much nobler character than Ney. Murat was generous and open; Ney partook of the *canaille*. Strange to say, however, Murat, though he loved me, did me more mischief than any other person in the world. When I left Elba, I sent a messenger to acquaint him with what I had done. Immediately he must attack the Austrians. The messenger went upon his knees to prevent him, but in vain. He thought me already master of France, Belgium, and Holland, and that he must make his peace, and not adhere to *demi-mesures*. Like a madman, he attacked the Austrians with his *canaille*, and ruined me: for at that time there was a negotiation going on between Austria and me, stipulating that the former should remain neuter, which would have been finally concluded, and I should have reigned undisturbed. But as soon as

Murat attacked the Austrians, the Emperor immediately conceived that he was acting by my directions, and indeed it will be difficult to make posterity believe to the contrary."

The bust of Napoleon's son had now been at the island thirteen days. It was generally known that it had arrived, and also that there were other presents for the imprisoned Emperor which were likewise detained. The Emperor was silent upon the subject. It was generally understood that the governor had threatened to break the bust of the idolized child to pieces, or to throw it into the sea. Sir Hudson Lowe, in his impotent defense, admits

"That at first he hesitated as to the course which his duty required him to take, considering the clandestine manner in which an attempt was thus made' to communicate with Napoleon, and he was inclined not to allow the bust to be forwarded until he had communicated with Lord Bathurst on the subject. Sir Thomas Reade, however, suggested that, as the bust was made of marble, so that it could not possibly contain any thing improper, it might be forwarded to Longwood at once; and *as its arrival had already become known*, Sir Hudson assented to the proposal."

The governor accordingly called on Count Bertrand, and informed him that "although the bust had come in a very irregular manner, yet, under the impression that it might be a thing acceptable to *him* who resided at Longwood (à celui qui résidait à Longwood), he would take the responsibility of landing it, if such was his wish." He said that the man expected five hundred dollars for the bust, which Sir Hudson Lowe thought was much more than it was worth. Such was the character of Sir Hudson Lowe.

General Bertrand immediately reported this conversation to the Emperor. Soon after, O'Meara was introduced. The Emperor mentioned the circumstances to him, and inquired,

"Did you know any thing about the statue?"

"I heard of it," O'Meara replied, "some days ago."

"Why did you not tell me?" the Emperor inquired.

O'Meara, much embarrassed, replied, "I expected the governor would have sent it up."

"I have known of it," said Napoleon, "for several days. I intended, if it had not been given, to have made such a complaint as would have caused every Englishman's hair to stand on end with horror. I would have told a tale which would have made the mothers of England execrate him as a monster in human shape. I have been informed that he has been deliberating about it, and also that his prime minister, Reade, ordered it to be broken. I suppose that he has been consulting with that little major (Gorrequer), who has pointed out to him that it would brand his name with ignominy for ever, or that his wife has read him a lecture at night about the atrocity of such a proceeding. He has done enough, however, to dishonor his name by retaining it so long, and by even allowing a doubt to exist of its being sent up. I do not know what he meant by saying that a hundred guineas was too much for the statue, whether he intended it as an insult or as a reflection upon us.

Surely no sum could be too much for a *father* to pay under similar circumstances. But this man has no feeling."

The Emperor afterward spoke of his own family. "My excellent mother," said he, "is a woman of courage and of great talent, more of a masculine than a feminine nature, proud, and high-minded. To the manner in which she formed me at an early age I principally owe my subsequent elevation. My opinion is, that the future good or bad conduct of a child entirely depends upon the mother."

June 11. The statue was sent to Longwood fourteen days after its arrival at St. Helena. It was a beautiful bust in white marble, about the natural size, and exceedingly well executed. It was placed on the mantel of Napoleon's contracted and dilapidated study, and there, hour after hour, the firm, unyielding, grief-stricken Emperor, alone and in silence, gazed upon the beautiful features of his idolized child. With inhumanity almost unparalleled, the father had been torn from his son, and there was no probability that the parent and the child would ever meet on earth again. The Emperor received no food, and left not his room as the hours of the day passed along. To no eye but that of God was the anguish of his bursting heart revealed, as he communed, in the solitary cell of his captivity, with the loved and the lost. At last he sent for Dr. O'Meara, and, standing before the bust, he pointed to it, and said, with deep emotion,

"Look at that! look at that image! Barbarous and atrocious must the man be who would break such an image as that. I esteem the man capable of executing or of ordering it to be worse than him who administers poison to another; for the latter has some object to gain, but the former is instigated by nothing but the blackest atrocity, and is capable of committing any crime. That countenance would melt the heart of the most ferocious wild beast. The man who gave orders to break that image would plunge a knife into the heart of the original, if it were in his power."

"He gazed on the statue for several minutes," says O'Meara, "with great satisfaction and delight, his face covered with smiles, and strongly expressive of paternal love, and of the pride which he felt in being the father of so lovely a boy. I watched his countenance narrowly, which I had an excellent opportunity of doing while he was contemplating attentively the beautiful though inanimate features sculptured on the marble. No person who had witnessed this scene could deny that Napoleon was animated by the tender affections of a father.

"Napoleon afterward," continues O'Meara, "vented his feelings about the alleged order for the destruction of the bust. When I endeavored to reason upon the uncertainty of the fact, and that it assuredly had not been given by the governor, he interrupted me by saying 'that it was in vain to attempt to deny a known fact. The statue to me,' continued he, 'was worth a million, though this governor contemptuously said that a hundred pounds was a great price for it.'"

In reference to Napoleon's warm and generous affections, Mrs. Abell makes the following remarks:

"I think his love of children, and the delight he felt in their society, and that, too, at the most calamitous period of his life, when a cold and unattachable nature would have been abandoned to the indulgence of selfish misery, in itself speaks volumes for his goodness of heart. After hours of laborious occupation, he would often permit us to join him, and that which would have fatigued and exhausted the spirits of others seemed only to recruit and renovate him. His gayety was often exuberant at these moments; he entered into all the feelings of young people, and when with them was a mere child, and, I may add, a most amusing one.

"I feel, however, even painfully, the difficulty of conveying to my readers my own impression of the disposition of Napoleon. Matters of feeling are often incapable of demonstration. The innumerable acts of amiability and kindness which he lavished on all around him at my father's house, derived, perhaps, their chief charm from the way in which they were done; they would not bear being told. Apart from the sweetness of his smile and manner, their effect would have been comparatively nothing. But young people are generally keen observers of character; and after seeing Napoleon in every possible mood, and in his most unguarded moments, when I am sure, from his manner, that the idea of acting a part never entered his head, I left him impressed with the most complete conviction of his want of guile, and the thorough amiability and goodness of his heart. That this feeling was common to almost every one who approached him, the respect and devotion of his followers at St. Helena is a sufficient proof. They had then nothing more to expect from him, and only entailed misery on themselves by adhering to his fortunes."

June 13. The Emperor, as usual when Dr. O'Meara was introduced, roused himself to vigor and cheerfulness. The conversation turned upon the possibility of his having sustained himself in France after the battle of Waterloo, in spite of the efforts of the allied powers.

"My own opinion was," said the Emperor, "that I could not have done so without having shed the blood of hundreds by the guillotine. I must have plunged my hands up to this in blood," stretching out one arm, and applying the finger of the other to his arm-pits. "Had the Legislative Body displayed courage, I might have succeeded; but they were frightened and divided among each other; La Fayette was one of the chief causes of the success of the enemies of France. To have given me a chance, I must have had recourse to the most sanguinary measures. The conduct of the Allies, in declaring that they waged war against me alone, had a great effect. Had it been possible to have rendered me inseparable from the nation, no efforts of the allied powers would have succeeded; but as it was, by isolating me, and declaring that if I were once removed, all obstacles to a peace would cease, people became divided in their sentiments, and I determined to abdicate, and remove, as far as I was concerned, every difficulty. Had the French nation guessed at the intention of the Allies, or that they would have acted as they have done since, they would have rallied round me; but they were overreached like the lambs in the fable, when the wolves declared they only waged war against the dogs; but the dogs once removed, they fell upon and devoured the lambs.

"There is a great difference of opinion," continued the Emperor, "as to what I ought to have done. Many were of opinion that I ought to have fought to the last. Others said that Fortune had abandoned me; that Waterloo had closed my career of arms for ever. My own opinion is, that I ought to have died at Waterloo—perhaps a little earlier. Had I died at Moscow, I should probably have had the reputation of the greatest conqueror ever known. But the smiles of Fortune were at an end. I experienced little but reverses afterward; hitherto I had been unconquered. I ought to have died at Waterloo. But the misfortune is, that when a man seeks the most for death, he can not find it. Men were killed around me, before, behind, every where, but no bullet for me."

June 28. Lord Amherst and his suite, who had been long expected, arrived on the 27th. To-day, accompanied by the governor, they called upon Count and Countess Bertrand. Napoleon afterward, speaking of the interview, said,

"The civilities of the governor are those of a jailer. When he came to Bertrand's with the embassador, he merely introduced him as Lord Amherst, and then, without sitting down or conversing for a moment like a gentleman, turned about and took his leave, like a jailer or a turnkey who points out his prisoners to visitors, then turns the key and leaves them together. Having come up with Lord Amherst, he ought to have remained for a quarter of an hour, and then left them."

CHAPTER XLII.
1817, July.

Arrival of the *Conqueror*—Malcolm—Validity of Napoleon's Title to the Crown—Breakfast with O'Meara—Story of the Bust—Letter to Mr. Radwick—The Presentation of Lord Amherst—Remarkable Conversation—Vigilance with which the Emperor was guarded—Captain Elphinstone—The Present—Cause of the War with Spain—Anecdote—Controversy with the Governor—Increasing Tyranny.

July 1. It was a beautiful day: not a cloud floated in the sky, and the serene yet brilliant atmosphere presented no obstruction to the vision. The Emperor was informed that an English ship of war, the *Conqueror*, was approaching the island. He walked out a few steps from his door to an elevation which commanded a view of the sea to watch the approach of the ship. Little Elizabeth Balcombe had that morning gone to Longwood, and she thus describes the scene:

"I recollect being at Longwood one beautiful day; the atmosphere had that peculiar lightness and brilliancy which in a great measure constituted the charm of the climate of St. Helena. The sea lay glistening in the sun like a sheet of quicksilver, the little merry waves bursting in sparkling foam at the foot of the stupendous rocks, and the exquisite soft verdure immediately surrounding Longwood formed a very pleasant contrast to the stern features of the rest of the island. It was one of those days in which the *past* and the *future* are alike disregarded; anxious thought is suspended for a moment, and the *present* alone is felt and enjoyed. I remember bounding up to St. Denis and asking for Napoleon. My joyousness was somewhat damped by the gravity with which he replied that the Emperor was watching the approach of the '*Conqueror*,' then coming in, bearing the flag of Admiral Pamplin. 'You will find him,' he said, 'near Madam Bertrand's, but he is in no mood for badinage to-day, mademoiselle.'

"Notwithstanding this check, I proceeded toward the cottage, and in a moment the whole tone of my mind was changed from gayety to sadness. Young as I was, I could not help being strongly impressed by the intense melancholy of his expression; 'the ashes of a thousand thoughts were on his brow.' He was standing with General Bertrand, his eyes bent sadly on the seventy-four, which was but yet a speck in the line of the horizon. The magnificent ship soon grew upon our sight, as, beating up to windward, silently yet proudly she pursued her brave career.

"The Emperor, after a long silence, commented on the beautiful management of the vessel. 'The English are kings upon the sea,' he said; and then, smiling somewhat sarcastically, added, 'I wonder what they think of our beautiful island; they can not be much elated by the sight of my gigantic prison walls!'"

NAPOLEON.

July 3. Admiral Pamplin, who was to succeed Sir Pulteney Malcolm, having arrived at the island a few days before in the *Conqueror*, was introduced to the Emperor by Admiral Malcolm. The appearance and address of the new admiral were not at all attractive. Speaking of the contrast, the Emperor said,

"Few men have so prepossessing an exterior and manner as Malcolm; but the other reminds me of one of those drunken little Dutch *schippers* that

I have seen in Holland, sitting at a table with a pipe in his mouth, a cheese, and a bottle of Geneva before him."

O'Meara dined with the Emperor *tête-à-tête* in his study. Napoleon was in cheerful spirits. In the course of conversation, he made some remarks on the late attacks made on the validity of his title to the crown.

"By the doctrines put forth by your government writers," said he, "upon the subject of legitimacy, every throne in Europe would be shaken from its foundation. If I was not a legitimate sovereign, William the Third was a usurper of the throne of England, as he was brought in chiefly by the aid of foreign bayonets. George the First was placed on the throne by a faction composed of a few nobles. I was called to the throne of France by the votes of nearly four millions of Frenchmen. In fact, the calling of me a usurper is an absurdity which your ministers will, in the end, be obliged to abandon. If my title to the crown of France was not legitimate, what is that of George the Third?"

The frugal dinner was served on a little round table. The Emperor sat on the sofa, and O'Meara in an arm-chair opposite. The Emperor was temperate, even to abstinence, seldom taking even a glass of wine. He often spoke of the convivial habits of the English, and of their custom of becoming merry over their wine. It was understood that the English officers at the camp often drank to excess. Playfully the Emperor said to O'Meara, "I should like to see you intoxicated. Marchand, bring a bottle of Champagne." Napoleon took one glass himself, and made O'Meara finish the rest, saying several times in English, "*Drink, doctor, drink!*"

July 4. The man who had brought the bust was an Italian. It was reported that it was executed by orders of Maria Louisa, and sent by her as a silent proof of her unchanged affection. Napoleon was sincerely attached to the amiable Maria Louisa. As he could neither write to his friends, nor receive letters from them, without submitting the correspondence to the eye of Sir Hudson Lowe, the Emperor, rather than submit to such an indignity, preferred to endure all the untold agony of entire non-intercourse with those he loved. His imprisonment thus became a living burial; for such a mind and such a heart, the most awful doom which imagination can conceive. He was exceedingly anxious to see Mr. Radwick, that he might, through him, receive some tidings from his wife and son. Count Bertrand earnestly plead with the governor to grant an interview; but the governor was inexorable. He would allow the Emperor to see Radwick, *but only in the presence of a British officer.* Napoleon was not a man to allow even the lacerated affections of his heart to torture him to submit to such an indignity. The man, guarded by Captain Poppleton, came to Longwood, but the Emperor declined seeing him in such a presence. Count Bertrand, however, by dictation of Napoleon, sent him the following letter:

"MR. RADWICK: Sir,—I have received the marble bust of the young Napoleon, and given it to his father. Its reception has given him the most lively satisfaction.

"I regret that it is not in your power to come and see us, and communicate to us details which would have the greatest interest for a father, and especially for one placed in such circumstances as he is.

"According to the letters forwarded to us, the artist values his work at £100 sterling. The Emperor has commanded me to put into your hands the sum of £300 sterling; the overplus is intended to indemnify you for the losses to which you have been exposed in the sale of your merchandise, by not having been allowed to send your goods on shore, and for the prejudice which that event may have raised against you, but which will secure you the esteem of every gallant man.

"Have the goodness to transmit to the persons who have paid him this obliging attention the Emperor's best thanks.

"I have the honor to be, &c., COUNT BERTRAND."

Soon after Lord Amherst's arrival, Dr. O'Meara dined with him at Plantation House. The doctor took occasion to say to the embassador that, if he went to Longwood with a view of seeing Napoleon, accompanied by the governor or any of his staff, he would certainly meet with a refusal, which, though far from the intention of Napoleon, might by others be construed into an insult; that if his lordship came up with only his own staff, there was but little doubt that he would be received, provided that Napoleon should be sufficiently recovered from a swelling in his cheek with which he was then afflicted. Lord Amherst assented to this arrangement.

Soon after this, Count Bertrand waited upon Lord Amherst, and informed him that Napoleon had been unwell for several days, and was at that moment suffering from ague in the face. He added, however, that if the Emperor should be in a state to see visitors before Lord Amherst's departure, he would receive him.

The friends of Napoleon guarded his interests with the utmost vigilance. They felt personally the insult cast upon France by the British ministry in the assertion that the Emperor of France, the most illustrious and beloved monarch earth had ever known, was but a *usurping general;* that the French people, his supporters, were but *rebels.* Consequently, the more the English ministers endeavored to degrade the Emperor, the more vigilant were his friends to surround him with every external testimonial of respect and homage. Count Montholon gives the following account of the presentation of Lord Amherst:

"Every thing had been prepared for Lord Amherst's audience as if the Emperor had been at the Tuileries. The presentation was performed by the grand marshal. One of Napoleon's suite was in the topographic cabinet, which served on this occasion as an ante-room. The valets de chambre, St. Denis and Noverras, were stationed at the doors of the ante-room and of the saloon in which the Emperor was. The suite of Lord Amherst was not to be presented till after the audience. Every thing was done as had been arranged. If Lord Amherst and his embassy had been received at the Tuileries in the most splendid days of the Empire, they could not have been more courteous and respectful, in manner as well as speech.

"The mission of this embassador to China formed the first subject of the conversation. Politics would not probably have been introduced at all had not Lord Amherst offered to transmit to the Prince Regent any requests which the Emperor might have to make to him.

"This offer aroused in the Emperor's mind the recollection of the perpetual outrages which daily poisoned his life.

"'Neither your king nor your nation have any right over me,' said he, in a tone of deep suffering. 'England sets an example of twenty millions of men oppressing one individual. Sylla and Marius signed their decrees of proscription in the midst of combats, and with the still bloody points of their swords; but the bill of the 11th of April was signed in the midst of peace, with the sceptre of a great nation, and in the sanctuary of the law.

"'The right of nations should at least have been the law of your ministers. But it would have paralyzed the savage hatred of some of them. They wanted the arbitrary right; they uttered falsehood to the Parliament; they pushed the audacity of falsehood so far as to say that they demanded the right of regulating my captivity, in order to treat me with more liberality than it was usual to grant to prisoners of war. And what use have they made of it? They have delegated this discretionary power to a man chosen for this among men of a character known by their preceding missions, and have said to him, "*If your prisoner escape, your career and your fortune are lost.*" Is not this telling him to abuse his power? Does not this interest all that is dear to man? A jailer in Europe can not impose restrictions according to his own caprice or panic terrors on the prisoner intrusted to his charge. He is obliged to confine himself to the execution of the regulations established by the laws or magistrates. There is but one means of taking from a prisoner all chance of evasion—to inclose him in a coffin. The Parliament which gave Charles I.'s head to the axe—the Convention which condemned Louis XVI. to die by the hand of the executioner, found excuses for their crimes in national interest. The bill of the 11th of April only serves the purposes of personal hatred. It will, sooner or later, be the shame of England. The Parliament which voted it forgot its sacred character, and, as a legislative body, committed a crime against English honor. I am not allowed to leave this unhealthy hut unless accompanied by a guard. I am forbidden to receive letters from my wife, my mother, or my family, except they have been read and commented on by my jailer.

"'But of what use are these odious restrictions here? What man of sense can admit the possibility of my escape, when numerous cruising vessels hover round the island; when posts are established at all points; when there are signals always ready to correspond with each other; when no vessel can approach or leave St. Helena without having been visited by the governor's agents; and, finally, when hundreds of sentinels are posted round the limits of this place from six in the evening till six in the morning?

"'But they do still more, if possible; they want me to deny a glorious fact—to acknowledge the shame of my country. They will have it that France had no right to place the imperial crown on my head; and pretend to wash away, by a decree of Sir Hudson Lowe's, the holy oil with which the vicar of Jesus Christ anointed my forehead. The name of General Bonaparte was the one which I bore at Campo Formio and at Luneville when I dictated terms of peace to the Emperor of Austria. I bore it at Amiens when I signed the peace with England. I should be proud to bear it still; but the honor of France forbids me to acknowledge the King of England's right to annul the acts of the French people. My intention was to take the name of Duroc. Your ministers, and their hired assassin, Sir Hudson Lowe, oblige me, by their ignoble intrigues on this subject, to retain the title of the Emperor Napoleon.

"'If your government denies my right to this title, it acknowledges implicitly that Louis XVIII. reigned in France at the time when I signed the peace of Amiens, and when the Lords Lauderdale and Castlereagh negotiated with my plenipotentiaries. It does more: it acknowledges that the Cardinal of York reigned in England when George III. signed the peace of 1783 at Versailles, and denies the royalty of Charles XIII. of Sweden. To assert this opinion would be to give instability to all thrones, and to propagate the germ of all revolution in every monarchy.

"'Your ministers were not contented with giving Parliament false information respecting my position. One of them said, in a numerous assembly in Ireland, that I had only made peace with England for the purpose of deceiving, surprising, and destroying. Such calumnies against a man suffering under their oppression, and held by the throat to prevent his raising his voice, must be disapproved by all men of truth and honor.

"'I always desired peace, and sincere peace, with England. I know of no rivalries which should prevent two great nations from coming to an understanding with each other, and from advancing conjointly toward the end aimed at by my government. I wished to fill up the abyss of revolutions, and to reconstruct, without shaking, the European edifice to the advantage of all, by employing kings to bestow on Continental Europe the blessing of constitutions—a blessing which your country as well as mine only acquired at the price of a fearful social commotion. England had nothing more to fear from me as soon as she would listen to me. If Fox had lived, the face of Europe would have been changed. His genius and his patriotism understood me. Every great and national idea vibrated in his soul. He died, unfortunately for England, unfortunately for the world. Not a cannon-shot would have been fired on the Continent after the battle of Austerlitz if Lord Lauderdale's negotiations had been continued. I repeat, that I always desired peace; I only fought to obtain it. The Congress of Vienna thinks it will secure this blessing to Europe. It is deceived. War, and a terrible war, is being hatched under the ashes of the Empire. Sooner or later, nations will cruelly avenge me of the ingratitude of the kings whom I crowned or pardoned. Tell the Prince Regent—tell the Parliament, of which you are a principal member, that I await, as a favor, the axe of the executioner, to put an end to the outrages of my jailer.'

"Lord Amherst heard with emotion these complaints of a great and deeply-wounded soul. He did not seek to conceal the interest which he felt in them. He promised to tell all to the Prince Regent, and respectfully offered his services to intervene with Sir Hudson Lowe.

"'It would be useless,' said the Emperor, interrupting him; 'crime and hatred toward me are equally in this man's nature. It is necessary to his enjoyment to torture me, like the tiger, who tears with his claws the prey whose agonies he takes pleasure in prolonging.'"

July 9. On the evening before the battle of Waterloo, an English officer, Captain Elphinstone, had been grievously wounded, and was lying stretched on the field in a hopeless condition. The Emperor happened to pass near him, observed his situation, and sent the surgeon in attendance on his person to make the necessary applications to stanch his wounds, from which the blood was copiously flowing. His natural goodness toward the wounded prompted him also to give him some wine from the silver flask which one of the chasseurs of the Guard always carried on service near his person. This providential assistance saved Captain Elphinstone's life.

The Emperor was at that time struggling with all Europe against him. His physical and mental energies were oppressed by cares and toils, such as no mortal ever sustained before. The night was darkening around him, and he was pressing on to the fatal field of Waterloo. His personal attention to the wounded Englishman, under these circumstances, is indeed an extraordinary proof of his humanity. The Hon. John Elphinstone, brother of the wounded officer, president of the East India Company's establishment in China, in gratitude to the Emperor for thus saving the life of a beloved brother, sent to St. Helena several small cases, containing a set of chess-men in ivory, of marvelously beautiful workmanship, a box of dice, another of counters, and two magnificent baskets of large dimensions, all exquisitely carved. Each of these objects was ornamented with the imperial crown, eagles, and letter N.

Sir Hudson Lowe delivered the letter announcing the arrival of these presents to Count Bertrand before he had opened the boxes and examined the contents; but when he saw engraved upon the chess-men the eagle, the crown, and the letter N., he hesitated as to the propriety of allowing *General Bonaparte* to receive gifts which recognized his having once been an emperor. When we reflect upon the circumstances of the case, that the Emperor had saved the life of a British officer, and that the brother of this officer had sent these presents as an acknowledgment of his gratitude for the noble act, we can not refrain from expressing our sense of the unutterable meanness of the governor. Count Montholon says that a month elapsed between the arrival of these presents and their being delivered to the Emperor. The governor intimates that they were detained but a few days. When they were delivered, they were sent, however, with an insulting letter. "He wrote to Bertrand," it is stated in his official documents, "saying *that if he were to act in strict conformity with the established rules, he ought to delay sending them; but that, as he had promised that the boxes should follow the letter, he had no alternative but to send them.*" We can not wonder that a magnanimous man like Napoleon should have despised Sir Hudson Lowe even to loathing. It must have been to him constant torture to be compelled to have any intercourse with such a spirit.

The exiled, captive Emperor could take but little pleasure in receiving gifts which had thus been soiled by the touch of the governor. But in his dreary chamber he endeavored to forget these outrages. In the evening he gathered his companions around him, and they passed a cheerful hour in examining and admiring the exquisite workmanship of the articles. "I will send," said he, "the work-basket to the Empress Maria Louisa, the box of counters to my mother, and the chess-men and superb board to my son."

In reference to these gifts, Mrs. Abell records the following pleasing incident:

"Early one morning, while I was wandering about the gardens and plantations at Longwood, I encountered the Emperor, who stopped, told me to come with him, and he would show me some pretty toys. Such an invitation was not to be resisted, and I accordingly accompanied him to his billiard-room, where he displayed a most gorgeously-carved set of chess-men, which had been presented to him by Mr. Elphinstone. He might well call them toys, every one being in itself a gem. The castles, surmounting superbly chased elephants, were filled with warriors in the act of discharging arrows from their bended bows; the knights were cased in armor, with their visors up, and mounted on beautifully caparisoned horses; mitred bishops appeared in their flowing robes; and every pawn was varied in character and splendor of costume, each figure furnishing a specimen of the dress of some different nation.

"Such workmanship had never before left China: art and taste had been exerted to the utmost to devise such rare specimens of skill and elegance. The Emperor was as much pleased with his present as I should have been with a new plaything. He told me he had just finished a game of chess with Lady Malcolm with these beautiful things, and that she had beaten him—he thought, solely from his attention having been occupied in admiring the men instead of considering the game. The work-boxes and card-counters were lovely, the latter representing all the varied trades of China minutely executed in carving.

"Napoleon observed that he thought the chess-men too pretty for St. Helena, and that therefore he should transmit them to the King of Rome. Another present which attracted my attention was a superb ivory tea-chest, which, when open, presented a perfect model of the city of Canton, most ingeniously manufactured of stained ivory; underneath this tray were packets of the finest tea, done up in fantastic shapes."

Lord Bathurst was a congenial spirit with Sir Hudson Lowe. He subsequently—September 18, 1817—wrote to the governor, approving of his having forwarded Mr. Elphinstone's present to Longwood "*under the circumstance of his having inadvertently given the assurance that it should be sent.*" He added, however, "I am so sensible of the inconvenience which may result from permitting *General Bonaparte* to receive any thing addressed to him as a sovereign prince, that I deem it necessary to instruct you that, in case of any present being hereafter forwarded to General Bonaparte to which emblems or titles of sovereignty are annexed, you are to consider that circumstance as altogether precluding its delivery, if they can not be removed without prejudice to the present itself."

July 11. The Emperor was busy in his study when Dr. O'Meara called. In the course of conversation, he remarked,

"If your Prince Regent were now to offer me a reception in England provided I would resign the throne of France, acknowledge myself a prisoner of war, and sign a treaty as such, I would refuse it, and prefer remaining here, although I have already abdicated, and therefore the first would be of no consequence. To sign a treaty acknowledging that the injustice of the English Parliament in detaining me as a prisoner of war in time of peace was lawful, I would never do. A treaty not to quit such part of England as might be allotted to me, nor to meddle with politics, and be subject to certain restrictions, I would gladly consent to, and, moreover, would desire to be naturalized as a British subject.

"The two grand objects of my policy were, first, to re-establish the kingdom of Poland, as a barrier against the Russians, that I might save Europe from those barbarians of the north; and next, to expel the Bourbons from Spain, and establish a Constitution which would have rendered the nation free, have driven away the Inquisition, superstition, the friars, feudal rights and immunities; a Constitution which would have rendered the first offices in the kingdom attainable to any person entitled to hold them by his abilities, without any distinction of birth being necessary. With the *imbecilles* who reigned, Spain was nearly useless to me; besides, I discovered that they had made a secret treaty to betray France. With an active government, the great resources which Spain possesses would have been made use of against England with such vigor that you would have been forced to make a peace according to liberal maritime rights. Also, I did not like to have a family of enemies so near to me, especially after I had discovered this secret treaty. I was anxious to dispossess the Bourbons; they were equally anxious to dispossess me. It mattered little whether my brother or another family were placed on the throne, provided the Bourbons were removed. In thirty or forty years, the ties of relationship would signify nothing when the interests of a kingdom were under discussion.

"It would," continued Napoleon, "have been a very easy matter to have made the French and English good friends, and love one another. The French always esteemed the English for their national qualities, and where esteem exists love will soon follow, if proper measures be pursued; they are very nearly akin. I myself have done much mischief to England, and had it in contemplation to do much more, if you continued the war. But I never ceased to esteem you. I had then a much better opinion of you than I now have. I thought that there was much more liberty, much more independence of spirit, and much more generosity in England than there is, or I never would have ventured upon the step I have taken."

July 18. Count Bertrand wrote a very cutting letter in reply to the insulting communication of the governor, in which he said, "We are not aware that we may not be permitted to possess any article on which there is a crown. If so, it would also be necessary to make new packs of cards, because there are crowns on those which are now used. The Emperor's linen, and the small quantity of plate still in his possession, are often taken to town. They are marked with a crown. The Emperor wishes for favor from no one, and will have nothing from the caprice of any person whatever. But he has a right to know the restrictions which are imposed upon him. I beg you, then, sir, to communicate to us these fresh restrictions. The Emperor charges me to protest against the existence of any restriction which shall not have legally been notified to him before being put into execution."

Sir Hudson Lowe, in his reply, remarks,

"The only object which I had in writing to you on the 8th of this month was to prevent a belief from being entertained that I tacitly acknowledged or approved of the imperial rank being recognized in the crown placed every where above the initial letter of Napoleon in presents sent to St. Helena, particularly by an English subject, and coming from an English factory.

"The person who sent these presents has his personal opinions, but I have the right of exercising my judgment in not permitting him to express them through me; and in forwarding the presents to their destination, without any other remarks than those contained in my letter, I did the utmost which could be required of me by the respect which the wishes or expectations of General Bonaparte demand from me."

Count Bertrand's letter, which was written the evening after the presents were received, excited vehemently the anger of the governor. The next day he saw Dr. O'Meara, and censured him for not defending more cordially the course pursued by the English ministers in their treatment of the Emperor. He denied most positively that he had ever thought of breaking the bust. In reference to this accusation, which was making much noise upon the island, the governor remarked to O'Meara,

"You do not appear to have testified sufficient indignation at what General Bonaparte said and did. You ought to have told him that he was guilty of a dirty action." He added that Bertrand had written him the most impertinent letter he had ever received, and deserved, for it, to be turned off the island. He also denied that Mr. Radwick had been prevented from landing at St. Helena to dispose of his goods. The governor requested O'Meara to repeat to General Bonaparte these remarks. Napoleon, annoyed by such constant petty vexations, listened to them with visible impatience, and then calmly said,

"Mr. Radwick declared before Madam Bertrand that he had been prevented from going on shore for several days, and, consequently, had been obliged to sell his little venture to Solomon or some other shop-keeper at half price, and had thereby sustained a great loss."

"This," Dr. O'Meara observes, "was an unquestionable fact, and notorious on the island."

O'Meara inquired, "What answer shall I return?"

For a moment the Emperor paced the floor in silence, apparently hesitating whether it were best to return any answer. Then suddenly stopping, he remarked with energy,

"Tell the governor that I am not obliged to render an account to my executioner. He addresses insinuations to me. This was the practice of the petty tyrants of Italy. This man seems to have no other object in view than to kill me by degrees. Some day or other his prince and his nation will be informed of his doings, and his wicked conduct will be known; and if he escape the justice of the laws which he violates, he will not escape that of the opinion of enlightened and feeling men. He is an unfaithful commissioner. He deceives his government, as is evident from the twenty falsehoods and calumnies in the speech of Lord Bathurst.

"His conduct with regard to the bust of my son, which is proved, is abominable, and of a piece with all his actions for the last twelve months. Till the end of December his conduct has been that of a man who would assassinate me. Since then, he has been somewhat more tranquil. I judge of men by their conduct. I do not read the hearts of men. God alone reads their hearts."

Then addressing himself to Dr. O'Meara in gentle reproach for continually annoying him with messages from the governor, he said,

"Leave me alone. Do your duty as a doctor, but do not stick pins into me. Let us speak of medicine, but do not torment me with those insinuations."

Afterward the Emperor remarked, "I informed Lord Amherst of the conduct pursued toward me. He declared that such were not the intentions of the bill; that the object of it was not to render worse, but to ameliorate my situation as a prisoner, and that he would not fail to make known the representations I had made to him to the Prince Regent, to Lord Liverpool, and to Lord Bathurst. He asked permission to report what I said to the governor. I replied, certainly. I told him that I had observed the governor taking him round the new road he had made, but that I supposed he had not communicated to him that I could neither quit it nor go into any houses, and that a prohibition had formerly existed which debarred me from speaking to such persons as I might meet. At this he was *beaucoup frappé*, greatly struck. He proposed that I should see the governor. I replied, 'Neither your prince, nor both of your houses of Parliament, can oblige me to see my jailer and my executioner.' I told him that he had pushed matters to such an extremity that, in order to leave nothing in his power, I had confined myself to my room, expecting that he would surround the house with sentinels. I left nothing for him to effect except violating my privacy, which he could not have done without walking over my corpse.* That I

---

* The Emperor was so firmly impressed with the idea that an attempt would be made forcibly to intrude on his privacy, that for a short time after the departure of Sir George Cockburn he always kept four or five pairs of loaded pistols and some swords in his apartments, with which he was determined to dispatch the first who entered against his will.

would not commit suicide, but would exult in being assassinated by an Englishman. Instead of drawing back, it would be a consolation to me in my last moments."

Dr. O'Meara reported this conversation to Sir Hudson Lowe. The governor was exceedingly angry and violent.

"After he had expended some portion of his wrath," says Dr. O'Meara, "I observed that I had attempted his defense to the best of my abilities, but that I did not think that he ought to be much surprised at Napoleon's not being on good terms with him, when he considered what material alterations had taken place in his situation since his arrival, all which tended to render Napoleon's situation more unpleasant. A long discussion now followed, during which I recounted to his excellency some of his own restrictions; among others, that one in which he prohibited Napoleon from speaking; at which he again became very angry, and insisted that it was not a prohibition—*it was only a request;* that it was not his fault if General Bonaparte did not choose to ride out. I took the liberty, then, of asking the following question:

"'Place yourself, sir, in Napoleon's situation: would you have availed yourself of the permission to ride out, coupled with the restrictions imposed upon him?'

"His excellency refused to reply to this question, which he pronounced to be an insult to him as governor and representative of his majesty. He concluded by telling me that '*I was not permitted for the future to hold any conversation with General Bonaparte unless upon professional subjects, and ordering me to come to town every Monday and Thursday in order to report to him General Bonaparte's health and his habits.*'"

July 21. Dr. O'Meara had another disagreeable discussion with the governor, and became so disgusted with his petty tyranny, and found himself exposed to such insults, that he requested to be removed from his situation as physician to Napoleon.

"Sir Hudson Lowe," he says, "took every opportunity of venting upon me all the ill-humor he could not personally discharge upon his prisoner; and I, perceiving that all hopes of accommodation between the parties had vanished when Admiral Malcolm departed, and that all my efforts to ameliorate the situation of the captive were fruitless, determined to confine myself as much as possible to my medical duties, and to avoid all unnecessary communication with a man who could avail himself of his irresponsible situation as a means of insulting an inferior officer."

CHAPTER XLIII.
1817, August.

Rumor of a Removal to Malta—Remarks upon the English Ministers—The Emperor's Birth-day—Fondness for Children—Blindman's Buff—Anecdotes—The Queen of Prussia—Malta—Interesting Remarks—Maria Louisa—The Restoration of the Bourbons—Dethronement of the Spanish Princes—Robespierre—Talleyrand—Fouché—Carnot.

August 10. A newspaper recently received from Europe mentioned a rumor that the Emperor was to be removed from St. Helena to the island of Malta.

"I can not credit it," said the Emperor, "for I should create less alarm in England than in Malta. The governor is exceedingly impolitic in treating me in such a way as to render me an object of sympathy to Europe. The greatest indignation will be excited by it. Nothing could have happened to lessen the English so much in the estimation of other nations. It will confirm them in the opinions of your government which the emigrants who returned from England have disseminated. They returned filled with hatred against your ministers, whom they accused of having acted in the most parsimonious manner, and descending to the most minute and unworthy details."

August 15. This was the Emperor's birth-day. He was forty-eight years of age. He was in a gloomy prison, and exposed to cruel insults. For a long time he had been closely shut up in his room, that he might escape the sight of his jailers, and that he might not expose himself to the indignity of being challenged and turned from his path by a sentinel. Though his health was rapidly declining, and, in the highest maturity of his powers, he was fast descending to the grave, he strove to beguile the weary hours by incessant intellectual occupation. For a long time he had risen at four o'clock in the morning, and had, with unremitted diligence through the day, devoted himself to reading and writing.

To-day, with cheerful countenance and affectionate smiles, he received his friends in his shabbily-furnished and rat-infested room. In celebration of the anniversary of his birth-day, they all dined together. Even the two babes of Madam Bertrand and Madam Montholon were brought in to receive the caresses of the Emperor. Napoleon became the playmate of the rest of the children, engaged heartily with them in their sports, and dismissed them all with a present. As he retired alone to his pillow after all had gone, the night wind sighed around his dreary abode, and the emotions struggling in his breast were revealed only to Him who is the friend of the captive and the avenger of the oppressed. Napoleon nobly reserved his griefs for himself, while he cheered his companions with cheerfulness and smiles.

We have often mentioned Napoleon's fondness for children, and the cordiality with which he entered into all their sports. While at the Briers, when the Emperor's spirits were not crushed as now by insult and outrage, he often, with great joyousness, became, as it were, himself again a child. Little Betsy Balcombe he often fondled upon his knee, and for her amusement the Emperor cheerfully consented to engage in infantile games. The following scene, described by her in after years, will be read with interest:

"I had often entreated the Emperor to give a ball, before he left the Briers for Longwood, in the large room occupied by him, and which had been built by my father for that purpose. He had promised me faithfully he would; but when I pressed him urgently for the fulfillment of his word, he only laughed at me, telling me he wondered how I could be so silly as to think such a thing possible; but I never ceased reproaching him for his breach of faith, and teased him so, that at last, to escape my importunities, he said that, as the ball was out of the question, he would consent, by way of *amende honorable*, to any thing I chose to demand to console me for my disappointment.

"I replied instantly, If you will play the game of blindman's buff, that you have so often promised me, I will forgive you the ball, and never ask for it again. He laughed at my choice, and tried to persuade me to choose something else, but I was inexorable; and, seeing his fate inevitable, he resigned himself to it with a good grace, proposing we should begin at once. My sister and myself, and the son of General Bertrand, and some others of the Emperor's suite, formed the party. Napoleon said we should draw lots who should be blindfolded first, and he would distribute the tickets. Some slips of paper were prepared, on one of which was written the fatal word 'la mort,' and the rest were blanks. Whether accidentally, or by Napoleon's contrivance, I know not, but I was the first victim, and the Emperor, taking a cambric handkerchief out of his pocket, tied it tightly over my eyes, asking me if I could see.

"'I can not see you,' I replied; but a faint gleam of light did certainly escape through one corner, making my darkness a little less visible. Napoleon then, taking his hat, waved it suddenly before my eyes, and the shadow and the wind it made startling me, I drew back my head.

"'Ah, leetle monkee,' he exclaimed, in English, 'you can see pretty well.' He then proceeded to tie another handkerchief over the first, which completely excluded every ray of light. I was then placed in the middle of the room, and the game began. The Emperor commenced by creeping stealthily up to me, and giving my nose a very sharp twinge; I knew it was he both from the act itself and from his footstep. I darted forward, and very nearly succeeded in catching him; but, bounding actively away, he eluded my grasp. I then groped about, and, advancing again, he this time took hold of my ear and pulled it. I stretched out my hands instantly, and in the exultation of the moment screamed out, 'I have got you—I have got you; now you shall be blindfolded!'" but, to my mortification, it proved to be my sister, under cover of whom Napoleon had advanced, stretching his hand over her head.

"We then recommenced, the Emperor saying that as I had named the wrong person, I must continue blindfolded. He teased and quizzed me about my mistake, and bantered me in every possible way, eluding, at the same time, with the greatest dexterity, all my endeavors to catch him. At last, when the fun was growing fast and furious, and the uproar was at its height, it was announced that some one desired an audience of the Emperor, and, to my great annoyance, as I had set my heart on catching him and insisting on his being blindfolded, our game came to a conclusion."

August 17. " Saw Napoleon at two o'clock," says Dr. O'Meara. " He was in extremely good humor, and very facetious, cracking jokes upon various subjects, and rallying me about a young lady in the island."

"When I made my triumphal entry into Berlin," said Napoleon, "the mother of the Prince of Orange, the sister of the king, was left behind, sick, in the upper apartments of the palace, and very badly off, having been abandoned without money, and neglected by almost every body. A day or two after my arrival there, some of her attendants came to ask for assistance, as they had not wherewithal to procure even fuel for her use. The king, indeed, had neglected her most shamefully. The moment it was made known to me, I ordered a hundred thousand francs [$25,000] to be instantly sent, and went to see her myself afterward. I caused her to be furnished with every thing befitting her rank, and we had frequent interviews together. She was much obliged to me, and a kind of friendship commenced between us."

Napoleon then spoke of the late Queen of Prussia in very high terms; said that he had an esteem for her, and that, if the king had brought her at first to Tilsit, it would, in all probability, have procured him better terms. "She was elegant, ingenuous, and extremely well informed."

O'Meara observed to the Emperor that his enemies had accused him of having treated her very barbarously.

"What!" said he, " do they say that I poisoned her too ?"

O'Meara replied, "No; but they asserted that you had been the means of her death, in consequence of the misfortunes which you had caused to befall her country."

"Why," replied Napoleon, " that grief for the fallen situation of her husband and her country, and for the losses they had sustained, and the humiliated state they were reduced to, may have accelerated her death, is very probable. But that was not my fault. Why did her husband declare war against me? However, instead of treating her barbarously, nobody could have paid her more attention or respect, or have esteemed her more, for which I received her thanks."

Napoleon then made some observations about Malta, an abode with which he declared he would be satisfied for some years, professing at the same time his disbelief of such being the intentions of government. He added, "The best thing the English government could do would be to make a kind of treaty with me, by which I would bind myself not to quit Malta for a certain number of years without the permission of the Prince Regent, with a condition that at the expiration of the time I should be received in England. This would save the nation six or eight millions of francs yearly. It would," added he, " have been much more honorable to England, and more humane, to have caused me to be shot on board of the *Bellerophon,* in the rage of the moment, than to have condemned me to be exiled to such a rock as this. They might have excused themselves by saying, 'It is necessary for the tranquillity of Europe to put this man out of the way.' This would have at once freed them from all alarm, and saved millions to their treasury, besides being much more merciful. It would have been more honorable, more consistent with policy, and, above all, more humane, to have caused me to be quietly shot on board of the *Bellerophon.* It would have been preferred by myself. I really think that Lord Bathurst imagined that, by a series of ill-treatment and humiliation, they would induce me to commit suicide, and, for that purpose, found his man. The very idea of this, if I ever had any thoughts of doing so, would effectually prevent my putting it into execution."

August 22. "Saw Napoleon," says O'Meara, "at twelve o'clock. He has continued to rise at four o'clock in the morning, and to employ his time in reading and writing. Pointed out to me that he had been obliged to cause his coat to be turned, as there was no green cloth on the island. 'The ministry,' said he, 'do not know how to separate the man from the situation. As First Consul, as Emperor, being at war with England, I did her as much harm as I could; but as plain Napoleon Bonaparte now, when all the world is at peace, what right have they to detain me as prisoner? It is a great nation going to war with one man.

"'The eyes of the English,' he continued, 'will soon be opened with respect to my character. They will see the folly and injustice of keeping me in this island; an island so bad that I can compare it to nothing else than the face of the wretch they have sent out as governor. This, and the enormous expense, will cause my removal.'"

O'Meara observed that he was afraid the present disturbed state of England would operate most powerfully against his being permitted to go to England.

"Bah!" replied the Emperor; "your ministers are not silly enough to believe that I would lose my character so far as to put myself at the head of a mob, even if the latter were willing to put a foreigner at their head, which is very unlikely. Even in France I refused to do it. I have too great a regard for the reputation I shall leave to posterity to act the adventurer. No, no, it is hatred, and the fear they have of the information I could give. They are afraid I should say *it was not true,** in reply to the histories of many political events which they have explained in their own way.

"What do you think," said he, "of all things in the world, would give me the greatest pleasure?" O'Meara was on the point of replying, removal from St. Helena, when he said,

"To be able to go about *incognito* in London and other parts of England, to the eating-houses, with a friend, to dine in public at the expense of half a guinea or a guinea, and listen to the conversation of the company; to go through them all, changing almost daily, and in this manner, with my own

* These words were spoken in English.

ears, to hear the people express their sentiments, in their unguarded moments, freely and without restraint; to hear their real opinion of myself, and of the surprising occurrences of the last twenty years."

O'Meara observed that he would hear much evil and much good of himself.

"Oh, as to the evil," the Emperor replied, "I care not about that; I am well used to it. Besides, I know that the public opinion will be changed. The nation will be just as much disgusted at the libels published against me as they formerly were greedy in reading and believing them. This," added he, "and the education of my son, would form my greatest pleasure. It was my intention to have done this, had I reached America. The happiest days of my life were from sixteen to twenty, during the furloughs, when I used to go about, as I have told you I should wish to do, from one *restaurateur* to another, living moderately, and having a lodging for which I paid three louis a month. They were the happiest days of my life. I was always so much occupied that I may say I never was truly happy upon the throne. Not that I have to reproach myself with doing evil while seated there; on the contrary, I restored fifty thousand families to their country, and the improvements I made in France will speak for themselves. I made war, certainly; of this there is no doubt; but in almost every instance I was either forced to it, or I had some great political object in view.

"Had I died at Moscow," continued he, "I should have left behind me a reputation as a conqueror without a parallel in history. A bullet ought to have put an end to me there; whereas, when a man like me dies in misfortune, his reputation is lessened. *Then* I had never received a check. No doubt afterward, at Lutzen and Bautzen, with an army of recruits and without cavalry, I re-established my reputation, and the campaign of 1814, with such an inferior force, did not lessen it."

O'Meara observed that the generality of the world was surprised that he had not made a peace at Chatillon, when circumstances were apparently desperate for him.

Napoleon replied, "I could not consent to render the Empire less than what it was when I mounted the throne; I had sworn to preserve it. Moreover, the allied powers each day brought forth some condition more inadmissible than on the preceding one. You may think it strange, but I assure you that I would not sign it now. Had I remained on the throne after the return from Elba, I would have kept the treaty, because I found it made, but I would not have made it myself originally."

O'Meara took the liberty of asking what he considered to be the happiest time of his life since his elevation to the throne.

"The march from Cannes to Paris," was his reply.

O'Meara ventured to express his surprise to Napoleon that the Empress Maria Louisa had not made some exertion in his behalf.

"I believe," replied the Emperor, "that Maria Louisa is just as much a state prisoner as I am myself, except that more attention is paid to decorum in the restraints imposed upon her. I have always had occasion to praise the conduct of my good Louisa, and I believe that it is totally out of her power to assist me; moreover, she is young and timorous."

August 24. The difficulty between Dr. O'Meara and Sir Hudson Lowe was rapidly approaching a crisis. In an angry and insulting interview, the governor demanded that the doctor should report to him every thing that was said or done in Napoleon's chamber. O'Meara refused thus to act the part of a spy over his patient. The conversation in the Emperor's chamber today turned upon the restoration of the Bourbons.

"Never yet," said Napoleon, "has there been so much political imbecility displayed by man as there has been by Lord Castlereagh. A king is forced upon the throne contrary to the wishes and to the opinion of the people, and then, as a mode of ingratiating himself with that people, and of conciliating them, he is compelled to make them pay contributions ruinous to the country. They have made the Bourbons the executioners of their people. (Then, again, those Bourbons have made a concordat with the Pope, which would not have answered in the tenth or fifteenth century. They have agreed to establish by degrees all the laws of the Church. What does this mean but the suppression of Protestantism and of all other religions except the Roman Catholic? You know that the Roman doctrine is, that out of the pale of the Church no one can be saved. It is, in fact, re-establishing all the old bigotry and superstition, and even the Inquisition, as that was one of the laws of the Church.)

"The Protestants must see that the intention of this concordat is to deprive them of the liberty of worship, and to tolerate no religion but the Roman Catholic. The Protestants will be worse than before the Revolution, at which time, if one of them wanted to marry, he was obliged to say that he was a Catholic. Though their churches were then in a manner tolerated, yet, if they frequently opened them, they were visited and tormented by the police. That priest-ridden king has been imbecile enough to give his consent to a measure that will ultimately cause the assassination of the priests. At one time I had myself the greatest difficulty in preventing the people from accomplishing it. Oh, those Bourbons! Well may the French say *they have learned nothing, they have forgotten nothing.* They rest upon a sleeping lion. I see France in a flame. I see rivers of blood flowing. You will behold a general massacre of the Bourbons take place; the old noblesse, the priests, and many an innocent Englishman and friend to liberty will pay the forfeit of his life to expiate the wicked policy of Lord Castlereagh. The imagination always exceeds the reality, and the great latitude given in the concordat to the king and to the priests to revive all the ancient superstition and intolerance will set France in a flame, and produce another revolution of '*red bonnets,*' and '*down with the priests.*'"

August 25. The Emperor received Dr. O'Meara in quite a glow of cheerful spirits. Speaking of the dethronement of the Spanish princes, he said,

"The fact is, that, had it not been for their broils and quarrels among themselves, I should never have thought of dispossessing them. When I saw those imbeciles quarreling and trying to dethrone each other, I thought that I might as well take advantage of it and dispossess an inimical family; but I was not the contriver of their disputes. Had I known at first that the transaction would have given me so much trouble, or that it would even have cost the lives of two hundred men, I never would have attempted it; but, being once embarked, it was necessary to go forward."

Speaking of the French Revolution, O'Meara asked the Emperor's opinion about Robespierre.

"Robespierre," replied Napoleon, "was by no means the worst character who figured in the Revolution. He opposed trying the queen. He was not an Atheist; on the contrary, he had publicly maintained the existence of a Supreme Being, in opposition to many of his colleagues. Neither was he of opinion that it was necessary to exterminate all priests and nobles, like many others. Marat, for example, maintained that, to insure the liberties of France, it was necessary that six hundred thousand heads should fall. Robespierre wanted to proclaim the king an outlaw, and not to go through the ridiculous mockery of trying him. Robespierre was a fanatic, a monster, but he was incorruptible, and incapable of robbing, or of causing the deaths of others either from personal enmity or a desire of enriching himself. He was an enthusiast, but one who really believed that he was acting right, and died not worth a sou. In some respects Robespierre may be said to have been an honest man.

"It was truly astonishing," added Napoleon, "to see those fanatics, who, bathed up to the elbows in blood, would not for the world have taken a piece of money, or a watch, belonging to the victims they were butchering. At the very time that Marat and Robespierre were committing those massacres, if Pitt had offered them two hundred millions, they would have refused it with indignation. They even tried and guillotined some of their own number, such as Fabre d'Eglantine, who were guilty of plundering.

"Not so Talleyrand, Danton, Barras, Fouché. They were mere actors, and would have espoused any side for money. Talleyrand is the most vile of agitators, corrupt, unprincipled, but a man of talent; an actor ready to sell himself and every thing to the best bidder. Barras was such another. When I commanded the army of Italy, Barras made the Venetian embassador pay to him two hundred thousand dollars for writing a letter, begging of me to be favorable to the republic of Venice. I never paid any attention to such letters. From my first career I always commanded myself. Talleyrand, in like manner, sold every thing. Fouché in a less degree. His traffic was in an inferior line. Of all the sanguinary monsters who reigned in the Revolution, Billaud de Varennes was the worst. Carnot is the most honest of men. He left France without a sou."

CHAPTER XLIV.
1817, September.

Influence of Libels—St. Helena chosen by Wellington—Remarks on Sir Hudson Lowe—Society of Ladies—St. Domingo—The Manuscript from St. Helena—Anecdote of the lent Horse—Ross Cottage—The Earthquake—Remarks on the Restrictions—Aristocratic Pride.

September 2. A vessel arrived bringing some European journals. One of the London papers contained a furious assault upon the Emperor. Napoleon, having read the fierce invective with perfect composure, calmly remarked,

" Scurrility and obloquy will now rather serve than injure me. These attempts to debase my character will now be unavailing, in consequence of the free communication of the English with France. The vast number of English who have had access to the Continent will long ago have discovered and published that I am not that monster I have been described in the English and French libels. They have found out their mistake, and will blush at the idea of having been so grossly deceived. I would desire no better vindication of my character than their opinion. The time for libels against me is past. A moderate criticism upon my actions, well managed, well written, and not too highly exaggerated, would be infinitely more injurious to me than all the furious diatribes in the Quarterly Review style."

A letter was also received by this ship, informing Count Bertrand that sixty thousand dollars had been deposited in the hands of Messrs. Baring, Brothers, and Co., of London, to his credit. As this money did not belong to the Emperor, the English ministers, who had already rifled Napoleon's trunks, did not venture to seize it.

In the course of conversation, the Emperor remarked,

" Have you ever heard that Lord Wellington was the person who first proposed to send me to St. Helena?"

" I have heard so," O'Meara replied, " but have not given the report any credit."

" If it be true," said the Emperor, " it will reflect but little honor upon him in the eyes of posterity."

September 3. When O'Meara called, he found the Emperor alone in his room, reading the Bible aloud. He spoke of the annoyances to which Count Bertrand was exposed in his endeavor to get bills, which Las Casas had left upon London, cashed, and remarked,

" Even the bills and salaries of the servants are minutely examined, and every trifling sum obliged to be accounted for. Useless vexations; as every man of sense must know that it would not be by means of any small sum that I could command here that I could escape; and that, though I have no money here, I have it at the extremity of my fingers. But this man has the rage to meddle in every thing. If he had his will, he would order me to breakfast at a certain hour, dine at another, go to bed at a time prescribed by him, and come himself to see it carried into execution. All will fall upon himself one day. He does not know that what passes here will be recorded in history. He sent a letter to Bertrand, in reply to the one written by him about the new restrictions, which convinces me, more than any thing he has ever yet done, that he is destitute of common sense. He avows his atrocious deeds. He says that he has authority to rip up the cover of a book, or to examine any piece of furniture in such a manner as to render it unserviceable either for ornament or utility, to search for letters. By his reasoning, he ought not to send up a loaf of bread, or a joint of meat, or a pair of shoes, as letters might be concealed in them, and frequently have been in the soles of the latter. Nothing but the publication of that letter is wanting to convince the ministers that he is an imbecile."*

September 4. The weather was exceedingly bad, the walls were drenched with moisture, and the Emperor was suffering from a severe cold. Still, he received Dr. O'Meara with his accustomed cheerfulness and smiles. He had fires built in his rooms to dispel the moisture, though the governor complained bitterly that so much fuel was consumed, and threatened to put the inmates of Longwood upon an allowance. The companions of the Emperor informed the governor that they were perfectly willing to pay for the wood themselves.

In the course of conversation with Dr. O'Meara, Napoleon remarked,

"Northern people require the bottle to develop their ideas; and the English appear, in general, to prefer the bottle to the ladies, as is exemplified by your allowing the ladies to retire from the table, while you remain for hours to drink. Were I in England, I should always leave with the ladies. If your object is to converse instead of to drink, why not allow them to be present? Surely conversation is never so lively or so witty as when ladies take a part in it. If I were an Englishwoman, I should feel very discontented at being turned out by the men to wait for two or three hours while they were guzzling their wine. Now, in France, society is nothing unless ladies are present. They are the life of conversation."

"One of the greatest follies I ever was guilty of was sending that army out to St. Domingo. I ought to have prevented the possibility of its being effected. I committed a great oversight and fault in not having declared St. Domingo free, acknowledged the black government, and, before the peace of

---

* In this long communication the governor says,

"Presents may be as obnoxious to the security of detention as a letter, and might require to be examined with a minuteness that would baffle any purpose of ornament or utility to be derived from them. A letter may be concealed under the squares of a chess-board, or the folds of a book cover, as well as in the lining of a waistcoat; and I am not necessarily called to place my trust in any person by whom they are sent.

"You ask if any regulation exists which prevents your possessing an article with a crown upon it. There is certainly, sir, no specific written regulation prohibiting any article with a *crown* on it reaching Longwood, nor to prevent your possessing an object with such a decoration upon it; but it was in this case the imperial crown over the initial of Napoleon, carved, gilt, or engraved on almost every article. His own abdication, the convention of Paris, and the acts of the British Parliament, supersede the necessity of any regulations upon that head."

Amiens, sent some French officers to assist them. Had I done this, it would have been more consonant to the principles under which I was acting. It would have done you incalculable mischief. You would have lost Jamaica, and your other colonies would have followed. Having once acknowledged them, I could not have sent an army out there during the peace; but after the peace I was continually beset with applications from proprietors of estates in the colony, merchants, and others. Indeed, the nation had *la rage* to regain St. Domingo, and I was obliged to comply with it; but had I, previous to the peace, acknowledged the blacks, I could, under that plea, have refused to make any attempts to retake it, in doing which I acted contrary to my own judgment."

Speaking of a work which had recently been published in Europe, entitled Manuscript from St. Helena, which attracted much attention, and which many attributed to the pen of the Emperor, Napoleon said,

"Notwithstanding many mistakes as to time and place, that would make a corporal in the old French army laugh, it was written by a man of talent, though in several passages he seems not to have had common sense. In some places, his assertion of the motives which actuated me is correct. What he says on the subject of my nobility is correct. What he says about my intentions and wishes to do away with every thing which had been established since Charlemagne is also right. That the nobility I formed was that of the people, is true, as I took the son of a peasant, and made him a duke or a marshal when I found that he had talents; that I wanted to introduce a system of general equality is true, and that every person should be eligible to every situation, provided he had talents to fill it, whatever his birth might be; that I wanted to do away with all the ancient prejudices of birth is also correct; that I labored to establish a government of the people, which, though rigid (*dur*), was still that of the people, is also true; that I ought to have deposed, for my own security, when I had it in my power, the house of Brandenburg, and all the ancient orders of sovereigns; and that they almost always combined against and attacked me, is also right.

"Probably I ought to have done so, and I should have succeeded. It is true that I wished to establish a government of the people. It is a work which will much displease the oligarchy, because they do not wish that any person except one of themselves should be eligible for any important situation. With *their* will, birth, and not talents or capability, should regulate the choice. A worse, a more despotic or unforgiving government than an oligarchy never existed. Offend them once, you are never pardoned, and no treatment can be too cruel for you when in their power. The pamphlet is written with that lightness peculiar to Frenchmen, and consequently contains many mistakes."

September 9. "One of the many instances of Napoleon's great good-nature," says Mrs. Abell, "and of his kindness in promoting my amusement, was on the occasion of the races at Deadwood. From having been, as was often the case, in arrears with my lessons, my father, by way of punishing me, declared that I should not go to the races; and, fearing that he might be induced to break his determination, lent my pony Tom to a friend of his for that day. My vexation was very great at not knowing where to get a horse, and I happened to mention my difficulty to Dr. O'Meara, who told Napoleon; and my delight may be conceived when, a short time after all our party had left the Briers for Deadwood, I perceived the doctor winding down the mountain-path which led to our house, followed by a slave leading a superb gray horse called 'Mameluke,' with a lady's side-saddle and housings of crimson velvet embroidered with gold. Dr. O'Meara said that, on telling the Emperor of my distress, he desired the quietest horse in his stable to be immediately prepared for my use. This simply good-natured act of the Emperor occasioned no small disturbance on the island, and sufficiently punished me for acting contrary to my father's wishes by the pain it gave me to hear that he was considered to have committed a breach of discipline in permitting one of his family to ride a horse belonging to the Longwood establishment, *and for which he was reprimanded by the governor!*"

In reference to this event, Dr. O'Meara, under the date of September 9, makes the following record:

"Races at Deadwood. The commissioners all present. None of the French from Longwood attended except the children and some of the domestics.

"During the interval between the heats, Sir Hudson Lowe sent for me, and asked if 'some of General Bonaparte's horses were not on the race-ground.' I replied in the affirmative. His excellency asked how they came there. I replied that I had borrowed the horses from General Gourgaud, one of which I had lent to Miss Eliza Balcombe, and the other to the surgeon of the *Conqueror.* Sir Hudson immediately broke out into not the most moderate expressions, and his gestures attracted the attention of many of the spectators. He characterized my having dared to lend any of General Bonaparte's horses without his (the governor's) permission to be the greatest piece of presumption he had ever witnessed. I observed that I had come to St. Helena to learn that it was a crime to borrow a horse for the use of a young lady, neither had I known that it was necessary to go to Plantation House to ask permission from him to borrow a horse belonging to the Longwood establishment. Sir Hudson replied that 'I had no business to form any opinion about it.'"

"There was so very little," says Mrs. Abell, "to vary the monotony of Napoleon's life, that he took an interest in the most trifling attempts at gayety in the island, and he generally consented to our entreaties to be present at some of the many entertainments which my father delighted in promoting. On one occasion, my father gave a fête to celebrate the anniversary of my birth-day at a pretty little place he possessed within the boundary of the Emperor's rides, called 'Ross Cottage.'

"When the festivities were at their height, we descried the Emperor riding along the hill's side toward the house, but on seeing such an assembly, he sent to say that he would content himself with looking at us from the heights above. I did not consider that this was fulfilling his promise of coming to the party, and not liking to be so disappointed, I scampered off to where he had taken up his position, and begged he would be present at our festivity, telling him he must not refuse, since it was my birth-day. But all my entreaties were unavailing. He said he could not make up his mind to descend the hill to be exposed to the gaze of the multitude, who wished to gratify their curiosity with the sight of him.

"I insisted, however, on his tasting a piece of birth-day cake, which had been sent for that occasion by a friend from England, and who, little knowing the strict surveillance exercised over all those in any way connected with the fallen chief and his adherents, had the cake ornamented with a large eagle; this, unluckily for us, was the subject of much animadversion. I named it to Napoleon as an inducement for him to eat the cake, saying, 'It is the least you can do for getting us into such disgrace.' Having thus induced him to eat a thick slice, he pinched my ear, calling me a saucy simpleton, and galloped away humming, or rather attempting to sing, with his most unmusical voice, 'Vive Henri Quatre.'"

September 22. During the night the island was agitated by quite a severe shock of an earthquake. The Emperor, speaking of it in the morning, said,

"At the moment of the first shock, I imagined that some accident had happened to the ship of war, the *Conqueror*, or that some powder-magazine on the island had exploded. At the second shock, however, I immediately perceived that it was an earthquake."

When it was mentioned to Admiral Pamplin, the new admiral at St. Helena, that the Emperor thought at first that some magazine had exploded, he remarked, "*Ay, ay, the d——d rascal supposed so because he wished it.*"

The character of this official may be inferred from the fact that he was living openly and shamelessly with a woman who was not his wife. Despots and aristocrats were Napoleon's *political* enemies, and men vulgar, profane, and debauched *socially* his foes. Napoleon would not combine with the despots of Europe and with the aristocrats of England to sustain political corruption, and he would not receive to his companionship such men as Pamplin and Lowe. The Emperor's *intimate friends* were always men of true nobility of character—such men as his brother Joseph, Caulaincourt, the noble Duroc, Desaix, and the serious and true Las Casas. He was compelled, in the wide reach of his empire, to avail himself of the energies of many an individual whose character was uncongenial with his own, but the earnest and pensive nature of the Emperor could find *fellowship* only with those whose sympathies were sincere and noble.

September 28. The Emperor, closely confined in his damp and mouldy room, deprived of air, of exercise, and of cheerful converse, was slowly but surely descending to the grave. His cheeks became pallid and emaciate, his limbs began to swell. Nervous pains gave him sleepless nights and days of suffering. Sir Hudson Lowe thought that he could thus torture him into submission to his arbitrary will. But the noble victim was inspired with a soul which no outrage or torture could vanquish. Dr. O'Meara, trembling for his patient, urged him to see a consulting physician.

Napoleon replied, "There is no necessity for it. If all the colleges of medicine in France and England were assembled, they would give the same advice as you have done, viz., to take exercise on horseback. I myself know, as well as any physician, what is necessary for me. It is exercise. Calling in Baxter to me would be like sending a physician to a man who was starving with hunger, instead of giving him a loaf of bread. As long as the present system is in force, I will never stir out. Would you have me render myself liable to be stopped and insulted by a sentinel, as Madam Bertrand was some days ago, at ten minutes past six in the evening, and while it was still daylight? If I had been in her place, it would have occurred, as the sentinel had orders to stop every body. It would have been a fine subject for this governor to have written upon to London, and to have stuck a caricature in the print-shops of Napoleon Bonaparte stopped at the gate, with a sentinel charging his bayonet upon him. Until matters are put on the footing they were in Cockburn's time, which were approved of by his government, or an equivalent given, I shall never stir out. To avoid the possibility of being insulted, I have shut myself up; and until I know to a certainty what restrictions there are, and by whom made, I shall not venture out, or expose myself to the caprice of my enemy. By prohibiting me to speak to such persons as I might meet, he offered to me the greatest insult which could be given to man. It is true that he has since taken it off; but if he has the power to make restrictions as he pleases, he may renew it to-morrow upon some pretext. To a man who has the power of doing what he likes, a pretext will never be wanting; for moral restrictions imposed by him upon a man like me have the same effect in imprisoning me as chains and irons on the legs would have upon galley-slaves. To robbers and galley-slaves, physical restrictions are imposed; to cultivated men, moral ones. There is not a little lieutenant in that regiment who would go out if subjected to the restrictions imposed upon me. I asked the embassador, 'Would you, my lord, go out under the restriction of not speaking more to any person you met than How do you do, unless in the presence of an officer? Would you go out under the restriction of not being able to move to the right or to the left of the road? Would you stir out under the obligation of coming in again at six o'clock in the evening, or otherwise run the risk of being stopped by sentinels at the gates?' He replied instantly, 'No! I should do as you do—I would remain in my chamber.' There are different ways of assassinating a man—the pistol, the sword, poison, or morally assassinating, as Castlereagh and Bathurst are doing to me. It is the same in the end, excepting that the latter is the most cruel. When the admiral, who was a man of blunt character, was here, you recollect what a different kind of life I led. I rode out four or five times a week, saw company, and even invited English officers, ladies, and others, to dine. In the admiral I had confidence. His word I believed, and not the slightest suspicion of sinister design ever entered my head. Though I disagreed with him, and thought he was a rough man, still I felt confidence in his character and in his integrity. Had I any intention of committing suicide, as this *geôlier* insinuates, I should have done it in the beginning, when, from not having been accustomed to it, I must have felt it most oppressive. Besides, if I intended it, a pistol would be my resource. I do not love a long war. What inconvenience ever occurred during Cockburn's time by my riding out? The intentions of the governor are to impose restrictions of such a nature, that I, without degrading my character, and rendering myself an object of contempt in the eyes of the world, must imprison myself; thereby, in the course of time, to bring on disease, which, in a frame impaired by confinement and the blood being decomposed, must prove mortal, and that I may thus expire in protracted agonies, which may have the appearance of a natural death. This is the plan, and is a manner of assassinating just as certain, but more cruel and criminal, than the sword or the pistol."

September 29. Napoleon was speaking of the attention devoted to the comfort of the soldiers in the French army, and particularly of the care bestowed upon the wounded. O'Meara remarked that in an English ship of war, at sea, during the winter, the seamen are better off than the officers, because the seamen can warm and dry themselves by the galley fire.

"And why can not the officers?" inquired the Emperor.

"Because," O'Meara replied, "it would not be exactly decorous for the officers to mix in that familiar way with the men."

"Ah!" exclaimed the Emperor, "that aristocratic pride, that rabid aristocracy! Why, in my campaigns, I used to go to the lines in the bivouacs, sit down with the meanest soldier, converse, laugh, and joke with him. I always prided myself on being the man of the people. You are the most aristocratic nation in the world. Had I been one of those petty princes in Germany, your oligarchy would never have sent me here; but because I am the man of the people—because I may say that I raised myself from the populace to the greatest height of power, without the aid of aristocracy or hereditary rights—because a long line of nobles or of petty princes did not distinguish my name—because, in fact, I was not one of them, they determined to oppress and humiliate me when in their power. The English people will understand that I am oppressed because I rose from the people, and in order to prevent any of them from presuming to elevate themselves to a level with the aristocracy."

CHAPTER XLV.
1817, October, November, and December.

Alarming Symptoms—The Restrictions relaxed—The Duke of Reichstadt deprived of his Inheritance—Napoleon's Command of himself—Libels—Continued Crimes of the Governor—The new House.

October 1. Serious symptoms of the liver complaint made their appearance. O'Meara urged that something must immediately be done, or the disease would terminate fatally. The Emperor replied,

"That would be truly a great consolation; but my death will be an eternal disgrace to the English nation, which has sent me to this climate to die under the hands of an executioner."

O'Meara remarked that he ought not to hasten his death by refusing to take proper remedies.

The Emperor solemnly replied, looking up, "That which is written is written. Our days are numbered."

October 3. The Emperor's increasing illness began to alarm the governor. He consequently wrote to Count Bertrand "that he would throw open to him (the Emperor) the whole of the space between Longwood and the new road, thus enabling him to traverse it on foot and on horseback in any direction he may choose. The same latitude, however, I do not feel myself warranted in extending to the officers and other persons of his family, except at the time they may be in immediate personal attendance upon him." O'Meara urged the Emperor to profit by this concession.

"It would only expose me," said he, "to more insults; for the sentinels do not know me, and every old soldier who wished to fulfill his duty so as to clear himself of all responsibility would say, '*Halte là!* Is General Bonaparte among you? Are you he? Oh, then, if you are he, you may pass.' Thus should I be exposed to daily insults, and be obliged to give an account of myself to every sentinel who thought it right to fulfill his duty properly. Besides, he has no right to impose more restrictions upon these gentlemen than upon me. By the paper which they have signed, they only agree to subject themselves to such restrictions as are or may be imposed upon me. Moreover, I do not recognize his right to impose any other restrictions than those made by Admiral Cockburn, which were approved of by his government, unless he shows that they are signed by the Prince Regent or by the ministers."

October 7. O'Meara found the Emperor very feeble, and informed him that the governor had intimated that Napoleon wished to kill himself.

"Had I intended this," Napoleon replied, "I would have fallen on my sword long ago, and died like a soldier. But to purposely kill myself by the slow agonies of a lingering disease, I am not fool enough to attempt. I never loved tedious warfare. But there is no death, however slow and painful, that I would not prefer to dishonoring my character. A man who was once capable of imposing the restrictions of the 9th of October and the 14th of March, is capable of laying them on again, or even worse, according to his caprice or his fears, real or imaginary. If I were to go out and be once insulted by a sentinel, it would have the effect of doing more injury to my health than six months' confinement. But this man is insensible to any moral feeling. He thinks that he has got some Corsican deserters or corporals to deal with. He is a melange of imbecility and stupidity. Before I had gone out a week, he would make some insinuations, as he perpetually does, to the commissioners, and say that I had abused the permission he had given."

November 2. Weary days of sickness and pain lingered slowly along, while the Emperor, in his close imprisonment, longed for the release of death.

Dr. O'Meara found him to-day reclining upon the sofa, with some newspapers lying before him. He was melancholy and languid. The governor, who was very careful to keep from the Emperor all good news, had sent him a paper containing the account that the Emperor's son had been disinherited from the succession to the Duchy of Parma.

"Now this intelligence," said Napoleon, "coming from another person, would be nothing; but as the governor invariably culls out all the news that might prove agreeable, which he retains at Plantation House, and sends whatever may wound my feelings, it is easy to see the motives by which he is actuated.

"You see," added he, with an emphasis, "that he lost no time in sending that news to me. I was always prepared to expect something of the kind from the wretches who compose the Congress. They are afraid of a prince who is the choice of the people. However, you may yet see a great change, that is, provided they continue to give him a good education, or that they do not assassinate him. If they brutify him by a bad education, there is little hope. As for me, I may be considered as dead—as already in the sepulchre. I am certain that before long this body will be no more. I feel that the machine struggles, but can not last.

"I," added he, "could listen to the intelligence of the death of my wife, of my son, or of all my family, without change of feature. Not the slightest sign of emotion or alteration of countenance would be visible. Every thing would appear indifferent and calm. But when alone in my chamber, then I suffer; then the feelings of the man burst forth.

"As to my son's being disinherited from the succession to Parma, it gives me little or no uneasiness. If he lives, he will be something. As to those contemptible little states, I would rather see him a private *gentleman*, with enough to eat, than sovereign of any of them. Perhaps, however, it may grieve the Empress to think that he will not inherit after her. But it does not give me the smallest trouble."

December 9. As the dreary weeks passed along, the Emperor was left unmolested in his dying chamber. Sir Hudson Lowe, however, was daily manifesting increased acrimony toward Dr. O'Meara, and was evidently determined to drive him from the island. The doctor resolutely refused to act the part of the governor's spy, and Sir Hudson Lowe was determined to replace him by a more pliant agent. In conversation to-day, something was said of the libels which had been published against the Emperor. Napoleon observed,

"Of all the libels against me with which your ministers have inundated Europe, not one will pass to posterity. When I was asked to write, or cause to be written, answers to them, I replied, Another victory, another monument is the true response. Besides, it would have been said that I paid for the writing of them, which would have been discreditable. Posterity will judge by facts. Calumny has exhausted all her poison on my person. I shall gain every day. When the first phrensy has passed away, I shall have for my enemies only the ignorant and the wicked. When there is not a trace of these libels to be found, the great works and monuments that I executed, and the code of laws that I formed, will go down to the most distant ages; and future historians will revenge the wrongs done to me by my contemporaries."

December 18. Under this date Dr. O'Meara makes the following record:

"Summoned to attend at Plantation House. As the reader must be already disgusted with the details of the manner in which the governor took advantage of his situation to insult and oppress an officer inferior in rank, because the latter refused to be his spy, I shall not fatigue him with any further account of the conduct practiced toward me on this day, than that my replies and refusals to disclose Napoleon's conversations caused me to be treated in a more outrageous manner than on the 18th of last month. The governor followed me out of the room, vociferating after me in a frantic manner, and carried his gestures so far as to menace me with personal violence.

"After this, orders were again given me to attend interrogations at Plantation House twice a week."

Thus, with Napoleon, darkly closed the year of 1817. His persecutors were becoming more and more implacable, and the chill glooms of the prison were settling in heavier folds over his dying bed. In dejection and pain, he passed most of the hours of his weary days and of his sleepless nights alone. The silence was only disturbed by the gambols of the rats, which had free range through his dilapidated hovel. The governor refused to erect the new house upon any of those spots which the Emperor had pointed out, but insisted upon placing it upon the bleak heights of Longwood. He ordered the foundations to be dug in the very garden of that shadeless, cheerless, storm-swept, unhealthy locality. This was an additional insult to the Emperor. To all these outrages he could only oppose silence and seclusion. It was three years before the new house was completed. But Napoleon was then gasping in death. His feet never crossed the threshold.

CHAPTER XLVI.
1818.

Sad Condition of the Emperor—Remarks on the French Revolution—O'Meara insulted by the Governor—Contrast between Lowe and Cockburn—New Instructions from Lord Bathurst—Portraits of Napoleon's Son—Dr. O'Meara again insulted by the Governor—Plans in the Invasion of England—Death of Cipriani—Gourgaud's Return to Europe—Departure of the Balcombes—O'Meara Imprisoned—O'Meara sent from the Island—Extension of Liberty—Dr. Stockoe.

January. "The year 1818," says Count Montholon, "began its course under sad auspices. Time, instead of alleviating the sufferings of our captivity, aggravated them every day, and the decline of the Emperor's health gave us serious uneasiness."

The Emperor remained secluded in his room, spending many hours every day in dictating the memoirs of his campaigns, and finding a melancholy pleasure in conversing with his friends. But little of his conversation during the month of January is recorded. On one occasion, speaking of the French Revolution, he said,

"The French Revolution was a general movement of the mass of the nation against the privileged classes. The nobles retained the higher and the inferior justice, and other feudal rights, under various forms; enjoyed the privilege of being exempt from the burdens of the community, and exclusively possessed all honorable employments. The chief object of the Revolution was to destroy those privileges and abuses, to abolish the manorial courts, suppress the remains of the ancient slavery of the people, and subject all citizens equally to bear the expenses of the state. It established equality of rights. Any citizen might succeed to any employment according to his talents. Before it, France was composed of provinces differently divided, and unequal in extent and population. They had a great number of legal customs and peculiar laws for the administration of civil as well as criminal justice. She was an assemblage of several states without amalgamation. The Revolution destroyed all those little nations, and formed a new one. There was one France with a homogeneous division of territory, the same civil and criminal laws, and the same regulation for taxes. There no longer remained any trace of the ancient privileges of the provinces, their ancient sovereigns, or ancient Parliaments. One half of the territory had changed proprietors. France presented the spectacle of thirty millions of inhabitants circumscribed in natural limits, composed of one class of citizens, and governed by one law, one regulation, one order. Subsequently the French nation established the imperial throne, and placed me upon it. No person ever ascended a throne with more legitimate rights. The throne of France was granted before to Hugues Capet by a few bishops and nobles. The imperial throne was given to me by the desire of the people, whose wishes were three times verified in a solemn manner."

Napoleon refused to have any intercourse whatever with Sir Hudson Lowe, and seldom mentioned his name or alluded to him in any way; but this brutal jailer daily became more malignant and tyrannical in his treatment of those who were the friends of the illustrious captive. Dr. O'Meara was exposed to every conceivable insult. Nothing but his intense and increasing affection for the Emperor induced him to retain a position which exposed him, a British officer, to such indignities. On the 2d of January the governor said, in an angry interview with the doctor,

"This is my office, sir, and there is the door leading to it. When I send for you on duty, you will come in at that door; but do not put your foot in any other part of my house, or come in at any other entrance."

"I calmly replied," says O'Meara, "that it was not for my own pleasure or by my own desire that I ever set foot in any part of his house, and, after suffering this paltry abuse of authority, departed."

On the occasion of the reception of some fresh insults, the Emperor said of Sir Hudson Lowe,

"I never look on him without being reminded of the assassin of Edward II. in the castle of Berkeley, heating the bar of iron which was to be the instrument of his crime. My nature revolts against him. In my eyes, she seems to have marked him, like Cain, with the seal of reprobation. This can not be a prejudice against the English nation, since Admiral Cockburn never inspired me with similar distaste. True, I had some complaints against him, but I always did justice to his honorable sentiments. I never felt the slightest distrust toward him; and I would willingly have bestowed my confidence on any medical man presented by him."

O'Meara, feeling heavily the immense responsibility which was resting upon him, entreated the Emperor to receive, as a consulting physician, Dr. Baxter, who was in Sir Hudson Lowe's employ. He represented the doctor as a man of irreproachable character and of distinguished talent.

"I believe," said the Emperor, "all the good that you tell me, and that I hear said of Mr. Baxter, but Mr. Lowe soils every thing that passes through his hands, and he wishes to make me consult Mr. Baxter, in order that he may then remove you, whom I have myself chosen, and be enabled to have such bulletins of my health written as it may suit him to forward to his government."

Sir Hudson Lowe received instructions from Lord Bathurst forbidding him any longer to communicate with *General Bonaparte* through Count Bertrand, for two reasons: first, because he was treating General Bonaparte with the respect due to sovereign princes, and, secondly, because Count Bertrand adopted an overbearing tone of authority. Heretofore, though the English officials refused to recognize the title of Emperor, the French were not prohibited from using that title; but now the command was given that no communication should be received from them in which that title was given to Napoleon.

February 16. Mr. Barber had arrived at St. Helena in the *Cambridge*, and opened a shop at Jamestown. He brought from Europe two portraits of Napoleon's son, thinking that it would be a gratification to the Emperor and his friends to receive them. Sir Hudson Lowe seized the portraits, and the bereaved father was never permitted to behold these lineaments of his idolized child.

February 18. Sir Hudson Lowe, in the exercise of petty tyranny for which we can scarcely find a parallel in the darkest page of history, strictly prohibited Dr. O'Meara from speaking to his patient *upon any subject whatever except his medical condition!* Dr. O'Meara records, under this day's date, the following interview with the governor:

"Sir Hudson Lowe then got up, and, looking at me in a menacing manner, said,

"'Upon your word of honor, sir, I ask you if you have had any other conversations with Napoleon Bonaparte than upon medical subjects for a month past.'

"I replied, 'Perhaps there may have been on other subjects not interesting.'

"'I do not allow *you*, sir,' he continued, 'to be a judge of whether they were uninteresting or otherwise. You have no authority for holding any communications with Napoleon Bonaparte unless upon medical subjects, and then only when sent to for that purpose. Have you had any communication with any other person of his family?'

"'Certainly, sir, I have had.' Without waiting to know whether those communications were medical or otherwise, he burst out with, 'You have no authority, sir, to hold any communication whatsoever with any of his family, who are subject to the same restrictions as himself, unless upon medical subjects, and then only when sent for, and when finished you are to leave them. You have no business to go among them unless for medical purposes. Have you, sir, had any communication with any of them unless upon those subjects?'

"I replied by referring his excellency to his own orders that I should not hold any other communication than medical with them.

"'This reply, sir,' said he, 'as usual, is not a direct one. You make it a practice to go to town when ships arrive, which I do not approve of. You go to collect news for General Bonaparte.'

"I answered 'that I was an English officer, and, as such, would not give up my rights; moreover, that I, as well as others, was desirous of purchasing the necessaries of life as soon as they were landed, and before any monopoly took place to increase the price. That, if he intended to prohibit me from going to town, I had to request orders to that effect in writing.' This Sir Hudson refused, saying, with a sneer,

"'The request is worthy of the place you came from, and the people with whom you associate. I do not think a person, under a pledge to Napoleon Bonaparte, ought to be received into company, and I do not approve of your going to town when ships arrive. You are suspected by me, sir.'

"I replied 'that I was under no other pledge to Napoleon than one which was tacitly understood in every society of gentlemen.'

"The governor said 'that it was presumption and insolence for me to dare to judge of the line of conduct his majesty's government had thought proper to pursue with respect to Napoleon Bonaparte.'

"I replied 'that I did not attempt to judge of that; that I merely mentioned what was the custom of society.'

"'You are a suspected man, sir—you are suspected by *me*.'

"'I can not help that, sir. It is a consolation to me, however, under such circumstances, to have the *mens conscia recti*.' This the governor said was a fresh insult, which he followed up by a volley of abuse."

February 19. The Emperor, speaking of his plans if he had succeeded in the invasion of England, said,

"I would have offered you a Constitution of your own choice, and have said, 'Assemble in London deputies from the people to fix upon a Constitution.' I would have called upon Burdett and other popular leaders to organize one according to the wishes of the people. I would have declared the Prince Regent fallen from the throne, abolished the nobility, proclaimed liberty, freedom, and equality. Think you that, in order to keep the house of Hanover on the throne, your rich citizens, merchants, and others of London would have consented to sacrifice their riches, their houses, their families, and all their dearest interests, especially when I had made them comprehend that I only came to sweep oppression away, and to give them liberty? No, it is contrary to history and to human nature. You are too rich. Your principal people have too much to lose by resistance, and your populace too much to gain by a change. If, indeed, they supposed that I wanted to render England a province of France, then indeed the national spirit would do wonders.

"But I would have formed a republic according to your own wishes, required a moderate contribution barely sufficient to have paid the troops, and perhaps not even that. Your populace would have been for me, knowing that I am the man of the people, that I spring from the populace myself, and that, whenever a man had merit or talent, I elevated him without asking how many degrees of nobility he had—knowing that by joining with me they would be relieved from the yoke of the aristocracy under which they labor. There is not a people in the world, not even the Prussian, worse treated. Excepting the obligation of serving as soldiers, the German populace are better off than yours.

"You have no more regard for yours than if they were so many Helots, and you treat them precisely as if they were such. To my lords and my ladies, to the aristocracy and the *gentlemen*, oh, indeed, you pay every kind of attention and regard; nothing can be too good for them; no treatment kind enough; but for your populace, bah! they are so many dogs: as your contractors said, when furnishing provisions to the French prisoners, 'It is too good for those French dogs.' You yourself, doctor, have a great deal of aristocratic pride in your head, and appear to look down upon your *common people* as if they were a race of inferior beings. You talk of your freedom. Can any thing be more horrible than your pressing of seamen? You send your boats on shore to seize upon every male that can be found, who, if they have the misfortune to belong to the populace—if they can not prove themselves *gentlemen*, are hurried on board of your ships, to serve as seamen in all quarters of the globe.

"And yet you have the impudence to talk of the conscription in France: it wounds your pride, because it fell *upon all ranks*. Oh, how shocking, that a *gentleman's son* should be obliged to defend his country, just as if he were one of the common people! and that he should be compelled to expose his body, or put himself on a level with a *vile plebeian!* Yet God made all men alike. Who form the nation? Not your lords, nor your fat prelates and churchmen, nor your *gentlemen*, nor your oligarchy. Oh! one day the people will revenge themselves, and terrible scenes will take place.

"That conscription," continued Napoleon, "which offended your aristocratic pride so much, was conducted scrupulously according to the principles of equal rights. Every native of a country is bound to defend it. The conscription did not crush a particular class like your press-gang, nor the populace because they were poor. It was the most just, because the most equal mode of raising troops. It rendered the French army the best composed in the world. The conscription would have become a national institution, instead of being regarded as a punishment or a servitude.

"Were you a nation," continued he, "of half savages, of poor wild mountaineers, or of ferocious shepherds like the Scythians, then, indeed, you might destroy your capital, and desolate your country, in order to stop the progress of an invader. Even if you were as poor, as wild, and as ignorant as the Spaniards, perhaps you might destroy some of your towns and habitations; but you are too rich and too selfish. Where is there one of you would say, 'I will destroy my house, abandon my property to be pillaged, my wife and daughters to be violated, my sons to be massacred! And for what? To keep the Prince Regent on the throne, and Lord Bathurst and the Archbishop of Canterbury in their employments of twenty thousand pounds a year. All this I will do against a man who offers terms, who proposes to give us a Constitution according to the wish of the nation.' No, no. It is more than could be expected from *man*. Pitt himself was well aware of it, and one of the means which he took to form the coalition against me was by asserting that a descent was possible; that if it were effected England would be conquered before twelve months; that then all the Continent would be at my mercy and my disposal; that, England once fallen, all was lost. This the King of Prussia told me afterward."

In further remarks upon the imperial government, the Emperor said,

"The system of government must be adapted to the spirit of the nation and to circumstances. In the first place, France required a strong government. While I was at the head of it, I may say that France was in the same state as Rome when a dictator was declared necessary for the salvation of the republic. Successions of coalitions against her existence were formed by your gold among all the powerful nations of Europe. To resist successfully, it was necessary that all the energies of the country should be at the disposal of the chief. I never conquered unless in my own defense. Europe never ceased to make war upon France and her principles. It was necessary for us to conquer under the pain of being conquered. Between the parties that agitated France for a long time, I was like a rider seated on an unruly horse, who always wanted to swerve either to the right or to the left; and, to make him keep a straight course, I was obliged to let him feel the bridle occasionally. The government of a country just emerged from a revolution, menaced by foreign enemies, and agitated by the intrigues of domestic traitors, must necessarily be rigorous. In quieter times my dictature would have finished, and I should have commenced my constitutional reign. Even as it was, with a coalition always existing against me, either secret or public, openly avowed or denied, there was more equality in France than in any other country in Europe.

"One of my grand objects was to render education accessible to every body. I caused every institution to be formed upon a plan which offered instruction to the public either gratis, or at a rate so moderate as not to be beyond the means of the peasant. The museums were thrown open to the people. My people would have become the best educated in the world. All my exertions were directed to illuminate the mass of the nation, instead of brutifying them by ignorance and superstition.

"Those English," added he, "who are lovers of liberty, will one day lament with tears having gained the battle of Waterloo. It was as fatal to the liberties of Europe in its effects as that of Philippi was to those of Rome; and, like it, has precipitated Europe into the hands of triumvirs, associated together for the oppression of mankind, the suppression of knowledge, and the restoration of superstition."

February 24. This day Cipriani, one of the Emperor's most devoted attendants, died, after a short but very violent illness. Napoleon wished to visit his sick-bed, but the doctor dissuaded him, as he feared the excitement might destroy all hopes of recovery. Cipriani was a man of remarkable natural strength of mind and great force of character. He was a strong Republican, and had yielded to the necessary establishment of the *Republican Empire*. His attachment to the Emperor was so enthusiastic that he left his own family in Rome that he might follow Napoleon to his gloomy prison. When the Emperor was informed of his death, he said, sadly,

"Where is his soul? Gone to Rome, perhaps, to see his wife and child before it undertakes the long, final journey."

As Cipriani was not buried within the limits allotted to the Emperor, Napoleon did not attend the funeral, as he would otherwise have done. He, however, as an expression of gratitude to the attention showed his remains, sent $125 to the clergyman who performed the burial service for distribution among the poor.

March. The month of March came and went enveloped in gloom. Funereal shades settled down, each day more dark and sombre, over the inmates of Longwood. General Gourgaud's health became so deplorable, and his spirits so utterly depressed, that it became necessary for him to return to Europe. He also hoped to make such representations there as to ameliorate the condition of the dying Emperor. General Gourgaud had the honor of a personal acquaintance with the Emperors of Russia and Austria, and had also been admitted to the intimacy of Maria Louisa. Hopes were therefore entertained that he might be enabled to make the truth known.

In no period of the Emperor's life does his imperial character shine more brilliantly than during the awful tragedy of St. Helena. His friends exerted their utmost energies to baffle the malignity of his foes. Napoleon opposed to all the hostile machinations of his enemies the sublimity of patience and seclusion, and the resistance of his renown.

Sir Hudson Lowe, in his pitiable defense, has endeavored to represent General Gourgaud as leaving St. Helena because he had become alienated from the Emperor, and wished to leave him. The following extracts from a letter addressed to Maria Louisa, but intended for the eye of all Europe, immediately upon his arrival in London, is a sufficient reply to all such calumnies:

"MADAM,—You will pardon the sad duty which I now fulfill by informing you that the Emperor Napoleon is dying amid the torments of the most frightful and prolonged agony. Yes, madam, he whom divine and human laws unite to you by the most sacred ties; he whom you have beheld an object of homage to almost all the sovereigns of Europe, and over whose fate I saw you shed so many tears when he left you, is perishing by a most cruel death, a captive on a rock in the midst of the vast ocean, at a distance of two thousand leagues from those he holds most dear, alone, without friends, without relations, without tidings of his wife or of his son, without consolation.

"Since I quitted the fatal rock, I had nourished a hope of being able to go to you, and of reciting his sufferings to you, in full reliance on the exertions which your generous soul was capable of undertaking; but in this I was deceived. I learned that no one who would recall the Emperor to your mind, describe his situation to you, and tell you the truth, was permitted to approach you; in a word, that you were in the midst of your court as in a prison. The Emperor himself thought this must be so. In his moments of anguish, when, in order to offer him some consolation, we spoke to him of you, he frequently replied, 'Be assured that if the Empress makes no effort to alleviate my situation, it is because she is surrounded by spies, who prevent her from learning what they make me suffer here.'"

Two only of Napoleon's companions now remained to cheer his captivity, Montholon and Bertrand.

The Balcombe family also departed from St. Helena in the same ship with General Gourgaud. The friendly relations existing between this excellent English family and the Emperor rendered them obnoxious to the governor. Mr. Balcombe consequently found it necessary to resign his situation. In the governor's official documents, it is said,

"Although Sir Hudson Lowe had no tangible cause of complaint against him (Mr. Balcombe), he was not without strong suspicion that his relations with Longwood were not limited to the ostensible duties of his office. His close intimacy with O'Meara, with whose conduct the governor was becoming daily more dissatisfied, of itself justified some jealousy of his actions."

The Emperor was not willing that his friends should suffer for their kindness to him. With his accustomed munificence, he presented Mr. Balcombe with bills upon London to the amount of fourteen thousand dollars, and also settled upon him an annual pension of twenty-four hundred dollars. In the letter which accompanied this gift, so characteristic of his noble heart, he wrote,

"I fear that your resignation of your employment in this island is caused by the quarrels and annoyances drawn upon you by the relations established between your family and Longwood, in consequence of the hospitality which you showed me on my first arrival in St. Helena. I would not wish you ever to regret having known me."

Mrs. Abell, who was then but a child, thus touchingly alludes to the parting interview:

"A day or two before we embarked, my father, my sister, and myself rode to Longwood, to bid adieu to the Emperor. He was in his room, surrounded by books, which had arrived a few days before. He seemed much depressed at our leaving the island, and said he sincerely regretted the cause. He hoped my dear mother's health would soon be restored, and sent many affectionate messages to her, she being too ill to accompany us to Longwood. When we had sat with him some time, he walked with us in his garden, and with a sickly smile pointed to the ocean spread out before us, bounding the view, and said,

"'Soon you will be sailing away toward England, leaving me to die on this miserable rock. Look at those dreadful mountains; they are my prison walls. You will soon hear that the Emperor Napoleon is dead.'

"I burst into tears, and sobbed as though my heart would break. He seemed much moved at the sorrow manifested by us. I had left my handkerchief in the pocket of my side-saddle, and seeing the tears run fast down my cheeks, Napoleon took his own from his pocket and wiped them away, telling me to keep the handkerchief in remembrance of that sad day.

"We afterward returned and dined with him. My heart was too full of grief to swallow; and when pressed by Napoleon to eat some of my favorite bon-bons and creams, I told him my throat had a great swelling in it, and I could take nothing.

"The hour of bidding adieu came at last. He affectionately embraced my sister and myself, and bade us not forget him; adding that he should ever remember our friendship and kindness to him, and thanked us again and again for all the happy hours he had passed in our society. He asked me what I should like to have in remembrance of him. I replied I should value a lock of his hair more than any other gift he could present. He then sent for Monsieur Marchand, and desired him to bring in a pair of scissors and cut off four locks of hair for my father and mother, my sister and myself, which he did. I still possess that lock of hair; it is all left me of the many tokens of remembrance of the great Emperor."

April 10. Sir Hudson Lowe sent a communication to Dr. O'Meara forbidding him to pass from the limits of Longwood. No reasons were assigned for this extraordinary measure by which a British officer was arbitrarily imprisoned. He was prohibited from holding any intercourse with the French save upon subjects connected with his profession. By his imprisonment within the limits of Longwood he was cut off from all intercourse with the English. Dr. O'Meara, thus insulted, immediately tendered to the governor his resignation as physician to Napoleon, and also wrote a letter to Count Bertrand, informing him of the circumstances which had compelled him to take this step. The Emperor, hearing of this, sent for the doctor to take leave of him. Taking his kind physician by the hand, he said, with much emotion,

"Well, doctor, you are going to quit us. Will the world conceive that they have been base enough to make attempts upon my physician? Since you are no more than a simple lieutenant, subjected to arbitrary power and to military discipline, you have no longer the independence necessary to render your services useful to me. I thank you for your care. Quit as soon as you can this abode of darkness and of crimes. I shall expire upon that pallet, consumed by disease, and without any assistance; but your country will be eternally dishonored by my death."

Dr. O'Meara was kept in confinement at Longwood twenty-seven days, without trial or accusation. During this time the dying Emperor received no medical advice, as he resolutely refused to accept another physician appointed by his brutal jailer.

In the mean time, Sir Hudson Lowe was detected in fabricating false bulletins respecting Napoleon's health, which were signed by a physician who did not see the Emperor. The detection of this duplicity, which was proved beyond all denial, created quite a sensation at St. Helena, and excited the indignation of the commissioners of the allied powers. Baron Sturmer said to Sir Hudson Lowe, " To provoke the resignation of the physician at Longwood by the rigors of military discipline, and, at the same time, to cause false bulletins to be drawn up by a medical man who did not see the Emperor, is to authorize a crime beforehand in case of the Emperor's death. I consider myself bound to protest against such measures."

In Sir Hudson Lowe's defense we read, " Baron Sturmer, the Austrian commissioner, was removed from St. Helena at the end of June, in consequence of his persisting in unauthorized communications with the French at Longwood."

After keeping Dr. O'Meara twenty-seven days in confinement, the Emperor during all this time receiving no medical advice whatever, for he would not receive to his sick-chamber a physician who came but as the creature and the spy of Sir Hudson Lowe, the governor, becoming alarmed by public sentiment at St. Helena, and by the indignant remonstrances of the commissioners, removed the restrictions from the insulted physician. O'Meara eagerly returned again to his suffering patient.

May 16. The governor, growing more and more irritable and malignant, issued a proclamation, which was placarded in all the most conspicuous places, interdicting all officers, inhabitants, and other persons from holding any correspondence or communication with the foreign persons under detention on the island.

The months of June and July passed sadly away, while the Emperor remained in his room with his books and his pen, his health rapidly failing, his limbs swelling, and a lingering and painful death dragging slowly on. He appeared cheerful with his friends, and seldom was any complaint heard to escape his lips. Those who loved him endeavored to shield him from the assaults of the governor; and the days at St. Helena were filled up with constant conflicts between Sir Hudson Lowe and all who had any sympathy with Napoleon. Wisely the friends of the Emperor refrained from annoying him with the recital of their incessant conflicts with their brutal jailer.

July 25. As Dr. O'Meara was returning to his room from the sick-bed of the Emperor, he received an order from Sir Hudson Lowe commanding him immediately to leave Longwood, and to hold no further communication whatever with *General Bonaparte*. " Humanity," says Dr. O'Meara, " the duties of my profession, and the actual state of Napoleon's health, alike forbade a compliance with this unfeeling command. I determined to disobey it, whatever might be the consequences."

O'Meara immediately returned to the Emperor and informed him of the order he had received. The Emperor replied solemnly,

"The crime will soon be consummated. I have lived too long for them. Your ministers are very bold. When the Pope was in France, sooner would I have cut off my right arm than have signed an order for the removal of his surgeon. When you arrive in Europe, you will either go yourself or send to my brother Joseph. You will inform him that I desire he shall give you the parcel containing the private and confidential letters of the Emperors Alexander and Francis, the King of Prussia, and the other sovereigns of Europe with me, which I delivered to his care at Rochefort. You will publish them, to cover with shame those sovereigns, and manifest to the world the abject homage which those vassals paid to me when asking favors or supplicating for their thrones. When I was strong and in power, they implored my protection and the honor of my alliance, and licked the dust from under my feet. Now, in my old age, they basely oppress, and take from me my wife and child. I require you to do this; and if you see any calumnies published of me during the time that you have been with me, and if you can say, 'I have seen with my own eyes that this is not true,' contradict them."

He then presented O'Meara with a superb snuff-box and a statue of himself, and said,

"On your arrival in Europe, make inquiries about my family, and communicate to the members of it that I do not wish that any of them should

ADIEU TO O'MEARA.

come to St. Helena, to witness the miseries and humiliation under which I labor. You will express the sentiments which I preserve for them. You will bear my affections to my good Louisa, to my excellent mother, and to Pauline. If you see my son, embrace him for me. May he never forget that he was born a French prince. Testify to Lady Holland the sense I entertain of her kindness, and the esteem which I bear to her." He then threw his arms around Dr. O'Meara's neck, warmly embraced him, and said, "Adieu, O'Meara. We shall never meet again. May you be happy."

As O'Meara left the Emperor's room, he was arrested by a British officer, taken as a prisoner to Jamestown, where he was placed on board a ship of war, and on the 2d of August he sailed for England. Sir Hudson Lowe, having thus got rid of Dr. O'Meara, immediately sent Dr. Verling to Longwood; but the Emperor, thus outraged, refused to receive a physician of Sir Hudson Lowe's appointing. For two months the Emperor, in consequence of the restrictions imposed upon him, had not been out of doors. He often passed hours of his sleepless nights alone, pacing his chamber in his dressing-gown. He uttered no complaints, but his friends could discern in his tottering frame and wasted cheek the indications of the anguish which consumed his heart.

"During more than two months," says Count Montholon, "the contest with Sir Hudson Lowe concerning the admission of an English physician into the service of the Emperor was incessant. To all his offers the grand marshal or I answered, 'Let us choose for ourselves, and place the person chosen in the same position as was at first enjoyed by Dr. O'Meara.'

"At length, on the 28th of September, no longer able to conceal from himself the rapid progress of disease caused by want of exercise, Sir Hudson Lowe enlarged the circle of our free walks, and left us for a time at rest. The Emperor's mind was less occupied by insults, which were not daily recalled to him. He gradually resumed his accustomed walks in his little garden, where it was easy for the orderly officer to get sight of him, either by day or by night, for the sentinels had orders to inform him as soon as they were certain that the Emperor had left his apartments.

"The Emperor again resumed his habit of work, and dictated some notes about his return from Elba."

For more than a year Dr. Verling remained at Longwood by the appointment of the governor, but Napoleon refused to receive a physician who was assigned to him as though he were a galley-slave, and without any regard to his own choice. Toward the end of December the Emperor's health again rapidly and alarmingly failed. In a moment of pain and peril, a month later, General Bertrand obtained permission of the Emperor to send for Dr. Stockoe, surgeon on board the *Conqueror*. The Emperor was ready to accept him as his physician, and Dr. Stockoe was willing to enter upon the duties of his office; but the fact that the Emperor had selected him, though he was an Englishman, and a surgeon on board an English ship, was his condemnation in the eyes of the governor. After a few calls at Longwood, he was prohibited from making any more visits, was tried and condemned by a court-martial for his sympathy with his dying patient, *and was punished for the crime by dismission from service.*

Such was the melancholy situation of the Emperor as the last hours of the year 1818 were tolled.

CHAPTER XLVII.
1819.

New Outrages—Departure of Madam Montholon—Noble Protest—Arrival of Dr. Antommarchi and the Ecclesiastics—Conversation with Antommarchi—The Books and the Portrait—Protest of Dr. Antommarchi—Corsica as a Retreat—Amiability of the Emperor—The Ancestry of Napoleon.

THE months of January and February of the new year came and went, bringing no change. Lord Bathurst now authorized Sir Hudson Lowe to compel General Bonaparte to exhibit himself twice a day to a British orderly officer.

"Should his system of seclusion," says this order, "render it necessary to adopt some compulsory mode, you will instruct the orderly officer to take proper measures for obtaining a view of his person."

Napoleon still kept secluded in his room, occasionally walking for a few moments in his garden, while his friends endeavored by all possible means to shield him from insult, and to keep the merciless governor at bay. The months of March, April, May, June, July, and August lingered slowly away in melancholy monotony. The gloom of a living burial brooded over Longwood. The Emperor, still refusing to accept Sir Hudson Lowe's physician, was suffering severely, and was evidently fast descending to the tomb. The governor had so far respected the dying sufferer as to refrain from intruding into his chamber by breaking down the door. Sir Hudson Lowe, that he might have his prisoner entirely to himself, was every day threatening to send away Count Bertrand and Count Montholon; but the firm soul of the Emperor, even by such torture, could not be brought to submission to this miserable tyrant.

The health of Madam Montholon was so utterly prostrated by the climate of St. Helena, that it was necessary, in order to save her life, that she should leave the island and return to Europe. Count Montholon, with devotion to his noble friend which must ever win the admiration of the world, still remained to cheer the captive in his hours of sickness and of sorrow. Early in July Madam Montholon sailed from St. Helena. The Emperor was much affected in taking leave of his kind companion. Sick and alone, she was to take the long journey to Europe. Love for the Emperor induced both husband and wife to submit to so painful a separation. As Napoleon bade her adieu, affection and emotion flooded his heart, and he burst into tears. He presented her, in parting, with some of the beautiful ivory ornaments which had been sent to him by Captain Elphinstone.

On the 29th of August Colonel Reade communicated to Counts Montholon and Bertrand that the orderly officer was commanded to *see* the Emperor every day, and to *force* his way into his sick-chamber if this were necessary; and that "if any opposition is attempted, those persons making this opposition will expose themselves to all the risk and danger which may follow, as well as to all other consequences which would result from such an act."

The Emperor dictated the following reply, which they were to present to the orderly officer if he insisted upon admission:

"You wish to violate the privacy of the Emperor's apartments, which have until now been respected, and which are under the protection of the law of nations, and of the strict decrees of your government. None but the Prince Regent or the Privy Council can make legal restrictions. They have been aware these four years that the Emperor's choice between an ignominious treatment and death is by no means doubtful. Alone, ill, debarred from all communication with the universe, or even with the English officers or inhabitants on this rock, he presents his throat to the poniards of his murderers. They need seek for no pretext.

"I reiterate that the Emperor would prefer the refuge of a tomb to ignominious treatment. He has sacrificed every thing, abandoned every thing, and reduced himself to the most miserable life, in order to satisfy the hatred of his enemies. If their vengeance is not yet disarmed, let them strike him down at a single blow. It will be a benefit, since it will put a termination to the agony which has lasted since the 11th of August, and in which pleasure seems to be taken in holding him under the knife."

Several days passed after this during which the Emperor remained unmolested, as Sir Hudson Lowe was not quite prepared to put him in chains, or to order a dragoon to shoot him down in his chamber. Napoleon was called a *prisoner of war;* but never before, in the history of civilized nations, was a prisoner of war so treated. On the 4th of September the governor informed Count Montholon that he had, by his communications, incurred the penalty of being sent to the Cape of Good Hope, there to await the ulterior orders of his government; that, as a last testimony of respect to General Bonaparte, he had refrained from putting this penalty into execution, but that it would be well for Count Montholon to keep this in mind.

The British government at last consented that the friends of Napoleon should send him another physician from Europe. The Emperor could have no correspondence with his friends, and knew nothing, except by rumor, of this arrangement. He was cut off from all intercourse with his kindred, as if he were consigned to the tomb.

September 19. Dr. Antommarchi, with two ecclesiastics, the aged Abbé Buonavita and the Abbé Vignali, arrived at St. Helena. Various circumstances led the Emperor to apprehend that this new physician was but a creature of Sir Hudson Lowe, to fulfill the functions of a spy. Counts Montholon and Bertrand, however, made favorable reports, and the Emperor decided to see the doctor and the ecclesiastics.*

---

* That the Emperor had some cause for apprehension in this respect is evident from the following dispatch from Lord Bathurst to Sir Hudson Lowe:

September 22. At two o'clock in the afternoon Dr. Antommarchi was admitted into the narrow and darkened chamber of the Emperor. It was his first interview. Napoleon was in his bed, and so little light penetrated the curtained windows that it was some time before the doctor could discern any object whatever in the room. The Emperor, perceiving this, in gentle tones requested him to approach his bedside.

He questioned him very minutely respecting his parentage, his past history, his motives for consenting to come to such a miserable rock, and his medical education. Satisfied with his answers, he said, frankly,

"You shall be my physician. Consider me as your father. Now give me some intelligence respecting my relations. Begin with my mother. She is not disheartened by adversity? She bears it with courage, resignation, and dignity? Does she receive company? Does she go out into the world? What kind of a life does she lead?"

"A very retired life," the doctor replied. "All her thoughts, her wishes, are at St. Helena. She only waits for a single word to brave the dangers of the sea, and to fold you in her arms."

"She has been all her life," said Napoleon, "an excellent woman, a mother unequaled. She has always loved me most tenderly. Does she often see her sons and Pauline? How are they? What do they say about me? State to me, with precision, all that every one of them has commissioned you to say to me. What did my mother say?"

"That she herself," Antommarchi replied, "her children, and her fortune are at your majesty's disposal; that, on the slightest intimation, she would give up all she possesses, even though she should endure the greatest misery."

This noble woman had transmitted to Napoleon a schedule of her property, praying him to hold at his command every thing which belonged to her. When some one represented that by this course she would reduce herself to absolute indigence, she replied, "*What consequence is it? When I am utterly destitute, I will take my staff and implore charity for the mother of Napoleon.*"

"And how is Lucien?" inquired the Emperor.

"Lucien had arranged with Joseph that they should each of them come and spend three years with your majesty, if you did not disapprove of it."

The British government would not allow Napoleon to be solaced by this act of fraternal kindness. Lucien applied, as we have before mentioned, to the British ministers, to be allowed to proceed to St. Helena, to share the captivity of his brother for two years, with or without his wife and children. He engaged not to occasion any augmentation of expense, and promised to submit to every restriction imposed upon his brother, or that might be imposed upon himself, either before his departure or after his return. This humane request was cruelly refused.

"You will find, I think, Buonavita a very harmless man. The surgeon is reckoned very intelligent, but I think will not be disposed to be troublesome, as he is apparently inclined to make advances to the government by preparing to dedicate the work he is completing to the Prince Regent."

"And how is Pauline?" Napoleon inquired.

"She only awaits the permission of your majesty to join you."

Napoleon smiled gratefully. These proofs of continued affection were gleams of joy to his imprisoned spirit. For a few moments there was entire silence. His heart yearned for his friends, but he could not endure the thought of calling them to share his misery. At length he sadly replied,

"No, I can not allow any of the members of my family to come and expose themselves to the insults of the English, and to witness the indignities which are offered me here. It is quite enough that I am obliged to endure them."

Napoleon then continued to make many minute inquiries respecting all the members of his family and of various personal friends, and then he dismissed his new physician. After the lapse of a few hours Napoleon sent for him again. The room was dimly lighted by a single wax candle. The Emperor was dressed, and reclining upon his sofa; Count Montholon and General Bertrand were with him. Napoleon immediately entered into conversation with his physician upon anatomy, physiology, and the phenomena of generation.

"His observations," says Antommarchi, "were learned, just, and precise, abounding with new views and ideas on the subjects he was discussing. He made me undergo a rigorous examination in the shape of a conversation which lasted above an hour. I was fortunate enough to answer his questions in a manner that satisfied him, and he expressed his satisfaction in very kind and highly flattering terms, after which he bade me retire."

At the close of a frank and touching interview with the two abbés, the Emperor said, "We have been too long deprived of the ordinances of religion not to be eager to enjoy them immediately, now that they are within our power. Hereafter we will have the communion service every Sabbath, and we will observe the fête-days recognized by the Concordat. I wish to establish at St. Helena the religious ceremonies which are celebrated in France. On these occasions we will erect a movable altar in the dining-room. You, Monsieur Abbé, are aged and infirm. I will select the hour which will be most convenient for you. You may officiate between nine and ten o'clock in the morning."

In the evening the Emperor was alone with Count Montholon. The count was not a religious man. He had frankly said, "In the midst of camps I forgot religion." Napoleon, with great joy, informed Montholon of his intention to attend mass the next day. He then uttered the following remarkable confession:

"Upon the throne, surrounded by generals far from devout — yes, I will not deny it — I had too much regard for public opinion, and far too much timidity, and, perhaps, I did not dare to say aloud, *I am a believer.* I said, *Religion is a power—a political engine.* But even then, if any one had questioned me directly, I should have replied, 'Yes, I am a Christian.' And if it had been necessary to confess my faith at the price of martyrdom, I should have found all my firmness. Yes, I should have endured it rather than deny my religion. But, now that I am at St. Helena, why should I dissemble that which I believe at the bottom of my heart? Here I live for myself. I wish for a priest. I desire the communion of the Lord's Supper, and to confess what I believe. I will go to the mass. I will not force any one to accompany me there. But those who love me will follow me."

General Bertrand was an avowed unbeliever, and often displeased Napoleon by speaking disrespectfully of sacred things. The Emperor was one day, about this time, conversing with him upon Atheism. "Your spirit," said Napoleon, " is it the same as the spirit of the herdsman whom you see in the valley below, feeding his flocks ? Is there not as great a distance between you and him as between a horse and a man ? But how do you know this ? You have never seen his spirit. No, the spirit of a beast has the endowment of being invisible. It has that privilege equally with the spirit of the most exalted genius.

"But you have talked with the herdsman, you have examined his countenance, you have questioned him, and his responses have told you what he is. You judge, then, the cause from the effects, and you judge correctly. Certainly *your* reason, your intelligence, your faculties are vastly above those of the herdsman. Very well ; I judge in the same way. Divine effects compel me to believe in a divine cause. Yes, there is a divine cause, a sovereign reason, an Infinite being. That cause is the cause of causes. That reason is the reason creative of intelligence. There exists an Infinite being, compared with whom you, General Bertrand, are but an atom ; compared with whom I, Napoleon, with all my genius, am truly nothing—*a pure nothing:* do you understand ? I perceive him, God, I see him, I have need of him, I believe in him. If you do not perceive him, if you do not believe in him, very well, so much the worse for you. But you will, General Bertrand, yet believe in God. I can pardon many things, but I have a horror of an Atheist and a materialist. Think you that I can have any sympathies in common with a man who does not believe in the existence of the soul ? who believes that he is but a lump of clay, and who wishes that I may be also, like him, but a lump of clay ?"

September 23. The doctor found Napoleon in bed, languid, appetiteless, and enduring severe pain. As Antommarchi was studying his symptoms, the Emperor's questions were unceasing. They were sometimes gloomy, and sometimes enlivened by pleasantry. " Goodness, indignation, and mirthfulness," says Antommarchi, " were alternately expressed by his words and his countenance."

"Well, doctor," said the Emperor, " am I yet destined to disturb for a long time the digestion of the rulers of the earth ? I think that they will not succeed in putting the fame of our victories under the ban of Europe. It will be handed down from age to age. It will proclaim the conquerors and the conquered ; those who were generous and those who were not ; and posterity will judge. I do not dread its decisions.

" You have given up every thing to come and attend upon me. It is but fair that I should also do something. I therefore resign myself. Let physic command. I submit to its decisions, and intrust myself into your hands. But, for that purpose, I think it right to give to you an account of the habits I have contracted, and of the affections to which I am subject." He then briefly mentioned his habits of life.

Upon Antommarchi expressing admiration of such uncommon temperance, the Emperor resumed,

"On our march with the army of Italy, I always had some wine, some bread, and a roasted fowl fastened to my saddle-bow. That provision sufficed for a whole day. I may even say that I often shared it with my suite. I thus saved time, and economized on the table for the field of battle. I eat fast, and masticate very little. My meals, therefore, do not consume much of my time. This is not what you must approve, I know. But, in the situation in which I am placed, what need I trouble myself about care and mastication? I am attacked with chronic liver complaint, a disease endemic to this horrible climate; I must fall a prey to it. I must expiate on this rock the glory I have shed over France, and the blows I have inflicted upon England. And see how they proceed! It is now more than a year since they have deprived me of all medical assistance! I have not been allowed to have a physician in whom I had confidence, and have been debarred from the right of trying the resources of art!

"It is an additional act of cruelty on the part of the English government to have selected for this office such a man as Sir Hudson Lowe. But iniquity seeks iniquity, and guesses where it is to be found. Ministers never meditate any atrocity without meeting with some corsair ready to assist them in the execution. I abdicated in favor of my son and of the Constitution, and freely and voluntarily bent my steps toward England, where I wished to live in retirement, and under the protection of its laws. Its laws! Does aristocracy know any law? Is there a crime it will hesitate to commit, or a right it will scruple to trample under foot? Its chiefs have all lain prostrate before my eagles. To some I gave crowns out of the fruit of my victories. I replaced others on their thrones, from which victory had hurled them. I showed clemency, magnanimity toward all, and all have betrayed me, deserted me, and basely contributed to rivet my chains. I am at the mercy of a freebooter."

"I endeavored," says Antommarchi, "to calm the Emperor's agitation. He had not been out for eighteen months. I represented to him the dangers to which he exposed himself by so prolonged a state of inactivity, and requested him not to remain pent up in his apartment, but to ride out and breathe the open air."

"No," said Napoleon; "insults have long confined me to these cabins, and now want of strength prevents me from leaving them. Examine that leg. I feel that it gives way under me. You feel too gently; press harder. Tell me whether Nature is in league with this Calabrian, and whether the climate will soon yield up to the minister the corpse which he waits for?"

September 25. The Emperor passed a cheerful night, and in the morning appeared in cheerful spirits. In conversation with Antommarchi, he inquired,

"Have you not brought me some books?"

"We have some, sire," Antommarchi replied, "but I do not know what they are. It was not I who purchased them."

"I warn you," said the Emperor, "that I will see every one of them."

"But, sire," said Antommarchi, "some libels may have slipped in among them."

"Poh!" said the Emperor, "the sun has no more spots. The herd of libelists has exhausted its pasture. Let me see every thing."

It so happened that at this moment a cart approached Longwood containing the boxes of books. "They are most welcome," said the Emperor. "I shall be relieved from the weight of a few hours. Let them be brought into the drawing-room. I will see them opened."

The boxes were brought in, broken open, and some books were taken out of them and handed to the Emperor. "No," said he, earnestly, "that is not what I want. Look into the box; examine it carefully: make haste! A package sent from Europe must contain something else. Books are not the first thing a *father* has to look at."

Napoleon was not disappointed. Soon a picture was found of his idolized son, which had been put in by Eugene. Tears immediately flooded the eyes of the Emperor. He gazed upon the beautiful lineaments of his boy long, silently, and earnestly, and pressed them with fervor to his lips. The attendants, moved by these outgushings of parental love, stopped their work, and stood in an attitude of religious awe. "Dear boy!" exclaimed the Emperor;

NAPOLEON RECEIVING THE PORTRAIT OF HIS SON.

"if he does not fall a victim to some political atrocity, he will not be unworthy of his father."

The unpacking was soon again resumed. As the books were taken out, Napoleon hastily examined them, and laid them aside. He was disappointed in not finding some important works which he hoped would have been sent him, particularly the celebrated historical work of the Greek historian Polybius, and Madam de Staël's "Germany."

"Why did you not devote," said he, "some four thousand dollars to make these purchases? My mother would have paid them, and you would have administered consolation to me by bringing me some books. If at least I had Polybius! But perhaps it will reach me from some other quarter."

The work did reach him, a short time before his death, through the kindness of Lady Holland. She was one among many thousand of the most generous spirits in England who mourned over the inhuman treatment of Napoleon.

Some bundles of newspapers were then taken out of the box. "Ah!" said the Emperor, "this will bring up the arrears of my information about the state of affairs. It is curious enough to see the wise measures which were to cancel the recollection of my tyranny! Poor Europe! what convulsions are preparing for it."

September 26. The Emperor passed a sleepless night, and endeavored to beguile the weary hours by reading the newspapers. As Dr. Antommarchi entered in the morning, Napoleon was looking upon the portrait of his idolized child, which he held in his hand.

"Here," said he, "place this admirable child by the side of his mother, there, nearer to the mantle-piece. You know her by her blooming looks. That is Maria Louisa. She holds her son in her arms. That other picture, do you know it also? It is the imperial prince. You do not guess what graceful hand held the needle that sketched this representation of his features. It was that of his mother. That picture before which you now stand is Maria Louisa again. The two others are portraits of Josephine. I loved her tenderly. You are examining that large clock. It served to wake the Great Frederick early in the morning. I took it at Potsdam. It was all Prussia was worth. Move the bust of the imperial prince to the left; it is too much to the right. The ornaments of my mantle-piece are, as you see, not very sumptuous. The bust of my son, two candlesticks, two gilt cups, two vials of eau de Cologne, a pair of scissors to cut nails with, and a small glass, are all it contains. This is no longer the splendor of the Tuileries. But no matter; if I am decayed in my power, I am not in my glory. I preserve all my recollections. Few sovereigns have immolated themselves for their people. A sacrifice so immense is not without its charms."

September 27. The Emperor passed another sleepless night, and had been reading for several hours when Dr. Antommarchi entered. "The dampness of the two rooms was excessive," says the doctor. "It attacked and destroyed every thing. The paltry nankeen which served as tapestry was hanging in rags against the walls. We took it down, and endeavored to place before the Emperor's eyes something more pleasing, by putting up, in its stead, some muslin we had purchased, and which we adorned with some fine birds of Egypt, of which we had a collection painted on paper. We grouped our paintings, and placed in the midst of them an eagle, which was to protect and guide them. 'Dear eagle,' said the Emperor, 'it would still soar on high if those whom it covered with its wings had not arrested its flight.'"

September 28. The Emperor was a little better. When Dr. Antommarchi called, and recommended a bath and more exercise, Napoleon said,

"While you were in bed, doctor, I was following your prescription. I had risen at daybreak, and was walking out to take a little fresh air. I am now turning over some ideas which have occurred to me respecting an operation in which my orders were not well executed."

"The flannel bag," says the doctor, "was on the ground, and Napoleon standing up, so that I had an opportunity of admiring his costume. It consisted of a white dressing-gown, a pair of very wide white trowsers with feet, red slippers, a Madras shawl around his head, no cravat, and the shirt collar open. I examined this singular dress. The Emperor perceived it, and said, laughing,

"Ah! I see what arrests your attention. And, to punish you for your want of respect for my dress, I close my door against your doings until tomorrow. I have some algebraical calculations to make."

October 3. The Emperor walked out into the garden, accompanied by Dr. Antommarchi. The following conversation took place:

"The climate," said Napoleon, "has been well chosen. It will not let its victim escape. But you—how do you find yourself in your situation? Are the eighteen hundred dollars assigned you sufficient to satisfy your wants?"

"I am too happy, sire," said Antommarchi, "in being near your person. I did not seek fortune. My only ambition has been to offer my services to your majesty."

"That is very well, my dear doctor," said the Emperor, "but to unite both things is better still. I give you what I gave at Paris. Circumstances are no longer the same, but for that very reason I wish your temporary salary to be equivalent to your wants. How long do you intend to remain here?"

"As long," said Antommarchi, "as my services are agreeable to your majesty."

"Do you know," said the Emperor, "that my surgeon is also the surgeon of the establishment? that, being alone, he must be at the same time surgeon, physician, and apothecary?"

"I know it, sire," Dr. Antommarchi replied. "I am devoted to you forever. Dispose of me as you may think fit."

"Well," said the Emperor, "I will not detain you more than five years on this rock. After that I will settle upon you a pension of fifteen or eighteen hundred dollars a year. You will then return to Europe, having enough to lead an independent life. You will be able to resume your anatomical labors, and will, in time, be ranked among the first physiologists of the age.

You are entitled to my gratitude, esteem, and affection for the sacrifices you have made for me."

October 4. The Emperor was very languid and dejected. He walked out with Dr. Antommarchi, and sat down upon a little green knoll beneath the shade of a tree. Before him was spread out an extensive scene of desolation and gloom. Barren volcanic rocks and blackened crags pierced the clouds with the monotony of dreariness.

"Ah, doctor," said Napoleon, "where is the fine climate of Corsica?" After a moment's pause, he continued, "Fate has not permitted me to see once more those sites endeared to me by all the recollections of my infant days. I intended to reserve to myself the sovereignty of that island, and I could have done so, but an intrigue, a moment of ill-humor, altered my choice, and I preferred Elba. Had I followed my first idea and retired to Ajaccio, perhaps I should not have thought of seizing again the reins of power. I should not have been vulnerable on every point. The promises made would not have been broken, and I should not be here. I had some idea of seeking refuge there in 1815. I was certain of uniting the opinions, wishes, and efforts of all, and I should have found myself in a condition to brave the malevolence of the allied powers. You know the inhabitants of our mountains! You know their energy, their perseverance, their courage, and with what a noble and undaunted mind they face the enemy!

"It was not, therefore, the sentiments of the population which gave me the least uneasiness; but it would have been said that I got out of the way —that I sought the port while all were perishing. I would not seek for a refuge while so many brave men were perishing. I resolved, therefore, to retire to America, and bent my steps toward England; but I was far from foreseeing on what horrible terms she grants her hospitality. I was also deterred by another consideration: once in Corsica, I did not fear the issue of the struggle; but I should have been in the centre of the Mediterranean; the eyes of France and Italy would have been turned toward me, and the effervescence would not have subsided. In order to secure their own tranquillity, the sovereigns would have been obliged to attack me, and the island would have been torn by war. I could not bear the idea of being reproached as the cause of its misfortunes.

"Ah, doctor, what recollections Corsica has left me! I still enjoy, in imagination, its sites and its mountains. Methinks I still tread its soil, and know it even by the odor it exhales. I intended to ameliorate its condition— to render it happy; in a word, to do every thing in its favor; and the rest of France would not have disapproved of my predilection. But our disasters came, and I could not carry into effect the plans which I had formed.

"But my enemies have had the art of making me waste my existence on the field of battle. They have transformed into the demon of war the man who desired only the blessings of peace. The nations have been deceived by the stratagem. All have risen, and I have been overpowered."

Antommarchi was greatly affected as the Emperor was speaking, and tears filled his eyes.

"What is the matter?" inquired the Emperor.

"Ah! sire," Antommarchi replied, "pardon my agitation; I can not control my feelings. The contrast is too striking."

"Doctor," said Napoleon, "our country! our country! If St. Helena were France, I should love even this frightful rock."

October 5. "I was not familiar," says Antommarchi, "with the forms of ceremony observed toward the Emperor, and endeavored to learn them, and to model my behavior upon that of the individuals who surrounded his person. None of us ever appeared before his majesty without being previously announced; and, in his presence, we were respectful and attentive, standing up uncovered, without presuming to approach or to put our hats on until invited to do so. Nobody addressed him unless in general conversation, in which case the Emperor listened, answered, animated the discussion, and enlivened it by his wit, showing himself at the same time brilliant, just, kind, and full of amenity.

"Napoleon was to us amiable and affectionate, seeking to centre in himself all our affections. His advice was that of a father, his reproaches those of a friend. In his anger he was impetuous and terrible, and would not brook contradiction; but, the fit over, he was all kindness and attention, and tried by every means in his power to console those whom he had ill treated. His actions, the tone of his voice, all expressed his kindly feelings, and manifested his regret. Every thing relating to these rules of general conduct was easily understood, and I had soon learned it. But etiquette has its forms, which it is impossible to divine. I did not know, for instance, that it forbade leaving the Emperor's room until ordered by him to withdraw.

"Napoleon had fallen asleep, and, fearful of disturbing him, I left the room, but I had not yet reached my own before he was awake again. He looked round, and not seeing me, rang the bell, and sent for me. I went back to him, and found him again asleep. He awoke a second time with a deep sigh, and, fixing his eyes upon me, said,

"'Oh! you are still here.'

"'Yes, sire, but I had gone away.'

"'Ah!' said he, rising, looking steadfastly at me, and taking me by the ear, laughing at the same time, "great Cape Corsican doctor, you leave me alone! you withdraw without my leave! You are a novice, and I forgive you; but neither the grand marshal nor General Montholon would have retired from my bedside until I sent them away.'

"I entreated him to excuse my ignorance. He again smiled and said, 'Ah! you are a novice.'"

October 8. The Emperor, feeling in better health, and his spirits reviving, sent for the children of General Bertrand. As they had not seen him for several days, they were overjoyed at the invitation. Full of glee, they hastened to his room, and began to play and sport around him. They made him the arbiter of their discussions, and appealed to him with all the affection and familiarity of children with a father. The lonely chamber of the Emperor became at once the scene of joyful tumults. The Emperor forgot his cares and his griefs, and played with his young companions with all the mirthfulness of a child. He kept them all to dine with him. He took the beautiful little Hortensia Bertrand by his side at the dinner-table. After dinner the noise and the frolic were resumed. At last they withdrew, having extorted from the Emperor the promise that he would see them again the next day.

"How happy," said the Emperor, after they had gone, "they all are when I send for them, or play with them! All their wishes are satisfied. Passions have not yet approached their hearts. They feel the plenitude of existence. Let them enjoy it. At their age, I thought and felt as they do. What storms since! But how much that little Hortensia grows and improves! If she lives, of how many young *élégans* will she not disturb the repose! I shall then be no more."

November 13. The Emperor had passed a good night, and was able to walk into the garden, whither Dr. Antommarchi accompanied him. He was very weak, and having sat down, he looked around him from right to left, and said, with a mournful expression,

"Ah! doctor, where is France and its cheerful climate? If I could but see it once more! If I could but breathe a little air that had passed over that happy country! What a specific is the soil that gave us birth! Antæus renewed his strength by touching the earth; and I feel that this prodigy would be repeated in me, and that I should revive on perceiving our coasts. Our coasts! Ah! I had forgotten that cowardice has taken victory by surprise; its decisions are without appeal.

"But the decrees of Fate are immutable, and every one must submit to his destiny. Mine was to run through the extremes of life, and I set out to accomplish the task allotted to me. My father was going to Versailles as deputy of the nobility of Corsica, and I accompanied him. We passed through Tuscany, where I saw Florence and the grand duke, and arrived at Paris. We were recommended to the queen; my father met with a most flattering reception, and I entered Brienne. I was happy; my ideas began to ferment. I felt a want to learn, to know, to push myself forward, and I devoured the contents of every book I could procure. In a short time I became the theme of universal conversation at the school; I was admired and envied. I felt a consciousness of my own powers, and enjoyed my superiority. Not that there did not already then exist some charitable souls who endeavored to embitter my satisfaction. I had, on arriving at the school, been introduced into a room, in which was a portrait of the Duke of Choiseul, and the sight of that odious man, who had sold my country, had drawn from me an expression of hatred and contempt. This was blasphemy—this was a crime sufficient to efface my success; but I allowed malevolence to vent itself, and applied to study with redoubled ardor and application. I saw what men are, and made my profit of the observation."

One day, as the Emperor was arranging a bed of French beans, he perceived some small roots, and began a dissertation upon the phenomena of vegetation. He analyzed them, and descanted upon them with his usual sagacity, drawing from them the conclusion of the existence of a Superior Being who presides over the wonders of nature.

THE EMPEROR A GARDENER.

"You do not believe in that, doctor," said he; "you physicians are above those weaknesses. Tell me, you who are so well acquainted with the human frame, who have searched it in all its turnings and windings, have you ever met the soul under your scalpel? Where does the soul reside? In what organ?"

At another time the Emperor was much interested in observing some ants who frequented a table in his bed-room upon which there usually stood some sugar. He was anxious that they should not be disturbed in their operations; he only now and then moved the sugar, following their maneuvers, and admiring the activity and industry they displayed until they had found it again.

"This is not instinct," said he; "it is much more—it is sagacity, intelligence, the ideal of civil association. But these little beings have not our passions, our cupidity. They assist, but do not destroy each other. I have vainly endeavored to defeat their purpose; I have removed the sugar to every part of the room; they have been one, two, or sometimes three days looking for it, but have always succeeded at last. The idea strikes me to surround the basin with water, and see whether that will stop them. Doctor, send for some."

But water did not stop them; the sugar was still pillaged. The Emperor then substituted vinegar, and the ants no longer ventured to approach.

"You see," said Napoleon, "it is not instinct alone that guides them, they are prompted by something else, but what I know not. However, be the principle which directs them what it may, they offer to man an example worthy of observation and reflection. It is only by perseverance and tenaciousness that any object can be obtained. Had we possessed such unanimity of views! But nations have their moments of forgetfulness and lassitude. Allowance must be made for the weakness of human nature.

"But how ridiculous," continued the Emperor, "are these new dogmas of legitimacy which they now seek to defend! What contradictions! Are these principles in conformity with Scripture, with the laws and maxims of religion? Are nations simple enough to believe themselves the property of a family? Was David, who dethroned Saul, a legitimate? Had he any other rights than those he derived from the consent of his nation? In France various families have succeeded each other on the throne, either by the will of the people or the votes of the Parliaments. The house of Hanover, which succeeded the prince which it dethroned, now reigns because such was the will of the ancestors of the present race of these touchy people, who thought this change of government absolutely necessary to the preservation of their interests and of their religious rites. Some of the old men still living have witnessed the efforts made by the last branch of the Stuarts to land in Scotland, where they were seconded by those whose ideas and sentiments were conformable to their own. The attempt was opposed, and the Stuarts repulsed by an immense majority of the people, whose new interests and opinions were opposed to those of that degenerate family."

December 31. For several months nothing had occurred to interrupt the monotony of the Emperor's existence. He had constructed a small garden near his windows, where he amused himself in the cultivation of vegetables and flowers. Almost all intercourse was cut off between the inmates of Longwood and the detested governor.

On the 31st of December Sir Hudson Lowe sent a note to Longwood informing Count Montholon that, "with the view of persuading *him*," for thus he designated the Emperor, "to take exercise on horseback, and of consulting the convenience of the persons belonging to *his* suite at Longwood, I have taken upon myself to make such additions to the circuit already granted as are explained in the annexed memorandum."

The Emperor could now ride out without being exposed to insult, and could return to his chamber without being challenged and questioned by a sentinel, even if his ride was prolonged a few moments into the grateful evening twilight. Thus, at the close of the year 1819, a faint gleam of sunshine penetrated the gloomy dungeon where the Emperor was immured.

CHAPTER XLVIII.
1820.

New-year's Day—Gardening Operations—Journal of the orderly Officer—Remarks on Waterloo and the Holy Alliance—Interview with the Daughter of Sir Hudson Lowe—Scenes at Fontainebleau—The Emperor's filial Affection—Birth-day Presents—Proposal for Escape—Aversion to Medicine—Public Works of the Emperor—The Fish-basin—Death of the Princess Eliza—Remarks on the Divorce—The Close of the Year.

January 1. The sun at St. Helena rose cloudless on the morning of the 1st of January, 1820. The Emperor received the customary congratulations of his friends with much apparent pleasure. "His manner toward us all," says Montholon, "was one of paternal kindness, and he assured us that it was long since he had felt himself so well." The enlargement of the limits, to which the governor had at last consented, led the Emperor again to seek exercise on horseback. This exercise recruited his health and revived his spirits. He rode frequently about five miles to a lawn in front of the house of Sir William Doveton, and there breakfasted, with his companions, under the shade of some trees. With health returned his recollections and anecdotes, and he resumed his dictations.

"A shelter from the disagreeable trade-winds," Count Montholon writes, "and a little shade from the sun, were two things the want of which, in our small degree of comfort at Longwood, was incessantly felt. The Emperor took up the idea of erecting both one and the other in the small gardens, and he was the first to set to work, giving us all the example of labor.

"It was a picture worthy of being represented by the most celebrated artists, to see the conqueror of so many kingdoms, him who had dictated laws to so many sovereigns, at dawn of day, with his spade in his hand, a broad straw hat on his head, and his feet clad in red morocco slippers, directing our labors, and those, assuredly more useful, of the Chinese gardeners of the establishment. In a few days he succeeded in this manner in raising two circular walls of tufts of bad grass, about eleven or twelve feet high, on a diameter of twenty yards, on a line with his bed-room and the library.

"The walls being finished, the Emperor had twenty-four large trees purchased, and caused them to be planted with two yards square of earth round their roots. The artillery company undertook the charge of transporting them to Longwood, with the help of several hundred Chinese.

"In this manner he created for himself a possibility of taking air and a little exercise at any hour of the day or night, without being annoyed by the sun or the presence of his jailers."

Captain Nicholls was at the time orderly officer at Longwood. He was entirely in the confidence of the governor, and performed his duties in such a manner as to secure his most cordial commendation. He kept his eye vigilantly fixed upon the inmates of Longwood, and reported to the governor every event which occurred. The following extracts from his journal will be read with interest:

"*January* 1. Sowerby saw General Bonaparte in his favorite garden to-day. He was out in the evening till gun-fire (nine o'clock), looking at the boys and others firing crackers.

"*January* 2. General Bonaparte was amusing himself with the pipe of the fire-engine, spouting water on the trees and flowers of his favorite garden.

"*January* 4. I saw General Bonaparte several times to-day, walking about the large garden. He still amuses himself by gardening, that is, superintending; however, he at times takes a watering-pot in his hands.

"*January* 5. General Bonaparte dined under the trees with Count Montholon.

"*January* 9. General Bonaparte was busily employed amid his valets gardening. He had on his head a large straw hat. He did not seem to mind a little rain which was falling.

THE EMPEROR GARDENING.

"*January* 10. I saw General Bonaparte this morning. He was amusing himself in one of his favorite gardens. His morning dress at present consists of a white gown and straw hat, with a long, broad brim. In the afternoon he appears out in a cocked hat, green coat, and white breeches and stockings. He walks a good deal most afternoons in Longwood garden, accompanied by either Count Montholon or Bertrand, and often pays a visit to the Bertrands in the evenings.

"*January* 12. This day the one-eyed cooper came up from Jamestown with a large tub, twelve feet wide, for General Bonaparte's favorite garden, to serve as a reservoir. The cooper told me that the general was very much pleased with the tub, and gave him a glass of wine in consequence with his own hand. The old cooper seemed highly delighted.

"*January* 18. I saw General Bonaparte in his little garden this morning. Counts Bertrand and Montholon busily employed measuring out more ground for the extension of the garden for the general. The general was out a good deal to-day. The day uncommonly fine.

"*January* 19. General Bonaparte was employed superintending the building of a sod wall. He had Count Montholon and all his valets hard at work. The young Bertrands carrying water to wet the sods as they were laid. The general's appearance was rather grotesque this morning. However, he appeared highly amused."

Thus lingered slowly away the months of January, February, and March. On one occasion, at the close of some very eloquent remarks upon the condition of Europe, the Emperor said,

"I had, I repeat, inclosed in a leathern bottle the wind of political storms. The bayonets of the English pierced it at Waterloo. I alone could proceed unattacked by storms to universal regeneration. It is no longer possible, unless by the aid of fearful tempests.

"What will be the result of the proceedings of the Holy Alliance? Europe will sooner or later form but two camps—kings and their followers on one side, nations and their interests on the other. It will no longer be divided by nationality into kingdoms, but will be divided by color, by opinion. Who would venture to predict the crisis, the effects of so many storms now piled heap upon heap on the European horizon? As to the issue, it is indubitable; for enlightenment never retrogrades but to advance more successfully. Nations and kings will regret me, and if ever my son is restored to the French, he may say to them, 'My father's thoughts were of you, on his rock in the midst of the Atlantic; I submit to your sanction the Constitution which he has left as a legacy to me, with his advice, for the grandeur and prosperity of our beloved country.'"

About this time Montholon records the following pleasing incident:

"A walk taken by the Emperor in the direction of Sandy Bay gave him an opportunity of catching a glimpse of Lady Lowe. He thought her very pretty, and could not forbear expressing his regret at not being acquainted with her. A few days afterward, Miss Susannah Johnson, the young and pretty daughter of Lady Lowe, ventured to come alone to Longwood, and begged me to show her the gardens newly created, as if by magic, by the manual labor of the Emperor. I had that moment left his apartment, when I saw Miss Johnson passing the barriers of our inclosure on horseback, and followed only by a groom. When this young girl suddenly arrived, therefore, and, springing lightly to the ground, explained her desire, asking me whether it were not possible to satisfy it, I, believing I might be certain of not meeting the Emperor in the garden, yielded to her wishes, and, offering her my arm, conducted her to the private gardens. We had scarcely gone a hundred paces, however, before, on making a turn in the covered walk, we found ourselves face to face with the Emperor, who, seated on a bench, appeared to be watching us. My surprise was great, but less so, I think, than the impression made on Miss Johnson. Her pretty face was lighted up with indescribable animation, and her looks expressed at once her timid embarrassment and her joy at seeing the Emperor. His manner toward her was amiable and kind. He had a plate of sweetmeats brought to her, appeared to take pleasure in showing her his gardening labors, said not a word which might remind her that she came from Plantation House, and, as she was taking her departure, plucked a rose, and offered it to her as a *souvenir* of what he termed *her pilgrimage.*"

April, May, June, and July passed slowly away, while the Emperor endeavored to beguile the dreadful monotony of Longwood by working in the garden, and by reading, and occasionally dictating to his friends.

July 20. The Emperor was reclining upon his sofa, languid and dejected. Dr. Antommarchi, in defiance of the infamous injunctions of Sir Hudson Lowe, conversed freely with his illustrious patient upon any subject which might interest his mind. Rome was mentioned. The noble mother of Napoleon was there in exile. A crowd of tender recollections rushed upon the mind of the affectionate and dying son. With a trembling lip he spoke of her maternal love, and of the care with which she had watched over his childhood. Turning his eyes to Dr. Antommarchi, he said,

"You, doctor, are very much attached to me. You care not for contrarieties, pain, or fatigue, when you can relieve my sufferings; yet all this is not maternal solicitude. Ah! mamma Letitia!" He could say no more. Weakened by sickness, his emotion overcame him, and, burying his face in his hands, he remained silent.

THE FISH-BASIN.

July 31. Even the bleak rocks of St. Helena looked cheerful this lovely day. The fish-basin was completed, and the Emperor, accompanied by all the children, went into the garden to put some fishes into the water which had thus been provided for them.

August 15. Another anniversary of the Emperor's birth-day had arrived. As usual, he gave presents to the children, and to all the members of the household. "He seemed heartily to share," says Montholon, "the noisy joy with which the munificence of his presents inspired the children. He appeared to be truly happy, as a good father might be in the midst of his family, when, at dinner, he was surrounded by our children, or when he amused himself by exciting their gayety, and drawing forth their little secrets.

"His great pleasure was to constitute himself a judge between them and us. He had accustomed them to this, and really I know not how we should have contrived to preserve our parental authority had he not always found means to adjudge us in the right, at the same time that he persuaded the children that his justice was impartial. But whenever the question agitated related to a piece of bread or jam, or a party of pleasure, his judgment was always in favor of the children."

About this time, a sea-captain returning from the East Indies proposed a plan to take the Emperor to America. When the Emperor was informed of it, he said,

"I thank the captain for his devotedness; but my resolution not to struggle against my destiny is immovable. I should not be six months in America without being assassinated by the Count d'Artois's creatures. Remember the Isle of Elba. Did he not send the *Chouan* Brulard thither to organize my assassination? Had it not been for the brave man whom chance had placed as marshal of the gendarmerie in Corsica, and who caused me to be warned of the condition of this Life Guardsman, who confessed every thing, I should have been assassinated. Every thing is written in Heaven. It is my martyrdom which will restore the crown of France to my dynasty. I see in America nothing but assassination or oblivion. I prefer St. Helena."

October 14. The Emperor was very feeble. Dr. Antommarchi advised the application of blisters.

"*Do you think, then,*" said the Emperor, "*that Sir Hudson Lowe does not torture me enough?* No physicking, doctor," he continued. "We are, as I have often told you, a machine made to live. We are organized for that purpose, and such is our nature. Do not counteract the living principle. Let it alone. Leave it the liberty to defend itself. It will do better than your drugs. Our body is a watch that is intended to go a given time. The watch-maker can not open it, and must, in handling it, grope his way blindfold and at random. For once that he assists and relieves it, by dint of tormenting it with his crooked instruments, he injures it ten times, and at last destroys it.

"You are aware, doctor, that the art of healing consists only in lulling and calming the imagination. That is the reason why the ancients dressed up in robes, and adopted a costume striking and imposing. That costume you have unadvisedly abandoned, and, in so doing, you have exposed the imposture of Galen, and no longer exercise the same powerful influence over your patients. Who knows," he continued, playfully, "whether, if you were suddenly to appear before me with an enormous wig, a cap, and a long train, I should not take you for the god of Health, whereas you are now only the god of Medicine?"

It is affirmed by the companions of the Emperor that he had but little confidence in the medical skill of the doctor. Antommarchi was an anatomical professor of some celebrity, but he had seen very little practice. The Emperor immediately perceived this deficiency, and, to spare the feelings of his kind physician, veiled his want of confidence in his medical adviser by magnifying his want of confidence in medicine.

October 22. The Emperor was quite cheered by a day of freedom from pain. He said to Dr. Antommarchi,

"When my health is once re-established, I shall restore you to your studies. You shall proceed to Europe, and publish your works. I will not suffer you to waste your existence on this horrible rock. You have told me that you do not know France. You will then see that country. You will see those canals, those monuments with which I covered it during the time of my power. The duration of that power has been like that of a flash of lightning. But no matter; it is filled with useful institutions.

"Yes, I have hallowed the Revolution by infusing it into our laws. My code is the sheet-anchor which will save France, and entitle me to the benedictions of posterity. Besides, there are the great public works. The Alps leveled! The plan of that undertaking is one of the first formed at the commencement of my career. I had entered Italy, and finding that the communications with Paris occupied a considerable time, and were attended with much difficulty, I endeavored to render them quicker, and resolved to open them through the valley of the Rhone. I also wished to render that river navigable, and to blow up the rocks under which it ingulfs and disappears. I had sent engineers to the spot. The expense would have been inconsiderable, and I submitted the plan to the Directory. But we were carried away by events: I went to Egypt, and nobody thought any more about it.

"On my return I took it up again. I had dismissed the lawyers, and, having no more obstacles in the way, we applied our hammers to the Alps. We executed what the Romans had not dared to try, and traced through blocks of granite a solid and spacious road, capable of resisting the efforts of time."

October 25. The Emperor, suffering extremely from pain, had at last consented to the application of blisters. Sadly he said to his physician,

"Can any thing be more deplorable than my present condition? This is not life; it is mere existence. My health will never be restored. Even my present situation must be precarious, and perhaps death will soon terminate my sufferings."

The doctor urged that if he would consent to follow the treatment prescribed, he would soon be better.

"You are a doctor," replied the Emperor, "and would promise life to a corpse if it would take pills. But I do not deceive myself. I feel that I am near my end. All the powers of the vital functions are concentrated on the spot which the blisters have excited."

October 26. The Emperor was worse. He sat before a large fire, endeavoring in vain to warm his shivering frame.

"In what a state am I!" said he to the doctor. "Every thing seems to weigh upon me—to fatigue me. I can scarcely support myself. You have not, among the resources of your art, any means of reviving the play of the machine?"

It was all this time supposed that the Emperor was suffering from the liver complaint. All the remedies were directed to meet that disease, which did not exist. (Though a cancer was devouring the Emperor's stomach, it is a remarkable fact that he seldom felt any pain there.)

November 5. The Emperor, while in the bath, found a transient respite from pain. In conversation, he passed in review the works which he had executed in Italy.

"I made roads from Pavia to Padua; from Padua to Fusina and Ponte Longo; from Sarravalle to Belluno and Cadore; and from Vicenza to Novarra. I dug the port of Malomocco; drained the valleys which terminate at Verona; threw bridges over the Adige; restrained the inundations of the Bacchiglione; raised dikes; reconstructed canals and aqueducts; and yet this was only the beginning of what I had planned for Italy."

November 6. The Emperor walked with a tottering step to the fish-basin. He often sat there for hours in silent thought, amusing himself by following the motion of the fishes, and throwing them crumbs of bread. Unfortunately, some mysterious disease suddenly attacked them: they struggled for a few moments, floated on the water, and one after another died. The Emperor was deeply affected by this incident.

"You see," said he, in touching tones of melancholy, "that there is a fatality attached to me. Every thing that I love, every thing that belongs to me, is struck. Heaven and mankind unite to afflict me."

From that moment neither weather nor sickness could prevent him from going daily to visit them himself. At last it was discovered that the fish were poisoned by the cement which had been used in the construction of the basin. A few were rescued alive and placed in a tub.

November 19. In the utmost extreme of lassitude and debility, the Emperor, as he returned from a short walk, threw himself upon his bed, and said to the doctor,

"What a delightful thing rest is! The bed is become for me a place of luxury. I would not exchange it for all the thrones in the world. What an alteration! How fallen am I! I, whose activity was boundless, whose mind never slumbered, am now plunged into a lethargic stupor, and must make an effort even to raise my eyelids! I sometimes dictated upon different subjects to four or five secretaries, who wrote as fast as words could be uttered. But then I was Napoleon. Now I am no longer any thing. My strength, my faculties forsake me. I do not live; I merely exist."

November 20. Dr. Antommarchi makes the mournful record, "The Emperor was absorbed in profound melancholy, and did not pronounce a single word."

December 16. The Emperor passed a night of extreme restlessness. After taking a bath, he endeavored to walk about the drawing-room, but his limbs bent beneath his weight, and he was obliged to sit down.

"See," said he, feeling of his legs, "they are exhausted; there is nothing left—mere skeletons. Every thing must have a term. I am fast approaching mine, and I do not regret it, for I have indeed no reason to be attached to life."

December 26. Newspapers arrived from Europe. The Emperor perused them with great avidity. They contained the intelligence of the death of the Emperor's sister Eliza. The tidings threw him into a state of stupor. He sat in his arm-chair, his head hanging down on his breast, motionless, in inexpressible grief. Deep sighs at intervals escaped him. The doctor entreated him to walk out into the open air. The Emperor silently consented. He rose with difficulty, and, leaning upon the doctor's arm, said, "I am very weak. My trembling legs can hardly support me." It was a lovely day. The Emperor walked as far as the summer-house, when his strength failed, and he sank down upon a bench which was near. After a few moments of silence, he spoke of the death of his sister, and said,

"You see, doctor, that Eliza has just shown us the way. Death, which

PORTRAIT OF ELIZA, THE SISTER OF BONAPARTE.

seemed to have overlooked my family, now begins to strike it. My turn can not be far distant. I have no longer any strength, energy, or activity left. I am no longer Napoleon. Your care is without avail against Fate. Its decrees are immutable, its decisions without appeal. The first person of our family who will follow Eliza to the grave is that great Napoleon who here drags on a miserable existence—who sinks under its weight; but who, however, still keeps Europe in a state of alarm. But as for me, all is over. My days will soon end on this miserable rock."

The Emperor returned to his room and to his bed. He began to converse about Maria Louisa and his idolized son. It was a painful subject, and Antommarchi endeavored to divert his thoughts.

"I understand you, doctor," said the Emperor. "Well, be it so. Let us forget, if indeed the heart of a father can forget." The anguish which the Emperor must have endured in being thus cruelly separated from his wife and child no words can express.

NAPOLEON WITH HIS WIFE AND CHILD.

December 1. The Emperor was increasingly ill. He complained of sharp internal pains resembling the stab of a penknife. Speaking one day of Josephine,

"My divorce," said he, "has no parallel in history, for it did not destroy the ties which united our families, and our mutual tenderness remained unchanged. Our separation was a sacrifice demanded of us by reason, for the interest of my crown and of my dynasty. Josephine was devoted to me; she loved me tenderly; no one ever had a preference over me in her heart. I occupied the first place in it, her children the next. And she was right in thus loving me, for she is the being whom I have most loved, and the remembrance of her is still all-powerful in my mind."

December 31. Under this date Count Montholon makes the following record:

"The night between the 31st of December, 1820, and the 1st of January,

THE EMBARRASSED INTERVIEW.

1821, was one of the last passed in intimate conversation on the recollections of a better time. The disease, which was some months later to deprive us of the Emperor, made, after this time, rapid progress. He daily felt himself less disposed to activity either of mind or body; a general feeling of fatigue oppressed him. He remained sometimes for hours listlessly seated in an easy-chair, and perfectly silent; he who before had passed the greatest part of the day in pacing the apartment, at the same time either dictating, or recalling recollections and collecting materials for his work. I now often remained standing for hours near him, expecting the termination of a phrase, or waiting till he should decide upon rousing himself from his state of torpor otherwise than by these few words, 'Well, my son, what have you now to say? What shall we do?' And it was only by reiterated entreaties, dictated by the convictions of a filial tenderness which he deigned to understand, that I was able to persuade him to take the air, either on foot or in the calèche; and this always revived him, until the crisis of the 17th of March, which was the prelude of his death."

CHAPTER XLIX.
1821, January to May.

Completion of the new House—Lady Holland—Phrenology—Departure of Buonavita—Progress of the Disease—Remarks to Dr. Arnott—The Emperor's Will—Atheism—The last Letter—The Dying-scene—Burial—Departure of the Companions of Napoleon.

THE commencement of the year 1821 found the Emperor rapidly sinking to the grave. Sir Hudson Lowe had at length nearly completed a new house for his captive, but a few rods from the miserable hovel where the Emperor had now been for five years imprisoned. But the captive had become wonted to his dungeon, and, in the extreme of debility and dejection, manifested no disposition to change his dying bed.

THE NEW HOUSE.

As all hope of relief expired, and the hour of death drew near, the Emperor thought more and conversed more respecting the future world. The ecclesiastics who had been sent to St. Helena were men of ordinary intellects and of limited information. Napoleon respected their sincerity, but, as companions, they were utterly valueless. The infirm old man, Buonavita, soon found it necessary, in consequence of his health, to return to Europe. The young man Vignali remained, and Napoleon undertook to guide him in his studies. It is deeply to be deplored that the Emperor had no Christian friend near him in whom he could repose confidence, and who could transmit a record of his religious thoughts in these sad hours. General Bertrand was an avowed unbeliever. Montholon was a "man of camps," generous, high-minded, but entirely thoughtless upon religious subjects. Antommarchi often wounded and displeased the serious-minded Emperor by his irreverence toward all serious things. Under these circumstances, it is singular that so much of the Emperor's religious conversations should have been preserved. We know that he was a daily and a careful reader of the Bible. We have his undoubted testimony that he became a cordial believer in Christianity, and that he understood and appreciated the way of salvation through faith in Jesus Christ.

The Emperor expressed frankly to Count Montholon his great disappointment in the utter incapacity of his spiritual advisers. "I want," said he, "a man of education and learning—a theologian with whom I can discuss the great topics of religion, and who can answer my questions on those religious subjects which require to be examined and sounded to their depths; one who is perfectly versed in the history of religion, and who is capable of acting as my guide in the perusal of the Scriptures—one able to convince and satisfy my mind."

Count Montholon also represents him as saying, "Voltaire himself asked for the consolations of religion before his death, and perhaps I also might find much comfort and relief in the society of an ecclesiastic capable of inspiring in me a taste for religious conversation, who might render me devout."

During the months of January and February but little occurred to interrupt the melancholy monotony of the dying chamber.

March 12. Lady Holland, with that compassionate interest which she unceasingly took in the fate of the noble captive, sent to the Emperor a package of books, with a bust containing divisions according to the craniological system of Gall. As the Emperor looked at the divisions, he said,

"We will talk on this subject when we shall have nothing better to do. As a resource, it will do as well as any other. And it is sometimes amusing to consider how far folly may be carried. Corvisart was a great admirer of Gall. He praised him, protected him, and used his utmost endeavors to push him up to me; but there was no sympathy between us. Such men as Lavater, Cagliostro, Mesmer, have never ranked very high in my estimation. I even felt a kind of aversion to them. Gentlemen of this description are all dexterous and well-spoken. They work upon that thirst after the marvelous which the generality of mankind experience, and give the coloring of truth to the falsest theories.

"Nature does not betray herself by her outward forms. She does not disclose her secrets; she conceals them. To judge and examine men upon such slight indications is the act of a dupe or of an impostor. The only way to know men is to see them, observe them, and put them to the test. To avoid falling into errors, they must be studied a long time and be judged by their actions; and even that rule is not infallible, and requires to be restricted in its operation to the moment in which they act, for we seldom act consistently with our genuine disposition. We give way to the transport or impulse of the moment, or are carried away by passion. And this constitutes what is called vice or virtue, perversity or heroism. Such is my opinion, and such has long been my guide. Not that I pretend to deny the influence of disposition and education. I think, on the contrary, that it is immense; but beyond that, every thing is but mere speculation and folly."

March 16. The Emperor's exhaustion was extreme. Languidly he raised his eyes, and said, "To what a state am I reduced! I, who was so quick, so active, can now scarcely raise my eyelids; but I am no longer Napoleon."

Madam Bertrand called in to the sick-chamber. She was also in very feeble health. The Emperor talked of walking out with her, and said,

"We will go out early. We will enjoy the fresh air of the morning. We shall gain appetite, and escape the influence of the climate. You, little Hortense, and myself are the greatest invalids. We must assist each other, and unite our strength to fight against the latitude, and deprive it of its victims."

This day the infirm old Abbé Buonavita took leave of the Emperor, as he was to embark for Europe. The Emperor said to Antommarchi,

"Accompany this good man to Jamestown. Give him every assistance and every advice so long a voyage requires. I should like to know that the good ecclesiastic were already arrived at Rome. Do you not suppose they will give him a favorable reception? At any rate, they owe it to me to treat him well; for, after all, without me, what would have become of the Church?"

March 18. A consultation of physicians was held, and but little hope was cherished of the Emperor's recovery. Speaking of the re-establishment of Christianity in France, Napoleon said,

"It was far from my wish to interfere in matters of divine worship. The Revolution had disturbed so many interests, that it was but fitting that religious opinions at least should be respected. I caused overtures to be made to the Pope. I proposed to him to join the French government, and use his influence to consolidate the internal tranquillity of the two states, and contribute to the advantage of both. I said to him,

"'The moment is arrived for executing an operation in which wisdom, policy, and true religion are equally interested, and in the performance of which they must equally concur. The French government has given permission to open anew the churches of the Catholic faith, and grants to that religion tolerance and protection. The priests will either take advantage of this first act of the French government, in the true spirit of the Gospel, by contributing to public tranquillity and preaching the true maxims of charity, which are the foundation of the religion of the Gospel, in which case I have no doubt that they will obtain a more special protection, and that this will be a happy commencement toward the attainment of the end so much desired; or they will pursue a totally different line of conduct, in which case they will be again persecuted and driven away.

"'The Pope, as the chief of the faithful and the common centre of faith, may have a great influence over the conduct of the priests; and he will, perhaps, think it worthy of his wisdom, and of the most sacred of all religions, to promulgate an order prescribing to the priests to obey the government, and do all in their power to consolidate the established Constitution. If that order be expressed in terms concise and favorable to the great end which it may produce, it will be a great step toward the re-establishment of order, and extremely advantageous to the prosperity of religion. The desire of being useful to religion is one of the principal motives that induce me to act.'"

March 20. The Emperor was suffering from acute internal pain and from a burning fever. Madam Bertrand came in, and to cheer her he made a great effort to throw off his dejection; but he soon sank down again in exhaustion, saying,

"We must prepare for the fatal sentence. You, Hortense, and myself are doomed to meet our fate on this miserable rock. I shall go first, you will come next, and Hortense will follow. We shall all three meet in the Elysian fields.

> " 'Mais à revoir Paris, je ne dois plus prétendre ;
> Vous voyez qu'au tombeau je suis prêt à descendre.
> Je vais au Roi des rois demander aujourd'hui
> Le prix de tous les maux que j'ai soufferts pour lui.' "

March 26. A physician of much celebrity arrived at the island, and the governor urged that he should see the Emperor. Napoleon raised his eyes languidly, and replied,

"In order to be a second edition of Dr. Baxter, and make false bulletins! Does the governor still want to deceive Europe, or is he already thinking of the autopsy? I will not have any man who is in communication with him. A consultation! What would be the use of it? Another physician would not see more than you do of what is passing in my body. Besides, whom should I consult? Englishmen, who would be inspired by Hudson? No! I will have none of them. I prefer letting the crime be accomplished. The stain resulting from it will be equal to all my sufferings."

Antommarchi still entreated for a consultation for his own sake. "Very well," said the Emperor, kindly, "I give my consent. Consult with the physician of the island whom you consider most skillful." Antommarchi immediately applied to Dr. Arnott, surgeon of the 20th regiment.

March 27. "Doctor," said the Emperor, kindly, "you must be quite exhausted. You are constantly disturbed, and have not a moment to sleep. I am not gone yet, and must take care of you; I will have a bed prepared for you in the next room."

He immediately gave the necessary orders, and then said,

"I am approaching my end. What effect do you suppose my death will produce in Europe?"

"Your majesty," said Antommarchi, "is the idol of the soldiers; they would be inconsolable. The nations would be at the mercy of kings, and the popular cause would be forever lost."

"Lost, doctor!" said the Emperor; "and my son! can you suppose that he will be forgotten? Will he have greater obstacles to encounter than I overcame? Did I start from a higher point? No, doctor! my son bears my name, and I leave him my glory, and the affection of my friends. It is not difficult to inherit my estate."

March 29. The hidden disease was making rapid progress. "That which is written is written," said the Emperor. "Can you doubt, doctor, that every thing that happens is written down? that our hour is marked, and that it is not in the power of any of us to take from Time a portion which Nature refuses us?

"To take medicine," said he, in a tone expressive of the utmost repugnance, "is, perhaps, beyond my power. The aversion I feel for medicines is almost inconceivable. I exposed myself to dangers with indifference—I saw death without emotion; but I can not, notwithstanding all my efforts, approach my lips to a cup containing the slightest preparation. True it is that I am a spoiled child, who has never had any thing to do with physic."

Then turning to Madam Bertrand, who was present, he said to her, "How

CHAMBER OF SICKNESS.

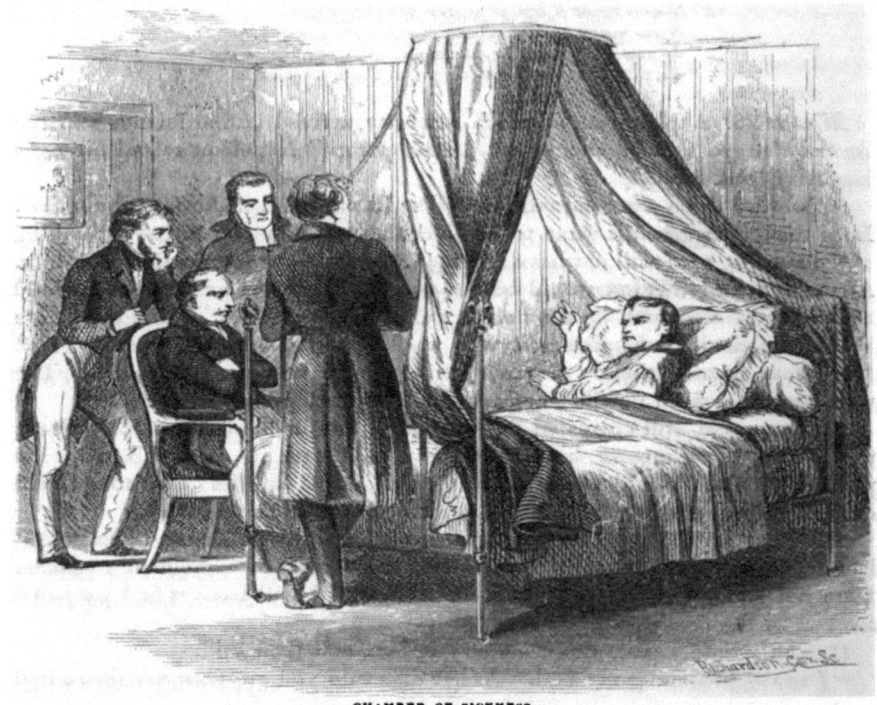

do you manage to take all those pills and drugs which the doctor is constantly prescribing for you?"

"I take them," Madam Bertrand replied, "without thinking about it, and I advise your majesty to do the same."

The Emperor then addressed the same question to Count Montholon, from whom he received a similar answer.

"I am, then," he added, "the only one who rebels against medicine. I will no longer do so. Give me your stuff." Receiving the cup in his hand, he immediately swallowed the nauseating dose.

April 8. The Emperor passed a night of dreadful suffering. At one time, overpowered with anguish, he was heard to exclaim, as he tossed upon his bed, "Ah! since I was to lose my life in this deplorable manner, why did the cannon balls spare it?"

April 14. The Emperor was a little more comfortable, and conversed with much animation with Dr. Arnott, whom we have before mentioned as the surgeon of the 20th regiment, and who had been admitted to the Emperor as consulting physician.

"Marlborough," said Napoleon, "was not a man who was narrowly confined to the field of battle. He fought and negotiated. He was at once a captain and a diplomatist. Has the 20th regiment got his campaigns?"

"I think not," the doctor replied.

"Well, I have there a copy of them," said the Emperor, "which I am glad to offer to that brave regiment. Take it, doctor; and you will place it in their library as coming from me."

Sir Hudson Lowe was guilty of the inconceivable brutality and insolence of ordering this book to be returned to *General Bonaparte.* He would not allow the regiment to receive the gift. "Dr. Arnott," says Lord Holland, indignantly, "was ordered to return the book, first, because it had not been transmitted through the Government House, and, secondly, because it was in the name of the Emperor Napoleon and not of *General Bonaparte.* Pitiful, narrow-minded malignity, disgraceful alike to the government and its agents."

Captain Lutzen, then the English orderly officer at Longwood, who was ordered to return the book, ventured to express some honest indignation in view of such an atrocity. For this crime he was immediately punished by dismission from office. The English officers at Longwood suffered about as much from the petty tyranny of Sir Hudson Lowe as did the French themselves.

April 13. The Emperor passed a very uncomfortable night, being drenched in the most profuse perspiration. "I changed the Emperor's linen," says Montholon, "seven times during the night, and each time both flannel and linen were perfectly steeped, and even the *Madras* which he wore on his head. He will not allow any light to be kept burning in his chamber, and only permits one wax candle to be left lighted in the next room.

"This morning, on awaking, the Emperor said to me, 'To-day I will dictate my last wishes to you; return at noon.' When I returned at the appointed hour, he requested me to bolt the door, and bid me write. He dictated for two hours uninterruptedly, and then asked me to read the dictation to him, saying kindly, 'Do you wish I should leave you more?' My emotion was too great to allow of my making any reply. He perceived this, and said, 'You may go and make a fair copy of what I have dictated. The day after to-morrow, which will be my good day, we will read it over again. You shall dictate it to me, and I will write.'"[*]

[*] The Emperor's will, which was very long and minute, and in which every friend was remembered, commences as follows:

"1. I die in the Apostolical Roman religion, in the bosom of which I was born more than fifty years since.

"2. It is my wish that my ashes may repose on the banks of the Seine, in the midst of the French people, whom I have loved so well.

"3. I have always had reason to be pleased with my dearest wife, the Empress Maria Louisa, and retain for her, to my last moment, the most tender sentiments. I beseech her to watch, in order to preserve my son from the snares which yet environ his infancy.

"4. I recommend to my son never to forget that he was born a French prince, and never to allow himself to become an instrument in the hands of the triumvirs who oppress the nations of Europe. He ought never to fight against France, or to injure her in any manner. He ought to adopt my motto—*Every thing for the French people.*

"5. I die prematurely, assassinated by the English oligarchy and its deputy. The English nation will not be slow in avenging me.

"6. The two unfortunate results of the invasions of France, when she had still so many resources, are to be attributed to the treason of Marmont, Augereau, Talleyrand, and La Fayette. I forgive them. May the posterity of France forgive them, as I do.

April 14. The Emperor requested Montholon to bring to him his will. He read over carefully what he had written, and dictated some changes. It has been said, very unfairly, "Napoleon bequeathed in his will a sum of money to the miscreant who attempted to assassinate the Duke of Wellington in Paris." The following is the item of the will:

"Two thousand dollars to the subaltern officer, Cantallon, who has undergone a trial upon the charge of having endeavored to assassinate Lord Wellington, *of which he was pronounced innocent.* Cantallon had as much right to assassinate that oligarchist as the latter had to send me to perish upon the rock of St. Helena. Wellington, who proposed this outrage, attempted to justify himself by pleading the interests of Great Britain. Cantallon, if he had really assassinated that lord, would have excused himself, and would have been justified by the same motives—the interest of France—to get rid of a general who, moreover, had violated the capitulation of Paris, and by that had rendered himself responsible for the blood of the martyrs Ney, Labedoyère, &c., and for the crime of pillaging the museums contrary to the text of the treaties."

Napoleon rewarded no assassin. He kindly remembered one who had been *falsely accused,* whom the tribunals declared to be *innocent,* and who, from known devotion to the Emperor, had suffered the anguish of imprisonment and trial.

April 15. The Emperor, now fully conscious that death was near at hand, passed nearly the whole of the day dictating his will. When Antommarchi entered, he found the carpet covered with papers which Napoleon had torn up.

"My preparations are made, doctor," said the Emperor; "I am going. It is all over with me. I know the truth, and I am resigned."

April 16. The Emperor was again employed upon his will until five o'clock. Such excessive application, in his exhausted state, seemed unnaturally to excite his mind. As Dr. Antommarchi entered, and manifested much uneasiness respecting the state in which he found his patient, Napoleon said,

"It proceeds from having been a long while engaged in business. I have written too much." Then placing his hand upon his stomach, he exclaimed, "Ah! doctor, what sufferings! what oppression! I feel at the left extremity of my stomach a pain which quite overpowers me."

April 19. About noon the Emperor arose from his bed, and took a seat in an arm-chair. He was free from pain, and appeared quite cheerful. Mon-

---

"7. I thank my good and most excellent mother; Cardinal Fesch; my brothers Joseph, Lucien, and Jerome; Pauline, Caroline, Julie, Hortense, Catharine, and Eugène, for the interest they have continued to feel for me. I pardon Louis for the libel he published in 1820; it is replete with false assertions and falsified documents.

"8. I disavow the 'Manuscript of St. Helena,' and other works, under the titles of 'Maxims,' 'Sayings,' &c., &c., which persons have been pleased to publish for the last six years. I caused the Duc D'Enghien to be arrested and tried, because that step was essential to the safety, interest, and honor of the French people, when the Count D'Artois was maintaining, by his own confession, sixty assassins at Paris. Under similar circumstances, I would act in the same way."

tholon read for some time to him, and all were cheered with the hope that the sufferer was getting better. As this hope was expressed, the Emperor looked around upon his companions with a placid smile, and said,

"My friends, you are mistaken. I am better to-day, but I feel, nevertheless, that my end is approaching. After my death, every one of you will return to Europe. Some of you will see your relations again, others their friends, and I shall join my brave companions in the Elysian Fields. Yes, Kleber, Desaix, Bessières, Duroc, Ney, Murat, Massena, Berthier, will all come to meet me. They will speak to me of what we have done together, and I will relate to them the last events of my life. On seeing me again, they will all become once more animated with enthusiasm and glory. We will talk of our wars with the Scipios, Hannibal, Cæsar, Frederick. There will be pleasure in that, unless," he added, smiling, "it should create alarm in the next world to see so many warriors assembled together."

At this moment Dr. Arnott came in. The Emperor received him with much affability. But, after a few moments' conversation, he said, in very solemn tones,

"It is all over with me, doctor. The blow is struck. I am near my end, and shall soon surrender my body to the earth. Bertrand, approach and translate to this gentleman what you are going to hear. It is the relation of a series of indignities worthy of the hand that has bestowed them. Express my full meaning. Do not omit a single word.

"I had come to seek the hospitality of the British people. I asked for a generous protection, and, to the subversion of every right held sacred upon earth, chains were the reply I received. I should have experienced a different reception from Alexander. The Emperor Francis would have treated me with more respect and kindness. Even the King of Prussia would have been more generous. It was reserved for England to deceive and excite the sovereigns of Europe, and give to the world the unheard-of spectacle of four great powers cruelly leagued together against one man. Your ministers have chosen this horrible rock, upon which the lives of Europeans are exhausted in less than three years, in order to end my existence by assassination.

"And how have I been treated since my arrival here? There is no species of indignity or insult that has not been eagerly heaped upon me. The simplest family communications, which have never been interdicted to any one, have been refused to me. No news, no papers from Europe have been allowed to reach me. My wife and son have no longer existed for me. I have been kept six years in the tortures of close confinement. The most uninhabitable spot on this inhospitable island, that where the murderous effects of a tropical climate are most severely felt, has been assigned to me for a residence. And I, who used to ride on horseback all over Europe, have been obliged to shut myself up within four walls in an unwholesome atmosphere. I have been destroyed piecemeal by a premeditated and protracted assassination. The infamous Sir Hudson Lowe has been the executioner of these atrocities of your ministers. You will end like the proud republic of Venice; and I, dying upon this dreary rock, away from those I hold dear, and deprived of every thing, bequeath the opprobrium and horror of my death to the reigning family of England."

The Emperor was much exhausted by this effort, and sank back almost fainting upon his pillow. He gradually fell into a peaceful sleep, and continued slumbering until about midnight. He then woke, and requested Count Montholon, who was sitting at his bedside, to send for the Abbé Vignali, saying, "Leave us alone, but return as soon as he shall have left me." The abbé remained an hour with the Emperor, and made arrangements for erecting an altar the next day by his bedside, and to administer the sacrament of the Lord's Supper to the dying Emperor. Montholon then returned to the room. He found the Emperor serene and thoughtful. After a few moments of religious conversation, Napoleon turned upon his pillow and again fell asleep.

April 21. The Emperor again sent for the Abbé Vignali, and gave him very minute instructions respecting the preparation of his body for burial, with all the customary religious ceremonies of the Catholic Church. Thinking that he perceived an expression of contempt upon the countenance of Dr. Antommarchi, he turned to him solemnly and said,

" Sir, you are an Atheist; you are a physician. Physicians believe in nothing, because they deal only in matter. I am neither a philosopher nor a physician. I believe in God. I am a Christian, a Catholic Christian. Be an Atheist, sir, if you will, but as for me, I wish to fulfill all the duties which religion imposes, and to receive all the consolation which it administers. It is not every one who can be an Atheist."

After the abbé had retired, the Emperor, again addressing the doctor, said,

" How can you carry it so far? Can you not believe in God, whose existence the greatest minds have believed?"

Antommarchi made some apology, saying that he had never doubted the existence of God. The Emperor replied,

" You are a physician. Those people have only to do with matter. They never will believe any thing."

"When we were visiting at Madam Bertrand's," says Mrs. Abell, "we always passed our Sundays as if at home, reading the lessons for the day, and observing the prayers, &c. One Sunday morning Napoleon came bustling in, and seeing me very earnestly employed reading aloud to my sister, asked what I was so intently engaged upon, and why I looked so much graver than usual. I told him I was learning to repeat the Collect for the day, and that, if I failed in saying it, my father would be very angry. I remarked,

" ' I suppose *you* never learned a Collect or any thing religious, for I am told you disbelieve the existence of a God.' He seemed displeased at my observation, and answered,

" ' You have been told an untruth; when you are wiser, you will understand that no one could doubt the existence of a God.'

"My mother asked him if he was a predestinarian, as reported. He admitted the truth of the accusation, saying, ' I believe that whatever a man's destiny calls upon him to do, that he must fulfill.' "

It is very evident that the Emperor believed in *human responsibility* as well as in the *foreordination of God*. Recognizing these truths as beyond the range of finite minds, he did not attempt their reconciliation. It is safe to say that every deep thinker is compelled to do homage to both of these truths.

April 24. "The Emperor has again," says Count Montholon, "spoken to me of his will. He thinks of adding to it several arrangements with which he will charge the Empress and Prince Eugène. His imagination is unceasingly employed in seeking to find resources from which to gratify his liberality. Each day brings to his mind the remembrance of some other old servant whom he would wish to remunerate."

Napoleon spoke of the different kinds of worship—of religious dissensions. "I had formed a plan," said he, "to reconcile all sects. Our reverses occurred too soon to allow me to carry that plan into execution. But I have at least re-established religion, and that is a service the results of which are incalculable."

General Bertrand, enraged by the insults which he had received from Sir Hudson Lowe, was determined to challenge him to a duel as soon as their mutual relations of jailer and prisoner should cease. In the governor's official documents it is stated, "It is pleasing to be able to mention that Napoleon, on his death-bed, earnestly begged Count Bertrand to use every means in his power, consistent with his honor, to effect a reconciliation with Sir Hudson Lowe, saying that he hoped that he would succeed, as he himself alone had been the cause of the differences between them. This was, at all events, stated by Madam Bertrand to Admiral Lambert, and she added that her husband was very desirous to fulfill Napoleon's dying wish."

April 26. The Emperor was pretty calm during the night, until about four in the morning, when he said to Count Montholon, with extraordinary emotion,

"I have just seen my good Josephine, but she would not embrace me. She disappeared at the moment when I was about to take her in my arms. She was seated there. It seemed to me that I had seen her yesterday evening. She is not changed; still the same, full of devotion to me. She told me that we were about to see each other again, never more to part. She assured me that—did you see her?"

"I took great care," says Count Montholon, "not to say any thing which might increase the feverish excitement too plainly evident to me. I gave him his potion and changed his linen, and he fell asleep; but, on awaking, he again spoke to me of the Empress Josephine, and I should only have uselessly irritated him by telling him that it was only a dream.

"The reading of an English journal," Montholon continues, "awakened in the Emperor's mind one of those terrible impressions against which his reason was powerless, but which always have their origin in a noble feeling. Unfortunately, Bertrand, in translating quickly, did not perceive that the article he was translating was an infamous libel against Caulaincourt and Savary, and when he would have stopped the Emperor made him proceed; then interrupting him suddenly, he cried, 'This is shameful!' He then sent for me, ordered me to bring out his will, opened it, and interlined the following words without saying a word to us:

"'I caused the Duc D'Enghien to be arrested and tried, because that step was essential to the safety, interest, and honor of the French people, when the Count D'Artois was maintaining, by his own confession, sixty assassins at Paris. Under similar circumstances, I would act in the same way.' Having written these few lines, he gave me back the will, and dismissed us by a sign of the hand."

In the evening he was in quite a stupor. As the doctor *urged* him to take some medicine, he pushed it away, and, suddenly rallying, said,

"Doctor, you ought to marry. I must arrange a marriage for you."

"For me, sire?"

"Yes, for you. You are too warm, too quick. You need something to calm your impetuosity. Marry, therefore, an English woman. Her iced blood will temper the fire which animates you, and you will be less tenacious."

"My object, sire," said Antommarchi, "was to administer relief to your majesty. I had no intention of doing any thing that might displease you."

"I know it, doctor," said the Emperor, immediately relenting, "and therefore your patient will be henceforward more obedient. Give me the medicine." He swallowed it at a single draught, and handing the cup to the doctor, said, "When a man has been guilty of irreverence toward Galen, it is thus that the sin must be expiated."

April 27. The Emperor passed a very painful night. A profuse perspiration rendered it necessary for him frequently to change his linen. He obtained scarcely two hours of sleep. At six o'clock in the morning Marchand came to relieve Count Montholon. The Emperor kept him busy several hours sealing with ribbons his will and codicils. He caused an inventory of his caskets to be made, and with his own hand wrote and signed, upon a pasteboard tablet, all the superscriptions on the envelopes.

While Marchand was making an inventory of the contents of the Emperor's caskets, the Emperor took from one of them a diamond necklace, and gave it to him, saying,

"Take this; I am ignorant in what state my affairs may be in Europe; the good Hortense gave me this before she left Malmaison, thinking that I might have need of it. I believe it to be worth two hundred thousand francs: hide it about your person. When you reach France, it will enable you to await the provision which I make for you in my will. Marry honorably; make your choice among the daughters of the officers or soldiers of my Old Guard: there are many of these brave men who are happy. A better fate was reserved for them, had it not been for the reverse of fortune experienced by France. Posterity will acknowledge all that I would have done for them had circumstances been different."

The Emperor then dictated the following letter, to be sent by Count Montholon to Sir Hudson Lowe, announcing his death:

"Monsieur le Governeur,—The Emperor Napoleon breathed his last on the ———, after a long and painful illness. I have the honor to communicate this intelligence to you. The Emperor has authorized me to communicate to you, if such be your will, his last wishes. I beg you to inform me what are the arrangements prescribed by your government for the transportation of his remains to France, as well as those relating to the persons of his suite. I have the honor to be, &c., Count Montholon."

THE EMPEROR DICTATING HIS LAST LETTER.

April 28. The physical prostration of the Emperor was extreme, yet his mind appeared to retain all its vigor. The tones of his voice were peculiarly gentle and tender as he addressed his friends. Calling Dr. Antommarchi to his bedside, he said,

"After my death, which can not be far distant, I desire that you will open my body. I insist, also, that you promise that no English medical man shall touch me. If, however, the assistance of one should be indispensable, Dr. Arnott is the only one whom you have permission to employ. I farther desire that you will take my heart, put it in spirits of wine, and carry it to Parma to my dear Maria Louisa. You will tell her that I tenderly loved her—that I never ceased to love her. You will relate to her all you have seen, and every particular respecting my situation and death. I particularly recommend to you carefully to examine my stomach, and to make a precise and detailed report of the state in which you may find it, which report you will give to my son. The vomitings, which succeed each other almost without interruption, lead me to suppose that the stomach is, of all my organs, the most diseased. I am inclined to believe that it is attacked with the same disorder which killed my father—I mean, a scirrhosis in the pylorus. I began to suspect that such was the case as soon as I saw the frequency and obstinate recurrence of the vomitings. I beg that you will be very particular in your examination, that, when you see my son, you may be able to communicate your observations to him, and point out to him the most proper medicines to use. When I am no more, you will go to Rome. You will see my mother and my family, and will relate to them all you may have observed concerning my situation, my disorder, and my death on this dreary rock."

From this effort his mind wandered away in the dreams of delirium.

April 29. The Emperor passed a night of burning fever. At four o'clock in the morning he requested Count Montholon to bring a table to his bedside, and he occupied himself two hours in dictating two projects, one on the destination of Versailles, the other on the organization of the National Guard for the defense of the kingdom.

"Astonishment," says Count Montholon, "has often been felt at the great faculties of the Emperor, which permitted him, on the eve of or on the day after a battle, which either was about to decide or had decided the fate of a throne, to sign decrees, and occupy himself with matters purely administrative; but these facts are far inferior to the one which we here attest. But five days later, all that remained of this sublime genius was a corpse, and yet his thoughts were still constantly directed toward the happiness and future prospects of France."

The Abbé Vignali was now called in. A movable altar was constructed at the bedside of the dying Emperor. All retired from the room except the abbé. The Emperor then, in silence and in solitude, received the sacrament of the Lord's Supper. After the solemn ordinance, Count Montholon, upon returning to the room, was struck with the placid and peaceful expression of the countenance of the Emperor.

The slumbers of the night were peaceful. As in the early dawn the Emperor opened his eyes, he said to his valet, in tones of peculiar gentleness and serenity,

"Open the window, Marchand. Open it wide, that I may breathe the air—the good air which the good God has made."

Dr. Antommarchi, when he entered, found the Emperor, though fast sinking, calm and rational. To his suggestion that a blister should be applied to the stomach, the Emperor replied, "Since you wish it, be it so. Not that I expect the least effect from it; but my end is approaching, and I am desirous of showing, by my resignation, my gratitude for your care and attention."

The feverish state of his stomach induced him to drink much cold water. With characteristic gratitude, he exclaimed, "If Fate had decreed that I should recover, I would erect a monument upon the spot where the water flows, and would crown the fountain, in testimony of the relief which it has

RESIDENCE AT LONGWOOD.

THE EMPEROR RECEIVING THE SACRAMENT OF THE LORD'S SUPPER.

afforded me. If I die, and my body, proscribed as my person has been, should be denied a little earth, I desire that my remains may be deposited in the Cathedral of Ajaccio, in Corsica. And if it should not be permitted me to rest where I was born, let me be buried near the limpid stream of this pure water."

May 1. The Emperor, though very feeble, spent two hours dictating to Count Montholon. He then sent for the Abbé Vignali, and, after a private interview with him, an altar was erected, and the prayers of the Church for the dying were offered.

May 2. The Emperor was in a raging fever during the night, and quite delirious. His wandering spirit retraced the scenes of the past, visited again his beloved France, hovered affectionately over his idolized son, and held familiar converse with the companions of his toil and his glory. Again the lurid storms of war beat upon his disturbed fancy as his unrelenting assailants combined anew for his destruction. Wildly he shouted, "Steingel, Desaix, Massena! Ah! victory is declaring. Run! hasten! press the charge! They are ours!" Suddenly collecting his strength, in his eagerness he sprang from the bed, but his limbs failed him, and he fell prostrate upon the floor.

At nine o'clock in the morning the fever abated, and reason returned to her throne. Calling the doctor to his bedside, he said to him earnestly, "Recollect what I have directed you to do after my death. Proceed very carefully to the anatomical examination of my stomach. I wish it, that I may save my son from that cruel disease. You will see him, doctor, and you will point out to him what is best to be done, and will save him from the cruel sufferings I now experience. This is the last service I ask of you."

At noon the violence of the disease returned, and Napoleon, looking steadfastly and silently upon the doctor for a few moments, said, "Doctor, I am very ill; I feel that I am going to die." He immediately sank away into insensibility. All the inmates of Longwood were unremitting in their attentions to the beloved sufferer. He was to them all, from the highest to the lowest, a father whom they almost adored. The zeal and solicitude they manifested deeply moved the sensibilities of the Emperor. He spoke to them in grateful words, and remembered them all in his will. As he recovered from this insensibility, he spoke faintly to his companions, enjoining it upon them to be particularly careful in attending to the comfort of the humble members of his household after he should be gone. "And my poor Chinese," said he, "do not let them be forgotten. Let them have a few scores of Napoleons. I must take leave of them also."

About eight o'clock in the evening the Emperor revived a little, and attempted to dictate to Marchand some testamentary arrangements in favor of his son and of the Princess Pauline; but he soon found that he was unable to control the wanderings of his mind.

May 3. The Emperor was in a burning fever, and during the night was quite delirious. With a convulsive movement, he rose up and endeavored to get out of bed. With difficulty he was induced to lie down again. A raging thirst consumed him, and he called often for orange water.

At two o'clock in the afternoon he revived for a moment, and said to those who were appointed the executors of his will, and who were at his bedside,

"I am going to die, and you to return to Europe. You have shared my exile, you will be faithful to my memory. I have sanctioned all good principles, and have infused them into my laws and my acts. I have not omitted a single one. Unfortunately, however, the circumstances in which I was placed were arduous, and I was obliged to act with severity, and to postpone the execution of my plans. Our reverses occurred. I could not unbend the bow, and France has been deprived of the liberal institutions I intended to give her. She judges me with indulgence. She feels grateful for my intentions. She cherishes my name and my victories. Imitate her example. Be faithful to the opinions we have defended, and to the glory we have acquired. Any other course can only lead to shame and confusion."

He then sent for the Abbé Vignali. All the rest retired; and the dying Emperor, for the second time, in silence and in solitude partook of the emblems of that Savior's love who was wounded for our transgressions, and who bore our sins in his own body on the tree. The Emperor then, with a serene spirit, fell asleep.

May 4. It was a dark and melancholy day; the rain fell in torrents, and a fierce gale howled over the drenched crags of St. Helena. Napoleon's favorite willow was torn up by the roots, and every tree at Longwood was laid prostrate in the mud. The elemental warfare disturbed not the quiet spirit of the dying Emperor, as, in his darkened chamber, he no longer resisted the approach of the King of Terrors.

THE STORM.

May 5. "The night was very bad," says Count Montholon. "Toward two o'clock delirium became evident, and was accompanied by nervous contractions. Twice I thought I distinguished the unconnected words, *France —armée, tête d'armée—Josephine;* at the same moment the Emperor threw himself out of his bed by a convulsive movement, against which I struggled in vain. His strength was so great that he threw me down, bringing me with him on the carpet. He held me so tightly that I could not cry out for help. Happily, Archambaud, who was watching in the next room, heard some noise, and hastened to assist me to replace the Emperor in bed. A few minutes afterward, the grand marshal and Dr. Antommarchi, who had thrown themselves on a sofa in the library, also entered; but the Emperor had already lain down again, and was calm.

"He seemed to be sleeping tranquilly when I left him at six o'clock in the morning, but I had scarcely had time to throw myself on my bed when some one came in haste to fetch me; the rattling in the throat—the forerunner of death—was beginning!

"When I approached the bed, the Emperor looked at me, and made me a sign to give him something to drink. But already his power of swallowing was gone, and it was only by means of a sponge wetted with sugared water that I was enabled to allay his thirst, by constantly pressing the sponge to his lips. From this moment until half past five in the evening, when he breathed his last, he remained motionless, lying on his back, with his right hand out of the bed, and his eyes fixed, seemingly in deep meditation, and without any appearance of suffering. His lips were slightly contracted, and his whole face expressed pleasant and gentle impressions.

"As the sun was setting, the Emperor quitted this earthly life, and I lost more than a father. I piously fulfilled the duty which his kindness confided to me—I closed his eyes.

THE DYING-SCENE.

"Immediately after his death, I wrote the letter which he had dictated to me on the 28th of April, announcing his death, and dispatched it to Sir Hudson Lowe, and at the same time I sent to inform Dr. Arnott and the orderly officer of the event. They came in to verify the fact, and both testified their respect and grief while obeying this sad duty. The head surgeon of the garrison and the head surgeon of the squadron then entered, and coldly laid their hands on the Emperor's heart. They only saw in this act the fulfillment of a formality—of a duty; and it did not even seem to occur to their minds that the heart which had just ceased to beat was that of one of those extraordinary and privileged men who appear once in a century, as manifestations of the great powers of the human mind. At seven o'clock in the evening, at the grand marshal's request, M. Marchand and I went to him for the purpose of drawing up the *procès-verbal* of the death of the Emperor, and of the delivery made to me by Monsieur Marchand of the testamentary acts, as well as of the envelopes containing the receipts for the deposits of money. I was obliged to stop, however, before their completion, for I felt exhausted with grief even more than with fatigue.

"So many cruel emotions were too strong for the female part of the family and for the children. Napoleon Bertrand fell down senseless while touching with his lips the ice-cold hand of the Emperor.

"*May* 6. The Abbé Vignali passed the night in prayer beside the Emperor's body. Bertrand and I fulfilled, by turns, the pious duty of watching. Marchand, although still very weak, also watched. The physicians, Antommarchi and Arnott, passed the night in a similar manner.

"This morning, at seven o'clock, Sir Hudson Lowe, followed by his whole staff, and accompanied by the French admiral, by General Coffin, and by the members of the council of government, as well as by the captains of the vessels then in the Roads, came to Longwood, and required me to admit him to see the body of the Emperor. All was ready for this sad ceremony. The Emperor lay on his camp bed in his little bed-chamber. Noverras, although exhausted by dysentery, had collected all his strength in order to shave him; and Marchand, with the assistance of St. Denis, had clothed him in the uniform of the mounted *chasseurs* of his imperial guard. The cloak which he wore at Marengo covered his feet, and a crucifix had been laid on his breast. The grand marshal stood on the right side of the bed, Marchand on the left, and the Abbé Vignali was engaged in prayer at the foot, when I admitted Sir Hudson Lowe, who had brought with him the Marquis Montchenu, commissioner of King Louis XVIII., and charged *per interim* with the functions of commissioner of the Emperor of Austria; Admiral Lambert, commander of the squadron; Brigadier General Coffin, commander of the brigade of land troops; Messrs. Brook and Thomas, members of the council of colonial administration of the island; two captains of the royal marine; and Drs. Mitchell, Short, Arnott, Burton, and Livingston, surgeons of the squadron, the garrison, and the East India Company.

"Sir Hudson Lowe bowed respectfully when I showed him the inanimate corpse of the Emperor, and his example was followed by all the persons of his suite. They all defiled before the bed with religious silence and respect.

"But scarcely had we quitted the chamber when Sir Hudson Lowe announced to me that the surgeons, by his orders, were about to proceed immediately to the post-mortem examination. I indignantly rejected the proposal, and summoned the grand marshal to my assistance; but our protestations would have been impotent against the will of the governor, had not the Marquis Montchenu added his opposition to ours, declaring that, acting in his double quality of commissioner of France and Austria, he protested against this illegal order, and claimed the execution of the regulations in use in the island with regard to interments.

"Sir Hudson Lowe was obliged to yield to the declaration made that the customs of St. Helena demanded that, unless symptoms of decomposition made their appearance, an interment should not take place before the expiration of twenty-four hours. It was agreed that this usage should be respected.

"The Emperor's death was unhappily but too certain. We could no longer entertain the slightest gleam of hope; and, nevertheless, our grief was sadly increased when, toward noon, Dr. Antommarchi declared to us that decomposition was making rapid progress, and that the necessity for proceeding to the examination and embalmment was urgent.

"Sir Hudson Lowe was informed of this state of things, and at two o'clock P.M., the English medical men, Short, Arnott, Mitchell, Burton, and Livingston, joined Dr. Antommarchi. The latter proceeded to the examination, in presence of the grand marshal, myself, and the persons belonging to the household of the Emperor; the governor was represented by the chief of his staff. This sad operation was performed in the topographic cabinet.

"Sir Hudson Lowe had signified to us that, conformably to the orders of his government, he forbade the embalmment of the body. But it was only at the moment that Dr. Antommarchi was proceeding to inclose the heart in a silver vase filled with spirits of wine, the Emperor having commanded us to take it to the Empress, that he sent a message declaring his opposition to this measure, and stating that no part should be thus preserved but the stomach, which was to be sent to England.

"This declaration gave rise to a warm discussion. All we could succeed in obtaining was, that the heart should be inclosed in a silver vase, in like manner with the stomach, and should be thus placed in the coffin. I also obtained permission to put into the coffin, in pursuance of an order received from the Emperor, a collection of gold money struck in his reign. The examination being terminated, the Emperor was again clothed in the dress of the chasseurs of the guard, and laid out on his camp bed in the chamber next to his usual bed-chamber. The bed was placed so as to face the glass door which opened to the little garden, and a crucifix was placed on his breast.

"The regiments of the garrison, and numerous detachments of the crews of the squadron, in full dress, but unarmed, defiled before his mortal remains. They all, officers, soldiers, and sailors, bent the knee to the ground on arriving opposite the glass door. Some of the officers entreated to be allowed the honor of pressing with their lips a corner of the cloak of Marengo, with which we had covered the Emperor's feet.

"The grand marshal, Monsieur Marchand, and myself surrounded the bed of the Emperor. The Abbé Vignali was engaged in prayer at the foot.

"*May* 7. This morning the whole Creole population came in procession to Longwood to pay a last testimony of homage and respect to the illustrious captive who had gained their love and admiration.

"At two o'clock in the afternoon, every thing being ready for placing the Emperor's mortal remains in the coffin which was to shut him from all eyes forever, we proceeded to the performance of this cruel duty.

"The following is the *procès-verbal* of it:

"*Procès-verbal of the placing in the Coffin.*

"This day, the seventh of May, one thousand eight hundred and twenty-one, at Longwood, island of St. Helena, the body of the Emperor, being clothed in the uniform of the *chasseurs* of his guard, was by us, the undersigned, placed in a tin coffin, lined with white satin, and having a pillow and mattress of the same. We also put into this coffin the heart, inclosed in a silver vase, surmounted by the imperial eagle, and the box containing the stomach; also a silver vase, engraved with the imperial arms, a cover of silver ditto, a plate ditto, six double Napoleons in French gold, four single gold Napoleons, a double silver Napoleon, and two Italian double Napoleons of gold.

"The first coffin, having been soldered in our presence, was placed in another of lead, which, after having also been soldered, was inclosed in a third coffin of mahogany.

"The coffin was placed on the camp bed, in the *chapelle ardente*, and covered with a pall of velvet, on which we spread the cloak which the Emperor had worn in every campaign since the battle of Marengo, after which we drew up and signed the present *procès-verbal*, the day and year above mentioned.

"(Signed),   COUNT BERTRAND.
                                               COUNT MONTHOLON.
                                               MARCHAND.

"*May* 9. Scarcely was the grave destined to receive the mortal remains of the Emperor completed by the military laborers, when the governor sent us information that the ceremony of interment was to take place at eleven o'clock precisely, and desiring that we might be in readiness at that hour.

"At ten o'clock A.M., the Abbé Vignali celebrated mass and the service for the dead.

"At eleven o'clock, the garrison being under arms and lining the way, the cortège quitted Longwood; the corners of the cloak were held by Count Bertrand, Count Montholon, Napoleon Bertrand, and Marchand; the Countess Bertrand and the whole of the Emperor's household surrounded the funeral car. The staff, and successively the whole garrison, followed in its rear.

"At noon, the almoner of the Emperor having blessed the grave dug at the fountain of Colbert, and the prayers being concluded, the coffin was lowered into the grave, amid the reports of salvos of artillery from the forts and the ships of the squadron.

"The grave was then filled in and closed with masonry in our presence, and a guard of honor placed beside it."

On the 27th of May, the surviving exiles of Longwood embarked for Europe. "Before we left the island," says Dr. Antommarchi, "we went to see, for the last time, the spot where Napoleon reposed. We bathed it with our tears; we surrounded it with violets and pansies, and bade *him* adieu forever. We took with us a few branches of the willow. The weather was fine;

NAPOLEON'S GRAVE.

not a cloud was to be seen. The wind filled our sails; the day was declining, and St. Helena was disappearing in the horizon. We waved a last adieu to that horrible rock."

INDEX.

ABDICATION, Napoleon's second, page 222.
Abell (Mrs.), testimony of, 290; remarks upon Napoleon, 571; interview with the Emperor, 579.
Abuse disregarded by the Emperor, 586.
Accounts, the Emperor's familiarity with, 95; revision of, 159.
Acorn (Golden), anecdote of, 158.
Alexander the Great, 481.
Alexander of Russia, 109, 150, 272; disappointed at Napoleon's second marriage, 273, 513; his designs on Constantinople, 534.
Algerines, their character, 430.
Ambigu (The), 536.
America the proper asylum for Napoleon, 221; treaty with, 285.
Amherst (Lord), his proposed interview, 558; presentation to the Emperor, 575.
Amiability, 62.
Amiens, rupture of the treaty with, 438; peace of, 472, 556.
Andreossi, 155.
Anecdotes of the Emperor, 19, 38, 59, 84, 103, 129, 136, 217, 238, 276, 386, 422, 585; of the court, 205.
Antommarchi (Dr.), arrival at St. Helena, 613; first interview with the Emperor, 614.
Antwerp, its works, 443.
Aristocracy, the support of monarchy, 308; its character, 470; remarks upon, 597.
Army, organization of, 75; its best discipline, 482, 465.
Atheism, Napoleon's views of, 549.
Augereau, 39, 42, 191.
Augusta (Princess), anecdote of, 108.
Austria, 220; her peril, 409.

Baden (Prince of), 216.
Baggage of the Emperor examined, 15.
Bailly (M.), his character, 258.
Balbi (Madam de), remarks upon, 320.
Balcombe (Mr.), his residence, 36.
" (Miss Elizabeth), Mrs. Abell, 51; receives a horse from the Emperor, 574; departure from St. Helena, 607.
Balcombe family, final interview with the Emperor, 608.
Barras, 246; his character, 247.
Barre (General), 207.
Bathurst (Lord), communication from, 148; his brutality, 416; his character, 486; his incorrect assertions, 564; letter to Sir Hudson Lowe, 579; commands that the Emperor should exhibit himself twice a week, 612.
Battle, fate of, 52; Napoleon sleeps on the field of, 121; dangers of, 127.
Belgians regret the victory of Waterloo, 546.
Bellerophon, the Emperor received on board of, 13.
Bergen-op-Zoom, its defense, 242.
Berlin Decree, its origin, 365.
Bernadotte, his hostility to France, 337; opinion of, 475.
Bernardin, 78.
Berthier (Marshal), 42.
Bertholet, his apostasy, 200.
Bertrand (General), 58; condemned to death, 321.
Bessières, 48; his death, 521.
Billaud de Varennes, 590.
Blockade, the right of, 337.
Blucher (General), 464.
Books, arrival of, 283.
Bossuet, his four propositions, 347.
Botanist (The), not permitted to see the Emperor, 538.
Bourbons, remarks upon the, 35, 90, 92, 385; their precarious situation, 375; their fanaticism, 446; deface public monuments, 493; anecdote of, 536.
Briers (The), description of, 32.
Broughton (Lord), Mr. Hobhouse, present to the Emperor from, 323.
Brumaire, its revolution necessary, 294.
Brune (General), 191.
Bulletins, correctness of, 127.
Bust of Napoleon's son, 569.

Cadastre, 96.
Cadoudal, his interview with the first consul, 231.
Cæsar, 53, 481.
Caffarelli, 196.
Cambacères, 45.
Campan (Madam), her establishment, 215.
Canals of France, 330.
Caricatures, remarks upon, 90.
Carnot, 46, 223, 249.
Caroline, Queen of Naples, 212, 448.
Carteaux (General), 23.
Castlereagh (Lord), 256; his slanderous assertions, 287; his hostility to liberty, 488; in Napoleon's power, 488; his weak policy, 537; his libel, 545.

INDEX.

Catharine of Russia, her character, 338.
Catholicism, remarks upon, 345.
Chance, remarks upon, 21.
Charette, his character, 458.
Chateaubriand, speech of, 237.
Chatham (Earl of), policy of, 256.
Chemical experiments, 386.
Chemistry, 75.
Cherbourg, works at, 301.
Chevreuse (Madam de), 230.
Cipriani, death of, 606.
Circumstances which had aided in the Emperor's career, 185.
Clay's (Henry) remarks upon Napoleon, 196.
Cockburn (Admiral Sir George), remarks upon, 61; interview with, 65; dines with the Emperor, 68; summary of his character and conduct, 145; rudeness of, 147.
Code Napoleon, 483.
Colonial system, remarks upon, 377.
Commissioners of the Allies, 276.
Condé (Prince of), 482.
Conscience, liberty of, protected by the Emperor, 444.
Conscription, remarks upon, 604.
Conspiracies, 20; of Cerachi, 130; of the fanatic of Schoenbrun, 131; of Cadoudal, 231.
Constant (M. Benjamin), his conversation with the Emperor, 115.
Constantinople, 170; remarks upon, 333, 452.
Convention, its history, 260.
Convents, remarks upon, 324.
Copenhagen, 255; attack upon, 265.
Corbineau (General), 80.
Cornwallis (Lord), character of, 256, 555.
Coronation by the Pope, 347.
Corsica, 228; remarks upon, 621.
Corvisart, 105.
Countenance not always true index to character, 225, 297.
Cromwell, remarks upon, 561.
Curates, usefulness of, 483.

D'Artois (Count), 35; anecdotes of, 154.
Danton, 590.
Decrés, 19, 196; anecdote of, 198.
Derlon, 53.
Desaix (General), remarks upon, 21, 53, 191, 510.
Dictation, manner of, 28, 71; recommenced, 240; Emperor's mode of, 275, 397, 399.
Dictatorship, necessity of, 288.
Diplomacy, English, 254.
Directory, measures of the, 250; remarks upon the, 253.
Dolgoruki (Princess), letters of the, 229.
Drama, remarks upon the, 459.
Drawing-room of the Emperor, the furniture of the, 70.
Dresden, Napoleon's situation at, 108; conference at, 156.
Dress, remarks upon, 299.

Dufresne, secretary of the Treasury, 95.
Dugommier, 25.
Duroc, character of, 81, 491.

Egypt, remarks upon, 19, 21, 127; campaign of, 315; plans for the improvement of, 550.
Elba, situation of the Emperor at, 143; return from, 536.
Eliza, sister of Napoleon, 448; her death, 633.
Elphinstone's (Hon. John) present to the Emperor, 578.
Emigrants, return of the, to France, 183.
Enghien (Duke of), 235; his execution, 499.
England, colonies of, 75; invasion of, 97; motives of, 114; animosity of the ministers of, 150; should be the friend of France, 152; the political interests of, 220; political condition of, 235; the slanders of, against Napoleon, 255; the unpopularity of, 255; national debt of, 378; regeneration of, 379; taxes of, 431; military ambition of, 431; depressed condition of, 564; invasion of, 528, 603; military power of, 563; state of, 564; character of the aristocracy of, 604.
English government, weakness of, as a military power, 280; desire to seize the Emperor's funds, 376; unrelenting cruelty of, 401.
English seamen, 433.
Etiquette, remarks upon, 275; of Longwood, 622.
Eugene (Viceroy), 53.
Europe, prospects of, 90, 141; histories of, 333.
European capitals, expenses of living in, 157.
Exmouth (Lord), expedition of, 430.

Family of Napoleon, 393.
Farewell to France, 17.
Farmer, conversations of Napoleon with, 61.
Fatalism, 400.
Faubourg St. Antoine, anecdote of, 423.
" St. Germain, anecdote of, 420.
Finances, administration of, 240.
Fish-basin, 630.
Fontainebleau, 143; remarks upon, 332.
Fortifications, remarks upon, 68; Longwood surrounded by, 484.
Fouché, 419, 590.
Fowling-pieces, the Emperor presented with, 67.
Fox, character of, 256.
France, prospects of, 141; division of, 219; manner of living in, 270; remarks upon, 277; arrangements made for the poor in, 311; peril of, 471; unsettled state of, 519.
Francis (Emperor), 42, 150.
Frederick the Great, his sword, 479.
French (The), natural character of, 107; fickleness of, 137; opposition to the Bourbons, 561.

Gall, remarks upon, 318.
Gaming, Napoleon's hostility to, 492.
Gantheaume, 196.
Gasparin, representative, 24.

INDEX.

Gasparin (representative), 24.
Gentilini, Napoleon's footman, 480.
Georges, 20.
Germans, hostility of the, toward the Emperor, 494.
Gibraltar, 68.
Gil Blas, 242.
Goldsmith, secret history of Napoleon by, 72.
Gourgaud (General), 58; return to Europe of, 606.
Government of Napoleon, energy of, 96.
Gracchi (The), 120.
Grant (Madam), 227.
Great men, causes of the success of, 481.
Greece, 110.
Gregoire, character of, 258.
Grouchy, 53; delay of, 553.
Guiche (Duchess of), 35.
Gustavus IV. of Sweden, 334; appeal to Napoleon of, 335.

Hamiton (Captain), presentation to the Emperor of, 154.
Hannibal, 481.
Hippocrates, 105.
Historical Atlas of Las Casas, 281.
History (Ancient), 120.
" (Roman), 121.
" very defective, 395; justice will be done the Emperor by, 444; difficulty of obtaining facts in, 497.
Hoche (General), 190.
Holland (Lord), protest of, 280; investigation of the treatment demanded by, 563.
Holy Alliance, remarks upon the, 625.
Hortense (Queen), 210.
Hostile biographers of Napoleon, 426.
House, preparations for building, for the Emperor, 206; remarks upon, 306.
Household (Imperial), composition of, 58.
Hulks, the English, 440.

Iliad of Homer, 188.
Imagination, effects of, 70.
Immorality, remarks upon, 434.
Imperial government, its efficiency, 455; a republic, 541; remarks upon, 605.
Imperial palaces, expenses of, 158.
" title refused by the English, 15, 581.
Incognito, the Emperor proposes to assume, 417; refused to the Emperor, 543.
India, the invasion of, 197.
" (East) fleet, 200; remarks upon, 453
Industry (French) encouraged, 285.
Infernal machine, 47, 462.
Inspector of reviews, post of, 390.
Institute, Napoleon a member of the, 192.
Institution, European, planned by the Emperor, 484.
Internal improvements, remarks upon, 329.
Iron railing, 548.
Italian republic, 471.

Jean d'Acre, 467.
Jerome (King of Westphalia), 213, 448.
Jesuits, dangerous principles of the, 446.
Jews, the Emperor afforded protection to, 446
Joseph (King of Spain), 212, 448.
Josephine, 52, 110; character of, 208.
Jourdan (Marshal), 428.
Junot, anecdote of, 27; Duke of Abrantes, 298.
Jurisprudence, remarks upon, 405.

King of Rome, anecdote of, 40; his prospects, 220.
Kleber, remarks upon, 22, 53, 207, 510.

Labaillerie, character of, 240.
Lacretelle, history of the Convention by, 257, 259.
La Harpe, writings of, 324.
Lannes, 48; last moments of, 80.
La Paux (M.), character of, 247.
La Perouse, shipwrecks of, 141.
Larrey (Baron), character of, 427.
Las Casas (Count), the new room for, 76; condition at court of, 282; arrest of, 505; examination of the papers of, 507; summary of the condition of, 515; sent to Europe, 524.
Las Casas (Immanuel), urged to groom his own horse, 103.
Lavalette (Count), 204.
Lavater, remarks upon, 318.
La Vendée, troubles in, 457.
Le Brun (Consul), 491.
Legion of Honor, remarks upon, 409.
Legitimacy, doctrines of, 574; remarks upon, 625.
Leopold (Prince), 469, 559.
Letitia (Madam), 212; letter from, 231; letter to the allies from, 525.
Letters, inspection of, 59; detention of, 236.
Libels, remarks upon, 21, 63, 599; upon the Emperor, 161, 199, 354, 554; Lord Castlereagh, 398.
Lieutenant, anecdote of, 239.
Little Corporal, anecdote of, 27.
Little Gibraltar, 24.
Liverpool (Lord), character of, 485.
Locke, system of, 486.
Lodi, 23.
Longwood, description of, 30; removal to, 56; plan of, 58; limits of, 70; remarks upon, 120; inmates of, 125; its great privations, 127; domestics of, examined, 163; its destitution, 257, 385; plans for enlargement of, 297.
Loudon (Lady), arrival of, 200.
Louis XVI., 46, 62.
" XVIII., 55.
" (King of Holland), 210, 392, 448.
Lowe (Sir Hudson), impertinence of, 141; presentation of, 144; the Emperor's opinion of, 144; Emperor's interviews with, 171, 201, 352; exactions of, 176; new requirements, 199; unreasonable exactions, 205; servant

arrested by, 215; remarks upon, 239; vexations of, 296, 305; the Emperor admits to an audience, 305; the insulting cruelty of, 323; the Emperor determines no more to see, 342; insolent message sent by, 355; vulgarity of, 383; annoyances continued by, 404; new exactions demanded of the French by, 406; new restrictions of, 410; exacts the "pound of flesh," 416; remarks of Napoleon upon, 508; quarrels with Dr. O'Meara, 581; Dr. O'Meara insulted by, 601.

Lower class, nations are formed of, 547.

Lyons, entrance into, 110.

Maintenon (Madam de), letters of, 376.

Malcolm (Sir Pulteney), Sir George Cockburn replaced by, 275; appearance of, 279; remarks upon, 280; a tent for the Emperor pitched by, 320.

Mallet, the affair of, 446.

Malta, 584.

Manning (Mr.), the arrival at St. Helena of, 566.

Manufactures (French), 75, 224.

Marchand, the valet, 71.

Maria Louisa (The Empress), 42, 101; envied by her mother-in-law, 108, 110; constraint of, 538.

Marine department, 196.

Market-woman, anecdote of, 422.

Marmont (Marshal), 42; betrays the Emperor, 127; defection of, 492.

Marriage, remarks upon, 243; independent of priests, 445.

Masonry, modern, 122

Massena (General), 39, 191; character of, 511.

Mathematics, the Emperor's fondness for, 74.

Medicine, the Emperor's distrust of, 51; remarks upon, 104, 242, 243.

Menou (General), 207.

Mesmer, remarks upon, 318.

Metternich, interview of Napoleon with, 152; the intrigues of, 274.

Meudon, institute of, 40.

Military school at Paris, 241; at St. Germain, 241; at St. Cyr, 241.

Ministry (English), warlike spirit of, 471.

" (of Napoleon), 491.

Mirabeau, remark of, 225.

Mohammed (of Voltaire), 160; character of, 160.

Molière, the Hypocrite of, 355.

Mollien (M.), character of, 240.

Monges, character of, 258.

Moniteur (The), testimony of, regarding Napoleon, 269.

Monks, the return of, to France, 278.

Montesquieu, 35; Madam, 40.

Montholon (Count), the Emperor's attachment for, 535.

Montholon (Madam), visit to, 71; return to Europe of, 613.

Montholon (Tristam), anecdote of, 296.

Moore (General), 207.

Moral courage, remarks upon, 53.

Morass, the Emperor mired in the, 66.

Moreau (General), remarks upon, 22, 53, 190; statue to, 231; his conspiracy, 234, 510; his death, 521.

Mosaic account scrutinized, 387.

Moscow, remarks upon, 15; its conflagration, 363; ought the Emperor to have died at, 447.

Moses, books of, 188.

Murat (King of Naples), 53; intelligence of the death of, 86; parallel between Napoleon and, 87; character of, 300, 466, 568.

Nantes (Bishop of), character of, 346.

Napoleon, anguish of, 33; charity of, 44; wounds of, 62; daily habits of, 68; disappointments of, 70; ability of, for mental exertion, 89; court of, 99; political designs of, 101; remarks upon the career of, 111, 169, 385, 631; accusation against, 126; candor and impartiality of, 136; his regret that he did not go to America, 137; private conversation of, 142; remarks upon the treatment of, 147; desires of, for peace, 152; message to the Prince Regent, 154; remarks upon the captivity of, 155; the wardrobe of, 156; proclamations of, to the army, 161; did not become a Mussulman, 162; parental influence of, 164; achievements of, 174; visit of Sir Hudson Lowe to, 175; deplorable condition of, 176; is invited to dine at Plantation House, 192; in the Council of State, 193; remarks on marriage by, 195; remarks on the governor's invitation to, 201; reading the Bible, 215; regrets his irritation, 236, 353; kindness of, 242; plan of life of, 243; alternatives presented to, 251; punning, 257; history will do justice to, 265; no engagements with Spain violated by, 265; second marriage of, 273, 479; care of wounded soldiers taken by, 292; return of, from Egypt, 293; assumption of government by, 293; paternal advice of, 318; appeal of, to Admiral Malcolm, 322; noble plans of, for France, 331; magnificent works of, 332; causes of the overthrow of, 340; angry interview of, with Sir Hudson Lowe, 352; reasons for retaining the title of Emperor, 366; review of the career of, 366; offers to pay his expenses, 376; large expenditures of, 383; intellectual activity of, 387; intense occupation of, 395; habits of, as Emperor, 396; mode of dictation of, 397; treasures of, 397; reply of, to libels, 399; refusal of, to see Sir Hudson Lowe, 413; proposal of, to assume incognito, 417; political principles of, 420; familiar habits of, 436; remarks of, on Sir Hudson Lowe, 549; aversion of, to war, 472; comprehensive plans of, 473; wounded, 475; love of the soldiers for, 475; the great principle of, "Equal rights for all men," 493; freedom of, from prejudice, 493; confidence of, in final reputation, 494; striking remarks of, 494; desire of, to

INDEX. 661

destroy the feudal system, 494; reasonable demands of, 513; causes of the rise of, 514; letter of, to Las Casas, 517; esteem of, for the English people, 532; newspapers withheld from, 536; Goldsmith's secret memoirs of, 552; libels upon, 554; habits of, 557; imperial title refused to, 581; the portrait of his son received by, 618; fondness of, for children, 623; opposition of, to medicine, 630; remarks of, upon medicine, 639; life of Marlborough presented to the 20th regiment by, 64; will dictated by, 641; remarks of, to Dr. Arnott, 643; sacrament of the Lord's Supper received by, 644; religious feelings of, 645; letter to Governor Lowe dictated by, 647; death of, 651; burial of, 655.

Narbonne (Count of), his character, 155.
Native country, charms of, 226.
Navy, 15; administration of, 390; remarks upon, 454.
Neapolitans, character of, 466.
Neckar (M. de), 76.
Ney (Marshal), 53; defense of, 55; trial of, 106, 191.
Nice, army of, 26.
Nichols (Captain), journal of, 627.
Nobility of Napoleon, reasons for the formation of the, 495.
Northumberland, 15; sailors of, return to Europe of the, 279.
Nuitz, interesting anecdote of, 326.

Œdipus, Greek tragedy of, 221.
O'Meara (Doctor), 58; idea of Napoleon, 540; social conversation prohibited between the Emperor and, 583; arrest of, 608; commission resigned by, 608; is banished from St. Helena, 609; final interview between the Emperor and, 610.
Orleans (Duke of), 55.
Oudinot (Marshal), 191.

Palm, execution of, 547.
Pamplin (Admiral), arrives at St. Helena, 573; vulgarity of, 573.
Paoli (General), 227.
Parliament (British), bill of, 275.
Paul and Virginia, remarks upon, 77.
Paul of Russia, plans of, 337, 534.
Pauline (Princess), marriage of, 187; extravagance of, 211, 448.
Pavia surrendered to pillage, 291.
Peace with England, Napoleon desired, 466.
Peasant woman, anecdote of, 100.
Pelletier, libels of, 541.
Persia, 170.
Peter the Great, remarks upon, 362.
Phrenology, remarks upon, 637.
Pichegru, arrest of, 233.
Picture of son received by the Emperor, 618.
Piedmont, remarks upon, 328.

Piontkowsky, arrival of, 66.
Pitt (William), policy of, 256; remarks upon, 452, 486.
Pius VII., goodness of, 349; arrest of, 350.
Plague, 105.
Plate of the Emperor broken, 387.
Poland, re-establishment of, 580.
Political designs of the Emperor, 21.
" economists, theories of, 284; Napoleon's views of, 284.
Political principles of the Emperor, 420.
Poniatowsky (Count), 460.
Poor rates of England, 310.
Poppleton (Captain), 206.
Pradt (Abbé de), libel of, 164; dismissed from embassy, 164.
Press, liberty of the, 269.
Prisoners, exchange of, 439.
Prisons of France, 314.
Protest, the Emperor's, 34; Napoleon sends Sir George Cockburn, 38; of the Emperor against the treaty of August 2d, 357; Emperor dictates, 613.
Protestantism, remarks upon, 345.
Protestants, Bourbons oppress, 589.
Prussia, King of, 274.
" Queen of, 271.
Public opinion, 45; influence of, 408.

Racine, works of, 485.
Raffles (Sir Stamford), arrival at St. Helena of, 208.
Reade (Sir Thomas), vulgarity of, 519.
Recamier (Madam), 94.
Regency, history of, 333.
Religion, remarks upon, 244; Napoleon's ideas of, 344; remarks upon, 616.
Renouard, the writings of, criticised, 93.
Reprisals, the Emperor restrained from, 440.
Restrictions at St. Helena, 523.
Revolution (French), 137, 140; situation of Napoleon at the commencement of, 227, 601.
Revolution, influence of, 92; remarks upon, 125; of France and England compared, 179; inevitable miseries of, 374.
Rewbel, (M.), 247.
Robespierre, 45; character of, 590.
Romance of Napoleon's life, 289.
Rousseau, new Eloise by, 237.
Rue de la Victoire, house in, 158.
Russia, retreat from, 168, 220, 460; campaign of, 364; vast designs of Napoleon against, 364; expedition to, 472; aggressions of, 562; best mode of checking its power, 559, 580.

Sailing of the convoy, 17.
Sailor, anecdote of, 68; (British), anecdote of, 557.
Santini, design of, to kill the governor, 323.
Savary, remarks upon, 274, 419.
Saxony, campaign of, 369.

Schoenbrun, fanatic of, 131.
School, female, at Ecouen, 241; at St. Denis, 241.
Scipio, 121.
Secret memoirs of Napoleon, 552.
Senate, character of, 37.
Sensibility, remarks upon, 391.
Sentinel, the Emperor aimed at by the, 71.
Serrurier, 39.
Ships, French, taken by the English, 560.
Sidmouth, Lord, character of, 486.
Sièyes (Abbé de), discomfited, 294; anecdote of, 419.
Slave, anecdote of a, 39.
Smith (Sir Sydney), 467.
Society, pleasures of, 242.
Soldiers, anecdote of, 154; of the English, 225; remarks upon, 253; English, 464.
Somnambulism, remarks upon, 319.
Soult (Marshal), 123, 191; anecdote of the wife of, 191.
Sovereigns, weakness and credulity of, 188.
Spain, Napoleon's designs for, 467.
Spaniards, 88.
Spanish princes, treatment of, 54; dethronement of, 589.
Staël (Madam de), character of, 341, 426.
Stephanie (Princess of Baden), 215, 217.
St. Bartholomew, massacre of, 373.
St. Domingo, remarks upon, 258; debt of, 389; error of Napoleon respecting, 592.
St. Helena, remarks upon, 14, 85; arrival at, 28; description of, 28; hopelessness of release from, 150; chances of leaving, 281.
St. Lawrence, contemplated colony of, 221.
Strange (Sir Thomas), visit to St. Helena of, 519.
Sturmer (Baron), sent from the island, 609.
Suffren (M. de), remarks upon, 453.
Sugar from beet-root, 75.
Suicide, remarks upon, 14, 596.
Summary of three months, 128; of April, May, and June, 1816, 290.
Sussex (Duke of), protest of, 280.
Syria, 128.

Talleyrand, character of, 138; intrigues of, 274; urges to peace, 340, 478, 549; anecdote of the wife of, 549, 590.

Talma, anecdote of, 94.
Taxes of England, 431.
Tilsit, interview at, 271; treaty of, 272.
Titles of honor, remarks upon, 305.
Toby, the Malay slave, 48.
Toulon, 23.
Toussaint, character of, 259.
Tragedy, influence of, 93.
Treasures of Napoleon, 397.
Treasury of France, 240; minister of, 391.
Treaty of August 2d, 171, 354; given entire, 356.
Tribunate, suppression of the, 37.
Tronchet, 193.
Tuileries, court of the, 229, 239, 382.
Turenne, 56, 482.

United States, purity of the ministry of the, 491.

Valley of Silence, 68, 83.
Vendemiaire, 140, 551.
Versailles, remarks upon, 331, 332.
Villeneuve (General), 207.
Voltaire, merits of, 161; comments upon, 221.

War (civil), fruits of, 313.
" (Russian), causes of, 165, 429.
" (Spanish), causes of, 187; remarks upon, 262.
Warden (Doctor), 199.
Water, destitution of, at St. Helena, 435.
Waterloo, carriage of Napoleon taken at, 107; the English will lament the victory of, 114; could France have been saved after the battle of, 132; official documents taken from the Emperor at, 155; dictation upon, 183; remarks upon, 432; ought the Emperor to have died at, 447, 490; plan of the battle of, 552; course to be pursued after the battle of, 571.
Weathercocks, description of, 199.
Wellington, St. Helena selected by, 490, 591.
Whitworth (Lord), misrepresentation of the interview with, 254; interview with, 556.
Widows of Napoleon's generals, 230.
Wilks (Governor), 67; Governor Lowe receives, 74; departure of, 151.
Williams (Miss), libel of, 123.
Wilson (Sir Robert), libels of, 204, 527.
Wright (Captain), remarks upon, 20.

THE END.

See — enquiries of Sidia — Voltaire —
Portrait of the father of Napoleon — 186
See — Napoleons remedy in case of sickness — 242
His ideas about religion — new line 243 = 2..
See Napoleons remarks religion — 34.
The Times have been sent ecca... ... l.
Napoleon to Longwood — 360
See His price of all kinds of food at St. H.. — 4.
              the Jesuits
Inquire for encouraging to H.. — 4..
See about the freeMasons — 4"5
about the Jesuits — 4—..
See difference of the 2 ...
Democracy and Aristocracy — 4.
See His idea on Conscription — 4..
Of the Clergy — new line 4..
I never was my own master — 4.
See of Massena by ...... — 5..
The brief cause of the last battle — not ... — 5..
See about Pierre ... ... 4.. ...
No ... ... — Portiers ... and .....
Dantons — Talleyrand — and the rest

Check Out More Titles From HardPress Classics Series In this collection we are offering thousands of classic and hard to find books. This series spans a vast array of subjects – so you are bound to find something of interest to enjoy reading and learning about.

Subjects:
Architecture
Art
Biography & Autobiography
Body, Mind &Spirit
Children & Young Adult
Dramas
Education
Fiction
History
Language Arts & Disciplines
Law
Literary Collections
Music
Poetry
Psychology
Science
…and many more.

Visit us at www.hardpress.net

Im TheStory
personalised classic books

"Beautiful gift.. lovely finish. My Niece loves it, so precious!"

Helen R Brumfieldon

★★★★★

UNIQUE GIFT

FOR KIDS, PARTNERS AND FRIENDS

Timeless books such as:

Kids

Alice in Wonderland • The Jungle Book • The Wonderful Wizard of Oz
Peter and Wendy • Robin Hood • The Prince and The Pauper
The Railway Children • Treasure Island • A Christmas Carol

Adults

Romeo and Juliet • Dracula

- **Highly** Customizable
- **Change** Books Title
- **Replace** Characters Names with yours
- **Upload** Photo (for inside page)
- **Add** Inscriptions

Visit
ImTheStory.com
and order yours today!

WS - #0021 - 201223 - C0 - 229/152/39 - PB - 9780371619056 - Gloss Lamination